THE GREENWOOD ENCYCLOPEDIA OF
INTERNATIONAL RELATIONS

THE GREENWOOD ENCYCLOPEDIA OF
INTERNATIONAL
RELATIONS

VOLUME III
M–R

CATHAL J. NOLAN

Executive Director
International History Institute
Boston University

GREENWOOD PUBLISHING
Westport, CT • London

Library of Congress Cataloging-in-Publication Data

Nolan, Cathal J.
    The Greenwood encyclopedia of international relations / Cathal J. Nolan.
        p. cm.
    Includes bibliographical references and index.
    ISBN: 0–313–30743–1 (set : alk. paper)—ISBN 0–313–30741–5 (v. 1 : alk. paper)—
ISBN 0–313–30742–3 (v. 2 : alk. paper)—ISBN 0–313–32382–8 (v. 3 : alk. paper)—
ISBN 0–313–32383–6 (v. 4 : alk. paper)
    1. International relations—Encyclopedias. I. Title.
JZ1160.N65 2002
327'.03—dc21   2002019495

British Library Cataloguing in Publication Data is available.

Library of Congress Catalog Card Number: 2002019495

ISBN: 0–313–30743–1 (set)
        0–313–30741–5 (vol. 1)
        0–313–30742–3 (vol. 2)
        0–313–32382–8 (vol. 3)
        0–313–32383–6 (vol. 4)

First published in 2002

Greenwood Press, 88 Post Road West, Westport, CT 06881
An imprint of Greenwood Publishing Group, Inc.
www.greenwood.com

Printed in the United States of America

The paper used in this book complies with the
Permanent Paper Standard issued by the National
Information Standards Organization (Z39.48–1984).

10 9 8 7 6 5 4 3 2 1

Sapere aude

For my children,
Ryan Casey and Genevieve Michelle

Contents

Maps follow page xxiii

Preface

"History," said the American industrialist Henry Ford, "is more or less bunk." Even the great eighteenth-century historian of the Roman Empire, Edward Gibbon, was only slightly more respectful: "history," he declared, is "little more than the register of the crimes, follies, and misfortunes of Mankind." So why bother to consult, let alone write, a multivolume work of international history and international relations such as this? Because history is—whatever Ford thought of it on his good days or Gibbon on his bad ones—the most important of all humanistic inquiries. For modern societies to live with the forces of nature that science has unleashed and that ideological folly or personal vanity threatens to deploy for destructive or oppressive purposes, they first must come to terms with history. Their leaders and citizens alike must understand the ways in which increased material knowledge brings social progress even as it expands conflict and opportunities for war. And they must appreciate that vanity and a lust for power among people of sustained ambition abides still near the center of public affairs and relations among nations and states. In sum, they must realize the profound truth of the matter-of-fact observation, which Albert Einstein once made, that politics is both more difficult, and ultimately far more important, even than nuclear physics.

This work presents readers with the essential continuity of events of their own day with the great ideas, leading personalities, and major developments of the past. Yet, how does any scholar determine what is a key event and who the leading individuals are or identify great-unseen forces and long-term trends that lead to tectonic shifts in the affairs of states and peoples? It is by now axiomatic that historians "know more and more about less and less." That is a particular problem for a work such as this, where the danger lurks of presenting a compendium of "interesting facts" and "more interesting facts," with little coherence and interpretive context. Had a simple compilation of facts been the aim of this work, it might have emerged instead as a multi-author effort wherein dozens of specialists were asked to present their findings about fairly narrow disputes. Instead, it is the work of a single author—albeit, one humbly grateful to hundreds of deeply learned and prolific specialists. Although such an approach presents dangers of interpretive error, it offers opportunities for an expansive exposition that may engage general readers to search out libraries of more specialized histories. Even so, in a work such as this it is more important than usual for readers to know the basis on which historical events and persons were selected for presentation, and the assumptions that underlie its author's judgments about their significance. These criteria and assumptions I have laid out in the paragraphs that follow.

LOGIC OF THE WORK

The first issue to be dealt with is objectivity. In the social sciences and academic history, objectivity springs from conscious emotional, intellectual, and personal detachment from the facts in order to permit them to "speak for themselves." Of course, that is precisely what facts never do. Historical, political, social, and economic statements and assumptions are laden with the values of observers and analysts, even those who honestly strive for detachment rather than merely make a humbug bow in its general direction. This problem is a by-product of the inherent uncertainty of knowledge in these fields. "If you would know history, know the historian" is also sound advice concerning economics and political science. In the final analysis, the best guard against subjective distortion of objective truth is a critical intelligence and skeptical, but not cynical, attitude toward intellectual authority. That does not mean that objective truth is impossible. It does mean, however, that it is hard to attain and that it must never be assumed. In writing this book, I have attempted to achieve a standard of objectivity, which is best summed up in the advice John Quincy Adams lent to all would-be writers of history. "The historian," Adams cautioned, "must be without country or religion." In addition, while alert to issues of human freedom in whatever era, which I must forewarn readers is a high personal value ("if you would know history . . ."), I have tried to avoid reading the values of the present into the past, the better to judge people and events in the light of the imaginative as well as real-world possibilities of their own day.

Passion is also disdained in the modern academy. Yet, it is mostly a virtue in historical writing. One must be scrupulous about facts, of course, and fair-minded. On the other hand, one should not be dispassionate about the Holocaust, or the crimes of Stalin or Mao, or the brutality of the génocidaires who carried out the Rwandan massacres. I have tried, and I hope that I have generally succeeded, to write "without country or religion" in assessing such matters, but that does not mean assuming a position of neutrality on the moral significance of salient people and events. A pose of studied disinterest about the qualities of communism or fascism relative to democracy, or the deeds of Tamerlane, or the meaning of terrorism, is necessarily feigned for any thinking and feeling human being. It is also itself a committed view, whether self-aware that it is so or not. Moreover, to take on a dishonest, because morally masked, position is, to paraphrase Talleyrand, worse than a crime: it would be a mistake. An affectation of detachment from lessons that history teaches about the human condition is both sterile and boring. It is far better for readers to encounter open judgments. On this point, I cleave to the wisdom of the British historian G. M. Trevelyan that in writing about and assessing historical actors and events "the really indispensable qualities [are] accuracy and good faith." Reconstructions of past events and motivations are as accurate as I have been able to make them, though I probably have made errors of fact and interpretation that will require correction in any subsequent edition of this work. As to the rest, I ask readers to accept that I have presented what I believe to be the facts of history, and drawn conclusions about the meaning of those facts, in good faith.

Concerning the comparative length of one entry with another, it is generally true that the further events recede from the present, the more history and historians compress their description. Ideally, that is done because more of the original dross, which always conceals the meaning of human affairs, has been burned away and the right conclusions drawn about what place in the larger story a given historical event or person holds. In reality, it probably more closely reflects a common tendency and need to fix all things in relation to one's own time and point of view. I have made what effort I can to correct for this habit, but I am sure I am as guilty of it as most. As to the length of the overall work, I may only plead in the spirit of Blaise Pascal that I would have written far less, but I did not have the time.

Analytically, this study starts from the straightforward observation that states have dominated international affairs for the past 350 years. Among the nearly 200 states of the early twenty-first century the vast majority are, at most, regional powers or just minor countries. Even so, smaller states sometimes have been quite influential in the larger course of world history, if sometimes solely as objects of aggression or imperial competition. And they are often interesting and important in their own right or concerning issues of regional significance. Thus, all countries currently in existence are covered in this work, as are a large number of extinct nations. Each is treated in an entry that at the least summarizes the main features of its national development and tries to situate the country in the larger contexts of time and region.

It remains true, however, that it is the most powerful states, the major civilizations from which they arise, and the wars in which they are involved that have been the major influences in world history. Even small changes within or among the Great Powers have a more important and long-term impact on world affairs than signal events within or among smaller countries. Comprehensive coverage is thus given to the foreign policies and interactions of the most powerful states and to the dynamics that drive them, including economic, intellectual, political, and social innovation or decay. This includes former Great Powers, now extinct or just declined from the first rank, dating to the Peace of Westphalia (1648) and emergence of the modern states system in seventeenth- and eighteenth-century Europe. Likewise, it is true that even lesser—whether in character or talent—individuals in charge of the affairs of Great Powers have a broad influence on world history and politics. Often, their influence has been weightier than that of even a moral or intellectual titan, if the latter was confined to a Lilliputian land. Therefore, individuals who might be reasonably judged as of little personal consequence are sometimes given their day in this work, owing to the indisputable public consequences of their choices, actions, or omissions while in command of the public affairs of major powers. More than one otherwise mediocre prime minister or president of a Great Power, or unrelieved and appalling dictator, has slipped into significant history via this back door, held ajar for them by the pervasive importance of raw power as a motive and moving force in the affairs of nations. For this reason, most leaders of major powers are profiled, including American, Austrian, British, Chinese, French, German, Indian, Japanese, Ottoman, Russian, and Soviet, along with key military and intellectual figures.

Even the Great Powers pursue grand plans and strategic interests within an international system that reflects wider economic, political, and military realities and upholds certain legal and diplomatic norms. A full understanding of world affairs—which is much more than just relations among states and nations—is incomplete without proper awareness of the historical evolution and nature of this international system (or international society), its key terms, ideas, successes and failures, and the role played in it by numerous nonstate economic and political entities. It is also crucial to appreciate that world affairs manifest cooperative as well as competitive and violent interstate relations and that, since the nineteenth century, complex international relationships have been mirrored in expanding numbers of regional organizations dealing with security, but also economic, social, legal, and even cultural arrangements. Besides the states on the world stage, other actors that demand attention include customs unions, multinational corporations, nongovernmental organizations, and an impressively expanding host—angelic and otherwise—of international organizations. As for individuals, prominent leaders from the lesser powers of Africa, Asia, Australasia, the Americas, and Europe are included according to whether they had a significant impact on international affairs beyond their nation's borders. If they had a major impact on their own society but not on wider affairs, mention of their role is usually made in the national reference alone. Also, United Nations (UN) Secretaries-General are listed, as are many individual Nobel Prize (for Peace) winners.

As with the unique role of the Great Powers, war as a general phenomenon—and great wars among major powers in particular—receives special attention. War is more costly and requires more preparation, effort, sacrifice, ingenuity, and suffering than any other collective human endeavor. There is no greater engine of social, economic, political, or technological change than war and the ever-present threat of war even in times of peace. Moreover, war and the modern state, and the larger international system, clearly evolved together since c. 1500, each greatly influencing the other. World wars—wars that involved most of the Great Powers in determined conflict—greatly compounded these manifold effects. Hence, world wars and protracted Great Power conflicts are covered in detail, including the *Seven Years' War*, the *French Revolution* and *Napoleonic Wars*, *World War I*, *World War II*, and the *Cold War*. Dozens of lesser wars, civil wars, rebellions, and guerrilla conflicts are also recounted, as they constitute a good part of international history and of influential national histories. In sum, war is a major part of international affairs and therefore a core subject of this book.

General developments of world historical significance are also covered, including *industrialization*, *modernization*, *telecommunications*, *total war*, and the *green* and *agricultural revolutions*. Straight historical entries include biographies, major battles, international economic history, national histories, and the history of general international processes and events. Entries attempt to summarize thousands of years when dealing with major civilizations, religions, or economic trends (though with numerous cross references), hundreds of years in the case of the Great Powers and precolonial, colonial, and post-independence history of newer nations. Most listings that are separate from national histories concern the modern era, though some go back much further. The focus is, once again, on the rise of the Great Powers and the course of world civilizations, their formative wars, and their diplomatic, political, and economic relations. This means that the progressive enlargement of the states system through imperial wars, colonialism, and the expansion of commerce and market economics beyond Europe to Africa, Asia, and the Americas has been covered.

In the interest of universality, a serious effort was made to cover regions that, objectively speaking, formed only tributary streams of the riverine flow of world history. Along with something of the flavor of their local histories, it is recounted how such areas were affected by their forced inclusion in the modern state system—often by the *slave trade* or overseas *imperialism*—and by international economic developments. This is particularly true for such areas as the Caribbean, Central America, and the associated states and dependencies of the South Pacific, which are often neglected in more straightforward narrative histories. Along with all modern states, also covered are all extant political entities, whether fully sovereign or not, including *associated states*, *city-states*, small *colonies*, *condominiums*, *dependencies*, *microstates*, and legal oddities such as the *Sovereign Military Order of Malta (SMOM)*. Lastly, a fair number of extinct polities are listed, including former empires, kingdoms, federations, failed states, and political unions, such as *Austria-Hungary*, the *East African Community*, the *Ottoman Empire*, *Senegambia*, the *Soviet Union*, and the *United Arab Republic*, among many others. Also included are colonial-era names and relevant descriptions of all newly independent nations.

Although most summaries are confined to the post-1500 period, national histories may include far distant events if these are generally deemed significant in the evolution and/or historical memory of modern nations or provide intimations of the scope and direction of a given people's posture toward the outside world. For instance, the founding and succession of China's divers dynasties receive extended coverage, partly because their accomplishments and failures importantly illuminate modern China's troubled response to external pressures and its twentieth-century struggle with foreign invasion and internal revolution and partly because China remains deeply cognizant of its long and rich history, and this fact has a strong influence on its contemporary foreign policy behavior. Major intellectual revolutions that have had global historical—including not only intellectual, but also legal and political—significance are also discussed, notably the *Renaissance*, *Protestant Reformation*, and the *Enlightenment*. Although these tumultuous upheavals were originally and primarily European phenomena, they ultimately had profound effects on all international relations down to the present day, such as in their contribution to the development of secularism and the ascendancy of the state as the central principle of political organization. All political revolutions of world historical significance are covered, including the *American Revolution*, the *French Revolution*, the two *Chinese Revolutions* of the first half of the twentieth century, and the several *Russian Revolutions*. Revolutions of more local or regional significance—such as the Cuban, Ethiopian, and Iranian—are also abstracted and their importance assessed.

STRUCTURE OF THE WORK

This work is organized alphabetically. Single-word entries are, therefore, easy and straightforward to locate. But it is not always obvious where a compound term should be listed. For ease of use by readers, compound entries are listed as they are employed in usual speech and writing, that is, in the form in which they are most likely to be first encountered by the average reader. For instance, *natural resources* and *strategic resources* appear, respectively, under N and S rather than R. If readers are unable to find an entry they seek under one part of the compound term, they should have little difficulty finding it under another component of the term or phrase. Additionally, the book is heavily cross-referenced (indicated by italics), with some license taken when cross-referencing verbs to entries, which are actually listed as nouns, such as *annex*, which leads to *annexation*. Readers would be well advised to make frequent use of this feature since cross-references almost always provide additional information or insight on the original entry. Rather than clutter the text unduly with italics, however, common references such as "war," "peace," "surrender," "negotiation," "defeat," "treaty," as well as all country names, have been left in normal font. Yet, all such commonly used terms and all countries have discrete entries. In rare cases, some common terms and specific countries are highlighted, indicating that they contain additional information highly relevant to the entry being perused. To avoid confusion or sending the reader on a fruitless cross-reference search, foreign words and phrases have not been italicized. If they are, then a specific cross-reference to the term or phrase is listed because it has a special and precise meaning for international relations. For example, a textual reference to "the domestic status quo" does not receive italics, whereas "after 1919, Britain was a leading *status quo power*" does, to inform readers that additional information exists under this specialized term. For ease of use, oft-cited acronyms are cross-referenced for quick referral. Thus, *UNGA* redirects browsers to *United Nations General Assembly*, and *WTO* refers readers to the *Warsaw Treaty Organization* and the *World Trade Organization*. Otherwise, entries that readers might have encountered elsewhere in acronym form appear here under the full name of the organization. If a reader does not know the formal title of an international organization, it may be easily located by scanning all entries under the first letter. Thus, if searching for *ECOSOC* without knowing what that acronym stands for, a reader should simply scan entries under E until he or she arrives at *Economic and Social Council (ECOSOC)*. Exceptions to this rule are foreign language acronyms commonly employed in English. These are listed under the acronym itself rather than under a foreign spelling, which is most likely unknown to the English language reader. Hence, the former Soviet security and intelligence agency is listed under *KGB (Komitet Gosudarstvennoy Bezopasnosti)*, rather than the obscure "Komitet."

Crises and wars are inventoried by conventionally accepted names. Readers unsure of a standard name for a war or crisis should simply check a country entry of any known participant. There they will find in the form of a cross-reference the precise term for the entry sought. This method is especially useful for the several wars that even now go by unusual names, or in some cases multiple names, or those conflicts with which a given reader may not be familiar. For instance, someone seeking information for the first time on China's several wars with Japan might reasonably assume that they are called "Chinese/Japanese War(s)" of some given date. In fact, these important conflicts are usually referred to, in English, as the *Sino/Japanese War(s)*. Looking under China or Japan will locate the appropriate cross-reference and guide the reader to the entry that is being sought. Likewise, the several wars involving Israel and various Arab states are listed chronologically under *Arab/Israeli War(s)*, rather than under politically loaded or parochial terms such as "Yom Kippur War" or "Six Day War," although these terms are listed and cross-referenced in consideration of readers who are used to them. In cases of special confusion or a recent change in nomenclature, a guiding cross-reference is listed. For example, the *Iran/Iraq War* was often called the *Gulf War* until that term was usurped by the media for use about the multinational conflict with Iraq over its 1990 invasion and annexation of Kuwait. Readers will find here the entry *Gulf War (1980–1988)*, which explains the shift and redirects them to the newly accepted name of *Iran-Iraq War (1980–1988)*. Below that appears *Gulf War (1990–1991)*, which synopsizes the UN coalition's war with Iraq. Some technical points are as follows:

1. For syntactical reasons, cross-references that begin with a country's name may appear otherwise in the text. For instance, the *invasion of Grenada* may appear in a given sentence, but the entry is found under *Grenada, invasion of*.

2. All civil wars are listed under the country name. Thus, *American Civil War* appears under A and not C. In this case, and some others, the advice of reviewers has been followed to cross-reference wars to their vernacular usages. This allows more general readers to easily find the entries they seek, but has the felicitous side effect of compelling chauvinists or jingoists, of whatever country or stripe, to locate their nation's most boastful conflicts by mere, even humbling, alphabetical order!

3. All dates are from the Common Era (C.E.) unless stated otherwise, in which case the standard designation B.C.E. (Before the Common Era) is used. In cases where ambiguity exists, C.E. is added to ensure clarity.

4. I have for the most part followed the practice of specialists in using the pinyin system for romanizing Chinese personal and place names. However, names that have long become familiar to Western readers under their Wade-Giles form have been left in that form, as in "Chiang Kai-shek" rather than "Jiang Jieshi," with a cross-reference to the pinyin form to avoid causing confusion for younger readers. In some special cases, the alternate form has been provided immediately in parentheses, but this has not been the preferred approach.

SPECIAL FEATURES

Biography

Recent trends in historiography emphasize interactions of whole populations and or social and economic forces. Yet it remains true, as Thomas Carlyle famously noted, that much of international history is accessible through stories of the lives of great men and women caught up in, and to some degree shaping, the tumultuous events of their times. Certainly that remains true of many, even most, states before the nineteenth century and of personal or "charismatic" dictatorships still. Significant lives may serve as beacons, illuminating history. The limitations of space in this work, however, meant that its compact biographies seldom attempt to explain the inner meaning of these extraordinary lives. Readers must explore full biographies to acquire that knowledge and psychological insight into their subject. This work is necessarily limited to the public importance of public lives and is mostly confined to the political sphere, with personal and psychological detail kept to a minimum. Even so, peculiar human elements have not been ignored where they are specially revealing and clearly relevant, as in the mysticism of Nicholas II, the cruelty of Amin, the erratic and callous disregard for life of Mao, the extreme overconfidence of Hitler, or the sadism and near-clinical paranoia of Stalin.

Diplomacy

Entries include key concepts such as *arbitration, conciliation, diplomatic immunity, good offices, mediation,* and *sphere of influence.* Major diplomatic conferences are described, including *Westphalia, 1648; Vienna, 1815; Paris, 1856; Berlin, 1878; Paris, 1919; Washington, 1922; Bretton Woods, 1944; San Francisco, 1945;* and *Helsinki, 1973–1975.* Practices of negotiation, diplomatic functions, and ranks and titles are included. Classic diplomatic terms such as *cordon sanitaire, raison d'état, rapprochement, Realpolitik, Weltpolitik,* and many others are defined and examples of their application provided.

Intelligence

A sampling of major intelligence agencies is included, among them *CIA, KGB, MI5/MI6, Mossad, NSA, STASI,* and *Sûreté,* as well as common terms, jargon, and slang from intelligence tradecraft.

International Law

Listed and defined are numerous international legal concepts, maxims, and specialized terminology, many with illustrative examples, including dozens of entries on subfields such as *international criminal law, international customary law, international public law, laws of war, recognition,* and *sovereignty.* Numerous treaties, from *arms control* to the *Space Treaty* to agreements on the *Law of the Sea* and *Antarctica,* are provided and their terms listed and explained. International law and the attendant politics of *human rights* issues are covered, including *female circumcision, citizenship, refugees, slavery,* and the *slave trade.*

International Organizations (IOs)

All major multilateral bodies and organizations are covered, dating back to the mid-nineteenth century. IOs proliferated with the founding of the *League of Nations* and the *UN.* This work includes entries on all specialized agencies, as well as key committees and commissions of the UN system. There is comprehensive coverage of regional organizations, including several failures, whether organized around economic, political, or security themes. Some prominent nongovernmental organizations are also listed.

International Political Economy

Major economic institutions, such as *GATT*, *IBRD*, *IMF*, and the *WTO*, and interstate economic associations, such as *ASEAN*, *CARICOM*, *ECO-WAS*, *EEC*, *EU*, *NAFTA*, *OECD*, and *OPEC*, have entries. Some historic multinational corporations have been added, such as the *East India Company* and the *Hudson's Bay Company*, and there are more general entries on foreign direct investment and related economic concepts and specialized language, such as *adjustment, balance of payments, debt rescheduling, deficit financing, First Tranche, free trade agreements, oligopoly,* and *structural adjustment*. Also, international economic history is well-covered in entries such as *world depressions*, the *Bretton Woods system*, the *agricultural revolution, industrialization,* and the *gold standard*.

Maps

Multiple maps are available to readers. Some cover world political divisions on a region-by-region basis. Others illustrate major historical conflicts or events, such as the occupation of Germany in 1945, expansion and contraction of the Japanese Empire, and U.S. intervention in Central America and the Caribbean. Some concern long-standing diplomatic and strategic controversies, such as the *Eastern Question* or the *Straits Question*.

Military History

Included are major concepts such as *envelopment, flanking, mobilization, strategy,* and *friction*. Also listed are entries on military ranks and units and a limited set of entries on major weapons systems, conventional and otherwise. Many wars are synopsized, including discussion of their course, causes, and effects. The crucially important events of *World War I* and *World War II* receive extended coverage. Pivotal battles over the past 500 years of world history are highlighted. Generals and admirals of special accomplishment or failure earned discrete biographical entries.

Political Geography

There are entries on every nation, colony, possession, and protectorate, as well as key geographical features, definitions of strategic regions and geographical concepts, and an overview of select geopolitical theories. Significant minority groups are described, such as *Fulani, Ibos, Karen, Kurds,* and *Zulu*. Some nonsovereign regions are cataloged, especially those with secessionist histories, including *Chechnya, Ossetia, Nagorno-Karabakh, Québec*, and *Shaba*. Country entries provide a synopsis history and description of major foreign policies pursued and alliances and may also list core international associations, population levels, and the quality and size of the national military.

Political Science

Included are major concepts, terminology, and translations into plain English of current thinking in this jargon-laden discipline, which also encompasses academic *international relations theory*. This embraces concepts and terms from theoretical subfields such as *dependency, deterrence, game theory, decision-making theory, just war theory, liberal-internationalism, Marxism, perception/mis-perception studies, realism, strategic studies*, and various *systems theories*. There are also intellectual sketches of key political thinkers on international affairs, among them *Hobbes, Bentham, Kant, Marx, Rousseau*, and *Adam Smith*.

Acknowledgments

Dr. Samuel Johnson noted, "The greatest part of a writer's time is spent in reading, in order to write; a man will turn over half a library to make one book." I am keenly aware of that truth and immensely grateful to the hundreds of specialists whose books and articles I have relied upon in such measure. I have not hesitated to add interpretations of my own in areas I know well or where it seemed to me that larger patterns in history were readily apparent and moral and other lessons might be fairly drawn. Even so, writing a work of history such as this is primarily an exercise in synthesis. In a work of this scale and nature, it is simply not possible for a single author to master the primary sources that are the raw ore from which the purer metals of historical truth must be smelted. Instead, my challenge has been to gain sufficient command of the specialty literature in order to provide enough detailed narrative that past events become comprehensible, while also communicating the differing interpretations to which those events may be subject.

If this were a normal monograph, my heavy intellectual debt would be documented in extensive footnotes. That has not proven possible here, since footnotes and related academic paraphernalia would have added several hundred more pages to an already overlong work. However, at the end of longer entries, I have cited direct sources and other recommended books—the latter for various reasons and not by any means always-interpretive agreement on my part. Also, I have added clusters of more general references upon which I have relied in entries of central importance, such as "*war*" or "*international law*" or "*Spanish America.*"

Finally, I have prepared and included a Select Bibliography of works consulted. Neither the end citations nor the bibliography are intended to provide a comprehensive listing of the many important works of specialized history available to scholars. My more limited purpose is to point general readers to a mixture of the best, along with the most recent, scholarship in different fields and to expose them to a variety of interpretive points of view. I fully appreciate that a broad work of this nature is necessarily a mere steppingstone to a far richer understanding of international history, which may be gleaned only from a wider reading of those specialized histories. If this work encourages readers to pursue that search for themselves, its purpose will have been achieved.

On a personal note, I need and wish to express my profound gratitude to those who have assisted me in completing this task. I have taken parts of the past seven years to write this work. In that time, I wrote or edited other books, but this one was always on my mind, its demands pervading my reading and thinking, its conclusions seeping into my teaching. My first thanks must go to my editor at Greenwood, Michael Hermann, who is simply the finest editor with whom I have ever worked. In addition to lifting from me all concerns about production values and the usual mundane matters that accompany production of any book, he has been a frequent and always constructive critic and adviser on issues of content.

Several of my colleagues at Boston University must wish that e-mail had never been invented or at least that I had never been introduced to the technology. For their patience with me and forbearance of my many inquiries, and for their counsel, collegiality, and friendship, I am ever appreciative. My thanks and gratitude to Erik Goldstein and David Mayers, both of whom have been extraordinarily supportive of my work. I look forward to many more years together as colleagues and friends, joined now also by my old colleague and friend from the University of British Columbia, Robert H. Jackson. William Tilchin has been prodigiously supportive of this project and as we have worked together on several other conference and book projects. He has read and commented on numerous entries, often saving me from error and always boosting my confidence whenever it sagged, usually during moments when I realized how absurdly huge a task it was that I had set myself. How may I express the fullness of my gratitude to my friend and colleague, William R. Keylor, with whom I had the privilege of cofounding the International History Institute at Boston University and with whom I am honored to work closely on a daily basis? Had I an entry in this book for "gentleman and scholar," it would simply read, "See Bill Keylor," because there would be no need to say more.

Few have read, commented on, corrected, and laughed at (usually in the places intended) more of the text than my dear friend and former colleague, Dr. Carl C. Hodge of Okanagan University College in Kelowna, British Columbia. I am grateful also for comments on selected entries by Dr. Charles Cogan, Senior Fellow at the John F. Kennedy School of Government at Harvard University; Professor Charles Neu, Chair of History at Brown University; and Professor Tom Nichols of the Naval War College. Many other scholars and specialists have read and commented on one entry or another. I have thanked them individually in private and now do so again here. Min Wu, of the International History Institute, has been particularly helpful in confirming and correcting Chinese personal and place names, as has Sijin Cheng of the Department of Political Science. To them, I also extend my sincere thanks.

My wife, Valerie, read all of the book in manuscript form and has been a constant and sage adviser on language, syntax, and Latin throughout its years of writing. As always, she has remained cheerful and supportive even as I spent far too many hours lost in a book on the Mauryan state in India, or Qing China, or Samori Touré, or ensconced in front of the computer. My children, Ryan and Genevieve, continue to fill our home with laughter, wit, and song. At ages eleven and nine, I am deeply grateful for their cheerful presence and companionship.

THE SPREAD OF WORLD RELIGIONS, c. 500 B.C.E.–600 C.E.

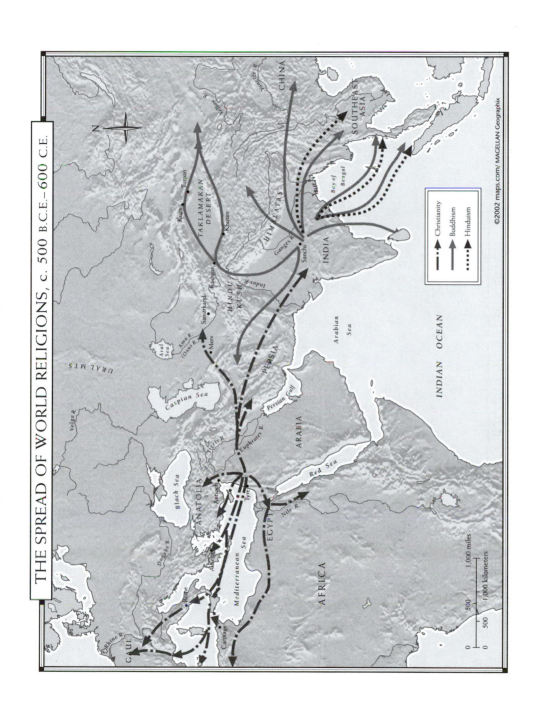

©2002 maps.com/ MAGELLAN Geographix

Legend:
- Christianity
- Buddhism
- Hinduism

CHINA

SOUTHEAST ASIA

INDIA

Sanchi

HIMALAYAS

Ganges R.

Indus R.

HINDU KUSH

Kashgar

Samarkand

TAKLAMAKAN DESERT

Turpan

Kuga

Khotan

URAL MTS

Aral Sea

Amu R.

Oxus R.

Merv

Caspian Sea

Volga R.

Dnieper R.

Black Sea

ANATOLIA

Antioch

Tyre

Tigris R.

Euphrates R.

PERSIA

Persian Gulf

ARABIA

Arabian Sea

Red Sea

Nile R.

EGYPT

AFRICA

INDIAN OCEAN

Bay of Bengal

Mecca

Mediterranean Sea

Athens

Rome

Carthage

GAUL

Rhône R.

0   500   1,000 miles

0   500   1,000 kilometers

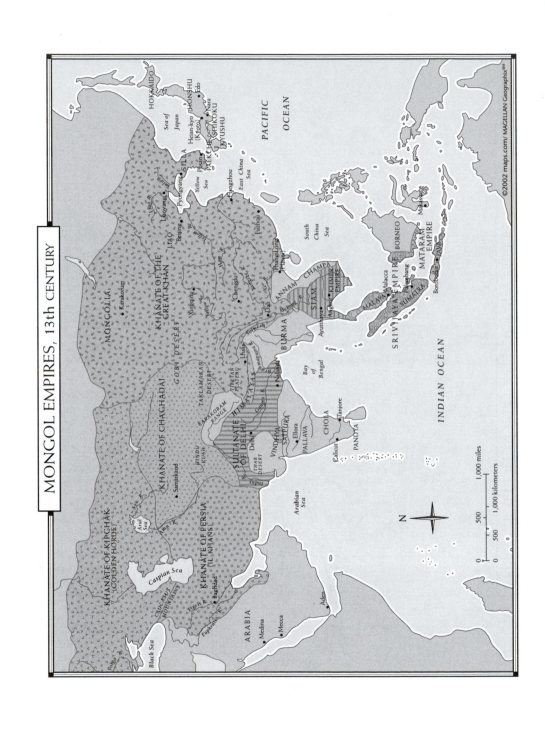

MONGOL EMPIRES, 13th CENTURY

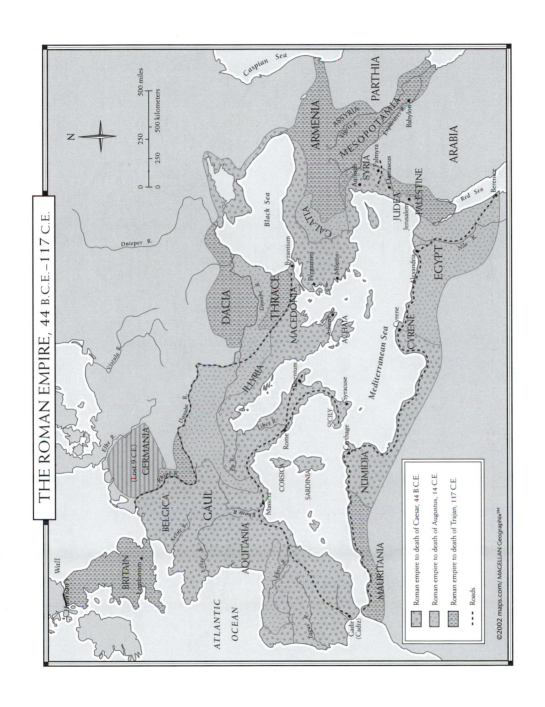

THE ROMAN EMPIRE, 44 B.C.E.–117 C.E.

Caspian Sea

PARTHIA

ARMENIA

ASSYRIA

Tigris R.

MESOPOTAMIA

Euphrates R.

Babylon

ARABIA

500 miles

500 kilometers

250

250

0

0

N

Black Sea

Dnieper R.

GALATIA

Antioch

SYRIA

Palmyra

Damascus

PALESTINE

Red Sea

Berenice

Byzantium

Pergamum

JUDEA

Jerusalem

Milletos

DACIA

Danube R.

THRACE

MACEDONIA

Athens

ACHAIA

Cyrene

Alexandria

CYRENE

EGYPT

Nile R.

Vistula R.

ILLYRIA

Mediterranean Sea

Danube R.

M.

Syracuse

Tiber R.

Brundium

Rome

SICILY

Carthage

GERMANIA

(Lost 9 C.E.)

Elbe R.

Weser R.

Po R.

CORSICA

SARDINIA

NUMIDIA

BELGICA

GAUL

Seine R.

Rhône R.

Massilia

AQUITANIA

Loire R.

MAURITANIA

Hadrian's Wall

BRITAIN

Londinium

Ebro R.

Tagus R.

Gadir
(Cadiz)

**ATLANTIC
OCEAN**

	Roman empire to death of Caesar, 44 B.C.E.
	Roman empire to death of Augustus, 14 C.E.
	Roman empire to death of Trajan, 117 C.E.
- - -	Roads

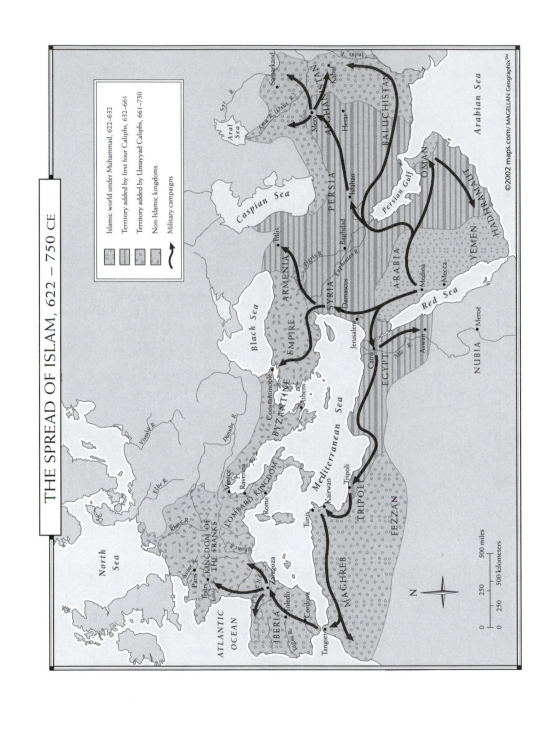

THE SPREAD OF ISLAM, 622 – 750 CE

Islamic world under Muhammad, 622–632
Territory added by first four Caliphs, 632–661
Territory added by Umayyad Caliphs, 661–750
Non-Islamic kingdoms
Military campaigns

©2002 maps.com/ MAGELLAN Geographix℠

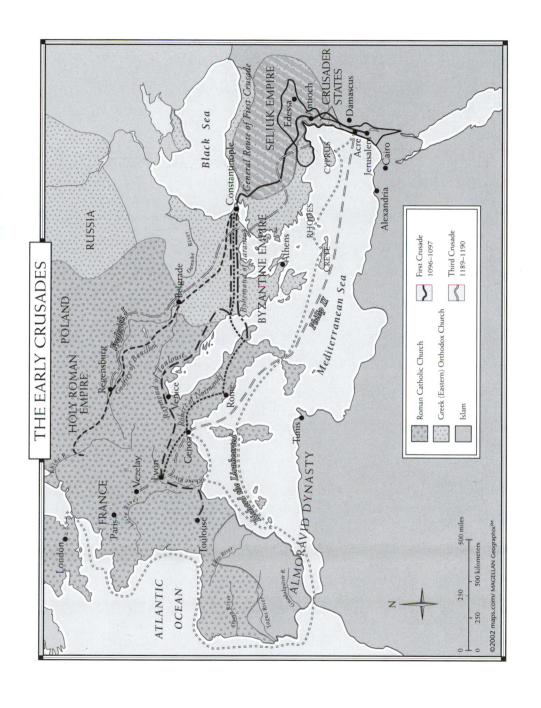

THE EARLY CRUSADES

ATLANTIC OCEAN

London

Paris

FRANCE

Seine River

Loire River

Vezelay

Lyon

Rhône River

Toulouse

Ebro River

Douro River

Tagus River

Guadalquivir R.

ALMORAVID DYNASTY

Tunis

Genoa

Venice

Rome

Robert of Normandy

Raymond of Toulouse

Godfrey of Bouillon

Mts.

Regensburg

Weser R.

Rhine R.

HOLY ROMAN EMPIRE

POLAND

RUSSIA

Belgrade

Danube River

Frederick I

Bohemond of Tarantum

Constantinople

BYZANTINE EMPIRE

Athens

Black Sea

SELJUK EMPIRE

General Route of First Crusade

Edessa

Antioch

CRUSADER STATES

Damascus

Acre

CYPRUS

Jerusalem

Cairo

Alexandria

RHODES

CRETE

Philip II

Richard the Lionhearted

Mediterranean Sea

N

0   250   500 miles

0   250   500 kilometers

©2002 maps.com/ MAGELLAN Geographix℠

	Roman Catholic Church	First Crusade 1096–1097
	Greek (Eastern) Orthodox Church	Third Crusade 1189–1190
	Islam	

EXPLORATION AND COLONIZATION, c. 1700

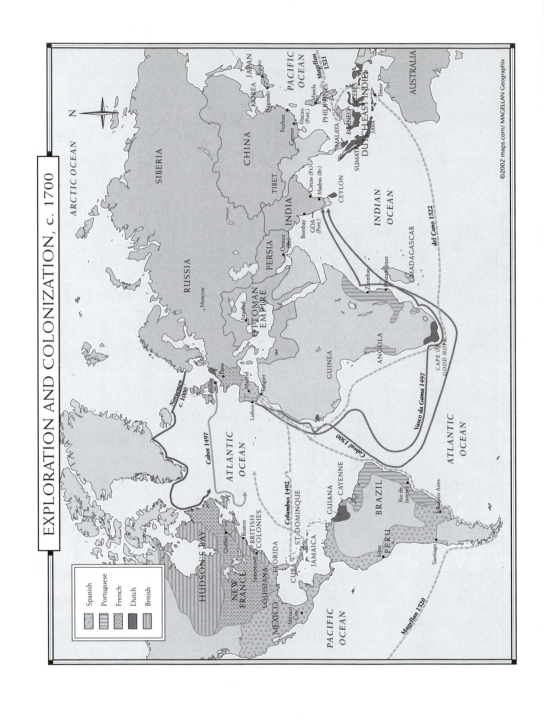

©2002 maps.com/ MAGELLAN Geographix

THE OTTOMAN EMPIRE, 1300–1924

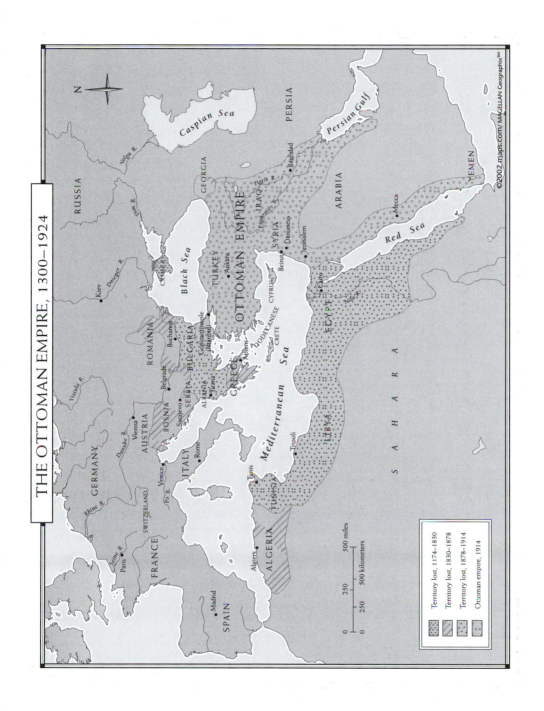

RUSSIA

Caspian Sea

PERSIA

Persian Gulf

volga R.

Dneiper R.

Kiev

Don R.

GEORGIA

Baghdad

Tigris R.

IRAQ

YEMEN

ARABIA

Euphrates R.

SYRIA

Damascus

Mecca

Black Sea

CRIMEA

TURKEY

Ankara

OTTOMAN EMPIRE

Beirut

Jerusalem

Red Sea

Visula R.

ROMANIA

Bucharest

BULGARIA

Constantinople (Istanbul)

CYPRUS

Cairo

Nile R.

EGYPT

Belgrade

SERBIA

Sarajevo

BOSNIA

ALBANIA

Tirana

GREECE

Athens

DODECANESE

CRETE

Danube R.

AUSTRIA

Vienna

Mediterranean Sea

LIBYA

SAHARA

Rhine R.

GERMANY

SWITZERLAND

Po R.

Venice

ITALY

Rome

Tripoli

Seine R.

FRANCE

Paris

Tunis

TUNISIA

Madrid

SPAIN

Algiers

ALGERIA

	Territory lost, 1174–1830
	Territory lost, 1830–1878
	Territory lost, 1878–1914
	Ottoman empire, 1914

500 miles

500 kilometers

250

250

0

0

250

N

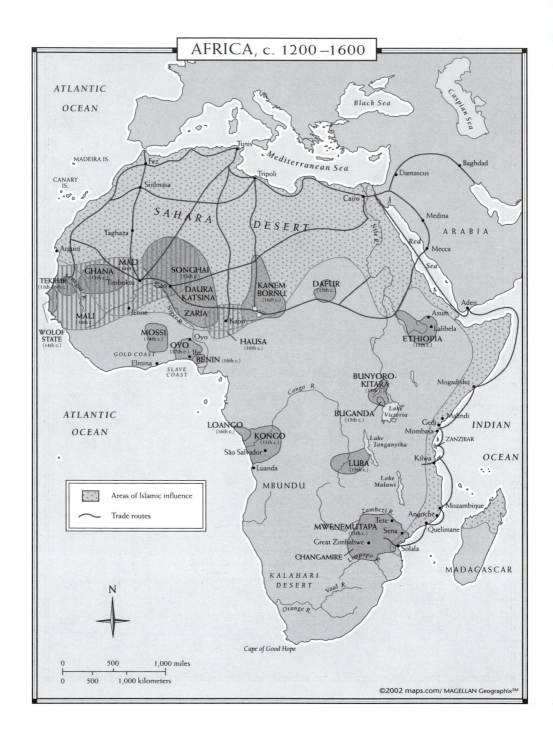

AFRICA, c. 1200–1600

ATLANTIC OCEAN

Black Sea

Caspian Sea

MADEIRA IS.

CANARY IS.

Fez

Tunis

Mediterranean Sea

Tripoli

Baghdad

Damascus

Cairo

Sijilmasa

S A H A R A   *D E S E R T*

Medina

ARABIA

Taghaza

Nile R.

Mecca

Red Sea

Arguin

GHANA
(15th c.)

MALI
(14th c.)

Timbuktu

SONGHAI
(15th c.)

Gao

DAURA
KATSINA

KANEM
BORNU
(16th c.)

DAFUR
(15th c.)

Aden

TEKRUR
(11th–16th c.)

MALI
(14th c.)

Senegal R.

Niger R.

Jenne

ZARIA

Kano

Axum

Lalibela

WOLOF
STATE
(14th c.)

MOSSI
(14th c.)

OYO
(17th c.)

Oyo

Ife

HAUSA
(16th c.)

ETHIOPIA
(13th c.)

GOLD COAST

Elmina

BENIN (16th c.)

SLAVE COAST

ATLANTIC OCEAN

Congo R.

BUNYORO-
KITARA
(15th c.)

Mogadishu

BUGANDA
(15th c.)

Lake Victoria

LOANGO
(16th c.)

KONGO
(15th c.)

Lake Tanganyika

Gedi

Mombasa

Malindi

INDIAN

ZANZIBAR

São Salvador

Luanda

LUBA
(15th c.)

Kilwa

OCEAN

MBUNDU

Lake Malawi

Mozambique

Angoche

Zambezi R.

MWENEMUTAPA
(15th c.)

Tete

Sena

Quelimane

Great Zimbabwe

Solala

CHANGAMIRE

Limpopo R.

MADAGASCAR

KALAHARI DESERT

Vaal R.

Orange R.

Cape of Good Hope

N

Areas of Islamic influence

Trade routes

| 0 | 500 | 1,000 miles |
| 0 | 500 | 1,000 kilometers |

©2002 maps.com/ MAGELLAN Geographix℠

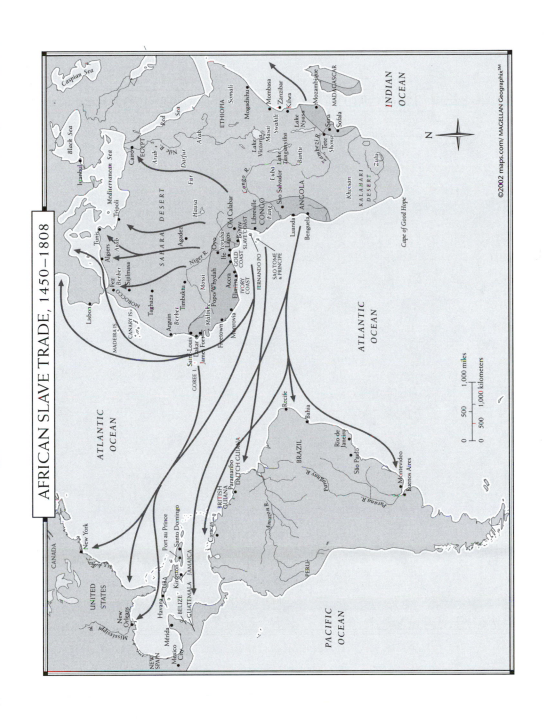

AFRICAN SLAVE TRADE, 1450–1808

©2002 maps.com/ MAGELLAN Geographix℠

THE GROWTH OF RUSSIA, 1598–1796

	Russia in 1584
	Acquisitions, 1584–1700
	Acquisitions, 1700–1772 (Primarily Peter the Great)
	Acquisitions, 1772–1796 (Catherine the Great)

0   300   600 miles
0   300   600 kilometers

FINLAND

Archangel

Ural Mountains

Baltic Sea

St. Petersburg

Pskov

Riga

Moscow

Kazan

Vistula River

Minsk

Smolensk

Warsaw

Kiev

Don River

Volga River

Dnieper R.

Odessa

Asov

Astrakhan

Caspian Sea

Danube River

Sevastopol

Black Sea

Caucasus Mts.

N

©2002 maps.com/ MAGELLAN Geographix℠

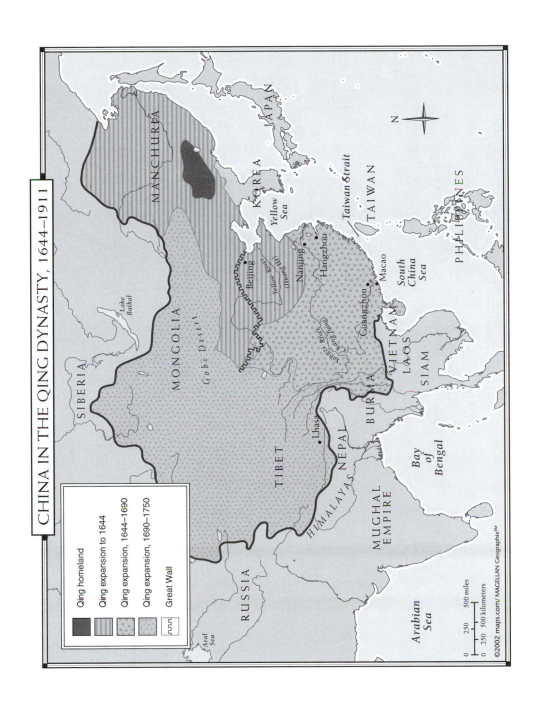

CHINA IN THE QING DYNASTY, 1644–1911

Legend:
- Qing homeland
- Qing expansion to 1644
- Qing expansion, 1644–1690
- Qing expansion, 1690–1750
- Great Wall

SIBERIA

Lake Baikal

MANCHURIA

MONGOLIA

Gobi Desert

KOREA

JAPAN

Yellow Sea

Yellow River (Chuang Ho)

Beijing

Nanjing

Hangzhou

Taiwan Strait

TAIWAN

Macao

Guangzhou

South China Sea

PHILIPPINES

Yangtzi River (Chang Jiang)

VIETNAM

LAOS

SIAM

BURMA

Lhasa

TIBET

NEPAL

HIMALAYAS

MUGHAL EMPIRE

Bay of Bengal

Arabian Sea

RUSSIA

Aral Sea

N

0   250   500 miles
0   250   500 kilometers

©2002 maps.com/ MAGELLAN Geographix℠

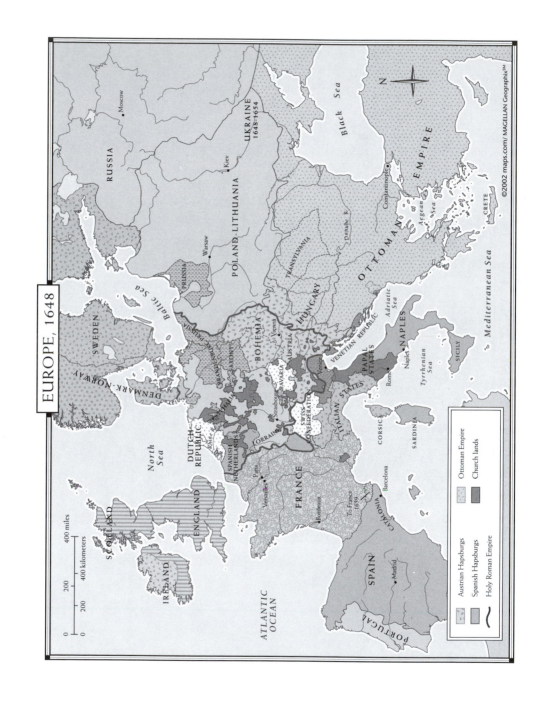

EUROPE, 1648

©2002 maps.com/ MAGELLAN Geographix℠

Legend:
- Austrian Hapsburgs
- Spanish Hapsburgs
- Holy Roman Empire
- Ottoman Empire
- Church lands

ATLANTIC OCEAN

North Sea

Baltic Sea

Mediterranean Sea

Black Sea

Adriatic Sea

Tyrrhenian Sea

Aegean Sea

SCOTLAND

IRELAND

ENGLAND

SWEDEN

DENMARK-NORWAY

RUSSIA

POLAND-LITHUANIA

UKRAINE
1648-1654

DUTCH REPUBLIC

SPANISH NETHERLANDS

FRANCE

SPAIN

PORTUGAL

CATALONIA

BRANDENBURG-PRUSSIA

PRUSSIA

SAXONY

BOHEMIA

BAVARIA

LORRAINE

SWISS CONFEDERATION

AUSTRIA

HUNGARY

TRANSYLVANIA

ITALIAN STATES

PAPAL STATES

VENETIAN REPUBLIC

NAPLES

CORSICA

SARDINIA

SICILY

CRETE

OTTOMAN EMPIRE

Moscow

Kiev

Warsaw

Paris

Versailles

Bordeaux

To France
1659

Barcelona

Madrid

Rome

Naples

Venice

Vienna

Prague

Strasbourg

Constantinople

Rhine

Danube R.

0   200   400 miles
0   200   400 kilometers

THE FRENCH AND INDIAN WAR, 1754–1763

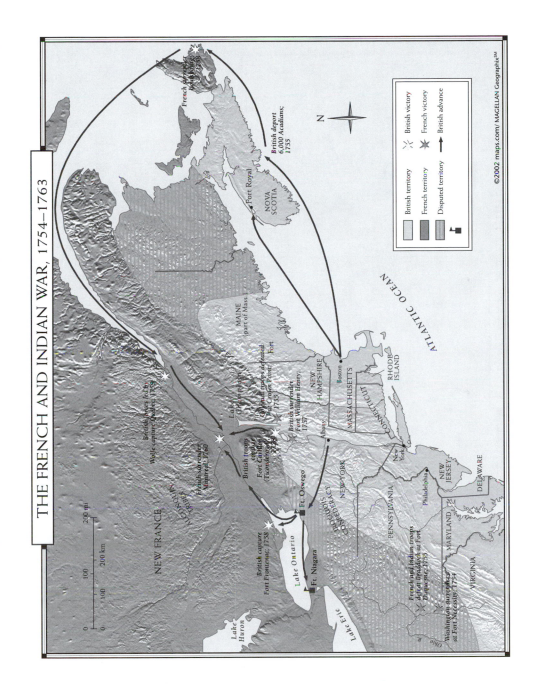

French surrenders Louisbourg, 1758

British deport 6,000 Acadians; 1755

Port Royal

NOVA SCOTIA

N

ATLANTIC OCEAN

British forces (c.)
Wolfe captures Quebec, 1759

British troops capture Fort Carillon (Ticonderoga) 1759

French surrenders Montreal, 1760

British capture Fort Frontenac, 1758

Lake Ontario

Ft. Oswego

Ft. Niagara

Lake Erie

Lake Huron

NEW FRANCE

IROQUOIS CONFEDERACY

Colonial troops defeated at Crown Point, 1755

British surrender Fort William Henry, 1757

Albany

NEW YORK

MAINE (part of Mass.)

NEW HAMPSHIRE

MASSACHUSETTS

Boston

RHODE ISLAND

CONNECTICUT

New York

PENNSYLVANIA

Philadelphia

NEW JERSEY

MARYLAND

DELAWARE

VIRGINIA

French and Indian troops defeat Braddock at Fort Duquesne 1755

Washington surrenders at Fort Necessity, 1754

Ohio R.

0   100   200 km
0   100   200 mi

British victory

French victory

British advance

British territory

French territory

Disputed territory

©2002 maps.com/ MAGELLAN Geographix℠

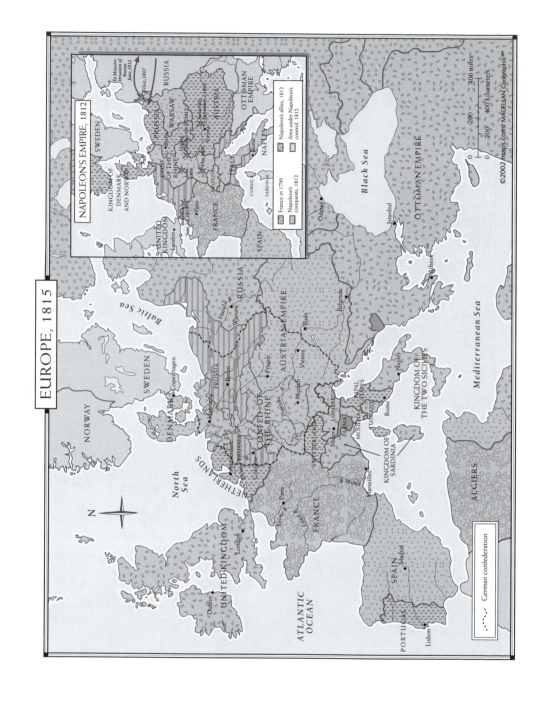

EUROPE, 1815

NAPOLEON'S EMPIRE, 1812

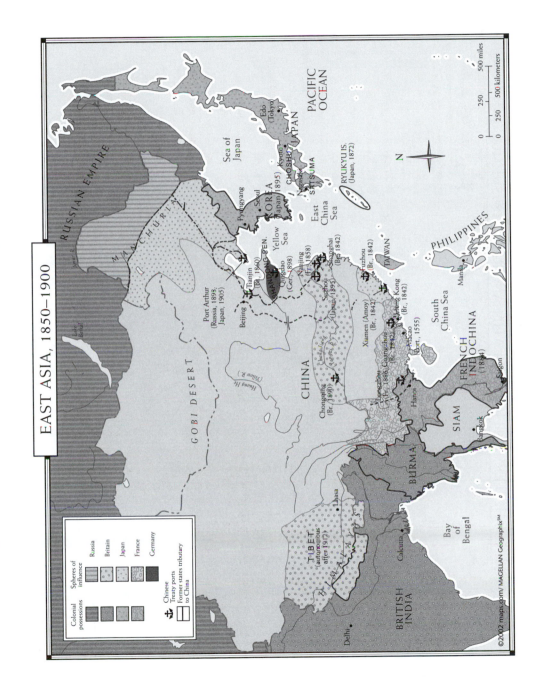

EAST ASIA, 1850–1900

U.S. INTERVENTION IN LATIN AMERICA, 1895–1940s

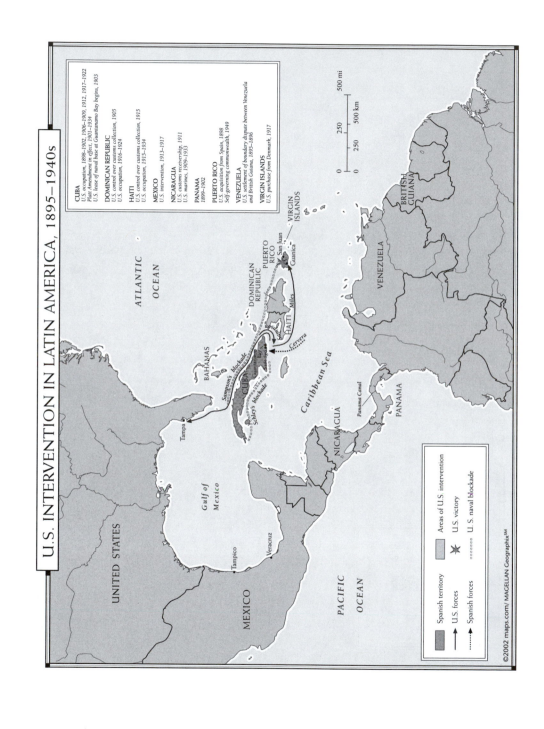

CUBA
U.S. occupation, 1898–1902, 1906–1909, 1912, 1917–1922
Platt Amendment in effect, 1901–1934
U.S. lease of naval base at Guantánamo Bay begins, 1903

DOMINICAN REPUBLIC
U.S. control over customs collection, 1905
U.S. occupation, 1916–1924

HAITI
U.S. control over customs collection, 1915
U.S. occupation, 1915–1934

MEXICO
U.S. intervention, 1913–1917

NICARAGUA
U.S. customs receivership, 1911
U.S. marines, 1909–1933

PANAMA
1899–1902

PUERTO RICO
U.S. acquisition from Spain, 1898
Self-governing commonwealth, 1949

VENEZUELA
U.S. settlement of boundary dispute between Venezuela and British Guiana, 1895–1896

VIRGIN ISLANDS
U.S. purchase from Denmark, 1917

Legend:
- Spanish territory
- U.S. forces
- Spanish forces
- Areas of U.S. intervention
- U.S. victory (★)
- U.S. naval blockade

©2002 maps.com/ MAGELLAN Geographix℠

JAPANESE EXPANSION IN ASIA, 1895–1941

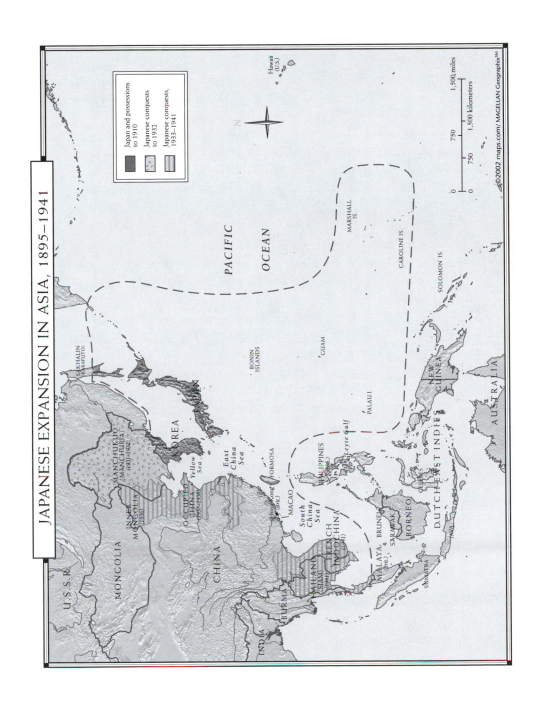

Japan and possessions to 1910

Japanese conquests to 1932

Japanese conquests, 1933–1941

U.S.S.R.

MONGOLIA

INNER MONGOLIA (1936)

MANCHUKUO (MANCHURIA) (1931–1932)

KOREA

OCCUPIED CHINA (1937–1938)

CHINA

Yellow Sea

East China Sea

FORMOSA

Hong Kong (Brit.)

MACAO

South China Sea

INDIA

BURMA

THAILAND (SIAM) (1941)

FRENCH INDOCHINA (1941)

MALAYA (Brit.)

SARAWAK

BRUNEI

BORNEO

SUMATRA

JAVA

CELEBES

DUTCH EAST INDIES

PHILIPPINES

Leyte Gulf

PALAU I.

GUAM

BONIN ISLANDS

PACIFIC OCEAN

Hawaii (U.S.)

N

MARSHALL IS.

CAROLINE IS.

SOLOMON IS.

NEW GUINEA

AUSTRALIA

SAKHALIN (KARAFUTO)

| 0 | 750 | 1,500 miles |
| 0 | 750 | 1,500 kilometers |

©2002 maps.com/ MAGELLAN Geographix℠

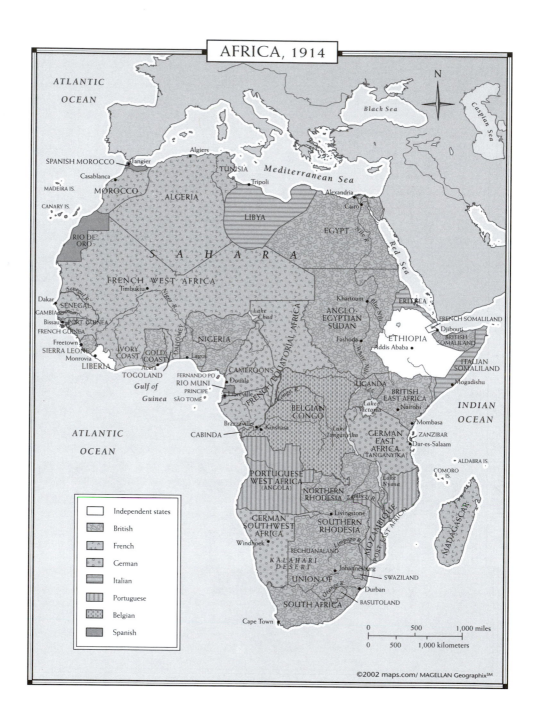

AFICA, 1914

ATLANTIC
OCEAN

Black Sea

Caspian Sea

N

SPANISH MOROCCO
• Tangier
Algiers •
TUNISIA
Mediterranean Sea
Tripoli •
Alexandria •
Cairo •

Casablanca •
MOROCCO

MADEIRA IS.

CANARY IS.

ALGERIA

LIBYA

EGYPT

Red Sea

RIO DE
ORO

S A H A R A

FRENCH WEST AFRICA
• Timbuktu

Khartoum •
ERITREA
FRENCH SOMALILAND

Dakar •
SENEGAL

Senegal R.

Niger R.

Lake
Chad

ANGLO-
EGYPTIAN
SUDAN

Blue Nile

White Nile

Djibouti •
BRITISH
SOMALILAND

GAMBIA
Bissau
PORT. GUINEA
FRENCH GUINEA

NIGERIA

Fashoda •

ETHIOPIA
Addis Ababa •

Freetown •
SIERRA LEONE
Monrovia •
LIBERIA

IVORY
COAST

GOLD
COAST

DAHOMEY

Lagos •

FRENCH EQUATORIAL AFRICA

ITALIAN
SOMALILAND

TOGOLAND

FERNANDO PO
RIO MUNI
PRINCIPE
SÃO TOMÉ

CAMEROONS
• Douala

UGANDA

Mogadishu •

Gulf of
Guinea

Libreville •

Congo R.

BRITISH
EAST
AFRICA

Lake
Victoria
• Nairobi

INDIAN
OCEAN

ATLANTIC
OCEAN

Brazzaville •
CABINDA

BELGIAN
CONGO
Kinshasa •

Lake
Tanganyika

GERMAN
EAST
AFRICA
(TANGANYIKA)

• Mombasa

ZANZIBAR
• Dar-es-Salaam

• ALDABRA IS.

PORTUGUESE
WEST AFRICA
(ANGOLA)

NORTHERN
RHODESIA

Lake
Nyasa

COMORO
IS.

GERMAN
SOUTHWEST
AFRICA

SOUTHERN
RHODESIA

Zambezi R.

• Livingstone

MOZAMBIQUE

PORT. EAST AFRICA

MADAGASCAR

Windhoek •

BECHUANALAND

Limpopo R.

K A L A H A R I
D E S E R T

• Johannesburg

SWAZILAND

UNION OF
SOUTH AFRICA

Orange R.

• Durban
BASUTOLAND

Cape Town •

SOUTH AFRICA

Legend

	Independent states
	British
	French
	German
	Italian
	Portuguese
	Belgian
	Spanish

0   500   1,000 miles

0   500   1,000 kilometers

©2002 maps.com/ MAGELLAN Geographix℠

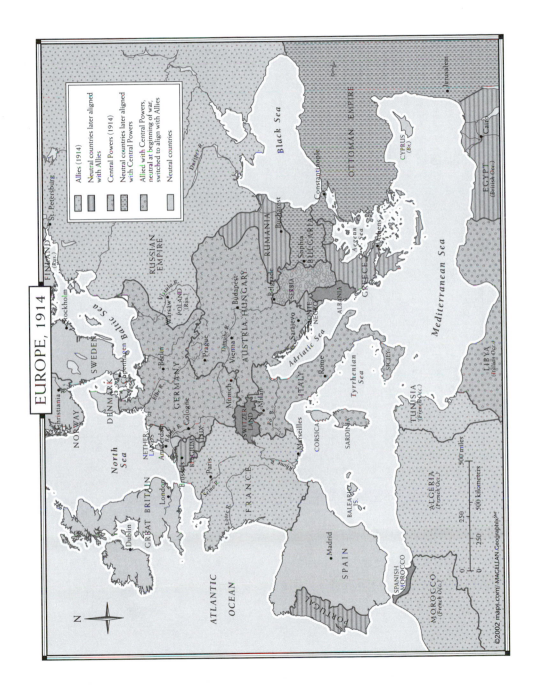

EUROPE, 1914

Legend:
- Allies (1914)
- Neutral countries later aligned with Allies
- Central Powers (1914)
- Neutral countries later aligned with Central Powers
- Allied with Central Powers, neutral at beginning of war, switched to align with Allies
- Neutral countries

FINLAND (Rus.)

St. Petersburg

SWEDEN

Stockholm

Baltic Sea

NORWAY

Christiania

DENMARK

Copenhagen

North Sea

GREAT BRITAIN

Dublin

London

NETHERLANDS

Amsterdam

BELGIUM

Brussels

LUX.

Paris

FRANCE

Seine R.

Loire R.

Rhône R.

GERMANY

Berlin

Cologne

Elbe R.

Rhine R.

Munich

SWITZERLAND

Milan

Po R.

Marseilles

CORSICA

SARDINIA

BALEARIC IS.

SPAIN

Madrid

PORTUGAL

SPANISH MOROCCO

MOROCCO (French Occ.)

ALGERIA (French Occ.)

TUNISIA (French Occ.)

LIBYA (Italian Occ.)

ATLANTIC OCEAN

POLAND (Rus.)

Warsaw

Vistula R.

Dnieper R.

RUSSIAN EMPIRE

Prague

Vienna

Danube R.

AUSTRIA-HUNGARY

Budapest

Belgrade

SERBIA

Sarajevo

MONTENEGRO

ALBANIA

ITALY

Rome

Tyrrhenian Sea

SICILY

Mediterranean Sea

Adriatic Sea

Aegean Sea

GREECE

Athens

RUMANIA

Bucharest

Sophia

BULGARIA

Black Sea

Constantinople

OTTOMAN EMPIRE

CYPRUS (Br.)

EGYPT (British Occ.)

Cairo

Jerusalem

N

500 miles

500 kilometers

0   250

0   250

©2002 maps.com/ MAGELLAN Geographix℠

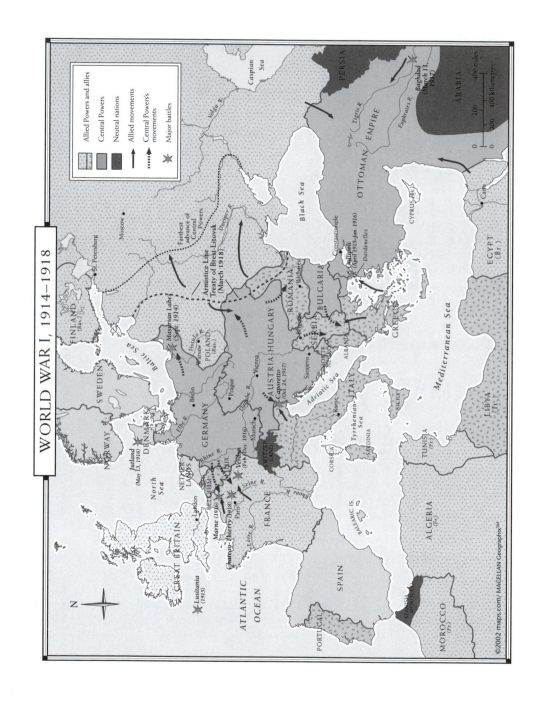

WORLD WAR I, 1914–1918

Legend:
- Allied Powers and allies
- Central Powers
- Neutral nations
- Allied movements
- Central Powers's movements
- Major battles

ATLANTIC OCEAN

NORWAY

SWEDEN

FINLAND (Rus.)

St. Petersburg

Moscow

North Sea

Baltic Sea

DENMARK

GREAT BRITAIN

London

NETHER-LANDS

BELGIUM

LUX.

GERMANY

Berlin

Prague

POLAND (Rus.)

Warsaw

Vistula R.

Tannenberg
Sept. 1914

Masurian Lakes
(Sept. 1914)

Volga R.

Dnieper R.

Farthest advance of Central Powers

Armistice Line
Treaty of Brest-Litovsk
(March 1918)

Jutland
(May 13, 1916)

Lusitania
(1915)

Marne (1914)
Château-Thierry (1918)

Paris

Loire R.

Seine R.

Verdun
(Feb.-Dec. 1916)

FRANCE

Rhine R.

Rhône R.

SWITZER-LAND

Munich

Danube R.

Vienna

AUSTRIA-HUNGARY

Caporetto
(Oct. 24, 1917)

ITALY

Rome

Corsica

SARDINIA

Tyrrhenian Sea

BALEARIC IS.

SPAIN

PORTUGAL

SPANISH MOROCCO

MOROCCO (Fr.)

ALGERIA (Fr.)

TUNISIA (Fr.)

Mediterranean Sea

LIBYA (It.)

Adriatic Sea

Sarajevo

MONTE-NEGRO

ALBANIA

SERBIA

Belgrade

ROMANIA

Bucharest

BULGARIA

GREECE

Constantinople

Gallipoli
(April 1915–Jan. 1916)

Dardanelles

Black Sea

OTTOMAN EMPIRE

Caspian Sea

PERSIA

Tigris R.

Euphrates R.

Baghdad
(March 11, 1917)

ARABIA

EGYPT (Br.)

Cairo

CYPRUS (Br.)

SICILY

N

0   200   400 miles
0   200   400 kilometers

©2002 maps.com/ MAGELLAN Geographix℠

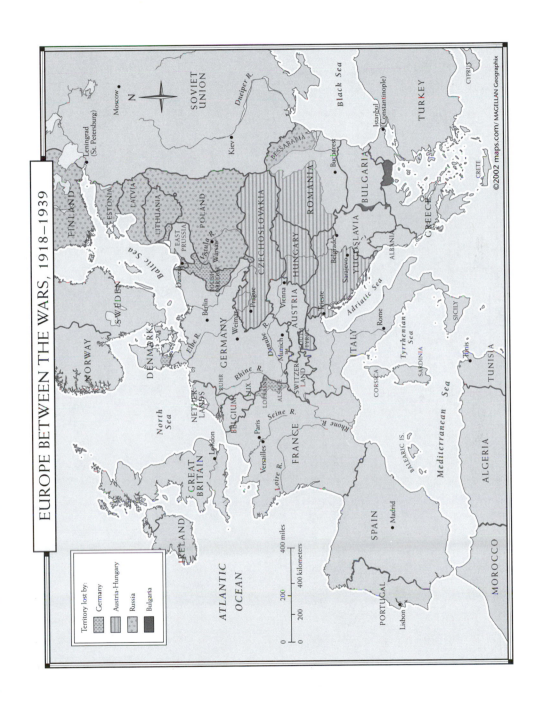

EUROPE BETWEEN THE WARS, 1918–1939

Territory lost by:

- Germany
- Austria-Hungary
- Russia
- Bulgaria

N

SOVIET UNION

Moscow

Leningrad (S. Petersburg)

Dneiper R.

Kiev

FINLAND

ESTONIA

LATVIA

LITHUANIA

EAST PRUSSIA

POLAND

Vistula R.

Danzig

Warsaw

POLISH CORRIDOR

Baltic Sea

SWEDEN

NORWAY

DENMARK

Berlin

Elbe R.

Weimar

GERMANY

Prague

CZECHOSLOVAKIA

Vienna

AUSTRIA

BESSARABIA

Bucharest

ROMANIA

HUNGARY

Trieste

S. TYROL

Munich

Danube R.

RUHR

Rhine R.

SWITZER-LAND

LORRAINE

ALSACE

LUX.

BELGIUM

NETHER-LANDS

North Sea

London

GREAT BRITAIN

IRELAND

ATLANTIC OCEAN

Paris

Versailles

Seine R.

FRANCE

Loire R.

Rhône R.

Belgrade

Sarajevo

YUGOSLAVIA

ALBANIA

BULGARIA

Black Sea

Istanbul (Constantinople)

TURKEY

GREECE

CYPRUS

CRETE

Adriatic Sea

Rome

ITALY

Tyrrhenian Sea

SARDINIA

CORSICA

SICILY

Tunis

TUNISIA

Mediterranean Sea

BALEARIC IS.

SPAIN

Madrid

PORTUGAL

Lisbon

ALGERIA

MOROCCO

0   200   400 miles

0   200   400 kilometers

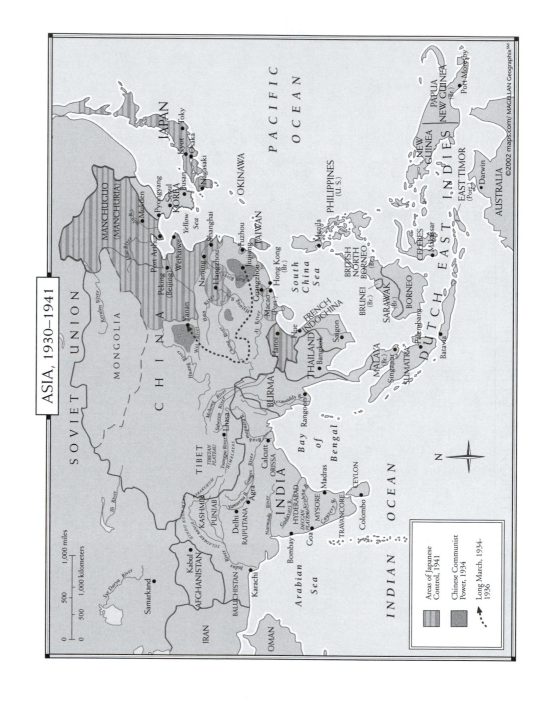

ASIA, 1930–1941

SOVIET UNION

MONGOLIA

CHINA

MANCHUGUO
(MANCHURIA)

JAPAN

KOREA

PACIFIC OCEAN

PHILIPPINES
(U.S.)

TAIWAN

Hong Kong
(Br.)

South
China
Sea

FRENCH
INDOCHINA

THAILAND

BURMA

TIBET

TIBETAN
PLATEAU

INDIA

Bay
of
Bengal

CEYLON

Arabian
Sea

INDIAN OCEAN

AFGHANISTAN

IRAN

OMAN

BALUCHISTAN

KASHMIR

PUNJAB

RAJPUTANA

HYDERABAD

DECCAN

MYSORE

TRAVANCORE

ORISSA

BRITISH
NORTH
BORNEO

BRUNEI
(Br.)

SARAWAK
(Br.)

BORNEO

MALAYA
(Br.)

SUMATRA

DUTCH EAST INDIES

CELEBES

NEW
GUINEA

PAPUA
NEW GUINEA
(Br.)

EAST TIMOR
(Port.)

AUSTRALIA

Tokyo
Kyoto · Osaka
Nagasaki
OKINAWA
Pyongyang
Seoul
Busan
Mukden
Port Arthur
Peking
(Beijing)
Weihaiwei
Yellow
Sea
Shanghai
Nanjing
Hangzhou
Yanan
Fuzhou
Jiujiang
Guangzhou
Macao
(Port.)
Hue
Hanoi
Bangkok
Saigon
Rangoon
Palembang
Batavia
Singapore
Lhasa
Calcutt
Agra
Delhi
Karachi
Bombay
Goa
Madras
Colombo
Kabul
Samarkand
Darwin
Port Moresby
Manila
Makassar

Huang River
Yangzi River
Xi River
Mekong River
Salween River
Irrawaddy River
Brahmaputra
Ganges River
Yamuna R.
Indus River
Narmada R.
Godavari R.
Krishna R.
Cauvery R.
Ili River
Syr Darya River
Kerulen River
Amur River
Yalu River
Tsangpo River
HIMALAYAS
KARAKORAM
SULAIMAN RANGE
HINDU KUSH
SULAIMAN RANGE

Areas of Japanese
Control, 1941

Chinese Communist
Power, 1934

Long March, 1934–
1936

1,000 miles
1,000 kilometers
500
500
0
0

N

©2002 maps.com/ MAGELLAN Geographix℠

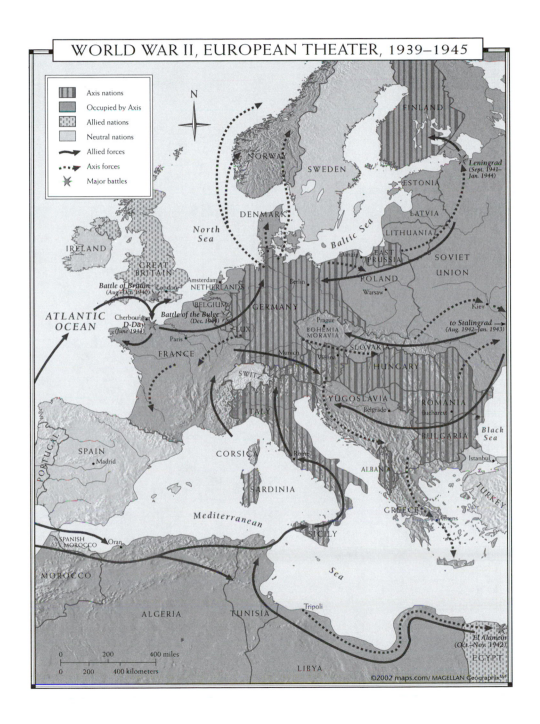

WORLD WAR II, EUROPEAN THEATER, 1939–1945

Legend:
- Axis nations
- Occupied by Axis
- Allied nations
- Neutral nations
- → Allied forces
- ⇢ Axis forces
- ✳ Major battles

N

FINLAND

NORWAY

SWEDEN

ESTONIA

Leningrad
(Sept. 1941–
Jan. 1944)

LATVIA

DENMARK

Baltic Sea

LITHUANIA

North
Sea

IRELAND

GREAT
BRITAIN

Danzig

EAST
PRUSSIA

SOVIET
UNION

Amsterdam

Berlin

POLAND

Battle of Britain
(Aug.–Oct. 1940)

London

NETHERLANDS

Warsaw

Kiev

BELGIUM

Battle of the Bulge
(Dec. 1944)

GERMANY

ATLANTIC
OCEAN

Cherbourg

D-Day
(June 1944)

LUX.

Prague

BOHEMIA
MORAVIA

to Stalingrad
(Aug. 1942–Jan. 1943)

Paris

FRANCE

Munich

Vienna

SLOVAKIA

HUNGARY

SWITZ.

YUGOSLAVIA

ROMANIA

ITALY

Belgrade

Bucharest

PORTUGAL

SPAIN

Madrid

CORSICA

Rome

BULGARIA

Black
Sea

ALBANIA

Istanbul

SARDINIA

TURKEY

Mediterranean

GREECE

Athens

SICILY

SPANISH
MOROCCO

Oran

Sea

MOROCCO

ALGERIA

TUNISIA

Tripoli

El Alamein
(Oct.–Nov. 1942)

EGYPT

LIBYA

0	200	400 miles
0	200	400 kilometers

©2002 maps.com/ MAGELLAN Geographix℠

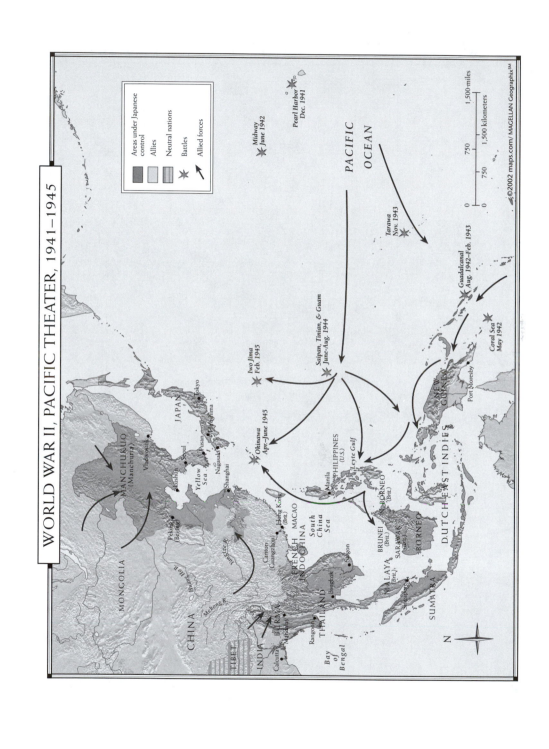

WORLD WAR II, PACIFIC THEATER, 1941–1945

Areas under Japanese control
Allies
Neutral nations
Battles
Allied forces

Pearl Harbor
Dec. 1941

Midway
June 1942

PACIFIC OCEAN

Tarawa
Nov. 1943

Guadalcanal
Aug. 1942–Feb. 1943

Coral Sea
May 1942

1,500 miles
750
0
1,500 kilometers
750
0

©2002 maps.com/ MAGELLAN Geographix℠

Iwo Jima
Feb. 1945

Saipan, Tinian, & Guam
June–Aug. 1944

Okinawa
Apr.–June 1945

MANCHUKUO
(Manchuria)

Vladivostok

JAPAN

Tokyo

Hiroshima

Lushun
Seoul
Pusan
Nagasaki
Shanghai

Yellow Sea

Peking
(Beijing)

Canton
(Guangzhou)

Hong Kong
(Brit.)

MACAO

South China Sea

PHILIPPINES
(U.S.)

Manila

Leyte Gulf

NEW GUINEA

Port Moresby

MONGOLIA

CHINA

Yellow R.

Huang Ho R.

Mekong R.

FRENCH INDOCHINA

Saigon

BORNEO
(Brit.)

BRUNEI
(Brit.)

SARAWAK
(Brit.)

BORNEO

DUTCH EAST INDIES

TIBET

INDIA

Calcutta

BURMA

Mandalay

Rangoon

THAILAND

Bangkok

MALAYA
(Brit.)

Singapore

SUMATRA

Bay of Bengal

N

INDEPENDENT STATES TO 1991

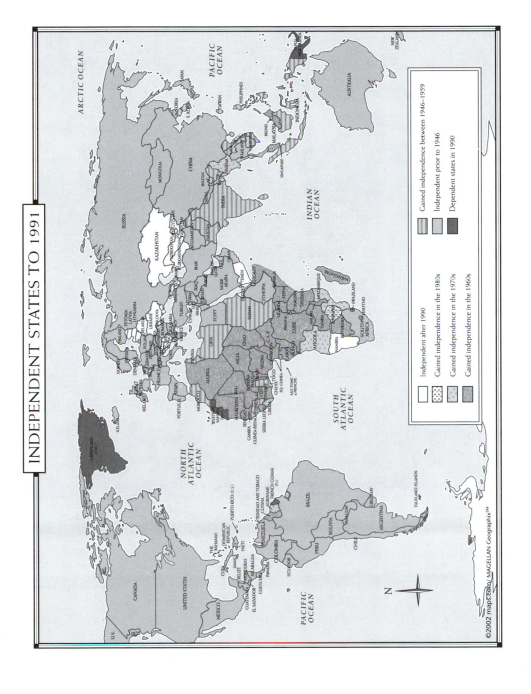

Legend:
- Independent after 1990
- Gained independence in the 1980s
- Gained independence in the 1970s
- Gained independence in the 1960s
- Gained independence between 1946–1959
- Independent prior to 1946
- Dependent states in 1990

©2002 maps.com / MAGELLAN Geographix℠

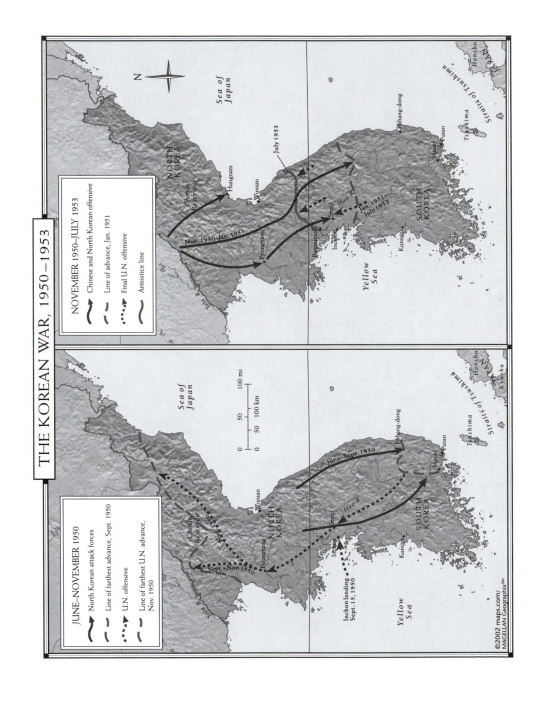

THE KOREAN WAR, 1950–1953

NOVEMBER 1950–JULY 1953

Chinese and North Korean offensive

Line of advance, Jan. 1951

Final U.N. offensive

Armistice line

NORTH KOREA

SOUTH KOREA

Sea of Japan

Yellow Sea

Straits of Tsushima

JAPAN

Honshu

Tsushima

Chosin Reservoir

Hungnam

Wonsan

July 1953

Pyongyang

Panmunjom

Seoul

Han R.

Inchon

Jan. 1951–July 1953

Kunsan

Pohang-dong

Masan

Pusan

Nov. 1950–Jan. 1951

Yalu R.

JUNE–NOVEMBER 1950

North Korean attack forces

Line of farthest advance, Sept. 1950

U.N. offensive

Line of farthest U.N. advance, Nov. 1950

NORTH KOREA

SOUTH KOREA

Sea of Japan

Yellow Sea

Straits of Tsushima

JAPAN

Honshu

Kyushu

Tsushima

Chosin Reservoir

Wonsan

Pyongyang

Seoul

Han R.

Inchon

Inchon landing Sept. 15, 1950

Kunsan

Pohang-dong

Masan

Pusan

June–Sept. 1950

Sept.–Nov. 1950

Nov. 1950

Yalu R.

0   50   100 mi
0   50 100 km

©2002 maps.com/
MAGELLAN Geographix℠

THE VIETNAM WAR, 1964–1975

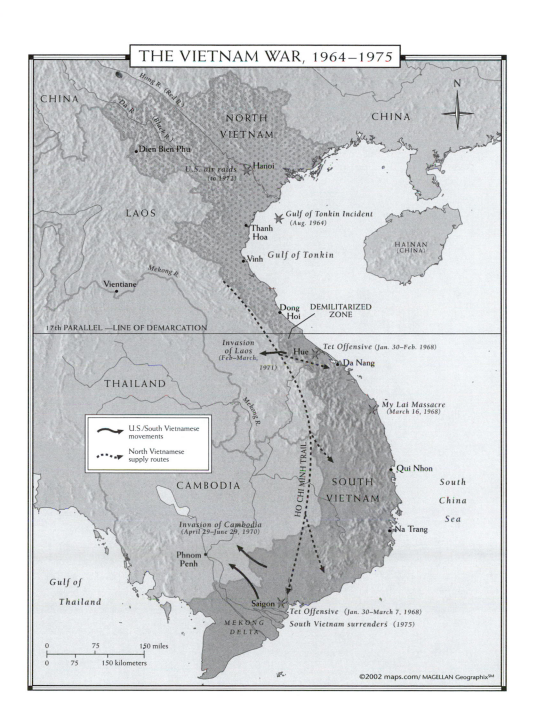

CHINA

Hong R. (Red R.)

Da R.

(Black R.)

NORTH
VIETNAM

Dien Bien Phu

U.S. air raids
(to 1972)

Hanoi

CHINA

N

LAOS

Gulf of Tonkin Incident
(Aug. 1964)

HAINAN
(CHINA)

Thanh
Hoa

Vinh   Gulf of Tonkin

Mekong R.

Vientiane

Dong
Hoi

DEMILITARIZED
ZONE

17th PARALLEL —LINE OF DEMARCATION

Invasion
of Laos
(Feb–March,
1971)

Hue

Tet Offensive (Jan. 30–Feb. 1968)

Da Nang

THAILAND

Mekong
R.

My Lai Massacre
(March 16, 1968)

U.S./South Vietnamese
movements

North Vietnamese
supply routes

Qui Nhon

South

CAMBODIA

HO CHI MINH TRAIL

SOUTH
VIETNAM

China

Sea

Na Trang

Invasion of Cambodia
(April 29–June 29, 1970)

Phnom
Penh

Gulf of

Thailand

Saigon

MEKONG
DELTA

Tet Offensive (Jan. 30–March 7, 1968)

South Vietnam surrenders (1975)

0   75   150 miles

0   75   150 kilometers

©2002 maps.com/ MAGELLAN Geographix℠

COLD WAR EUROPE, 1946–1990

N

NATO Alliance

Warsaw Pact Nations

ICELAND

ATLANTIC
OCEAN

North
Sea

NORWAY
Oslo

SWEDEN
Stockholm

FINLAND
Helsinki
Leningrad

IRELAND
Dublin

UNITED
KINGDOM
London

DENMARK
Copenhagen

Riga

Vilnius
Minsk

SOVIET UNION

NETHERLANDS
Amsterdam
Rhine R.

Berlin
EAST
GERMANY

Warsaw
POLAND
Vistula R.

Kiev

BELGIUM
Brussels
Bonn
LUX.
Seine R.
Paris
Loire River

WEST
GERMANY

Elbe River

Prague
CZECHOSLOVAKIA
Bratislava
Danube River
Vienna

FRANCE
SWITZ.
Geneva

Munich
AUSTRIA
HUNGARY
Budapest

Kishinev

ROMANIA

Po River

SPAIN
(Joined NATO in 1982)

Belgrade
YUGOSLAVIA
Sarajevo

Bucharest

BULGARIA
Sofia

PORTUGAL
Lisbon
Madrid

Tiber R.
Rome
ITALY

Skopje
Istanbul

ALBANIA
(Withdrew from
Warsaw Pact in 1968)
Tirana

TURKEY

GREECE
Athens

Mediterranean Sea

0   200   400 miles

0   200   400 kilometers

ALGERIA

©2002 maps.com/ MAGELLAN Geographix℠

THE GULF WAR, 1991

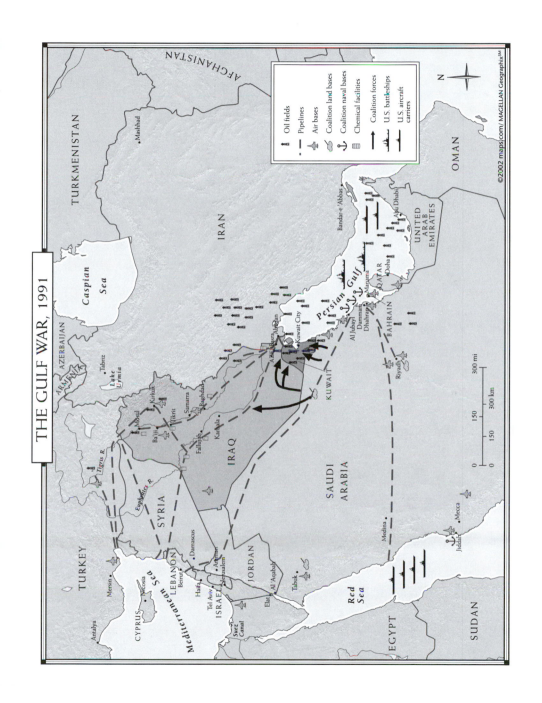

Legend:
- Oil fields
- Pipelines
- Air bases
- Coalition land bases
- Coalition naval bases
- Chemical facilities
- Coalition forces
- U.S. battleships
- U.S. aircraft carriers

©2002 maps.com/ MAGELLAN Geographix℠

300 mi

300 km

150

150

0

0

M

Maastricht Treaty (1991). "Treaty on European Union." Agreed to December 1991; in effect as of November 1, 1993. It was the culmination of the proposals of the *Single European Act* aiming at creation of a fully integrated *common market*, free of *tariffs* and restrictions on movement of *capital* and *labor*. It enhanced the *supranational* aspects of the *European Community* (EC), renaming it the *European Union* (EU). It tried but failed to promote the *Western European Union* (WEU) for collective defense, but did locate a "Common Foreign and Security Policy" (CFSP) in the WEU. It also called for a unified *currency* by 1997–1999, which led to adoption of the euro. Its passage provoked a sharp popular reaction in several countries that caught Europe's governmental *elites* by surprise: in Denmark, a *referendum* narrowly rejected Maastricht, which passed in a second referendum after concessions were made; in Britain, Maastricht provoked a party and parliamentary revolt within the *Conservative* caucus; in France, the majority favoring Maastricht was far smaller than expected; and in Germany, too, the treaty faced a hard constitutional challenge. Maastricht thus revealed profound tensions within the European Community over the pace and the purpose of political and *monetary union* and suggested to some that a *two-speed Europe* solution should be adopted. *See also Amsterdam Treaty (1997); deepening versus widening.*

Macao. A Portuguese colony on the south China coast, established as a trading outpost by Portuguese merchants in 1557. *Kangxi* ordered all Chinese to leave Macao during the 1660s, when he blockaded it as part of an effort to reduce the last *Ming* holdouts on *Taiwan*. He tried to ban the Portuguese from Macao, but local officials connived at their continuing presence, and it subsequently became their main base in China. In 1974, after a *revolution* in Portugal, Macao achieved local *autonomy*. After the return of *Hong Kong* to China in 1997, Macao was the last piece of foreign-occupied Chinese territory. It was returned to China at the end of 1999.

MacArthur, Douglas (1880–1964). U.S. general. MacArthur served in the Philippines in 1903 and then as an aide to his father, who commanded the Pacific theater, 1905–1906. He was an aide to *Theodore Roosevelt*, 1906–1907. He served in Kansas and then as an instructor, 1908–1912. He was appointed to the *general staff*, 1913–1917. He participated in the Veracruz expedition sent into Mexico by *Woodrow Wilson* in 1914. He fought in France during *World War I*, then served with occupation forces in the *Rhineland*. He returned to the Philippines, 1922–1925 and 1928–1930. In 1932 he led an armed expedition that cleared encamped, unemployed veterans from Washington, D.C. In 1935 MacArthur retired from U.S. service to succeed his father as commander of the Philippine Army. Recalled to the colors, he put on a vigorous defense of the Philippines but was pushed back to *Corregidor* and *Bataan* by the Japanese by March 1942. He pledged, partly as a genuinely torn and honorable commander who did not wish to abandon troops he was ordered to leave behind, and partly with characteristic egoism, "I [not we] shall return." He was then made supreme commander of all *Allied* land forces in the Southwest Pacific theater, 1942–1945, by *Franklin Roosevelt*.

MacArthur bridled under the knowledge that it was Admiral *Chester Nimitz*'s naval forces that controlled overall strategy and that Washington viewed the Pacific theater as less important compared with the fighting in Europe. His forces became bogged down in heavy jungle fighting in New Guinea, which they eventually retook from the Japanese. MacArthur then participated in the Nimitz's inspired "island-hopping" campaign, which led to invasions of islands in the Moluccas and Carolines but isolation of large Japanese garrisons on other islands. Some wanted to hop over the Philippines as well, but MacArthur won that fierce argument in the Allied *war council*. In 1944 he commanded the invasion of the Philippines, wading ashore, twice, to ensure the newsreels caught the historic moment. Fighting continued there well into 1945, perhaps detracting from a more rapid advance toward the Japanese *home islands*. His troops also invaded Borneo and Okinawa. He was planning the Allied invasion of Japan when news came of *Hiroshima, Nagasaki*, and Tokyo's *surrender*. MacArthur accepted the formal Japanese surrender in Tokyo Bay aboard the USS Missouri on September 2, 1945. Appointed to head the *occupation* as *Supreme Commander, Allied Powers (SCAP)*, MacArthur enjoyed the powers—if not the formal status—of a Roman proconsul. He moderated demands for retribution, most controversially by refusing Allied demands that *Hirohito* be tried as a war criminal. With firm benevolence MacArthur imposed a democratic and antimilitarist Peace Constitution on Japan, working closely with *Yoshida Shigeru*, and oversaw the *reverse course* in American policy in Asia in the formative years of the *Cold War*. In a storied and deeply controversial career, in which his military reputation was later seriously challenged, his work in Japan remains his greatest achievement.

Recalled to active duty at age 70 during the *Korean Conflict*, MacArthur took command of United Nations forces in the middle of a desperate defensive campaign to save what was left of South Korea from complete conquest by *Communist* North Korea. The UN hold in Korea was reduced to the "Pusan pocket." MacArthur stabilized the defense and then undertook his single greatest military feat: an extraordinary amphibious landing at *Inchon*, 200 miles behind North Korean lines. He then crossed the 38th parallel at the head of UN forces. Under instructions not to tangle with Chinese forces suspected of having crossed the North Korean border, and to report any contacts with the Chinese "volunteers," MacArthur instead loudly and publicly advocated forceful unification of Korea while lying to President *Truman* about reports of Chinese troop concentrations as UN forces approached the Yalu River. MacArthur's forces were nearly overwhelmed when 300,000 Chinese suddenly attacked, pushed the UN forces back, and poured south. After a second retreat, he turned the tide and recaptured Seoul by mid-March. When MacArthur went public with demands that the war be brought home to China, with *nuclear weapons* if need be (he asked for thirty-four bombs to be used on China), Truman had enough of this insubordination and reckless conduct and fired MacArthur on April 11, 1951. The decision was greatly unpopular in the United States at the time, but later was seen by most as deeply wise and courageous, not least because it rescued the principle of civilian primacy over the military. MacArthur returned to a New York City ticker tape parade and widespread adulation. He told supporters in Congress: "In war there is no substitute for victory," but after a somewhat inept run at the presidency MacArthur just faded away into quiet retirement.

Suggested Readings: Richard Finn, *Winners in Peace* (1992); Michael Schaller, *Douglas MacArthur* (1989); Michael Schaller, *American Occupation of Japan* (1985); Stanley Weintraub, *MacArthur's War* (2000).

Macartney mission (1793). A diplomatic mission by Lord George Macartney, in behalf of the *East India Company,* to the Emperor *Qianlong* in China in 1793. Macartney arrived in a British *man-of-war*, which was calculated to impress the Chinese court. Once he got there, Macartney refused to perform the *kowtow*, merely bending a knee as he might to his own king. He was sent away empty-handed except for a message to King *George III* that China required none of his country's goods and declined to establish *diplomatic relations*. In 1816 another East India Company mission was rudely rebuffed. China's foreign trade thus continued confined to the *Cohong system* until it was forced open on the most unfavorable terms by the *Opium Wars*, the *Treaty of Nanjing* (1842), and other *unequal treaties. See also East India Company; Qianlong emperor.*

Macedonia. Macedonia occupies the mountainous buffer region between Greece and the rest of the Balkans. It took its place briefly but spectacularly on the world stage with Philip II (382–336 B.C.E.), who conquered Greece after the *Peloponnesian War* (431–404 B.C.E.), and his son, *Alexander* of Macedon (the Great), who ruled Greece in the fourth century B.C.E. and conquered much of the known world. Subsequently, Macedonia suffered the gifts and vicissitudes of the two great empires that came and conquered, and then ebbed their strength away over the centuries in the eastern Mediterranean and Balkans: the *Roman Empire* and the *Byzantine Empire*. For five centuries after 1380 Macedonia was an *Ottoman* province. It was targeted by Bulgarian annexationist designs in the 1870s and joined to Bulgaria in the *Treaty of San Stefano* (1878), but returned to Turkey at the *Congress of Berlin* (1878). It was the prize sought by all during the *First* and *Second Balkan Wars*. Macedonia was incorporated into the new state of *Yugoslavia* after *World War I*, though a portion remained in Greece and another in Bulgaria. In 1946 it became a republic within the Yugoslav *federation*. It broke with what was left of Yugoslavia (Serbia and Montenegro) in 1992. Greece blocked it from *European Community* and United Nations recognition, on the grounds it has a province of the same name and fears Macedonia's historic claim to that province. Athens agreed to UN membership for Macedonia on condition its flag not fly outside the UN building, as it is the emblem of Alexander of Macedon. The UN solution to this almost surreal dispute was to use a formula pioneered by the *International Monetary Fund*, to wit: admit Macedonia under the cumbersome, but temporary, name "Former Yugoslav Republic of Macedonia," with the problem of terminology to be worked out with Greece later. In 1993 it became the 181st member of the United Nations. A few months later, 300 U.S. troops arrived as UN peacekeepers to deter any Serbian *aggression*. Like other tenuous, new countries in Europe, it asked to join *NATO*. In 1994 Greece imposed an *embargo* and closed off Macedonia's access to the port of Salonika. The *European Union* responded by taking Greece to the *European Court of Justice*. Tensions also arose with Serbia (Yugoslavia) over a *frontier dispute*. In 2001 spillover fighting from *Kosovo* disturbed Macedonia's northern *frontier*. NATO brokered a disengagement agreement and dispatched troops to monitor its implementation.

Machel, Samora (1930–1986). President of Mozambique, 1975–1986. He was the field commander of FRELIMO, a nationalist *guerrilla* movement, during its fight with Portugal from 1964 to 1974. He became president when FRELIMO's political leader, Eduardo Mondlane, was killed by a mail bomb. Machel governed from a doctrinaire, *Marxist* perspective, and his *expropriations* of foreign companies alienated many in the West. However, he was seen as a hero by many others in southern Africa for these same expropriations and for his support of the ANC. Faced with South African economic *sabotage* and military *incursions*, he accommodated to geopolitical reality and signed the

Nkomati Accord (1984) with the *apartheid* regime. He was killed in a suspicious plane crash in 1986, just inside South African territory.

Machiavellian. (1) Philosophical: Akin to the principles of *Niccolò Machiavelli*, in particular his emphasis on expediency over absolute conceptions of morality and his pessimism about the quality of human nature and the dim possibilities for success of schemes of social organization that do not rely ultimately on fear and force. (2) Pejorative: Unscrupulous and dishonest; excessively cunning and full of intrigue; merely self-interested, without higher purpose.

Machiavelli, Niccolò di Bernardo (1469–1527). Florentine political thinker. Like Jonathan Swift, he has been more often misinterpreted and vilified for his honesty than understood or appreciated for his insight. He is surely the only human whose name is regularly used as an adjective to depict the moral character of Satan, often qualified as a demon of *Machiavellian* cunning, duplicity, and low morality. Some regard Machiavelli as the founder of *political science*—in its classical concerns with governance, *power*, *ethics*, and *diplomacy*, not its modern and mostly sterile preoccupations with arcane methodologies and self-referential "theorizing." He lived in greatly turbulent and violent times. Italy was torn by clashing armies of the *city-states* and then overrun by foreign invaders (France in 1493, followed by Spain), and diplomacy was a prime instrument of *statecraft* in a battle for survival that was red in tooth and claw, to paraphrase Tennyson. When the *Medici*, the ruling family of Florence, fled in 1493, the path of opportunity opened to him and he was appointed secretary of The Ten, the new governing council of the Florentine Republic. He held that position to 1512, organizing the Florentine *militia* (he paid a great deal of attention to the problem of citizen armies versus *mercenary* forces and to military problems in general) and undertaking many lesser diplomatic missions, including to Caesar Borgia in 1502. Upon the restoration of the Medici, Machiavelli was arrested, imprisoned, and tortured (1513). He spent the remainder of his adult life seeking public office and longing to return to the practical exercise of power, but was not trusted by the Medici and was given only minor historiographical and diplomatic missions after 1519.

Machiavelli's thinking reflected those realities. His most famous, and still widely read, works are "De Principatibus" ("The Prince," published after his death and later condemned by Pope Clement VIII and other clerics), the "Art of War," and "Discourses on Livy." In military terms, he lived in a transitional time between the agrarian-based *feudal* structures and armies of Europe and newly professional formations: mercenaries and the *cavalry*-heavy "condottieri" of *Renaissance* Italy, whom Machiavelli held in contempt, which were made possible (and then necessary) by the expansion of money economies. This fundamental transformation of the social and economic basis of military power lay at the heart of his conception of the emerging state, and thus of his political thinking as well. As a military theorist and organizer, Machiavelli was determined to displace the unsteady and untrustworthy condottieri and foreign mercenaries with a conscripted civic militia, whose far greater loyalty and reliability would permit Florence more independence in the conduct of its diplomacy and further stabilize its polity. His frank writing about the new nature of warfare—he disassociated thinking about war from ethics or religious purpose, concentrating instead on its factual bases in economics and politics—startled and shocked a population not aware that an end was coming to, and thus yet not inured by brutal disregard for, the abstract but shared moral order sustained by the *res publica Christiana*. Thus, Machiavelli did not waste praise on the ideal condition of peace, the assumed universal good of the *ancien régime* of Medieval Europe, or ritual incantations of old doctrines about *just war*. He wrote instead of more pagan, that is Roman, qualities in the making of war: courage, ferocity, duty, and love of country. In this way, Machiavelli moved European discourse about war from a Medieval preoccupation with the idea of the Christian way of war, combat as the instrument and revelation of God's purposes on Earth as divined by the Church or at least the good conscience of a Christian knight, to the modern idea of republican war, of war for and by the secular state not for high ideals but for what *Richelieu* would later call *raisons d'etat*. Machiavelli tried out his new military theories in a drawn-out siege of rival Pisa, with only mixed success. Empirically, he simply was wrong about militia—or at least, he was several centuries ahead of the times. In Machiavelli's lifetime, and for another 200 years after that, mercenaries, not the conscript armies he envisioned and proposed, dominated the European battlefield.

As a political thinker, Machiavelli was truly exceptional. He laid out an understanding of politics rooted in a profound fear of *anarchy*, which upheld expedience by rulers in choice of means as a regrettable but unavoidable requirement of successful political action, dictated by the underlying wickedness and venality of the governed. He accepted the equivocal nature of public, as opposed to personal, moral judgment, maintaining what *Max Weber* would later call an "ethic of consequences" as the true political ethic, much to be preferred and indeed admired as compared with an "ethic of intentions," which Machiavelli thought weak and foolish (imprudent). He wrote: "Since love and fear can hardly coexist . . . it is far safer to be feared than loved." This emergent nature of the modern state, as based fundamentally on its capacity to make war, first became apparent in the Italy of Machiavelli's lifetime, and he was the first to apprehend it. Less widely recognized, Machiavelli wished for the successful, and if need be ruthless, exercise of power not for its own sake or in a vacuum of values. Instead, he yearned to see princely power advance specific causes he regarded as having inherent moral content, including *republicanism* and the *liberation* of Florence—and even all Italy—from foreign control. He is justly famous for his depiction of the workings of power in the real world. His awareness of the *balance of power*, and intuitive recognition of how the lust for power curls naked and expectant beneath the covers of the most silken idealism, was instinctive, instructive, and brilliant. *See also disarmament; Frederick the Great; friction; Hugo Grotius; Thomas Hobbes; Immanuel Kant; Napoleon I; realism;* Realpolitik; *Jean-Jacques Rousseau; Sébastien le Prestre de Vauban.*

Suggested Readings: John R. Hale, *Machiavelli and Renaissance Italy* (1960); John R. Hale, *War and Society in Renaissance Europe, 1450–1620* (1986); Peter Paret, *The Makers of Modern Strategy* (1986).

machine gun. A belt-fed, water- or air-cooled, automatic weapon that delivers a devastatingly sustained and high rate of fire. Several types were introduced late in the nineteenth century by American inventors who lent their names to early models (Browning, Gatling, Lewis, Maxim, and others). It was first used extensively in combat by the British during the *Zulu Wars*, but the early models often jammed, and some commanders eschewed them. The machine gun came into its own as a weapon of *Great Power* warfare during the *Russo-Japanese War* (1904–1905), where it was heavily used and to great effect. By the early twentieth century one machine-gun crew deployed the equivalent firepower—and over a much longer range—of a company of riflemen from the *Franco-Prussian War* (1870–1871) or a full battalion firing muskets during the *Napoleonic Wars*. Germany relied on machine guns to stop the initial French advance along the Chemin de Dames in 1914, and it thereafter became the dominant defensive weapon of *World War I. See also* élan vital; *revolution in military affairs; trench warfare.*

Machtpolitik. "Power politics." A celebration of conflict among *nations* as the forceful assertion of national will, as embodied in the *state*. Distantly related to *Realpolitik*, this notion soberly recognized that the German Empire was constructed by force of Prussian arms. It also reflected a romantic view of martial virtues and belief that international struggle was morally redemptive. For example, *Helmut von Moltke* (the elder), principal architect of Prussia's *victories* over Denmark (1864), Austria (1866), and France (1870–1871), once said in Machtpolitik vein: "war is a link in the divine order of the world." *See also militarism; social Darwinism.*

Machtstaat. "Power state." In *Nazism*, and more generally in German history, an exaltation of the *state* as a *reified*, organic whole, with a moral force and worth unto itself that far exceeded that of any individual. This view of the state underlay much of the Nazis' appeal to extreme *nationalism* and lent support to their *assertive* and then *aggressive* foreign policy.

Mackenzie-Papineau Rebellion (1837). *See Durham Report; William Lyon Mackenzie.*

Mackenzie, William Lyon (1795–1861). Canadian rebel and Scottish-born MP. He joined forces with French Canadian rebel Louis-Joseph Papineau (1789–1871), who objected to the *union* of the Canadas and to British government in *Québec*. Their joint *rebellions* in *Upper* and *Lower Canada* failed. Mackenzie formed a rebel government in Buffalo, New York, and with aid from Irish-Americans launched cross-border raids from a base in the Niagara region. In *retaliation*, a Canadian military raid of some fifty men sank a rebel ship, the Caroline, while it was berthed in American waters (December 29, 1837), killing one U.S. *citizen*. Hotheads on both sides called for war, and relations deteriorated badly before cooler minds prevailed. By 1840 the Caroline Affair had petered out into stiff *diplomatic protests*. The episode deepened Canadian suspicions that Americans secretly wished to annex Canada (most did not, in fact); it also left unsettled U.S. claims for *reparations*, adding another load to the desultory cargo of Anglo-American relations. *See also Durham Report*.

Mackinder, Halford (1861–1947). British geographer who posited the geographical *pivot of history* and ideas of the *Heartland* and *World Island*, from which he derived the rule: "Who rules east Europe commands the Heartland; who rules the Heartland commands the World Island; who rules the World Island rules the world." His theory was most influential in Germany, where it affected Imperial *war plans* and later fed into *Nazi* ideas about *Lebensraum*, though he personally had no sympathies in that direction. He also influenced American naval *strategy* between the wars and during the early *Cold War*. However, he failed to account for the fact that the following powers controlled much of the "Heartland" without dominating the world: Tsarist Russia, 1815–1917; Nazi Germany, 1941–1944; and the Soviet Union, 1920–1941, 1945–1991. Most glaringly, his theory could not explain why a naval power such as the United States was completely separate from the "World Island," yet was the *preponderant power* for most of the twentieth century. In his later work he also badly neglected *air power*. *See also geopolitics*; Geopolitik; *rimland*.

MacMahon, Marie Patrice (1808–1893). French general. Governor of Algeria, 1864–1870; president of France, 1873–1879. He fought in Algeria and in the *Crimean War*. His entire army, along with himself and Emperor *Napoleon III*, was defeated and captured at *Sedan* during the *Franco-Prussian War*. He held France together after this defeat, savagely crushing the *Paris Commune* and trying vainly to restore a monarchy. He was then elected president of the *Third Republic*. He refused to stage a monarchist *coup* and instead stepped down in 1879.

MacMillan, Harold (1894–1986). British statesman. Minister of defense, 1954–1955; foreign secretary, 1955; prime minister, 1957–1963. He coordinated British diplomacy in North Africa during *World War II* and helped negotiate the *Austrian State Treaty* after it. As prime minister, he sought to play a role as *mediator* between Moscow and Washington. He was ineffective because he took office as Britain's influence began to plummet after the *Suez Crisis* and because he was so personally and politically close to U.S. leaders. In 1960 he spoke in South Africa of the "winds of change" (that is, *decolonization*) sweeping that continent and Asia. While that remark has been cited as a perspicacious and daring warning, it may also be seen as just a pithy observation of unfolding events. *See also Nikita Khrushchev; Partial Test Ban Treaty.*

macroeconomics. A subfield of economics that analyzes large-scale *indicators* and processes, such as a nation's total foreign *debt, GDP, GNP, money supply, balance of trade,* and *balance of payments.*

macropolitics. Analyses that attempt to view political and economic affairs from the vantage point of the *international system* as a whole. *See also balance of power; dependency theory; hegemonic stability theory; Marxism; systems theory.*

macroregion. An area of dense, central population, industry, and trade, surrounded by and influencing a wider, more rural area of weaker and dependent economic development. The idea is most prominently used by some Sinologists to explain China's economic history, as distinct from the overlay of its administrative (governmental) structures during either the Imperial or *Communist* eras.

Madagascar. This large island off Africa's Indian Ocean coast was uninhabited into the first millennium. It was then settled by Malays and Polynesians, who sailed there from Borneo and other southeast Asian islands in ocean-going canoes assisted by monsoon winds. Trade later developed with *Swahili Arabs* of the African coast, and this drew African settlement to the island. Once France established plantations on nearby Réunion and Mauritius, slaves were taken from Madagascar. This local *slave trade* stimulated political consolidation by the hitherto fragmented Malagasy: as happened also on mainland Africa, small coastal states and tribes with first access to firearms raided and sold their inland neighbors into *slavery.* Out of this prolonged contest the Hova state of Merina, under Namipoina (r. 1787–1810), emerged to dominate and conquer most of the central plateau. Under Radam I (r. 1810–1828), about two-thirds of Madagascar paid homage to Merina, which for the rest of the century was governed by a sequence of queens. In 1820 Christian *missionaries* arrived. In 1835 the mission schools were closed by the Hova elite, which feared external influences. In 1861 a Hova succession struggle turned violent. Missions were again allowed after 1868, and by the end of the century most Malagasy had converted. In 1885 the first in a series of Merina-French wars broke out, each furthering French domination. Madagascar thus became a French *protectorate* in 1885, though Merina disputed this claim. France sent a large force to the island in 1895 and declared it a formal *colony* in 1896. Resistance to French rule continued for years. During *World War II* it was occupied by Britain and the *Free French*. In 1945 it was made an *overseas territory*. In 1946–1947 rice riots led to open rebellion, which France repressed with ruthless ferocity. Madagascar then gained *autonomy* in 1958 within the *French Community* and full *independence* in 1960 as the Malagasy Republic (the name was changed back to Madagascar in 1975) under the moderate nationalist leader and first Prime Minister, Philibert Tsiranana. Unrest at continuing French *colons* economic dominance led to a *coup* in 1972 and a radical regime, which *nationalized* French property and sought closer ties with China. In 1979 all foreigners were expelled. In 1990 the regime cracked, a victim of its own radicalism and mismanagement, and a multiparty system was reintroduced. Peaceful elections were held in 1993.

Madeira. This uninhabited Atlantic island was settled by Portugal in the 1420s. Its plantations were the first to be worked by imported African *slaves*, an example that later spread to tropical plantations in the Americas. *See also Canary Islands.*

Madison, James (1751–1836). U.S. statesman. Secretary of state, 1801–1809; *Republican-Democratic* president, 1809–1817. He was among those who saw success in the *American Revolution* as requiring a strong central government, but preferred this to be Congress rather than the *executive* power favored by *Alexander Hamilton*. He was involved in the *Louisiana Purchase* and in the *embargo* imposed by *Jefferson*, 1807–1809, with whom he had cofounded the *Democratic Party* in 1792. As secretary of state and as president, Madison looked to "republican" or Jeffersonian (that is, economic) substitutes for *force* in foreign policy. Facing the chaos and danger of the *Napoleonic Wars*, in which American citizens were *impressed*, ships seized, and trade interfered with, he failed to prepare the nation for war or to provide an effective *deterrent* to Britain and France. For 12 years he searched for a form of peaceful coercion, a "republican alternative" to war, and thought he found it in a denial of trade. What he failed to realize was that Britain and France were locked in a mortal combat in which trade (Britain's *blockade* versus the French *Continental System*) had become, as it had been for the *mercantilists*, a weapon of war, not a tool of peacemaking. Moreover, he wrongly regarded Britain as the greater threat to the United States, partly because its ships were the most evident and its blockade the most effective. He did not seem to grasp the long-term threat to the United States should France achieve *hegemony* over Europe. Most important, his policy of bluff and bluster failed because the United States remained a small and weak nation, without a real navy or other armed means to enforce its threats.

Instead of accommodating to that reality and compromising on claims of *neutral rights*, Madison chose to shout loudly at London, although all he carried was a gentleman's walking stick, when his adversary had the rather more impressive club of the *Royal Navy*. With the country ill-prepared and virtually unarmed, he asked Congress for a *declaration of war*, commencing the *War of 1812*. Hoping for a quick seizure of *Upper Canada* so he could trade it back to Britain for maritime concessions, he authorized an *invasion*. It fizzled, though American troops did manage to burn the Upper Canada parliament in York (Toronto). The next year, battle-hardened British troops, veterans of the *Napoleonic Wars*, invaded the United States and in retaliation burned the White House in Washington. Madison fled the city, to wander the Virginia countryside for three days. Worse might have come had not the *Treaty of Ghent* been agreed: before the *Hundred Days* in Europe, the British were beginning transfers of troops from France, amid public calls for vengeance against the former, upstart *colony* that had attacked while they fought (as it was thought in London) to defend international liberties from the great tyrant in Paris. From the U.S. point of view, victory in the *Battle of New Orleans*— actually irrelevant to the outcome of the war and to the peace, which had already been made—meant that "Mr. Madison's War" might be proclaimed a triumph, even a "second war of independence." It was no such thing. It was more a close escape from the consequences of a disastrously naïve and ideological diplomacy, which having blundered into war was fortunate not to have had a draconian peace imposed upon the land.

Suggested Reading: J. C. A. Stagg, *Mr. Madison's War* (1983).

Mafeking, Siege of (1899–1900). One of several *sieges* of garrison towns by the *Boers* during the *Second Boer War*. The siege at Mafeking became a cause célèbre in the British press until it was lifted and the Boer Army crushed. That forced the Boers into shifting from *conventional warfare* to *guerrilla* tactics, which prolonged the war. In a quaint holdover from an earlier era of warfare, fighting during the siege always stopped on Sundays.

Maghreb. "al-Maghrib" ("The West"). The western half of North Africa, populated mainly by *Berber* peoples. It includes modern Algeria, Libya, Mauritania, Morocco, and Tunisia, as well as *Ceuta* and *Melilla*. Before the twentieth century, its life revolved around major coastal cities, supported by interior hinterlands that sustained nomadic tribes. In the twelfth century, it was united under the Almohad *Caliphate*, which also ruled Muslim Spain. However, it subsequently broke into three parts under rival Berber dynasties: the Hafsids, the Wadids, and the Marinds. The city-states of the Maghreb all were termini of the trans-Saharan trade and buyers of *sudanese* military *slaves* into the mid-nineteenth century. *See also Barbary States; Ifriqiya; Tripoli.*

Suggested Reading: J. Abun Nasr, *A History of the Maghreb* (1971).

Maghreb Union (UMA). A loose regional association of Algeria, Libya, Mauritania, Morocco, and Tunisia. It was founded in 1989 to coordinate policy on matters of regional interest and to negotiate with the *European Union*.

Maginot Line. A French system of fortification-in-depth from Belgium to the Swiss border, built between 1929 and 1934 and representing perhaps the purest form of military *deterrence* in the twentieth century. It was named for André Maginot (1877–1932), minister for war. Belgium also fortified, but independently of France and in front of the Maginot Line, along the Meuse River. In 1936 Belgium renounced its security treaty with France and returned to reliance on a formal, legal *neutrality*, which would fail, again, in 1940. France deemed the *Ardennes* impassible to *armor*, but also recoiled at the expense of extending the Line and the logistical difficulties of constructing fortifications in the densely populated area on the Franco-Belgian border. That left 250 miles of exposed front, which invited a *flank* attack. When the test came, in the *Battle of France*, the Maginot fortifications worked: where assaulted, they stopped the German advance. However, the main *Panzer* thrust went around the Line, through the "impenetrable" Ardennes and across the Belgian frontier. French guns in fixed positions were circumvented and many failed to fire a shot against the invader. Hundreds of thousands of defenders surrendered after offering just token resistance, and some not even that. As a result, the *British Expeditionary Force* (BEF) was cut off and thrown back and had to be evacuated from *Dunkirk*. *See also fortification; Great Wall; Schlieffen Plan; Sébastein le Prestre de Vauban.*
   Suggested Reading: J. M. Hughes, *To the Maginot Line* (1971).

Maginot spirit. A mood of *defeatism* pervading France between the world wars that in a real sense had begun with the *French Army mutiny* of 1917. This mood was symbolized and reinforced by the exclusively defensive posture of French security policy, represented by the *Maginot Line*, which was contrary to a long French military tradition of offensive warfare. The idea that France could never again take the offensive against Germany paralyzed its diplomats and army, contributed to the *appeasement* policy of the 1930s, led directly to the *Phony War*, and presaged French collapse and *surrender* in 1940.

Magyars. (1) Native Hungarians. (2) The Hungarian landed *aristocracy*. The original Magyars were barbarian invaders from Central Asia whose swarms of mounted archers raided and overran much of central Europe in the tenth century. They were beaten by Henry and Otto of Saxony at Merseberg (933) and Lechfield (955) and, later, by the *Teutonic Knights*. They were beaten back from Italy as well and by the twelfth century settled in what is today Hungary.

Mahan, Alfred Thayer (1840–1914). American naval strategist and founder of modern naval strategic theory. He wrote enormously influential books on the idea of *sea power*. His great work, "The Influence of Sea Power Upon History, 1660–1783" (3 vols., 1890–1892), which he conceived as the counterpart to *Jomini*'s work on land warfare, greatly shaped naval thinking, naval strategy, and naval procurement policy for most naval powers for at least another half-century. He argued that, contrary to theories emphasizing *land power*, the dominant powers in the modern age were sea powers with strings of overseas bases, possessions, and markets, which took advantage of the efficiency and uninterrupted advantages of sea transport and travel. Just as Jomini downplayed the importance of technological changes on land, Mahan maintained that, despite advances in weaponry and armor, the principles of naval strategy and warfare remained constant and that dominant power was linked to martial and commercial command of the seas and their great *trade routes* and overseas markets (trade protection and interdiction). Again like Jomini on land, Mahan emphasized the need for concentrating forces at sea to deliver stunning, decisive blows at critical junctures. Some have attributed to his theories the interest of Germany and Britain in twentieth-century naval dominance (Great Britain, given its long history of sea power, hardly needed encouragement). Others point to U.S. interest in a large *battleship* navy and acquisition of overseas bases, as conceived and carried out by *Theodore Roosevelt* in the period of rapid imperial expansion during and after the *Spanish-American War*. That almost certainly exaggerates Mahan's influence: Roosevelt appears to have arrived at "big navy" views independently of, and indeed earlier than, Mahan. Still, Mahan's work is known to have influenced *Winston Churchill*, as first sea lord, and *Kaiser Wilhelm II*. His greatest influence was probably posthumous: the U.S. and NATO policy of *containment* during the *Cold War* that set up a circle of alliances around the Soviet Union, linked by naval bases and forces sustained by sea power, owed something to Mahan. *See also geopolitics; Trafalgar.*

mahdi. "Divinely Guided One." A title taken by numerous historical figures claiming to be the embodied fulfillment of the messianic tradition in *Islam*, especially, but not solely, within the *shi'ite* branch. The tradition looks to a temporal—but divinely anointed—ruler, a foreordained leader who will bring a final reign of righteousness to the world through revelation of the "hidden imam" and a final social transformation. This eschatological vision of history kept the Faithful on their toes, constantly on the lookout for a sign of the arrival of the mahdi and the beginning of the transformation to a more just and godly society. The best known (in the West) claimant of the title was the Sudanese Mahdi of Dongola, Muhammad Ahmed bin Abdallah (1840–1885). In 1881 he proclaimed himself the mahdi, and within two years overthrew Egyptian control of Sudan. In 1885 he took Khartoum, where his "ansar," or disciples (known alternately to the British as "whirling dervishes" and more disparagingly as the "Fuzzy-Wuzzies"), clashed bloodily with a British expedition, besieged and eventually killed *Charles "Chinese" Gordon* and his garrison, and thus helped topple *Gladstone*'s government. His successor ruled northern Sudan for another 13 years until defeated by a British expedition under Kitchener at the bloody slaughter—which it was, more than it was a battle—at *Omdurman* (1898). His great-grandson, Sadiq al-Mahdi, set up a *theocracy* in Sudan in 1986. In 1980 a Chadian *refugee* was acclaimed mahdi by his followers in Nigeria, and 10,000 died in religious bloodletting. Another claim led to hundreds of deaths in *Mecca* in 1979; and so on.

Mahmud II (1785–1839). Ottoman sultan, 1808–1839. His authority was repeatedly challenged by *Mehemet Ali* of Egypt. Mahmud fought a losing war with Russia, 1809–1812, losing *Bessarabia* to Russia. He lost control of Serbia and Greece after the *Greek War of Independence, 1821–1829*, including the destruction of his fleet at *Navarino*. He lost a related war to Russia, 1827–1828, and might have been destroyed and lost even *Constantinople* had not the other *Great Powers* intervened. He lost Syria and Palestine to Mehemet Ali in the 1830s. In response to these setbacks, he sought to stem the decline of the *Ottoman Empire* through modernizing reforms and destruction of the *Janissaries*. His was a radical effort, comparable to *Peter the Great*'s in its symbolic banning of traditional clothing and many social habits. While the reforms provided elements of modernization, they alienated important elites. The Ottomans thus remained reliant on external props—first British, later German—to remain intact and in power over their sprawling and fractious empire.

***Maine*, USS, sinking of (1898).** This U.S. *warship* was blown up, cause still unknown, along with 260 sailors, in Havana Harbor on February 15, 1898. The slogan, "Remember the Maine!" became a rallying cry of the *yellow press*, calling for *intervention* in Cuba against Spain, and a *casus belli* for launching the *Spanish-American War*. Theories about the cause of the explosion vary from a faulty boiler (in which case the U.S. casus belli was spurious) to a mine or torpedo planted either by the Cubans to draw the United States into their rebellion, or by the Spanish, for unclear motives—in the unlikely event the Spanish were responsible, that would have to rank among the more stupid decisions of the nineteenth century.

mainland China. A mostly archaic term used to refer to the People's Republic of China to distinguish it from *Taiwan (Republic of China)* without signaling which China the speaker recognized as more *legitimate*. *See also* expulsion; *two Chinas policy.*

Majapahit. A syncretic *Hindu-Muslim* kingdom on Java during the fourteenth and fifteenth centuries. It maintained extensive claims on several of the larger islands, including *Kalimantan* and *Sumatra*, and was a substantial regional naval power. It was the major state in the Indonesian archipelago encountered by European traders.

Maji-Maji Rebellion (1905–1906). *See Tanganyika.*

Majlis. An *Islamic* parliament, notably that of Iran, but also in several other Muslim countries.

majority rule. (1) A basic principle of representative government, resting legitimate authority in the expressed will of an adult majority, with respect for rights of minorities. (2) A term for government by black majorities, which followed transition from white-minority or colonial regimes in former Portuguese Africa, Rhodesia, Namibia, and South Africa from c. 1975–1990. (3) A decision-making device in which *multilateral* decisions within *international organizations* are taken by majority vote, rather than under the *unanimity rule*. *See also elitism; popular sovereignty; power sharing.*

Major, John (b. 1943). British prime minister. He succeeded *Margaret Thatcher* in an internal party coup; to the surprise of most observers (and pollsters), he also won the next general election. He led Britain during the *Gulf War*, and was a strong supporter of tough United Nations resolutions on Iraq and later consistent enforcement. After wavering on the *Maastricht Treaty*, he put his career and his government on the line in July 1993, threatening his own party with a snap election it would surely lose if his backbenchers failed to ratify Maastricht. That maneuver briefly undercut earlier criticism about political weakness. He authorized secret talks with the *IRA* in 1993 and signed a breakthrough agreement with the Republic of Ireland regarding *Ulster.* Party opposition (partly based on class prejudice about his lack of advanced education), a public dullness, and exhaustion with sixteen years of Tory rule ended his stint as prime minister.

Malabar coast. The southwestern coast of the Indian subcontinent.

Malacca. A small Muslim state founded in the fourteenth century. It was conquered by the Portuguese in 1511 (by Alfonso de Albuquerque), after which it became a center of the *spice trade*. It was captured by the Dutch in 1641. It was held by the British, 1795–1802 and 1811–1818, during and after the *Napoleonic Wars*. It became a British colony from 1824. It was occupied by Japan during *World War II*. It became part of the Federation of Malaya in 1957.

Malacca Straits. A strategic and heavily traveled waterway located between Malaysia and Sumatra.

Malagasy Republic. The former name of Madagascar, 1960–1975.

Malan, Daniel François (1874–1959). South African prime minister, 1948–1954. Malan was a coarse racist convinced that he knew directly the will of the deity and that God insisted on separation of the races. He introduced legal *apartheid* to South Africa after leading the *National Party* to electoral victory. The country was thus set face against the prevailing winds of *self-determination* and *decolonization*. Several decades of deepening isolation from the *community of nations* followed. *See also Fredrik Willem de Klerk; Nelson Mandela.*

Malawi. The Malawi ("Fire People") were organized into small, decentralized *tribute* states from about the fifteenth century. Arab slavers raided the Bantu of Malawi in the nineteenth century. The *slave trade* was eradicated and the British Central African Protectorate, later called "Nyasaland," was proclaimed in 1891, partly at the behest of *missionaries* who wished to keep *Cecil Rhodes* out of the area. Nyasaland was joined to the *Central African Federation*, 1954–1963. It gained its independence in 1964 as "Malawi," and became a *republic* in 1966 under Hastings Banda Kamuzu (1900?–1997), prime minister, 1964–1971, and then president-for-life. He bought *peace* for his regime at the price of much accommodation of South African interests and considerable repression at home. Although a *frontline* state, Malawi mainly kept a low foreign policy profile and stayed out of the many *regional wars*, although it was compelled to absorb large numbers of *refugees* from neighboring Mozambique. After a severe drought and much public unrest against the Banda government, 1992–1993, many donor nations suspended aid. A *referendum* in 1993 called 63 percent for a pluralist democracy. In May 1994, the aged Banda was thrown out in Malawi's first multiparty election.

Malaya. The Malay peninsula was dominated by *Hindu* kingdoms in the second half of the first millennium, including the Kingdom of Langkasuka, centered on Kedeh. The Sri Vijaya state dominated much of the peninsula, in rivalry with Kedeh, from the eighth through the thirteenth centuries. For the next several centuries Malaya was a locale of diverse minor states; a crossroads of Hindu, *Muslim*, and Chinese cultures; and a battleground for more powerful foreign invaders from Java, Aceh, and Siam, and from the seventeenth century, also from the Netherlands' colony at Batavia (Jakarta). In 1641 the Dutch took *Malacca* away from the Portuguese (who had conquered it in 1511). The Bugis, a Sulawesi people, now joined the fray, capturing the sultanate of Johor at the tip of the Malay peninsula in 1721. The British arrived in 1786, in form of the *East India Company* (EIC), which established a base at Penang. From 1791 the EIC paid *tribute* to the sultan of Kedah. In 1819 "John Company" founded *Singapore*, and in 1824 the Company acquired Malacca from the Dutch. Penang, Malacca, and Singapore were thereafter jointly administered as the Straits Settlements. Siam also invaded the Malay peninsula at this time, overrunning and overseeing Kedah, 1821–1841. Britain and Siam then jockeyed for control, with Britain securing full control by 1867. In 1896 four Malay states were formed into the Federated Malay States under a British resident general. Five more Malay states were joined to the Federation by 1914. The next signal event occurred when the British garrison at Singapore was overwhelmed by a Japanese attack early in *World War II* and surrendered to *Yamashita* on February 15, 1942. The colony was not liberated until 1945. In 1946 the British established a composite colony of all their Malay holdings, leading to sharp ethnic conflicts among the peninsula's ethnically Chinese, Indian, and Malay populations. In 1948 Britain instead established a *protectorate* (Federation of Malaya), 1948–1957, as a looser constitutional arrangement wherein its nine Malay colonies were joined administratively to Penang and Malacca. A *Communist* rebellion ("The Emergency") began in 1948, which it took British and *Commonwealth* troops a decade to repress. Malaya was an independent republic, 1958–1963. It then joined with *Sabah, Sarawak*, and Singapore to form *Malaysia*.

Malayan Emergency (1948–1958). *See Malaya.*

Malay archipelago. The Southeast Asian island group comprising the principal islands of Borneo, Celebes, the Moluccas, the Philippines, Sumatra, Timor, and many smaller islands.

Malaysia. A Federation of Malaysia, amalgamating *Malaya, Sabah, Sarawak* and *Singapore*, was formed in 1963. Singapore departed the Federation in 1965 to become an independent *city-state*. Tunku Abdul Rahman (1903–1990), prime minister of Malaya, 1957–1963, was prime minister of Malaysia, 1963–1970. His was a voice for moderation, whether of internal ethnic conflicts between Chinese and Malays or interstate conflict. He oversaw the founding of the Malay and then Malaysian Republic. The latter *union* was met by Indonesian hostility in the *Konfrontasi*. There was also tension with the Philippines. Malaysia was a founding member of ASEAN, through which it sought to insulate itself from the war in *Indochina*, and in which it prospered. Even with the departure of Singapore, Malaysia remained ethnically divided between Malays and Chinese. It lays claim to some of the *Spratlys*. Mahathir bin Mohamad became prime minister in 1981. Under his leadership, which grew increasingly authoritarian by the 1990s, Malaysia steered a more confrontational course with the West, though mostly on symbolic issues rather than on matters of trade or security. Despite its relative poverty and weakness, in the late 1980s it was prominent in an unsuccessful drive by a *Third World* coalition to open the *Antarctic* to mineral exploitation on the basis of the *common heritage principle*. When the *Cold War ended*, Malaysia repeatedly raised strenuous objections to Western notions of *human rights* at the *World*

Human Rights Conference, and, in general, while discriminating against its Indian and Chinese minority communities. In 1993 it announced it would increase defense spending from 2 to 6 percent of the gross national product over the next 10 years, to keep pace with the new Asian *arms race*. It experienced a severe economic contraction, 1997–1998, during the *Asian financial crisis*. It responded uniquely in the region, rejecting *International Monetary Fund* loans, *tied aid*, and *structural adjustment* advice, and instead imposing draconian fiscal and currency controls. Meanwhile, Mahathir Mohamad gave vent to absurd *anti-Semitic* explanations of the currency speculation and crisis, deflecting all charges of his own government's mismanagement of the economy. In 2000 he purged his closest rival on trumped-up sex and corruption charges.

Suggested Reading: Barbara Andaya and Leonard Andaya, *A History of Malaysia*, 2nd ed. (2001).

Maldives. Formed of some 2,000 islands, this archipelago is populated primarily by Muslims, with an independent history dating back 1,000 years. It was made a British *protectorate*, 1887–1965, but enjoyed limited *autonomy* after 1948. In 1965 it resumed a status as an independent *sultanate*. In 1968 it became a *republic*. In 1988 India's intercession prevented an invasion by a ragtag band of *mercenaries* from succeeding.

Malenkov, Georgi Maximilianovich (1902–1988). Premier of the Soviet Union, 1953–1955. He helped *Stalin* destroy the *kulaks* and was always close to the great dictator after 1930. He joined the *Politburo* in 1946. He succeeded Stalin as party secretary in 1953, but within weeks was relegated to a figurehead position. Thereafter, he suffered repeated demotions. In 1957 he was expelled from the *Central Committee* and eventually was made a *non-person*.

Mali Empire. This great inland Muslim *empire* ruled a huge swath of West Africa for centuries. It was founded by *Mande* peoples who expanded all through the thirteenth century, conquering non-Mande peoples as well, to the new termini of the trans-Saharan *trade route*, which ended at Timbuktu and Gao. Mali's *Islamicized* ruling class, whose power rested on a large army (perhaps 100,000 troops and 10,000 *cavalry*) exacted *slaves* and *tribute* from *Songhay*, which it had cut off from control of the Saharan trade routes, as well as from the Wolof of Senegal and other areas and peoples. Mali's capital, Timbuktu, hosted a great Muslim university ("madrassa"). After 1360 the Keita *dynasty*, which governed Mali, fell prey to internal rivalry and a resurgence of Songhay power, and Songhay and the Wolof broke away. Timbuktu fell to the *Tuareg* in 1433, while Songhay forced Mali back to the valleys of the Gambia and Nile rivers. Mali survived, but in severely truncated form and as a much poorer and less powerful state. In the late sixteenth century Moroccan power was ascendant. It utilized early coastal access to firearms to expand deep into the desert and seized control of the ancient caravan (salt, gold, and slave) trade. A major Moroccan expedition, 1590–1591, conquered Songhay, including portions of the old Mali empire, so that Morocco governed a vast desert and *tributary* and slave-raiding empire stretching to Timbuktu and Jenne. Mali was thus ruled from far-off Morocco until the nineteenth century. Then a great upheaval erupted in the deep desert in the form of several *jihads*, including by the *Tukolor empire*, which were part of a larger Islamic revival that also stirred the *Fulbe*. However, this effort at religious and political unification ran into superior French military forces penetrating from the coast under instructions to consolidate the French Empire in West Africa.

Suggested Readings: J. F. A. Ajayi and Michael Crowder, eds., *History of West Africa*, 2 vols. (1974); N. Levtzion, *Ancient Ghana and Mali* (1973).

Mali, Republic of. Upon the French conquest of Senegal and the interior of much of West Africa and defeat of *Samori Touré*, this area was renamed "French Soudan." In 1898 it was incorporated into *French West Africa*. In 1946 it was declared an *overseas territory*, but in 1958 it became *autonomous* within the *French Community* as the "Soudan Republic." In 1959 it attempted a *union* with Senegal (the "Mali Federation") but this quickly broke up and it changed its name to Mali, after the ancient empire, in 1960. It withdrew from the *Communauté Financière Africaine* (CFA) currency zone, 1962–1967, with disastrous results. In 1968 a coup ended civilian government in Mali. In 1985 an old dispute with Burkina Faso over the Agache border region revived, leading to military clashes. This desperately poor, desert country, along with the rest of the *Sahel*, suffered through three decades of drought in the late twentieth century. That destroyed its economy, made *refugees* of many of its *citizens*, and kept its politics unstable—including fighting with the Tuareg in the mid-1990s over land expropriation and cultural repression, which led to more dislocated populations of refugees. A *one-party state* until 1992, Mali's subsequent elections during the 1990s did not inspire either internal or international confidence in the results.

Malplaquet, Battle of (1709). *See War of the Spanish Succession.*

Malta. This island state is strategically located in the middle of the Mediterranean. As such, it was successively part of several ancient Mediterranean empires, including those of the Phoenicians, Greeks (ancient and *Byzantine*), Carthaginians, *Roman*, and Arab (*Islamic*). The *Normans* conquered Malta in the late eleventh century, and it became a key base of Christian armies (and pilgrims) heading for the *Holy Land* during the *Crusades*. When the Crusader state in *Jerusalem* fell, its defeated knightly defenders retreated to Cyprus and Malta, which was ruled by the *Sovereign Military Order of Malta*, 1530–1798. The *Habsburgs* and *Ottomans* struggled over Malta, 1564–1565, when the

Knights resisted a siege by 20,000 Ottomans. *Napoleon* captured Malta on his way to invade Egypt in 1798, ending rule by the Knights. The British *block-aded* and captured Malta from the French in 1800. It was to be restored to independence under terms of the *Treaty of Amiens*, but, when that ill-fated peace broke down, Malta was annexed by Britain (1814). It thereafter became the main British naval base in the central Mediterranean and was second only to *Gibraltar* in strategic importance. In the 1920s and 1930s Britain warded off demands by *Mussolini* that Malta be ceded to Italy. From 1940 to 1943 it stood against constant Italian and then German air attacks and played a vital role in disruption of the *Axis* sea *supply lines* in north Africa. It was next used in launching the *invasions* of Sicily and Italy. The population of the entire island was later given a decoration for valor. Malta gained independence in 1964 and became a *republic* in 1974. Britain closed its naval base in 1979, ending a 180-year presence, and Malta became *nonaligned*. From 1980 to 1985 it was involved in a *dispute* with Libya over *oil* exploration within conflicting claims to *Exclusive Economic Zones*, in which Libya used its navy to prevent Maltese drilling. The dispute was resolved by a compromise in 1985. In 1989 Malta declared itself a *nuclear weapons–free zone*. In 1994 the *European Union* advanced Malta's position on a membership waiting list.

Malthus, Thomas Robert (1766–1834). English economist. He argued that optimism about the perfectibility of the human condition, such as character-ized the *Enlightenment*, was misplaced because of the *law of diminishing returns*. Instead, he said, there was a tendency in nature for *population* to increase faster than the production of *food* and other essentials of human existence. In his famous "Essay on the Principle of Population" (1798), published an-onymously, he wrote: "Population, when unchecked, increases in a geomet-rical ratio. Subsistence increases only in an arithmetical ratio." He thought that population, left unchecked, would double every 25 years, a fact that should shatter *Enlightenment* hopes, as in the writings of *Rousseau*, for human social and moral progress. The inevitable result must instead be the ride of the "Four Horsemen of the Apocalypse": *war, disease, famine,* and death. Un-happily for Malthus' good name, he described these grave misfortunes as "pos-itive checks" on human population—although he did not take any joy from this gloomy forecast and was by all accounts in his personal affairs an amiable and pleasant man. Nonetheless, his reputation—like Jonathan Swift's and *Machiavelli's*—ever after suffered from misplaced accusations of supposed mis-anthropy. More deservedly, he was criticized for opposing minimum wage laws and poor relief. More happily, Malthus' predictions were not fulfilled because agricultural and technological advances—from draining swamps to new crop varieties to vast increases in worker *productivity* attendant on *industrialization*—along with widespread birth control in more prosperous societies, changed the basic equation by accelerating economic *growth* and limiting population. This "demographic transition" was oft repeated elsewhere: as societies grew richer and healthier, their populations boomed for a generation or so, then leveled off, and finally started to decline. Latter-day *Malthusians* sometimes converted Malthus' observations into a raw justification for social inaction concerning poverty, public health, and starvation. Charles Darwin was influenced in another direction, toward his remarkable theory of natural selection as a response to population increase and competition for scarce food supplies. *See also agricultural revolution; green revolution; growth; logistic; population.*

Malthusian. A shorthand term used to describe the dire possibility that population increase in the *Third World* tends always to exceed *food* supply, leading to *famine* and other social and political disruptions, including *revolution* and *war*. Critics point out, with considerable justice, that a sole focus on reproduction deflects attention from underlying economic and social problems, which may be more important to long-term *population* control. *See also Thomas Robert Malthus; zero population growth.*

Malvinas. *See Falkland Islands.*

Mamluks. Also known as Mamelukes. The term meant "owned," or "*slave*," but carried the additional connotation of "white male slave." This was because most Mamluks were Central Asian–Turkic slaves who, starting in the ninth century, were imported to Syria and Egypt by Muslim *caliphs* (the Abbasids) to reinforce then-failing Arab armies all over the empire. The Mamluk specialty was mounted archery. A Mamluk slave dynasty ruled large parts of northern India for a time after 1206. The Mamluks were brought to Egypt by *Salāh-ed-Dīn* (Saladin, 1137–1193), who overthrew the Berber Fatamids in all but name and replaced their army with loyal Mamluk soldiers. From 1250, after crushing a French *Crusading* army under Louis IX, a Mamluk rebellion left them in control of Egypt. This period is conventionally divided in two: rule by the Bahri (River) Mamluks, 1250–1382, and by the Burji (Citadel) Mamluks, 1382–1517. In 1260 the Mamluks defeated the *Mongols* in Galilee. The next year the Abbasid caliphate moved to Cairo from Baghdad, which had fallen in 1258. The Mamluks actually benefited from Mongol disruption of northern *trade routes*, which diverted goods into Mamluk ships plying the Indian Ocean and Red Sea. They expanded into *Alwa*, in southern *Nubia*, pushing that Christian state further south after 1316. The Mamluks also governed Palestine and Syria until 1400, when a Mamluk army was beaten at Aleppo by *Tamerlane*, and Syria was lost to them for a time. It was later recovered, as Tamerlane's "empire" fell apart upon his death.

Because the children of Mamluks were originally forbidden to become knights, the Mamluks continually drew fresh supplies of Turkish-Russian slaves to renew their military formations. The Mamluks failed to adapt to the *gunpowder revolution*. They thus lost Syria again and Egypt, too, to the *Janis-*

saries, the firearm-bearing troops of the Ottomans, 1516–1517. The Mamluks thereafter became vassals of the Turkish empire, governing Egypt in the name of the Ottomans to 1798. Though numbering just 10,000–12,000 at their peak, they remained among the most feared militaries of the Middle East. As the Ottomans declined after the sixteenth century, Mamluk power slowly revived, even as the Mamluks—cut off from their old supply of Turkish and Slavic slaves—evolved into a hereditary caste. Internal instability invited foreign intervention, however. In 1798 some 6,000 Mamluk *cavalry* were slaughtered in less than an hour, in the shadows of the Pyramids, by *Napoleon*'s cannon and infantry. The French lost just 30 men, decisively proving that the once-feared power of centuries past was no match for the rising power of industrial Europe. In 1811 *Mehemet Ali* finished off the Mamluks in a carefully planned massacre of their leaders.

Suggested Readings: David Ayalon, *The Mamluks and Naval Power* (1965); Thomas Phillip and Ulrich Haarmaan, eds., *The Mamluks in Egyptian Politics and Society* (1998).

managed trade. Where *states* agree to mutual *quotas* and other mechanisms to control the flow of trade. A synonym is *directed trade*. It is often just a euphemism for *protectionism*. *See also fair trade; free trade.*

Manchester School. A nineteenth-century school of economic theory that argued for British leadership in establishing international *free trade* and adopted a *laissez-faire* attitude on questions of both economics and social reform. Its main figures were John Bright (1811–1889), organizer and member of one of the original Peace Societies and anti–Corn Law activist, and Richard Cobden (1804–1865), the quintessential apostle of *free trade*.

Manchukuo. "Land of the Manchus." A Japanese *puppet state* set up in occupied *Manchuria*, 1932–1945. *Pu Yi*, the last *Qing* emperor of China, was installed as emperor. Only the *Axis* states recognized it. Ordinary Japanese migrated there in substantial numbers, even though Chinese *guerrilla* resistance continued for years. Japan also invested heavily, though to little gain, including by the *zaibatsu*. Manchukuo was overrun by Soviet forces at the end of *World War II*.

Manchuria. The historic homeland of the *Manchus*, and three northeastern provinces of *Imperial China*—Liaoning, Heilongjiang, and Jilin. Some object to the use of "Manchuria," insisting on referring to this territory solely as part of China. Manchuria was the home to semi-nomadic Jürchen peoples who repeatedly launched invasions of China proper, but in more recent centuries was itself invaded and fought over by nearby *Great Powers* (Japan and Russia). Part of Manchuria was briefly occupied by the *Han Empire*. From 1122 to 1234 Jürchen warriors ruled northern China ("Jin empire"). After their retreat, they took subsidies from the *Ming*. Bridging the sixteenth and seventeenth centuries, *Nurgaci* laid the foundation for the Manchu conquest of China as he consolidated Manchuria and reorganized it as a martial state. The *Qing* emperors forbade Chinese settlement there, marking the line with a willow ditch that ran the length of the border. Russians penetrated Manchuria economically and built roads and rails across the territory toward the end of the nineteenth century. They occupied it directly after the *Boxer Rebellion*. Japan seized part of Manchuria in the *First Sino-Japanese War*, but was forced to return it by the *Triple Intervention*. Japan then attacked Russia in Manchuria in 1904 during the *Russo-Japanese War*. The region was returned to China in the *Treaty of Portsmouth*, with both Japan and Russia retaining transit rights and garrisons. In 1906 Japan built the Manchurian Railway, enabling the *Guandong Army* to fully penetrate and live off the region. This also ensured ongoing conflict with China. In 1907 Japan and Russia secretly divided Manchuria into north and south *spheres of influence*, a de facto division that persisted into *World War I*, when Japan issued its *Twenty-one Demands* (1915) and the *Russian Revolutions of 1917* focused Russian attention on internal crisis. Japan seized upon Russian defeat in World War I and its subsequent severe internal divisions to increase its own presence in Manchuria, further infiltrating its politics, economy, and national life. In 1931 the Japanese staged the *Mukden incident*, invaded Manchuria, and set up a *puppet state* called *Manchukuo*. Manchurian and Japanese units were bloodied by the *Red Army* along the Amur River in August 1939 in a punishing border clash that helped convince Tokyo to attack *Pearl Harbor* rather than into *Siberia*. Manchuria was liberated from Japanese occupation by the Red Army in 1945 and returned to Chinese control. Given the messy end of *World War II* in Asia, caused in part by very late Soviet entry into that theater of operations and partly by *Stalin*'s ambiguous ambitions, the border between Russia and China in Manchuria was not agreed upon. This engendered a prolonged conflict that fed into and aggravated the *Sino-Soviet split*. See also *biological warfare*; *Treaty of Peking*.

Suggested Reading: Yoshihisa Matsusaka, *The Making of Japanese Manchuria, 1904–32* (2000); Louise Young, *Japan's Total Empire* (1998).

Manchurian incident. *See Mukden incident.*

Manchus. An *Inner Asian* people known as Jürchen ("Jin Empire"), when they ruled north China in the twelfth century, but renamed "Manchu" by *Nurgaci*. *See also Qing dynasty; Song dynasty.*

mandate of heaven. The central Chinese Imperial governing doctrine, probably originating during the Zhou dynasty (1040–256 B.C.E.), arguing from *Confucian* principles that even an *autocrat* is bound by moral forces and the social compact that guides an entire community. In turn, that idea sustained the core myth of Chinese political theory (that is, of *autocracy*); to wit: that notwithstanding the absence of representative institutions in China, the emperors (or later, *Communist* or other dictators) governed from a mandate given by the people, which demanded personal virtue and benevolent administration from rulers. Dynasties maintained the mandate by having the emperor ("Son of Heaven") ritually observe an imperial cult of ancestor worship and other rituals on a daily basis, erecting temples, maintaining an effective and established state religion, keeping domestic order and upholding the laws, and securing the frontier from barbarian invasions. The mandate was claimed by each new dynasty, and later regimes. Each claim was contested, but also usually accepted once confirmed by the fact that overt resistance was finally crushed. *See also enlightened despotism; Kangxi emperor; popular sovereignty; prestige.*

mandate territories. *Colonies* and other territories taken from the *Central Powers* and administered under Article 22 of the *Covenant of the League of Nations* by appointed states as diverse as Australia, Britain, France, Japan, and South Africa. There were three kinds: Class A: limited mandates, expected to advance to *independence* (Iraq, Palestine, Transjordan); Class B: indefinite mandates, to be governed like colonies (Tanganyika, Togoland, South-West Africa); Class C: indefinite mandates, to be governed as if they were indistinct from the *metropolitan power*, with little thought of independence (a number of minor territories, including most former German colonies in the South Pacific). They later became United Nations *trust territories*. States that were not members of the *League of Nations* negotiated separate *recognitions* of League mandates. As with *Yap Island*, this process did not always go smoothly. Whereas most literature treats the mandate system as mere cover for the usual "spoils of war going to the victor," in fact it is best viewed as a moderate and reasonable, because achievable, compromise between the continuing realities of *imperialism* and the new ideal of *self-determination*. It also fit within a broader redefinition of imperial administration then underway within the *British Empire* especially, and to a lesser degree also within the *French Empire*. This new view, clear in British policy by 1923, was one of distant but ultimate realization of self-government on the model of the *Dominions*.

Mande. A general term for several West African peoples of common linguistic stock. Some Mande broke away from the *Ghana Empire* in the twelfth century, and a Mande invasion made a *tributary* of Ghana in the thirteenth century. Others founded the new empire of *Mali*. With the rise of *Songhai*, former Mande soldiers, known as "Mane" (originally, stateless armed marauders comparable to the Yaka in Congo or *mercenary* bands in France during the *Hundred Years' War*), set up several petty kingdoms in West Africa. In general, the Mande peoples and cultural influences expanded along the river systems of West Africa, especially the Gambia and the Niger.

Mandela, Nelson (b. 1918). South African nationalist. He was a principal organizer of the *African National Congress (ANC)* in the 1950s, facing arrest and trial several times. He was arrested, tried, and finally imprisoned on Robben Island, 1962–1990, becoming the most famous *political prisoner* in the world. As his sentence lengthened, his stature and reputation for integrity grew apace. Released by *F. W. de Klerk* in 1990 in order to facilitate a negotiated and peaceful end to *apartheid*, he instantly became the spokesman for black civil rights and an international symbol of moral and political rejection of apartheid. By mid-1993 all of apartheid's pernicious legal forms had been abolished, and agreement was reached to hold free and fair, multiracial elections in May 1994. Mandela became South Africa's first truly democratically elected president. He served from 1994 to 1999. He was awarded the *Nobel Prize* for Peace, jointly with de Klerk, in 1993. In the late 1990s he was repeatedly involved in efforts to mediate civil and political struggles, and wars, among neighboring African states, including Burundi, Rwanda, and Congo.

Suggested Reading: Anthony Simpson, *Mandela* (1999).

maneuvers. *Tactical* exercises essayed to test equipment and troops and gain simulated experience of large-scale operations in wartime. They can be air, land, or naval exercises.

Manhattan Project. The code name for the Anglo-American *atomic bomb* project during *World War II*. Although German scientists were the first to split the atom, and the German atomic bomb program enjoyed an early lead, *Hitler's* expulsion of Jewish academics from the universities led to a mass exodus of leading physicists to the United States and a fatal retardation of the subsequent Nazi effort. In 1939 *Albert Einstein*, the most prominent of these extraordinary refugees, wrote to President *Franklin Roosevelt* informing him that a *fission* bomb was possible. This led to a top-secret research project, which accelerated in importance, budget, and military interest after *Pearl Harbor*. From 1942 it drew upon resources and facilities at the University of Chicago, Oak Ridge in Tennessee, and *Los Alamos* in New Mexico. It was supervised by Gen. Leslie R. Groves, who worked closely with *J. Robert Oppenheimer*, and included *Edward Teller* among its dozens of brilliant scientists. The British and Canadians folded their research into this effort, which at its height employed more than 120,000 people. Scientists in the Manhattan Project, as this high-priority military research program was code-named, saw themselves in a race against German scientists working at *Peenemünde*. Their success in that race was aided by deliberate targeting for heavy bomber attack of atomic research centers in German-occupied Europe, including a heavy water facility in Norway and the main labs at Peenemünde.

After the war, interrogations of captured German scientists revealed that their research was several years away from making a bomb—though this was not known at the time. This gap resulted partly from Hitler's fixation on making breakthroughs in conventional weaponry (such as rockets, jet aircraft, and snorkel equipment for his *U-boat* fleet), partly because Nazi ideology steered even scientific research in peculiar directions, and from the sheer brilliance of the team assembled under the Manhattan Project code name. The American team—again with British and émigré help—was the first to test an atomic bomb, on July 17, 1945. The Soviets were not included in the research program or informed about the new weapon until after the successful test; the bomb was detonated during the *Potsdam* conference, when *Truman* told *Stalin* about the new weapon. In fact, Stalin had well-placed spies in position inside the program the whole time (*Klaus Fuchs* and *Julius Rosenberg*) and knew a great deal about the Project. The first two operational bombs were code-named "Little Boy" and "Fatman." They were dropped on Japan on August 6th and 9th, 1945, destroying most of *Hiroshima* and *Nagasaki*, respectively. Its goal accomplished, the Manhattan Project was disbanded in 1946. *See also Minatom.*

Suggested Reading: Richard Rhodes, *Making of the Atomic Bomb* (1986).

manifest destiny. An 1840s notion that it was the historic destiny of white, democratic, Protestant American civilization to expand over the width and breadth of the North American continent. That such was the will of Providence, it was said, was manifest in the endless bounty and evident success of the United States and its character as a self-governing society of free men— slaves and women were simply overlooked in this flattering self-appraisal. Besides, the vast and rich lands of the west were empty, more or less—Indians also did not count in these assessments. When Indians forced whites to take notice, by resisting *conquest*, it was argued that they should forfeit the land anyway because most did not till and exploit it to create wider prosperity, as Providence clearly intended. Similarly, Mexican claims to *Texas, California,* and the Pacific coast were swept aside, as that people were said not to enjoy divine favor; after all, they were *Catholic*, nonwhite, and ill-governed. The idea of a manifest national destiny became immensely popular, rising to its peak after the *Mexican-American War* as a post facto justification for expansion at a neighbor's expense. A version peculiar to the South also claimed Cuba, with its 400,000 slaves; in 1856 supported *William Walker* and his filibusterer expeditions to Nicaragua; and at the extreme dreamed of an empire of slavery stretching over all of the Gulf of Mexico, Central America, and most of Mexico itself.

The doctrine was not applied to Canada, however, by any but the most extreme. That British *colony* was mostly peopled by whites and seen as reasonably democratic, albeit curiously ill-governed and stubbornly anti-republican. Not of minor account, it was also closely defended by Britain. That was an uncomfortable, decisive fact, but one that hardly could be admitted in polite, expansionist company while discussing the marvelous unfolding of a divine plan for an "empire of Liberty" in the *New World*. The idea of manifest destiny in its original form did not survive the *American Civil War*, which it helped bring about through encouraging over-rapid acquisition of vast new western territories, which then broke the old compromise over *slavery* by forcing the question of admission of new states to the union as either *free soil* or *slave states*. However, the basic impulse that gave rise to it found continuing expression in the looser but also deeper notion of an American moral and political "exceptionalism," born of republican institutions. It also fed into justifications mouthed in defense of additional *Indian Wars* in the 1870s and 1880s. *See also Andrew Jackson; Thomas Jefferson; mission; mission civilisatrice; James Polk; white man's burden.*

Suggested Readings: Frederick Merk, *Manifest Destiny and Mission in American History* (1963); Tony Smith, *America's Mission* (1994); Ernest Tuveson, *Redeemer Nation* (1968); Albert Weinberg, *Manifest Destiny* (1935).

manned penetrator. Military *jargon* for a piloted aircraft, as opposed to drones, assigned to penetrate enemy defenses and press home an attack on selected targets.

Mannerheim, Carl Gustaf Emil von (1867–1951). Finnish field marshal and statesman. He served in the Russian *cavalry*, 1889–1917, seeing action in the *Russo-Japanese War* and *World War I*. He led Finnish *Whites* in Finland's war of independence against Russia in 1918, capturing *Karelia* for Finland. He was president of Finland, 1919–1920. He headed Finnish defenses, designing the *Mannerheim Line* of fortified positions in the Karelian isthmus. He led the army in another war against Russia, the *Finnish-Soviet War*, 1939–1940. He agreed to an anti-Soviet *pact* with Germany, and fought Russia again, 1941–1944. He was reelected president on August 4, 1944. He signed an *armistice* as the *Red Army* advanced, in which Finland agreed to switch sides and enter the war against Germany. He resigned as president in 1946, age 80, and retired.

Mannerheim Line. Finnish defensive positions on the *Karelia* isthmus and peninsula, named for *Carl Mannerheim*, which held the Soviets up for three months during the *Winter War. See also fortification.*

man-of-war. The largest *warship* during the age of sail. First built by the Portuguese, it was a mobile *artillery* platform capable of bringing to bear multiple decks of cannon in a devastating broadside or *bombardment. See also sloop-of-war.*

Manstein, Erich von (1887–1973). German field marshal. In the judgment of many military historians, the best German general of *World War II*. Manstein planned the invasion of France in 1940 that circumvented the *Maginot*

Line. He would have commanded the invasion force had the *Luftwaffe* won the *Battle of Britain* and *Hitler* invaded the United Kingdom. Instead, he moved to the *eastern front*, where he led a corps during *Barbarossa* that nearly took *Leningrad.* From 1942 to 1944 he commanded in south Russia, capturing the Crimea and trying, but failing, to relieve the German 6th Army at *Stalingrad.* He might have defeated the Russians at *Kursk* had Hitler not delayed the attack. During the retreat through Poland which followed, Manstein showed an unmatched competence in conducting a controlled, fighting withdrawal. Hitler hated retreat of any kind, even a successful strategic one, and dismissed him in March 1944. After the war he was tried by the British and was sentenced to 18 years, but was released in 1953.

Maoism ("Mao Zedong Thought"). The ideas and practices of *Mao Zedong* and of foreigners who took up the banner of Maoism. Derived partly from Mao's autodidactic study and *sinification* of *Marxism* and *Leninism,* and in part from his and China's *Confucian* heritage, Maoism called for *democratic centralism* within the *Communist Party*; an agrarian and peasant rather than urban and *proletarian* political base, with land reform that aimed more at securing peasant loyalty than rural liberation or improved yields; class struggle against landlords and the "national bourgeoisie"; and national communism, or revival of China as a *Great Power* and expulsion of foreign influences, but all under Communist Party (that is, Mao's personal and imperious) control. *See also collectivization; Four Cardinal Principles; Gang of Four; Franz Fanon; Great Leap Forward; Great Proletarian Cultural Revolution; Hundred Flowers Campaign; mass line; Nepal; people's war; Red Guards; reeducation;* Sendero Luminoso.

Maori. The *indigenous people* of New Zealand, formerly of Polynesia. *See also Maori Wars; tribe; Treaty of Waitangi.*

Maori Wars. The first Maori encounter with Europeans was with the sailors of *James Cook*'s expedition, which landed in 1769 on the islands that were later to be known as New Zealand. The Maori apparently regarded these first Europeans—who arrived in extraordinary sailing vessels and bore remarkable weapons—as supernatural beings, but with additional contact the delusion quickly passed. In 1772 and 1773 there were violent clashes, and some Maori ate the crew of Cook's sister ship, the Adventurer. As more Europeans arrived, and with them new diseases and sources of internecine strife, fighting and occasional massacres (by both sides) occurred. The First Maori War broke out in 1843. It began as a rebellion caused by colonial disregard for land settlements the Maori had accepted in 1840 in the *Treaty of Waitangi.* British troops suppressed the rising. The Second Maori War lasted ten years, 1860–1870. It was a *guerrilla* campaign undertaken mainly on North Island. Again, the central issue was conflict over native land claims and unbridled white settlement. With British help, the settlers ultimately imposed their will on the Maori. *See also New Zealand.*

Suggested Reading: James Belich, *The New Zealand Wars* (1986).

Mao Zedong (Mao Tse Tung, 1893–1976). "The Great Helmsman." *Communist* guerilla leader, Chinese revolutionary, and tyrant. In terms of sheer number of lives lost and disrupted, Mao's revolution was the most deadly and disastrous social experiment in all human history. Mao was the son of a prosperous farmer. He became active in revolutionary politics, 1911–1912, while an orderly in a local *militia* unit. He then returned to school until 1918. In 1919 he became a school teacher in Hunan. He was attracted to the *May 4th Movement*, but soon turned in frustration to *Bolshevism*, class warfare, and violent revolution. In 1921 Mao served as a delegate at the founding conference of the Chinese *Communist Party* (CCP) in Shanghai. He joined (to infiltrate) the *Guomindang* in 1923. He fled arrest, to Canton, in 1925. Now a committed *Leninist*, he was still obscure enough to survive the slaughter of Communists by *Chiang Kai-shek* in the *Shanghai massacres* of April 1927. He fell out with fellow Communists on the *Central Committee* and was censured by them after leading a failed uprising in Hunan in September ("Autumn Harvest Uprisings").

Mao retreated to the Jinggang Mountains, where, after killing a few landlords and experimenting with doctrinaire Communist organization, he encountered sharp opposition from more established peasants. He adapted both his policies and tactics, dropping his most radical schemes for land reform and allying with local bandit leaders to emerge in 1928 as founder and principal leader of the *Jiangxi Soviet*. At Jiangxi, Mao also confirmed a lifelong pattern toward women: theoretically and legally liberating them (as from arranged marriages), but in fact and personally subordinating them as virtual "*comfort women*" subject to his personal appetites and the desires of loyal male cadres. Mao solidified his position in the Party during the *Long March*, in which he displayed a talent for innovative *guerrilla* tactics. Most important was his deep and original appreciation (entirely contrary to orthodox *Marxist* doctrine and extant Soviet practice, which argued for concentration on organizing the urban proletariat) of peasant grievance as the real and historical springboard to revolutionary power in China. Once in *Yenan*, Mao concentrated on Party work and developing national communism, while *Zhu De* commanded the *Peoples' Liberation Army* (PLA) and *Zhou Enlai* handled *diplomacy* during much of the *Sino-Japanese War* (1937–1945) and resumption of the *Chinese Civil War* after 1945. After a series of carefully planned Party *purges*, Mao became chairman of the Communist Party and then of the People's Republic of China (PRC) upon its founding on October 1, 1949.

Thereafter, Mao increasingly concentrated power in his own hands, growing evermore corrupt and detached from reality as he did so. After the *Korean Conflict*, the CCP continued to expand apace, but the PLA was partly demobilized. Mao explained: "Every communist must grasp the truth: 'political power grows out of the barrel of the gun.' Our principle is that the Party commands the gun and the gun shall never be allowed to command the Party." One of his first acts was to consolidate the *revolution* by *radical* land reform, a *collectivization* of the Chinese peasant masses modeled on *Stalin's* brutal treatment of the *kulaks*, in which peasants were forced onto Peoples' Collectives. That draconian and brutal coercion of the peasantry took over a decade to complete, led to enormous social and economic dislocation and a major *famine*, and cost by some estimates more than 25 million lives. Early in 1950 Mao made an extended visit to Moscow—his first ever trip outside China—to consult with Stalin, whom Mao greatly admired and emulated with his own *cult of personality*. In general, Mao thought it necessary to replicate the stages through which Soviet development had already progressed under Stalin's guiding (and bloody) hand, though he hoped to achieve communism in China in a more compressed time frame than was the plan in Moscow. In the 1990s it was confirmed, from Soviet archives, that Mao came under strong pressure from Stalin to back North Korea and later to approve massive Chinese *intervention* in the *Korean Conflict*. When he did order the PLA to intervene, he did so from a combination of ideological and nationalist impulses. He hoped to support North Korea, but also hoped that by killing hundreds of thousands of American troops China would gain respect as a world power. Lastly, he hoped to serve the Sino-Soviet alliance in which he still firmly and genuinely believed.

By the mid-1950s, however, Mao's stark disdain for the post-Stalinist Soviet Union was evident, as was his penchant for direct confrontation with the United States, as in the *Quemoy and Matsu crises*. Mao considered Soviet *revisionism* about Stalin, as in the *secret speech* given by *Khrushchev* in 1956, not merely wrong, but a threatening example to his own *cadres*. His only other trip outside China, made once again to Moscow in 1957, did not go well. By 1958 he was fully estranged from the new leadership in Moscow, charging it with *revisionism*, and the *Sino-Soviet split* was well advanced. His effort to woo Chinese intellectuals with the *Hundred Flowers campaign* ended in further revelation of his extremely narrow tolerance for dissent and his cunning about exposing opponents. This pattern recurred on a far more massive scale later, during the *Great Proletarian Cultural Revolution*.

Mao's policies were: emphasis on the central role of the peasant in a sinified, *Marxist-Leninist* model of *development*, but underwritten by a *fascistic* (there is no other, or better, word for it) stress on collective will and heroic commitment by the masses; *permanent revolution* (he called it "continuing revolution"); radical egalitarianism in theory, emperor-like rule by himself in fact; collectivization of agriculture; total state control of capital accumulation and allocation and of the labor supply; rejection of *peaceful coexistence*; dictatorship by the Communist Party; and dictatorship over the CCP by himself as a latter-day *Manchu* in all but name; *peoples' war*; *cultural revolution*; and the ill-conceived and disastrous schemes of the *Great Leap Forward*. Taken together, these policies not only savaged the peasantry, they cost China enormously in the longer term by taking it down a thirty-year path of foregone growth and distorted development.

Politically, Mao thrived on chaos. Temperamentally, he was a puritan romantic, a *Jacobin* who judged social and political behavior by moral zeal and purity of ideological intent rather than practical outcome. He little understood economics, viewing deep problems of lack of agricultural and industrial *modernization* as amenable to military-style commands and methods of *mobilization*. Mao cared nothing for the welfare of individuals: he once shocked his doctor by saying he hoped the United States would use *nuclear weapons* to kill 20–25 million Chinese, merely so that the turpitude of capitalist nations might be revealed. Mao was responsible for tens of millions of deaths: the exact number remains unknown, but likely exceeded the totals of even *Hitler* and Stalin, possibly combined. This awful consequence arose from his ineptitude, technical and political ignorance, and moral indifference to the suffering of others—all compounded by ruthlessness and a willingness to commit mass murder in the name of class struggle.

Mao was a visionary who sought national independence and national communism, but also a rigid dogmatist who instead delivered a colossal personal tyranny and an ever-shifting *party line*. He was clever and charismatic, but also a bloody tyrant who ruled well within the long tradition of imperial *autocracy*. As he aged he rotted into a moral monster, utterly corrupted by his almost total power. His most radical policies were all later undone—for the clear betterment of more than a billion Chinese—by *Deng Xiaoping* and his more moderate successors. Yet, Mao's greatest achievement—reunification of China and expulsion of direct foreign interference from its national life—stood, as brutally accomplished as it was. *See also biological warfare; Gang of Four; Lin Biao; Mongolia; Nazi-Soviet Pact; Red Guards.*

Suggested Reading: Mao Zedong, *Quotations of Chairman Mao* (1965; 1972); Maurice Meisner, *Mao's China and After* (1986); Jonathan Spence, *Mao Zedong* (1999); Shu Zhang, *Mao's Military Romanticism* (1995).

maquiladoras. *See export processing zones.*

Maquis. *See Resistance.*

marabouts. Muslim holy men—often former hermits or sharifs—of the *Maghreb* and Saharan West Africa, who in the sixteenth through nineteenth centuries led prolonged *jihads* to purify the religious life of coastal cities (such as Algiers) and to plunder their wealth.

Marathas. Originally, western Indian peasants who lay outside *Mughal* control, in Maharashtra, and constructed their own state from the mid-seventeenth century, utilizing firearms technology to eventually establish a powerful Marathan kingdom in the *Deccan*. Under Shivaji Bhonsle (1627–1680) they tentatively, and then directly, challenged Mughal power, *plundering* Surat in 1664, provoking *Aurangzeb* to a furious counterattack by *Rajput* troops. After a temporary setback, in 1670 the Marathas again *pillaged* Surat and faced and defeated a Mughal army. In 1674 Shivji proclaimed Maratha an independent kingdom. Intermittent fighting with the Mughals continued. In 1688 Shivaji's successor, Shambuji Bhonsle, was captured and taken before Aurangzeb to be butchered, while the emperor's army restored Mughal authority over Maharashtra. However, the Marathas turned to *guerrilla warfare* in 1700 under the executed king's brother, Rajaram Bhonsle, and then his warrior widow, Tara Bai. They harassed and harried Aurangzeb's armies, or fortified multiple positions and thereby forced the Mughals to lay in sieges. This lasted for the remainder of Aurangzeb's reign, tying him down in prolonged and costly campaigns.

In 1702 Tara Bai led 50,000 Marathas against Hyderabad, sacking the city and ruining Mughal trade. Upon Aurangzeb's death a civil war broke out among the Marathas over the succession, with Tara Bai eventually losing out to her dead husband's nephew, Shahu (d. 1749). In 1718 the collapse of Mughal *legitimacy* and power was so near complete that an alliance with the Marathas was made which elevated them essentially to the role of guarantors of a hollowed-out throne upon which perched a succession of powerless emperors. Shahu aggressively expanded the Maratha kingdom. He attacked north against the Mughals in Malwa and Gujarat, and even raided Delhi in 1737, to collect a ransom for the Mughal emperor. And he attacked south against Nizam and Hyderabad. After 1740 the Marathas expanded boldly into Rajasthan, Delhi, and the Punjab and raided into Bengal. After 1750 they began to encounter European troops—French and English—in the company of their enemies. Maharashtra was overrun by more traditional invaders of India, however: Afghans crushed the Marathas at *Panipat* (1761). Maharashtra was then overrun by troops of the British *East India Company* in two sharp wars, 1775–1782 and 1803–1805, and a last rebellion was put down in 1818.

Suggested Readings: John Keay, *India: A History* (2000); Burton Stein, *A History of India* (1998); Stanley Wolpert, *A New History of India*, 6th ed. (2000).

March 1st movement (1919). *See Korea.*

march on Rome (1922). A central event in the history of Italian *fascism*, inspired by *D'Annunzio*'s assault on *Fiume*, but one inflated in the retelling far beyond its import or heroic content (which was minimal). Rather than a dramatic march to capture the capital, it was more of a hesitant shuffle by *blackshirts* while *Mussolini* negotiated for control of the government from a weak king and inept opposition. Mussolini actually arrived in Rome by train, better rested and in advance of more pedestrian fascists. Still, the episode greatly impressed *Adolf Hitler* and partly inspired his own *Beer Hall Putsch*.

Marco Polo (Lugouqiao) Bridge incident (July 7, 1937). Near Beijing, shots were exchanged between a Chinese garrison and Japanese troops on *maneuvers* (permitted under the *Boxer Protocol*) after a Japanese soldier went missing. The Japanese troops were part of an international garrison based in the city by right of *servitude* under certain equally hated *unequal treaties*. The initial Japanese attack was repulsed and China, fearing a wider confrontation for which it was not prepared, formally apologized. On July 27th Japan attacked in force anyway—*Guangdong Army* officers had long looked for a pretext to attack—and quickly overran the ancient Marco Polo (Lugouqiao) bridge and surrounding territory. Thus began the *Second Sino-Japanese War*, or the China War, as it is known in Japan. By 1938 virtually all of the fertile lands that could be reached by *railway*, and all the major coastal cities of China, were under a brutal Japanese *occupation*. *See also Tōjō Hideki.*

Marcos, Ferdinand (1917–1989). Dictator of the Philippines, 1965–1986. He falsely claimed to have led the *resistance* against Japan, though this did not prevent *Lyndon Johnson* from decorating him years later. His first term as president saw increasing repression. In 1969 he won a second term, and his corruption and repression deepened. In 1972 he declared *martial law*. It was not lifted until 1981. Although oppressive, Marcos' regime was never the equivalent of brutal martial law states elsewhere. Although domestic opposition grew, his strong ties to the United States and the *strategic* importance of the Philippines meant there was little more than rhetorical pressure from Washington to re-establish democracy. Things began to fall apart after Marcos had the principal (and principled) opposition leader, Benigno Aquino, murdered as he stepped off a plane in Manila. The *Reagan* administration threw its support to the opposition at a critical moment in 1986, and with this and by "peoples' power," Marcos was forced from office and out of the country. He was replaced by his murdered rival's widow, *Corazón Aquino*. The corruption of Marcos' regime—Marcos and his cronies stole billions—was symbolized by revelations about his wife's (Imelda, a former beauty queen) extreme hoarding, including a shoe closet containing 3,000 pairs of shoes in a nation where too many children grew up barefoot. Marcos spent his final days in Hawaii. In 1993 Imelda was permitted to re-inter his remains in-country.

mare clausum. "Closed sea." A navigable body of water enclosed by, and therefore under the sole *jurisdiction* of, a single state.

mare liberum. "Free sea." A navigable body of water open to all nations, under the *jurisdiction* of none. *See also freedom of the seas; Hugo Grotius; neutral rights.*

mare nostrum. "Our sea." A Roman boast about the status of the Mediterranean. For the *Roman Empire,* it was not an idle gloat. It was a strategic condition sought and most nearly achieved by the British in the nineteenth century. *Mussolini* used the term, quite inaccurately, in reference to his presumed control of the Adriatic before *World War II.*

Marianas Islands. Colonized by Spain after 1688, *Guam* was ceded to the United States and the other islands sold to Germany in 1899. They were seized by Japan in 1914. In 1921 they became a Japanese *mandate territory,* but were administered as though they were an integral part of the Japanese Empire. During *World War II,* they were captured by the United States and after the war were administered as part of the *Trust Territory of the Pacific Islands.* In 1975 a United Nations *referendum* led to *commonwealth status* for the Northern Marianas, in association with the United States. In 1990 the Security Council ended the trusteeship, and the population (43,000) became U.S. *citizens.*

Maria Theresa (1717–1780). Archduchess of Austria and Queen of Hungary and Bohemia, 1740–1780. After 1756 she ruled jointly with her son, *Joseph II.* Upon her birth her father, Charles VI, drafted a document called the Pragmatic Sanction, which guaranteed the Imperial (*Holy Roman Empire*) succession to his daughter, although the Imperial crown itself was forbidden to women and would go to her consort. Charles VI's efforts to gain international acceptance of the document required numerous diplomatic and territorial concessions that encouraged a view that Austria was weakening. It was widely thought that Maria Theresa was unready and unfit and would be a weak ruler. She was not. In 1740 she marshaled the country's resources and vehemently refused to accept the naked *aggression* against Austria of *Frederick the Great,* who attacked and annexed *Silesia.* She always called Frederick "that wicked man," but over time, to counter him she would mimic him, building military academies and making war in the new way he had devised. She led the Austrian *Habsburgs* in the long *War of the Austrian Succession* and remained Frederick's greatest enemy for more than 30 years. She was involved in the *diplomatic revolution* of 1756 that precipitated the *Seven Years' War.* She also joined in the 1772 *partition of Poland.* Frederick said accurately of her, she was "always weeping, and always annexing." He, on the other hand, while ever enlightened was always despotic, and annexed without tears.

Mariel boat lift (1980). Hundreds of thousands of *boat people* left Cuba for the United States, many voluntarily, others under compulsion. Cynically included by the *Castro* government were several thousand criminals and mentally ill people. These were *interned* in the United States and returned to Cuba in an *immigration* agreement signed in 1987. In 1994 the *Clinton* administration agreed to offer 20,000 immigrant visas per year to Cubans, via lottery and conventional application. In a break with precedent, the

United States also pledged to forcibly return to Cuba any escapees intercepted at sea.

marines. Naval troops, as opposed to regular *infantry*. Historically, marines were lightly armed soldiers who arrived at the battlefield via marine transport. Nowadays, they are as likely to sport heavy firepower and to be air-lifted into combat.

marine sovereignty zone. *See territorial sea.*

maritime frontier. The limit to a state's *sovereign* claim of *jurisdiction*, extending from the coast out to sea. *See also baseline; Exclusive Economic Zone; straight baseline; territorial sea.*

maritime law. *See law of the sea.*

market economy. One in which, in theory, the forces of supply and demand and private economic interests are given relatively free reign as to *production*, distribution, and consumption of *goods and services*. Of course, in the real world even *OECD* market economies reflect a significant degree of nonmarket activity and influence, such as government intervention through *protectionism*, regulation, and/or *subsidy* to specific sectors or industries. *See also capitalism; command economy; five-year plans;* laissez-faire; *mixed economy; planned economy; reform liberalism.*

Marlborough, John Churchill, Duke of (1650–1722). British general; ancestor of *Winston Churchill.* After seeing minor actions on land and at sea, he enlisted in an English regiment in the service of *Louis XIV.* He was in multiple actions during Louis' war against the Netherlands. During the English Civil War he was loyal to James II and commanded the Royal Army at Sedgemoor (July 6, 1685). He grew disillusioned with James, however, and embraced *William of Orange* and Queen Mary when they landed at Torbay in 1688. He fought for William against Louis XIV during the *War of the League of Augsburg.* He helped plan William's campaign in Ireland, which eventually culminated in the Protestant victory at the *Battle of the Boyne,* and secured the southern half of the island before falling out with his king. In 1700, restored to favor, he commanded the English Army in the Netherlands. He achieved his greatest victories during the *War of the Spanish Succession,* notably at *Blenheim* (1704). He also achieved victories in Flanders (1707–1710). He was recalled to England in 1710, partly to clear a path to negotiations with France. He is widely regarded as the greatest of English generals of the time, and even of all time.

Marne, Battles of. Two great battles of *World War I* are generally known by this name. Separated by almost four years, in both cases they marked the high tide of the German advance in the west.

(1) First Marne (September 7–19, 1914): This crucial battle took place within sight of Paris, after *Moltke* and his corps commanders altered the *Schlieffen Plan* by turning the *Reichswehr* onto a new, improvised path of advance to the west of the city, a move starkly warned against by *von Schlieffen*. The arrival of French reinforcements by rail and any and all other means of transport, including 600 taxis commandeered in Paris, lent the Allied counterattack on the exposed German flank the popular name "battle of the taxis." The French, commanded by *Ferdinand Foch*, and the *British Expeditionary Force* (BEF) thereby outnumbered the Germans—something never foreseen in the Schlieffen Plan. Their counterattack forced a German retreat and abandonment of the strategic objectives and timetable laid out in such detail by von Schlieffen. Had Germany won, World War I might have been radically foreshortened and the history of the twentieth century vastly different. As Schlieffen foresaw and feared, but never resolved, insurmountable logistical difficulties meant it always had been impossible for the German Army to amass the preponderant force necessary to overwhelm Paris, a massive fortified city that acted as a breakwater to slow and stop the German advance. That check to Berlin's grand *war plan* compelled a German retreat to defensive lines and to an order to all units to dig in along the Marne and Aisne rivers. This led to the so-called *race to the sea*, which terminated at the coast, and propelled all sides into the unanticipated horror of *trench warfare* for the next four years.

(2) Second Marne (July 15–20, 1918): This failed thrust into the Allied sector was the third prong of the great German spring offensive of 1918, their last offensive action in World War I. It carried the Germans across the Marne River before they were thrown back in unredeemable defeat and sullen *mutiny*. A massive Allied counterattack beginning in August brought home the depth of that defeat to *Ludendorff*, and thence to the civilian leadership, by mid-September. The political and moral consequences for the founding of the *Weimar Republic*, out of chaotic defeat and national humiliation caused by the military failure of the Reichswehr in the final months of the war, were enormous. *See also stab-in-the-back.*

Maronite Christians. A distinctive Christian sect in Syria and Lebanon from the eighth century C.E. During the *Crusades*, they re-established ties with the *Catholic Church*. During the period of French colonial occupation of Lebanon, the Maronites were both a privileged minority and a mainstay of the colonial regime. They were deeply engaged in the Lebanese Civil War in the 1980s.

Maroons. "Cimarrones." Former black slaves, and their descendants, brought to the *New World* by the Spanish but who escaped into the forests of Central

America and the Caribbean and established free communities in hiding. During the long Anglo-French-Spanish contest for dominance in the Caribbean in the sixteenth through eighteenth centuries, Maroon *pirates* sometimes formed alliances with English *privateers*, including Sir Francis Drake (c. 1540–1596), to fight the Spanish.

marshal. *See military ranks.*

Marshall, George Catlett (1880–1959). American statesman. Chief of staff, 1939–1945; secretary of state, 1947–1949; secretary of defense, 1950–1951. As a young officer he saw action in the Philippines, 1902–1903. He served as a staff officer in France during *World War I*. He was a key planner under General *Pershing* during the American offensive at Saint-Mihiel on the *western front* in 1918. He handled his duties masterfully and was named chief of operations for the American First Army. After the war, he served with *occupation* forces in the *Rhineland*. Back in the United States, he became an aide to General Pershing until 1924. He saw a tour of duty in China in 1927 and then was an army instructor until 1932. In 1938 he headed the War Plans Division of the general staff. As chief of staff, he undertook preparations for *World War II*, rapidly expanding the army from its 1938 strength of just 200,000. After *Pearl Harbor*, Marshall was intimately engaged in all wartime military *strategy* as *Franklin Roosevelt*'s main advisor on military affairs. He attended all the key wartime conferences, including *Tehran, Yalta,* and *Potsdam*. He was the top U.S. military advisor during the war, shaping overall strategy in both the Atlantic and Pacific theaters. In 1945 *Harry Truman* sent him to China to *mediate* a peace between *Chiang Kai-shek* and *Mao Zedong*. As secretary of state from January 1947, he backed the *Truman Doctrine* and conceived the *Marshall Plan*, which was likely his single greatest achievement—in a lifetime of historic achievements. He was instrumental in keeping U.S. forces out of the *Chinese Civil War*. He opposed early *recognition* of Israel, but was overruled by Truman, on the advice of *Clark Clifford*. Marshall was centrally involved in organizing the *Berlin airlift*, the creation of NATO, and planning in the *Korean Conflict*. Despite his extraordinary record of decades of exceptional and patriotic achievement, he was absurdly accused by Senator *Joseph McCarthy* of having *Communist* sympathies. With far more justice, Marshall was awarded the *Nobel Prize* for Peace in 1953, the only professional warrior ever to receive it.

Suggested Readings: Robert H. Ferrell, *The American Secretaries of State and Their Diplomacy: Marshall* (1966); Forrest Pogue, *George C. Marshall* (1987).

Marshall Islands. Made a German *protectorate* in 1886; in 1921 they became a Japanese *mandate territory*. During World War II they were *occupied* by the United States and, after 1947, administered as part of the *Trust Territory of the Pacific Islands*. They rejected a 1969 offer of *commonwealth status*, opting instead for *free association*, signing a compact in 1982, ratified by *referendum* in 1983. The United Nations *Trusteeship Council* endorsed the change, and in 1990, the Security Council formally ended the *trusteeship*. While efforts were made to diversify foreign relations, the United States continued to perform most *consular* and diplomatic functions in the Marshall's behalf. In 1991 the Marshall Islands joined the United Nations. *See also Bikini Atoll; Eniwetok.*

Marshall Plan. See *European Recovery Program.*

Marston Moor, Battle of (July 2, 1644). *See Oliver Cromwell.*

martial. Warlike; pertaining or disposed to *war. See also militarism.*

martial law. The imposition of strict military controls over a *civilian* population by a national government during an emergency, during or after a *coup*, or by a foreign army setting up an *occupation. See also state of emergency.*

Martí, Jose (1853–1895). Cuban revolutionary leader against Spanish colonial rule. Martí's pamphlets, plays, and poems did much to inspire Cuban national resistance to Spain. In 1895 he led an armed rebellion that aimed at independence, but he was soon killed. The rebellion continued after his death, however, ultimately leading to the *Spanish-American War* (1898) and then to Cuban independence. His example was cited by *Castro* as an inspiration for his own armed assault on Cuba in the 1960s, and thereafter Martí's revolutionary and nationalist aura was wrapped around the *Communist* regime.

Martinique. An *overseas department* of France, located in the West Indies. It has been a French possession since 1635 (Spain had never bothered to settle it).

Marxism. The philosophical system, *grand theory*, and *ideology* originating in the analysis of *history* and industrial capitalism undertaken by *Karl Marx*. It has since evolved into a greatly diverse set of theories and speculations about the main topics of *politics*, philosophy, and the social sciences. Like *Christianity* and *Islam*, Marxism falls within the apocalyptic tradition of Western thought. It too foresees a new millennium of eternal peace and perfect justice in the future, but only after a cataclysmic final conflict with the forces of evil. Its basic premise is the use of Hegelian logic (the *dialectic*) to study history and arrive at "laws" of "historical materialism" by which the material (economic) base of any given society determines and "explains all historical events and ideas" (*Engels*). Thereby, Marx famously "stood Hegel on his head" by substituting material interests for reason as the ultimate reality in the dialectical process. Thus, for Marx, in every historical epoch the dominant class (*thesis*) is determined by the underlying material basis of society (the *mode of pro-*

duction), but also inevitably confronted by another class, generated by the prevailing system of economic relations and representing an opposing idea of social organization (*antithesis*); the clash that results produces a breakthrough to a higher level of human social life (*synthesis*); this forms a new thesis—a class-based idea, moving not just in, but also shaping history itself—that is opposed by a new antithesis, and so on.

Subordinate ideas include the argument that the "superstructure" of social and political forms, customs, ideas, and relations is determined by the "economic base" of human life. The superstructure then reinforces and reproduces the relations of production that brought it into being. This relationship advances through knowable stages, from primitive or "natural communism" to *slavery, feudalism, capitalism,* and *socialism,* until it reaches its culmination in the liberation of the human body and spirit under mature *communism,* though Marx himself had little to say about the form that this idealized communist society might take. Only then could the tyranny of the *state,* cruelly necessary during the penultimate period of the *dictatorship of the proletariat,* "wither away" and each person be returned to the naturally harmonious condition wherein one would take only what one needed (would not hoard the "surplus" produced by the labor of others) and willingly give back to society the best one had. Marx claimed that, unlike *utopian socialism,* his—also patently utopian—vision was actually "concrete" and "scientific." Indeed, he said it was rooted in the "iron laws of history," which he had discovered via processes of reasoning (*dialectical materialism*).

The orthodox Marxist thesis may be reduced to a core proposition and an attendant faith: in all lands and times hitherto, the state and the means of production have been controlled by the strongest and wealthiest classes. But take heart, for history is knowably progressive, the achievement of communism will mean the *end of history* (defined as class conflict), and it will usher in a material, earthly utopia of perfect social and moral justice in a classless and global society of proletarian fraternity. As a speculative vision and faith, that promise proved highly attractive to a great many people. It is essential to comprehend this point, that at its core Marxism was a heart-felt cry of moral pain and outrage against real-world oppression and injustice, wrapped in huge intellectual pretensions that drew in lesser intellectuals but also masked its core emotional appeal to a great many ordinary people who could not follow, and did not care about, its more arcane doctrinal disputes. Its emotional appeal and leveling vision is the main reason it was so attractive to so many millions, especially the poor and poorly educated, for it was in fact alluring to many and this historical fact must not be overlooked. On the other hand, for this same crucially important reason, among others, everywhere it was implemented revolutionary Marxism quickly led in practice to broad social disaster—as despoiled utopian idealism always does—and to a willingness among its adherents to apply *terror* and accept mass death if that was the necessary price to be paid for the final triumph of just revolution.

Marx's followers took various of his theories in a variety of new directions. The *Bolsheviks* first looked to *permanent revolution* to counteract the effects of *uneven development* they said was the product of capitalism and then turned to *socialism in one country* as a *Stalinist* adjustment to the fact that revolution had not occurred, as most had anticipated it would, in the advanced capitalist countries. After the *Shanghai massacres* of 1928, Chinese Communists were more heretical (or innovative): they worked directly among the mass of the peasantry, rather than with China's tiny urban working classes, and used peasant—not industrial worker—grievances, civil war, and nationalist sentiment as the springboard for their revolution. So, too, did communist movements in *Vietnam* and other largely peasant, *Third World* societies. Surely among the greatest ironies produced by this vast body of naïve speculation that looked forward to the end of the nineteenth-century state, which was to wither away along with the destruction of capitalism, was the actual construction in the twentieth century of *totalitarian* societies that elevated the state to a previously unknown plane of domination in human and social relations.

As for international relations, orthodox Marxism said very little. *Lenin* cobbled together an unoriginal and historically parochial thesis on *imperialism* that did not stand the test of time, but that nonetheless animated much of the Soviet Union's foreign policy, as in its material and ideological support for *wars of national liberation*. Otherwise, the basic international premise of Marxism was that politics among nations would cease to exist (the *end of history*) along with nations themselves, as all class antagonism dissolved in a universal socialist brotherhood. In fact, during the twentieth century, communist states several times went to war with each other, as well as with nonsocialist states. Then virtually all collapsed. Practical recognition of Marxism's many flaws by Marxists (many others saw fatal problems right away, in the original work) first occurred in the *revisionism* of *Eduard Bernstein*, which later evolved into the one successful political form Marxism took: *social democracy*. Harder intellectuals, such as the Bolsheviks or *Rosa Luxemburg*, among others, clung to cherished orthodox myths much longer. West European Marxists only partially and with great reluctance abandoned Marx's sterile utopian aesthetics, as when Antonio Gramsci (1891–1937) sought to escape Marxism's deterministic prison and attach it instead to popular consent and grassroots activism. For most, the break did not come until *Stalin* signed the *Nazi-Soviet Pact* in 1939, and revelations about the nature of the GULAG *Archipelago* leaked out. Even then, committed Marxists retreated into explanations of how the Soviet Union and other avowedly Marxist states "weren't really Marxist." Some settled on the astonishing thesis that these societies were actually examples of *state capitalism*.

In light of such obduracy, which has the ring of faith rather than reason, as *John Maynard Keynes* once put it: "It must always remain a portent to historians . . . how a doctrine so illogical and so dull can have exercised so powerful and enduring an influence over the minds of men, and through them, the events of history." *See also Albania; Salvador Allende Gossens; Berlin Wall; Benin; bourgeoisie; Brezhnev Doctrine; Bulgaria; Cambodia; Cambodian genocide; Cambodia-Vietnam War; Fidel Castro; China; class struggle; Cold War; collectivization; COMECON; COMINTERN; Communist Manifesto; Communist Parties; critical theory; Cuba; Czechoslovakia; dependency theory; East Germany; economic determinism; Ethiopia; Eurocommunism; First (Second, Third, Fourth) International; five-year plans; Franz Fanon; grand theory; Grenada; Erich Honecker; Hungary; ideology; Industrial Revolution; Khmers Rouges; labor theory of value; Laos; Leninism; liberation theology; lumpen proletariat; Mao Zedong; Maoism; Marxism-Leninism; means of production; Mensheviks; Robert Mugabe; national liberation; New Economic Policy; Nicaragua; party line; peaceful coexistence; permanent revolution; people's war; Partai Kommunis Indonesia (PKI); Poland; Pol Pot; Popular Front; Prague Spring; proletarian revolution; reeducation; rehabilitation; Rumania; Russia; Russian Revolutions (1905, 1917); secularism; Sino-Soviet split; Sino-Vietnam War; social fascism; Solidarity; Soviet bloc; soviets; surplus value; Tito; Leon Davidovich Trotsky; Trotskyites; vanguard; voting with their feet; war communism; Max Weber; Yemen; Yezhovshchina; Yugoslavia.*

Suggested Readings: Marshall Berman, *Adventures in Marxism* (1999); A. James Gregor, *The Faces of Janus: Marxism and Fascism in the Twentieth Century* (2000); Sidney Hook, *Marxism and Beyond* (1983); Maurice Meisner, *Marxism, Maoism, and Utopianism* (1982).

Marxism-Leninism. Adaptations of basic *Marxism* made by *V. I. Lenin*, which emphasized the role of a ruthless *vanguard* party in establishing the *dictatorship of the proletariat*. The essential Leninism in Marxism-Leninism was the concept of the vanguard. Lenin saw such a party as necessary because, unlike Marx, he had no faith in the spontaneous acquisition of revolutionary consciousness on the part of the *proletariat*. Lenin was disgusted by what he saw as the betrayal of the cause, for example, by the Fabians and the trade union movement in embracing parliamentary reform in Britain, and similar adjustments proposed by *Social Democrats* on the Continent such as *Jaurès* in France and *Bernstein* in Germany. Moreover, he was deeply shocked by what he viewed as a betrayal of the Left by the German and French (and other) trade unions in July and August 1914. The union leadership, and most members, in each *belligerent* nation had endorsed national *war aims, conscription,* and voluntary enlistments, all for *nationalist* reasons, rather than sit out *World War I* or work to bring down their governments. Lenin therefore turned *Marx* on his head by proclaiming that a true vanguard party did not have to await the production of the proletariat by *capitalism* to succeed at *socialist* revolution: it could take advantage of the calamity of the Great War to seize power in even so backward a state as Russia. The war, said Lenin, was the bastard child of *imperialism*. Such imperial conflicts only hastened the day the capitalist edifice would come crashing down, this in contrast to Marx's stress on internal *revolution*.

That was Lenin's most important—though not his original—idea: by focusing on imperialism as a projection of *class struggle* to the world stage Lenin gave Marxism an international dimension, which Marx had almost completely ignored. He also provided the impetus for the Soviet Union to move down the path of support for *wars of national liberation*. That turned out to be a dead end, but one littered with corpses and broken nations, and a path taken for which Lenin and his inapt and historically parochial theory of imperialism must share some blame. This body of doctrine drew as well upon the dizzyingly adaptable, or perhaps better and more accurately said, callously expedient, policies and practices enacted by Lenin and the *Bolsheviks* within Russia, ranging from *war communism* and the *Red Terror* to the *New Economic Policy* and the treatment of the "nationalities question." During the *Cold War*, Marxist-Leninist doctrine repeatedly led Soviet and other Communist leaders into romantic—and, very often, also extremely bloody—commitments and conflicts that did not survive underlying and countervailing pressures of national histories, international realities, or basic human nature. *See also Leninism; Marxism.*

Suggested Readings: V. I. Lenin, *State and Revolution* (1917); V. I. Lenin, *Imperialism: The Highest Stage of Capitalism* (1916).

Marxism–Leninism–Mao Zedong Thought. *See Mao Zedong; Maoism.*

Marx, Karl (1818–1883). German philosopher. He enthused over the *Revolutions of 1848*, for which he coauthored with *Engels* the most famous pamphlet in history: "The Communist Manifesto." Much of his life was spent in political exile in London, researching and writing his magnum opus, "Das Kapital," in the Reading Room of the British Museum. He was essentially a millenarian thinker. Although he learned from *Hegel* to despise the backward "Oriental civilizations" of India and China as outside the main flow of history, he nonetheless hoped and thought that the *revolution* in Europe would be sparked by the *Indian Mutiny*. It was not. He similarly expected a mass uprising in China during the *Second Opium War* to cascade until it brought the revolution to Europe. Once more he was bitterly disappointed. Yet again he thought world revolution had arrived with the *Paris Commune*, and again he was disappointed.

Marx founded the *First International* to work directly for revolution, but angry personal rivalries with, and his deep and constant intolerance of, other "men of the left" destroyed it. Reflecting with perspicacity on what even he recognized as the peculiar obtuseness of many of those who became fanatical devotees of his ideas, he once said: "I am not a Marxist." Among his more pithy aphorisms: "Religion . . . is the opium of the people" (1844). "Capitalist production begets, with the inexorability of a law of nature, its own negation" (1859). "From each according to his abilities, to each according to his needs" (1875). No passage better captures Marx's astonishing naïveté, while also illustrating the attractiveness of his moral vision to so many trapped in insecure occupations of ill-pay and worse conditions, than the following famous selection from his "German Ideology," wherein he waxed poetic about the coming *communist* society. This will be a society, he promised, wherein "nobody has one exclusive sphere of activity, but each can become accomplished in any branch he wishes." It would be a perfect and wholly liberating society, which "regulates the general production and thus makes it possible for me to do one thing today and another tomorrow, to hunt in the morning, fish in the afternoon, rear cattle in the evening, criticize after dinner, just as I have a mind, without ever becoming hunter, fisherman, shepherd or critic." Who would not wish to live as a communist, if that was what it really meant? Many Marxist cadres later concluded that anyone who opposed such a glorious, millenarian vision must be a *reactionary* or a *counterrevolutionary* and should be dealt with accordingly and ruthlessly. *See also Mikhail Bakunin; Vladimir Ilyich Lenin; Mao Zedong; Marxism; Marxism-Leninism; Pierre Joseph Proudhon; Josef Stalin; Max Weber.*

Suggested Readings: Sidney Hook, *Marxism and Beyond* (1983); David McLellan, *Karl Marx* (1974); Maurice Meisner, *Marxism, Maoism, and Utopianism* (1982).

Masai. *See Kenya.*

Masaryk, Jan (1886–1948). Czech statesman and son of *Tomáš Masaryk*. Ambassador to Berlin, 1925–1938; foreign minister, 1939–1948 (*government-in-exile*, 1939–1945). He resigned the ambassadorship to protest the rape of Czechoslovakia at *Munich*. After *World War II* he wanted to accept *Marshall Plan* aid, but *Stalin* prevented that. Still in office after the *Communist* coup in 1948, he either fell or was hurled to his death from a window in the Foreign Ministry.

Masaryk, Tomáš (1850–1937). Czech statesman. A member of the Austrian legislature in the 1890s, he came late in life to Czech nationalism outside an imperial framework. He was an admirer of Western democracy and sought help from the *Allies* and a promise of *recognition* of Czech independence. In 1917 he went to Russia, where he organized the *Czech Legion*. He then traveled to the United States, where he may have influenced the views of *Woodrow Wilson*, who at the least accepted Masaryk's claim to head an independent Czechoslovak republic. He became its first president, 1918–1935.

Masina (1818–1862). A Muslim empire located around the great bend of the Niger River. Its brief rise was based on *cavalry* forces into which all eligible males were *conscripted*. *See also Fulbe Empire.*

Mason-Dixon Line. The boundary surveyed by Charles Mason and Jeremiah Dixon, 1763–1767, mainly between Pennsylvania and Maryland. It was widened in the popular imagination to become the marker between North and South, free and slave, in the tense period before the *American Civil War*. It survived that war as a metaphor for Southern cultural uniqueness from the rest of the United States.

massive retaliation. A *strategic doctrine* most closely associated with *John Foster Dulles* and *Eisenhower*. It held that any Soviet *aggression* would be met with the full nuclear retaliatory capability of the U.S. arsenal. Critics said that this doctrine severely limited options, as it appeared to lack credibility. Eisenhower clove to it as a means of avoiding any war. It gave way to the idea of *flexible response* under *Kennedy*. *See also brinkmanship; war-avoidance strategy; war-fighting strategy.*

mass line. A *Maoist* doctrine (reminiscent of aspects of *Confucian* bureaucratic practice) that instructed Party members to learn directly from listening to peasant grievances and then develop policy to address those problems. Although superficially pragmatic and reformist, its real aim was to reinforce *democratic centralism* and Mao's own emperor-like dictatorship.

mass production. The production of standardized, interchangeable goods by machine, mechanical power, and, later, also assembly line. Among the first rudimentary examples was the Dutch shipbuilding industry of the sixteenth century. The development of new power sources, technologies, and organizational principles, especially during the nineteenth century and after, permitted manyfold increases in world *productivity*. As such, mass production was one of the cardinal features of *industrialization* and helped transform the material basis of the daily lives of a growing percentage of the human population. A marked departure was development of the *American system of manufactures*. Additional advances made by Henry Ford (1863–1947) in the U.S. automotive industry—principally the assembly line—were quickly copied worldwide. That unintentionally helped make possible both mid-twentieth century *totalitarianisms* and mass war machines, along with the successful waging of *total war* (hot and cold) by well-armed and affluent democracies that defeated them at mid-century and again before the century's end. *See also Battle of the Atlantic; economies of scale; Lend-Lease.*

"master race." *See* Herrenvolk; *National Socialism; racism.*

Masurian Lakes, Battles of. (1) First (September 2–28, 1914): A badly outnumbered Russian army, nearly broken by its defeat at *Tannenberg*, conducted a tough fighting retreat, avoided *Hindenburg*'s efforts to complete its encirclement, and after six bloody days extricated itself from an exposed position. It then counterattacked at the end of the month, drove the Germans back, and retook much of the ground lost two weeks earlier. (2) Second (January 31–

February 21, 1915): This extraordinary lakes region (nearly 3,000 lakes break up the countryside) was the scene of a second great Russo-German battle, in 1915. The Russian attack was beaten back, with heavy casualties on all sides. Second Masurian Lakes is sometimes called the "Winter Battle."

mature economy. In classical economic usage, one that runs a *balance of payments* (and, in particular, a *current account*) surplus and is a net exporter of *capital*. This *model* is at odds with the recent practice of a number of *OECD* countries, most notably the United States, which in the 1970s to 1990s ran current account deficits and were net importers of capital. *See also developing nation.*

Mau-Mau rebellion. *See Kenya.*

Maurice of Nassau (1567–1625). *See Eighty Years' War (1566–1648); Gustavus Adolphus; revolution in military affairs.*

Mauritania. In the eleventh century, part of this broad territory was incorporated into the ancient empire of *Ghana.* That empire was succeeded by *Mali.* The Portuguese arrived off the coast in the 1440s on their way to locate the *Gold Coast* and points farther south. They were followed, as elsewhere in West Africa, by the Dutch, English, and French. From the mid-nineteenth century much of contemporary Mauritania was governed as part of the composite French colony of *Senegal.* This drought-stricken area became a distinct French *protectorate* in 1903, toward the end of the *scramble for Africa,* though it was not *pacified* for some years after that. In 1920 it was merged with *French West Africa.* It gained *autonomy* within the *French Community* in 1958 and *independence* in 1960. Mauritania is racially and religiously divided between Muslim Arabs (Moors) and Christian and animist blacks. The latter historically were slaves of the former. This animosity has been reflected in tensions over foreign policy and international *alignment,* whether with Arab states, within the *OAU,* or with France. The Moors still hold political power and have declared Mauritania an Islamic republic. In 1976 it upheld a claim, along with Morocco, to *Western Sahara*; in 1979 it abandoned this claim in the face of effective *POLISARIO* resistance. In the 1980s, relations with Morocco deteriorated over the latter's interference in internal Mauritanian politics. In the 1970s and 1980s Mauritania participated in a *World Bank* irrigation scheme involving nine countries. This raised land prices near the rivers, and in 1989 violence exploded between displaced black fishermen and farmers and Moorish speculators. The dispute led to a border war with Senegal after Mauritania stripped 60,000 blacks of *citizenship* and *deported* them to Senegal (they were ethnically Senegalese). Quixotically, Mauritania supported Iraq diplomatically during the *Gulf War,* leading the United States and other *donor nations* to suspend *development assistance*. The subjugation of the country's black population continued to draw international criticism on *human rights* grounds into the early twenty-first century.

Suggested Reading: J. F. A. Ajayi and Michael Crowder, eds., *History of West Africa*, 2 vols. (1974).

Mauritius. Located in the Indian Ocean 400 miles east of Madagascar and 800 miles from the coast of Africa, this island was uninhabited, other than for a Dutch military outpost, until Dutch settlers began to arrive from 1638. France seized it in 1721 and began settling it with French farmers. The French also imported African slaves from *Zanzibar* or Madagascar to serve its growing plantation economy. This contributed to the racially mixed (*Creole*) population to which the majority of Mauritians belong. In 1810 Britain took possession and, having banned the *slave trade*, imported poorly paid Indian laborers instead. This practice continued after the British abolished *slavery* itself within their empire (1833). Mauritius remained a colonial backwater into the 1950s, when agitation for *independence* arose. It became independent in 1968, an occasion marked by ethnic rioting among African-Creoles and *Hindus*. In 1970 it set itself up as an export-processing zone. In 1971 it declared a state of emergency in response to a *general strike*. After a brief, authoritarian interregnum, democracy was restored in 1976. In the 1970s and 1980s, Mauritius took advantage of the *Lomé Conventions* and made itself into an important off-shore banking center, and in general its economy launched into rapid growth. Its one outstanding international dispute is a claim to the *British Indian Ocean Territory* (Chagos archipelago), including *Diego Garcia*, where the United States maintains a naval and air base. Interethnic rioting in 1999 again threatened its young, and still fragile, democracy.

Mauryan Empire. *See India.*

Maximilian, Ferdinand Joseph (1832–1867). "Emperor of Mexico," 1864–1867; brother of *Francis Joseph*. He was placed on the Mexican "throne" by *Napoleon III*. He was left to his own, rather poor, devices when the United States threatened to *intervene* and the French withdrew military support. Refusing to flee, he was captured by *Juárez* and shot.

Suggested Reading: Joan Haslip, *The Crown of Mexico* (1971).

maximizing. *See game theory.*

Maya. An Amerindian civilization centered on Guatemala and the Yucatan peninsula. Like the ancient Egyptians and other imperial peoples, the Maya were pyramid builders. They were governed by a hierarchical theocracy in which warrior queens often played key roles and human sacrifice and cannibalism was commonplace, especially after the tenth century C.E. The Maya lived in a decentralized culture organized not as a single great *empire* but a system of many *city-states*, all engaged in competitive expansion to some degree, and therefore often at war. There is much more to be learned about these cities, but it is already known—mainly from archeological evidence and textual studies—that they included Calakmul (the largest and most important in the sixth and seventh centuries), Caracal, Copan (a local *hegemon*), Dos Pilas, Naranjo, Palenque, Piedras Negras, Tikal (an ancient rival and ultimate victim of Calakmul), Tonina, Quirigua (which rebelled against Copan), and Yaxchilan. The Mayan economy was limited by reliance on hoe agriculture (no draft animals). It also employed *slave labor*, but it was sufficiently sophisticated to sustain a large population and multiple social classes from the fourth to ninth century C.E. Mayan city-state politics was likely marked by intense rivalry and constant warfare, comparable to politics in the Greek *city-state system* or the Italian *Renaissance*. In the tenth century a small Mayan empire emerged in northern Yucatan, centered on the city of Chichén Itzá. About 1200 it was succeeded by a lesser state, Mayápan, which also disappeared before the Spanish arrival. *See also Aztec; Inca.*

Suggested Readings: Daniel Drew, *The Lost Chronicle* (2000); Simon Martin and Nikolai Grube, *Chronicle of the Maya Kings and Queens* (2000).

Mayaguez affair. *See Gerald Ford.*

May Day. May 1st, a date widely celebrated by organized labor to honor and advance workers' solidarity, outside Canada and the United States, which celebrate Labour/Labor Day in September. *Soviet bloc* countries made use of the holiday to display industrial and military might in the form of factory and military parades, to impress the home folks, frighten the neighbors, and in hope of enhancing their *prestige*. May Day parades were attended by foreign *military attachés* and other diplomats and closely observed by *Sovietologists* and *Kremlinologists*.

May 4th movement. At the *Paris Peace Conference*, on April 30, 1919, it was decided by the *Big Four* that Japan should retain possession of *Shandong*, rather than return this former German *leasehold* to China. On May 4th China was shaken by mass demonstrations by students from a number of universities and colleges who first met to vote resolutions at Beijing University and then gathered at Tiananmen Square to demonstrate against the decision, but also in favor of "awakening the masses" in China about the foreign threat to the country's political, economic, and cultural integrity. As one result, China did not ratify the treaties negotiated at Paris. This demonstration was followed by a massive *boycott* of Japanese goods by Chinese *nationalists*. Most importantly, the May 4th movement inspired many students and intellectuals to social and political activism and to literary and journalistic engagement with cultural and social issues, thereby bringing these classes to the forefront of organization and resistance to foreign *concessions*, as well as helping to politicize most matters of taste and culture. "May 4th movement" later became shorthand for a larger cultural reexamination, and also in many ways a rejection, of Chinese Imperial and *Confucian* traditions. *Mao Zedong* was an early disciple, but soon abandoned the peaceful methods of May 4th to embrace *Leninism* and violent revolution and join the then-foundling Chinese *Communist Party*.

Suggested Reading: Vera Schwarcz, *The Chinese Enlightenment* (1986).

May 30th incident. *See Shanghai massacres.*

Mayotte. It has been an *overseas department* of France since 1976, when its *Catholic* population voted in a *referendum* to merge with France rather than remain with the largely *Muslim*, and newly independent, *Comoros Islamic Republic*.

Mazarin, Jules (1602–1661). French statesman. Educated by *Jesuits*, he began his diplomatic career as papal nuncio at the French court, 1634–1636. He became a *naturalized* French subject and joined the French diplomatic corps. That fact may have helped him convince *Vauban*, whom Mazarin found a *prisoner of war* in the Spanish service, to join the French Army. Mazarin was made a cardinal by the influence of *Richelieu*, by whom he was also anointed successor as advisor to the old king during the *Thirty Years' War* (1618–1648). That was a great conflict in which Richelieu had finally intervened, but did not live to see brought to a successful finish. When Louis XIII died, Mazarin effectively ruled during the regency period of *Louis XIV*; he likely was, but may not have been, the queen-regent's lover. He oversaw the triumph of French arms and diplomacy in the *Peace of Westphalia*. Thereafter he became embroiled in the civic unrest of the Frondes, 1648–1653. Those plots, riots, and rebellions were mostly a delayed reaction against the centralizing policies of his predecessor, retarded by the need to maintain unity until the war in Germany was won. They were provoked when Mazarin ordered the arrest of all refusing to pay new taxation he had introduced and were fed as well by widespread rumors that he was personally corrupt. First was the "Frondes parlementaire," in 1648, a bloodless call for reform that was mostly defused by 1649. In 1650 the "Frondes princière" went further: it involved outright rebellion by the nobility and even treacherous alliance with Spanish troops in the border regions. Mazarin raised a royal army and put down the princes, but he was effectively exiled from Paris during the later Frondes, 1650–1653. Upon his return to favor and to power he allied France with *Cromwell* by surrendering Dunkirk to the English (1653). In 1659 he finally ended the long war with Spain, in victory, and dictated the terms of the *Treaty of the Pyrenees*. In general, Mazarin solidified the policies of his great predecessor—whom he rivaled in power and actually surpassed in administrative efficiency and talent. Like Richelieu, he always elevated the interests of the crown above all else, which was both his great achievement and the cause of most of his troubles. He died a hugely wealthy man, who bequeathed much to France in the form of his famous library and the Mazarin Bible. *See also Edict of Nantes.*

Mazzini, Giuseppe (1805–1872). Italian patriot and *liberal* revolutionary. He witnessed the failed uprising in *Piedmont* in 1821 and became dedicated to the *nationalist* cause. He was arrested in 1830 in Sardinia. A thorough idealist, who scorned all moderation and was endlessly engaged in conspiracy in favor of a unified Italy, through his tireless campaigning and voluminous writings he more than anyone prepared Italy psychologically and politically for unification. His practical schemes were less successful, however. In Marseilles, he founded the *Young Italy* movement. When he appealed to the king of Piedmont to lead the national cause, *Metternich* had him banished from Italy (1831). The next year he was also barred from France. In 1834 he organized a failed invasion of *Savoy*. From exile in Switzerland, his writings exerted an influence on liberal and nationalist revolutionaries all over Europe. In 1837 he moved to London, where he lived in poverty for many years. In 1844 he won a privacy case against the British government, which had been opening his mail and sharing it with various rulers in Italy. During the *Revolutions of 1948* he was fully involved in Lombard politics, coordinating closely with *Garibaldi*, who years before had joined the Young Italy movement. In March 1849, he headed a triumvirate governing the Roman Republic. Within a month, French troops ended that state of affairs. From exile in London he fomented rebellion in Mantua (1852), Milan (1853), Genoa (1857), and Leghorn (1857). He worked with *Kossuth* and other failed revolutionaries from 1848 for Europe-wide republicanism and support for revolution in Italy. In 1859 he opposed Piedmont's alliance with *Napoleon III* of France and war on Austria. That year, he threw his support behind Garibaldi in the latter's march on Sicily and Naples. He disliked and distrusted *Cavour* (the feeling was mutual). He finally broke with Piedmont in 1862. He was then arrested and imprisoned. Messina elected him, in protest, four times to the Italian Assembly. He was again an exile in Switzerland, again expelled, and again arrested, in 1870. He died at Pisa in 1872.

McCarthyism. Making charges of disloyalty and *treason* against high officials, especially of secret attachment to *communism*, but based less on fact than on mere association with known Communists, circumstantial evidence, or no evidence at all. The term is often—and too loosely—used as a substitute for the wider Red Scare, which swept certain circles in the United States after *World War II*. It derives from the scurrilous practices of Senator Joseph McCarthy (R-Wisconsin) and his staff and supporters, notably his assistant Roy Cohn, whom McCarthy appointed chief counsel to the Government Committee on Operations of the Senate. During 1952 and 1953 McCarthy, who was personally mendacious and utterly reckless, rode a campaign of slander and smear, disguised as patriotism, out of political obscurity to national prominence. He charged that the *State Department* was riddled with Communists, and went so far as to—quite absurdly—accuse *George C. Marshall* of being soft on China and, by extension, on communism. In fact, in the 1990s it was publicly revealed that intelligence intercepts showed Soviet access to U.S. secrets and penetration of U.S. agencies had been much greater during World War II than it was in the 1950s, when many Soviet agents had been recalled by Moscow or were simply left inactive.

As McCarthy's popularity rose, *Truman* delayed facing him down, as did *Eisenhower*. Some spoke out, however: *Dean Acheson* strenuously defended the State Department and, much more problematically but mostly from personal loyalty, also *Alger Hiss*. The increasingly wild, alcoholic McCarthy was eventually censured by the Senate, without ever identifying a single Communist agent in the government. However, his fall from media and political grace did not take place before a wave of Red-baiting hysteria destroyed hundreds of reputations and careers, many of people entirely innocent of the charges made, and spread fear into the arts, the media, and the professions. The real causes of this phenomenon were, of course, much bigger than the excesses of a single rogue senator with a fifth of bourbon rather than evidence in his valise. They had to do with widespread fear and uncertainty over the "loss of China" to the Communist camp in 1949, with Soviet detonation of an *atomic bomb* well ahead of expectations (also in 1949), and with how badly the *Korean War* was going after China's sudden, massive, and stunning intervention in November 1950. For many, such catastrophic setbacks in the early years of the *Cold War* were quite bewildering and required villains (that is, scapegoats) in order to be explained and understood. McCarthy tapped into this rich vein of fear and confusion, to then set off explosive charges that treason and conspiracy were behind all the ills of American foreign policy.

Although his specific charges were groundless and rash, and his prosecution of them feckless, McCarthy was not entirely wrong on the larger issue. It was, of course, true that Soviet spies were operating in the United States and within the high councils of other Western governments, just as the reverse was also true. What was pernicious and poisonous about McCarthyism, therefore, was not the making of charges of *espionage*, or even disloyalty or treason, as such. It was the insistence of accusers on deciding the guilt of the accused by mere association, or even just innuendo, and the attendant failure of elite opinion to stand against and condemn such unprincipled, indeed un-American, star-chamber procedures. In the end, McCarthyism seriously damaged U.S. interests by making it less acceptable among many American intellectuals to be avowedly anti-Communist—a pose dating at least to the trial of the *Rosenbergs*. In that respect McCarthy was among the best friends the

KGB ever had, as one high-ranking KGB defector later conceded. It should also be remembered that, although McCarthyism was an unfortunate aberration from the norms of American justice, the entire episode paled in comparison to the state of constant *terror*, denunciation, and regular mass *purges* by which all Communist states were governed before, during, and after the Cold War.

Suggested Readings: Richard Fried, *Nightmare in Red* (1990); Arthur Herman, *Joseph McCarthy* (1999); Alan Weinstein and Alexander Vassiliev, *The Haunted Wood: Soviet Espionage in America—the Stalin Era* (1999).

McCarthy, Joseph (1909–1957). *See Dean Acheson; Dwight Eisenhower; George Catlett Marshall; McCarthyism; Harry S Truman.*

McClellan, George B. (1826–1885). *See American Civil War; Abraham Lincoln; Winfield Scott.*

McCloy, John Jay (1895–1989). U.S. statesman. Despite his "outsider" origins (a trait he shared with *George Kennan*), he built connections across the political divide based upon his identity as a *Republican* internationalist and his cooperation with *Democrats*. He was assistant secretary of war in *Franklin Roosevelt*'s administration during *World War II*. He rose on his own merits to become one of the *Wise Men* of American foreign policy during the *Cold War*. His most important role came as U.S. high commissioner to Germany, 1949–1952, during its early transition to liberal-democracy. He worked closely with *Adenauer*, ensuring Germany's readmittance to the club of *civilized states*, its *integration* into Europe, and (though after his departure) also its full membership in *NATO*. He was criticized for not rigorously pursuing *denazification*, but that needs to be judged as against the successful reintegration of a newly democratic West Germany into the western family of nations. As one of the Wise Men, he advised successive presidents on policy toward Germany and the Soviet Union, as well as on *disarmament* and the *Vietnam War*.

McKinley, William (1843–1901). *Republican* president of the *United States*, 1897–1901. He defeated *William Jennings Bryan* in the 1896 election, a campaign fought over "free silver" versus the *gold standard*. As America emerged from the effects of a *world depression*, McKinley kept up a high *tariff* wall and worried about immigration depressing the labor markets. Like Grover Cleveland, McKinley wished to avoid foreign entanglements that would impede rapid recovery from the *depression*, which ended in 1893. The problem of Cuba was intractable, however, and drew him into the *Spanish-American War*. McKinley's great failure was his inability to resist the pressures of an aroused *public opinion* and Congress, both of which wanted war with Spain in 1898 as newspapers printed reports sympathetic to Cuban rebels and the USS *Maine* mysteriously blew up in Havana Harbor. McKinley feared the public would punish his party electorally if war was not forthcoming, and so he gave it war. Americans thereby acquired Puerto Rico, Guam, and the Philippines (where they faced a continuing insurrection from Filipino nationalists under Emilio Aguinaldo), all as a result of a pugnacious crusade to free Cuba, accompanied by something approaching national innocence about the consequences of such self-indulgent exercise of great power. McKinley also annexed *Hawaii* in 1898 and began to maneuver for a *sphere of influence* in China. Many were left baffled, but also impressed, at how a "splendid little war," as *Elihu Root* called it, in "America's backyard" had made the United States a Pacific and imperial power. In the end, McKinley would be reelected on the basis of a return to prosperity, more so than for his administration's stunning victory over Spain. Still, his was the most *expansionist* administration since *Polk's*, before the *American Civil War*. Less spectacularly, McKinley protested to the Tsar about mistreatment of Jews, who were flooding into the United States in ever larger numbers and in destitute conditions. He was also concerned about Russian expansion in Asia and leaned toward Japan's cause in *Korea* and *Manchuria*. He was assassinated in Buffalo, New York, on September 14, 1901, by an anarchist. *Theodore Roosevelt*, his vice president, succeeded him.

Suggested Readings: Louis L. Gould, *The Presidency of William McKinley* (1981); Ivan Musicant, *Empire by Default* (1998).

McMahon Line. The *boundary* between Tibet and India, marked out by the British, Chinese, and Tibetans in 1914 on the principle of the highest watershed. It was never *ratified* by China, which regarded it as an unjust British imposition. Beijing negotiated an agreement on the line with Nepal and Burma in 1960 and 1961 and with Pakistan in 1963. India refused to accept China's interpretation or claims. The line was overrun by Chinese troops during the *Indo-Chinese War* of 1962.

McNamara, Robert Strange (b. 1916). U.S. secretary of defense, 1961–1968; president of the *World Bank*, 1968–1981. Under *Kennedy*, he promoted *flexible response* as a replacement doctrine for *massive retaliation*. He supported *intervention* in Vietnam and was a principal advocate of using massive bombing to coerce the Democratic Republic of Vietnam (North Vietnam) into a settlement. Overconfident and morally careless, he tried to apply his Harvard Business School background and *econometrics* training to running the war. He developed the idea of a "body count" of North Vietnamese Army and *Việt Cong* dead as a measure of whether the war was being won or not, without proper regard for important intangibles such as the *national morale* of both the South and North Vietnamese. Deeply ignorant of Vietnam's history and blinded by a naive faith in *quantitative analysis*, he was one of the key decision-makers who took America into costly, unnecessary conflict and failure in Vietnam. He grew disillusioned during 1967, called for a halt to the bombing, and resigned in 1968. At the World Bank he was instrumental in adding poverty alleviation to the list of funding criteria. Despite deep unpopularity among Vietnam veterans and others, he continued to write and speak adamantly about U.S. foreign policy.

Suggested Readings: Robert McNamara, *In Retrospect* (1995); George C. Herring, *America's Longest War* (1979); David Kaiser, *American Tragedy* (2000); Andrew Rotter, *Path to Vietnam* (1987).

means of production. (1) In *Marxism*, the factors, especially *labor* and *capital*, essential to the production of goods. (2) A synonym for *technology* in the broadest sense. *See also mode of production.*

measures short of war. Unilateral, diplomatic, or forceful actions essayed by a state in defense of its legal rights, to wit: imposing a pacific *blockade*, making a *diplomatic protest*, severing *diplomatic relations*, proclaiming an *embargo*, carrying out an *occupation*, or making a *retorsion* or *reprisal*. *See also self-help.*

Mecca. This ancient city located in modern Saudi Arabia is capital of the *Hejaz* and spiritual center of the *Islamic world*. Mecca is forbidden to non-Muslims, but millions of Muslims visit it annually during the *haj*. It was long a commercial center and thus a crossroads also of religious interaction—before Muhammad it hosted numerous local cults, as well as communities of Nestorian Christians and Jews, to all of whose practices and doctrines Muhammad was exposed as a youth growing up in Mecca. In 622 he fled the city, where he and a handful of early followers were not initially welcomed. This was a seminal event in the founding of Islam: the Hegira. He later returned, with an army, from Medina. Always revered, Mecca has not always been respected, as *fundamentalists* have on occasion challenged more moderate, even temporal, Muslims for control of Islam's holiest sites. It was captured by the *Ottoman Empire* in 1517 and added to their claims to the *caliphate*. During the *Wahhabi* revolt it fell into rebel hands, 1803–1813, until retaken by *Mehemet Ali*'s son, nominally in behalf of the Sultan in *Constantinople* but really for the benefit of his Egyptian vassal. For generations, Mecca was overseen by *Hashemite* sharifs under the authority of the Ottomans. That ended when *Ibn Ali Hussein* was defeated by *Ibn Saud* in 1924, laying the basis for incorporation of Mecca into the new state of Saudi Arabia. In November 1979, fundamentalist followers of a self-proclaimed *mahdi* seized the Grand Mosque. Hundreds were killed in the fighting that followed, during which the Mosque was damaged, to the dismay of the faithful. The *Iranian Revolution* brought new trouble to Mecca, as Iranian *shi'ites* repeatedly violated the strict prohibition on political activities during the haj. In 1988 some 400 disorderly Iranians were killed by Saudi police in a riot-cum-bloodbath that deeply embittered Saudi-Iranian relations.

mechanical majority. (1) The position enjoyed by the United States in the *United Nations General Assembly* during the 1950s, when it could count on nearly automatic voting support from allied European states and friendly Latin American countries. (2) The position enjoyed by *Third World* states in the United Nations General Assembly after c. 1965. *See also G-77; Nonaligned Movement.*

Médecins sans Frontières (MSF). This humanitarian organization (a non-governmental organization) was founded in 1971 by *Red Cross* doctors determined to bring medical relief to victims of *war* and *crimes against humanity* as soon as possible, whatever the political circumstances or personal danger. It arose directly from broad French national and governmental support for Biafran *secession* during the *Nigerian Civil War.* It subsequently spoke against *human rights* abuses in numerous situations in which governments and even the Red Cross remained silent, and it focused international attention on overlooked humanitarian crises and issues. It thereby also intervened directly where traditional *international law* would defer to the states concerned. It may be reasonably argued, on both sides of the issue, as to whether this is a good or bad thing for the long-term evolution of a more humane and law-governed world. In 1999 it was awarded the *Nobel Prize* for Peace.

mediation. When a third party tries to reconcile states engaged in a *political dispute.* Unlike *arbitration,* there is no promise of a binding solution, but contrary to *good offices* the mediator does offer real, substantive proposals aiming at a solution.

Medici. The wealthiest, most powerful, and ruling family in Florence during the Italian *Renaissance.* Their money came from banking; their dictatorial power, from their control of Florence. The family produced two French queens, four popes, and dominated much of the political and cultural life of the Renaissance. *See also Henri IV; Martin Luther; Machiavelli.*

Mediterranean Agreement (1887). Austria-Hungary, Britain, Italy, and Spain secretly agreed to consult on ways to defend the *status quo* in the Mediterranean. The understanding aimed at preventing either France or Russia benefiting from any change in the status of *Ottoman* holdings. *Bismarck* knew about and approved of the agreement, even while signing with Russia the *Reinsurance Treaty,* which ostensibly advanced Russian interests in the *Straits Question.* The Agreement lapsed in 1892.

Mediterranean Sea. It is enclosed by Africa, Europe, and western Asia and is therefore of enormous *strategic* and commercial importance. For much of the eighteenth and nineteenth centuries it was effectively controlled by Britain, which held *Gibraltar* closely and worked to close the *Bosporus* and *Dardanelles* to Russia. After construction of the *Suez Canal* the Mediterranean became even more important. It was the scene of major naval commitments in *World War I*, and again during *World War II*, and in the *Cold War*. Today a major threat is pollution, requiring *multilateral* action from the many states that share its waters. *See also* mare nostrum; *Mediterranean Agreement; Straits Question.*

Suggested Readings: Michael Grant, *From Rome to Byzantium* (1998); Michael Grant, *Ancient Mediterranean* (1969); Peregrine Horden and Nicholas Purcell. *The Corrupting Sea* (2000).

megaton. One million tons of TNT equivalent, a measure developed to account for the energy released by, and destructive impact of, *nuclear weapons.* *See also kiloton.*

Mehemet (Mehmed) Ali (1769–1849). (Turkish: Mehemet; Arabic: Muhammad; therefore, also known as "Muhammad Ali"). Viceroy of Egypt, 1805–1848. This Macedonian *mercenary* leader arrived in Egypt in 1801 at the head of an Albanian military mission in the wake of *Napoleon*'s destruction of the *Mamluks.* In 1805 he rose to become governor (pasha), nominally under the *Ottomans* but de facto independent of external control. From this position he dominated the history of North Africa and the Red Sea region for nearly 50 years. Mehemet Ali displayed exceptional ability and daring and grew in power and independence of the Ottoman *sultans.* In 1811 he ruthlessly suppressed surviving Mamluk power by massacring hundreds of their leaders and scattering the rest. His adopted son was then sent to clear Arabia and *Mecca* of the *Wahhabi* revolt, while he laid the basis for his own dynasty and for Egypt to emerge as a modern state. These embroilments in the sultan's problems mostly entangled him with European powers, however, and did little to advance the cause of Egyptian autonomy. On his own account, Mehemet Ali conquered *Nubia* and central Sudan, 1820–1822, *plundering* both for black male *slaves* for his army (black females were sold across the Red Sea).

Mehemet Ali founded Khartoum in 1824 as a base for slave-raiding and to mark off and administer his southern empire. During the campaign in the south his son overthrew the *Funj Sultanate* (1821). In later decades sudanic slaves were extracted under the "zeriba system" of fortified camps of slave raiders who fanned into Central Africa south of Khartoum at his behest. They scourged the entire Nile-Congo region under powerful *slave traders* and *warlords.* Zeriba raiders remained active for decades after Mehemet Ali's death, into the late 1870s, highly disrupting the region and ensuring a heritage of deep Arab-Black animosity in Sudan. Back in the Mediterranean, from 1821 Mehemet Ali sent an army to aid the sultan fight the *Greek War of Independence,* including occupying for a time the island of Crete. He sent his fleet, too, in 1828, but it was sunk at *Navarino.* He turned openly against the sultan, seizing long-promised lands in Palestine and Syria, 1831–1833, where his son routed an Ottoman army at Koniya (1832), upon which the *Sublime Porte* ceded Syria to Mehemet Ali as a *tributary* province of the Empire. He took still more territory, 1839–1841, but then was forced by the *Great Powers* to cede Syria back to the Ottoman Empire, which Britain was propping up as a bulwark against Russia in the *Great Game*. In exchange, his family became hereditary rulers of Egypt, and he retained control of Sudan. Meanwhile, he went slowly mad. It is notable that even at the height of his power Mehemet Ali never sought full independence for Egypt. Still, arguments abound over whether he was an early Egyptian nationalist or should be seen as part of a broader Ottoman tradition of powerful provincial governors ("notables," or "ayans," or "derebeys"). His success inspired much imitation, including by the *Qajar* in Persia.

Suggested Reading: Khaled Fahmy, *All the Pasha's Men* (1997).

Meiji Restoration (1868). *See Japan: Meiji Restoration; It Hirobumi; Sun Yatsen; Ieyasu Tokugawa.*

Meir (Myerson), Golda, née Mabovitch (1898–1978). Israeli ambassador to the Soviet Union, 1948–1949; foreign minister, 1956–1966; prime minister of Israel, 1969–1974. Born in Ukraine (Kiev), she migrated to *Palestine* in 1921 and worked for the *Jewish Agency* before *independence*. She later helped found the Israeli Labor Party. As foreign and prime minister she cultivated ties with the emerging nations of Africa. Her greatest success came in securing Israel's ties to the United States (she enjoyed a close working relationship with *Richard Nixon*). She was in office during the *War of Attrition*, 1969–1970. She was criticized by some for being caught unawares by the start of the *Fourth Arab-Israeli War* and did not survive postwar votes on nonconfidence in her government.

Melanesia. One of the subdivisions of *Oceania*, consisting of the *South Pacific* island groups northeast of Australia, including New Guinea, whose *indigenous peoples* are ethnically distinct from *Polynesians*.

Melanesian Spearhead Group (MSG). It was formed in 1986 by Papua New Guinea, the Solomon Islands, and Vanuatu to support *decolonization* demands of French South Pacific *territories*, to distance themselves from Australia, and to work for *rapprochement* with Indonesia. Fiji at first declined to join, but did later. It is also expected that a *Kanak* government on *New Caledonia* would do the same. The exclusive character of this group threatened to divide the *South Pacific* along *Melanesian-Polynesian* lines. In 2001 MSG membership was Fiji, Papua New Guinea, Solomon Islands, Vanuatu, and New Caledonia's main independence movement, the Kanak Socialist National Liberation Front.

The 2001 summit caused great controversy in New Caledonia and with France, when it was announced that the Kanak Front would host it.

Melian Dialogue. *See Peloponnesian War.*

Melilla. A Spanish *enclave* inside Morocco, captured by Castile in 1497. Its future status is tied to Spain's lingering efforts to reclaim *Gibraltar* from Britain. It and *Ceuta* are the last European possessions in Africa. *See also Morocco.*

Memel (Klaipėda). This Baltic seaport was a member of the *Hansa*. After *World War I* it became a *condominium* governed by the *League of Nations*, 1919–1923, when it was wrested away by (then mostly landlocked) Lithuania. Its possession was demanded for Germany by *Hitler* in 1939. In the wake of his successful incorporation of the *Sudetenland* into the Reich, the Lithuanians did not argue. It was overrun and *annexed* by the Soviet Union in 1945. It is located today within independent Lithuania, renamed as Klaipėda.

Mensheviks. "Minority." The moderate faction of the Russian Social Democratic Party, against which *Lenin* led the *Bolshevik* split in 1903 and formally parted company in 1912. The main points at issue were Lenin's insistence on dictatorship within the party (*democratic centralism*), as well as by the party over the state come the *revolution*; his deviation from orthodox *Marxist* views in arguing for a *vanguard party* versus awaiting the inevitable role of the *proletariat* to play its part on the stage of history; and his call for an *insurrection* by the *soviets* in 1917 to take advantage of the chaos brought about by *World War I*. The more orthodox Mensheviks argued that a *bourgeois* democratic revolution must of historical necessity precede any proletarian revolt and that without this prior bourgeois revolution it was not possible to proceed directly to creation of a *socialist* state. During the *Russian Revolution of 1917* some Mensheviks joined a coalition government with the Kadets and SRs. Other Mensheviks governed Georgia, 1918–1921. After the *Russian Civil War* these old comrades of the Bolsheviks were briefly tolerated and then savagely repressed. Many who had avoided imprisonment or internal exile to tsarist *Siberia* died instead in the socialist *GULAG* of the Soviet Union, the "workers state" erected by the Bolsheviks.
Suggested Reading: Abraham Ascher, ed., *The Mensheviks in the Russian Revolution* (1976).

Menzies, Robert (1894–1978). Australian statesman. Prime minister, 1939–1941, 1949–1966. Both good and lucky at politics, he led Australia into *World War II* and later dominated its political life. He was ousted in 1941 but returned to office in 1949 for 16 uninterrupted years, during which he shifted Australia under an American security umbrella, joining *ANZUS* and *SEATO*. He used the *Cold War* to build a national economy and define Australia's place in the world as a western state within Asia. He was uncomfortable adapting to changes in the *Commonwealth* after c. 1957, reflecting in his speech and policies the racial attitudes of many Australians of that day. He thus kept *aboriginal* questions suppressed and maintained a "White Australia" immigration policy. In 1965 he sent the first Australian troops to fight in the *Vietnam War*. He retired undefeated, but also mostly out of touch with changes that were necessary and impending.

mercantilism. Mercantilist "theories" were not systematic. Instead, they were a loose, sixteenth through eighteenth century set of practices that treated *politics* as superior to *economics* and saw competition among states over access to, and the distribution of, wealth as the main current in the world *political economy*. Still, there were discernible general characteristics. In essence, mercantilism was a continuation of war and statecraft by economic means. It was concerned with state control (*power*) in all its manifestations, domestic and foreign, in particular with concentration of military and financial power—which were, of course, even then intimately related—in central hands at the pinnacle of the state. It therefore was concerned with building up national institutions that served to enhance the power of the state, or *sovereign*, as against private and subnational forces and interests. That meant, in practice, supporting newly professionalized armies and navies, along with deploying and enforcing a more efficient tax collection system that oversaw and regulated commerce, and maintenance of all physical facilities (docks, seaside warehouses, repair facilities) necessary to sustain the new *standing armies* and permanent navies that were growing out of the *revolution in military affairs*.

In economic terms, mercantilists assumed that a fixed amount of world trade and wealth existed, and therefore argued for a national policy of accumulating wealth by maintaining a favorable *balance of trade* through high *tariffs* and by hoarding precious metals because they thought that trade and hoarded bullion (see *bullionism*) translated into enhanced national power; and in an age of *mercenary* armies and still primitive state finances, that point had real merit. If one did not possess colonies that produced *gold* or silver—and Europe had few gold or silver deposits left—accumulating bullion through trade was essential, although *piracy* was also a real option and was turned to as such by several states, most notably England. The idea that power correlated to trade that accumulated bullion initially stimulated growth in trade, but over time hampered development of an international trading system by creating excessive reliance on monopolies and export *subsidies*, which were then countered by other states introducing protectionist measures. The "theory" also drove creation of colonial *empires* as sources of rare metals, markets for exports, and supports for political *self-sufficiency*. Mercantilism thus exacerbated interstate conflict while encouraging low domestic consumption and leading to high *inflation*. It did not survive the rebellion of the American *colonies* against its strictures, the rise of national armies during and after the *French Revolution*, or the *Industrial Revolution* and *liberal* trade regime of the mid-nineteenth century promoted by Great Britain. Late nineteenth-century German nationalist economists tried to revive the term ("merkantilismus") to refer positively to state-directed development of national economies; they were not successful outside Germany. Mercantilism's international antonym, and successor, was *free trade*.

Although mercantilism is often identified with service to *absolutist* states, the types of regime it served varied widely, from absolute monarchies such as France under *Louis XIV* and finance minister *Jean-Baptiste Colbert*, to the Dutch Republic (which was never as exclusive concerning trade as was England, France, or Spain), and even parts of the *Hansa*. In the late eighteenth century the term acquired a lasting pejorative meaning, largely from the writings of *Adam Smith*. In first describing established economic practices in order to criticize them, Smith systematized them into what he called "the mercantile system." The impact and triumph of his own economic ideas soon froze this pejorative sense in place, thereby somewhat falsely raising mercantilist practices to the level of economic "theory." *See also autarky; colonialism; comparative advantage; convoy; East India Companies; Alfred Thayer Mahan; neo-mercantilism; physiocrats; Seven Years' War; War of Jenkins' Ear.*

Suggested Reading: Eli Heckscher, *Mercantilism* (1965).

mercenaries. An international, professional soldier or sailor—usually an officer—who fights for fee or *plunder*, not for a national or political cause or because he is a *conscript*. Historically, mercenaries have been important carriers of military skills across borders and among nations. Mercenaries have been around as long as war itself: they marched alongside, as well as against, the legions of the late *Roman Empire*; the *Song* emperors of China employed them in the twelfth century; they guarded great trans-Saharan *trade routes* for the empires of *Mali* and *Songhay*; and they fought for and against the crusader states of the *Holy Land*. The *Aztec Empire* was built by a people who began as for-hire soldiers to the more advanced *city-states* of the central Mexican Valley, who then founded their own city and callous and bloody imperium. In parts of Medieval Europe primogeniture ensured that many young men were forced to turn to arms to earn a living. This produced the necessary forces to eventually defeat the *Vikings* and other warlike invaders and raiders, with the later surfeit of warriors produced by a whole society structured for war sent off to fight the *Crusades*. By the thirteenth century, independent mercenary bands ("companies") were commonplace, and a social and economic scourge, especially in France during the *Hundred Years' War*. Much of the *Reconquista* was fueled by mercenary impulse, a need for armies to live off the land. The hard methods and cruel attitudes learned by Iberians while fighting Moors were then applied in the *Americas* by mercenary *conquistadores*. Mercenaries ("condottieri," or foreign "contractors") played a major part in the wars of the *city-states* of the Italian *Renaissance* and, along with French "gen d'armes" and Swiss pikemen ("pas d'argent, pas de Suisses"), filled out the armies of *Charles V, Philip II*, and their many enemies during the *Wars of Religion* of the sixteenth and seventeenth centuries.

For a century or more, mercenary dominance of the European battlefield led to fewer battles but much longer wars, conditions that best satisfied the interest of military professionals in prolonged but also cautious and relatively nonsanguinary service. During the *Thirty Years' War* many soldiers and top officers were mercenaries, notably on the *Habsburg* side under *Wallenstein*. Not all of these were *Catholics* (Wallenstein himself was an agnostic mystic). They came from Scotland, England, Ireland, the Swiss cantons, and the many over-run and warring German states. When *Gustavus Adolphus* intervened in the war to save the *Protestant* cause, his Swedish Army was actually comprised of nearly 80 percent mercenaries wrapped around a core of well-trained Swedish conscripts. A century later, *Frederick the Great*'s peacetime armies were still about 50 percent mercenary, with the rest conscripts. Hessian mercenaries fought for England in the *American Revolution*. Bought soldiers entered an era of obsolescence with the French *levée en masse*. The advent of modern *nationalism* finished them for good within Europe after that, as they were displaced by new conscript and national armies and thus played a decreasing role in *Great Power* warfare, though the British employed German, Swiss, and Italian mercenary legions in the *Crimean War*, and *Gurkhas* everywhere after the *Indian Mutiny*, and the *French Foreign Legion* fought in nearly all France's wars. The role of mercenaries in the Great Power wars of the twentieth century was minimal.

Outside Europe, however, mercenaries continued to play a significant role in warfare. During the nineteenth century they helped reunite Vietnam and establish the Nguyên dynasty in 1802. The *Qing* employed mercenaries under *Gordon* during the *Taiping Rebellion* when their own *banner troops* failed. The French Foreign Legion helped carve out and then hold a new *French Empire* in Africa and Indochina, aided by African mercenaries in the *Tirailleurs Sénégalais*. All other European empires in Africa, too, were largely won by African mercenaries under European officers. In lesser conflicts in the twentieth century, too, they plied their trade, especially in the numerous African wars that followed decolonization. They were particularly active in the *Congo crisis* and the *Nigerian Civil War*. Some mercenaries attempted coups or takeovers of entire countries, including the *Maldives, Seychelles*, and *Comoros*. In response to this, an article was introduced to the Additional Protocol #1 (1977) to the 1949 *Geneva Conventions* that changed the definition of *prisoner of war* to include guerrillas ostensibly conducting *wars of national liberation*, but also specifically to exclude mercenaries from any international legal protection whatever. This was aimed mainly at white mercenaries then based in South Africa, where several mercenary companies were established. In 1998 these closed shop, as the new majority black government passed stern antimercenary laws. Nothing was done to curtail other Africans from taking up the gun, however. After 1998 a wave of brutal mercenary recruits in the pay of various parties, comprised mainly of Hutu "génocidaires" fresh from acts of tribal butchery of 800,000 Tutsi in Rwanda, swept over the Great Lakes region of Central Africa after the Rwandan genocide. They greatly exacerbated the Tutsi-Hutu conflict in Burundi, and contributed to the fall into *anarchy* by Congo. *See also Afghan-Soviet War; Bosnian War; Janissaries; Lebanon; Mamluks; Mercantilism; Papua New Guinea; pirates; privateer; Samori Touré; Switzerland.*

Suggested Readings: M. Mallet, *Mercenaries and Their Masters* (1976); David Shearer, *Private Armies and Military Intervention* (1998).

merchant marine. The fleet of civilian ships that carries a *nation*'s trade. *See also freedom of the seas; Navigation Acts; navy; privateer.*

"merchants of death." A rhetorical pejorative referring to all arms manufacturers and exporters. The crude idea that the "merchants of death" are the primary cause of *wars*—that arms manufacturers promote conflict to create markets for their goods—was widespread in the 1930s, even among professional historians, concerning the root causes of *World War I.* A strikingly naïve version was contained in George Bernard Shaw's "Major Barbara." It was widely believed in the United States in select circles during the *Vietnam War* and again concerning *proxy wars* during the *Cold War.* Indeed, it can be located in some form in reporting, historical literature, or film, about nearly every modern conflict. *See also military industrial complex.*

Mercosur. Southern Cone Common Market. A *free trade* association set up in 1991, building upon an earlier Argentine-Brazilian agreement and taking advantage of a continental turn toward *democracy* after the *Falkland's War* and *debt crisis.* It sought to combine the larger economies of Argentina and Brazil with the smaller economies of neighboring Paraguay and Uruguay. Its immediate aim was to create a *customs union* among member states; its ultimate declared aim was to set up an inclusive South American Free Trade Association (SAFTA), modeled on *NAFTA* but aiming to go beyond even that agreement's regional benefits. In 1996 Chile joined as an associate member, and Bolivia became an observer. Further progress stalled in the late 1990s as Brazil entered *recession* and Argentina suffered through a major currency crisis.

mestizos. "Mixed (race)." Racially blended people descended from Spanish *conquistadores* and settlers who married Indian women, and later also Africans, and who today form the majority of the Latin American population.

metastrategy. *See game theory.*

metropolitan power. (1) The dominant or imperial power in a colonial relationship. (2) The home or original country of a *multinational corporation. See also crown colony.*

Metternich, [Prince] Klemens (1773–1859). Austrian statesman, though not of Austrian nationality. Foreign minister, 1809–1848; chancellor, 1821–1848. Metternich first worked for the small German state of Westphalia, but entered Austrian service in 1801 as *minister* in Dresden (Saxony). In 1803 he was appointed minister to the Prussian court in Berlin, and in 1805 (after *Austerlitz*) he moved to Paris. Foreign minister from 1809, he appeared to accept the French alliance, even arranging a *dynastic marriage* to connect *Napoleon* to the House of *Habsburg*: the wedding of Napoleon and Maria Theresa, daughter of the Austrian Emperor, was a consummation of the diplomatic art by which the crafty Metternich lulled Napoleon while Austria again prepared for war and waited for the moment to strike. That came in 1813 after the *retreat from Moscow.* Metternich helped form the *Quadruple Alliance* and directed Austrian policy during the *War of the Fourth Coalition.* Highly active and even dominant at the *Congress of Vienna*, he worked to prevent Prussian domination of Germany, forestall displacement of Austrian influence from north Italy, prevent a Prussian-Russian war from breaking out over yet another *partition of Poland*, foil Russian territorial ambitions in Poland (in this latter task, he failed), and cooperate with *Castlereagh* to restore the *balance of power* to its pre–*French Revolution* preeminence as the guiding principle of European interstate affairs.

Subsequently, Metternich presided over the *Congress system* and within the *Concert of Europe* and pandered to *Alexander II*'s interest in the *Holy Alliance* without fully endorsing its goals or interventionist ambitions. He oversaw the so-called Metternich system, wherein conservative monarchs and social classes cooperated to maintain balance of power diplomacy on a pan-European basis, but also to repress *liberal* reform in home affairs and suppress outbreaks of *nationalism* seen to threaten the very existence of a multinational empire such as Austria. He was therefore widely seen by liberal reformers and revolutionaries as the principal *reactionary* of the age. Even so, this reputation for reaction is sometimes overdone. Metternich was not principally responsible for Austria's police state, for instance, because he was never permitted (as a foreigner) to guide Austria's domestic affairs. After 1815 his diplomacy focused on growing turmoil and nationalist sentiment in Italy, from which he banished *Mazzini* in 1831, and on the *Eastern Question* as it pertained especially to the *Balkans.* Metternich negotiated the *Münchengrätz Agreements* (1833) with *Nicholas I*, proposing a partition of the *Ottoman Empire* should it collapse and mutual guarantees of their extant occupation and partition of Poland. He kept an interest in Germany, but left intra-German politics more to *Prussia* than had his predecessors, reflecting the fact that Austria's position there had in fact been weakened by the great events of 1792 to 1815. His office as chancellor, and his "system," were alike overthrown by the *Revolutions of 1848*. Metternich went into exile in England, but returned in 1849 to play—from his retirement in a Rhenish castle—the role of *elder statesman* to the whole of conservative Europe.

Suggested Readings: Henry Kissinger, *A World Restored* (1957); Paul Schroeder, *The Transformation of European Politics, 1763–1848* (1994).

Metz. A French fortress that witnessed battles between French and German forces in 1870 (*Franco-Prussian War*), 1918 (*World War I*), 1940, and 1944 (*World War II*). In the last battle, the French were joined by other *Allies*.

Mexican-American War (1846–1848). After the United States annexed *Texas* in 1845, relations with Mexico deteriorated rapidly and severely. President *James Polk*, who decided on war as the best means of acquiring *California* after a half-hearted attempt to buy the territory, sent troops into a disputed area (March 1846) in a clear *provocation* to Mexico, then deeply internally divided (some states would refuse to participate in the war). When the Mexican Army under *Santa Anna* was dutifully provoked and attacked (April 1846), Polk asked Congress to *declare war*. He was opposed by the *Whigs*, but rode a cresting wave of public support into the conflict. (Among the Whigs was a young congressman, *Abraham Lincoln*, who challenged Polk's *expansionism* and belligerence without success.) The resulting military clash was among the most one-sided victories in American history. *Zachary Taylor* defended the Texas border and then invaded northern Mexico (May–September 1846), while a small expedition was sent to secure California. Taylor faced Santa Anna and a large Mexican force at Buena Vista (February 1847). Behind Santa Anna, U.S. forces commanded by *Winfield Scott* landed and captured Veracruz (March 1847), in the first amphibious operation ever launched by the U.S. Army, and then moved inland to take Mexico City (April–September 1947). The fall of its capital and defeat of its army forced upon Mexico the onerous terms of the *Treaty of Guadalupe Hidalgo*. The extent of its national humiliation left Mexico permanently embittered toward its large neighbor and pushed Santa Anna from power. In the short-term, America's victory soon turned to ashes in the mouth: within a decade the newly acquired lands asked for statehood and admission to the Union, raising the great and fatal question of *slave state* versus *free soil*, which hastened the awful carnage of the *American Civil War*. Longer term, however, the war left the United States unchallenged as leader in North America and launched it as a Pacific power as well. Many of the young officers who first saw action in Mexico—including *Grant*, *Lee*, and *Sherman*—would later face each other during the Civil War. *See also manifest destiny.*

Suggested Readings: John Eisenhower, *So Far From God* (1989); Norman Graebner, *Empire on the Pacific* (1955); David Pletcher, *The Diplomacy of Annexation* (1973); John H. Schroeder, *Mr. Polk's War* (1973).

Mexican Revolution (1911–1920). The *Díaz* dictatorship staggered to its end facing multiple uprisings. In the north, the bandit leader *Pancho Villa* organized a peasant uprising, while *Emiliano Zapata* led Indian peasants in a southern revolt, and in central Mexico liberals and constitutionalists fought the old guard of the social and political order. Díaz fled Mexico in 1911, but the new leadership failed to satisfy Indian or peasant demands and fell out among themselves. *Woodrow Wilson* ordered U.S. intervention in 1913, helping to bring the constitutionalists to power in Veracruz with direct intervention by U.S. troops (April 1914). Opposing the constitutionalists was Army Chief Victoriano Huerta and the landed oligarchy. In all, perhaps one million died as armies ranged north and south over Mexico, in a paroxysm of bloodletting, rape, and massacre. Huerta was essentially finished by July 1914. Then the constitutionalists violently argued about the social and economic meaning of the revolution. *Venustiano Carranza*—who was less than devoted to social revolution—had emerged as leader of the northern constitutionalists and became president, 1915–1920.

Carranza was opposed by Villa and especially by Zapata after it became clear his dedication to *agrarian reform* was fairly shallow. In November 1914 Carranza left Mexico City for Veracruz, and Villa occupied the capital, where he was soon joined by Zapata. The U.S. supplied Carranza with weapons, which gave him a distinct advantage. Villa retired to the north, but was pursued, and at the Battle of Celaya Villa's forces were defeated by Carranza's. Back in the north country, Villa's army fell apart and, although he kept up an intermittent *guerrilla* campaign for several years, he never again threatened to take power. Meanwhile, Zapata withdrew his forces from Mexico City to his home province of Morelos. Thus began a period of continuous civil war, though at a lesser scale of violence than from 1913 to 1915. Carranza alienated Wilson in 1917 by his (entirely defensible) refusal to take Mexico into *World War I*. A fairly radical constitution was passed in 1917, severely and clearly separating church and state, breaking up and redistributing some larger landholdings, and granting some workers' rights. These gains were consolidated during the 1920s, but the social revolution many hoped for was stymied and the revolutionary myth instead was made to serve the Institutional Revolutionary Party, which governed Mexico to the end of the twentieth century.

Suggested Readings: Samuel Brunk, *Emiliano Zapata: Revolution and Betrayal in Mexico* (1995); Alan Knight, *The Mexican Revolution*, 2 vols. (1990); Frank McLynn, *Villa and Zapata: A Biography of the Mexican Revolution* (2000); Robert Quirk, *The Mexican Revolution, 1914–1915* (1963).

Mexico. Among the earliest known Amerindian civilizations in Mexico was the Olmec culture inhabiting the Gulf coast of North America. To the south, in the Yucatan peninsula, *Mayan* civilization crept upward from Central America. The Maya flourished between the fourth and ninth centuries C.E. before collapsing mysteriously, leaving few traces beyond magnificent, abandoned *city-states*. Among later, less spectacular Amerindian cultures in what is now Mexico were the Toltecs (centered on the city of Tula) and Mixtecs; their states were already in decline, however, by the twelfth century. A ruthless warrior tribe, the *Aztecs* (Mexica), overran much of central Mexico in the fourteenth century, just before the arrival of Europeans. The Aztec Empire collapsed suddenly, between 1519 and 1521, falling with spectacular speed and relative ease to Spanish marauders led by *Cortés*, but more to his host of allies among other Indians keen to overturn the Aztec tyranny. Unfortunately, what replaced that native tyranny was mass death, mostly from unintentionally imported diseases but also from intentionally cruel Spanish exploitation. New Spain's *audiencia* was established in 1527. It was the first Spanish court on the mainland of the Americas and remained a key institution of Mexican governance throughout the colonial period. Also during the colonial period, Mexico City (built on top of the Aztec capital, Tenochtitlan) became one of the great urban centers anywhere in the *New World*— providing some grace amid the squalor and exploitation of Spanish rule, and much squalor amid the privilege and grace of its urban life. In the 1540s major silver deposits were discovered in the north, drawing the Spanish conquest there. Still, the upcountry conquest of Mexico took the Spanish until about 1600. Local discontents were legion, but remained local: in the eighteenth century there were more than a hundred minor uprisings in various states of Mexico, but none coalesced into a major Indian rebellion. A sharp repression by the audiencia from 1808 drove dissent underground, where it built pressures toward a later explosion. This came in the critical year for almost all *Spanish America*, 1810. This time, local revolt proved a spark that ignited the tinder of a national rebellion, as Creole nationalists and republicans and Indian peasants alike took full advantage of Spain's entanglement in the *Peninsular War* in order to express and advance their grievances against the status quo.

The rebellion that broke out in Mexico in 1810 drew upon multiple sources. At first it was led mainly by *Creole* elites in the cities, though it found its original expression in leadership by the radical country priest Miguel Hidalgo y Costilla (1753–1811), who issued the "grito de Dolores" ("cry of Dolores") on September 16, 1810, and started a march across Mexico hoisting a statue of the Virgin of Guadalupe at the head of his procession. The claims of this rising were heartfelt, and the justice of their demands and grievances— an end to Indian *tribute*, abolition of *slavery*, land reform and redistribution, and only later, also independence from Spain—has left Mexico with a popular legacy of admiration for their heroism and principles. In fact, Hidalgo's revolt was little more than a *jacquerie*. On September 23rd, his peasant and Indian mob reached the provincial city of Guanajuato, where it revealed a definite racial component to the uprising by indiscriminate killing of Creoles and Spaniards. In October the "army of the poor," numbering perhaps 85,000, took Morelia (Valladolid) and then turned toward Mexico City. A battle was joined with Creole *militia* on October 30th, but actual fighting rather than *sacking* and *pillage* did not appeal to many of Hidalgo's recruits, who therefore returned home with their *plunder*. On January 17, 1811, the remnant of Hidalgo's dwindling force was crushed in another battle with the Creole militia at Guadalajara. Hidalgo was later caught trying to flee to the United States and was executed.

Grassroots rebellion continued, however, under another parish priest, and a mule driver's son, Jose Maria Morelos y Pavón (1765–1815). An early supporter of Hidalgo, he organized a small army in 1811 and in early 1813 took Acapulco, but then was defeated and forced into a protracted defensive war. He was captured only in 1815. He was convicted by the Catholic Church of heresy and by New Spain of treason and was shot (December 22, 1815). Not all Mexicans approved of rebellion and some fought to retain the tie to Spain, notably most conservative and devoutly Catholic Creoles. In 1812 a *liberal* constitution was proclaimed in Spain itself by the Cortes in Cadiz. This formed up sides in Mexico, of supporters and opponents of liberal reform. Adding to the resentment and turmoil, the Spanish continued to insist upon *mercantilist* trade relations with Mexico. Independence was proclaimed in 1822 after a proposal by Augustín de Iturbide (1783–1824), who had helped defeat Morales, for a separate Mexican monarchy. Support for Iturbide built during 1821, and he quickly crushed the opposition. In July 1821, the Spanish garrison in Mexico City *mutinied* against the viceroy. In September, the last Spanish troops surrendered to Iturbide and the new Spanish Captain-General, with whom Iturbide had met and arranged a settlement; thus the rebellion ended with a whimper rather than an explosion. Mexico had not so much rebelled against an empire, as sensibly left a rickety structure that was collapsing anyway.

Mexico was dominated by *Santa Anna* for the next several decades. It lost Texas to *secession* and then had *California* and other sizeable territories north of the Rio Grande stripped from it upon defeat in the *Mexican-American War*. In 1855 Mexican liberals under *Juárez* drove Santa Anna from power. La Reforma (a brimming, liberal movement among Mexico's ruling classes) climaxed in a new and progressive constitution in 1857. Unfortunately, this liberal turn in the road led to the War of the Reform among Mexicans, of which *Napoleon III* took advantage to invade and impose upon Mexico the "empire" of *Maximilian*. War against the French continued until 1867, when the republic was restored. From 1876 to 1911 there was relative peace and prosperity under *Porfirio Díaz*. That period was followed by the huge turmoil of the *Mexican Revolution* (1911–1920) and U.S. intervention. The revolution comprised a series of agrarian and constitutionalist uprisings under leaders as varied as *Venustiano Carranza, Pancho Villa,* and *Emilio Zapata*; it ended in *civil war* among the victorious revolutionaries and in the dictatorship of Plutarco Calles (1877–1945), 1924–1928. Preoccupied with internal conflict, Mexico stayed out of *World War I*. From 1929 to 1999 Mexico was ruled by a single party, the Institutional Revolutionary Party (PRI), which kept up a leftist rhetoric while running statist (*import-substitution*) and social conservative, but also anticlerical, policies. As a result of the *Great Depression*, from 1934 to 1940 the PRI under Lázero Cárdenas (1895–1970) instituted *agrarian reform*, which ended the semi-feudal "latifundia" and *nationalized* the *oil* industry (1937). *Camacho Ávila* continued these reforms. He also took Mexico into *World War II*, declaring war on the *Axis* in 1942, but playing a minor role and contributing few forces.

Mexico incrementally *modernized* during the 1950s and 1960s, utilizing steady oil revenues. It ran up enormous *debt* through excessive borrowing in the 1970s. In 1968 a draconian police and military response to riots in Mexico City left hundreds dead and the country shaken. Under Luis Echeverria (1970–1976), Mexico followed a more activist (and leftist) diplomacy in regional affairs. In the 1980s, too, it tried to *mediate* conflicts in Central America that threatened to destabilize its southern regions. Its economic crisis came to a head in 1981 and it was compelled to seek massive international financial assistance. In 1993 Mexico joined *NAFTA*. On January 1, 1994, an uprising of *indigenous people* took place in southern Mexico (Chiapas). Its declared, and proximate, cause was the NAFTA accord, but its root causes lay buried in the deeper soils of rural poverty, discriminatory landholding laws, and central government neglect. In 1997 a massacre of Chiapas Indians demonstrated that the crisis was far from resolved. That year, Mexico also joined the OECD, signed a *free trade* agreement with Colombia and Venezuela, and again received massive international financial assistance and debt relief. In 1999 the PRI was defeated by a conservative businessman, Vincente Fox, as Mexico witnessed its first peaceful and democratic transition of power since the Revolution.

Suggested Readings: Jan Bazant, *A Concise History of Mexico, From Hidalgo to Cárdenas, 1805–1940* (1977); Hugh Hamill, *The Hidalgo Revolt* (1966); Enrique Krauze, *Mexico* (1998).

Mfecane (1816–1828). "Time of Troubles" or, alternately, "The Crushing." (Zulu: Mfecane; Sotho: Difaqane) Sparked by the astonishingly brutal military *imperialism* of the *Zulu*, but arising primarily from population growth and land hunger among the *Nguni* peoples of southern Africa, it was launched against the other Nguni tribes, 1816–1828, by the Zulu under the leadership of *Shaka*. The Nguni had been migrating south for years, mostly at the expense of San and Khoi. Then they encountered better-armed *Boers* migrating northward from *Cape Colony*. This blocked southward migration and increased already enormous pressure on the Nguni to find grazing lands to support their rapidly growing population. Two Nguni tribes, the Swazi and Zulu, responded to the crisis in like manner: they developed tight military structures and launched aggressive wars against their neighbors, driving all others from the grazing lands. This was the root cause of the Mfecane. It took on its peculiarly destructive and bloody character, however, owing to the driven and indeed also twisted personality of Shaka, who instituted a condition of permanent warfare in the region. Perhaps a million were killed, while several million Nguni were displaced by the expanding Zulu. By some estimates 15,000 square miles were rendered devoid of human life so the Zulu could camp and graze their cattle there. Some Zulu generals broke with Shaka, joining but also driving the mass of refugees away from his lands. Other tribes mimicked the Zulu military formations in order to defend themselves, or to conquer others in order to survive: the Sotho moved into Transvaal and Botswana in the 1820s; parts of modern *Zimbabwe* were overrun from 1832 by displaced Nguni (the Ndebele) under a former Zulu general; other displaced Nguni regiments raided in the 1840s as far north as the southern shore of Lake Victoria and as far east as the Lozi Kingdom on the Zambezi. Two tribes fended off the Zulu: the Swazi settled in what became Swaziland, and the Basuto founded and defended Lesotho. Back in the original lands, whole areas were depopulated and thus left ripe for Boer and British expansion and conquest later in the nineteenth century. *See also Great Trek; Swaziland.*

MI5/MI6. The twinned British *intelligence* and security services. MI5 handles *counterintelligence* and counterterrorism within Britain; MI6 operates overseas and is the intelligence-gathering and *covert action* branch. Its early concerns were preserving the *British Empire* from "subversive" *nationalists* and countering the *Bolshevik* threat. Both concerns were overwhelmed by the advent of *Hitler* in Germany. British intelligence reacted slowly at first, still concentrating on Moscow at the cost of monitoring Berlin. It recovered, to enjoy its finest hour during *World War II*, when it greatly contributed to British and Allied victory. On the other hand, it failed to block Soviet penetration of the British team (*Klaus Fuchs*) involved in the *Manhattan Project*. During the *Cold War*, British intelligence worked closely with the *Central Intelligence Agency* and other American intelligence agencies to gather information and conduct operations, though the relationship was not without its suspicions and rivalries. In the late 1940s, both supported Ukrainian resistance to the reimposition of Soviet rule. In 1950 it was involved in a failed effort to overthrow *Enver Hoxha* of Albania. Afterward, this "cowboy" era of covert operations declined in favor of analysis. Then the British secret service was racked by scandal and controversy, as it was discovered it had been deeply penetrated by multiple Soviet *moles*. The most damaging scandal was over identification of a high-profile ring of spies for the Soviet Union known as the "Cambridge Comintern," bound to each other by their homosexuality, alienation, and recruitment at the University of Cambridge. Two of the group—Guy Burgess and Donald Maclean—defected to Moscow just before they were uncovered, with the help of a third mole, Kim Philby. A fourth friend, Anthony Blunt, eventually was caught and confessed, but his confession was kept secret by the "old-boy network" until the 1980s, and Blunt was even allowed to continue to serve as the Queen's personal art curator. Persistent rumors about a fifth man in the ring led to identification in 1990 of John Cairncross. In the 1980s MI6 cooperated closely with the CIA in the highly successful training (in Scotland) and arming of the Afghan *mujahadeen* and in running information-gathering networks out of Pakistan.

Suggested Readings: G. Borovik, *The Philby File* (1994); Stephen Dorrill, *MI6* (2000); *Jane's Intelligence Review* (1991–).

micro credit. A *development* strategy in which tiny loans are granted to the very poor to start up small businesses. As opposed to welfare, this fosters entrepreneurial behavior and self-reliance rather than passive dependence.

microeconomics. A subfield of *economics* that looks at the market behavior of individuals and enterprises, especially as to how this affects *supply*, demand, and production costs.

Micronesia. The "little islands." A subdivision of *Oceania*, consisting of island groups north of the equator and east of the Philippines: the *Carolines*, *Marianas*, *Marshalls*, and remaining small *trust territories*.

Micronesia, Federated States of (FSM). Germany bought these South Pacific islands from Spain (1898). They were invaded by Japan (1914), which from 1920 oversaw them as a *mandate territory* of the *League of Nations*. During *World War II* the four islands that make up the Federated States of Micronesia (Kosrae, Pohnpei, Truk, and *Yap*) were *occupied* by the United States. Later administered as part of the *Trust Territory of the Pacific Islands*, they rejected a 1969 offer of *commonwealth status*, opting instead for *free association* with the United States. They signed a compact in 1982 (ratified by *referendum* in 1983), which granted *autonomy* but left the United States in charge of *defense*. The United Nations *Trusteeship Council* endorsed the change, and in 1990 the *Security Council* ended the trusteeship. In 1991 Micronesia joined the United Nations, where it is one of the smaller members in terms of population and resources.

microstates. Formerly "dwarf states." Tiny nations with an extremely small area and/or population: *Andorra*, *Dominica*, *Kiribati*, *Liechtenstein*, *Monaco*, *Maldives*, *Nauru*, *San Marino*, and *Tuvalu*. See also *associated states*.

Middle East. Looking from Western Europe from the eighth century C.E., the Middle East was the great *Muslim* domain stretching from India to Persia, the Arabian desert, Syria, Palestine and Egypt. It refers now mainly to the states clustered near the eastern Mediterranean: Egypt, Iran, Iraq, Israel, Jordan, Lebanon, Saudi Arabia, the Gulf States, Syria, and Turkey. Some usages include Cyprus, Libya, and the *Maghreb*.

Suggested Reading: Efraim Karsh, *Empires of the Sand* (1999).

middle power. One not ranked among the *Great Powers*, but whose *capabilities*, interests, and *influence* clearly rank it ahead of small powers. In 1945 Canada led an effort to obtain official recognition of this term and status within the United Nations, but was rebuffed by all the Great Powers. "Middlepowermanship" is thus more of a national (or elite) state of mind than a formal ranking. It also implies a *multilateral* slant to foreign policy and a readiness to perform tasks according to one's *functional* abilities, including *mediation, good offices, advisory services*, and so forth. Canada and Sweden rank among (unofficial, self-described) middle powers in part because that is how they view themselves, which makes the ranking something of a self-fulfilling prophesy through sustained efforts to live up to it. Of course, this also involves a considerable craving for *prestige*. Poland, Argentina, and similarly sized states might rank as middle powers according to fairly objective measures of power, should they seek to play a wider international role in the twenty-first century than they did for most of the twentieth.

Midway, Battle of (June 4–5, 1942). The decisive naval engagement in the Pacific in *World War II*. After the *Doolittle raid* on Tokyo, the Japanese were determined to capture *Midway Island*, which they saw as the outer sentry of the U.S. Navy based at Pearl Harbor in Hawaii. The American and Japanese fleets never sighted each other, making Midway the first major sea battle decided solely by naval *air power*. While the U.S. island airport and base was heavily pounded, American fliers sank four Japanese *aircraft carriers*, while losing just one of their own. The victory turned the tide of the *Pacific War*. Before Midway, Japan's carrier force was the largest in the world, outnumbering the U.S. fleet in the Pacific 10 to 3. Midway evened the military balance and, indeed, forced Japan onto the defensive within just six months of its great successes at *Pearl Harbor, Singapore, Hong Kong*, and elsewhere. Subsequently, the United States out-built Japan in all classes of carriers and aircraft and carried the fight into the Japanese *home islands*. *See also Battle of the Atlantic; Jutland; Leyte Gulf; Chester Nimitz; Trafalgar; Yamamoto Isoroku.*

Midway Island. This North Pacific island was acquired by the United States in 1867. Because it has no *indigenous* population, it is administered by the U.S. Navy, which still maintains an important base there. *See also Battle of Midway.*

MIG. A series of Russian-built *fighters* named for the Russian aircraft designers Mikoyan and Gurevich. In the 1960s and 1970s the MIG-21 became the most widely used military aircraft in the world. By 2001, the most advanced model was the MIG-31.

migration. The voluntary relocation of people within or across national borders. Involuntary migrants are called *refugees*. Migration occurs for climatological (drought, flood), social, or economic (escaping discrimination at home or seeking better opportunities elsewhere) reasons, but ethnic conflict and *human rights* violations also greatly contribute. Migration poses major questions of *immigration* policy, *indigenous peoples'* rights, regional *development*, and international as well as internal race relations. Cheap transportation (canals, railways, steamships) greatly spurred international migration beginning in the early nineteenth century. Some 60 million Europeans left that continent between the *Napoleonic Wars* and *World War I*, with the outflow peaking at about one million per year by 1914; 40 million of these migrated to North America between 1850 and 1914. Many more tens of millions migrated within Europe, from rural areas to the cities, from one economic region to another, from Germany to Poland and Russia, and so on. The *Great Depression*, *World War II*, and the *Cold War* all impeded international migration, which dropped to just 50,000 per year between 1930 and 1945 and became more heavily political rather than economic in inspiration. The end of the Cold War sped up international flows once again. With the end of empire, 1945–1975, millions of Indians and Africans independently sought entry to Western Europe, where they were joined in the 1990s by East Europeans freed to move by the fall of communism. Similarly, millions of economic migrants from Central America, Cuba, Haiti, and Mexico migrated to the United States in the second half of the twentieth century, overcoming most efforts to stem the flow.

Migration tends to overwhelm political boundaries over time, but states nonetheless seek to at least channel it in directions that serve their perceived interests. This has been especially true of empires, which sought to direct external migration to recently conquered areas. Such policies brought British to *Cape Colony* and the *White Highlands* in Africa and elsewhere in the vast *British Empire*, and French *colons* to the four corners of the earth. Similarly, some 25 million Russians migrated from Russia to conquered lands within the boundaries of the Russian empire. With the collapse of the Soviet Union they found themselves politically stranded in the *near abroad*. Similarly, Chinese internal migration over the centuries naturally ran from the arid north and west to the more fertile south. This was reversed by force and policy during the *Communist* epoch. At the close of the twentieth century, however, as internal controls eased, Chinese internal migration again ran from the poor north to the advanced south and from the peasant interior to the urban coast. As before in Chinese history, this caused severe regional tensions and problems of uneven internal development. Similarly, within the continental United States, migration historically has tended to flow from the northeast coast to the southwest. *See also passport.*

militarism. This term is very often used loosely and nearly always in the pejorative. (1) A spirit or habit of mind that regards the rigors and virtues of military life as both an individual and national ideal. It endorses hierarchical political and social organization, calls for self-sacrifice for the greater good, and accepts warfare as inevitable, perhaps even desirable, and as both inculcating and requiring strong civic virtues and heroic leaders. Unlike *feudalism*, in which military virtues were confined to a single, warrior class, militarism calls for infusing the whole society with a martial spirit. A sure sign of militarist politics is when civilian leaders appear in uniform. In many countries and cultures, such celebration of a sacralized state or nation occurred when loyalty to organized religion faded or was swept aside by some revolutionary idea. (2) Maintaining a large military, even when doing so absorbs too much of the material wealth of a nation, dominates politics, and corrupts the economy. *See also demilitarization; fascism; Imperial Way; kokutai; levée en masse; militarization; National Socialism; pacifism; Potsdam Declaration; social Darwinism; Third World; World War I; World War II.*

militarist. A person who espouses a policy or exhibits a spirit of *militarism*.

militarization. (1) To suffuse a population with a spirit of *militarism*. (2) To enlist or equip a region with military supplies. During the nineteenth century a huge multiplication of force took place in Europe. This resulted in the first instance from a large increase in the population, which made it possible to have much larger armies as the decades passed. In addition, the *agricultural revolution* made these armies healthier and the *Industrial Revolution* made them better armed. In combination, the overall expansion of the economy made it possible for states to raise more taxes and to use these funds to sustain larger armies and navies and institute permanent *conscription*. Finally, new and more destructive weapons became available with the harnessing of steam power, better smelting processes to make steel and alloys, the invention of breechloading rifles and guns, and the invention of TNT and nitroglycerine. During the second half of the twentieth century, most of the rest of the world replicated the European experience, so that upon entering the twenty-first century humanity was more heavily militarized than at any prior point in its history. *See also demilitarize; feudalism; Pax Romana; revolution in military affairs; total war.*

military attaché. *See attaché.*

Military Conversations (1906–1914). Talks between the British and French *General Staffs* (also including the Belgians) that aimed at increasing army cooperation in the event of *war* with Germany. Naval talks did not begin until 1912, and with Russia not until June 1914. This was as close as these powers came to *alliance* before September 1914, when in the aftermath of *hostilities* a formal *pact* was signed. *See also* Entente Cordiale; *Triple Entente.*

military government. (1) A domestic *regime* in which the military has seized power and rules by issuing decrees enforced by draconian punishments. (2)

A temporary legal situation during an *invasion* or *occupation*, where the local population is placed under foreign military authority. *See also Berlin; Lucius Clay; Douglas MacArthur; martial law.*

military-industrial complex. A phrase first used by President *Dwight D. Eisenhower* in his 1961 Farewell Address. He warned the American people not to permit their most important national decisions to be skewed by the narrow, special interests of "an immense military establishment and a large arms industry . . . new in the American experience. . . . We recognize the need for this development. Yet we must . . . guard against the acquisition of unwarranted influence, whether sought or unsought, by the military-industrial complex." This fear largely reflected Eisenhower's small-town, *Republican Party*, and fiscally conservative values, which were threatened by the need for a large peacetime military to prosecute the *Cold War*. The phrase was later used to refer to the symbiotic relationship between certain industries (automotive, steel, chemical, aeronautic, and, later, computer and space) and military decision-makers in most major powers. It was subsequently used as a pejorative, often without due discrimination. *See also "merchants of death"; Minatom; People's Liberation Army.*

military law. (1) A synonym for *martial law.* (2) The discrete code of professional and legal conduct applied to serving officers and troops, but not civilians.

military necessity. A moral argument claiming that a waiver of normal ethical guidelines is warranted if one cannot avoid violating such rules when carrying out the destruction of a legitimate *military objective. See also collateral damage; just war.*

military objective. Any target the loss or damage of which will reduce the military performance and/or capabilities of the enemy. *See also collateral damage.*

military ranks. Military ranks vary from country to country and over time. Some are not recognized in certain armies or navies. In general, however, they are:

In most armies: (1) private: a soldier of any of the three lowest grades; (2) corporal: a *noncommissioned officer* of the lowest rank; (3) sergeant: a noncommissioned officer above corporal (sergeant-major is the highest grade within the sergeant classification, as well as the highest grade of noncommissioned officer); (4) lieutenant: the lowest class of ranks of *commissioned officers*; (5) captain: above lieutenant, in command of a company; (6) major: above captain, in command of a battalion; (7) colonel: a rank forming several grades between major and general, usually in command of a brigade; (8) general: several grades of officer of the second highest rank (first in the United States), usually in command of a division or larger unit; (9) marshal: the highest possible rank, ranging in Britain, Germany, and some other armies to a grade of field marshal. In the modern French Army "Maréchal" was not a rank but a state title conferred on victors. Retired by France after the *Napoleonic Wars*, it was revived in 1916 and awarded to *Joffre* to spare him the humiliation of losing actual command. The United States does not use this rank.

In most air forces: (1) flight commander: an officer in charge of a flight; (2) group commander: an officer in charge of a group; (3) wing commander: an officer in charge of a wing of aircraft. Note: for the composition of a flight, group, or wing, see *military units*, below.

In most navies: (1) sailor: equivalent to private; (2) warrant officers: all noncommissioned officers; (3) ensign: the lowest ranked commissioned officer; (4) lieutenant: ranked above ensign; (5) commander: the third tier of officer grades; (6) captain: an officer in command of a *warship*, ranking below admiral; (7) admiral: several grades of the highest rank, peaking at fleet, rear, or grand admiral in some navies; usually commanding a fleet. *See also brevet promotion; flag officer; officer; officer corps; petty officer.*

military revolution. *See revolution in military affairs.*

military science. Professional study, undertaken mainly by an *officer corps*, of the causes and nature, but especially of the tactics and stratagems, of *war*. *See also Karl Maria von Clausewitz; Antoine-Henri Jomini; Niccolò di Bernardo Machiavelli; Sébastien le Prestre de Vauban.*

military spending. All spending on *arms*, *logistics*, and support (housing, uniforms, food, and pay) of military personnel. Global military spending is a major sector of the world economy, valued at many hundreds of billions of dollars per year.

military units. These units varied greatly in size and firepower over the centuries and vary from country to country. In general, however, they are:

In most armies: (1) squad: the smallest group into which regular soldiers are organized; (2) platoon: three or four squads under the command of a junior *officer*; (3) company: four or more platoons and a headquarters (in the *artillery*, this is called a battery); (4) battalion: four to five companies and a field headquarters; (5) brigade or regiment: three battalions and a regimental headquarters; (6) division: this innovative unit dates to the *revolution in military affairs* of the *Napoleonic Wars*, when it was comprised of 12 battalions of infantry and 12 of artillery (12,000 muskets and 72 field guns); it later consisted of three brigades or regiments and a divisional headquarters, with combat support personnel, artillery batteries, and transport units attached; (7)

corps: two or three divisions, a corps headquarters, field hospitals, transport, and so on; (8) army: two or more corps, a major headquarters with support staff, whole divisions of artillery, and often control of air units as well.

In most air forces: (1) flight: the smallest air unit, often used for specific missions or routine patrolling; (2) squadron: the foundation unit of an air force; (3) group: two or more squadrons and a substantial headquarters; (4) wing: a large unit, though varying in size and number of aircraft from air force to air force, and war to war; (5) division: the largest manageable air formation.

In most navies: (1) squadron: a small unit of two or more ships, assigned to a specific patrol or mission; (2) flotilla: two or more squadrons of ships, up to a small fleet; (3) fleet: the largest naval unit under the command of a single officer, usually an admiral. An alternate meaning of "fleet" is the total naval forces of a nation, as in "the Japanese Fleet."

militia. (1) A military *reserve*, called up only during emergencies. (2) A private military force. (3) A nonprofessional army *mustered* from citizen volunteers. *See also guerrilla war*; levée en masse; *partisans*; *people's war*; *Resistance*; *skirmishers*.

Milošević, Slobodan (b. 1941). Serb dictator. Thuggish, sleazy, and thoroughly corrupt, he came to power in part because *Tito* unintentionally cleared the path for a character like him by *purging* reform-minded Serbian *Communists* in the 1970s. He consolidated his personal grip on power, 1987–1988, around an expedient conversion to *nationalism* as *Yugoslavia* began to break apart. He clearly counted on a deliberate policy of *war* to keep him in power as the federation disintegrated. He aided Serb *militia* in their aggressive and often savage fight for *territory*, and he supported their *ethnic cleansing*, in Croatia and *Bosnia* through the mid-1990s. The early successes of Serbian arms, and *NATO*'s desire to negotiate any deal over Bosnia that would forestall a threat to alliance cohesion, allowed Milošević to slip "peacemaker" clothes over his wolflike policies even as fighting continued in Bosnia, 1993–1994. When NATO finally intervened with force in Bosnia, he shifted his attention to *Kosovo*, where ethnic Albanians were beginning to resist the iron grip he maintained on the province. In the second half of the 1990s Milošević's policy of serial *aggression* brought international disapprobation and *sanctions* down upon Serbia. He thereby gave Serbs *hyperinflation*, consumer shortages, deepening poverty, *secret police*, and many thousands of dead, in the effort to retain power for himself and his cronies and in the name of delivering *Greater Serbia*. In 1999 Milošević led Serbia into war with NATO over stepped-up ethnic cleansing in Kosovo. When he lost that historic province, he was ousted. In 1999 he was indicted for *war crimes* by the International Tribunal in The Hague. He was defeated in Serbian elections in 2000 by a public that yearned for a more normal national life after a decade of war and nationalist hysteria. The next spring in 2001 he was arrested—over the violent resistance of die-hard supporters—on charges of corruption. In July 2001, he was deported to The Hague to stand trial for war crimes, including for authorizing acts of *genocide*. He refused to answer questions or in any way to recognize the jurisdiction of the court, proffering only the demonstrably absurd defense that he had worked his whole career to maintain peace in the region and always in defense of Serbia against putatively aggressive neighbors and enemies. The trial continued into 2002.

Minatom. Code-named "Ministry for Medium Machine Building" during the *Cold War*, afterward renamed Ministry of Nuclear (Atomic) Energy, or Minatom. It was the top-secret *nuclear weapons* research arm of the Soviet state and later a somewhat more open ministry of the post-Soviet Russian government. It was set up by *Lavrenti Beria* in 1942 to begin a crash research program into building a Soviet *atomic bomb*. It quickly expanded into *missile* and other related weapons research, design, and manufacture. In its early work, at least, it drew heavily upon information obtained through *espionage* by *Klaus Fuchs* and others within the *Manhattan Project*. Relying on *slave labor* from the GULAG, Beria built a vast complex of secret cities, some reaching populations of scientists, engineers, and their families numbering more than 100,000 without appearing on Soviet maps. This *elite* lived pampered lifestyles and enjoyed great prestige within the *nomenklatura*, supported by state funds and GULAG labor in return for top-secret weapons work. At least 10 large cities were constructed, and perhaps more, with Minatom's total population reaching c. 800,000. Nearly 90 secret Minatom installations and weapons factories were publicly identified after the *Cold War* ended. At one, Arzamas-16, *Sakharov* worked on the Soviet *hydrogen bomb*. Upon development of *ICBMs* by the United States, the system was spread out over Russia's vastness owing to fear of a *first strike*. Minatom kept its disasters secret too: it presided over numerous nuclear accidents, several larger than *Chernobyl*. In 1957 nearly half a million people were irradiated by an accidental release of radioactive material; they were never informed of their danger. On April 6, 1993, at Tomsk, a major accident occurred. It was immediately reported by Russia to its neighbors, unlike the long and deadly delays that had attended Chernobyl.

mine. An indiscriminate, passive, explosive weapon intended to be triggered by contact with, or in the proximity of, an enemy target, whether a person, vehicle, ship, or satellite. *See also ADM; ASAT; land mine; land mine treaty; sea mine.*

minesweeper. A (sometimes unarmed) small *warship* used to clear *sea mines* from shipping lanes.

Ming dynasty (1368–1644). The Ming defeated and ended the *Yuan dynasty* of the *Mongols* and reunited China in 1368, establishing their dynasty under a former leader of the Red Turban Rebellion, Zhu Yuanzhang, who captured Nanjing in 1356. He broke with the Red Turbans (a *White Lotus* Buddhist sect) to claim descent from the *Song*. In 1368 he proclaimed the Ming dynasty and took the reign name *Hongwu* (r. 1368–1398). Ming China experienced a surge in population growth, to 130 million by the fifteenth century. Hongwu governed from Nanjing, with great cruelty and paranoia. After a civil war among the Ming, the third Emperor, Yongle (r. 1402–1424), moved the capital to Beijing. He also commissioned seven spectacular transoceanic voyages by Admiral Zheng He, 1405–1433. Ming ships, merchants, and ambassadors spread into Asia and as far afield as eastern Africa, opening markets and establishing trade colonies nearly 100 years before *Columbus* sailed to America in much flimsier craft. These contacts importantly influenced local histories, but soon faded from memory in China: in 1433 another Ming emperor forbade trade expansion and banned ocean-capable ship-building; in 1436 he imposed a *Tokugawa*-like isolation on China, abandoning its considerable lead in *sea power* and ending its participation in the *Age of Exploration*. Within 150 years European vessels would take command of the world's sea routes, and fleets of *wakō* pirates from Japan would ravage China's coast. Worsening matters, the Ming penalized differential economic growth in the coastal regions, since they saw this as threatening central control and imperial unity. This policy stifled any possibility of emergent *capitalism* by redirecting mercantile wealth and investment into land.

Late Ming China decayed under the baleful influences of a stifling Confucian bureaucracy and fatal insulation from the emerging centers of world trade and technological innovation, which had shifted from Asia to Europe. In 1449 a Ming emperor was captured by Mongol raiders, who subsequently advanced on Beijing. After 1474, the now-terrified Ming rebuilt and extended the *Great Wall* to fortify themselves from further raids. Ming decline was hastened by the 48-year-long rule of the *Wanli* Emperor (r. 1572–1620), who progressively withdrew from public responsibilities, leaving these to corrupt and tyrannical cadres of eunuchs. *Hideyoshi*'s two Japanese invasions of Korea in the 1590s, which the Ming opposed with diplomacy and then with force, were costly in lives and national treasure and destabilized China even further. For many years Wanli withdrew from administering China. In a system in which all power flowed from the top, that resulted in administrative paralysis and widespread corruption and factionalism in the imperial court. Tax revenues fell, army mutinies and desertions threatened, damaging *inflation* set in with the arrival of large amounts of monetary metals with the new European seaborne trade, and to the north *Nurgaci* threatened with a *Manchu* army.

In 1630 Li Zicheng and Zhang Xianzhong emerged as principal *warlords* commanding huge rebel armies controlling significant parts of China, which was additionally ravaged and destabilized by outbreaks of epidemic disease and *famine*. Continuing internal political divisions—especially between the scholar-elite and Wanli's out-of-control eunuchs—and desertions by key generals contributed to Ming displacement by the Manchus (*Qing dynasty*). The end came in 1644, when Li Zicheng attacked Beijing with a vast army (hundreds of thousands strong), proclaimed himself emperor, and moved to crush General Wu Sangui, who in desperation asked the Manchus for military aid. As the dynasty collapsed around him, the last Ming emperor hanged himself just outside the *Forbidden City* (April 1644). Into this chaos, Nurgaci's successors brought the Jürchen, organized into a well-trained mass army in the *banner system*, invited through the Great Wall into China. Wu and the Manchus together took Beijing (June 1644), and the Manchus claimed the *mandate of heaven*. Fighting continued for another seventeen years against Ming diehards and pretenders, but the dynasty was never restored.

Suggested Reading: Jonathon Spence and John Wills, *From Ming to Ch'ing* (1979).

minimax principle. *See game theory.*

minimizing. *See game theory.*

minimum deterrence. Forestalling an attack with limited rather than massive retaliatory force. What constitutes a minimum deterrent in the real world is, of course, more a matter of art than political or military science. *See also credible threat.*

minimum winning coalition. *See game theory.*

minister. (1) A member of the *executive*, with full *cabinet* rank. (2) The usual title of *ambassadors* until well into the nineteenth century.

minister plenipotentiary. *See envoy extraordinary.*

ministers resident. A class of *diplomats* below *ambassador* and *envoy extraordinary.*

Ministry of Trade and Industry (MITI). Japan's super ministry charged with coordinating foreign economic policy, domestic industrial policy, and business *growth* as Japan recovered from *World War II*. It aided in coordinating private research and development with public and private financing. It also acted as management consultant. Its influence was very great, but sometimes was exaggerated to the point that MITI became feared by some foreigners. Its role was much greater in the first few decades of postwar recovery than when Japan developed an increasingly sophisticated and complex economy. In 1993–1994 MITI announced a policy shift partway from support for large conglomerates toward encouraging *venture capital* firms.

Suggested Reading: C. Johnson, *MITI and the Japanese Miracle* (1982).

Minorities Treaties. On the insistence of *Woodrow Wilson* and other *liberals*, the post–*World War I* settlement included clauses in special treaties with the new states of East and Central Europe granting full rights to ethnic and religious minorities, to be guaranteed by the *League of Nations*. There was considerable popular concern in the United States for the treatment of Jews in Poland and Rumania. For France and Britain, it was hoped that guarantees of minority rights to the Germans cut off by *Versailles* from Germany proper might help Weimar accept the larger settlement. Germany itself, therefore, was not required to grant such rights to its own minorities. *See also Volksdeutsche.*

Minuteman. (1) A member of the *militia* in the *American Revolution*. (2) An ICBM first deployed in the 1960s; it formed the core of the land-based U.S. *nuclear deterrent.*

Miranda, Francisco de (1750–1816). South American revolutionary. A controversial adventurer, he drew deeply from republican wells in United States after 1776, and France, 1792–1794, where he even commanded revolutionary troops. In 1806 he organized a small force (fewer than 200) to try to foment a rebellion against Spain in Venezuela, his native land, but this came to naught. Upon Venezuela's declaration of *independence* in 1810 he returned to take command of its small army, and in 1812 he was briefly an effective national leader. In 1812 he surrendered to the Spanish, an act that may have been unavoidable but that nonetheless earned him contempt from *Bolívar* and others. He died in a Spanish prison. *See also Marquis de Lafayette.*

mirror images. In *misperception* theory, the propensity of *decision makers* to see an opponent just as one is seen by that opponent (as hostile, aggressive, uncompromising, and so forth). In one of the more trite uses of this idea, which is otherwise not without merit as a description of one possible psychological state during a *crisis*, it was suggested by some that the *Cold War* could be reduced to the self-reinforcing perceptual image U.S. = S.U. *See also moral equivalence.*

MIRV. *See multiple independently targetable reentry vehicle.*

misperception. The inability to accurately perceive or interpret incoming information, particularly concerning an opponent's intentions. Some argue that misperception is a key cause of failures of *deterrence*, and therefore a proximate cause of *war*. *See also causation; cognitive dissonance; crisis; decision-making theory; fact-finding mission; image; levels of analysis; mirror images; rational choice theory; rational decision-making.*

missile. Any projectile weapon, whether ballistic or guided. Modern missiles have ranges from hundreds of yards to many thousands of kilometers. The larger, "smarter" ones have highly developed, controllable thrust engines, inertial guidance systems, and extensive heat shielding. See *ABM; ballistic missile; BMD; bus; cruise missile; hardening; ICBM; launcher; MIRV; missile technology control regime; SDI; smart weapons; terrain contour matching; V-1 and V-2 rockets; warhead.*

missile gap. *See Dwight Eisenhower, John Fitzgerald Kennedy; SPUTNIK.*

Missile Technology Control Regime (MTCR). This *regime* to voluntarily constrain export of *ballistic missiles* and their component parts was set up in 1987 by Britain, Canada, France, the United States, and West Germany. By 1995 an additional 20 states adhered. Some states wanted to move to a global condition of zero ballistic missiles (ZBM), including a robust ban on test flights. The MTCR remained a weak, porous instrument of little practical effect.

missing in action (MIA). A designation used of soldiers who cannot be located among the dead, wounded, deserted, or captured. After a suitable period has passed, they are (usually correctly) presumed dead. Suspicion about unreturned MIAs from the *Vietnam War* (in which there were more than 10,000 official U.S. MIAs) prevented *rapprochement* between the United States and Vietnam into the 1990s. That reflected deep distrust on the part of many Americans toward the Vietnamese regime, as well as their own government. The belief was fed by occasional reports, true or not, of sightings and concealed information, including a spectacularly misleading and reckless statement about sightings of American prisoners of war in the Soviet Union made by *Boris Yeltsin* in 1993. At another level, refusal to admit that most MIAs were probably deceased represented a deeply naïve, however human and understandable, unwillingness to accept that a war of industrialized destruction fought in a tropical jungle does not easily give up its dead. Note: Vietnam (the Republic of Vietnam [South Vietnam] and Democratic Republic of Vietnam [North Vietnam] alike) suffered many times more MIAs in the same war.

mission. (1) A diplomatic endeavor undertaken by an official below the rank of *ambassador*; (2) a field activity essayed by some international organization; (3) an outpost promoting religious conversion, operated by *missionaries. See also trade mission.*

missionaries. Most major religions have at some point in their history sent out missionaries to proselytize for converts, as well as made conversions directly by conquest and force. Chinese emperors, *Hindu* potentates, and *Muslim* sultans and holy warriors all engaged in missionary conversion, whether for political or religious reasons, or more often both. The *Christian Crusades* and the Iberian *Reconquista* were in part driven by missionary impulses. In more modern times, during the process of European *colonization* of Africa, Asia, and the Americas, religious orders (such as the *Jesuits*) set up overseas missions to proselytize, and sometimes also to provide general education and medical relief among the newly (or about to be) conquered. These did varying amounts of good or evil and met with dissimilar levels of acceptance or resistance, ranging from mass conversions to violent rejection, murder, or expulsion. Perhaps their greatest effect on international relations was to provide a psychological link—through popular stories of heroism, charity, and self-sacrifice—between ordinary Europeans and the idea of empire as a redemptive, Christianizing and civilizing *mission*.

Christian missionaries were killed or expelled, and then barred, from Japan by the *Tokugawa shoguns*. They were similarly restricted in China under the *Qing* and before, during, and after the *Chinese Revolutions* of 1911 and 1949. In 2000, the announced intention of the *Vatican* to canonize 120 martyred Catholic missionaries from earlier periods in China's history damaged efforts to re-establish *diplomatic relations* with Beijing. In the nineteenth century, Vietnam persecuted Catholic missionaries and local converts, providing an excuse for French intervention. The *Orthodox Church*, too, historically dispatched missionaries to Central Asia, *Siberia*, and *Russian America*. After the *Cold War*, American evangelicals, along with thousands of young Mormons, set up missions within most former *Soviet bloc* nations. Indeed, the rapidly expanding Mormon Church far surpassed the more static Catholic Church in the number of missionaries it supported. In the late twentieth century, Christian denominations also competed vigorously for converts from each other in Central America and Africa, with inroads made into established *Catholic* populations by *Protestant* evangelicals, while in eastern Europe and Russia clerics of the Orthodox faith fretted and protested over possible Catholic evangelism under the guidance of *John Paul II*. *See also Boxer rebellion;* encomienda; *footbinding; Hawaii; Toyotomi Hideyoshi;* jihad; *Korean Conflict; Madagascar; Malawi;* mission civilisatrice; *Nagasaki;* requerimiento; *rites controversy.*

Suggested Readings: Roger Beck, *Christian Missionaries and European Expansion, 1450 to the Present* (1999); Jack Beeching, *An Open Path: Christian Missionaries, 1515–1914* (1980); Philip Carman, *The Lost Paradise: The Jesuit Republic in South America* (1976).

mission civilisatrice. "Civilizing mission." Closer to the idea of *white man's burden* than to *manifest destiny*, this concept of a peculiar French mission grew from a conviction that French culture was the highest expression of Western civilization. That implied an obligation to carry enlightenment to what were seen as less civilized, non-European peoples (having lost the Revolutionary and *Napoleonic Wars*, 1792–1815, the French had given up trying to civilize the English, Germans, Italians, and other nearby barbarians). Where necessary—and curiously, it was usually found necessary—this grand mission was to be accomplished via *colonialism* to provide the benefaction of French governance (and manufactures) and was accompanied by *missionaries* to Christianize and save the heathen or to teach him the glories of the French language, literature, and law. Over time, as *informal empire* became *direct rule* and territorial governance, the conceit developed that the *French Empire* should seek *assimilation* of native *elites* into the full beneficence of French culture and civilization.

In short, the idea of a civilizing mission to Africa, Asia, and Polynesia merely clothed as a noble venture a core imperial policy, which otherwise might have discomfited the sensitive back home by exposing itself as a naked commercial and geopolitical undertaking. This sense of deep cultural self-confidence—which peaked just before *World War I*—was fatally undermined in France, and among other imperial states, by the two world wars and the *Great Depression* of the first half of the twentieth century. In addition, those cataclysms undercut France's (and again, also all of Europe's) material ability to maintain overseas empire. In addition, the idea of mission was attenuated from within by its own limited success. After *World War II*, articulate, educated colonial elites employed the core notions of French civilization—ideas of *self-determination* and *democracy* and the great slogan of *liberté, égalité, fraternité*—to demand liberty from French rule, *sovereign* equality for their nations with France, and brotherhood as they chose to define it according to their own distinct national cultures and traditions. *See also* négritude.

mission creep. When the original, limited mission undertaken by an *intervention* or *peacekeeping* force expands into new and more difficult tasks under the pressure of unfolding events. For example, the U.S. military entered Somalia in 1992 to provide basic security for *famine* relief efforts, but it was soon drawn into policing and nation-building roles and even into Somalia's ongoing clan warfare. The United Nations intervention in Bosnia also experienced mission creep in 1993, as did the 1994 U.S. intervention in Haiti. *See also nongovernmental organization.*

mission, sense of. All great empires, civilizations, and nations have developed a sense of historic mission, which their people, or at least their *elites*, felt called upon to perform. In some cases, such notions served as moral justification for self-interested elite policies—imperial expansion or regional dominance—which were only loosely supported by the populace and were generally found distasteful if dished out in the unpalatable form of their plain interests. The common denominator of senses of national mission is an altruistic cloak that covers the naked pursuit of *dynastic* or *national interests*, but is yet light and attractive so as to beguile many into genuine belief in its more noble aspects. Thus, Chinese emperors sought *Sinification* of conquered provinces, the *Roman Empire* felt compelled to expand to bring the *Pax Romana* to barbarian nations, and Christians were blessed by priests, bishops, and popes as they made war to recover the Holy Lands, even though they detoured into sacking *Constantinople* (and *Jerusalem*) and erected personal fiefdoms (the *Crusader* states) in the Middle East. Muslim imperialists matched such propaganda blow-for-blow with their concepts of *Dar al-Islam* and *jihad*.

Spanish and Portuguese empire-builders argued—and many sincerely believed—that the *New World* was God's gift and that they were doing "His work" in conquering it and enslaving the Indian population in the *encomienda system* wherein, they told themselves, native souls would be saved for Christ even as native bodies were broken by hard labor in the fields or mines of Iberian masters. Meanwhile, Spanish and Austrian *Habsburg* kings and emperors thought that they too were working directly for the deity by seeking hegemony over the *Old World*. Over the next several centuries, *missionaries* helped provide a psychological link—through popular stories of their heroism, charity, and self-sacrifice—between ordinary Europeans and the idea of empire as a redemptive, Christianizing, and civilizing mission. In the nineteenth century, France cleaved to a sense of *mission civilisatrice*, Britain shouldered the *white man's burden*, Americans pursued their *manifest destiny*, and Russians advanced *pan-Slavism* even where other Slavs asked them not to. The British sense of mission came to include a powerful sense of obligation to end the *slave trade* and then to end slavery itself. On occasion, this meant establishing *direct rule* in the African interior where African rulers continued to engage in traditional slave-raiding and held open slave markets. That was not the case within the French Empire, where indigenous slavery was tolerated much longer.

In the twentieth century, the United States finally engaged militarily and diplomatically with the wider world and developed an expanded sense of mission to accompany its new role. By 1917 it deemed it necessary to "make the world safe for democracy" and sought to do so rhetorically, and usually though not always also sincerely, over most of the remainder of that century. Other twentieth-century ideas of mission were more sinister: Japan coined mock-imperial slogans such as "*Asia for Asians*" and the "*Greater East Asia Co-Prosperity Sphere*," the Nazis ranted that the *Third Reich* served the highest possible morality (race superiority), and Soviet leaders boasted that in subverting neighboring states and crushing their own subject populations they were doing the great work of *historical materialism* and the dialectic. At the start of the twenty-first century a resurgent China insisted upon completing a historical and cultural mission of reunification of its ancient empire—including several areas, such as Tibet, occupied by non-Han peoples and others, such as Taiwan, which had developed an independent national consciousness—on the principle of "One China, One Culture." *See also Hernando Cortés; Adolf Hitler; imperialism; Mao Zedong; pan-Africanism; pan-Arabism; Philip II; seisen; Third Rome; World War I.*

mita system. "Time labor." *See also* encomienda.

Mitteleuropa. (1) German, for Central Europe. (2) The nationalist dream of a German-led superstate in *Central Europe* and the *Balkans*. Not all Germans shared this vision of a united *Volksdeutsche* in a single *Reich*. Notably, *Bismarck* rejected the notion as romantic, far-fetched, and dangerous. It was taken up by *Wilhelm II*, however, and was an article of faith for *Nazis*.

Mitterrand, François Maurice (1916–1996). President of France's *Fifth Republic*, 1981–1995. An active *resistance* fighter during *World War II*, he was a stubbornly independent politician in the 1950s as he worked for a grand coalition on the left. From 1954 he served in cabinet, including as justice minister, and supported ferocious repression during the *Algerian War of Independence*, condoning torture and terror killings by French forces. He rode an electoral alliance with the *Communist party* into the presidency, but split with the Communists in 1984 when economic reality forced him to reverse his program of *nationalization* and high *deficit spending*. Also in 1984, he met Chancellor *Kohl* of Germany—with whom he already had an excellent working relationship—at *Verdun*, in a ceremony of reconciliation between France and Germany. After 1986 Mitterrand was a much diminished figure, as the socialists lost their majority in the National Assembly. Yet, he was personally reelected in 1988. He kept up a pose of supreme independence during the *Cold War*, yet cooperated with *NATO* missile deployments necessary to counter Soviet SS-20s and was always a strong proponent of the *force de frappe*. He adjusted quickly to German reunification, supporting *Maastricht*, proposing a Franco-German *EUROCORPS*, and increasing cooperation with the United States in the *Security Council*. He led France in a major contribution to the *Gulf coalition*. In 1994 he encouraged a French *rapprochement* with NATO, and NATO enforcement of *no-fly zones* in Bosnia. He never wavered, however, from a belief that Europe needed to find its own voice in security affairs that was fully independent of the United States.

mixed arbitral tribunal. An international tribunal composed of representatives of all parties to a *legal dispute*, as well as a mutually acceptable third party.

mixed economy. An economy with features drawn from theories of both *socialism* and *capitalism*; or better, one in which there developed historically—and for reasons of both ideology and the failure or economic unprofitability of selected private enterprises (passenger rail or ferry service, utilities, war-related production)—a mixture of private ownership and production alongside governmental ownership of selected sectors or industries. This is actually the situation in most advanced, industrial societies. *See also command economy; five-year plans; liberalism; planned economy; reform liberalism.*

mixed motive game. *See game theory.*

MNC/MNE. *See multinational corporation/enterprise.*

mobile launchers. Any surface means by which *missiles* may be transported (to protect them or move into firing range) and launched.

mobility, in warfare. *See air power; armor; Blitzkrieg; cavalry; fortification; Mongols; Napoleonic warfare; Panzer; Rapid Deployment Force; Rapid Reaction Force; revolution in military affairs (RMA); trench warfare; sea power.*

mobilization. To assemble the armed forces so that they are ready for active service. It involves calling up *reserve* units, checking and preparing equipment, arranging transportation, moving troops closer to the likely locales of combat, putting units on alert status, issuing marching orders, and the like. This takes planning and time. *See also American Expeditionary Force; mobilization crisis.*

mobilization crisis (June 28–August 4, 1914). On June 28th *Francis Ferdinand*, heir to the Austrian throne, was assassinated in the Bosnian capital *Sarajevo*. The assassin was a 24-year-old Serb *fanatic* (Gavrilo Princip, 1894–1918) who had help from the Serbian *secret police*. Unwilling to act alone, out of fear of Russia, on July 5th Austria consulted with Germany. Vienna was promised Berlin's full support for whatever actions it might choose to take—this was the infamous *blank check*. Having written it, *Wilhelm II* departed on his yacht for Norway (July 6th), while Austria delivered an *ultimatum* to Serbia consisting of multiple conditions and intended to court rejection, expiring in the early evening of July 25th. Serbia was willing to concede nearly every point, but then received a late guarantee of support from Russia. Serbia then attached conditional acceptance to six points, rejected the most important—the right of Austrian police investigation of the assassination—and *mobilized* its army. Austria was by this time intent on humiliating Serbia. *Conrad von Hötzendorf*, chief of the Austrian general staff, had wanted to attack Italy when it was stricken by an earthquake at Messina in 1907; now he and others of like mind wished to take advantage of the Serbians' foolhardy provocation in killing the Archduke to attack Serbia. Vienna thus cited Sarajevo's qualified acceptance of its ultimatum as a *casus belli* and *declared war* on Serbia on July 28th. Fighting did not begin immediately, as full Austrian mobilization on the Serbian front required another two weeks to complete. The Austrian declaration thereby set in motion an intense week of real crisis in which the Great Powers scrambled first to avoid a general war and then to position themselves for it.

Thus began the descent into *World War I*, a war the likes of which the world had never seen. Russia had already partly mobilized and now ordered full mobilization against Austria. Tsar *Nicholas II* was told he had to mobilize against Germany too, as the plans and timetables were too complex to alter and delay might bring defeat should Germany enter the war. He reluctantly agreed to mobilize against his German cousin, Wilhelm II, then faltered and cancelled the order on July 29th. Fearing that even a partial Russian mobilization would upset the fine timetable of the *Schlieffen Plan, Moltke* secretly urged full Austrian mobilization and sought Germany's as well. On July 30th the Tsar responded to frantic entreaties from his advisers and reordered full mobilization. Germany sent an ultimatum to Russia on July 31st demanding that all mobilization stop. Meanwhile, Berlin sought assurances from France that it would not support its Russian ally in case of war, as it was bound to do by treaty, and from Britain that it would remain *neutral*. It got neither. France and Germany therefore both ordered full mobilization on August 1st; Germany declared war on Russia two hours later. On August 2nd, Berlin sent out its final ultimatum—to neutral Belgium, demanding a right to transit its territory en route to France. When this expired the next day, German troops crossed into Luxembourg and invaded Belgium, putting into operation the first steps in the Schlieffen Plan; that day, Germany also declared war on France.

On August 4th Britain sent Germany an ultimatum, demanding it withdraw from Belgium by midnight that day and respect the *Treaty of London* (1839). And it at last announced its decision to support France—London's prolonged, irresponsible silence in July had greatly contributed to overall tensions. Russia, France, Belgium, and the *British Empire* were thus all at war with Imperial Germany by midnight, August 4th. Austria declared war on Russia the following day. Britain and France declared war on Austria on August 12th. Most of the main players were by now assembled, and the carnage commenced (though not, at first, in Serbia). Italy, Turkey, the United States, and various smaller powers would enter the war later, each for reasons peculiar to its interests and circumstance, and not all willingly.

Note: The phrase "July Crisis" suggests a superficial causation, wherein rigid *war plans* appear to have made war inevitable in 1914. As A.J.P. Taylor once pointedly noted, the really interesting question is why the crisis was not stopped before it led to war, when other more serious crises in 1912 and 1913 had been. After all, Austria wanted a war only with Serbia; Russia had not wanted war at all, but felt required to support Serbia for reasons of *prestige*; Germany had not wanted war, but was prepared to risk it to support its Austrian ally; France supported Russia out of fear of isolation against Germany; and Great Britain vacillated through most of July, failing to make its interests and intentions clear early enough to have a real *deterrent* effect in Berlin and Vienna.

Suggested Readings: John Keegan, *The First World War* (1999); Hew Strachan, *The First World War* (2001); Hew Strachan, ed., *World War I* (1999).

Mobutu Sese Seko, né Joseph Desiré (1930–1997). *See Congo crisis.*

Moctezuma II (c. 1470–1520). Also known as Montezuma II. The last *Aztec* emperor (r. 1502–1520). From the beginning of his reign he continued the Aztec tradition of expansion of an already vast military empire via conquest of neighboring Indian cities and tribes. This continued right up to his fateful encounter and dealings with *Cortés*, which helps explain why the Spanish were able to muster so many anti-Aztec Indian rebels, who hated the Aztec Empire and were happy, at first, to see it fall. He was overthrown, and either murdered or killed in a struggle, in 1520. One of his descendants served as viceroy, 1697–1701. *See also Aztec Empire*; conquistadores; *Mexico*.

model. In economics and social science, an *abstract* representation of a set of (supposedly) causally related *variables*.

mode of production. In *Marxism*, the general organization of a society, and especially of *labor*, for the production of *goods*. It is marked out by a *dialectical* process of progressive historical stages reflecting successive dominant classes, thus: *slavery, feudalism, capitalism, socialism*, and finally *communism*, which is supposed to be classless. Everything else—from the form of government to the international legal character of the state to geopolitics and the ideology of the ruling class—is part of the far less important "superstructure," which rests ultimately on, and is produced by, the underlying mode of production at any given historical moment. This is an extreme *reductionist* view that does not properly account for the behavior of social and political classes in fact and ignores the crucial role of *technology* and moral and political ideas in fomenting structural change. Moreover, Marx also specified a nonchronological mode of production, which he called "Asiatic." In that geographical deviation from the "laws of history," he revealed both the limitations of his analytical system and the limiting and common prejudices of other Europeans, perhaps especially the bourgeoisie of his day. *See also production; Max Weber.*

modernization. An inherently controversial idea among political scientists, but generally taken by political economists to mean the process of changing traditional societies into modern (industrial, urban, and more secular) economies and societies. It is more than just the process of development of *infrastructure*. It includes the fundamental transformation of traditional attitudes, habits of mind, and patterns and institutions of authority. Thus, it is not universally seen as desirable. Until *World War II*, and for some analysts still, modernization was often read as a near synonym for *westernization*. This tendency arose from a *convergence* thesis (common to *Marxist* thinking, but foreign to most comparative historians) posing that in achieving modern *development* all societies must and would move toward social structures and economic *modes of production* first achieved in the *capitalist* West. *See also* *agrarian reform; agricultural revolution; conservatism; end of history; Enlightenment; feudalism; fundamentalism; French Revolution; globalization; global village; green revolution; indicators; industrialization; interdependence; international political economy; liberalism; Marxism; multinational corporation; Peter I; postmodernism; rising expectations; secularism; Smithian growth; stages of growth; technology; transnational.*

Suggested Readings: Cyril Black, ed., *The Modernization of Inner Asia* (1991); Jan De Vries and Ad Van Der Woude, *The First Modern Economy* (1997); Immanuel Hsu, *Rise of Modern China*, 4th ed. (1990); Marius Jansen, *The Making of Modern Japan* (2000); W. Morse, *Alexander II and the Modernization of Russia* (1962); Chie Nakane and Shinzabur Oishi, eds., *Tokugawa Japan: The Social and Economic Antecedents of Modern Japan* (1990); Kenneth Pomeranz, *The Great Divergence: Europe, China, and the Making of the Modern World Economy* (2000); John Rundell, *Origins of Modernity: Social Theory from Kant to Hegel to Marx* (1987); Jonathan Spence, *The Search for Modern China* (1990).

Mogul (Mughal) Empire. *See India.*

Moldavia and Wallachia. *See Danubian principalities; Rumania.*

Moldova. This territory was progressively absorbed by the *Ottoman Empire* from the fifteenth century to become a battleground *frontier* between the Ottomans and the rising power of Russia. From the late eighteenth century (1792–1812), Moldova was annexed in stages by the Russian Empire, except for *Bessarabia.* The Russian part of this region straddled the outer border of the empire, along the Dniester River. It was merged with ethnically Rumanian Bessarabia after that area was annexed to the Soviet Union by *Stalin* in 1940. The next year the whole region was *occupied* by Rumania, which had joined the *Axis alliance* with *Nazi Germany.* The Russians retook Moldova and Bessarabia in 1944 and merged them into a single "autonomous republic" (with some territory passed to Ukraine) within the USSR. After a failed *coup* attempt in Moscow in August 1991, Moldova declared *independence.* However, this was not accepted by *Red Army* units still in-country and not *recognized* until, along with most other *successor states* of the old Soviet Union, it was set loose by the *extinction* of that state on December 25, 1991. Within a few months fighting erupted in eastern Moldova, or *Trans-Dniestra.* Ethnic Ukrainians and Russians feared Moldova's Rumanian speakers wanted to merge with Rumania and sought to secede (as the Trans-Dniester Republic) and rejoin Russia or Ukraine; they had help from the (now renamed) Russian 14th Army. Russian troops remained in the area, as did *CSCE* monitors, in 1994. An ethnically Turkish area had been given *autonomy* in 1994 and looked to offer a model for Trans-Dniestra. The stakes were raised by a *referendum* held in 1995, which supported independence from Moldova. Desultory fighting continued as an accord was worked out that gave Trans-Dniestra autonomy within the Moldavian union in 1997. Russia withdrew all troops from Moldova in 2001.

mole. Slang for *penetration agent.*

Molotov, Vyacheslav Mikhailovich, né Scriabin (1890–1986). "Mr. Nyet." Soviet premier, 1930–1941; deputy premier, 1941–1957; foreign minister, 1939–1949 and 1957; ambassador to Mongolia, 1957–1960. His adopted name meant "The Hammer." From 1921 onward he was one of *Stalin's* closest supporters. He helped direct the *collectivization* of agriculture, *liquidation* of the *kulaks,* and artificial *famine,* which killed millions (especially in Ukraine) in the 1930s. And he again did bloody work during the *Yezhovshchina.* In his memoirs and end-of-life interviews he never expressed regret for these actions. Rather, he defended them vehemently, even while recalling that had Stalin lived another year, he might not have. The measure of Molotov's abject sycophancy came during the *purges,* when Stalin ordered him to divorce his Jewish wife and have her sent to a labor camp; he complied without question, but took her back when the old tyrant died. He negotiated the *Nazi-Soviet Pact* with *Ribbentrop* in 1939 and in 1941 secretly discussed with *Hitler* the option of a four-power pact with Italy and Japan. These conversations could not overcome a serious German-Soviet dispute over the status of Finland. It was Molotov who, with Stalin in hiding and in near collapse mentally, announced to the Soviet population that the nonaggression pact had failed and that Hitler had launched *Barbarossa,* his great attack on Russia. Molotov was present at all the major conferences of *World War II* (*Tehran, Yalta, Potsdam*) and signed various *postwar* treaties with *Soviet bloc* allies/vassals. With Stalin's death, Molotov's power waned, despite his briefly forming part of a ruling troika. His last major act was to negotiate for the Soviet Union the *Austrian State Treaty* in 1955. Seen as a rival by *Khrushchev,* he was shunted aside, all the way to political death as ambassador to *Outer Mongolia.* The indignities continued when he was stripped of party membership in 1962 (it was reinstated in 1984). *See also Lavrenti Pavlovich Beria; GULAG; Maxim Litvinov; Andreai Vyshinsky.*
  Suggested Reading: Vyacheslav Molotov, *Molotov Remembers* (1993).

Molotov cocktail. A crude *incendiary* weapon, usually homemade from gasoline, detergent, and rags. It was named after *Vyacheslav Molotov.*

von Moltke, Helmuth (1800–1891). German field marshal and strategist. He was from Mecklenburg, and hence not a Prussian: his father was an officer in the Danish service, and Moltke was himself a Danish cadet. A student and disciple of *Clausewitz,* who was director of the War College when Moltke entered it in 1823, he joined the Prussian *general staff* in 1833. In 1835 he was sent to Turkey as a military attaché to the *Sublime Porte,* where he disobeyed orders by joining the Turkish service in order to fight *Mehemet Ali* of Egypt in 1839. Back in Prussia, he studied the use of *railways* (and personally invested in them), Germany's developing road system, and the telegraph in warfare. He rejoined the general staff in 1846. He became an aide to the future Kaiser, *Frederick III*, and traveled extensively in Russia, Britain, and France. He was made chief of staff to *Otto von Bismarck* in 1857. He reorganized and professionalized the Prussian Army and general staff, devised new war plans, and commanded in lightening victories over Denmark (1864), Austria (1866), and France (1870–1871), in which his use of railways and telegraph played a major role. Like Bismarck, after 1871 he became cautious, even fearful, over Germany's exposed position and the possibility of a *two-front war*. He proposed a defensive posture should war come: Germany should hold against France, while attacking Russia only in its Polish provinces, and even then just to gain territory for a later trade in return for acceptance of the *status quo ante bellum*. *See also Paul Hindenburg;* Machtpolitik; *Alfred von Schlieffen; strategic envelopment.*

von Moltke, Helmuth (1848–1916). Chief of the German *general staff*, 1906–1914; son of the elder *Moltke*. He just missed seeing action in the *Franco-Prussian War*. Afterward, he held a series of increasingly important staff positions, including as an aide to his father. In 1906 he succeeded *Alfred von Schlieffen* as chief of the general staff. He spent the next eight years adapting the *Schlieffen Plan* to changing circumstances, especially the growing weakness of his Austro-Hungarian ally. He repeatedly exceeded his authority during the *mobilization crisis* of 1914, making war more likely. During the opening offensive of *World War I*, with the German Army within 25 miles of Paris, Moltke altered the path of the advance, dangerously exposing the army's flank to a French counterattack at the *First Battle of the Marne*. He was dismissed from active command after his interference contributed to failure of the German offensive in the west (though the real, logistical cause of failure was built into the Schlieffen Plan itself), which in turn led to a prolonged *two-front war*, the very thing his father and other German strategic planners had feared since 1871.

Suggested Reading: Otto Friedrich, *Blood and Iron* (2000).

Moluccas. *See Indonesia; Spice Islands.*

Monaco. Bordering the southeast Mediterranean coast of France, this *microstate* (principality) is barely one-half square mile in *size*, and yet has remained more or less independent for three centuries by adapting to whatever was the prevailing political wind in a given age. It was a Spanish *protectorate*, 1542–1641, under French domination, 1641–1793, and was then annexed to France, 1793–1815. It was restored by the *Congress of Vienna* as a protectorate of *Piedmont-Sardinia* until 1861, when it was transferred back to French "protection" as a reward for *Louis Napoleon*'s support for Italian unification under the crown of Piedmont. Its main industry is *tourism*.

monarchy. A political system in which legal authority is vested in the person of a *sovereign*. While *republicanism* has outstripped monarchism as the preferred government for most societies in the last two centuries, there are still monarchies among the states: all of Europe except France and Switzerland in 1914, about one-fourth of all states in 2001. Most of these were constitutional monarchies, where the monarch had strictly constitutional and ceremonial, and even largely touristic, functions. Yet, kings still ruled directly in several countries, notably in the Middle East, Africa, and Nepal. *See also absolutism; autocracy; nonintervention; popular sovereignty.*

monetarism. A theoretical challenge to *Keynesian economics* that stresses a return to *laissez-faire* models, but with the government continuing to intervene to moderate extreme fluctuations in the *business cycle* and control *inflation* via control of the money supply and a reduction in discretionary government spending. In contrast to Keynesianism, monetarists tend to view the government as destabilizing naturally self-regulating private markets, rather than as an essential stabilizer and constant intervener in those markets. *See also Ronald Reagan; stagflation; supply-side economics; Margaret Thatcher.*
   Suggested Reading: Charles Kindleberger, *Keynesianism vs. Monetarism* (1985).

monetary policy. A *macroeconomic* device that aims at controlling the *balance of payments* or levels of *inflation* or unemployment by means of interest rates and limiting the money supply.

monetary standards. A monetary standard tries to define the value of a *currency* in terms of a known amount of a substance of more permanent value, such as monetary metals. Internationally, monetary standards permit easy conversion of all (or most) other currencies at stable, predictable rates. Precious metals usually served as the standards. The English term "pound sterling" derived from the Medieval standard of a literal pound of sterling silver. An alternate standard arose during the *Age of Exploration*: the *guinea*, which was a *gold standard* based upon gold coins minted from West African gold mined on the Guinea coast. The term stuck even after more of Europe's gold came from the treasure troves of the *Aztec* and the *Inca* and then from the gold mines (and ultimately more important, the silver mines) of the Americas. England remained on silver until the *Napoleonic Wars*, but thereafter shifted to a gold standard. Most other European economies cleaved to a bimetallic standard (gold and silver) during the nineteenth century. In 1865 France, Belgium, Italy, and Switzerland attempted to erect a common silver standard (the Latin Monetary Union), partly to resist Britain; they were later joined by Spain, Serbia, and Rumania. When Germany adopted the gold mark in 1871 after its victory in the *Franco-Prussian War*, other nations were compelled to move onto a gold standard too. The United States was on a bimetallic standard before the *American Civil War*, but switched to a gold standard in 1879. The *secular trend* in declining gold prices after 1873 caused deep unease with gold and spurred, among other things, the triple presidential candidacies of *William Jennings Bryan*. Russia and Japan went onto gold in 1897. Monetary standards broke down during and after *World War I*, as several failed attempts were made to return to gold. From 1945 to 1971 the *Bretton Woods system* secured an international return (excluding the *Soviet bloc*) to a gold standard backed by the "full faith and credit" of the U.S. dollar. The United States went off the gold standard in 1971, as part of the *Nixon shocks* to the world economy, and since then no global monetary standard has existed. Instead, the world's major currencies *float* against each other.

money market. International *hard currency* markets where lending tends to be short-term and contract volume is high. *See also capital market.*

Mongolia. A region in north *Inner Asia* comprising the modern state of Mongolia, but also the province of Inner Mongolia in China and the former Tuva Autonomous Soviet Republic in Russia. The modern state was a Chinese province known as Outer Mongolia, 1691–1911, with the conquest taking from 1691 to 1697. In the 1730s the Ili of western Mongolia broke into rebellion, but this was suppressed by 1735. In 1911, with tsarist assistance, Mongolia broke away from China during the great chaos of the *Chinese Revolution* (1911). It immediately fell prey to *warlords*, leading to chaos, which local *Communists* rode into power with Soviet aid in the early 1920s, when it was renamed the Mongolian People's Republic and became the first Communist state beyond the Soviet Union. Its independence was disputed until 1950, when the new People's Republic of China government in China and the Soviet Union signed a joint guarantee of Mongolian independence, forced on *Mao* during his extended visit to Moscow. Mongolia spent the rest of the *Cold War* as a quiet backwater. In 1990, during the breakdown of the *Soviet bloc*, it held its first open elections, in which the old Communist authorities cross-dressed into nationalist clothing and won handily. After 1990 Mongolia experienced a revival of traditional culture, including a *revisionist* celebration of the great khans. In 2000 and 2001 its nomadic herdsmen were devastated by a drought and then by severe winters ("zud") that killed millions of their animals. *See also Mongols.*

Mongols. The most expansive empire in world history (the Chinggisid Empire) was carved out by Mongol khans during the twelfth to fourteenth centuries, a feat of arms and transcontinental devastation, which in one sense launched world history. In the end, however, the Mongol empire was one merely of *conquest* and *plunder* of more advanced and civilized peoples, not one of independent building or lasting achievement. Mongol military formations swept over *Eurasia*. Their success derived from superb mounted archers, superior battlefield communications and tactical coordination, and utter ruthlessness in dealing with any who resisted. Mongol tribes were first united by Chinggis (Ghengis, or "Mighty Ruler") Khan (1162–1227) in 1206. They overran north China between 1217 and 1223 and conquered the Jin Empire in 1234. They defeated the *Song* in 1279 under Kublai Khan (1214–1294) and ruled all China as the *Yuan dynasty* until 1368, when they were ousted by the *Ming*. In the span of three generations after Chinggis, they conquered much of the known world, overrunning most of Russia and Central Asia, deeply frightening Western Europe and interrupting the *Crusades*, and defeating the Persian and Abbasid Empires of the Middle East; Baghdad fell to the Mongols in 1258. They failed to overcome the *Mamluks* of Egypt, however, losing in Galilee in 1260. And although the dominant *land power* of the Age, they were not adept with *sea power*. In Chinese junks, Mongol hordes tried to invade Japan in 1274 and 1281 and were repulsed by bad weather and determined defenders. They also tried, and failed, in the late thirteenth century, to conquer from the sea Burma, Java, Siam, and Vietnam.

A wave of Turkic invaders had conquered north India ahead of the Mongols—the Khaljis, who took control of Delhi in 1290. The Muslim state they established beat back a Mongol invasion out of Afghanistan during the first decade of the fourteenth century, though not without seeing Delhi partially sacked and plundered. In this sense, the Turkic invaders of India may have preserved it from even worse depredations by the Mongols, deflecting them instead into Ukraine and southern Russia. Various Mongol hordes ruled Central Asia until defeated by *Tamerlane*, and the Mongol Golden Horde ruled the Caucasus, Ukraine, and southwestern Russia from the thirteenth to the fifteenth century, though it was on the defensive after a major defeat in Russia in 1380. In all these places barbarism, cruelty, and the fundamentally parasitical nature of Mongol warrior culture worsened local despotic traditions and held back ideas and social forces that might have advanced civilization and hastened modernity. The great Russian poet Alexandr Pushkin said of the Mongols, contrasting Russia's misfortune with the encounter between *Islam* and the West after the seventh century, that they were "Arabs without Aristotle or algebra." Their passing as a major power was unmourned virtually anywhere, save in Mongolia. *See also black death; Han; Inner Asia; kamikaze; Manchus; Silk Road.*

Suggested Readings: S. Adshead, *Central Asia in World History* (1993); R. Amitai-Preiss and David Morgan, eds., *The Mongol Empire and Its Legacy* (1999); Leo de Hartog, *Ghengis Khan* (1989); Luc Kwanten, *Imperial Nomads: A History of Central Asia, 500–1500* (1979); J.

Langlois, ed., *China Under Mongol Rule* (1981); David Morgan, *The Mongols* (1986); Paul Ratchnevsky, *Ghengis Khan* (1992); Morris Rossabi, *Khubilai Khan* (1988).

monism. The doctrine that *international law* and *municipal law* are inseparable or part of the same legal order. Note: Advocates of this doctrine may hold one or the other superior. *See also dualism.*

Monnet, Jean (1888–1979). French diplomat and economist. He served in the *League of Nations*, 1919–1923, and was head of the National Planning Council, 1945–1947. His chief contribution was to press for the idea of *integration* of the French and German economies through the *Schuman Plan*, on the way to a wider *European Community*. He was a major figure in the founding of the *ECSC*, serving as its president, 1952–1955.

monopoly. When one firm controls the license, production, or transport, and thus effective pricing, of a *commodity* or *service. See also East India Companies; monopsony; oligopoly; "seven sisters."*

monopsony. A market in which only one buyer exists, and thus effectively sets the price; this is often the case with large government procurement contracts. *See also monopoly.*

Monroe Doctrine. A statement of U.S. opposition to extra-hemispheric *intervention* in the Americas. It implicitly linked U.S. policy to Britain's, despite explicit pronouncements about avoiding *entangling alliances* and maintaining *isolation* from Europe's affairs. It was drafted by *John Quincy Adams* and announced by President *James Monroe* on December 2, 1823. It said: "The American continents . . . are henceforth not to be considered as subjects for future colonization by any European power. . . . We should consider any attempt on their part to extend their system to any portion of this hemisphere as dangerous to our peace and safety." It was stimulated by a threat from the *Holy Alliance* to reinstate the Spanish *monarchy* in the newly independent Latin American *republics*. A secondary interest was Russia's hint that it would expand its holdings in northern *California*. Monroe's declaration that the *Americas* should be off-limits to *colonialism* by any European power was not a new idea. Nor were the other two principles of the Doctrine new: *nonintervention* in American affairs and *noninterference* by the United States in European affairs. After all, Americans had long believed in the incompatibility of the political systems of the *Old* and *New Worlds*. Moreover, the Monroe Doctrine exhibited a characteristic American (and perhaps, democratic) habit of wrapping immediate self-interest in a blanket of abstract principle, claimed as universal.

Most European powers were angered by Monroe's declaration and held it in contempt as the preposterous claim of a minor power. However, British support for Latin independence was another matter. It was, in fact, the *Royal Navy* that defended Latin America from intervention, and the threat may not have been great in any case. *George Canning* openly claimed this when he later boasted to Parliament that in guarding the fragile Latin republics: "I called the New World into existence to redress the balance of the Old." And John Quincy Adams admitted as much in private when arguing for the declaration, saying: "It would be more candid as well as more dignified to avow our principles explicitly to Russia and France, than to come in as a cockboat in the wake of the British *man-of-war*." The crisis passed, the South American states were soon recognized generally, and in 1825 a U.S. accord with Russia marked out the *Northwest Frontier*.

The Monroe Doctrine was thereafter mostly ignored, until it gained some real teeth with emergence of the United States as a *Great Power* after the *American Civil War*. That was also the first time it was tested, when the French tried to reenter North America by installing *Maximilian* in Mexico. (*Polk* had invoked it toward the *Oregon Question*, but to little real effect.) It was invoked repeatedly in the late 1890s. In the early twentieth century the *Roosevelt* and Lodge Corollaries amended it, respectively, to authorize unilateral use of force if that was necessary to preempt Great Power intervention in the hemisphere and to extend its prohibition to non-European powers (that is, Japan). It was again repeatedly invoked before *World War I* to explain and justify American interventions in the Caribbean and Central America. At *Woodrow Wilson's* behest, it was given special international legal status in the *Treaty of Versailles*. It was reasserted before *World War II* and during the *Cuban Missile Crisis*. Yet, that crisis also breached the Doctrine by leaving a Soviet base in Cuba. Increasingly seen as anachronistic by Latin American states, it belongs more to history than to policy, though it is still ritualistically invoked in public debate and potentially may be withdrawn from the archives and deployed, should some future purpose appear to warrant re-issuance. *See also Simón Bolívar; Calvo clause; Drago Doctrine; Alexander Hamilton; isolationism; near abroad; Organization of American States; Platt Amendment; Rio Pact; sphere of influence*.

Suggested Readings: Frederick Merk, *The Monroe Doctrine and American Expansionism* (1966); Gaddis Smith, *Last Years of the Monroe Doctrine* (1994).

Monroe, James (1758–1831). U.S. statesman. Secretary of state, 1811–1817; secretary of war, 1814–1815; *Republican-Democratic* president, 1817–1825. He began the negotiations that led to the *Rush-Bagot Treaty*, which *demilitarized* the Great Lakes. That was part of his larger effort to improve U.S. defenses in the wake of British invasion during the *War of 1812*. He provided for a larger army and coastal fortifications. He was a Virginia slave owner, who yet opposed retaining *slavery* in America (as threatening to the Union) and agreed with *Jefferson* that the solution was to ship all the slaves back to Africa. He therefore facilitated a settlement of freed slaves in West Africa. That was the beginning of *Liberia* (the name means "Freedom"), with its capital Monrovia. He was also an avid expansionist. He obtained the Floridas and settled a long simmering border dispute with Spain over *Louisiana*. His native *republicanism* and democratic instincts encouraged him to early *recognition* of the new republics in Latin America, but he held back upon the advice of Secretary of State *John Quincy Adams* until their viability was established. He then issued the *Monroe Doctrine*, drafted by the more-than-able Adams.

Monrovia bloc. *See Organization of African Unity.*

Mons, Battle of (August 1914). *See Battle of the Frontiers.*

Montagnards. (1) "Mountain People." French term for the Thái, Muong, and Meo tribes of the highlands of central Indochina. For centuries they formed a buffer between the Kinh of coastal and delta Vietnam and the Siamese and Khmers to the west. They fought the Black Flags in the *Tonkin Wars*. Many fought fiercely against *Communist*, and Vietnamese, rule in the several Indochinese wars of the 1950s–1980s. (2) The Montagnards, who formed the "Mountain" during the *French Revolution*, were mostly *Jacobin* deputies who sat on the left wing of the *Convention*.

Montenegro. A distinct principality from the fourteenth century, Montenegro utilized its mountainous terrain to ward off the *Ottomans*, gaining *de facto* independence in 1799. Reconquered in 1852, it gained *de jure* independence upon its *recognition* by the *Great Powers* in 1878. It participated in both the *First* and *Second Balkan Wars*. During *World War I* it fought in support of Serbia, with which most Montenegrins share language and religion. It was overrun and *occupied* by Austria in 1915. Its annexation to *Greater Serbia* was accepted at the *Paris Peace Conference*, and it became part of *Yugoslavia*. There was fierce *guerrilla* fighting there during *World War II*. Upon the breakup of Yugoslavia it remained tenuously attached to Serbia. In 2000 it played a key role in the political demise of *Slobodan Milošević*.

Montevideo Convention on the Rights and Duties of States (1933). The standard legal codification of statehood. It defined a *state* as an entity with a permanent *population* and a definite *territory* under the effective control of a single government. *See also recognition; sovereignty.*

Montezuma II. *See Moctezuma II.*

Montgomery, Bernard Law (1887–1976). "Monty." British field marshal. As a young officer, Montgomery fought in *World War I* with the *British Expeditionary Force* (BEF) and was severely wounded at *First Ypres* (November 1914). After recovering, he saw action again at the *Somme* in 1916, *Arras* (April 9–

15, 1917), and *Third Ypres* (1917). From 1929 to 1937 Montgomery served in *Palestine*, Egypt, and India. He returned to Palestine in 1939 to oversee antiguerrilla operations. He fought in Flanders in 1940, conducting a superb rear-guard action as the BEF retreated to *Dunkirk*. Less gloriously and successfully, Montgomery helped plan the *Dieppe raid* (August 19, 1942), earning the lasting and bitter resentment of the relations of the thousands of Canadian troops killed or captured there to so little gain. In North Africa Montgomery took command of Eighth Army, with his headquarters in Egypt, with orders to prepare a counterattack against German and Italian forces. He defeated *Rommel* and the Afrika Korps decisively at *El Alamein*, thereby gaining the respect of Australian and other Commonwealth troops and emerging as Britain's major public hero.

Montgomery's armies won again in Sicily. However, he was subsequently heavily criticized by American military leaders (though only in private during the war) for his—in their view—excessive caution during the *Normandy campaign*. This, along with sheer egoism, may have contributed to the excessive ambition of Montgomery's subsequent bloody and unsuccessful attempt to cross the Rhine in one swoop, in a great failure to secure Antwerp as a base of supply before going "a bridge too far" at Arnhem in the Netherlands. That failure damaged his military reputation and lessened the confidence of his superiors. Montgomery's personal and professional rivalry with *George Patton* and the grave exasperation he caused *Eisenhower* (who at least considered sacking him) was legendary. However, Montgomery is considered by most military historians to have commanded particularly well during the *Battle of the Bulge*. Montgomery led the British Army across the Rhine in March 1945 and accepted the surrender of north German forces in May. He was by all accounts a supreme egoist (he once sat for a portrait while his men were engaged in battle in September 1944) of ascetic temperament, who was compulsively driven to self-justification and to blame others for mistakes he made. He became chief of the British *general staff* after the war and was deputy commander of *NATO*, 1951–1958. Despite Allied criticism, during the war Montgomery was, and remained thereafter, a revered hero to most British. There is no consensus among historians on the overall quality of his generalship. North American historians by and large take a slightly jaundiced view, whereas British military historians are more admiring.

Montreux Convention (1936). Turkey called an international conference to adjust the *Straits Question*, fearing Italian ambitions in the region. It was agreed that Turkey could remilitarize the Straits in exchange for allowing all light foreign *warships* to pass through during peacetime. At *Potsdam* it was agreed to revise the convention in favor of the Soviet Union, but the Soviets then demanded full control of the Straits from Turkey and exclusion of the British. The United States sent a flotilla to Turkey to *show the flag* and signal its objections, and the Soviets backed down.

Montserrat. A tiny British island *colony* in the West Indies (Leeward Islands). Its settler population was largely Irish, who began to arrive in good numbers in the mid-seventeenth century. It developed a planter economy, employing *slave labor*. In 1997 the island economy was destroyed, and most of its population forced to flee, by a massive volcano.

mood theory. Recognizing that most people pay little attention to public affairs, let alone foreign policy, this body of social science "theory" about *public opinion* attempts to gauge broad "moods" rather than more precise measurements. It has more to do with academic trends (indeed, moods) than public ones and is about as useful to real-world *statecraft* as a mood ring. *See also national morale.*

Moon Treaty. Agreement Governing the Activities of States on the Moon and Other Celestial Bodies. Originally proposed by the Soviet Union in 1971, this treaty was then delayed over Soviet reluctance to accept the *common heritage principle*. It was finally agreed that neither the surface nor the subsurface of the moon are to be subject to exclusive or territorial claims by any state. The treaty also seeks to prevent the moon from becoming an area of interstate conflict. A resolution endorsing the treaty passed the *United Nations General Assembly* unanimously in 1979. It was opened for signature in December that year and came into force in 1984. Very few states signed it, however, as most space-capable nations indicated that they would not do so. *See also Outer Space Treaty.*

Moors. The mixed Berber and Arab peoples of North Africa, who once ruled much of Spain and the *Maghreb*. The last Moorish kingdom on the Iberian peninsula, *Granada*, was defeated by *Castile* in 1492. Thereafter, a terrible persecution of Jews and Muslims followed, under the Catholic *Inquisition*. *See also Ferdinand and Isabella; Philip II.*

moral equivalence. (1) The view that both sides in the *Cold War* were equally culpable, and indeed evil, in their propagation of the conflict. Some analysts who adopted this view were led to purely structural explanations of the conflict in which the role of *volition* and the *normative* realm in general were curtly, even cavalierly, dismissed. (2) The striking of a similar pose of faux *objectivity* about any other international or political conflict. *See also mirror images; totalitarianism; triumphalism.*

moratorium. A delay or suspension of some action, such as *nuclear weapons* testing or *debt* repayment, undertaken either unilaterally or in tandem with other *states*. It is a device used to test the efficacy of certain arrangements in the absence of a *treaty* and to test political will. If successful, it may lead to the greater permanence of a formal treaty. Or it may be abused as a *propaganda* ploy by an insincere government. *See also Partial Test Ban Treaty (1963);* *whaling.*

Moravia. An Austrian province taken by Czechoslovakia in 1918, an action confirmed by the *Treaty of St. Germain* (1919).

la mordida. "The bite." In many Latin societies, a bribe required to conduct business. *See also* baksheesh; dash; guanxi.

Moresby Treaty (1822). *See Zanzibar.*

Morgenthau Plan. Henry Morgenthau (1891–1967), U.S. secretary of the treasury, 1934–1945, proposed "pastoralization" of Germany after *World War II*, partly to ensure it would not rise again as a military threat and partly to punish Germans for what many among the *Allies* believed was their willing collaboration with the *Nazi* regime. *Roosevelt* signed on briefly in 1944, and the Soviets and some French were enthusiastic. The plan was leaked before war's end, which played into *propaganda* by *Goebbels* aimed at mass mobilization of the German people for *total war*. In fact, the plan was soon rejected by those of cooler blood and wiser perception, who saw that it would require a permanent Allied *occupation* to enforce and an expensive need to feed, clothe, and house the destitute civilian population it was sure to create. Also, by March 1945 even Roosevelt was growing concerned about *Stalin's* intentions and realized that so draconian a treatment of Germany stood to render its postwar population susceptible to the lure of *communism* by leaving it impoverished and hopeless.

Moriscos. *See Ferdinand and Isabella; Inquisition; Philip II; Spain.*

Moroccan Crisis, First (1905–1906). Secret agreements among Britain, France, and Spain to *partition* Morocco led to German plans to split the *Entente Cordiale* by demonstrating to France that the British *alliance* was unreliable. Germany was also eager to strike while Russia was in the throes of the *Russian Revolution* (1905) and before it recovered from the *Russo-Japanese War* (1904–1905). Kaiser *Wilhelm II* put ashore in *Tangier* and declared support for Moroccan *independence*. This was a deliberately provocative act that resulted in a real *crisis*. Britain moved to support France. The crisis was resolved, partly with the able mediation efforts of *Theodore Roosevelt*, but not on the terms the Germans anticipated. *See also Algeciras Conference (1906); scramble for Africa.*

Moroccan Crisis, Second (1911). *See Agadir.*

Morocco. From the eleventh to mid-thirteenth century, North Africa and southern Spain were ruled by a *Berber* dynasty (Almohads) based in Morocco. The Marinds succeeded the Almohads in 1248 and moved the imperial capital to Fez. By the fifteenth century, Morocco entered a long decline related to, and paralleling, the rise of rival Portuguese and Spanish naval power that circumvented its erstwhile monopoly on the trans-Saharan trade in *gold* and *slaves*. In 1415 Portugal took *Ceuta*, and in 1471 the Portuguese took *Tangier*. In 1472 Wattazid viziers seized the *sultanate* from the Marinds. At the start of the sixteenth century, Portugal took control of several Moroccan ports. Morocco might have become a mere coastal colony had not radicalized Muslims from the desert interior, led by *marabout* sharifs of the Atlas Mountains, expelled the Portuguese and the Wattazid "usurpers" by 1550. The sharifs soon divided, as holy men are wont to do, some to ally with Christian Portugal; others, with the distant *Ottoman Empire*, in a succession struggle and civil war that ended only with a climactic Battle of the Three Kings in 1578. The winner soon died but his brother, Mawlai Ahmad al-Mansur (r. 1578–1603), proved a spectacular success. He introduced firearms and *mercenaries* to the army, moved the capital to Marakesh, and began to expand into the desert to seize control of the caravan trade. He sent a large military expedition through the deep Sahara, 1590–1591, to conquer the distant *Songhay Empire* at Gao, Jenne, and Timbuktu. Songhay's medieval army succumbed to the Moroccans' superior military technology, despite outnumbering them by 20 to 1. Briefly, Morocco thus governed a vast desert and *tributary* empire, stretching as far as Timbuktu and Jenne. The tie to Morocco was broken in 1618, when the fruits of conquest failed to meet expectations, but the "Moors of Timbuktu" remained in power in distant isolation.

After Ahmad, Morocco succumbed to another succession crisis, from which it did not emerge until the 1660s when a new dynasty of marabout sharifs, the Alawids, took charge. In the interim, its military colony in former Songhay broke away. Under Mawlai Ismail (r. 1672–1727), Moroccan power was increasingly based on black military slaves (he built a slave army, the Abid, numbering up to 150,000 troops). Upon his death, as so often occurred in medieval or premodern states, the system fell apart: the economy declined and recourse was taken to the old trade, *piracy*. Successive losses to interior tribes reduced Morocco to a Muslim princedom (one of the *Barbary States*) by the early nineteenth century. It never fell under Ottoman control, however. Because it also did not enjoy Ottoman protection, under Sultan Mawlai Suleiman (r. 1792–1832) it pursued a policy of *isolation* from European and Mediterranean quarrels: Moroccans were forbidden to leave or to consort with Christians or cooperate with British antislavery laws.

After 1832 Morocco supported the resistance of Abd al-Qadir (1808–1883) to the French occupation of Algiers. This provoked a strong French retaliation in 1845, in which Morocco's outdated forces were badly bloodied. In 1859–1860 Morocco was invaded by Spain over the issue of Moroccan raids into *Ceuta* and *Melilla*. The war ended with a large *indemnity* forced on Morocco, which ultimately brought it under international financial supervision. In the interior, small marabout rebellions were commonplace. Under Sultan Mawlai al-Hasan (r. 1873–1894), Moroccan troops put down marabout revolts and extended central authority into the Atlas Mountains and northern Mauritania. By 1905 Morocco was a target of French colonial ambitions, which made it the locale and stimulus for two dangerous *Moroccan Crises* before *World War I*. Its new and young sultan, Abd al-Aziz (r. 1894–1909), sought to Europeanize the country, provoking civil war between the cities and elite and the more devout and semiautonomous desert tribes of the Atlas Mountains. In 1912 Morocco was *partitioned* between France and Spain, with Tangier made a *free city*. Coastal and urban Morocco (notably Rabat and Casablanca) was rapidly *modernized* under French rule, though the interior tribes remained unreconciled even to French efforts to accommodate *indirect rule* with local Berber chiefs.

France—in the person of Hubert Lyautey, resident-general from 1912 to 1925—thus inherited the sultan's problems with desert dissidents, with whom fighting continued in the Atlas Mountains until 1934. Lyautey attempted to institute *indirect rule* over the country, but ended by being drawn evermore deeply into its internal affairs, thereby depleting Morocco's extant institutions of *legitimacy*. France was also drawn into the *Rif Rebellion*, 1921–1926, led by Abd-el Krim (1881–1963), who declared a Rif Republic and smashed a Spanish army at Anual. He was overthrown and captured by a Franco-Spanish force in 1926, and foreign rule resumed. Moroccan colonial units would later fight in the *Spanish Civil War* in support of *Franco*. The French helped bring Sidi Muhammad to the sultan's throne in 1927, in the expectation he would prove pliable. Beginning during *World War II*, he instead led a nationalist political revival. In 1953 Muhammad was deposed by the French, an act that united most Moroccans behind his legitimacy. In 1955 he returned from *exile* in Madagascar. The next year France and Spain withdrew from their respective zones of occupation, and Morocco became independent, incorporating Tangier, with which it was reunited.

In 1957 Morocco invaded the Spanish *enclave* of Rio de Oro (*Spanish Sahara*), but was repulsed. Muhammad next claimed part of Mauritania, but was rebuffed by France. The Spanish *enclave* of Ifni was added in 1969. In 1975, 350,000 Moroccans staged a "Green March" into the Western Sahara to assert Morocco's claim to that territory. The next year, when Spain withdrew, Morocco annexed a mineral-rich part of the *Western Sahara*, partitioning it with Mauritania. That embroiled it in a protracted war with *POLISARIO*. In 1979 Mauritania quit the war, and Morocco occupied the whole of Western Sahara. A *cease-fire* was signed in 1990 under United Nations auspices, but peace remained elusive. The war isolated Morocco from its neighbors and within the *OAU*, from which it withdrew in 1984. Its pro-Western policies during the *Cold War* assured it of United States support. Domestically, Morocco entered the twenty-first century still so poor it employed extensive child labor bordering on slavery. It also continued its illegal occupation of Western Sahara.

Suggested Readings: Monir S. Girgis, *Mediterranean Africa* (1987); Douglas Porch, *The Conquest of Morocco* (1982); I. William Zartman and William Habeeb, eds., *Polity and Society in Contemporary North Africa* (1993).

Mossad. Hebrew: "Institute." The Israeli civilian *intelligence* agency, founded in April 1951, by *David Ben Gurion*. It was formerly known as the Central Institute for Coordination and the Central Institute for Intelligence and Security. Its main concerns are *humint, covert operations,* and countering *terrorism*. Its focus is, of course, on Israel's Arab neighbors, as well as Iran and other more distant hostile states. Mossad assisted Jewish *refugees* escape repressive regimes, including Syria, Iran, and Ethiopia. It is known to have successfully penetrated high levels of several Arab governments and to operate as well in Europe, the *CIS* region, and the United States, or wherever else Israel's *national interests* are deemed to be at stake. In 1960 Mossad successfully kidnapped *Eichmann* from Argentina. In the 1970s, and later, it tracked down and assassinated members of the *Black September* terrorist group who had murdered Israeli athletes at the Munich *Olympic Games*. In the process, it also killed an innocent Algerian waiter working in Norway, who was mistaken for a terrorist. Israel later paid *compensation* for this act to the man's family. In 1986 it kidnapped an Israeli who was abroad and who had revealed facts about Israel's *nuclear weapons* program. It assassinated key *Palestine Liberation Organization* leaders, including Abu Jihad in Tunis in 1988. And it probably killed Gerald Bull, a Canadian scientist of little to no morality beyond a driven need to build a "super gun," and who was doing so (illegally) for *Saddam Hussein* in Iraq; he was killed in Brussels in 1990. From the 1990s Mossad was active in countering *Hezbollah, Hamas,* and the *Intifada*. Mossad's greatest failure was its lapse in security that permitted the assassination, on November 15, 1995, of Prime Minister *Yitzhak Rabin* (by an Orthodox Jew, Yigal Amir). A failed effort to assassinate a leading Hamas figure in Jordan, where Mossad had developed close working relations with King *Hussein*'s regime, was another embarrassment. It required Mossad's chief, Danny Yatom, to resign in 1998.

Suggested Reading: *Jane's Intelligence Review* (1991–).

Mossadegh (Mosadeq) Muhammad (1880–1967). Prime minister of Iran, 1951–1953. In 1925 he opposed the *accession* of the first Shah, and all his public life he objected to foreign control of Iran's *oil* industry and assets. In 1951, shortly after becoming prime minister, he *nationalized* the Anglo-Iranian Oil Company. He was overthrown in a *coup* that had support from *MI5* and the *CIA*, who saw him as a *Communist* stooge. In fact, he was an anti-Communist nationalist whose main interest was to restore Persian pride and *prestige*, which meant shucking off control by outside powers. He is looked upon by some Iranians as a symbol of what might have been: a nationalist leader who could have avoided the extremes of both the *Pahlavis* and the *Ayatollah Khomeini*. Others see him as an emotionally and politically unstable character.

most-favored nation (MFN). This status, when included as a clause in a treaty governing trade, meant that trade must occur on the same *tariff* levels granted to one's most-favored trading partner. It thus encouraged progressive tariff reduction, but also aimed at avoiding creation of separate trade blocs. The term most-favored nation was first used in a *commercial treaty* between *Frederick the Great*'s Prussia and the infant United States in 1786. The principle became a mainstay of *free trade* in Asia, where it also served as a powerful wedge into China's (and Japan's) *internal affairs*, such as under the *treaty port* system after 1842 as established in the *unequal treaties* of *Nanjing* and *Wanghia* and others. As multiple agreements were signed among trading nations, and as the United States came to dominate world trade after 1900, the MFN principle became standard fare in most commercial agreements. Yet, MFN was always a misnomer, as under *GATT* (and even outside it) most trading partners enjoyed MFN. It did not, therefore, imply special preferences so much as mean that no uncommon discrimination was permitted. For example, if Australia permitted imported cars from Korea or other countries to enter at a 10 percent tariff, then it could not impose a higher tariff on Japanese cars, if Japan also enjoyed MFN status. If Australia revoked Japan's MFN, it could then apply whatever tariff it liked, subject only to Japan's ability to retaliate. Once the vast majority of countries adhered to new international trade rules codified after 1945, the term "MFN" lost its original meaning. Indeed, after 1974 it was more often misunderstood by legislators, journalists, and especially the public, to imply that some special status was being granted to a foreign trade partner. In fact, by 1998 only six U.S. trade partners did not have MFN status: Afghanistan, Cuba, Laos, North Korea, Vietnam, and China—all Communist countries or, in the case of Afghanistan, a state that sponsored *terrorism*. This misperception was a real problem in U.S. trade relations after passage of the *Jackson-Vanik Amendment* (1974), which applied to trade with the *Soviet bloc*, but also China. In 1998 free traders in Congress quietly removed the term "MFN" from all trade legislation, substituting the more accurate and deliberately less inflammatory "*normal trade relations* (NTR)."

Mountbatten, Louis (1900–1979). British statesman; grandson of Queen *Victoria*; uncle of Queen Elizabeth II. Mountbatten owed most of his career to royal attachments, rather than particular merit. He was amiable and shallow, but not without personal courage. He served on a *torpedo boat* during *World War I*. During *World War II* he was made director of combined operations by *Churchill*. He helped plan—with *Montgomery*—the disastrous *Dieppe raid* (August 19, 1942), for which many Canadians still hold him blameworthy. He worked until 1943 planning for the invasion of Europe and then was assigned to command in Southeast Asia. He gained a solid reputation in the Burma *campaign*, 1944–1945. He accepted the Japanese *surrender* in Southeast Asia, briefly using armed Japanese *prisoners of war* to keep order in Indochina and Indonesia. From March to August 1947, he was the last British viceroy of India. He oversaw independence for India and Pakistan, after concluding that *partition* of *Bengal* and the *Punjab* from India was required given the intransigence of *Ali Jinnah* and the level of communal violence. He then insisted that partition of the subcontinent take place according to a strict timetable. He performed this awful but necessary task well enough that he was asked to become India's first governor general. He held a naval command in the Mediterranean in the mid-1950s. While on holiday off the Irish coast in 1979, he was killed by the *Irish Republican Army* when his boat was blown up, along with his innocent grandson and another innocent teenage boy. He had been targeted as a symbol of the hated *British Empire* (the IRA operatives were not that bright, and so rather out-of-date) and as a prominent member of the Royal Family. This cowardly act actually steeled British resolve not to bend to IRA terrorism.

Mozambique. The port of Sofala was an outpost of *Swahili Arab* trade for centuries before Portuguese traders first landed on the Mozambique coast in 1497 (Vasco da Gama). In 1505 an expedition was sent from *Goa* to oust the Arabs, which was accomplished by c. 1515. Portugal subsequently colonized the area, trading with *Great Zimbabwe* but also acting as *pirates* with regard to Arab shipping further north. In 1575 the Portuguese signed a treaty with the Mwene Mutapa permitting them to mine, trade, and bring in *missionaries*. The interior remained in the hands of various Shona states (Kiteve, Mandanda, Manyika, Mutapa, and, in the seventeenth century, Barwe and Butwa), with Portugal sometimes interfering in local politics, but mostly concentrating on coastal trade and their protracted competition with the small Muslim powers of the region. This relationship between coast and interior survived into the late nineteenth century. It was only during the *scramble for Africa* that the Portuguese moved decisively inland to stake territorial claims, which forestalled other European claimants; in so doing they also extended an essentially *feudal* economic and political structure to the *hinterland*. Portuguese immigration continued even after *World War II*, when most other European states were preparing to abandon their African empires. By the 1960s about 130,000 white *settlers* (not all were Portuguese) were in-country, and most were prepared to fight to retain their farms and privileges. A *guerrilla war* began in 1964, led by the *Marxist-nationalist* FRELIMO. Along with several other colonial wars Portugal had to fight in Africa, this helped bring about the collapse of the Portuguese dictatorship in 1974. Mozambique therefore became independent in 1975, under FRELIMO Army commander, then President, *Samora Machel*. Until 1980 it faced repeated border *incursions* from Rhodesia, and until a 1984 accord was signed it was raided by South African troops and had to fend off guerrilla attacks sponsored by Pretoria. The war cost many lives and the economy virtually collapsed; this was followed by a protracted *civil war*. Former guerrilla leader Joaqum Alberto Chissan (b. 1939) became president in 1986. During the civil war he opened negotiations with South Africa in an effort to undercut its support for his opponents. Besides *famine, civil war,* and internal *refugees*, Mozambique was hard hit by the spread of *AIDS*. A *peace* agreement was reached at the end of 1992, supported by a team of 7,000 observers and troops from the United Nations. During the 1990s Mozambique began to recover from the war, but in 2000 and again in 2001, devastating floods literally washed away much of the progress made.

Suggested Reading: Gervase Clarence-Smith, *The Third Portuguese Empire, 1825–1975* (1985).

Mubarak, Muhammad Hosni (b. 1928). President of Egypt 1981– . Head of the air force, 1969–1975; vice president, 1975–1981. He succeeded *Anwar Sadat*, beside whom he was seated when the assassins struck on October 6, 1981. A supporter of the *Camp David Accords*, he oversaw the return of the final third of the *Sinai* in 1982. He was a strong supporter of the *Gulf coalition* in the *Gulf War*, committing significant forces, but also arranging a quid pro quo whereby $10 billion in debt was forgiven by the United States. In 1993 he began all-out repression of Egypt's *Muslim Brotherhood*. He was repeatedly reelected (1987, 1993, 1999), though no fair observer could say the process was genuinely democratic. He was deeply frustrated with the lack of further progress in the peace process, especially after the outbreak of the *Intifada* ripped the process from more moderate hands on both sides.

Mugabe, Robert (b. 1924). *See Zimbabwe.*

Mughal Empire. *See India.*

Muhammad II (1432–1481). "The Conqueror." This great sultan achieved a long-desired goal of the *Ottoman Empire*: capture of the *Byzantine* capital of *Constantinople*. He accomplished the feat in 1453 after a two-year siege. In a remarkable maneuver, he transferred his fleet of some 80 warships overland, since the *Bosporus* was blocked by the Byzantines. He did so by means of a greased plank road more than a mile long, along which the ships were towed. The fleet then bombarded the city from one side, while Muhammad's land-based *artillery* pounded it from the other. He allowed his troops to *sack* the city, with much loss of life (and international respect), before settling upon it as his new capital. In 1456 he invaded Serbia, laying siege to Belgrade. He overran Serbia by the end of 1458 and turned his attention to Greece and the Aegean Islands, 1458–1460. He conquered Bosnia, 1463–1464. He began a long war against Venice in 1463 and penetrated into Croatia and Dalmatia by 1468, the same year he reconquered Albania. He was attacked by Persia in 1473, in alliance with Venice. He rolled up the Venetian towns on the Adriatic coast, then threatened north Italy during the 1470s—bringing additional fear to, and pressure on, the divided *city-states* of the Italian *Renaissance*. He was stymied at Rhodes, however, in 1479, by the Knights of St. John. He captured Otranto in 1480. He died while campaigning in Persia. In addition to martial success, Muhammad made important advances in the codification of Ottoman law.

Muhammad Ali. *See Mehemet Ali.*

mujahadeen. "Holy warriors." *Islamic* fighters who are, think they are, or just say they are engaged in a *jihad. See also Afghan-Soviet War; Central Intelligence Agency; MI5/MI6; Taliban; terrorism.*

Mukden (Shenyang) incident (September 18, 1931). Free-lancing *militarists* of the *Guandong Army* staged an explosion on the *railway* line that they controlled at Mukden. Falsely claiming they had been attacked by the Chinese garrison from the city, they invaded *Manchuria.* The commander of Japanese units in Korea chimed in by attacking across the Chinese border on his own initiative. Once engaged, these officers pleaded necessity to their (nominal) superiors in Tokyo and extant commitment of forces and proceeded with their planned conquest. This rank *aggression* deeply angered the Western powers, the United States in particular, but consumed with the *Great Depression* and abiding memories of *World War I* they did nothing. By early 1932 Japanese troops controlled all Manchuria. When a *fact-finding* mission (the *Lytton Commission*) sent by the *League of Nations* mildly criticized this action, Japan withdrew from the League and set up the *puppet regime* of *Manchukuo.* The civilian government in Tokyo was angered by the lack of advance consultation by the army, but did not act to curtail its *aggression* and refused to renounce it. Manchuria later became a base camp for Japan's invasion of the Chinese heartland. *See also Hoover-Stimson Doctrine; Kellogg-Briand Pact; Nine Power Treaty; Tōjō Hideki.*

mullah. In *Islamic* nations, this is a title of respect for persons learned in the *sharia* law.

Mulroney, Martin Brian (b. 1939). Canadian prime minister, 1984–1993. After the *Trudeau* years of intermittent confrontation with the United States over energy, *investment*, and even *security* policy, and a long, futile search for a "Third Option" for Canada's trade and foreign policy, Mulroney reoriented the country toward continentalism. He institutionalized this basic change in the *Canada–United States Free Trade Agreement* and with *NAFTA*. He enjoyed close relations with two presidents (*Reagan, George H. Bush*). He took Canada into the *Gulf War*, but only as a minor player serving *logistical* and *blockade* functions until the air war was nearly at an end, when Canadian pilots were at last allowed to engage the enemy. As the *Cold War* ended, Mulroney announced a pullback of troops from *NATO* deployments in Europe and an upper limit to Canada's traditional *peacekeeping* service. In 1990 he overturned decades of hesitation and took Canada into the *OAS*. Domestically, he joined all other prime ministers in failing to resolve the problem of *secessionist* sentiment in Québec. Despite his substantial achievements, he left office deeply unpopular over federal tax policy, the constitutional impasse, and elements of his leadership style. His Conservative Party was nearly eliminated from Parliament in ensuing elections, and the conservative coalition in Canada broke apart for a full generation.

multiethnic. A state or other political community composed of two or more *ethnic groups*, for example, Canada, India, Indonesia, and most African states. With rising *immigration*, even once homogenous states are becoming multi-ethnic, for example, Germany and France. Some countries resist such pressures with tight immigration laws and discriminatory social practices, for example, Australia, Canada, United States, Japan, and others, at various times. *See also nation.*

multilateral. Any interaction taking place among more than two *states*.

multilateral aid. *Development* aid channeled through and administered by *international organizations*, such as the *International Bank for Reconstruction and Development, International Monetary Fund*, or various *regional banks*.

multilateral diplomacy. Diplomacy conducted by large numbers of *states*, often in public, as opposed to *bilateral* and secretive *negotiations*. *See also conference diplomacy; public opinion.*

Multilateral Trade Negotiations (MTN). The various rounds of the *General Agreement on Tariffs and Trade* (GATT), of which the most important were the *Kennedy, Tokyo,* and *Uruguay Rounds*.

multinational corporation/enterprise (MNC/MNE). A firm with production, marketing, and distribution facilities located in several countries and highly flexible in moving around *capital, goods,* and *technology* to match market conditions. It is also said to "think globally," or have no specific loyalty in making these decisions, which are based instead on questions of *economies of scale*, taxation policy, and *repatriated* profits. This feature has led to criticism from *host countries* about insensitivity to local needs and interests. There are also complaints, on occasion, about MNC interference in domestic political affairs. They have existed for centuries: the *Medici* bank dominated the economy of the Mediterranean in the fifteenth century; the *Fugger* bank was dominant in Central Europe in the sixteenth century; the *Rothschild* banks became genuinely international in reach in the nineteenth; the British *East India Company* governed India during the seventeenth and eighteenth centuries, while its Dutch counterpart ran much of Indonesia at that time, and the *Hudson's Bay Company* explored and controlled much of Canada and the Pacific Northwest of the United States.

Modern MNCs proliferated in the twentieth century, starting from bases in the United States and Europe but eventually becoming truly global in their reach, and later also in their origin, as Japanese, Korean, South African, and other MNCs matured. From the 1960s, some effort was made to develop an international code of conduct for MNCs, but the most effective measures proved to be those adopted unilaterally. The expanding wealth and role of MNCs stems from the very processes that produce modern economic benefits, as well as global *interdependence*. This causes tension with national governments that are losing *autonomy* and local economic control to larger market forces. More enthusiastic advocates of MNCs see this decline in effective *sovereignty* as both inevitable and a good thing. They argue that it increases the quotient of human welfare by promoting interconnected growth and political homogenization. Fiercer critics, frequently drawing upon *dependency theory*, see MNCs as extending the tentacles of capitalist domination, producing hierarchical rather than interdependent relations and promoting private power and gain at the expense of public welfare.

Most governments have learned to take a pragmatic, middle view and road: they encourage MNC *investment* within whatever national guidelines they are able to impose, adjust to global economic and technological shifts by merging their bargaining power through regional economic *integration*, and slowly open to wider benefits through moves toward regional and global *free trade*. By 2001 there were some 40,000 MNCs—broadly defined—operating among larger, *OECD* economies. Together, these firms had gross sales nearly equal to the GNP of the United States. *See also Andean Common Market*; chaebol; *foreign direct investment; internalization theory; portfolio investment; product cycle theory; transnational*; zaibatsu.

Suggested Readings: Robert Reich, *The Work of Nations* (1991); Paz Estrella Tolentino, *Multinational Corporations: Emergence and Evolution* (2000).

multinational empire/state. A political entity composed of several *nations*, though most often organized to greatly advantage a dominant *ethnic group* (Germans in *Austria-Hungary*, Serbs in *Yugoslavia*, or Russians in the *Soviet Union*). Multinational empires dominated world history over the past 500 years. With the passing of *colonialism* and of the Soviet Union, that era appears to be at an end.

multiple independently targetable reentry vehicle (MIRV). When a single *launcher* carries a *bus* that delivers two or more *warheads* to different targets. Its introduction in the 1970s eroded *SALT I* and seriously complicated *arms control* talks.

multipolarity. A metaphor, borrowed from magnetism, depicting a distribution of *power* in the *international system* where three or more *Great Powers* of roughly equal strength act as poles of attraction and repulsion for smaller powers. Each has preponderant influence over lesser powers within a *sphere of influence* and seeks to repel all other Great Powers from its zone. Some theorists maintain that a system with five powers, or poles, is the most stable; others argue for one or for two (almost no one argues for three). Yet, all such abstract, theoretical preferences are ahistorical, parochial, and superficial. The widely held view of five as the optimum number is based upon European experience after 1660, and especially the example of the *Concert of Europe*. Similarly, a theoretical preference for a single *preponderant power* overseeing international order has no historical referent other than to the position of the United States after *World War II* and again after 1990. Nonetheless, it is frequently presented with over-easy reference to the *Roman Empire* or *Imperial China*. In fact, Rome and China each ruled but a corner of their world, faced powerful enemies, and were ultimately overrun. Even in the case of the United States, for decades after 1945 American influence was foreclosed from large sections of the world's economy, politics, and land surface. Lastly, to abstract from the *Cold War* a firm generalization about the supposed inherent stability of any *international system* with two dominant powers is crude *determinism*. Among other things, it ignores the vivid possibility that another such conflict could have a quite different outcome (as could have the Cold War itself), depending on real choices made by *decision makers*, the virulence of ideological or other competition, altered *technology* or other circumstance, or dumb chance. *See also bipolarity; tripolarity; unipolarity.*

Münchengrätz Agreements (1833). *Metternich* and *Nicholas I* met and agreed to act in concert should the *Ottoman Empire* collapse and be *partitioned* and to guarantee each other's Polish territory against *rebellion*. A follow-up pact drew in Prussia for a *declaration* of intent to come to the aid of any *sovereign* faced with a *liberal* or *radical* revolt. *See also Holy Alliance.*

Munich analogy. Any analogy, whether accurate or not, that seeks to compare a policy problem or a crisis situation to the *Munich Conference*. Such analogies are usually invoked to remind leaders to bear in mind the main lesson of Munich, taken to be that *appeasement* will only whet the appetite of an *aggressor* and require later payment of a much higher price in blood and treasure. *See also containment; Korean Conflict; Dean Rusk; Vietnam War.*

Munich Conference (September 29–30, 1938). This infamous conference was called to address a building crisis between *Nazi Germany* and Czechoslovakia, in which Germany mobilized preparatory to an attack on the Czechs. It was attended by *Neville Chamberlain*, prime minister of Great Britain; *Édouard Daladier*, prime minister of France; *Benito Mussolini*, prime minister of Italy; and *Adolf Hitler*, *Führer* of Germany. Also present were, inter alia, *Ciano, Göring, Hess, Himmler*, and *Ribbentrop*. Munich is permanently associated with the utter failure of the West's policy of *appeasement*, which grew out of a sense in Britain that the *Treaty of Versailles* was indeed onerous and unjust to Germany and from France's realization that without major allies supporting a tough policy against German *revisionism* it could not alone resist a German assault on the Treaty. It also sprang from a lingering war-weariness among the victors of 1918, compounded by domestic social unrest and the huge challenge of recovery from the *Great Depression*. Munich was Chamberlain's third trip to Germany to persuade Hitler not to use force in Europe. This time, he and Daladier agreed that the price of peace would be paid by the Czechs: the *Sudetenland* was cravenly handed over to Hitler and other parts of Czechoslovakia went to Hungary, Rumania, and—most foolhardily—Poland (which partitioned Czech *Silesia* with Hitler), with no consultation whatever with the Czech or Soviet governments, which were vitally interested in the outcome. What was left of the Czech state was "guaranteed protection" by the four signatories. Chamberlain flew home to proclaim "peace with honor" and was received with great acclaim. The accolades lasted only until March 1939, when Hitler moved into the rump of Czechoslovakia, finally shocking the West into all-out preparations for war. Munich stunned the Soviets. *Stalin* ceased sending security feelers westward, sacked *Litvinov*, and moved to make a separate deal with Hitler. Major consequences of Munich were thus the *Nazi-Soviet Pact* and the subsequent outbreak of *World War II*, with the great anti-German coalition of *World War I* shattered by mutual suspicion. *Winston Churchill* said of Munich and appeasement: "The German dictator, instead of snatching the victuals from the table, has been content to have them served to him course by course." *See also Little Entente; Munich analogy; Treaty of Amiens.*

Suggested Readings: Telford Taylor, *Munich* (1979); Igor Lukes and Erik Goldstein, eds., *The Munich Crisis, 1938* (1999).

Munich Putsch. *See Beer Hall Putsch.*

municipal law. Domestic law, *sovereign* and distinct from *international law.*

munitions. Matériel used in war: equipment and supplies, but especially *arms* and ammunition.

Münster, Treaty of (January 30, 1648). A *peace treaty* between *Habsburg* Spain and the *Netherlands*, through which an end was made to the "Revolt of the Netherlands," or *Eighty Years' War* (1568–1648). Dutch *independence* was accepted by Madrid, and limited freedom of religion was granted to Spaniards conducting business in the Netherlands and vice versa. It also formed part of the general settlement in Europe constituting the end game to the *Thirty Years' War* and the *Peace of Westphalia*.

Murat, Joachim (1767–1815). Marshal of France; king of Naples. One of *Napoleon I*'s key marshals and also his brother-in-law, this son of an innkeeper was rewarded for both positions with an Italian throne (1809). He was a *Jacobin* during the *French Revolution*. He joined Napoleon in time to deliver the "whiff of grapeshot" that propelled his new master to power. He fought in Italy, 1796–1797, and in Egypt and Syria, 1798–1799. He backed Napoleon again in the *coup d'etat* of "18 Brumaire" (November 10, 1799). He married Caroline, Napoleon's sister, in 1800. He fought in nearly all of Napoleon's major victories, including Marengo (June 14, 1800). He was promoted to marshal in 1804. He captured Vienna in 1805, and fought brilliantly at *Austerlitz*. In 1806 he captured Warsaw from the Prussians. On February 8, 1807 he led the largest *cavalry* charge of the century, at Eylau: 10,000 French horse charged through the Russian line, overran the *artillery*, and charged back again. He had less success in Spain in 1808. He then changed places with Napoleon's brother Joseph and became king of Naples. In 1809 he attacked the British in Sicily. He reluctantly left Naples to command the French cavalry during Napoleon's ill-conceived invasion of Russia in 1812 and lost most of his men (and even more disastrously, irreplaceable cavalry mounts) on the awful *retreat from Moscow*. He fought for Napoleon again at *Leipzig*. In 1814 he made a *separate peace* with the Allies to save his throne. He rallied to his old commander during the *Hundred Days*. He was defeated by the Austrians and returned to France. After Napoleon's second abdication Murat tried to reclaim his throne. This time he was arrested by *Restoration* authorities, tried for *treason*, and shot.

Muscat and Oman. *See Oman.*

Muscovy. *See Ivan III; Russia.*

musket. *See gunpowder revolution; infantry; Napoleonic warfare; revolution in military affairs; rifled-bore; smooth-bore.*

Muslim. A believer in *Islam*. *See also ayatollah*; *caliph*; *fundamentalism*; haj; imam; *Iranian Revolution*; *Ismaili*; *Mecca*; mullah; *Muslim Brotherhood*; *shi'ia Islam*; *sultan*; *sunni Islam*; *Wahhabi*.

Muslim Brotherhood. A *fundamentalist* movement within *Islam*, founded in Egypt in 1928 by Hassa al-Banna (1906–1949). It has engaged in assassination of *secular* Arabs and other *Muslims* as part of a campaign to substitute the *sharia* for secular law and political authority in Muslim countries. For this it has been banned in several countries (in Egypt, as early as 1954). Al-Banna was himself assassinated by the Egyptian government in retaliation for the killing of a prime minister. While its radicalism and antisecularism have earned it disapprobation internationally, its promotion of grassroots public works and Islamic revival earned it a substantial following among the poor, notably in Algeria, Egypt, Sudan, and Syria.

Muslim League. The political party that founded *Pakistan*. It was formed in 1905–1906 in the wake of *Curzon's* partition of Bengal. Until *World War I* the League represented mostly *elite* Muslim merchants and landowners in a cozy relationship with British officials and was disregarded by most Indian Muslims. In 1912 it moved away from collaboration and called for *Home Rule*, though thereby it still accepted India as having some place within the *British Empire*. World War I proved a turning point, as India's Muslims found themselves unwillingly at war with the *Ottoman Empire*, which joined the *Central Powers* against Britain. The League was swept up in the *kalifah movement* until abolition of the Ottoman caliphate in 1924. It split from alliance with the *Congress Party* of India, led by *Mohandas Gandhi*, in 1920. In 1930 the League first mooted the idea of a separate Pakistan for Muslims. It was rescued from obscurity by the *Round Table Conferences* and the ambitious leadership of *Muhammad Ali Jinnah*. Still, in 1937 it failed to win a majority of even those seats reserved to Muslims under the *India Act* of 1935. Afraid that a Hindu Rāj might replace the British Rāj, Jinnah and the League lobbied all-out for Pakistan. In 1946 Jinnah's call for direct action initiated a week of mass killings in Calcutta, launching what was in effect a war of secession by Pakistan. The Muslim League was the dominant party in Pakistan after independence. By the late 1960s, however, it was displaced by the Awami League in *East Pakistan* and faced a growing challenge from the Pakistan People's Party in *West Pakistan*.

Mussolini, Benito (1883–1945). "Il Duce" ("The Leader"). Dictator of Italy, 1922–1943. Mussolini's political career was spent in pursuit of martial and imperial greatness for the Italian nation, rather an irony given that as a young man he fled Italy (1902) to avoid military service. Mussolini abandoned his early, radical *socialism* for the crudest *militarism* and *nationalism* with the outbreak of *World War I*, in which he enlisted and was wounded, in the buttocks, in 1917. By the end of the war he moved to embrace a new radicalism: *fascism*. That appealed to his appetite for power, *social Darwinism*, and deeply *racist* view of the world, a view that profoundly—and adversely—influenced his diplomacy and strategic planning in later years. Mussolini borrowed *irridentist* and other nationalist ideas freely and heavily from *Gabriele D'Annunzio* and was deeply influenced in both political tactics and style by that zealot's seizure of *Fiume*.

Mussolini became prime minister in 1922 after the so-called *march on Rome*; he was outright dictator from 1925. He settled the Italian state's dispute with the *Vatican* in the *Lateran Treaty* and *concordat* of 1929. He proudly claimed of his fascist *revolution*: "We have buried the putrid corpse of *liberty*." Though one is tempted to dismiss his foreign policy as mere bombast from a balcony (his favored locale for public strutting), it was in fact opportunistically *expansionist*, cost many lives, and in the end left Italy a shattered and occupied nation. That resulted from failing to adjust his imperialist sights as Nazi Germany rose, relying on what was only a façade of Italian military power, exercising high-risk *brinkmanship*, and worst of all, launching a series of failed wars parallel to those waged by *Hitler*.

Mussolini tried to take *Corfu* in 1924, but backed down. He invaded Ethiopia in 1935, starting the *Second Abyssinian War*, and pursued a long and brutal campaign of repression in *Tripoli* (Libya). In 1936 he signed the *Axis* pact with Hitler and intervened in the *Spanish Civil War*. Mussolini took Italy out of the *League of Nations* in 1937. After that, he fell increasingly under Hitler's personal influence in what one historian aptly called "the brutal friendship." He joined Italy to the *Pact of Steel* in 1939, the same year he invaded Albania. Mussolini treacherously attacked France as German tanks were rolling through Paris in 1940. He reportedly said: "I need 1,000 dead to sit at the peace table." What he got was humiliation: four French divisions held off twenty-eight Italian divisions, surrendering less than two miles of front and losing eight killed to 5,000 Italian dead.

Mussolini next invaded Greece, again in 1940 and again losing badly. Once more, his military had to be bailed out by Hitler's forces. This debacle forced Hitler into increased confrontation with Britain in the Balkans and in North Africa at a time when he was preparing to invade the Soviet Union, thus further thinning his forces and delaying the attack on Russia. It represented, therefore, Mussolini's single most important influence on the course of the war. His prestige, though not his pomposity, was greatly diminished by these repeated martial humiliations. Mussolini consistently overestimated the capabilities of the Italian armed forces, which continued to suffer from poor and outdated equipment and low morale throughout the war. They were easily thrown out of East and North Africa, 1941–1942, mainly by the British. And his *declaration of war* on the United States was deeply unpopular with the millions of Italians who had extended family in America.

Mussolini lost Sicily and southern Italy in 1943 to invading Anglo-

American forces. With the *Allies* moving on Rome he was dismissed by his own fascist inner circle, including his son-in-law, *Count Ciano*. Arrested in a palace *coup* led by *Pietro Badoglio*, whom Mussolini had once appointed governor of Libya, he was imprisoned, but then was freed by German paratroopers in a daring *commando* raid. Still suffering from a fatal attraction to Hitler, he was installed as a tattered Nazi puppet in north Italy. Captured by *partisans* in 1945 while trying to flee Italy (disguised in a German uniform), Mussolini was *summarily executed* on April 28th—just two days later his "friend" in Berlin blew his own brains out. Mussolini's body, and that of his murdered mistress, Clara Petacci, were taken to Milan and there hung by the feet and left for public display and vile personal abuse in the Piazza Loreto.

Suggested Readings: MacGregor Knox, *Mussolini Unleashed* (1982); D. Mack Smith, *Mussolini* (1982).

mustard gas. A liquid blister agent (bis-sulfide) that turns into a noxious yellow gas when exposed to air, hence the name. It blinds and scorches the lungs and flesh of any who encounter even minute particles. It was first used at *Passchendale* in 1917. It was a hated and much-feared weapon among troops in the trenches of *World War I*, when it was known by advocates as the "king of gas weapons." Yet, it proved so entirely indecisive militarily that, despite stockpiling, it was not used by any side in *World War II*.

muster. To assemble troops for battle. To muster in/out means to enlist/discharge from the military.

mutatis mutandis. "With the required changes made." An operational assumption commonly made in economic and statistical analysis.

mutilated victory ("vittoria mutilata"). A famous complaint by Italian supernationalists about Italy's putative mistreatment by the other *Allied and Associated Powers* at the *Paris Peace Conference*. The charge was powerfully made by *D'Annunzio* and echoed through Italian politics in the postwar period, undermining stability by its damnation of those who took Italy into *World War I*, but to such little apparent final purpose or accomplishment. The main charge was that Italy had been denied its just demand for *Fiume*, along with other *Italia irredenta* territories promised in the secret *Treaty of London* of 1915. The Treaty of London was published by the *Bolsheviks* in 1918, to the dismay of Britain and France, and provoked deep anger and opposition to Italy's claims on the part of *Woodrow Wilson*. In fact, the terms of the Treaty were kept at Paris: Italy received everything promised in the Treaty of London by Britain and France. It was denied its additional demand for *Fiume*, which had not been included in the Treaty because, although *Clemenceau* and *Lloyd George* felt duty-bound to give *Orlando* everything they had promised, they joined Wilson in denying Fiume to Italy. On that point,

Orlando had stormed out of the conference, returning later only to sign the several *peace treaties* legally ending the war. *See also stab-in-the-back; victory.*

mutiny. Any revolt of soldiers (or marines, militia, or sailors) against the legally constituted military authorities that normally command them, and usually implying violence against *officers*. Mutiny plays a neglected and mostly unheralded role in world affairs, given that its occurrence usually reflects a deteriorating state of *national morale*, and not just military disaffection, and considering that any rebellion by armed forces may pose a major internal threat to a government suffering from a crisis of *legitimacy*. When mutiny arises on a large-scale among *frontline* troops, it may lead to *defeat* or other disaster. It was more common in the era of mercenary armies and ineffective war finance than among modern, national armies; but it still occurs. During the *Eighty Years' War* (1566–1648) the Spanish Army of Flanders mutinied forty-six times between 1572 and 1607, mainly over not being paid as a result of *Philip II*'s frequent bankruptcies and chronic shortage of capital and similar habits by his son. Mutinies on all sides were common during the *Thirty Years' War*. Even great military reformers such as *Gustav II* and *Cromwell* faced mutinies. After 1630, mutinous rebellions by *Ming* troops opened the door to the *Manchu* invasion of China.

Serious mutinies occurred during the *Napoleonic Wars*, including two British naval mutinies (Spithead and Nore) of 1797, in the face of possible French invasion, which were put down only by a combination of reforms and executions. Troops in both American armies mutinied during the *American Civil War*, including at Shiloh (April 6–7, 1862). The *Indian Mutiny* (1857–1858) faced Britain with perhaps the gravest challenge in its imperial history. A mutiny by the Chinese military in 1911 finally persuaded the *Qing* that they must abdicate. In 1914, after the first bloody battles of *World War I*, elements of the Indian Army mutinied in Rangoon and Basra. Other units mutinied in Singapore in 1915 and some on the *western front*, from where they were reassigned to the Middle East. In 1917 widespread mutiny among tsarist troops forced Russia onto the defensive, and when the disaffection reached the Navy too, it led to the *Russian Revolutions* of 1917. Elements of the British Army mutinied in 1917 on the western front. A simultaneous but more widespread *French Army mutiny* brought down the government in France and momentarily threatened the Allied war effort. German soldiers on home leave and sailors in Kiel ordered on a suicide mission against the *Royal Navy* mutinied in October 1918, hastening the fall of the *kaiser* and signing of the *Armistice*.

In 1946 the Royal Indian Navy mutinied in Bombay. Shore positions were heavily bombarded by mutinous warships, with some 80 ships and 20 shore stations experiencing some degree of mutinous unrest. This further encouraged Britain toward acceptance of Indian independence. In 1956 a mutiny in the Hungarian Army sparked the *Hungarian Uprising*, which led to massive Soviet *intervention*. A 1958 mutiny in the French Army in Algeria shook the

French Republic to the core. In 1964 the newly independent states of Kenya, Tanzania, and Gabon all were wracked by army mutinies, which required Britain and France to intervene to restore order and civilian rule. Mutiny may also take an insidious, individual or small-unit form: during the *Vietnam War* low morale among American *conscripts* sometimes led to incidents of "fragging," a euphemism for wounding or killing one's own officers if they were too aggressive in pursuing the enemy. Mutiny very often is confined to one or more units and does not spread: before the *Tiananmen massacre* in China, elements of the PLA refused to carry out orders to suppress the demonstrators. Similarly, several units of the *Red Army* refused orders to support the *coup* against *Gorbachev* in August 1991. *See also Algerian War of Independence; Clemenceau; French Foreign Legion; Jutland; Kronstadt mutiny; Pitcairn Island; Russian Revolutions; Tang dynasty; voting with their feet; war communism.*

mutual assured destruction (MAD). *See assured destruction; deterrence; Strategic Defense Initiative (SDI).*

Mutual Force Reduction (MFR) Talks. Negotiations that began in 1973 between *NATO* and the *Warsaw Pact* concerning *conventional weapons* and reducing troop levels. The talks went virtually nowhere until the end of the *Cold War*, when agreement was reached across the board on massive conventional cutbacks.

Mwata Kazembe and Mwata Yamvo. *See Lunda.*

Myanmar. *See Burma.*

My Lai massacre (March 16, 1968). American GIs under Capt. Ernest Medina entered a cluster of hamlets called My Lai 4, looking for *Viêt Cong*. They *tortured* the men for information and then murdered between 200 and 500 unarmed men, women, and children. When the story broke, it reinforced a growing perception that the *Vietnam War* had gone terribly wrong and was tragically corrupting America's young men along with its national life and politics. Twenty-five men originally were charged, but only six faced court-martial. Five were acquitted. Just one, Lt. William Calley, was convicted. He was sentenced to life, saw this reduced to 20 years hard labor, overturned on appeal, and reinstated. He was then paroled in 1975. The trial was most notable for the court's rejection of the defense of *superior orders*, a decision implicitly upholding the precedent of the *Nuremberg war crimes trials.*

N

nabob. An English corruption of the Hindi *nawab*.

NAFTA. *See New Zealand-Australia Free Trade Agreement; North American Free Trade Agreement.*

Nagasaki, atomic bombing of. On August 9, 1945, Nagasaki experienced the second use of an *atomic bomb* in wartime: a *plutonium* device code-named Fat Man was air-burst over the city by the U.S. Air Force. Thus was a second major city of the Empire of the Rising Sun illuminated by the elemental power of the sun at the dawn of the Nuclear Age. The blast and firestorm killed 40,000–60,000 outright (one Japanese study suggests closer to 75,000), with perhaps 100,000 more dying lingering, painful deaths in the months and years that followed. The attack came just three days after the first atomic bomb had been dropped on *Hiroshima* and a single day after the Soviet Union entered the war in the Pacific, attacking and driving back the Japanese Army in Manchuria and northern China. In combination, those events broke all remaining will to resist, which was already wavering among most Japanese, other than the most fanatic, after years of wartime privation, death, and *thousand bomber raids*.

What has since emerged in the historical literature is that the atomic bombs persuaded Japan's military leaders that, because the Allies possessed such awesome weapons, they would not need to invade the Japanese home islands. Therefore, the final and bloody defense of Japan—which the militarists had hoped might be used to extract concessions from the Allied powers—was no longer a viable option, and the Japanese military leadership decided on *surrender* instead. On August 10th, the first formal peace feelers were sent out, and on August 15th Japan agreed to *terms*. On September 2, 1945, representatives of Imperial Japan signed the instrument of surrender to the Allied powers aboard the American battleship U.S.S. Missouri in Tokyo Bay, in the presence of Allied representatives and a number of liberated *prisoners of war*, including commanding officers who had experienced the *Bataan death march*.

Suggested Readings: Richard B. Frank, *Downfall: The End of the Imperial Japanese Empire* (1999); Martin Sherwin, *A World Destroyed* (1987).

Nagasaki, port of. From the sixteenth century this ancient port served as Japan's "window on the West." Iberian traders were followed by *Jesuits*, Dominicans, Augustinians, and other *missionaries*. In 1597 *Hideyoshi* turned on the missions and had 26 Franciscans crucified in Nagasaki. After 1641 Westerners were strictly confined to the artificial island of *Deshima*. In 1635 Chinese had been confined to Nagasaki, which thereafter was the hub of an important China trade in the seventeenth and eighteenth centuries, although this was restricted after 1790. Restrictions ended with the *Meiji Restoration* in 1868.

Nagorno-Karabakh. An ethnically Armenian *enclave* of some 200,000 souls, located entirely within post-Soviet Azerbaijan. For centuries it was governed by Armenian princes until being conquered by Russia. During the chaos of the Russian collapse in the summer and fall of 1917, it tried to join Armenia, which was breaking free of the Russian Empire, but was prevented from doing so by Azerbaijan (with aid from Turkey). In 1918, with the collapse of *Ottoman* power, it tried again to join Armenia, which was then briefly independent. This time it was prevented by Britain from consummating the *union*. In 1920 the Soviets re-established Russian control. In 1921 the *territory* was ceded to Soviet Armenia, but within days protests from Soviet Azerbaijan overturned the decision. *Stalin* enforced a false peace on the region, setting the modern borders in 1936. In 1963 anti-Azeri riots broke out. In 1988 *Gorbachev* agreed to consider a transfer to Armenia, and the Assembly in Nagorno-Karabakh voted 110 to 17 to accept such a transfer. However, the Soviet committee studying the question bent to Azeri pressure and said no. Sectarian riots then broke out across the region, generating fears of *genocide*, as anti-Armenian *pogroms* began in Baku. Soviet troops tried unsuccessfully to intervene in 1988 and 1989, after sporadic fighting began.

In January 1989, Gorbachev placed the enclave under direct administration from Moscow. That was opposed, and he quickly reversed the decision. In 1990 the Soviets occupied Baku, site of recent massacres of Armenians. By early 1991 the Russians could no longer enforce peace, and when the Soviet Union collapsed at the end of the year, they ceased trying. A conflict that had been limited to rifle fire and sporadic violence became supplemented by tanks, *artillery*, aircraft and the full apparatus of interstate war as Armenia and Azerbaijan emerged as independent states and the *Armenia-Azerbaijan War* spread and widened. Russia mostly stayed out of the conflict. Turkey and Iran, on the other hand, threatened *intervention* if Armenia attempted *annexation*. The enclave was 80 percent Armenian before fighting began. By 1994 *ethnic cleansing* raised that figure to 95 percent, when a *cease-fire* was agreed and monitors introduced by the *Organization for Security and Cooperation in Europe*. Six years of fighting had killed 30,000 and driven one million inhabitants out of the enclave, leaving it governed by an unrecognized ethnic Armenian regime while also retarding economic development in the former Soviet republics. Desultory fighting continued through the 1990s. In 1999 Azerbaijan's president, Geidar Aliev, and Armenian president Robert Kocharian began direct talks jointly mediated by the United States and Russia. *See also Nakhichevan.*

Nagy, Imre (1896–1958). Prime minister of Hungary, 1953–1955, 1956. He was purged from the *Communist Party* in 1955 on charges of *Titoism*. He returned to power in 1956 and with *János Kádár* stepped up the changes—notably, an end to forced *collectivization* on the *Stalinist* model—that led to the *Hungarian Uprising*. When the *rebellion* was crushed by the Soviet Union he was arrested, in violation of a promise of safe conduct, and was later shot (this fact was kept secret for two years).

Nakhichevan. A noncontiguous part of Azerbaijan, forming an Azeri *enclave* between Armenia and Turkey. In 1924, Nakhichevan was made an autonomous republic within the Soviet Union, whereas *Nagorno-Karabakh* was made an Autonomous Oblast. During the *Armenia-Azerbaijan War*, fighting spilled into this area (1992). In 1993 rebel Azeri from the enclave fought a brief *campaign* against the Azeri government, ostensibly to protest its poor management of the war with Armenia. In 1998 *oil* exploration began in the expectation of discovery of major fields.

NAM. *See Nonaligned Movement.*

Namibia. Formerly *German Southwest Africa*, a German colony, 1883–1915. From 1904 to 1907 a revolt by the Herero was savagely repressed by the German governor—*Hermann Göring's* father—costing the lives of two-thirds of the Herero people (the *Herero-Nama War*). The colony was invaded by British and South African troops during *World War I*, after which it was *mandated* to South Africa by the *League of Nations* (1920). White settlement, mostly German, continued between the wars, with Africans segregated on "reserves" of barely habitable desert land. In 1946, with the *extinction* of the League, South Africa refused to transfer Namibia to the authority of the United Nations *Trusteeship Council*. In 1960 an *independence* movement, the South West African People's Organization (SWAPO), was founded. In 1966 it moved to *guerrilla* attacks aimed at pressuring Pretoria into conceding independence, with support from the *frontline states*. That same year, the United Nations rescinded the mandate. In 1971 the *International Court of Justice* ruled that South Africa's continued refusal to grant UN authority over Namibia was illegal. A United Nations Contact Group comprising Canada, Britain, France, Germany, and the United States was formed to negotiate a settlement. In 1980–1981 South Africa invaded southern *Angola* in a bid to eliminate SWAPO bases. Subsequently, and with tacit U.S. support, it linked elections in Namibia to withdrawal of Cuban troops from Angola. Final settlement came when Cuba pulled out in 1988 and South Africa, itself about to undergo massive change, conceded independence to Namibia. *Apartheid* was ended in Namibia on May 13, 1989, preparatory to that territory becoming fully sovereign on March 21, 1990. In 1993 *Walvis Bay* was ceded to Namibia. SWAPO retained power through the 1990s. As *Congo* disintegrated after 1997, Namibia was one of several regional states that intervened in its civil war.

Nanjing (Nanking), Rape of (1937). On December 13, 1937, Nanjing, the capital of *Nationalist China*, fell to the Japanese *Guandong Army* during the opening phase of the *Second Sino-Japanese War*. Over the next seven weeks Japanese troops ran amok, cruelly and systematically slaughtering at the very least 100,000—and more likely close to 300,000, which is the official Chinese figure—men, women and children. This was no spontaneous collapse of discipline: under orders from the high command, Japanese troops raped and *pillaged* and then burned the city. This utter barbarism—repeated many times on a smaller scale throughout Japanese-occupied Asia over the next eight years—shocked international opinion (even *Nazi Germany* made a humbug protest), damaged the overseas image of Japan, where public celebrations of the fall of the city were held, and further hardened American attitudes toward Tokyo's thrust into China. After the war, commanding general Matsui Iwane was tried and hanged by the *Tokyo war crimes tribunal* for atrocities and *war crimes* committed in Nanjing. *See also Spanish Fury.*

Suggested Readings: Joshua Fogel, ed., *The Nanjing Massacre* (2000); Masahiro Yamamoto, *Nanking* (2000).

Nanjing (Nanking), Treaty of (August 29, 1842). This was the first of the *unequal treaties* and was far and away the most important international agreement in modern Chinese history. It ended the *First Opium War*, ceded *Hong Kong* to Britain, designated five coastal cities as *treaty ports*, compelled *reparations*, and imposed a low tariff on British goods. In exchange, the British would withdraw from the cities they occupied and reopen access to the *Grand Canal*. The treaty thereby ended the *Cohong* trade system, which had confined foreign traders to Guangdong (Canton). Moreover, by explicitly eliminating both the forms and *kowtow* language of *tributary* relations, it forced China into the modern—but also European and *Great Power*–dominated—*international system* of *diplomatic relations* and *international law*. For all those reasons, it marked the beginning of China's long obeisance to foreign powers and of its agonizing internal fragmentation. It was quickly copied by other foreign trading and imperial powers in accordance with the *most-favored-nation* principle, which the British inserted into a supplementary agreement with China in 1843. *See also Macartney mission.*

Nansen, Fridtjof (1861–1930). Nansen earned fame as an Arctic explorer, but his life changed with *World War I*. In 1920 he served as Norway's delegate to the *League of Nations*, where he embraced the full *liberal peace program*. On behalf of the League he oversaw repatriation of a half-million German and other *prisoners of war* stranded by the *Russian Civil War* in the disintegrating Russian Empire. The *Red Cross* asked Nansen to oversee *famine* relief to the Soviet Union, a task in which he cooperated with the *American Relief Administration*. As *High Commissioner* for Refugees he issued passports in his own name to 1.5 million *stateless* refugees who had fled the *Russian Revolution*. These "Nansen passports" were recognized by 50 states and greatly facilitated resettlement. In 1922 Nansen was awarded the *Nobel Prize* for Peace; in 1938 the Prize went to the Nansen Office for Refugees. He next aided the exchange of 1.5 million Greek refugees who fled Turkey after 1922, for 400,000 Turks in Greece. He tried to help Armenians establish a national homeland, but without success. *See also Vidkun Quisling.*

Nantes, Edict of (1598). This royal edict was issued by *Henry IV* to permit *Protestant* worship in predominantly *Catholic* France and thereby bring an end to the Wars of Religion that had divided the country, and hamstrung its foreign policy, for 30 years. It granted to the *Huguenots* the key port city of La Rochelle as a stronghold and retreat, along with nearly 100 other fortified towns. It also gave them their own courts. This was a major breakthrough for religious tolerance on the part of the state, which presaged the grand settlement in all of Europe, with minor exceptions, that French statesmen (and cardinals of the Church) such as *Richelieu* and *Mazarin* would apply to end the wars of *Protestant Reformation* and Catholic *Counter Reformation* a half century later in the *Peace of Westphalia*. The military terms of the edict remained in effect until Richelieu took La Rochelle back from the Huguenots (1628). Its religious terms were observed until *Louis XIV* revoked the edict in 1685. That caused a mass exodus of the Huguenots from France. As with the expulsion of the Jews from Spain in 1492, this arrogant act sharply weakened the national economy by cutting it off from its more entrepreneurial members, and led them as refugees to strengthen Louis' foreign enemies. *See also Peace of Augsburg; Peace of Westphalia.*

Napoleon I (Bonaparte), né Napoleone Buonaparte (1769–1821). Military despot; emperor of France. Napoleon was born into the minor nobility of Corsica shortly after the island was annexed by France from Genoa. He was educated as a cadet in the French *artillery* school, 1779–1784, and ever after he referred to his artillery as "my daughters." This was one key to Napoleon's rise to power: he would use his skill with artillery to gain favor by destroying the enemies of France and of the *French Revolution*, and to keep power by innovative use of cannon on the battlefield. Napoleon joined the *Jacobin* club in Grenoble, but his commitment to political ideals never seemed to amount to more than a search for personal advantage. In 1789 he plunged into Corsica's politics, but he parted company with Corsican nationalism when it clashed with his career and family interests. He and his family fled Corsica in June 1793 for Marseilles. This experience with island revolution gave Napoleon a lifelong distaste for the mob but also an acute awareness of its potential. In September, Napoleon accepted a republican commission and excelled during the siege of Toulon, where he was bayoneted superficially. Toulon had been betrayed to the *Royal Navy* by a monarchist admiral, and Napoleon's leading role in recovering it to France and the Revolution brought him to national attention.

In 1794 Napoleon was put in charge of French artillery in Italy. As a Jacobin, he was briefly imprisoned following the death of *Robespierre*, whose brother had been Napoleon's patron. On his release Napoleon was offered a command in the West Indies, which he refused, wishing to remain near the center of affairs in Paris. Therefore, on October 5, 1795 (13 Vendémiaire), he was present, able, and willing to use his cannon to deliver "a whiff of grapeshot" into a Paris mob in an act of simultaneous revolution and repression that was a portent of things to come. In the short run, his career moved even closer to the center of the national stage. In 1796 Napoleon began to spell his name in the French rather than the Italian fashion, as he headed off to command a floundering republican army in Italy. He quickly achieved a series of rapid and daring victories over Austria and Piedmont, demonstrating a driving will and speed on the battlefield that made him superior to all opposing generals. As a result of this Italian campaign, Nice and Savoy were annexed to France, and Napoleon personally proclaimed the "Lombard Republic." That was the first of a series of French *protectorates* he established: within a year, France controlled the "Cisalpine" and "Romagna" republics, and the "Helvetic Republic" in Switzerland (the city of Geneva was annexed). In 1797 Napoleon personally opened direct peace talks with Austria, which withdrew from the war after signing the *Treaty of Campo Formio*. That left only Great Britain still at war with France.

Facing the barrier of the Royal Navy, Napoleon next led a brash and foolhardy expedition to Egypt to cut Britain's route to India and strangle its trade. En route, he captured Malta. Within a day of arriving in Egypt he captured Alexandria (July 2, 1798). Within three weeks he had destroyed the *Mamluk*

Army, ending centuries of Mamluk dominance of Egypt, and took Cairo (July 22, 1798). His triumphs proved impermanent: in the interim, *Nelson* had destroyed the French fleet at *Abukir*, cutting off Napoleon's *line of supply* and retreat. Isolated, he marched into Syria in 1799, but he met fierce *Ottoman* resistance and was compelled to withdraw. Meanwhile, the War of the Second Coalition began in Europe, threatening France itself with invasion. Napoleon abandoned his sick and wounded soldiers in Egypt, just as he would later abandon them in Russia and again on the bloody fields at *Waterloo*, and returned in secret to France, arriving on October 9, 1799. Napoleon took power in a *coup d'etat* on 18 Brumaire (November 9, 1799), with the considerable aid of his brother, Lucien, who intervened at a decisive moment and turned the debate. Napoleon set in motion major reforms, including introduction of universal manhood suffrage. He was not a true reformer, however, instead using the plans of sincere reformers to consolidate his personal power and position. His real intentions were revealed when, under cover of a liberal constitution endorsed by *plebiscite,* he set up a tight dictatorship and a highly centralized state with himself as first consul.

While Napoleon consolidated his hold on power he offered peace to Britain (December 1799), but the offer was rejected. Facing a new coalition, as always Napoleon chose to attack first. He defeated the Austrians decisively at Marengo (a small battle by later standards, in which Napoleon commanded just 16,000 men) on June 14, 1800, isolating Britain. In July 1801, he signed a *concordat* with Pope Pius VII. In March 1802, he concluded the *Treaty of Amiens* with Great Britain, and briefly Europe was at peace. Made first consul for life in August 1802, again by a rigged plebiscite, Napoleon also accepted the presidency of the puppet Italian Republic. Now came the great reforms of his Consulate. He changed the shape of government by establishing the French prefecture system, founded colleges and reformed education, and established the Bank of France and the Legion of Honor. Reform of the law was next, leading to the hugely influential Civil Code of 1804 (renamed the Code Napoleon in 1807), which constitutes his greatest and most positive legacy. Napoleon next turned a failed assassination attempt against him into a political murder of his own: he ordered kidnapped and executed a distant candidate for the empty French throne, the Duke d'Enghien, who was innocent of the charge of conspiracy brought against him. This scheme was launched not only to clear the way to make his own rule hereditary but also to signal that the gains of the French Revolution were permanent. On December 2, 1804, in the great medieval cathedral of Notre Dame de Paris, Napoleon crowned himself *emperor* of the French. Consciously aping Charlemagne, he took the crown from a pope's hands (Pius VII, who had been summoned from Rome) and placed it on his own head. Then he crowned as empress his cool bride, Josephine.

Napoleon grew restless for war, for which he appeared to have a deep psychological need, along with a need to dominate all around him, whether individuals or whole nations. Indeed, it may be doubted whether he had any truly serious political ideas or long-term objectives beyond personal gratification and aggrandizement: he invariably succumbed to short-term political ends and a driven need to test again his great talent for conceiving of military campaigns as a strategic whole. He was unusually aggressive by nature, although personally capable of great charm. His foreign policy was almost always one of war, interrupted by tactically beneficial truces that he broke whenever he chose, without regard for the severe damage this did to his or France's ability to conduct future negotiations or achieve a stable peace. Without Napoleon in charge of the affairs of France for some 15 years, it is highly likely that the *balance of power*—a concept utterly alien to him but closely supported by the moderate *Talleyrand*—would have been restored many years earlier than it was (1815), and at a much reduced cost in blood and treasure to France and to its enemies.

This time, Napoleon provoked war by repeatedly interfering in the *internal affairs* of Germany, Holland, and Switzerland. With tensions mounting through 1804, Britain refused to evacuate its naval base on Malta as it had agreed at Amiens. In London, *Pitt* returned to power and formed a new anti-French coalition in response to provocations such as the annexation of Piedmont-Savoy, Napoleon's coronation as king of Italy, and launch of a 20,000-man expedition to restore French rule (and *slavery*) in Haiti. The War of the Third Coalition resulted and saw Napoleon's greatest victories. Again, he struck first, defeating the Austrian Army under General Mack at Ulm (October 17, 1805), where he took 33,000 prisoners after only the barest minimum of fighting. Napoleon's plans to invade Britain were blocked by Nelson's spectacular victory at *Trafalgar*. Napoleon learned of this crushing defeat of his Franco-Spanish fleet in November while in Vienna, which he had occupied. It was a bitter and crucial strategic blow that would haunt him the rest of his life. For the moment, however, he had other battles to fight. On December 2nd Napoleon achieved his single greatest (and favorite) victory, by routing the combined armies of Austria and Russia at *Austerlitz* (December 2, 1805). Austria was finished, knew it, and sued for peace. In the Treaty of Pressburg (1806), Vienna recognized Napoleon's Italian claims, even ceding the Venetian and Dalmatian lands it had acquired at Campo Formio.

With Austria out of the war, Napoleon utterly reordered Germany, launching the myth of the *revolution on horseback*. He erased 120 sovereign entities dating to the *Peace of Westphalia* or before, eliminated the *Holy Roman Empire* once and for all, and established a puppet state (the Confederation of the Rhine) as a French protectorate. Hoping to settle with Britain, Napoleon offered to return Hanover—the home state of the English dynasty—to London. All this was too much even for cautious, *neutral* Prussia, which joined Pitt's coalition in October 1806. Thus began the War of the Fourth Coalition. In just a few weeks Napoleon destroyed the Prussian Army, at *Jena* and Auerstädt, both fought on October 14, 1806. By the end of October, Napoleon had occupied Berlin, and by early 1807 he controlled most of Prussia and Germany. He was set back on his heels by the Russians at Eylau (February 8, 1807), but he smashed the Russian Army at Friedland (June 14, 1807). That compelled the tsar to agree to a broad *spheres of influence* arrangement, negotiated at *Tilsit*. This was the high point of Napoleon's career. After Tilsit, victories would be fewer, harder fought, and harder won, and his defeats would mount.

Napoleon's power was drained by *Wellington's* strategy of *attrition* in the *Peninsular War*. He was unable to keep even his minor allies in line with the economically oppressive and unbalanced *Continental System*, and he failed to consolidate earlier conquests into his ever-growing empire. Austria prematurely rose against French hegemony in 1809, starting the War of the Fifth Coalition. After early coalition victories, the French won decisively at the two-day Battle of Wagram, July 5–6, 1809, where Napoleon's swollen forces numbered 160,000. Peace with Austria came a week later and was affirmed by Napoleon's *dynastic marriage* to Marie Louise, daughter of the Austrian emperor. That diplomatic act was consummated by the crafty *Metternich* to win Napoleon's confidence while Austria again prepared for war and waited until the moment ripened. Metternich did not have to wait long: in a reckless gamble at best, and an arrogant and irrational act of spectacular egoism at worst, Napoleon invaded Russia.

Napoleon crossed the Niemen, his Rubicon, on June 24, 1812. The Grand Armée that accompanied him contained some 600,000 men, about half of whom were French and half sullen conscripts from allied or occupied lands, who began to desert almost immediately. Napoleon captured Smolensk, then fought to a bloody and costly tactical draw at *Borodino*, some 70 miles in front of Moscow. The Russians—soldiers and civilians, and the tsar and his court—abandoned Moscow to the French. Instead of pursuing and finishing off the wounded Russian Army, Napoleon billeted the Grand Armée in the ruins of Moscow, which the Russians had evacuated and razed by fire as they fell back. Napoleon had badly extended his lines of supply, and Paris was so far to the rear that an attempted coup against him by a half-madman nearly succeeded in his absence. News of the coup attempt and of fresh defeats in Spain reached him outside the smoldering ruins of the Russian capital (he had been compelled to abandon the *Kremlin* by the choking smoke of the burning city). In other words, his vaunted strategic view and control of war was breaking down.

Napoleon thus made the fateful decision to *retreat from Moscow*. As the retreat by the Grand Armée turned to rout, and as he had done once before in Egypt, he abandoned his army, leaving it this time to the untender mercies of Russia's winter, and to Cossacks and *partisans*. He narrowly escaped personal capture in a daring river crossing under fire. As he and the Grand Armeé ran, the Allies assembled the Sixth Coalition to finish him off. Napoleon reached France, saw to it that his power base was not directly threatened, hastily conscripted a new army, and marched it into Germany to meet the Allies, who were advancing only slowly as they confirmed their coalition and *Alexander I* paused to subdue Poland within the Russian empire. In Germany, the converging armies finally met and fought it out at the colossal, three-day-long *Battle of Leipzig* (October 16–19, 1813). Napoleon was decisively defeated by the numerically superior multinational force that had gathered to crush him, and which now also fought in the fashion he had taught Europe. He retreated well and in style, but he now paid the full price of his earlier errors: bereft of the cavalry mounts he lost in Russia, he lost the battle; and given his prior disregard for law and treaties, he reaped a whirlwind of contempt and rejection of his every entreaty and peace offer by any and all of the advancing powers. Napoleon was thus compelled to abdicate (April 6, 1814) and went into exile on *Elba*.

There, Napoleon waited until he sensed division among the powers gathered at the *Congress of Vienna*, and then audaciously returned to France (March 1, 1815), launching the spectacular episode of the *Hundred Days*. Once more, he brought mass death to France and Europe, but this time his tenure was mercifully short, ending with his final defeat at *Waterloo* (June 18, 1815). Napoleon abdicated for the second time on June 23rd and was exiled again, this time to distant *St. Helena*, where he remained for the rest of his life under constant British guard. Decades later, Napoleon's corpse was disinterred and returned to Paris, where it still lies in state to excite the imagination of French schoolchildren and cause more foolish adults to mourn the passing of empire.

Domestically, Napoleon first completed, then stabilized, and finally betrayed the great principles and reforms of the *French Revolution*. He left a legacy of authoritarian *Bonapartism* to compete with government by parliament (parlement) in France. Yet he also codified French law, confirmed the end of legal and economic *feudalism* and the revolutionary transfer of wealth and power to the bourgeoisie, and helped (largely unwittingly or at most instrumentally, to serve short-term ends) transplant liberal constitutional ideas to Italian, Swiss, and German soil. He personally revolutionized *warfare*, and in so doing also accelerated the ongoing centralization and *modernization* of the state all over Europe. In the longer term, and perhaps most importantly, his rejection of *limited war* in favor of utter victory and hegemony posed such an absolute threat to the European state system that it provoked a new concept of *international security* based on consultation, cooperation, and a conscious *balancing of power*. That idea took hold among the Great Powers in direct reaction to Napoleon as the embodiment of the aggressive thrust of the French Revolution and led directly to the several moral and political advances of the *Congress System* and the *Concert of Europe*. *See also George Jacques Danton; Frederick the Great; George Friedrich Hegel; Napoleonic warfare; Napoleonic Wars; Friedrich Nietzsche; Pripet marshes.*

Suggested Readings: Michael Broers, *Europe Under Napoleon* (1996); Peter Hofschröer, *1815: The Waterloo Campaign* (1998); Georges Lefebvre, *Napoleon*, 2 Vols. (1969); Martyn

Lyons, *Napoleon Bonaparte and the Legacy of the French Revolution* (1994); Alan Schom, *Napoleon Bonaparte* (1997).

Napoleon II, Bonaparte (1811–1832). "King of Rome" 1811–1814; son of *Napoleon I* and Marie Louise of Austria. When his father was overthrown (in part by *Metternich* and by his grandfather, the Austrian emperor) in 1814, the son was taken to Vienna to be raised as an Austrian prince. Although Bonapartists accepted him as heir to the Empire, he was sickly and died young. Napoleon never saw him, or Marie Louise, after 1814.

Napoleon III (1808–1873). Also known as Louis-Napoleon. Emperor of France, 1852–1870; nephew of *Napoleon I*. He twice tried to seize power (1836 and 1840), but his scheming was treated mildly by those who feared his uncle's ominous legend. He was elected president of the *Second Republic* in 1848, but three years later launched a *coup*; one year after that he proclaimed the *Second Empire*, on December 2nd—the anniversary of his uncle's self-coronation. He said, "The Empire is peace." He had an erratic and vainglorious personality, and within two years he joined in the *Crimean War* against Russia, more to appease Britain than to defend French interests. He began French penetration of Indochina in 1857. He schemed constantly over Italy. The *Franco-Austrian War* (1859) was a turning point, straining relations with the pope and with French Catholics. He next proclaimed *Maximilian* as the emperor of Mexico in a costly and foolhardy adventure, starting in 1862, but later abandoned him in the face of Mexican resistance and American threats of intervention. Napoleon was outwitted by *Bismarck* during the *Seven Weeks' War* and was destroyed by him during the *Franco-Prussian War*. He was captured at *Sedan*, and his regime collapsed. He spent his final years in brooding exile in Britain. His only son was killed fighting for Britain against the *Zulus*, ending the main Napoleonic line. *See also International Telegraph Union.*

Napoleonic warfare. More than anything, *Napoleon's* martial success came from his emphasis on mobility on, and even more importantly, on the way to, the battlefield. He did not succeed because of any technological superiority—the weapons of his era were broadly similar to those of the time of *Louis XIV*—but due to his superior tactical insight and innovations and his cunning exploitation of political differences in the opposing alliances he nearly always faced. He had an uncanny ability to choose just the right ground to meet the enemy, and he used line and column formations in innovative combinations to create local superiority over his foes. On the march he dispersed his troops into separate corps and divisions—a formation he devised that was adopted by all later armies—rather than sticking to the somewhat ponderous Frederickian drill and regimental battle formations used by other armies, especially those of Prussia. This enabled French armies to move rapidly down multiple roads, to meet again at the point and moment of a decisive battle, rather than crawling with the baggage and supply trains along a single highway. In addition, he insisted on his troops *living off the land* to further speed movement. As he famously observed about the importance of *logistics* and of *requisition* of supplies in the field, "an army marches on its stomach."

This principle of "la guerre nourrit la guerre" ("war feeds itself") dated in European warfare to the innovations of *Frederick the Great* during the *Seven Years' War* (1756–1763), but Napoleon perfected it as the key underpinning to the use of *combined arms* and speed of attack. He used *cavalry* alternately like a rapier to scout or *flank* the enemy, then in battle as a blunt and brutal shock force to smash gaping holes in the opposing lines at critical points and moments in a given battle, into which his *infantry* were then dispatched to exploit the wound in the enemy's line and divide and defeat him in detail. Meanwhile, the cavalry broke through to threaten from the rear and to cut up the enemy's supply trains. The breaking up of what had been unitary artillery formations into divisions that combined with infantry and cavalry was another of Napoleon's key innovations. The use of concentrated cannon fire from mobile *field artillery*, along with light infantry skirmishers to break up the enemy lines and formations, permitted his heavy columns to strike with unexpected suddenness and overwhelming local force. There is no denying Napoleon's commanding and inspirational presence among French troops on the field of battle: *Wellington* himself said it "made a difference of forty thousand men."

Napoleon was further aided in the early years by the revolutionary élan of his troops and by a qualified merit system for choosing commanders: every foot soldier, he told them, "carries a marshal's baton in his knapsack." For most of his career he commanded highly motivated troops who knew he would reward merit displayed in battle. He was thus blessed with able commanders, whereas opposing armies might be led by tactical dolts who happened to be some aristocrat's son or nephew. Moreover, he promised and delivered great *plunder* to his troops, to his political supporters, and to France. This was an ancient device for motivating troops and was an equally ancient stimulus to war. This more than anything revealed that Napoleon had no new political ideas to offer Europe. After his consulate period, all he gave France and Europe was more war and further military occupation, ever more conquest for decreasing gain, packaged in his personal intoxicating brilliance—although for many, this was enough.

Over time, however, others learned how to mimic Napoleon's tactics and how to defeat them and him. The Prussians were the first to do so. Wellington was the second. By 1809 Napoleon no longer enjoyed all his earlier advantages, and he began to show signs that he did not know how to adjust to the use of his own tactics, or other countermeasures, taken against him. Fundamentally, this was because the underlying structural changes wrought by the *French Revolution*—changes of mass mobilization and ideological commitment on the part of ordinary soldiers, the tiger on whose back he had ridden to mastery of France and of Europe—were taking at least partial hold in other countries, with the exception of England, which retained an eighteenth-century structure in its army all through the Napoleonic Wars. This eroded France's initial great military advantage, as in later years Russians, Prussians, and others also put the *nation-in-arms*—mass armies, inspired by nationalist spirit—into the field. With the added problem of *war weariness* in France, Napoleon's martial empire became increasingly unstable. At *Borodino* in particular, but also at other later battles, Napoleon lost huge parts of his army by frontal assaults that made little or no gain. At *Waterloo*, his last battle, he was tentative and indecisive, and he showed none of his old daring or verve. Admirers attribute this to physical illness that day, which may indeed have played a role.

The legend of Napoleon's facility with movement to and on the battlefield would fixate much military thinking in later decades, even as the *rifled-bore* musket and cannon, widespread by 1850, rendered his tactics obsolete by extending the range of effective defensive fire. Napoleon might have adjusted to this change. Other military men, however, dazzled by his early success—which was elevated to a pseudoscience of war by fawning admirers like *Jomini*—for the most part failed to take notice. That oversight contributed to many futile, bloody charges and offensives in the *Crimean War*, again in the *American Civil War*, and most horribly during *World War I. See also* Blitzkrieg; *siege warfare; Schlieffen Plan; tirailleurs; trench warfare.*

Suggested Readings: Charles Esdaile, *The Wars of Napoleon* (1995); Gunther E. Rothenberg, *The Napoleonic Wars* (1999).

Napoleonic Wars. The Wars of the *French Revolution* and the Napoleonic Wars overlapped in the War of the Second Coalition. Partly for convenience sake, all the conflicts are listed together here, although the War of the First Coalition was not dominated by the exploits of *Napoleon* until it was nearly over. In reality, too, they represented a nearly continuous struggle among nations: between France and its allies (albeit under the exclusive leadership of Napoleon after 1799) and shifting coalitions of anti-French interests cobbled together and sustained financially by Britain. Together, they formed the greatest warfare—in terms of numbers of dead and the scale of combat—seen in Europe since the barbarian invasions 1,000 years before. The war between Britain and France was also a true *world war*, spanning several continents and oceans and with lasting significance for the fate of nations in all four corners of the earth. Intertwined with this prolonged Anglo-French war, which lasted from 1792 to 1815 with just a few months of peace—more accurately *cease-fire*—in 1802 and again in 1815, was a series of *Great Power* wars between France and, at some point or other, every other Great Power in Europe. The United States was drawn into war with Great Britain, 1812–1814, as a direct result of the greater conflict in Europe. Finally, once the war in Europe spread to Iberia, its impact was felt throughout the Spanish and Portuguese empires in the Americas as well and led to an additional 15 years of wars of independence as Latin Americans broke away to form independent states and a new regional states system.

(1) War of the First Coalition (1792–1797): Revolutionary France, led by the *Girondins*, declared war on Austria (April 20, 1792). In July, Prussia joined Austria, and they were joined over the next two years by Britain, the Netherlands, Spain, Naples, the Papal States, and Piedmont-Sardinia. To everyone's surprise, French armies crossed the Rhine and captured Frankfurt and Mainz, beating the Prussians at Valmy and the Austrians at Jemappes. At this moment, France was riven by real (as well as imagined) *counter-revolutionary* plots and was gripped by great fear of monarchical retribution and a peasant and *Catholic* revolt in the *Vendée*. With the king's execution and ever more radical policies driven by the *sans culottes* of Paris, officers who once served the Revolution loyally now changed sides; others conspired to deliver French cities to the British or to Austria. Finally, the coalition armies won a series of victories. Into 1794 this combination of internal and external threats propelled the Revolution into its most radical phase, *The Terror,* under *Robespierre* (who actually opposed the war). It also stimulated the *levée en masse,* however, which called one million French to the tricolors and put the *nation-in-arms.* That, and superior generalship by the French overall (and the young Napoleon in particular), enabled France to hurl back the professional armies of the invading monarchies and then take the offensive in 1794. France conquered Naples, the Netherlands, Piedmont, and the Papal States. It forced Spain out of the war in 1795 and Prussia, too, in the Treaty of Basle (1795). Napoleon invaded northern Italy in 1796 and forced the Austrians to terms in 1797, in the *Treaty of Campo-Formio.* That ended the First Coalition, leaving only Great Britain still at war with France.

(2) War of the Second Coalition (1798–1801): Britain was joined in its dogged war against France—and France's enforced ally Spain—by Austria, Naples, Portugal, Russia, and Turkey. Napoleon invaded Egypt but was isolated there by the defeat of his fleet at *Abukir Bay* (August 1, 1798). He forayed into Syria, then scurried back to Europe in secret and in disguise to secure his political future. By 1801 the English defeated the remnant of the French army he had abandoned to its fate in the Middle East. On his return to France he quickly reengaged in Naples, which was easily defeated. Arguments within the Second Coalition then led to Russia's withdrawal in 1799. Napoleon next fell upon the Austrians, defeating them at Marengo (June 14, 1800), his first truly great and classically "Napoleonic" victory (sudden, stunning, and decisive), and again at Hochstadt, also in June. Turkey withdrew from the war in 1800. Napoleon knocked Austria out in January 1801 by virtue of one of his more brilliant campaigns. Meanwhile, Prussia and Denmark attacked and overran Hanover, while Spain invaded Portugal. Russia, Denmark, Prussia, and Sweden then formed the new *League of Armed Neutrality,* but this was challenged by the *Royal Navy* in the *Battle of Copenhagen.*

In 1801 Spanish and French forces compelled Portugal to resign the contest. With *William Pitt* briefly out of office over the question of *Catholic emancipation*, Britain made peace with France at *Amiens* in March 1802. Napoleon's renewed aggressions, this time in Germany, brought Pitt back into office and Britain back to war with France by 1803.

(3) War of the Third Coalition (1805–1806): The wily Pitt again brought Austria and Russia into an alliance against Napoleon and also encouraged Prussia to *mobilize*, although it did not join the fray. As always, Napoleon struck first, met a divided enemy, and inflicted a military *defeat in detail* that would shatter the Third Coalition. An Austrian army under Mack was quickly surrounded and humiliated at Ulm (October 17, 1805), where Napoleon took 33,000 Austrian prisoners mainly through superior maneuver and position, with hardly an exchange of cannon fire or musketry on the field. Meanwhile, Britain permanently secured itself from the threat of invasion by the extraordinary and decisive naval victory, under the final command of *Horatio Nelson*, over the combined French and Spanish battle fleets off Cape *Trafalgar* (October 21, 1805). Napoleon was dismayed, but he consoled himself by occupying Vienna (November 13, 1805). Austria scrambled to concentrate its remaining forces and to join them with advancing columns of Russians, whose divisions had finally arrived in south central Germany after a long march from Poland. Prussia remained *neutral*; the British Army was not engaged or a serious factor. The significance of Trafalgar was made clear just two months later, when 30,000 more Allied troops were lost to Napoleon when a second Austrian army was destroyed on the hillsides and frozen lake at *Austerlitz* (December 2, 1805) along with much of the army of their Russian ally. The Austrians had no choice but to sue for peace, which came at Pressburg three weeks later. That treaty detached Austria from the Third Coalition. The Russians retreated, fighting stubbornly as they fell back all the way to the Niemen River in Poland. Britain was left unconquered in its island security, but isolated once more, other than for the retreating Russians, and still at war with a French Empire that now straddled most of the continent.

(4) War of the Fourth Coalition (1806–1807): In 1806 Prussia finally joined the anti-French alliance, at the worst possible moment. It was deeply concerned that Napoleon's victory over Austria at Austerlitz had left France the effective master of the Rhineland and southern Germany. When Napoleon added to that injury the follow-up threat to treat central Germany as an exclusive French *sphere of influence*, Berlin decided for war. The Prussian Army had been so long at peace that its reputation as the best-trained and most professional army in Europe, won on the battlefields of *Frederick the Great*, was long untested and now revealed to be wholly out of date. Again, Napoleon struck first and hardest. He and his marshals stunned Prussia and Europe into submission by destroying the celebrated Prussian Army in two great engagements, *Jena* and *Auerstädt*, fought on the same day, October 14, 1806. At the end of October the French Army occupied Berlin, which burned

in consequence. By early 1807 Napoleon controlled Prussia and most of Germany, and Austria was a wounded and frightened state. Napoleon was briefly set back on his heels by the Russians at Eylau (February 8, 1807), but he smashed a Russian army at Friedland (June 14, 1807). That compelled Tsar *Alexander I* to accept the fact of French domination of Europe in the *Tilsit* agreements, when he met Napoleon on a barge in the middle of the Niemen. Britain was once again left alone in its determined opposition to French *hegemony* over Europe, without any ally from the Baltic to the Mediterranean.

(5) War of the Fifth Coalition (1809): Frustrated by his inability to invade Britain and deal with his greatest enemy where it lived, Napoleon tried to fully strangle British trade instead with his *Continental System*. That provoked war with Portugal. When he tried to force his brother onto the Spanish throne, rebellion against French arrogance broke out in Spain. Although the Spanish Army was quickly brushed aside by his marshals, Napoleon soon found himself facing a new kind of war, one neither he not his marshals ever overcame: Spanish *guerrillas* wore down the French garrison army, while in the Portuguese highlands an English force under *Wellington* fought a brilliant defensive campaign. Napoleon was increasingly troubled by the "Spanish ulcer," as he later called this *Peninsular War* in Iberia. In 1809 Austria rose against French hegemony, confident of English subsidies but overconfident in its chances. The move was premature. This was the kind of war at which Napoleon excelled. After an early Austrian victory at Essling, he won decisively—although at a high cost in men—at Wagram (July 5–6, 1809). Austria was now forced to formally accept French predominance in Europe. Its subservient, virtually *tributary* relationship to France included commitment of Austrian troops to Napoleon's war and a permanent reduction in the size of its army. This pact was sealed when *Metternich* arranged the *dynastic marriage* of the Austrian emperor's daughter, Marie Louise, to the Corsican upstart and would-be dynast, Napoleon. In secret, however, Metternich awaited the ripening of the moment when Austria might rise up again, to rid itself of the French and to rid Europe of Napoleon. Meanwhile, Britain fought on at sea, strangling French trade and squeezing every Continental economy, and occasionally raiding the coast. Most of Europe sought to evade the strictures of the Continental System, and smuggling abounded, aided and abetted by the British. Meanwhile, the "ulcer" in Iberia continued to bleed the French Army white.

(6) War of the Sixth Coalition (1812–1814): Better known as the War of the Grand Alliance. When Tsar Alexander announced that Russia would no longer abide by the Continental System, as agreed at Tilsit, Napoleon did the only thing he knew how when facing opposition to his will. He invaded Russia—his single gravest error—in the summer of 1812, with his Grand Armée of more than 600,000 men, of whom most were unwilling allied conscripts and only 270,000 were French. He captured Smolensk, advanced through Russian *scorched earth* to fight a savage battle at *Borodino* (September

7, 1812), and staggered from there to occupy Moscow. He now had badly extended *lines of supply*, and the Russian winter threatened. Indeed, Paris was left so far to his rear that a quixotic coup attempt nearly succeeded in his distant absence. News of the abortive coup, and of fresh defeats of his armies in Spain, reached Napoleon even as Moscow smoldered and all discipline in the Grand Armée dissolved. He decided to *retreat from Moscow*. The Russians now forced him to take the same northern route by which he had come, where there was no shelter or forage left for man or mount. As retreat turned into panicked rout, he hurried back to Paris, leaving most of his Grand Armeé behind to be killed by winter or by Cossacks, *partisans*, and encircling Russian armies: Napoleon left more than 300,000 dead in Russia and another 200,000 captured.

As Napoleon raced for Paris to raise a new army the Allies cobbled together a Sixth Coalition. This last and greatest of the anti-French alliances was assembled by *Castlereagh*. His diplomacy and Napoleon's spectacular defeat in Russia brought Britain into alliance with Austria, Prussia, Sweden, and Russia, as well as smaller German states, including erstwhile French allies such as Bavaria, Saxony, and Würtemburg. Napoleon reached Paris, then led a new army of 145,000 men into Germany to face the Allies; but these were mostly raw recruits, and he had almost no cavalry, having left far too many dead mounts in Russia (some eaten during the retreat). He was decisively defeated at the three-day *Battle of Leipzig*. He fell back to Paris in another brilliant (but this time also losing) fighting retreat. Meanwhile, *Wellington* smashed Napoleon's last Spanish army at Vitoria (June 1813) and invaded France from the south. The armies of the Grand Alliance, headed by Alexander I and the king of Prussia, entered Paris on March 31, 1814. Napoleon abdicated two weeks later (April 11th), and the *Restoration* began.

(7) The Hundred Days (1815): The Allies were magnanimous, in retrospect foolishly so. Napoleon was exiled to the small Mediterranean island of *Elba*, from whence he returned for the stunning, bloody, yet essentially foreordained failure of the *Hundred Days*, which ended at *Waterloo* and led to his second and final abdication. In the end, Napoleon had been defeated by Britain's impenetrable island security and unmatched prosperity and naval power, by *nationalist* reaction to French occupation and raw economic exploitation, and by the ever-growing excesses of his personal and military hubris. *See also Congress of Vienna; French Revolution; Napoleonic warfare; Horatio Nelson; Michel Ney; Quasi War; Charles Talleyrand; War of 1812.*

Suggested Readings: T. C. W. Blanning, *The French Revolutionary Wars, 1787–1802* (1996); Charles Esdaile, *The Wars of Napoleon* (1995); David Gates, *The Napoleonic Wars, 1803–1815* (1997); Gunther E. Rothenberg, *The Napoleonic Wars* (1999).

narco-terrorism. Use of *terrorism* techniques by *drug cartels*, with the aim of intimidating the civil authorities into abandoning antidrug policies.

narodniki. "Go to the people (narod)." A Russian populist and reformist movement in the *Slavophile* tradition that arose in the wake of the *Crimean War.* It was most active in the 1870s when several thousand idealistic students, deeply influenced by *Alexander Herzen*, went forth to hundreds of villages to persuade rather bemused peasants to emancipate themselves. They were alternately ignored or informed on. Subsequently, Russian radicals increasingly turned to violent, direct action. Note: In the 1920s, similarly idealistic young Chinese students went into the countryside to educate the peasants, with about as much effect. In the 1960s nearly 16 million Chinese students, many of them former *Red Guards*, were sent down to the country not to teach but for "*reeducation*" through labor and for punishment.

Suggested Reading: A brilliant portrait of the narodniki is contained in Ivan Turgenev's novel *Virgin Soil* (1877).

Narva, Battle of (November 30, 1700). A major battle at the start of the *Great Northern War* (1700–1721) in which the 18-year-old Swedish king *Charles XII* deployed an army of just 9,000 men to defeat a Russian army of 40,000 under the 28-year-old Tsar *Peter I.* The Russians were poorly drilled and led, had inefficient and antiquated *artillery*, and were low on supplies after a month-long siege. Charles landed at Pernau in late October, and on November 30th (November 19th on the old calendar) he attacked a stretched-out Russian line at Narva, penetrating it easily and breaking up the Russian formations when the ill-motivated Russian conscripts fled the field, leaving 8,000 to 10,000 of their fellows dead upon it. Peter sought an end to the war, but Charles—perhaps feeling the oats of his victory, and because he was a youth who apparently enjoyed war for its own sake—instead struck south into Germany and Poland, leaving Peter to recover, reform, and retrain his army.

Nassau Agreement (December 18, 1962). *Harold Macmillan* met *John Kennedy* in the Bahamas (such *summit* locales were among the pleasant perks of *empire*), where they agreed to arm British *submarines* with nuclear-tipped *missiles.* When he vetoed the entry of the United Kingdom into the *European Community, Charles de Gaulle* cited the agreement as an example of Britain still being unready for membership in the European club, because it was too close to the interests of the United States.

Nasser, Gamel Abdel (1918–1970). Egyptian statesman. Prime minister, 1954–1956; president, 1956–1970. He was one among several leaders of the *coup* that overthrew *Faruk* and the Egyptian monarchy. His policy sprang from a vision of Egypt as the heart of three mutually reinforcing cultures: *African, Arab,* and *Islamic.* Of these influences, his *pan-Arabism* predominated. He broke with the *West* in 1955, seeking and securing arms and diplomatic support from the *Soviet bloc*, including assistance in building the *Aswan Dam.* He played a key role in founding the *Nonaligned Movement at Bandung*. He *nationalized* the *Suez Canal*, which precipitated the *Suez Crisis*. He emerged from the *Second Arab-Israeli War* that followed as a figure of repute throughout the *Third World* and as the leading statesman and public figure in the Arab world. In the name of pan-Arabism he attempted *union* with Syria, 1958–1961, but it failed. Although he was nowhere near the Hitlerian figure that *Anthony Eden* sometimes thought he was, Nasser certainly was a ruthless dictator determined to dominate the Arab world. His assertion of personal and Egyptian leadership of the whole Arab world won him more enemies than allies, however, as when he sent 70,000 troops into Yemen from 1962 to further a "Nasserite" revolution there, provoking wide opposition from other Arab states in the Gulf. He led Egypt into the *Second* and *Third Arab-Israeli Wars*, gaining enormous *prestige* from the first conflict but losing much of what he had gained in the second. His last days were spent conducting the *War of Attrition*.

Suggested Reading: R. W. Baker, *Egypt's Uncertain Revolutions Under Nasser and Sadat* (1979).

Natal. The abolition of *slavery* in the *British Empire* (1833) led to the importation of Indian "coolie" labor to Natal and also led to the *Great Trek* of the Boers under Andries Pretorius (1799–1853) out of *Cape Colony* into Natal. A Boer republic was set up in 1839 and was annexed by Britain in 1845. When Natal's whites were granted "self-government" in 1893 they moved to stop Indian immigration. The suffering of the Indian community launched the career of a young lawyer, *Mohandas Gandhi*. Natal was incorporated into the *Union of South Africa* in 1910.

nation. "Nation" is often loosely used in lieu of *state* or *nation-state*. It is a fluid concept, but it has two main meanings. (1) A self–conscious, imagined (but nonetheless real) political community composed of those who share ethnicity, language, and possibly also a common religion and/or culture, but who may or may not possess a legally *sovereign* state; e.g., *Kurds* or *Palestinians*. (2) A political community that need not share common race, language, or culture but has a *recognized* and defined *territory* and government derived from historical circumstance, which it defends with a display of some degree of common purpose: for example, Belgium, Canada, or India. Such nations may contain one or more regional identities or subnationalities, which, under different circumstances, could themselves constitute nations. Most nations possess—or if they do not, they quickly seek to develop—a romanticized, even largely invented, tradition that celebrates a pantheon of legendary and/or historical heroes, purveyed by oral history, literature, film, and other propaganda. *See also empire; nationalism; tribe.*

Suggested Reading: Edward Mortimer and Robert Fine, eds., *People, Nation, and State* (2000).

national. *See citizen; nationality; statelessness; subject.*

national bank. *See banking; central bank.*

national debt. The debt of a national government, not the total of all debt held by all levels of government of a nation. It is therefore smaller than the *public debt*. The first-ever national debt, as distinct from the personal debt of the king and crown, was identified by England in 1693. Separation of royal debt from the common national debt was forced by Parliament on the English Crown after a century of bloody civil war and revolution. The concept took longer to catch on in countries where representative government had less hold, and *absolute monarchs* or dictators continued to reach into the public purse at will and from need. In the history of the *British Empire* the national debt was a critical advantage Britain enjoyed over its Continental rivals, Spain in the seventeenth century and France during the eighteenth century. Where the British government could borrow in wartime and pay *debt service* after the peace, Spanish and French kings repeatedly faced the choice of either raising taxes to pay for their wars (which threatened to provoke domestic rebellion and always brought new demands from the nobility for representation) or being forced into royal bankruptcy and to the peace table on unfavorable terms.

national front. Governments with the participation of all (or nearly all) parties, formed to deal with a war or other national crisis. Such governments were assembled in Britain and elsewhere during the *Great Depression* and again in *World War II*. They reflect a public demand and a real need to submerge normal partisan politics beneath genuine concern for *national security* in wartime or during another vital endeavor. Note: This is not the same as a *Popular Front*. Also, it is a term seldom used in or about the United States, where "bipartisanship" is the preferred nomenclature, although without implying an emergency situation.

national income. The total income accrued from production of all *goods and services* by a national economy. This figure is usually smaller than the *Gross National Product*, with the *Gross Domestic Product* falling between these other two aggregate numbers.

national interest. A conception drawn from classical *realism*, where it means, in its rawest form, national survival. Once this minimum and *vital interest* is secured, other national interests may be addressed by foreign policy. In this sense, "national interest" is a much wider term than "vital interest," although this important distinction is often lost in heated discourse. In fact, even the narrow classical meaning is far more expansive than is sometimes depicted by its critics. Thus, the national interest includes security for a nation's institutions, population, and even cultural values—by whatever measures improve its (absolute and relative) *power* position vis-à-vis other states in the military, political, economic, or other realm. For realists, the cardinal moral virtue upheld by leaders pursuing the national interest is held to be *prudence*, and the yardstick of final judgment is a successful outcome (a utilitarian standard) rather than personal righteousness or purity of motive (a deontological standard). More sophisticated usages add pursuit of enlightened self-interest in *international security*, *peace*, and *distributive justice* as components of the national interest, insofar as these goals might help create a wider environment in which the nation is more secure. It was *Lord Palmerston* who in 1848 first imbued the idea of the national interest with a permanence beyond ideology or sentiment: "We have no eternal allies and we have no perpetual enemies. Our interests are eternal and perpetual." Similarly, *Winston Churchill* said of the Soviet Union's attitude toward the outbreak of *World War II* in Europe, "I cannot forecast to you the action of Russia. It is a riddle, wrapped in a mystery, inside an enigma; but perhaps there is a key. That key is Russian national interest."

However, it is important to note that this narrow, classical, and even classroom sense is not the way the term is generally used in daily discourse on world affairs or concerning a given nation's foreign policy. Instead, there is a nearly inescapable tendency to frame virtually any momentarily favored interest or policy option put forward by a government, or by an interest group competing for policy attention, as an element of the national interest. That is done whether suggested policy serves a truly common and permanent (that is, national) interest or merely a special or even private interest overdressed in grandiose pretensions. For example, does a given *casus belli* truly represent a national grievance or merely a powerful sectoral one? Or is a *free trade* agreement or heavily *protectionist* legislation in the nation's interest, or mainly in the interest of specific groups (say, exporters in the first case, and inefficient industries in the second)? Despite—or rather, because of—this ambiguity, debate over what specific interests are also national interests, and whether they are so in the short term or the long term, is at the center of nearly all discussion of foreign policy. *See also internationalism*; raison d'etat.

nationalism. Loyalty and devotion to a *nation*, and/or to the *state* or *nation-state* that houses it. Nationalism frequently shades into *chauvinism*, in which one's nation is exalted above all others. It became a force of political construction in the fifteenth century, building larger communities in previously decentralized and loosely cohering regions. Later, it became a force of destruction as well, tearing apart *multinational empires*, dividing established states by encouraging subnationalisms, and blocking advancement to greater regional or global *integration*. As a modern, mass phenomenon, nationalism dates to the *French Revolution* and notably to the *levée en masse*. The subsequent occupation of Europe by French armies spread ideas about nationality, but it was *Napoleon's* imposition of raw economic exploitation in the *Continental System*, and conscription of conquered peoples to serve the French Army, that stimulated nationalist reactions in several countries, starting with the *Peninsular War* in Spain and Portugal.

During the remainder of the nineteenth century the new force of nationalism—as a reaction to external threats to traditional self-governance—contended with the antinationalist interests of the *Great Powers*, which were also multinational empires. The Great Powers mostly ignored national questions at the *Congress of Vienna*, quietly or tacitly agreeing to suppress nationalist outbreaks by subject peoples in their respective "backyards" (Britain in Ireland, Austria in Italy and the Balkans, Russia in Poland). One exception was Prussia, whose backyard was Germany, and which increasingly contended with Austria and with Rhenish and other regional German nationalisms for the hearts and minds, and attendant political loyalties, of what would become a single German nation—although a conservative, not a revolutionary empire—under the guiding hand of *Bismarck*. The *Holy Alliance* thus intervened to crush outbreaks of liberal-nationalist rebellion in Italy and Iberia, and Russia even thought as well to act outside Europe. It failed to do so, however, where Britain stood in the way for other reasons: Latin America. There, from 1810 to 1825, an entire continent broke free of imperial control and into diverse and quarrelsome new nations.

As the nineteenth century progressed and the great multinational empires further centralized, nationalism—often newly wed to liberalism—emerged as the key challenge to internal repression and to the international order of the *Concert of Europe*. The *Eastern Question* repeatedly forced the powers to face the reality of new nations emerging along ethnic lines, whatever that meant for the *balance of power* and the old principle of *compensation*. So, too, did the *Revolutions of 1848*, although in some cases, such as Hungary, one set of national demands canceled out several others. The *American Civil War* showed, to those with eyes to see, that nationalism might be enormously destructive as well as creative. Yet the main pattern remained one of nation-building. The late nineteenth century thus saw a redrawing of the map of Europe by the *Risorgimento* in Italy, unification of Germany under *Bismarck*, and a further unraveling of the Ottoman Empire so that the new nations of Bulgaria, Montenegro, Serbia, and Rumania slipped free. Outside Europe the great imperial powers at first ignored or repressed national or ethnic identity, as when they divided Africa at the *Berlin Congress* or carved up China with *unequal treaties*. Meanwhile, Indian national sentiment was growing in response to consolidation of British power after the *Indian Mutiny*. In China, intense national feeling broadened despite the corrupt *Qing* dynasty, due to resentment of the unequal treaties and broadened foreign assertions of *extraterritoriality*. It exploded with the *Boxer Rebellion* in 1900 and the *Chinese Revolution* of 1911.

This pattern of nationalism taking shape as a violent response to foreign occupation and exploitation was repeated in dozens of other colonized areas during the twentieth century. The crisis mounted before 1914, as revealed by the *Balkan Wars*. It reached fruition in 1918: *World War I* ripped apart three multinational empires, freeing many formerly captive nations, creating new ones from whole cloth (*Czechoslovakia* and *Yugoslavia*), and enormously encouraging colonial peoples the world over to likewise demand *independence*. In partial response, the British devolved powers to the *White Dominions*. Even the mostly humbug *mandate system* recognized this fact. From *Zionists* to the *May 4th Movement* in China, to the *Congress Party* in India, nationalists made demands that were accelerating variations on a theme: *Home Rule*, or *self-determination*, or outright national independence. The Irish were the first to assert the claim successfully by force of arms (and by changing public opinion within the colonial power), winning the *Irish War of Independence* by 1921. Within four decades, following the greater cataclysm of *World War II*, most of the rest of the colonial world followed suit. In the interim, nationalism within several of the Great Powers had taken on a twisted and disturbed shading. In many countries, nationalists embraced race theories drawn from *social Darwinism* and bad continental philosophy. In Italy, Germany, and Japan (and Spain, Rumania, and elsewhere) *fascists* developed ideologies of devotion to the nation, defined now in spurious "racial" terms, and to the state or even an individual leader—reified as the embodiment of the nation. In Germany this led to horrific new depths of discrimination against minorities and then to a war of extermination and industrialized *genocide*. The defeat of fascism in World War II came at the price of empire for such old and expansive imperial powers as France and Great Britain and for lesser imperial powers such as the Netherlands and Belgium.

A wave of nationalism (as well as *pan-Africanism*) swept over the African continent after WWII—although it is important to distinguish between traditional ethnic nationalism, in which loyalties flowed according to the older notion of *tribe*, and modern or state-focused nationalism, which developed only rarely in Africa and in most cases only at the elite level. The British freed their colonies more or less gracefully by c. 1960; the French fought and lost the *French-Indochina War* and the *Algerian War of Independence* before they, too, bowed to new realities and withdrew from much of their overseas empire. Everywhere nationalist leaders, sometimes blending their nationalism with *communism*—which briefly appeared to be on the side of the weak and colonized—rejected *imperialism* and asserted national rights, in arms where necessary. Still, for the most part *decolonization* was peaceful: the 1960s–1980s ushered in quiet independence for much of Africa and Asia. An exception was the Portuguese Empire, where multiple rebellions flared until 1975, and South Africa and Rhodesia, where white settler communities resisted the winds of change. The captive nations of the *Soviet bloc* broke free in 1989, and most of those within the *Soviet Union* did so in 1991. *Yugoslavia* broke up far more violently, however. Despite a greatly expanded world population of nearly 200 sovereign states by 2000, including some astonishingly small *microstates*, national questions lingered in international relations. Indeed, what constitutes a nation and who may claim self-determination became questions of new import as forces of *globalization* made local ethnic identities appear more attractive than many older national ones. Nationalism in the early twenty-first century was thus still capable of flaring into horrific violence. And it could threaten otherwise successful states with breakdown via the ballot box, as in Belgium and Canada. *See also Biafra; Bosnia; Chechnya; Chinese Revolution; cosmopolitan values; culturalism; East Timor; Eritrea; Greater Serbia; Hô Chí Minh; irredentism; jingoism; Katanga; Kashmir; Kosovo; Mao Zedong; National Socialism; patriotism; secession; Taiwan; Tibet.*

Suggested Readings: Akira Iriye, *Cultural Internationalism and World Order* (1997); MacGregor Knox et al., eds., *German Nationalism and European Response, 1890–1945* (1985); Edward Mortimer and Robert Fine, eds., *People, Nation, and State* (2000); Norman Naimark, *Fires of Hatred* (2001); Salim Rashid, ed., *The Clash of Civilizations? Asian Responses* (1997); Jaime Rodríguez, *The Independence of Spanish America* (1998).

Nationalist China. All of modern China, 1928–1949; Taiwan alone, 1949– . Republican China dates from the fall of the *Manchus* in 1911 to the ascendancy of the Communists in 1949. *See also China; Chinese Civil War; Chinese Revolution; Guomindang; Second Sino-Japanese War; Taiwan.*

Nationalists, in China. *See China; Chiang Kai-shek; Chinese Civil War; Chinese Revolution; Guomindang; Second Sino-Japanese War; Taiwan.*

nationality. The legal tie between *states* and firms, vessels, or persons, deciding to which states duties and rights are owed or held by such persons, vessels, or firms. States have broad powers to define and restrict their grant of nationality. However, with regard to individuals, new limits on this power evolved in the second half of the twentieth century in response to the actions of *Nazi Germany* in stripping Jews of their nationality under the *Nuremberg Laws* and later, also of South Africa under *apartheid* to strip blacks of their nationality within the Union of South Africa and Namibia. These extreme cases speeded along a more general and historic elevation of individual *human rights* in international law that began in the nineteenth century and sprang from revived notions of *natural law* and efforts to regulate the new destructiveness of industrialized warfare. Concerning firms, the occupation of most of Europe by the Nazis and their economic compulsion of foreign firms during World War II changed the wartime test by which nationality is determined by most states from the old method (domicile) of identifying the country that hosted the headquarters of a *multinational corporation* (MNC), to a new test (control) of which state effectively ordered the behavior of the MNC. *See also Bancroft Conventions; Bantustans; citizenship; dual nationality; effective link;*

expatriation; flag of convenience; indefeasible allegiance; jus sanguinis; jus soli; *naturalization; statelessness.*

nationalization. To take under state control and ownership a property or enterprise that was previously privately owned. It is usually confined to industries or resource sectors thought to be key to *national security* or economic independence. To avoid being mere *expropriation*, it should be accompanied by fair *compensation. See also neoliberalism; privatization.*

national judge. A Justice of the *International Court of Justice* who sits on a case involving the state of his or her nationality. *See also chambers of the Court.*

national liberation, wars of. "la guerre révolutionnaire." (1) Wars fought by a *nation-in-arms,* or some portion thereof, to establish political independence for a colony or to otherwise free a *nation* from foreign control. Such wars, usually conducted by *nationalists* organized as *guerrillas,* grew more common in the twentieth century as formal colonialism waned but some *metropolitan* states nonetheless resisted the change. The first was the *Irish War of Independence.* The term, which was endorsed by the *Soviet Union* (see #2, below) was used during the *Cold War* to describe anticolonial struggles for independence that had a *Marxist* or some other leftist slant. These were usually small-scale guerrilla affairs, but they turned into larger wars according to specific colonial circumstances, such as in the *Algerian War of Independence,* the *French-Indochina War,* and the *Vietnam War.* Ironically, the last such war of the Cold War era was fought against the left: the *Afghan-Soviet War.* (2) A Soviet *strategic doctrine,* drawing on *Lenin's* view of *imperialism,* calling for support for anticolonial *insurgencies* as threatening the supposed weakest link in the chains of *world capitalism.* Although *Khrushchev* openly endorsed the concept, it was an idea already rooted in Soviet notions of *class struggle* and the putative common interests of all workers. It was also a resort to which the Soviets were driven by the logic of *peaceful coexistence. See also Brezhnev Doctrine;* colons; *decolonization; Franz Fanon;* Intifada; *just war tradition; Marxism-Leninism; resistance; Reagan Doctrine; self-determination.*

national missile defense (NMD). *See ballistic missile defense (BMD).*

national morale. The degree to which a population supports a government's *foreign policy.* It is a broader idea than *public opinion,* as even the most absolute dictatorships must take it into account. When it collapses it does so with terrific speed and major consequences, such as when Russian morale collapsed during *World War I* or when Iranian morale fell at the end of the *Iran-Iraq War.* When it is high—such as in France during the years of the *French Revolution* and under *Napoleon,* in the Democratic Republic of Vietnam (DRV, or North Vietnam) during the *Vietnam War,* or in Afghanistan during the *Afghan-Soviet War*—it enhances military power and *diplomacy* by helping the *state* marshal the full resources of the *nation*. When it is low, such as when France endured the *Maginot spirit*, it may fatally undermine a more forceful diplomacy precisely when strength is urgently required. *See also mutiny*.

National Party (South Africa). The all-white, predominantly *Afrikaner* party that won power in 1948 and introduced *apartheid*. It held power from 1948 to 1993. It was opened to black membership in 1992, but for obvious reasons it struggled with recruitment of new members, even while losing white voters to even more extremist parties like the Herstigte Nasionale. *See also African National Congress; Louis Botha; Pieter Botha; Fredrik Willem de Klerk; James Hertzog; Daniel Malan; Nelson Mandela; Jan Christian Smuts*.

national security. Foreign policy issues pertaining, directly or indirectly, to matters of defense of a given country. *Alliances, conscription,* overseas commitments, military expenditures, procurement policies, and *strategic doctrine* are all obvious components of national security. Less plain, but perhaps no less vital, are considerations about the economic underpinnings of national *power* such as *competitiveness, deficit spending,* and *productivity. See also international security*.

National Security Agency (NSA). The largest and best-funded U.S. *intelligence service*. Founded in 1952, and headquartered at Fort Meade, Maryland, it is mainly concerned with collection and analysis of *sigint* and *elint*. Less well known than the much smaller *CIA*. An anonymous (could it be any other way?) wag once said that the initials NSA really stood for "No Such Agency." During the *Cold War* it sent *U-2* spy planes over the Soviet Union and even tunneled under the Soviet embassy in Washington. The tunnel was betrayed to the *KGB* by an FBI agent, who was not caught until 2001. It supplemented military intelligence during the *Vietnam War*. Among its ongoing responsibilities are *satellite*, telephone, and computer surveillance.

National Security Council (NSC). A subdivision of the *executive* branch in the United States, set up in 1947 as an advisory body to the president on all matters relating to *national security*. It brings together the top U.S. foreign-policy officials, including by statute the president, vice president, and secretaries of state and defense, and nonstatutory members such as the *Joint Chiefs* and director of the *CIA*. The NSC became increasingly important during the *Cold War* as a policy-making and coordinating body, outstripping in influence and public profile even the *Department of State*. Its single most important directive was *NSC-68*.

National Security Council Directive #68 (NSC-68). Issued in April 1950, it was the most influential policy statement in U.S. *Cold War* diplomacy. Its principal drafter was *Paul Nitze*, who used dramatic, even sinister, language not usually encountered in internal memoranda or diplomatic analysis in portraying the *Soviet Union* as fundamentally bent on *aggression* and relentless expansion, which was necessary to sustain the *Communist* system at home. *Containment*, already the watchword of Washington's political and economic policy in Europe and Japan, was thereby given a new militarized and global twist. NSC-68 went on to sanction the use of almost any available means to defend the interests of the democracies. It was different from the X *article* and the *Long Telegram* in its tone, the scope of the threat it depicted, and its contention that a Soviet offensive against the West had become global. Just months later North Korea attacked South Korea, in apparent confirmation of NSC-68's warning. The Cold War thus moved center stage to Asia. Before long its impact would be felt on every continent except *Antarctica*.

Suggested Readings: John L. Gaddis, *Strategies of Containment* (1982); John L. Gaddis, *We Now Know* (1997); Ernest May, *American Cold War Strategy* (1993).

national security state. The idea that national life is grossly distorted in *states* that are involved in sustained international *tension*, such as characterized the *Cold War*, because of the requirement to divert social spending and national energies to matters of *national security* and military exigency. *See also military-industrial complex; Minatom.*

National Socialism. *See Nazism.*

National Technical Means of Verification (NTM). All nonhuman, non-*multilateral* means of *verification* of *arms control* agreements that remain in the hands of a single country: *satellites*, radar, *listening posts*, and so forth. *See also elint; sigint.*

national treatment. (1) In *international law*, the requirement to treat foreign *nationals* by the same legal rules and standards afforded to the nation's own *citizens.* (2) Under *GATT* and *World Trade Organization* rules, once a product has been imported it is supposed to be treated (regulated, taxed) no less favorably than its domestically produced competitor(s).

nation-building. A process whereby external powers supply financing, technical advice and assistance, diplomatic support, and above all military security to fragile regimes in formerly war-torn countries that are attempting to overcome factionalism, *tribalism*, and ethnic enmities and instead develop or return to a civil society and shared political institutions. The term gained currency during the 1990s at the *United Nations* and through promiscuous usage by the *Clinton* administration in reference to international reconstruction efforts in Haiti, Bosnia, and Kosovo. On a grander scale, the United States (and in some cases, also Great Britain and France) engaged in nation-building, then known as stabilization and reconstruction, in Japan, Germany, Italy, and a dozen other nations after *World War II*. Comparable efforts—including erection of economic *infrastructure* and cultivation of new political institutions—were a feature of the *mandate* and *trustee* systems set up after 1919 and 1945, respectively. In addition, during much of the twentieth century a number of colonial powers, most notably the British in West Africa, undertook a sustained—albeit paternalistic and in the end also largely unsuccessful—effort to prepare some of their larger colonies for eventual *sovereign* independence.

nation-in-arms. Mass armies, usually made up primarily of conscripts but clearly inspired by nationalist spirit. This was a phenomenon first clearly seen during the *French Revolution* with the *levée en masse*. For its hugely important effects, *see also Napoleonic warfare; Napoleonic Wars; nationalism; revolution in military affairs; total war.*

Suggested Reading: Paul W. Schroeder, *The Transformation of European Politics, 1763–1848* (1994).

nation-state. "état nation." It is a malapropism, although quite common, to use "nation-state" as a synonym for *state*; it is less common (but very French, and that is the language in which the term originated) to use it for *nation*. This draws on and alludes to the modern state and nation-building phase of European history wherein the old *feudal* order was displaced by centralized political authority (*sovereigns*) after c. 1350 (*Hundred Years' War*) in England and France, and post-*Renaissance* elsewhere in Europe, except for Italy and Germany, where the process was not completed until the nineteenth century. Neither the process nor the term is universal, however, if taken to imply that all states are or should be coterminous with nations: even most European states, original home of the concept, are polyglot ethnic communities. The confusion arises from the fact that, on the whole, one ethnic group tends to dominate in any given state (other than explicitly *multinational* states), to impose and uphold its values as national ones, and to project its own image internationally. Thus, in Great Britain the English historically dominated the Irish, Scots, and Welsh, although at different times and to different degrees; France marginalized and to a degree assimilated its *Basque*, *Norman*, and other minorities; whereas in the *Balkans*, in Eastern Europe, and in Russia, most states remain ethnic patchwork quilts. Similar situations abound in Asia, where non-Han Chinese and Tibetans have been largely repressed in China, Punjabis dominate the other peoples of Pakistan, no one group controls India, and the Persians of Iran control large Azeri and Kurdish minorities. In Latin America the culture of *indigenous peoples* has, in many countries, been crushed under imported *Iberian* traditions. And in Africa, it has long been common for myriad ethnic groups to live together in a single state, but it has been rare for *public goods* to be allocated equitably. The result, too often, has been ferocious conflict that blends aspirations to social, ethnic, or economic justice with opposition to existing state boundaries. *See also city-state.*

NATO. *See North Atlantic Treaty Organization.*

natural frontiers. A term of art asserting that this or that international *boundary* should be set according to a state's "natural frontiers," usually determined by sharply distinct physical features such as coastlines, major rivers, mountain ranges, and water basins. It can also be twisted into an imperial claim, as was the case with *Louis XIV* and again with *Napoleon I*, both of whom claimed as France's "natural" frontiers such markers as the Rhine and the Pyrenees, and then occupied adjacent territories in ways resisted by the neighbors as unwanted and unnatural acts.

naturalization. A national legal process with international legal implications, conferring rights of *nationality*, usually meaning the full rights of *citizenship*, at least in countries where citizens have rights against, and not just duties to, the state. This may or may not involve renunciation of previous and existing citizenship, and may or may not extend to children, depending on bilateral agreement between the states involved in a given case. Most states historically held to a doctrine of *indefeasible allegiance*. After 1867, however, the United States gained increasing international acceptance for a right of *expatriation*, a campaign in which it was supported by other *immigrant* nations. *See also Bancroft Conventions; jus sanguinis; jus soli.*

natural law. In *international law* and moral reasoning, an approach holding that rules governing individual and social relations may be divined—through the application of reason—from universal principles that inhere in the "natural order" ("human nature" or "the mind of God"). Rules and principles so discovered are universal and thus are higher than (and binding on) individuals and political communities, whether in the absence of or in addition to man-made or *positive law*. This approach underlay much of the classical tradition in international law. In revived and amended form, it also informs modern concern for *human rights* and the *just war tradition*. *See also Hugo Grotius; jus naturale; popular sovereignty; Emerich de Vattel.*

natural resources. Wealth inherent to the territory and *internal waters* of a country: *land*, mineral ores, *oil*, productive soil, fresh *water*, *fisheries*, forests, and so forth. For most of human history animal and *slave* muscle power, supplemented by water power where available, was the main source of productive energy. With *industrialization*, the adaptation to fossil fuels such as coal and, much later, also ground oil (and then *uranium*) changed the shape and productive capacity of advanced economies and the nature of the relationship between *labor* and *production*. Today, it is a basic assumption in analysis of the sources of *power* that access to key natural resources is crucially important to the strength of a given economy. At the start of the twentieth century coal accounted for 75 percent of world energy production. One hundred years later it had been displaced by oil, nuclear power, and other forms of energy as *population* and *migration* pressures compelled greater application of science and technology to the fruitful exploitation of natural resources. On international aspects of evolving natural resource exploitation, *see also Antarctic Treaty; common heritage principle; development; Exclusive Economic Zone; landlocked states; Moon Treaty; New International Economic Order; Outer Space Treaty; power;* res communis; *Seabed Treaty; UNCLOS III.*

Nauru. It was a German colony from 1888 until 1914, when it was captured and *occupied* by Australia during *World War I*. After the war it became a *mandate territory* jointly administered by Australia, Great Britain, and New Zealand. Japan occupied Nauru, 1942–1945, after which it was made a United Nations *trusteeship territory*, under the same three powers as before. It became a *republic* and a *special member* of the Commonwealth in 1968. Rich in phosphates, it was the only island state in Polynesia to give others foreign aid in the 1970s and 1980s. The phosphate deposits were soon exhausted, however. In 1993 Australia paid *compensation* for earlier mining practices that had left 80 percent of the atoll uninhabitable. This Micronesian *microstate* is the smallest independent microstate in the world, with a combined (native and foreign) population of c. 12,000 in 2001. Nauru declined full membership in the *United Nations* until 1999, but it joined as the United Nations began to consider the problems of small island states.

naval power. *See sea power.*

Navarino, Battle of (October 20, 1827). As the *Greek War of Independence* continued and the *Ottoman Empire* refused to accept independence for Greece, a combined fleet of British, French, and Russian *warships* met in battle with the Turkish fleet of *Mahmud II*, which had combined with the still larger Egyptian fleet of *Mehemet Ali*. The Turkish and Egyptian fleets were annihilated, with heavy loss of life. This action was much criticized on *Realpolitik* grounds in Britain, where concern over the *Eastern Question* (and what would shortly thereafter be called the *Great Game* in Central Asia) was on the rise, and hence concern was waxing that the Ottoman Empire not be weakened to Russia's advantage. Navarino was a major setback for Mehemet Ali, but even more for Mahmud II. It drove the former from the Greek war, to re-fix his sights on the latter's holdings in Syria and Palestine.

Navassa. An uninhabited island discovered by *Columbus* in 1504, about 40 miles southwest of Haiti. The United States took control in the mid-nineteenth century (1857) under its Guano Islands Act (1856), which authorized ship captains to claim as *territorium nullius* any uninhabited islands rich in guano (nitrates). U.S. interests then mined the guano for several decades, and a coast guard station was established there but later abandoned. The American claim and occupation conflicted with a prior historic claim made by Haiti. In 1998 this dispute reemerged as the United States sought to declare the island a protected area to preserve its coral reefs.

"navicert" system. A credentials system for the *merchant marine* developed by Britain as a means of assurance that goods shipped by its merchants or by *neutrals* did not end up in enemy ports. It involved inspection of cargoes and issuance of letters of assurance that the *ultimate destination* was friendly or neutral territory. The United States began to use a similar system, calling the credentials navicerts, in early 1916.

Navigation Acts. Laws designed to compel national trade to make use of the host country's *merchant marine*. Most seafaring nations passed such laws, but the most important historically were a series of acts of the English parliament. These were crucially important in developing the early *law of the sea*, as well as supporting English naval and commercial maritime predominance. The first was passed in 1381. A more enforceable version, passed by *Cromwell* in 1651, was aimed directly at the Dutch monopoly over the Baltic and North Sea carriage trade. It led to the first of the *Anglo-Dutch Wars*. England's victory over the Dutch meant that English interpretations of sea law, as enshrined in the Navigation Acts, came to dominate the development and codification of international maritime law that followed. The Acts, which required all goods imported to England to be carried on English ships, were also a deep irritant in relations with the American colonists during the *American Revolution* and with the United States before, during, and after the *War of 1812*. They were opposed by *Adam Smith* as a lingering *mercantilist* provision.

navy. (1) Originally, all ships, of any kind, belonging to a single nation. (2) Today, all *warships* and auxiliary military (support and supply) ships operated by a *sovereign* power; the officers, crews, *high command*, and *strategic doctrine* they develop and follow; and all supporting enlisted and civilian bureaucracy. *See also Age of Exploration; aircraft carrier; Anglo-German naval arms race; blockade; Dreadnought; galleys; gunpowder revolution; ironclads; laws of war; London Conference; merchant marine; piracy; privateer; Royal Navy; sea power; submarine; warship; Washington Conference.*

navy yard. A government-operated shipbuilding and repair dock that services ships of the *navy*.

nawab. A traditional Indian title translatable as "viceroy," or one who exercises powers as the deputy of a higher *sovereign*.

Nazi Germany. The 12-year period in German history from January 1933, when *Adolf Hitler* became chancellor, to May 1945, when the Nazi leadership committed suicide, surrendered, or escaped abroad and Germany was compelled to accept *unconditional surrender* and *occupation* by the *Allies of World War II*. See also *Germany; Sonderweg*.

Nazi Party. See *Nazism*.

Nazism (National Socialism). Political, social, economic, and racial doctrines of the Nationalsozialistische Deutsche Arbeiterpartei, or National Socialist German Workers' Party (NSDAP), nicknamed the Nazi Party or just "Nazis" by the press and its enemies—the *Weimar* press similarly called Socialists "Sozis" and Communists (Kommunists) "Kommis." Under *Adolf Hitler*, the NSDAP instituted a terror state in Germany and Austria (the *Third Reich*), 1933–1945. The Nazi Party had roots in the *Freikorps*. The Party failed to take power in Bavaria in the *Beer Hall Putsch* (1923) and was briefly banned. It remained a minor, regional party until 1929, when it gained a mass following in face of the onset of the *Great Depression*. In 1930 it took 18 percent of the vote and 130 seats in the *Reichstag*. In 1932 it won 37 percent of the vote and 230 seats, making it the largest party in Germany. In November 1932 its vote fell to 33 percent. Within months of Hitler becoming chancellor in 1933, the NSDAP was the only legal party left in Germany. Membership in the Party, and at least public endorsement of its propaganda and agenda, thus became a prerequisite of career advancement. During *World War II* it had some 4.5 million members.

The tenets and key characteristics of Nazism were assertion of the racial superiority and consequent right of "*Aryans*" to first European and then world dominance; *anti-Semitism* and anti-*communism*; subjugation of the individual to the group, of all class conflict to a single national purpose, and of the Party and nation to the *Führerprinzip*; supremacy of a *totalitarian* state; ruthless political will, utterly unrestrained by conventional morality or the rule of law (coupled with a perverse insistence on making even the most foul atrocity formally legal); denial of all civil rights, and even of humanity for some, up to and including *slave labor* and physical extermination for "lesser races," such as *Slavs* and *Gypsies*, but especially the Jews; glorification of *militarism*, of physical activity over things intellectual, and of Germany's pre–*Christian* history, heroes, and myths; destruction of non-Aryan, and hence "decadent," art and literature; assertion of cultural and racial superiority of the *Volksdeutsche*; unification of all German Volk in a single, enlarged Germany; *Lebensraum* for the "German people" at the expense of the peoples of East European states and of the Soviet Union and its diverse peoples; and surrender to the personal and supreme will of Adolf Hitler. See also *concordat; death camps; denazification; Karl Adolf Eichmann; fascism*; Geopolitik; *Gestapo; Joef Goebbels; Herman Göring*; Herrenvolk; *Rudolf Hess; Heinrich Himmler; Historikerstreit;*

Holocaust; Kristallnacht; *Krupp family*; Mitteleuropa; *nationalism*; *neo-Nazism*; *Night of the Long Knives*; *Nuremberg Rallies*; *Nuremberg Laws*; *Nuremberg trials*; Schutzstaffel; Sicherheitsdienst; Sturmabteilung; Untermenschen.

Suggested Readings: Ian Kershaw, *The Nazi Dictatorship* (1985); Ian Kershaw, *Hitler*, 2 vols. (1999, 2000); Dietrich Orlow, *History of the Nazi Party*, 2 vols. (1969–1973).

Nazi-Soviet Pact (August 23, 1939). Formally called the Russian-German Treaty of Nonaggression, it was negotiated and signed by *Ribbentrop* and *Molotov*. Only part of it was published, that portion stipulating a 10-year *nonaggression* agreement and pledging *neutrality* should either party go to *war* with a third state. That alone shocked the world, including many a loyal *Nazi* and *Communist* who had been told they were each other's mortal enemy. Some Communists in the West burned their Party cards that day; those who did not were confirmed as slavishly doctrinaire or blindly loyal to the *party line*. More important, the Pact opened the way for *Hitler* to launch his *Blitzkrieg* on Poland two weeks later. The *pact* also contained a secret *protocol* agreeing to a fourth *partition of Poland* and to divide Eastern Europe into German and Russian *spheres of influence*. Germany took western *Poland* and *Lithuania*, while the Soviets were granted control of *Bessarabia*, *Estonia*, *Finland*, *Latvia*, and eastern Poland and agreed to supply Germany with *food* and other resources on advantageous terms. An addendum at the end of September traded eastern Poland to Germany in return for Lithuania. The immediate victim was Poland, attacked first by German and then Russian armies moving to a prearranged *partition* line. The fallout did not end there. A Soviet attack followed on Finland, in the *Winter War*. While Germany was occupied in France and the *Low Countries*, May–June 1940, the Soviet Union completed its acquisition of the *Baltic States* and Bessarabia, all of which it annexed.

Hitler's purpose in agreeing to the pact was to clear the way to the destruction of Poland and to avoid a *two-front war*. Yet he always intended to attack Russia in the end. *Stalin's* purposes are less clear. Until the very hour of the German attack on Russia on June 22, 1941, he continued to send trainloads of supplies to Germany and to refuse to countenance any reports that it was preparing to attack. It seems likely that his main motives were to simultaneously avoid a war with Germany for which the Soviet Union was not ready and to turn Hitler westward in the hope that the draining slaughter of *World War I* might be repeated, so that all his enemies to the west might destroy each other. [This view was shared by *Mao*, who welcomed the Pact as gravely damaging to the "international reactionary bourgeoisie," by which he meant Britain and France.] The unexpectedly rapid collapse of France changed everything, however. It left the Soviet Union to face the onslaught of *Barbarossa* less than two years after it signed the pact, without a continental *ally*. Less directly, the pact made the Japanese cautious about provoking Russia and thus helped turn them southward toward *Indochina*, the Philippines, and

Pearl Harbor. Postscript: The secret protocol was uncovered when American troops captured the Nazi archives in 1945. For decades, the Soviet Union denied it ever signed such an agreement with the mortal enemy it ended by fighting so bitterly and at enormous cost in lives and national treasure in what Russians call the *"Great Patriotic War."* In 1991, however, the *Kremlin* at last accepted the authenticity of the German documents. The *KGB*, on the other hand, said it was "still looking" for the Russian-language copy, which, it was implausibly asserted, had been misfiled.

"near abroad." (1) A Russian term for the other *successor states* to the old *Soviet Union*. Relations with these states are viewed by Moscow as distinct from relations with other foreign states. This is because of historic links through the old Russian and Soviet *empires*, the contemporary fact that some 25 million Russians live in the near abroad, *propinquity*, and because Russia regards these areas as being within its historic *sphere of influence*. The idea may yet amount to a modern, Russian version of the *Monroe Doctrine*. (2) A Swedish rejoinder to the Russian claim of special rights in the *Baltic states*, in which Sweden announced in 1994 that its traditional neutrality would not inhibit its *intervention* to prevent Russian reassertion of imperial claims to the Baltic region. *See also* cordon sanitaire.

Near East. (1) Archaic: Looking from Western Europe, the Near East historically referred to North Africa and what is today called the *Middle East*. The term sometimes included the Ottoman-occupied *Balkans*. (2) Modern sense: Looking from Western Europe, the core Turkish lands, excluding the Arab Middle East.

near-nuclear states. Those states suspected of trying to achieve a *nuclear weapons* capability, and those thought to have done so in secret. They included, at various times, Argentina, until it signed bilateral and multilateral *nonproliferation* agreements and opened itself to *IAEA* inspections in the late 1980s; Brazil, whose *civilian* government renounced, also in the late 1980s, a secret nuclear weapons program undertaken earlier by that country's long-standing military regime; Iran, which sought to build or purchase nuclear weapons at least from the early 1980s, driven by its conflicts with Iraq, Israel, and the United States; Iraq, whose nuclear weapons program was severely retarded by an Israeli preemptive strike on its nuclear research facilities (June 7, 1981) and was further slowed by international inspections in the wake of defeat in the *Gulf War*; Taiwan, until 1987 when a CIA *mole* in the Taiwanese military research program stole vital documents that prevented completion of its development of nuclear weapons; North Korea, which in 1993 refused *IAEA* inspectors and renounced the *NPT* but also agreed to a bilateral agreement on nonproliferation with the United States and South Korea; and South Africa, which early in 1993 announced that it had in fact secretly built six bombs in the 1980s but had just as secretly dismantled them before rati-fying the NPT in 1991. Israel is widely thought to have about 200 nuclear warheads, and by most analysts is now considered a *nuclear state*. India and Pakistan were numbered in the near-nuclear group for many years. India first tested an *atomic bomb* in 1974, but until 1998 Delhi denied that it kept any weapons in stock. In 1990 the *CIA* said it regarded Pakistan as already nuclear capable, triggering a suspension of all aid under domestic U.S. legislation. In May 1998, India and Pakistan field tested multiple warheads of varying *yield* in a zealous, even frenzied, tit-for-tat display of nuclear capability. All indus-trialized states with advanced civilian nuclear technology are also "near-nuclear" states in the sense that, if their security interests were severely threatened, they could produce some form of nuclear weapon in relatively short order.

necessary representation. In *international law*, acceptance of the fact that corporate entities such as *states* or *MNCs* must act through individuals.

necessities of war. *Derogation* from accepted international moral standards under the claim that the requirements of making *war* force a waiver of those standards. *See also standards of civilized behavior.*

necessity. When exceptional circumstances lead to waiver of the otherwise illegal character of an act. This assertion is made by *belligerents* as a *justification* for breaches of customary legal obligations they take in the prosecution of a *war*. *See also angary.*

negotiation. In international relations, discussion of *disputes* by diplomatic representatives of the parties involved, with the aim of resolving such disputes peacefully, whether in an informal understanding or a formal *treaty*. *See also diplomacy.*

négritude. A celebration of the heritage of the black peoples of the world (not just of sub-Saharan Africa) whose cultural origins lay in Africa. Follow-ing the wave of *independence* for African nations in the 1960s it fed into *pan-Africanism*, to which it was closely related. It was promoted by *Léopold Senghor*, Aimé Césaire of Martinique, and Léon Damas of French Guiana, among oth-ers. Senghor, in his twin capacities as respected poet and president of Senegal, was its leading light. Its advocates were anticolonial, but they tended also to be *conservative* in their views of how independent black societies should be organized and governed and tended to favor the *West* in the *Cold War*. They celebrated native traditions and values against French policies of *assimilation* while maintaining a basic respect for Western culture, institutions, and po-litical thought. Its core creed was to ask Africans to assimilate what was good from the West into their own traditions and national lives, rather than be assimilated by and to the West. *See also Franz Fanon;* mission civilisatrice; Rassemblement Démocratique Africain.

Nehru, Jawaharal (1889–1964). "Panditji" ("Teacher-guide"). Indian statesman. Prime minister, 1947–1964. Son of a leading nationalist, Motilal Nehru, and a close confidant and admirer of *Mohandas Gandhi*, he rose easily within the leadership ranks of the *Congress Party*, especially after the *Amritsar massacre* (1919). He became its youngest president, at age 40, in 1929. Handsome, sophisticated, intellectually brilliant, and regal in nature and bearing, yet a devoted *democratic socialist*, he was a winning aristocratic complement to the Mahatma's intense political focus on the Indian peasantry. He vehemently opposed *Ali Jinnah* for his raw sectarianism and—in Nehru's view—reactionary social policies. In 1945 he defended *Indian National Army* officers on trial for *treason* in Delhi. He headed an interim government from September 2, 1946, until formal independence. This, and Gandhi's dejected withdrawal, positioned him as the main Congress leader during the *partition* negotiations of 1947, although he was neither *Hindu* nor *Muslim*, but a confirmed agnostic. On independence he served as both prime minister and minister of foreign affairs. He had large dreams, but few resources to carry them out. He guided India through the *First Indo-Pakistani War* and sent troops into *Hyderabad* in 1948. He later oversaw the occupation of *Goa* and all remaining French and Portuguese *enclaves*. He converted India into a republic in 1950, expanded its democracy by extending the franchise to include all adult Indians, legally abolished *untouchability*, and did much to improve the legal and economic lot of lower-*caste* women. His economic program was less than effective, however, being based on overly centralized management of *industrialization* and *five-year plans*. He was a key founder of the *Nonaligned Movement* and hoped for Asian unity and Indo-Chinese friendship. He was therefore rudely shocked by the harsh reality of Mao's China, especially when he stumbled into the *Indo-Chinese War* in 1962. His daughter *Indira Gandhi* and his grandson *Rajiv Gandhi* followed him into the prime ministership. Neither had his intellect or personal depth or achieved his high moral stature.

Suggested Readings: S. Gopal, *Jawaharal Nehru*, 3 vols. (1975–1984); Stanley Wolpert, *Nehru* (1997).

ne judex ultra petita partium. "A judge must not award more than the aggrieved party has claimed." Legal maxim guiding *damages*.

Nelidov Project (1896). Seriously considered but never tried, this was a secret Russian plan to seize the *Bosphorus*; it was devised and proposed by Ambassador Alexander Nelidov.

Nelson, Horatio (1758–1805). British admiral. During the *American Revolution* he served in *convoy* escorts in the Americas. While in the Mediterranean during the early *Napoleonic Wars*, he started a famous affair with Lady Hamilton, wife of the British ambassador to Naples. In 1794 he lost an eye during a fierce battle against the French off Corsica. For the next two years he harried the French in the Mediterranean. He excelled against the Spanish fleet, after Spain joined the war on the side of France. In 1797 he *blockaded* Cadiz, losing his right arm from wounds suffered in battle. Nelson was responsible for the two greatest naval actions of the period. In 1798 he destroyed a French fleet of nearly 400 vessels anchored at *Abukir* Bay, thus stranding *Napoleon* and his army in Egypt; during the engagement, he was wounded for a third time. In 1799 he blockaded southern Italy, where Naples had fallen to the French. He was reprimanded for ignoring a sailing order from a superior but was given a command in the Baltic in 1801. He again disobeyed a direct order during the *Battle of Copenhagen*, but this time it was clear that his was the better course of action and had won the victory. Nelson was thus given command of the Baltic fleet. He retired during the brief *Peace of Amiens* and went to live with the Hamiltons south of London. In 1803 he was recalled to command the Mediterranean fleet, whose main job was to bottle up the French fleet and prevent it from escorting an invasion of England. For nine months in 1805 Nelson pursued a French and Spanish invasion fleet, to the French West Indies and back to Europe, where he finally located his enemy at Cadiz. He engaged and largely destroyed both enemy fleets at Cape *Trafalgar*, on October 21, 1805. Standing on the deck of the H.M.S. Victory, Nelson was killed by a French sniper just as the great battle—among the most decisive in all naval history—was won.

nemo judex in re sua. "No one [state] can judge [its] own cause."

neocolonialism. The idea that the former colonial powers exercise indirect control of their former possessions, either through economic domination or by co-opting local *elites* (in *dependency theory*, the *comprador class*), and by occasional military *intervention*. A looser usage refers to skewed economic relations that either continue or reinforce the structural *dependency* of parts of the *Third World*. The term is used to portray unequal economic relations as a result of deliberate policy by the *North*, including those areas where traditional economic analysis views economic weakness in the *South* as deriving primarily from onsite inefficiencies, lack of *infrastructure*, and other local causes.

neoimperialism. The domination of one *nation* by another through indirect and informal control of its core economic and political operations. For most analysts, this must be deliberate to be imperialistic; otherwise it is seen as a structural feature. The more doctrinaire tend to see all unequal economic relationships as imperialistic, whatever their actual socioeconomic or historical origin. *See also colonialism; imperialism.*

neoliberalism. (1) In economics, an approach to *development* that arose in response to the demonstrable failure of efforts at *import substitution* in many *Third World* countries. It stressed a return to international financial and capital markets and a renewed emphasis on export of *cash crops* and manufactured goods that partook of a country's *comparative advantage*. In addition, trade and economic integration was embraced on both regional and global levels, and some formerly *nationalized* industries were *privatized*. (2) In international relations theory, a late–twentieth-century revival, in denser academic form, of classical liberal ideas about presumed positive correlations between *democracy*, *international organization*, *free trade*, and *peace*.

neo-Malthusian. Advocacy of control of *population* growth, usually by contraception or sterilization, based on dire projections of populations outstripping local and/or global resources. Harsher critics of the *Food and Agricultural Organization (FAO)* and the *World Food Program* argue that the approach to hunger and *famine* taken by those agencies is neo-Malthusian, in that it focuses on reducing population, increasing food availability, and providing temporary food *aid*. They suggest that *poverty* rather than population is the real cause of famine, and pose as an alternative programs that aim at poverty reduction. *See also Indira Gandhi; Thomas R. Malthus.*

neomercantilism. (1) Modern belief in that aspect of *mercantilism* that sees shifts in *power* among *nations* as driven by a recurring cycle of ascendancy and decline of economic *hegemons*. (2) When *states* aggressively pursue a trade surplus, leading to trade deficits among their partners. Japan was accused of this in the 1980s, but all major exporters practiced it (or would like to) in key portions of their economy, especially automobiles, steel, computer chips, and *agriculture*. *See also Common Agricultural Policy (CAP); Great Depression; Ministry of Trade and Industry (MITI); voluntary export restraints.*

neo-Nazism. Characteristic or celebratory of some or all of the tenets of *Nazism*, but subsequent to the moral, political, and physical defeat in *World War II* of *Nazi Germany*. It became a major social problem in Germany after reunification in 1990, feeding off higher unemployment and anti-immigrant anger in the former *East Germany* especially. This led to a deterioration of Germany's foreign image, and to strained relations with Turkey, after Turks and other foreign citizens were killed by neo-Nazi street thugs. Neo-Nazi political parties also emerged in other countries, notably Austria. *See also fascism.*

neorealism. "Structural realism." A social-science triumph of abstract theory over reality, heavily garnished with *jargon* and pretensions to having uncovered universal laws of interstate behavior. It emphasizes the *structure* of the international system as the key determinant of *state* action and views all states in *game theory* terms as "maximizing," *rational actors*. In general, this body of theory de-emphasizes the realm of free choice available to *statesmen* through emphasis on the large-scale structures of international relations that supposedly arise in response to a basic problem of *anarchy*. Its main accomplishment was to focus academic attention on *international political economy* questions in a way that classical *realism* seldom did. It was heavily and justly criticized, however, for neglecting social dimensions of international politics, the insights of classical realism and the *classical school* into abiding international political patterns, the moral and cooperative concerns of *liberal-internationalism*, and even more radical views of the global economic system upheld by *dependency theory*. At its worst, this rigid method of analysis tended to crude *determinism*, proved to be mostly intellectually sterile, was certainly irrelevant to policymaking, and was often spectacularly self-referential and self-indulgent. On the other hand, that hardly mattered outside the academy, since no decision maker ever paid this peculiar social science approach the slightest attention. *See also postmodernism.*

Suggested Readings: Robert Keohane, *Neorealism and Its Critics* (1986); Kenneth Waltz, *Theory of International Politics* (1979).

Nepal. This mountainous *Hindu* kingdom was the birthplace of the *Buddha* and has a royal tradition dating back 2,500 years. It was dominated by the *Gurkhas* from the eighteenth century, and was governed by the Shah dynasty. The Gurkhas invaded *Tibet* in 1790, but they were defeated there two years later by *banner troops* sent in by the *Qing* emperor *Qianlong*. In 1792 it was forced into *tributary* status by China, and it paid tribute in five-year installments until 1908. To preserve its isolated, mountain independence from further Chinese encroachment it forged an *alliance* with Britain in the nineteenth century, at the price of sending many Gurkha sons to fight and die as *mercenaries* in distant British wars. From 1950 to 1990 its traditional absolute *monarchy* underwent relaxation and some reform. Bir Bikram Shah Deva Birenda (1945–2001), king from 1972, steered a careful course of *nonalignment* in the *Cold War*, as well as between Nepal's giant neighbors, India and China. Nevertheless, India blockaded landlocked Nepal in the 1990s, ostensibly to punish it for weapons buys from China, but possibly to destabilize it and bring the Nepalese *Congress Party* to power. In 1990 an opening to multiparty democracy was initiated after bloody riots, as the mostly benevolent Birenda accepted to become a constitutional monarch. Elections were held in 1991. From 1996, *Maoist* guerrillas launched terror attacks in the countryside that destabilized Nepal and slowed further *modernization*. Stunning and bewildering the nation, on June 2, 2001, King Birenda, his wife, and six other members of the royal family were shot dead by Crown Prince Dipendra, who then shot himself.

Nerchinsk, Treaty of (1689). Negotiated by the *Kangxi emperor*, with the aid of *Jesuit* interpreters, it set the border of China with Russia after a half-decade of *frontier* warfare and in the shadow of a common threat from *Inner Asian* tribes in what is today western China. It was signed as between two *sovereigns*, which was a huge departure from China's usual insistence on at least the fiction of *tribute system* in their external relations, and it was different from any arrangement made with other Western powers. It thus showed that the *Qing* understood that Inner Asian and northern relations with other *land powers* were a thing apart from relations with what they still saw as upstart *sea powers* encountered along the coast. In 1727 a supplementary treaty (Kiakhta) was signed that established a clearer border, trading posts, and rights, and permitted the Russian *Orthodox Church* to build and worship in Beijing. *See also banner system.*

nerve agents and weapons. *Chemical agents*, often in gaseous form, that kill or immobilize by attacking the nervous system of people or animals, resulting in fatal paralysis, heart failure, or seizures. Chemically related to pesticides, nerve agents are absorbed through the skin, eyes, intestinal tract, or lungs. They are generally colorless and odorless. Death may take anywhere from a minute to an hour or two, depending on exposure levels, and results from suffocation due to paralysis of the respiratory system. Early work on nerve agents was done by German researchers at IG Farben, who developed the first agent, Tabun, a pesticide derivative, in 1934. Subsequent research led to more than 2,000 derivative nerve agents, including new classes such as Sarin (1938) and Soman (1944), produced by scientists working for *Hitler*. Nazi Germany built a nerve agent factory and produced thousands of tons of Tabun and other agents during *World War II*, but most of these were somewhat unstable. The Nazi stockpiles were captured by the *Allies* in 1945. In the 1950s American scientists produced a series of more stable agents, each 10 or more times as deadly as Sarin, and thus ranking with *plutonium* as being among the most toxic substances known to science. Research advanced further in later years in many countries.

Nesselrode, Karl Robert (1780–1862). Russian statesman. Foreign minister, 1822–1856; chancellor, 1845–1862. He advised *Alexander I* at Paris in 1814 and played a lead role at the *Congress of Vienna*. He was not an adventurer, by any means. Instead, he sought to restrain the vaulting ambitions of some in the *pan-Slavism* movement and to curb Russian eagerness to control the *Balkans*. He thus conciliated Turkey, opposed the *Crimean War* as unnecessary, and opposed further expansion into Asia (*Siberia* and *Manchuria*). As a *conservative*, he also endorsed *Metternich's* system, approving of military intervention to repress *nationalism* and *liberalism* in Poland (1831) and Hungary (1849).

Net Domestic Product (NDP). The GDP minus *depreciation* of *capital goods* used in production. *See also Net National Product (NNP).*

Netherlands. Historically, the *Flanders* region of Western Europe, roughly corresponding to modern *Belgium, Luxembourg,* and the *Kingdom of the Netherlands. See also Austrian Netherlands; Low Countries; Spanish Netherlands.*

Netherlands Antilles. An *overseas territory* of the *Kingdom of the Netherlands,* consisting of two island groups in the West Indies.

Netherlands East Indies. A former Dutch colony that later formed the core territories of Indonesia.

Netherlands Guiana. Archaic name of Suriname.

Netherlands, Kingdom of. Two-thirds of the modern Netherlands is land reclaimed from the sea over the centuries by dike building and drainage, hence the saying, "God made the world, but the Dutch made Holland." The *Low Countries* came under *Habsburg* rule in 1477 when a *dynastic marriage* gave Burgundy to the Habsburgs. During the *Reformation* the main Dutch provinces converted to *Protestantism* and emerged as a leading maritime and commercial center. William the Silent, Prince of Orange (1533–1584) assumed the main leadership role in the early phase of the "Netherlands Revolt," which mushroomed into the *Eighty Years' War* (1566–1648). With formation of the defensive and anti-Spanish Union of Utrecht (1579), seven Dutch provinces split away from the old Spanish Netherlands (the tie to Spain was repudiated in 1581) to eventually emerge as a new state called the United Netherlands. Fully independent by 1648, and also by that year the greatest trading nation in the world, the Dutch expanded boldly into southeast Asia under the auspices of their *East India Company* (VOC). During the seventeenth century they dominated the Baltic and North Sea trade and were a principal naval power.

The Netherlands was also the first nation to undergo a modern *agricultural revolution.* It was long a sanctuary of free thinking and *free trade,* and it welcomed religious and political refugees from all over Europe: Jews from Spain after 1492, Protestants from Bohemia and southern Germany after 1520, and *Huguenots* from France on revocation of the *Edict of Nantes* by *Louis XIV* in 1685. The United Netherlands, or Dutch Republic, was a key opponent of the hegemonic ambitions of *Philip II,* fighting and ultimately winning the Eighty Years' War (1566–1648). In the mid-seventeenth century it broke with England, fighting the *Anglo-Dutch Wars* in 1652–1654 and 1665–1667, then united with the English to fight the *Dutch War* (1672–1678), the first of several great contests against the ambitions and pretensions of Louis XIV. In the process, the Dutch emerged as major proponents of *freedom of the seas* and *neutral rights*. Under *William of Orange* the Netherlands forged an alliance and a union with England that successfully blocked France by 1713. The Dutch Republic preserved its independence until 1795, when *Napoleon* over-ran it and made his brother king. The Netherlands was *annexed* outright by France in 1810, with the brother abdicating in the French emperor's own favor. The *Congress of Vienna* sanctioned recreation of the Kingdom of the Netherlands, then comprising modern *Belgium* and *Luxembourg* as well as the modern Dutch states.

In 1830 Belgium seceded, over Dutch objections. Belgian independence was accepted in the *Treaty of London* (1839). The Dutch constructed a large and wealthy overseas empire, mainly in *Southeast Asia*. They had a lasting impact on the region, beginning with the *slave trade* in the seventeenth and eighteenth centuries, moving to an antislavery stance and overseeing a tran-sition to free labor economies in the nineteenth and twentieth centuries. Back home, Luxembourg became an independent grand duchy in 1890, when the male line in the Netherlands failed and it was decided that a woman could not succeed to the dukedom. *Neutral* in *World War I*, it escaped that holocaust (indeed, it had not been in a war since the secession of Belgium). Neutrality in *World War II* did not prevent a German *invasion* and *occupation*, mainly because Dutch territory presented an easy invasion route around Belgian de-fenses. During the war some Dutch embraced *fascism*, accepting *Hitler's* in-vitation to join as invited ethnic cousins, and fellow "*Aryans*," in his "higher cause." Most bitterly resented the occupation, and the Dutch *resistance* and public welcomed and assisted the *Allied* armies of liberation in 1944. A sen-timental relationship with Canada dates from this period, because the Dutch royal family took refuge there but mainly because it was the Canadian First Army that did much of the bitter fighting that liberated the Netherlands in 1944 and 1945. The Dutch fought to restore their empire and against inde-pendence for *Indonesia* until 1949. Afterward, they faced occasional *terrorism* from South Moluccan nationalists. Otherwise, after World War II the Neth-erlands enjoyed peace and great prosperity as a member of NATO and the *European Union*. *See also Deshima; freedom of the seas; Hugo Grotius.*

Suggested Readings: Jonathon Israel, *Conflicts of Empires* (1997); Jonathon Israel, *The Dutch Republic* (1995); Jan De Vries and Ad Van Der Woude, *The First Modern Economy* (1997); Charles Wilson, *The Dutch Republic* (1969).

Netherlands New Guinea. An archaic name for *West Irian*.

Net National Product (NNP). The *GNP* minus *depreciation* costs of *capital goods* used in production. The reasoning behind this figure and the *NDP* is an effort to arrive at working assessments of what is available for consumption and production, after subtracting from the gross figures what is necessary just to maintain the productive capacity of the economy. *See also System of Na-tional Accounts (SNA).*

Neuilly, Treaty of (November 27, 1919). Drafted at the *Paris Peace Conference*. Bulgaria was not treated as severely as the other *Central Powers* by this treaty, out of fear of creating a new unstable situation, and possibly war, in the *Balkans* such as that preceding *World War I*. Bulgaria lost minor territories to Greece, Rumania, and Serbia, had to pay some *reparations*, and was limited to a *self-defense* force.

neutral. (1) Any state not a *belligerent* when a *war* is ongoing, or a member of an *alliance*. (2) States such as Cambodia, Ireland, Finland, or Sweden that historically proclaimed they would not side with any military or political alliance. *See also Nonaligned Movement.*

neutralism. A political stance of *neutrality* toward a given conflict, but without the full legal ramifications incurred by a formal status (as during a war) or declaration. This term evolved after the *Cold War* as a substitute for *nonalignment*.

neutrality. (1) A foreign policy stance of rejection of adherence to any formal *alliance*. This was a permanent status and attitude proclaimed by some (e.g., Belgium to 1949, Siam, Sweden, Switzerland) and imposed on others (e.g., Austria, Finland). (2) The legal status of any state not involved in a given *war*, granting that state *neutral rights and duties* such as freedom to trade and freedom from hostile military action, but carrying with it obligations to be impartial toward all *belligerents* and to restrain one's own nationals from taking direct part in hostile acts. In post-1945 legal theory and general diplomatic practice, the traditional right to assert neutrality is restricted for members of the *United Nations* in cases that invoke their Charter obligation to uphold *binding resolutions* of the *Security Council*. That is because the United Nations is effectively a "universal alliance" bound by treaty law, and no member of an alliance may be neutral as to its policies. *See also armed neutrality; blockade; Theobald von Bethmann-Hollweg; hot pursuit; League of Armed Neutrality; Neutrality Acts; nonalignment.*

Neutrality Acts (1935–1940). A series of acts by which the U.S. Congress prohibited all loans or credits or sales of war matériel to all *belligerents*, no matter what the cause or war. Thus was rejected the moral premise of *collective security*, and indeed of prudential foreign policy, that said it was wise and proper to make distinctions between *aggressor* nations and their victims. As a result, the United States gave no aid to China in the opening years of the *Sino-Japanese War*, to Ethiopia in the *Abyssinian War*, or to Republican Spain (which American Catholics opposed anyway) in the *Spanish Civil War*. In 1939 Congress partly lifted the ban to help Britain. This had the unintended side effect of also helping Japan in its *aggression* against China. That was so because to avoid the *World War I* dilemma of American ships being sunk while carrying goods through *war zones*, Congress stipulated that foreign powers must collect the goods themselves ("cash and carry"). This the British and Japanese could do, but Germans and Chinese could not. When Congress sought to correct its mistake by selective legislation aimed at denying war matériel to Japan (aircraft, steel, and oil), Tokyo viewed these selective *embargoes* as hostile acts.

neutralization/neutralized states. (1) An agreement between *belligerent powers* to exclude a given *territory* from war, such as the Persian Gulf waters in the *Iran-Iraq War*. (2) The involuntary assumption of *neutrality* by a state, imposed by outside powers, as in the cases of Switzerland (1815), Belgium (1831), Congo (1885), Austria (1955), and Laos (1962).

neutral rights and duties. The concept of rights and obligations of neutral *states* in time of *war* evolved as a set of practical and legal *norms*, laid out in several *conventions* in the nineteenth and early twentieth centuries, but was heavily weighted toward British interpretations owing to that country's long predominance and preeminent *sea power*. However, in *World War I* these finely defined legal rights were severely eroded, and before and during *World War II* they were nearly totally ignored by all sides. They were respected only toward the larger neutrals, such as the United States, and then only as a prudential matter when such a powerful neutral insisted on its legal rights and backed its claims with *force*. The 1945 creation of *United Nations Charter* obligations to assist resistance to *aggression* qualified the conception of neutral rights in theory, but less so in practice. These rights and duties are outlined below.

(1) In general: by the rules of the *Treaty of Washington* (1871), the *Hague Conventions* (1907), and other such agreements, neutrals must exercise "due diligence" and exercise all "means at their disposal" to ensure that their *territory* is not used by *agents* of *belligerents* or their own *citizens* to wage war or otherwise directly aid *combatants* (for example, by gathering *intelligence*). Neutral governments may not sell or export *arms* to belligerents. (However, the sale of arms or other supplies by private persons is not prohibited.) Legal *blockades* must be respected, whether enforced on land or at sea; there is no such thing as an aerial blockade, at least in law. Neutrals retain the right to use force to defend their just neutral claims without this being taken as an act of war or declaration of belligerency.

(2) On land: Neutral territory is held to be inviolable. Recruitment of neutral nationals by belligerents is forbidden, although individuals may travel abroad and then enlist. If soldiers or citizens (other than diplomats or the sick or wounded) of belligerents arrive on neutral soil, the neutral is obliged to *intern* them.

(3) At sea: *Territorial waters* are also inviolable. Neutrals may prohibit belligerent *warships*, should they so choose, from their waters and/or their ports.

Yet *innocent passage* may be permitted. However, warships may not abuse neutral waters to seek refuge from combat or *capture*. The United States added the proviso before World War II that all belligerent *submarines* were barred, except in cases of *force majeure*, when they were required to travel surfaced. Nor may enemy vessels transfer to a neutral registry or *flag*. Otherwise, at sea the laws of blockade are the main guideposts to neutral rights.

(4) In the air: A convention drafted in 1923 has never received sufficient *ratifications* to enter into effect. Nonetheless, certain customary rules apply that parallel rules for land and sea warfare: neutral airspace is inviolable, crews and aircraft must be interned, and so on. *See also armed neutrality; Belgium; Bosnia; Burma; Cambodia; Continental System; contraband; embargo; Laos; Lusitania notes; navicert system; neutrality; Panama Declaration; ultimate destination; Sweden; Switzerland; undeclared submarine warfare; Quasi War; War of 1812.*

neutral zone. (1) A *buffer* area between states that has been *demilitarized* by *treaty*. For example, (a) Iraq–Saudi Arabia: The zone was created by the Treaty of Mohammura in 1922 and confirmed in 1938, but divided by mutual agreement in 1975. (b) Kuwait–Saudi Arabia: Set up in 1922 and confirmed in 1963, the zone was *partitioned* in 1966 but not abrogated. The Kuwaiti half was occupied by Iraq during the *Gulf War*. (2) An area agreed to by *belligerents* that is declared off-limits to *acts of war* to afford protection to civilians, often under international supervision by the *Red Cross* or *United Nations. See also safe haven.*

neutron bomb. An "enhanced radiation weapon" (a small *hydrogen bomb*) that destroys life by releasing a massive shower of neutrons and other short-lived radiation, and with greatly reduced *blast effects*. It was designed by *NATO* for battlefield use. After the destruction of large military formations (for example, a *Warsaw Pact* armored spearhead advancing into West Germany), NATO troops could have moved into and used the bombed area without suffering radiation poisoning; *collateral damage* to *civilian* areas due to blast and longer-lived radiation would also be greatly reduced. If used on cities such a weapon would kill people but leave most property intact. This characteristic—which was a possibility but was not the intended use of the neutron bomb—led some critics to portray it as inherently evil, more so than other types of *nuclear weapons*. That reaction baffled those who pointed out that a standard nuclear weapon would both kill people and destroy their homes and would also render the surrounding land poisoned and uninhabitable for years. Highly effective in *propaganda* terms, the Soviets dubbed it the "perfect capitalist weapon" and worked hard to prevent its deployment. Faced with aroused public opposition, particularly in Western Europe, *Jimmy Carter* backed away from production or deployment in 1978. That damaged the U.S. reputation for leadership within NATO and hurt *Helmut Schmidt* politically, as he had expended a great deal of *political capital* supporting the project. *Ronald Reagan* resumed production in the 1980s, with the weapons being stockpiled rather than deployed in the field. In 1988 China tested a neutron bomb, and in 1999 it publicly acknowledged construction of an arsenal of these weapons. By 2001 several more *nuclear states* either had or were developing similar capabilities.

Neuve-Chapelle, Battle of (March 10–12, 1915). The British, reinforced by units of the *Indian Army*, attacked the "shoulder" of the German salient near *Ypres*. After initial penetration of the German lines, the gap was closed. British casualties were heavy (nearly 12,000 to Germany's 8,600). The offensive later continued at Artois.

Nevsky, Alexander (1220–1263). Prince of Novgorod. *See also Livonian Order; Russia.*

New Caledonia ("Kanaky"). It was charted by *James Cook* on his Antarctic voyage. It was acquired by France in 1853. The chain comprises the large island of the same name and its *dependencies:* the Loyalty Islands, Isle of Pines, Huon Islands, and the Chesterfield Islands. It was used as a French penal *colony*, 1864–1896. The Kanaks revolted in 1878 and again in 1917. It was occupied by the United States during *World War II*, 1943–1945, then returned to France. After it rejected *independence* in a 1958 *referendum*, in which non–Kanaks swayed the vote, it became an *overseas territory* of France. It is an important repository of minerals, particularly nickel. Relations between French workers and settlers and the Kanak population were hostile in the 1980s. In 1988 some devolution of power was agreed to, and a referendum on *self–determination* was set for 1998. However, when the date arrived it was instead agreed that the colony would be provided with considerable additional *autonomy* and any referendum would be postponed for another 15 years. New Caledonia is a member of the *Pacific Islands Forum (PIC)*. Some PIC members support observer status for Kanaks. Kanak parties are also shadow members of the *Spearhead Group.*

New Deal. *See Franklin D. Roosevelt.*

New Delhi. *See Delhi.*

New Economic Policy (NEP). Limited, market-style reforms introduced by *Lenin* in March 1921 to alleviate the distress and dislocations caused by the *Russian Civil War, famine,* and *war communism.* It replaced compulsory seizure of agricultural produce with a more limited tax, permitted privatization of small-scale industries, and promoted a national electrification program. It lasted until *Stalin* introduced the first *five-year plan* in 1929. By opening internal trade and reducing the role of bureaucratic brokers it eased the immediate food shortage in 1921 (which had caused a desperate famine and forced the *Bolsheviks* to appeal to the West for food and other aid), but it did not reverse the centralized control of the economy the Bolsheviks had inaugurated. In the 1980s *Mikhail Gorbachev* proclaimed that he was returning to Lenin's NEP example with his *perestroika* reforms; perhaps that was the reason they failed. *See also American Relief Administration.*

Newfoundland. "The Rock." Discovered by the Genoese John Cabot in 1497 while on an English commission, Newfoundland became England's first *colony* in the Americas, although for more than two centuries it was run almost exclusively to exploit the rich fishing grounds of the Grand Banks (settlement for other purposes was initially forbidden but occurred anyway, under awful conditions for most settlers) and to train English seamen in the stormy ways of the North Atlantic. Newfoundland's native population was hunted down and wholly exterminated, after which mainly Scots and Irish settlers eked out a rough existence from coastal fisheries tied to the European trade, isolated from the mainstream of North American development. During the sixteenth and seventeenth centuries it played a part in the long, worldwide naval and colonial confrontation between England and France, with the French establishing a base at Placentia, from whence they raided English settlements. It was secured formally by Britain in the *Treaty of Utrecht* (1713). In the 1750s the first *Codfish War* was fought off the Newfoundland coast by England and France. Conflict occurred again during the *Seven Years' War (1756–1763)* and when France allied with the United States during the *American Revolution.* In 1824 it was finally made a formal colony within the *British Empire.* In 1832 a local assembly was permitted. During the remainder of the nineteenth century it progressively evolved toward more local *autonomy.* It rejected confederation with Canada in 1867. In 1927 a British court awarded Newfoundland control of the large mainland area of Labrador. It lost its autonomous status in 1934 after a total economic collapse. It fought in *World War I* and *World War II* within the *British Empire* forces, taking heavy losses. After a close *referendum,* it joined Canada in 1949. In the 1980s it began development of the offshore Hibernia oil fields. *See also Rodney.*

New France. All French *colonies,* possessions, and claims in North America. *Acadia* (Nova Scotia) and Hudson's Bay were lost to England in the *Treaty of Utrecht* (1713); *Québec* was captured during the *Seven Years' War,* and its loss to Britain was confirmed in the *Peace of Paris* (1763); the *Louisiana Territory* was surrendered to Spain, also in 1763, although it was later briefly recovered before being sold to the United States. *See also French and Indian War (1754–1760); French and Indian Wars (1689–1763); Indian Wars; Iroquois Confederacy; King George's War; King William's War.*

Suggested Reading: W. J. Eccles, *The French in North America, 1500–1783* (1998).

New Galicia. Northern Mexico during the colonial period. It had a regional capital at Guadalajara.

New Granada. A vast region of South America, evolving from a vague geographical description and imperial aspiration in 1538 to a composite Spanish *colony* comprising present-day Colombia, Ecuador, Panama, and Venezuela. It was elevated to a viceroyalty first in 1718, but the attempt failed. It was elevated again in 1739. In 1781 a major revolt broke out that forced the government to concede most rebel demands, which largely concerned heavy imperial taxation and attempts at centralized reform. The viceroy was deposed by the independence revolt in 1810. It was reconstituted as the core of *Simón Bolívar's* dream of a much larger state of *Gran Colombia*. Ecuador and Venezuela broke away in 1829–1830, however, forming separate states. From 1830 to 1886 Colombia—then still incorporating modern Panama—was known as the Republic of New Granada.

New Guinea. The large South Pacific island divided between *Irian Jaya* and *Papua New Guinea*. It was first encountered by Spanish explorers, sailing from Mexico, in 1528.

New Hebrides. A Pacific group, charted by *James Cook* on his Antarctic voyage. From 1906 to 1980 it was an Anglo-French *condominium*. *See also Vanuatu.*

Ne Win (b. 1911). Burmese dictator, 1962–1988. Trained by the Japanese, he became chief of staff in the Army of *Aung San*, and thus he too fought against the British, 1943–1945, and with them against the Japanese in 1945. In 1958 he was appointed prime minister during a domestic crisis. After a *coup* in 1962 he expelled all foreigners (helping to destroy much of the economy in the process) and imposed a rigid *autarky* on Burma. He *nationalized* most major industries and established a *one-party state*. This turned Burma from a promising new nation upon its independence into one of the world's poorest and most ineptly governed countries. He was forced out in 1988 after massive street demonstrations. His colleagues restored military control but did not return him to power.

New International Economic Order (NIEO). A 1970s campaign by the *Non-aligned Movement* to so radically reform the world market economy as to effectively replace it with centrally managed policies on a global scale, taking great account of questions of *distributive justice* and of *reparations* for *colonialism* in the form of massive *aid*. Supporting reforms included demands for guaranteed prices and markets for *commodities*, heavy regulation of *multinational corporations (MNCs)*, *technology transfers*, alterations to *International Monetary Fund (IMF)* and *International Bank for Reconstruction and Development (IBRD)* voting rules, and expanded access to private *capital* funds by *Least-Developed Countries (LDCs)*. The program never really extended beyond *resolutions* in the *United Nations General Assembly* and the *United Nations Conference on Trade and Development (UNCTAD)*, although marginal changes were made to the lending policies of the IBRD and the IMF. There followed a decade of rhetorical confrontation amidst a crisis of deepening *debt* and *oil shocks*. By the mid-1980s the *debt crisis* led to a new pragmatism about mutual interests between the G-77 and the *OECD*.

New Laws (1542). *See Hernando Cortés; encomienda system; Francisco Pizarro; slave trade.*

New Left. An intellectual/political movement prominent in the United States and Western Europe in the 1960s. In foreign policy terms, it viewed the *Cold War* and *Vietnam War* as the outcome of putatively aggressive, expansionist, imperialistic, and even "racist" American policies. The New Left advocated radical international wealth redistribution through foreign aid, an end to the Cold War via *disarmament*, up to and including unilateral disarmament by the Western states, and general encouragement of *isolationism* within America as a form of domestic *containment* of the United States itself, which New Left historians and analysts viewed as the true "evil empire." *See also Wisconsin School.*

newly independent states (NIS). A term used widely in the 1990s that by definition was destined to a short shelf life: it referred to all the *republics* formed out of the former *Soviet Union*, not just those that joined the *CIS*.

newly industrialized countries (NIC). Countries with economies previously at *LDC* levels of output, which later achieved or approached *OECD* levels of production and wealth, largely through *export-led growth*. *See also Asian Tigers; Group of Twenty.*

newly industrialized economies (NIE). A synonym for *newly industrialized countries.*

"new military history." Military history written about strategy, tactics, and battles, but with one *Clausewitzian* eye on the impact war clearly has on society and culture and the other on the impact society and culture surely has on war.

"new monarchies." A term often employed about the newly centralized, strong national monarchies of Western Europe that first began to take shape in England and France during the *Hundred Years' War* (1337–1453). Also identified in this group are Spain upon the *dynastic marriage* of *Ferdinand and*

Isabella. They are said by those favoring the term to have shared a novel (just how novel it was is the subject of strenuous debate) sense of royal authority and a more effective and more centralized *bureaucracy* and system of taxation and law. *See also Augsburg, Peace of; Holy Roman Empire.*

New Order. *Hitler's* nightmare vision of a "racially purified" social and political order in Europe, and perhaps the world, centering on an ascendant *Third Reich* and its so-called *Aryan* "racial" allies. This idea fed directly into plans for *conquest*, especially of Russia, and to the *Holocaust. See also fascism; Nazism.*

New Orleans, Battle of (January 8, 1815). Due to a delay in news crossing the Atlantic of the *peace treaty* signed at *Ghent*, this needless battle was fought after the formal end of the *War of 1812*. American troops defended against and routed a large British force; the British lost 2,000 killed, whereas the Americans lost 13 men. The main effect of the battle was to inspire a nationalist legend that would one day bring *Andrew Jackson*, the American commander, to the presidency.

New People's Army (NPA). Filipino *Communist* guerrillas who took up the old fight of the *Huks* in the 1970s, gaining support from the peasantry due to the repression of the *Marcos* regime and the slow pace of land reform. They were most active on Mindanao and Negros Island, but were also active in Quezon Province and the Cordillera and Bicol regions of Luzon. In the late 1980s their organization and activity faltered, undercut in part by the reformist government of *Corazon Aquino*. However, a desultory NPA *insurgency* continued into the twenty-first century, becoming indistinguishable from broad peasant grievances in the isolated mountain country of the Philippines.

new protectionism. The rise of *nontariff barriers* against more efficient foreign competition, including *anti-dumping laws*, *voluntary restraint agreements (VERs)*, *quotas*, *procurement policy*, and odd customs and environmental standards. These challenged the *General Agreement on Tariffs and Trade* (GATT), as they were not easily regulated and their impact was harder to assess. Still, some rules against them were added to the *Uruguay Round* and incorporated into the *World Trade Organization* (WTO). The multiplication of such practices is a testament to the success of the GATT process and the WTO, and of regional *free trade areas*, in reducing *tariff* barriers to *free trade*.

New Spain, Viceroyalty of (1535). The Mexican and Central American territory conquered by Spain in the first half of the sixteenth century, which hosted one of two Spanish *viceroys* in the *New World*, in Mexico City. "New Spain" as a geographical and administrative expression thus stopped short of Panama (then part of Colombia) and excluded all holdings in South America, which was then known to the Spanish as *Peru*, and which hosted the other viceroy in Lima. It also included the Philippines. *See also* audiencia; *Aztec Empire*; *Black Legend*; *Christopher Columbus*; conquistadores; *Council of the Indies*; encomienda; *Maya*; real patronato; requerimiento.

New World. Sometimes misread by Americans to mean solely the United States, historically this term referred to the *Americas* as a whole. From the time of *Columbus*, it connoted to Europeans easy and fabulous riches, vast space and vaster opportunity, and fresh starts in culture, commerce, and politics. For generations of later Americans the expansive bounty of their brave new continental empire sustained a quasi-religious sense of living in a "New Eden," which Providence supposedly set aside for them alone to perfect a redemptive national mission of a new type of enlightened politics and society. *See also Indian Wars; manifest destiny; Monroe Doctrine; New Spain; Old World; slavery.*

New World Information and Communication Order (NWICO). A *Third World* proposal made within *UNESCO* in the mid-1970s. It aimed at international regulation of news gathering and reporting to correct a putative bias toward Western interests and perspectives. Its declared intent to license journalists meant that for most Western countries the NWICO arrived stillborn. It showed no more sign of life in the post–*Cold War* world than it did in the ideologically contentious 1970s and 1980s, as historically Western notions of freedom of information ascended almost to the plane of acceptance as international moral and political values and were at the least seen by many non-Westerners to have real economic utility in an information age.

"new world order." (1) A cliché phrase usually used after some apparent tidal shift in world politics to indicate that modifications in the *balance of power* and other *international security* and economic matters are underway. The changes usually turn out to be less dramatic than they may at first appear. (2) A slogan (as opposed to a concept) repeatedly used by *George H. Bush* to describe massive changes in world politics that were in fact occurring after the collapse of the *Soviet bloc*. For also suggesting that the shape of this world order would reinforce *liberal* economic, political, and security norms extant in American foreign policy and embedded in international law, Bush was accused by some of "triumphalism" and exaggeration. (3) Historically, "new world orders" necessarily follow the failure of a *Great Power's* effort to establish *hegemony* (the *Habsburgs*, arguably, in 1555 and certainly by 1648; France in 1713 and again in 1815; Germany and Japan in 1945; the Soviet Union in 1991). Or they follow the collapse of a given imperial order or other international order, which leaves old opponents and new *successor states* alike unsure of the real distribution of power among them.

New Zealand. Originally settled by the *Maori* from Polynesia, the first European to chart these islands was Capt. *James Cook* (1729–1779), who circumnavigated and charted them in 1769–1770. British settlers arrived in number during the 1820s–1840s. They were granted *autonomy* within the *British Empire, 1853–1856*. In 1843 and again from 1860 to 1870, the *Maori Wars* were fought, ending with British and settler domination over the Maori. *Federation* with Australia was considered, and rejected, in 1901. In 1907 it became a *Dominion* within the Commonwealth. Despite being among the most strategically secure of populated places on earth, it was automatically a belligerent in *World War I*, by virtue of its inclusion in the Empire, when Britain *declared war* on the *Central Powers*. Its contribution to ANZAC forces saw bloody defeat at *Gallipoli*. Although the *Statute of Westminster* applied also to New Zealand, full *independence* did not come until 1947.

In *World War II* New Zealand again fought on the British and Allied side. After the war it slowly emerged that the threat from Japan had awakened New Zealanders from their colonial doldrums and complacency and brought home to many the reality that their country's future was as an Asian power rather than as a European ethnic and cultural outpost in Asia. New Zealand thus became more committed to a foreign policy focused on the Pacific. It also switched from being under the protection of the British, which had slipped in the first days of the war as the *Royal Navy* "legions were recalled" to protect the home country, and moved instead under an American security umbrella by joining *ANZUS* and *SEATO*. New Zealand sent troops to fight in the *Korean Conflict* and, much more controversially, also in the *Vietnam War*. From the mid-1970s New Zealand tended to see its Pacific interests as less than fully compatible with *Great Power* involvement in the region. It objected, in particular, to American, British, and French nuclear tests, with a serious breach in relations occurring over French *covert action* in the *Rainbow Warrior incident*. This changing viewpoint reflected its *location*, the growing political activism of its large Polynesian and Maori minorities, a more open *immigration* policy, and a general liberalization of society along with a new form of complacency about physical threats to its independence.

New Zealand maintains commitments to the *Cook Islands*, *Niue*, and *Tokelau*, which it has administered since 1925. It also administers the Ross Dependency in the *Antarctic*. From 1975 it pushed for the South Pacific *nuclear weapons free zone* (NWFZ). The next year, New Zealand began a major reorientation of its defense and foreign policy toward the South Pacific, confirming this in a 1987 defense White Paper. It lent *good offices*, and a warship, to Papua New Guinea to assist in negotiating a *cease-fire* in the *Bougainville insurgency*. In 1980 it backed a Regional Trade and Economic Cooperation Agreement. Under Prime Minister David Lange, 1984–1989, its assertive antinuclear policy pleased domestic and regional opinion but brought repeated conflict with France, the end of ANZUS, and a downgrading of New Zealand's relations with the United States. In 1990 Auckland set up a regional export assistance program. More than two-thirds of its *foreign aid* goes to the region. The United States resumed high-level political talks with New Zealand on regional affairs in 1994. New Zealand also has differences with Japan on *fishing* and *whaling* policy.

Suggested Readings: James Belich, *Making Peoples: A History of the New Zealanders, from Polynesian Settlement to the End of the Nineteenth Century* (2001); Colin Davis and Peter Lineham, eds., *The Future of the Past* (1991); Geoffrey W. Rice, ed., *Oxford History of New Zealand*, 2nd ed. (1992).

New Zealand–Australia Free Trade Agreement (NAFTA). Agreed to in 1965, it began a slow process of *tariff* reduction between these South Pacific neighbors. In 1982 a deeper and more comprehensive Closer Economic Relations (CER) agreement was reached, which progressively moved the pair closer to genuine *free trade*.

Ney, Michel (1769–1815). Marshal of France. Arrogant and often reckless, like his master, Ney, the son of a barrel-maker, was *Napoleon's* greatest marshal. He was at his most reliable when carrying out orders, but he seldom proved capable of independent command. He was a major figure in several of the *Napoleonic Wars*, from 1805 to 1815, during which time he also did much to promote the career of the young Swiss military theorist *Jomini*. Ney did well against the Austrians, Russians, and Prussians, but he more than met his match in Spain during the *Peninsular War*. He fought well at *Borodino* and commanded well again when left behind by a scrambling—indeed fleeing—Napoleon to oversee the final stages of the disaster that was the *retreat from Moscow*. During the great defeats of 1813 and 1814 that followed, he at times considered suicide. Instead, he chose to turn against Napoleon, persuading other French marshals to do likewise. Ney retained his titles (a better fate than suicide, surely) in the *Restoration* by being the first marshal to demand Napoleon's abdication and by serving in the *Bourbon* Army, 1814–1815. At the start of the *Hundred Days* he promised *Louis XVIII* to bring Napoleon to Paris "in an iron cage," but when his own troops cheered and embraced their old emperor, Ney ("loyal and neutral in a moment," "Macbeth," Act II, scene iii) again expediently changed masters and offered Napoleon his sword. After *Waterloo*, during which he was almost killed four times, his avowals of a second rediscovery of well-hidden royalism were quite properly dismissed. He was arrested, tried for *treason*, and shot.

Nguni. Several related peoples of southern Africa: the Pondo, *Swazi*, Thembu, *Xhosa*, and *Zulu*. They were mostly stateless into the eighteenth century. *See also* Mfecane; *Shaka Zulu*.

Nguyên Cao Kỳ (b. 1930). South Vietnamese general. He led the *coup* that overthrew *Diem*, heading a *junta* that then took power. He introduced land reform and rural development programs, but he became deeply entangled in controversy with *Buddhists* and used heavy force to repress dissent in Dà Nang and Huê. He was later criticized in the United States for his conduct of the war. His retort was that Americans were guilty of heartless abandonment of the Republic of Vietnam (RVN, South Vietnam) during the collapse of 1975, when they (but also he) fled, along with the human *flotsam and jetsam* of the RVN regime. He became a businessman in America. *See also Nguyên Vãn Thìêu.*

Nguyên Vãn Thìêu (b. 1923). General, president of the Republic of Vietnam (RVN, South Vietnam), 1967–1975. He participated in the *coup* that overthrew *Diem*. He thereby achieved the pinnacle of power in the RVN just before the *Tet Offensive*. He did little about the vast corruption of RVN government and society. That weakened the war effort and wore down the morale of the ARVN, as well as that of its U.S. ally. He reluctantly adapted to *Nixon's* policy of *Vietnamization* of the war, and he fought on after the United States pulled out in 1972. In March 1975, he made the spectacular error of ordering withdrawal of ARVN troops from the Central Highlands and two northern provinces. That led to a complete military collapse by most ARVN units, although some fought most bravely and under desperate conditions. Thìêo Taiwan to escape the People's Army of Vietnam (PAVN) armies that swept into and over the RVN, an outcome and military failure he bitterly blamed on the United States, charging it with faithlessness and reckless abandonment in the *Paris Peace Accords*. *See also Nguyên Cao Kỳ.*

Nian Rebellion (1851–1868). A major, prolonged, mostly peasant uprising in north China roughly coterminous with the *Taiping Rebellion*. The Nian were far less well-organized or centrally led than the Taiping, like whom they were ultimately repressed with savage violence. Instead, they formed multiple groupings that came together in alliance from 1852 under Zhang Luoxing, a local landlord with bandit and smuggling credentials. They also were, unlike the Taiping, essentially nonideological. Their grievances were more vague but also more local, so that their numbers grew dramatically after 1855 when large-scale flooding in northern China displaced and destituted many peasants. For awhile, the Nian organized into a *banner troop* system of their own. Later, they proved adept at *guerrilla warfare* tactics, remarkably similar to those that would be employed by *Mao* and Chinese *Communists* during the *Chinese Civil War* of the twentieth century. In combination, the Nian and other rebellions occurring in the 1860s (the Taiping and others by western Muslims) nearly toppled the *Qing* dynasty. Although the Nian were ultimately crushed, their revolt gravely weakened both the Qing and China. See also *Great Fear*; jacquerie; *Pugachev rebellion; Túpac Amaru II.*

Suggested Reading: Elizabeth Perry, *Rebels and Revolutionaries in North China, 1845–1945* (1980).

Nicaragua. Conquered by Spain in 1522, its Mosquito Coast was infested with English *pirates* from the 1630s to the 1780s, when they were driven out by the Spanish. It was part of the *Captaincy-General of Guatemala* until that larger region gained independence in 1821, coincidentally with the independence of *New Spain* (Mexico). It then broke from Mexico to join a short-lived federal experiment called the *Central American Union, 1824–1838*, but left that troubled association on its breakup in 1838. The *filibusterer William Walker* (1824–1860) caused a good deal of trouble in Nicaragua in 1860 but on the intervention of several Central American armies he was overthrown and shot. Nicaragua conquered the coastal Mosquito Indians in the 1890s. The first U.S. *intervention* in 1909 led to the overthrow of the dictator José Zelaya. For 10 years Zelaya had been ignored while waging petty wars against neighboring Honduras and El Salvador, but then he made the mistake of threatening American interests. An attempt was made to regulate Nicaraguan customs, but the U.S. Senate rejected the idea. In 1912 U.S. marines quelled a new uprising, and 100 were stationed there to discourage rebellion. The marines were pulled out in 1925, but they returned almost immediately when a civil war broke out. Augusto Sandino (1896–1934) continued to fight for six years after a United States–brokered peace in 1927, giving birth to the original *Sandinistas*. Sandino was murdered in 1934 while negotiating a cease-fire. The marines left in 1933 under the *Good Neighbor policy*.

Nicaragua was thereafter ruled by a family of dictators headed by *Anastasio Somoza*, 1936–1956, and then his two sons, 1957–1979. After 1961 several formerly separate peasant and left-wing *guerrilla* movements organized into the Frente Sandinista de Liberación Nacional (FSLN), a new "Sandinista" movement. The rebels overthrew *Anastasio Somoza Debayle* (1928–1980) in 1979. They then split into a faction that favored a constitutional democracy and a *Marxist* faction, led by *Daniel Ortega*, which soon took control. At first the revolution was greatly popular as its land reforms won allies among the peasantry. The middle classes grew increasingly alienated, however, with more doctrinaire policies of *expropriation* of private property and repression of civil rights. Many fled to Mexico or Miami, where they lobbied the United States for *intervention*. The *Reagan* administration supplied and sustained an *insurgency* by *Contra* guerrillas, mined Nicaragua's ports in 1984, and placed an *embargo* on trade, loans, and credits. With the end of Soviet *aid* what was left of the economy collapsed in 1988, and Ortega agreed to hold internationally supervised elections in 1990.

The Sandinistas lost the election to Violeta Barrios de Chamorro, a centrist supported by the United States, but they retained a respectable share of the vote. That allowed them to negotiate a *power sharing* coalition with President Chamorro in which they retained control of the police and army, in a tense *national front* government. The Contras and excess Sandinista troops were *demobilized*, and U.S. aid and trade resumed. In 1993 guerrilla attacks were launched by small groups of former Contras and Sandinistas, sometimes in opposition to each other but sometimes allies in adversity, alike protesting the failure of an earlier promise to provide land in exchange for both sides laying down their arms. Ortega and the Sandinistas were defeated again in 1996, by José Arnoldo Alemán and the Liberal Alliance. In November 1998, Hurricane Mitch killed thousands and did great economic damage. *See also Iran-Contra affair; Reagan Doctrine.*

Suggested Reading: Thomas W. Walker, *Nicaragua: The Land of Sandino*, 3rd ed. (1991).

Nicholas I (1796–1855). Tsar of Russia 1825–1855. A harsh *reactionary* and *anti-Semite*, he succeeded his brother, *Alexander I*, and began his reign by repressing the *Decembrist revolt*. He continued his predecessors' policy of expansion at the expense of Turkey and Persia. He closed Russia to foreign influence, opposed mass and higher education, and enforced brutal domestic *ukase*, especially against the Jews (he was an *anti-Semite*), but also against *Catholics, Protestants,* and *Old Believers*. He contemplated *emancipation* of the serfs but lacked the vision or courage to carry this out. Yet he was also a devoted bureaucrat whose steady policies some see as building toward the great reforms of his successors. In foreign policy, he crushed revolts in Poland (1830–1831), where he then attempted *Russification*, and in Hungary (1849). He negotiated the *Münchengrätz Agreements* (1833) with Metternich, regarding the *Eastern Question*. He fretted over re-establishment of the French Empire under *Napoleon III* and determined that it was high time to finish off Turkey. He thus pressured Turkey into declaring war in 1853, leading not to triumph but to the great disaster for Russia of the *Crimean War* with Britain and France, during which he died in his bed, on March 2, 1855. His motto: "Orthodoxy, Autocracy, Nationality." *See also Alexander I; Alexander II; Catherine II; Ivan III; Nicholas I; Nicholas II; Peter I.*

Suggested Readings: W. Bruce Lincoln, *Nicholas I* (1978, 1989); Nicholas Riasonovsky, *Nicholas I* (1959).

Nicholas II (1868–1918). Tsar of Russia, 1894–1917. A weak, indecisive, and unpopular tsar who came under the influence of mystics, especially his wife and *Rasputin*. He called the first *Hague Conference* in 1899 to try to end an *arms race* Russia could not afford. His regime was shaken by the loss of the *Russo-Japanese War*, after which he waved at reform in public while privately supporting arch-*reactionary* and *anti-Semitic* groups behind the scenes. He moved Russia into *tacit alliance* with France and Britain after 1907 and secretly patched relations with Japan over *Manchuria*. He took personal command of the Russian armies in 1915, and so was blamed for the awful defeats of 1916. He abdicated after the *February* (*March Revolution*) in 1917. His entire family, including several small children as well as personal servants, was murdered by the *Bolsheviks* in July 1918. In 1992 newly opened *KGB* files revealed that the order for the atrocity came from *Lenin*, a fact that had been denied for three-quarters of a century. The bodies were exhumed from an unmarked grave and forensically identified in 1993. In 2000, prelates of the *Orthodox Church* voted unanimously to canonize Nicholas and his family— not so much for his years of misrule as for suffering death at the hands of the now utterly discredited Communists. *See also Alexander I; Alexander II; Catherine II; Ivan III; Vladimir Ilyich Lenin; Nicholas I; Peter I; Josef Stalin; Peter Stolypin; Serge Witte.*

Suggested Readings: N. Fero, *Nicholas II* (1991); T. G. Stavrou, ed., *Russia Under the Last Tsar* (1969).

NIEO. *See New International Economic Order.*

Nietzsche, Friedrich (1844–1900). German philosopher. He hated everything to do with *bourgeois* society, "Christian morality," and—ironically, given the followers he inspired—the German state and fashionable *racist* views about the putative superiority of "*Aryans.*" Among other ideas, he developed the notion of a philosophical *elite*, a revolutionary vanguard led by the "Superman" (Übermensch—the so-called blond beast), a perfectly free creature unimpressed and unrestrained by conventional political morality, who despised all weakness and rejected all encumbrances such as law or consideration for others. As a historical example of what he intended he pointed admiringly to *Napoleon I*. Later, *Hitler* and other Nazis developed this and other of his notions into the corrupt *Führerprinzip*. Some have traced other ideas in Nazism and *fascism* to his writings, in particular Hitler's garbled idea of Nietzsche's "will to power" as the ultimate moral principle, which for Hitler took the form of a view of German history to be driven forward by his own "iron will." Nietzsche had no time for *nationalism* in any traditional sense, instead unwittingly bequeathing to fascism a loose concept of a racially and morally superior class of men of amoral will and historic destiny. The Nazis also took their antagonism to Christianity from Nietzsche. He was no anti-Semite, however; that special perversion was all theirs, and Hitler's. Nietzsche went insane during the last 11 years of his life.

Suggested Readings: Friedrich Nietzsche, *Thus Spoke Zarathustra* (1885); *Beyond Good and Evil* (1886).

Niger. The *Tuareg* established a state with its capital at the oasis city of Agadez, in modern central Niger, in the eleventh century. From there, they controlled one of the great trans-Saharan *trade routes*, using *slave labor* to mine the salt that upheld the desert trade. Southern Niger was settled by the *Hausa*, whereas central Niger was ruled by *Songhay*, and later by *Bornu*. At the turn of the nineteenth century Niger was overrun by the great *jihad* of the *Fulbe* under *Uthman dan Fodio*. At the *Conference of Berlin* (1884–1885) it was agreed that France should control Niger. This impoverished desert region became a French *colony* after French forces moved into the area and attacked and captured several *Tuareg* cities, 1898–1899. Niger's Hausa and Fulbe populations were quickly subjugated, but intermittent fighting continued even after the fall of Agadez against fierce Tuareg nomads, into the 1920s. Niger was made part of *French West Africa* in 1922. Parts of northern Niger remained mostly outside French control, and under that of the Tuareg, until after *World War II*. It received *autonomy* within the *French Community* in 1958, and outright *independence* in 1960. Niger maintained a poor but quiet national life as a *client state* of France, staying out of major wars in neighboring Nigeria (1967–1970) and Chad (1966–). Like its neighbors, it was devastated by the great drought that afflicted the *Sahel* in the 1970s, leading to internal migration to its towns and cities by impoverished peasants and prompting a 1974 coup. Discovery of *uranium* led to higher export earnings in the 1980s, mostly retained through corruption at the *elite* level. The deep desert Tuareg also occasionally clashed with the government. More coups followed, in 1996 and 1999, leading to suspension of *foreign aid* programs by several donor nations.

Suggested Reading: F. Fuglestad, *A History of Niger, 1850–1960* (1983).

Nigeria. The Nok culture of c. 500 B.C.E. was the oldest recorded civilization in what is today Nigeria, Africa's most populous modern nation (nearly one in every five Africans is Nigerian). Ancient enmities scar the area's history. For centuries *Yoruba* kingdoms in the southwest warred among themselves, feeding the transatlantic *slave trade* with their *prisoners of war* and sometimes also their own people. The major Yoruba kingdom was Oyo, which extended into what is today Togo and warred also with the *Kingdom of Benin*. To the east the *Ibo* (Igbo) and riverine tribes remained relatively isolated behind a screen of mangrove swamps along the coast and the Niger delta to the west. In the north, the dominant *Hausa* converted to *Islam* in the thirteenth century C.E. and established a full-blown *city-state* system based on a slave agricultural economy. The Portuguese explored the Yoruba coast, reaching Lagos in 1486. This area was later called the Slave Coast after the principal cargo carried from it. The English took over the bulk of the slave trade by c. 1600 and controlled it until its abolition (in British law, although not immediately in fact) in 1807. In the early nineteenth century the expansionist *Fulbe Empire*, under *Uthman dan Fodio*, conquered the Hausa and other northern peoples. Later in the nineteenth century Fulbe southward expansion was stopped by the tsetse fly, which bore sleeping sickness to their *cavalry*, and by the advancing and technologically superior British, whose own imperial bite proved the more lethal to Fulbe ambitions.

British steamers penetrated the "Oil Rivers," then the source of palm oil, now of crude oil, finally navigating the Niger into the interior in the 1860s. Lagos was made a protectorate in 1851 in return for an end to the slave trade.

Britain claimed the territory around the port of Lagos as a *crown colony* in 1861, after which penetration and claims to the interior followed in due course. In 1885, in response to the French annexation of Dahomey (1883) and the German annexation of Togo (1884) and Kamerun (1884), Britain proclaimed an *Oil Rivers Protectorate* over the Niger delta. The British then moved rapidly north via the Niger River from their Oil Rivers base. They penetrated Hausaland, commercially as well as militarily, from 1886 in the form of the Royal Niger Company, owned and operated by George Goldie. In 1898 London began to take direct control of northern Nigeria, piece by piece. After 1900, under *Lugard*, the British proclaimed two Nigerian *protectorates*, one in the south (Lagos and Oil Rivers were merged), under *direct rule*, and one in the north, where they used the local *sultan* and *emirs* to run a system of *indirect rule*. Kano was taken by force in 1902. On numerous occasions atrocities were carried out by British and native levies against resistant northern villages. Fighting continued in the Hausa/Fulbe lands into 1906. These two colonies were administratively fused in 1914 to form Nigeria. Even so, a quiet war of conquest continued in eastern Nigeria until 1918, largely unreported and unnoticed by a British public preoccupied with news of the *western front* in Europe, where the British Empire was ostensibly fighting to preserve the "rights of small nations."

Nigerians served in the British Army in both world wars. After *World War II* the demand for independence grew apace with the wider *decolonization* movement. In 1954 Nigeria was united under a federal constitution. In 1960 it gained its independence when the British handed power essentially to a northern political party that represented the interests of the Fulbe emirs. Part of *Cameroon* then was joined to Nigeria in 1961. In 1963 the federation was divided into three administrative regions, but federal power remained vested in the north. Tension among the major tribes was only exacerbated by rising oil revenues, as oil reserves were concentrated in the Ibo-dominated east. In 1966 President Nnamdi Azikwe ("Zik"), an Ibo chief and long-respected nationalist leader, was deposed in a *coup* in which Alhaji Abubaker Tafewa Balewa (1912–1966), the prime minister from the north, was killed. His murder was deeply resented by northern Muslims. The next year, massacres of some 30,000 Ibo were carried out in the north by Hausa-Fulbe stirred to a murderous frenzy by demagogic leaders. That led the eastern region to secede, along with all its oil reserves, and proclaim independence as Biafra. That sparked the *Nigerian Civil War*.

After the federal victory in 1970 under General Yakubu Gowon (1966–1974), the nation reconciled and avoided a widely feared genocide against Biafrans. There followed a decade of boom, arising from *OPEC* oil price rises in 1973 and 1979. Nigeria spent its billions unwisely, and corruption rose to staggering levels. A series of military coups was interrupted in 1979 when General Olesgun Obasanjo handed power back to elected civilians. However, a government led by a northern Muslim, Shehu Shagari, proved even more corrupt than the officer corps and was cast aside by a coup in 1983. Two years later another coup brought General Ibrahim Babangida to power. He provided stability and redressed some of the country's economic problems by de facto adhering to (he refused to actually sign) a *stabilization program* designed by the *International Monetary Fund* (IMF). In 1991 the national capital was moved from the lively coastal Yoruba city of Lagos to a dispiriting planned city in the interior, Abuja. Elections were held in June 1993. Babangida then indulged a flair for opéra bouffe: he canceled the results even though international observers said they were free and fairly arrived at, once it became clear that Moshood Abiola, a Muslim Yoruba with genuine national appeal, would win. New elections were called, from which the previous candidates were banned from participation. Abiola was jailed (his wife was later murdered) and Babangida was replaced by General Sani Abacha, who proceeded to run the most corrupt, incompetent, and repressive government in Nigerian history.

Nigeria staggered from worsening political instability and economic decline, which hamstrung its ability to play the role of Africa's natural leader to which it aspired. And yet, as its domestic situation deteriorated and it fell under international *sanctions*, it did finally begin to play a constructive role in regional affairs. In the 1990s it *mediated* a long-standing conflict in Chad, took the lead in *armed intervention* in civil wars in Liberia and Sierra Leone, and joined UN *peacekeeping* efforts in Cambodia, Somalia, and the former Yugoslavia, all under the worst, most corrupt, and widely despised regime in its history. In 1998 Abacha was said to have suffered a heart attack during a coup attempt; few believed the story, and even fewer mourned his passing. Internationally supervised elections were held in 1999. Obasanjo, who had been jailed by Abacha, won handily.

Suggested Readings: R. A. Adeleye, *Power and Diplomacy in Northern Nigeria, 1800–1906* (1972); J. F. A. Ajayi and Michael Crowder, eds., *History of West Africa*, 2 vols. (1974); Michael Crowder, *The Story of Nigeria*, 4th ed. (1978).

Nigerian Civil War (1967–1970). After a coup in Lagos dominated by young *Ibo* officers, in 1966 and 1967 northern Muslims, mainly *Hausa* and *Fulbe*, massacred about 30,000 Ibo civilians living and working in the north. Tens of thousands of Ibo refugees sought safety in the southeast region, their historic tribal homeland. When that region, which contained most of Nigeria's known *oil* reserves, subsequently seceded (May 30, 1967) under the name Biafra, *civil war* broke out. After a brief Biafran offensive, the superior numbers and resources of the Federal Nigerian forces led to a grinding war of *attrition*. Biafra was *blockaded* and slowly compressed. As the world was confronted with pictures of starving Biafran children in a shrinking *enclave*, the response was mixed. Most African states supported the Federal side, with only four members of the OAU recognizing Biafra (Côte d'Ivoire, Gabon, Tanzania, and Zambia), and that mainly in a last-minute attempt to save lives. France gave minimal support to Biafra out of flirtation with the idea of dividing Nigeria, which was more populous than all *francophone* nations in West Africa combined. The United States and the Soviet Union did not become directly involved. Both supported the Federal side, however, thus insulating the civil war from the *Cold War* and leaving the decisive role to the old colonial power, Britain. The United Kingdom fully supported the Federal side diplomatically and with financial and military aid and arms sales. Most Arab states also supported the Federals, which they (correctly) perceived as sustaining Muslim interests. Several private aid agencies, notably CARITAS, and some *mercenary* forces, came to Biafra's assistance. A highly successful *propaganda* campaign waged by Biafra and the aid agencies suggested that a war of *genocide* was being waged against the Ibo, many of whom were *Christian* (largely *Catholic*), generating extensive public protests in Western countries. The war dragged on until 1970, pushing even Vietnam off the television screens on a few nights, but mostly it was waged outside the mainstream of world affairs. In the end, the Ibo were hemmed into a pocket around their capital, Enugu. When it, too, gave way, hostilities ended abruptly. One million died, mostly by starvation. To Nigeria's lasting credit there was a relatively generous *peace*, as Ibos were more or less reintegrated into Nigerian society—although deep hostility and resentment lingered for decades. In 1982 the young (32 in 1966) and charismatic Biafran leader, Colonel *Chukwuemeka Ojukwu*, was pardoned and allowed to return to Nigeria. *See also* Médecins sans Frontières.

Suggested Readings: John de St. Jorre, *The Nigerian Civil War* (1972); John Stremlau, *The International Politics of the Nigerian Civil War* (1977).

Night of the Long Knives (June 30–July 2, 1934). A weekend of killing without even the pretense of legality, when *Hitler purged* Ernst Röhm (1887–1934) and the *Sturmabteilung* (SA), using *Himmler's* new and more sinister *Schutzstaffel* (SS) to do the deeds of murder. Several hundred were killed (the exact figure is unknown, but it may have reached over 1,000) that night and later. Some were vaguely socialist and loyal to Röhm over Hitler; others were the victims of some private score settled by an SS murderer. Among the dead were a number of homosexuals, including Röhm, who had been specially targeted for that reason. The official excuse for the purge was that Röhm was planning a *Putsch*; he was not, although there was a left revolutionary wing within the SA. Its real purpose was to placate the *Wehrmacht*, which was worried that the SA sought to displace it, and German industrialists, who worried about the radical socialist doctrine espoused by a portion of the SA. It thereby cleared the way to Hitler's assumption of the presidency with the support of the Wehrmacht and German capitalists. Within months Hitler became commander-in-chief, besides being chancellor of the *Reich*, and made the officer corps eat their servility in public by swearing a loyalty oath to him, personally. In the years that followed, many homosexuals—especially in the armed forces—would be summarily executed or deported to the *death* *camps*, although some secret homosexuals were tolerated in high positions in the Nazi Party all through the *Third Reich*. Hitler personally gave the bloody night its name. While it shocked many in the West it was well received in Germany, where the SA was despised. Also, *Stalin* reportedly admired its verve and decisiveness.

Nile, Battle of (1798). *See Battle of Abukir Bay (1798).*

Nimitz, Chester (1885–1966). Nimitz was chief of staff to the U.S. *submarine* fleet during *World War I*. After *Pearl Harbor*, he was promoted to admiral and replaced H. E. Kimmel (1882–1968), who had been singled out for official blame for the failure of December 7th, as commander of the Pacific Fleet. Three months later he became overall commander of U.S. forces in the Pacific theater, including of land forces commanded by *Douglas MacArthur*, who deeply resented this subordination. Nimitz blocked the Japanese advance at the *Battle of the Coral Sea* and then struck a fatal blow to the Japanese fleet one month later at *Midway*. His greatest contribution to victory was insistence on an "island-hopping" strategy that isolated Japanese strong points as the Americans advanced through the Gilbert Islands (1943), the Marshalls (1944), and the Marianas (1944). He wanted to bypass the Philippines and drive straight to Japan, but that prospect appalled MacArthur. In the end, Nimitz's ships carried MacArthur's invasion force to the Philippines, fighting the desperate *Battle of Leyte Gulf* off the central part of the archipelago. Nimitz directed the desperately fought invasions of *Iwo Jima* in February 1945 and *Okinawa* on April 1, 1945. He began planning for all-out invasion of the Japanese home islands, but this became unnecessary with the *atomic bomb* attacks on *Hiroshima* and *Nagasaki* and the Japanese *surrender* on September 2, 1945. Nimitz served as a UN observer in *Kashmir*, 1949–1951.
    Suggested Reading: See his (with E. B. Porter) *Sea Power: A Naval History* (1960).

Nine Power Treaty (1922). Negotiated at the *Washington Conference*, it internationalized the principle of the *Open Door*, at least concerning China. It was signed by all powers with significant Asian interests: Britain, Belgium, China, France, Italy, Japan, the Netherlands, Portugal, and the United States. It guaranteed China's administrative and *territorial integrity* and formally rejected Japan's *Twenty-one Demands*. The treaty was an attempt to make long-standing American principles binding on all major Asian powers (except the Soviet Union, which was absent). Japan subsequently returned the *Shandong* leasehold to China. In 1937, when a conference was called to discuss Japan's direct attack on China, the Japanese contemptuously stayed away, and the conclave solved nothing.

Nine Years' War. *See War of the League of Augsburg.*

Ningxia. A semi-*autonomous* region in north central China, populated mainly by Muslims (hui).

Nitze, Paul (b. 1907). U.S. *Cold War* strategist. During *World War II* he served on the U.S. Strategic Bombing Survey (1944–1946). He was not influential in the early stages of the Cold War, until he succeeded *George F. Kennan* as head of the *State Department's* policy planning staff, 1950–1953. Then he had a major impact, exerted at first through the crucially important policy paper *NSC-68*, which he wrote in 1950 before the start of the *Korean Conflict*. Subsequently, he remained a powerful, hard-line anti-Soviet voice within the inner circles of U.S. policy. He was secretary of the Navy (1963–1967) and deputy secretary of defense (1967–1969). He served on the U.S. delegation to the *Strategic Arms Limitation Talks* (1969–1973) and was assistant secretary of defense (1973–1976). He raised a powerful voice in opposition to *ratification* of SALT II (1979) and subsequently served as President *Ronald Reagan's* chief negotiator of the *Intermediate Range Nuclear Forces (INF) treaty* (1981–1984). In 1984 he became Reagan's special adviser on *arms control*. Even when not in office, he was one of the *Wise Men* who regularly advised presidents of both parties.

Suggested Readings: David Callahan, *Dangerous Capabilities* (1990); John Gaddis, *Strategies of Containment* (1982); Paul Nitze, *From Hiroshima to Glasnost* (1989).

Niue. Formerly called Savage Island. A British *protectorate* from 1900, this *microstate* was annexed to the *Cook Islands* by New Zealand in 1901. Since 1974 it has been *autonomous* in *free association* with New Zealand; its people are also New Zealand *citizens*. In fact, three times as many Niueans live in New Zealand as in Niue. Note: Niue is not a *United Nations* or *Commonwealth* member, nor is it recognized by all states as fully independent.

Nixon Doctrine. A retrenchment from global security commitments, brought about by the *Vietnam War* and *Richard Nixon's* sense that the globalization and militarization of *containment* policy had taken U.S. diplomacy off course. The doctrine established that the United States henceforth would support those fighting local *Communist* movements but would not itself become directly involved in the fighting, and by implication, was prepared to let some minor countries fall to the other side in the *Cold War*. It thus globalized the principle of *Vietnamization* (localization of conflicts, with U.S. support limited to logistics and matériel) then being pursued in Southeast Asia, rejected the *domino theory*, and sought to refocus American resources and attention on the *strategic* regions of Europe and Asia and thus return containment to reliance on the great Western advantages in economic and political *linkage* rather than brute military force.

Suggested Reading: Edward Litwak, *Détente and the Nixon Doctrine* (1984).

Nixon, Richard Milhous (1913–1994). U.S. vice president, 1953–1961; *Republican* president, 1969–1974. As vice president under *Dwight D. Eisenhower*, 1953–1961, Nixon was a prominent international traveler. His most famous trips were to South America in 1958, where he was met by hostile, stone-throwing crowds in Caracas; and to the Soviet Union in 1959, where he took part in a televised "kitchen debate" (it took place in an industrial showplace featuring kitchens) with Premier *Nikita Khrushchev*. They argued over the respective merits of Soviet *communism* and American-style *capitalism* and *democracy*, with Nixon making a strong impression on the folks back home. He was defeated in the extremely close 1960 presidential race by *John F. Kennedy*. He next lost the gubernatorial race in *California*, and his political career appeared to many to be over. Then came the *Vietnam War* and disintegration of the national *Democratic Party*. Nixon secured the 1968 Republican nomination and was elected to serve in the White House.

Working intimately with *Henry Kissinger*, Nixon's immediate aim as president was to wind down the war in Vietnam. He hoped thereby to reorient *containment* policy to its original purpose—blocking Soviet political advances into the key *industrialized* centers of Asia and Europe, with primary reliance on political support and economic inducements to allies rather than direct military force against the Soviet Union or its proxies. Despite a noted career as an anti-Communist, Nixon did not view foreign policy through as colored an ideological prism as many anticipated (and as a few still suggest). Instead, he took a *Realpolitik* approach as often as not. There was an important exception to this, however: Nixon feared losing the war in Vietnam, mainly for what it would mean to him politically, and he also appeared unable to learn from the prior French or American experience in Indochina. That led him to continue and then expand *Johnson's* bombing campaign, and later to widen the ground war into Cambodia and Laos. Convinced that he could end the war in Vietnam without losing it, Nixon stepped-up *Vietnamization* and *pacification* to enable a phased U.S. withdrawal, while conducting simultaneous peace talks with the Democratic Republic of Vietnam (DRV, North Vietnam) in Paris. He understood that he needed cooperation on this from China and the Soviet Union, the only states capable of bringing sufficient pressure to bear on the DRV, to get Hanoi to cooperate in allowing an American pullout. Therefore, Nixon developed *détente* with the Soviets after 1970 and made his extraordinary breakthrough trip to China in 1972. To both he offered the lure of American trade and credits, but conditioned on an acceptable settlement in Vietnam. And taking advantage of the *Sino-Soviet split*, to China he implicitly offered a counterbalance to the regional preponderance of the Soviet Union. Nixon kept up pressure on the DRV by continuing to heavily bomb the north as well as People's Army of Vietnam (PAVN) bases in Cambodia and Laos, and ultimately by invading Laos and Cambodia (1970) to physically cut the *Hô Chí Minh Trail*—actions for which he was severely but not always fairly criticized at the time or since. More problematically, he authorized several new rounds of bombing of DRV cities (Operations Line-backer I and II), including a so-called "Christmas bombing" in 1972, which he claimed forced the DRV back to the peace table in Paris.

Nixon's overall foreign policies of détente with the *Soviet bloc* and *rapprochement* with China were not designed merely to end the Vietnam War, however. They aimed as well at a lasting reduction in tensions with Moscow, and with the Communist world more generally, and at real *arms control* and a limit to Soviet *adventurism* in regional conflicts. He also sought to appease growing Western European (especially West German) demands for a new *Ostpolitik* toward the East bloc. He was a strong supporter of Israel, yet he played tough with Tel Aviv (and Moscow) in the *Fourth Arab-Israeli War*, when the Soviets threatened to intervene directly to support their Egyptian ally. He supported *Reza Pahlavi*, viewing the Shah's Iran as an island of *stability* (it turned into something of an Atlantis in 1979) anchoring the whole Middle East. On economic policy, he shifted from *Keynesian* social spending toward fighting *inflation*, and then *stagflation*, and took the United States off the *gold standard* and raised tariffs in the "*Nixon shocks*" of August 15, 1971. His second term was hamstrung and then destroyed by the *Watergate scandal*. Nixon was the only president to resign (August 9, 1974), which he did to avoid impeachment and likely removal from office. *See also Jackson-Vanik; Nixon Doctrine; SALT I; Shanghai communiqué.*

Suggested Readings: Stephen Ambrose, *Nixon* (1987); Joan Hoff, *Nixon Reconsidered* (1994).

Nixon shocks (August 15, 1971). In the spring of 1971 there was a run on the dollar and the United States first showed a trade deficit. Gold stocks were in decline, and *stagflation* was developing. *Nixon* suddenly announced, without consulting major allies, a new economic policy that radically transformed the international monetary system. He took the United States off the *gold standard*, thereby devaluing the dollar, and imposed a surcharge on all imported goods. Thus ended the *Bretton Woods* era. It came to its close for two main reasons: (1) The fixed *exchange rate* system that had been agreed to in 1944 could not withstand inflationary pressures on the U.S. economy arising from both the *Vietnam War* and *Lyndon Johnson's* expensive "Great Society" social programs. (2) The *strategic* interest that originally gave U.S. leaders the political will to sustain the Bretton Woods system had declined, then disappeared, as Western Europe and Japan achieved economic recovery and emerged as major competitors. *See also International Monetary Fund (IMF).*

Nkrumah, Kwame (1909–1972). *Gold Coast* prime minister, 1957–1960; president of *Ghana*, 1960–1966. He was the best-known African statesman of his time and was a worldwide champion of *decolonization*. He exerted influence over leaders as diverse as *Nyerere* and *Lumumba*. However, he distrusted the surrounding *Francophone* African nations and resented other African leaders as rivals to his own dominance of the continent's news and politics and *pan-African* leadership. Domestically, his regime disintegrated under a weight of corruption and inefficiency that grew apace with Nkrumah's personal megalomania and political repressiveness—a phenomenon masterfully portrayed in Ayi Kwei Armah's novel "The Beautiful Ones Are Not Yet Born" (1968). Nkrumah was overthrown while visiting Hanoi in 1966. He died in a Rumanian sanatorium. *See also OAU.*

NKVD (*Narodnii Kommissariat Vnutrennikh Del*). "People's Commissariat of Internal Affairs." The Soviet *secret police*, 1934–1954, including during the *Yezhovshchina*. Previously, it was known as the *CHEKA* and then as the *OGPU*. In 1954 it was renamed the *KGB*. It was responsible for millions of deaths among the *kulaks* during forced *collectivization*. *See also Lavrenti P. Beria; Comintern; Josef Stalin.*
   Suggested Reading: Robert Conquest, *The Soviet Police System* (1969).

Nobel Prizes. Highly prestigious international awards generated from the estate of Alfred Nobel (1833–1896), a Swedish *munitions* manufacturer who became fascinated by controlled explosions while working in his father's nitroglycerine factory. Nobel made his money from the sale of dynamite and blasting jellies to the mining industry, and of smokeless gunpowder (lyddite, cordite, melinite) to munitions manufacturers. He left a large share of his estate to fund prizes in chemistry, literature, medicine, peace, and physics, granted in most years since 1901. In 1969 a controversial "memorial prize" was added for *economics*. Because economics is not considered by everyone to be a subject that rises much above informed speculation, its deliberately distancing title is "Central Bank of Sweden Prize in Economic Sciences in Memory of Alfred Nobel." Whereas other prizes are awarded only to individuals, singly or with others, the Nobel Prize for Peace also may be given to institutions and organizations. Before *World War I* it was given mainly to parliamentarians and activists in the movement for international *arbitration*. With *World War II* it widened to include advocacy of *human rights* as an underpinning of lasting peace. After 1960 it was more often awarded to persons or organizations beyond the original concentration in North America and Europe, and on a broadened definition of peace that went far beyond attempts to resolve internecine or interstate conflicts. During the first century of granting Nobel peace prizes, 1901–2001, the *United Nations* or associated agencies received the peace prize 14 times. It was reserved (not awarded) 1914–1916, 1918, 1923–1924, 1928, 1932, 1939–1943, 1948, 1955–1956, 1966–1967, and 1972. *See also African National Congress; Amnesty International; Kofi Annan; Oscar Arias; Aung San Suu Kyi; Menachem Begin; Willy Brandt; Aristide Briand; Ralph Bunche; Austen Chamberlain; Winston S. Churchill; Dalai Lama; Fredrik Willem de Klerk; Albert Einstein; famine; "fog of war"; Mikhail Gorbachev; Dag Hammarskjöld; Cordell Hull; International Committee of the Red Cross; Inter-*

national Labor Organization; Frank B. Kellogg; Henry Kissinger; Land Mine Treaty; Lê Đúc Thọ; Nelson Mandela; George C. Marshall; Médecins sans Frontières; Fridtjof Nansen; peacekeeping; Lester B. Pearson; Theodore Roosevelt; Elihu Root; Anwar Sadat; Andrei Sakharov; Sato Eisaku; Alexandr Solzhenitsyn; Gustav Stresemann; United Nations High Commission for Refugees; UNICEF; Lech Walesa; Woodrow Wilson.

Nobunaga Oda (1534–1582). In 1560 this Japanese *warlord* defeated a massive army sent by the Ashikaga *shoguns* against his domain. He then allied with *Ieyasu Tokugawa*. For several decades the *Unification Wars* raged. Nobunaga and Tokugawa defeated their northern enemies at Anegawa (1570). Nobunaga then sought to unify all Japan under his rule, which rallied other *daimyo* against him. He took Kyoto in 1568 but did not claim the shogunate. In 1573 Nobunaga encircled and burned much of Kyoto to punish a rebellious shogun. He then brought pressure on the emperor to resign. At Nagashino (1575) he used a corps of musket men to route his enemies. Nobunaga also ruthlessly persecuted *Buddhists*, crushing their sectarian armies as he had those of the daimyos. Having conquered one-third of Japan by 1582, he was betrayed by a vassal daimyo. Defeated in battle, Nobunaga committed seppuku (ritual suicide by disemboweling). His destruction of Buddhist military power and reduction of provincial fortifications greatly advanced military and political unification of Japan.

no-fly zone. A ban on military, or even all, flights in a given area, enforced by *multilateral* action. Southern and northern Iraq were so designated in 1991 to prevent *Saddam Hussein* from attacking *shi'ites* in the South and *Kurds* in the North. Bosnia was declared a no-fly zone by the UN *Security Council* in October 1992 to prevent the resupply of Serb *militia*. NATO was selected to enforce the zone, its first-ever combat duty.

noise. In *intelligence*, when significant incoming signals picked up by *agents* or a *listening post* cannot be identified due to a blizzard of misleading signals and other information. *See also disinformation.*

nomads. *See Arabs; Aryans; Byzantine Empire; China; Fulbe Empire; Inner Asia; Islam; Mongols; Roman Empire; Sahara Desert; Tamerlane; Tartars; Tuaregs.*

no-man's-land. A *World War I* term for the space between enemy trenches, which neither side controlled, but both patrolled. Pock-marked with millions of shell holes and marked out by dense barbed-wire borders, it was hundreds of sinuous miles long but at most a few thousand yards wide on the *eastern front*, and no more than a few hundred yards wide on the *western front*. It was regarded by troops of all armies with fear and loathing. It was the locale of the greatest exposure to enemy fire once troops went "over the top" of the trenches, toward awful suffering and terrible death. *See also Battle of Loos; trench warfare.*

nomenklatura. "Task-schedulers." Originally, the top 5,000 or so *Communist Party* officials in the *Soviet Union* whose appointment was controlled by the party's central organs. After 1928 that meant they were beholden to *Stalin,* who had used his administrative position to take control of the party, 1924–1928. The most powerful were regional party secretaries who controlled lower levels of the *apparat,* on which the center depended to implement its policies. Later the term came to include all highly placed and privileged members of the bureaucracy, party, and military in all *Soviet bloc* countries.

nonaggression pact. A *treaty* between or among states that is far less than an *alliance,* and instead simply declares that no signatory will attack another. In any given case its reliability is dependent on *good faith.* Some pacts outline *spheres of influence* agreements; others approximate the terms of, and are close synonyms for, *friendship treaties. See also Nazi-Soviet Pact.*

Nonaligned Movement (NAM). A mainly, though not exclusively, *Third World* movement started at *Bandung* in 1955. Its major themes were anti–*colonialism,* opposition to *racism,* and formal *neutrality* toward the *Cold War,* and initially to U.S. efforts to ring the Soviet Union with defensive alliances of Third World states such as *CENTO* and *SEATO.* It brought together those poorer states that wanted to raise economic and social issues onto the agenda of *international organizations,* where larger powers were preoccupied with Cold War security concerns, as in promoting the *NIEO* in the 1970s. It suffered a chronic lack of unity and effectiveness born of the following factors: (1) Some of its members were clearly supporters of either the American or the Soviet camp (the Philippines and Cuba, respectively) and acted as Trojan horses for the agendas of the *superpowers.* (2) Differences in levels of *development,* ideology, and regional animosities among members were too great for the NAM to present a genuinely united negotiating front. (3) The rise of *OPEC* and the southern *NICs* exacerbated these differences and divided the movement over the issue of *oil shocks* and commodity *cartels.* By the early 1990s, with the original purpose of the NAM fading into irrelevance and regional animosities resurfacing, the movement was adrift, even though its shell and form were kept intact by its many members.

nonalignment. From the practice of the *Nonaligned Movement,* a diplomatic stance of not taking sides in a conflict between two formal *alliances,* especially where one involves former colonial powers. Nonaligned states were often quite activist and not necessarily even-handed, sometimes proposing *mediation* and at other times commenting directly and one-sidedly on the merits of disputes during the *Cold War*, whereas traditional neutrals assumed formally balanced and quieter postures. *See also alignment; neutralism; neutrality.*

nonbelligerency. Legal *neutrality* toward a given *war*, whether this sentiment is real or feigned in practice. It is almost more a political than a legal term. *See also Battle of the Atlantic.*

noncombatant. (1) In *international law*, a *neutral* state. (2) In the *just war tradition*, a *civilian*. The distinction between combatants and noncombatants rarely correlates to "guilt" and "innocence" in making war. In the medieval period in Europe, a simple declaration of *guerre mortelle* sufficed to permit slaughter of prisoners, women, and children. The just war tradition sought to make a clear distinction for noncombatants that was subsequently obliterated by the movement toward *total war*. Thus, workers in a munitions or tank factory—even while asleep in their homes with their families—became legitimate targets of ground or aerial bombardment on the logic that they directly contributed to the enemy war effort. *See also air power; carpet bombing; strategic bombing; terrorism; war crimes.*

noncommissioned officer (NCO). An enlisted person ranked above private, but not holding a commission (a certificate of presidential or other formal authority). *See also military ranks.*

noncompliance. Failure by a *state* to observe terms of a *treaty*, *Security Council* resolutions, or some other legal obligation.

nonconcessional loans. *See hard loans.*

noncontraband. *Goods* without military utility (such as vaccines) destined for an enemy port, which may not be seized under the law of *blockade*. *See also contraband.*

nondiscrimination. *See most-favored-nation.*

nongovernmental organizations (NGOs). Private organizations involved in activities that have *transnational* implications or international memberships; for example, *Amnesty International; Greenpeace; Médecins sans Frontières;* or the *Red Cross.* NGOs first importantly appeared on the scene in the nineteenth century, when the Red Cross, international lawyers associations, and early Peace Societies contributed to the drafting of several international conventions on the *laws of war.* They were active again at the *League of Nations* and at the *San Francisco Conference* that formally founded the *United Nations.* By 1990 there were some 6,000 NGOs engaged in international activity, but by 2001 there were more than 26,000. That paralleled developments in many advanced countries. For instance, in the United States there were thought to be more than two million domestic NGOs by the end of the twentieth century. Many NGOs are now comfortably integrated into the daily operation of the *international system* and are increasingly utilized by states to fulfill humanitarian and other functions that they may (and frequently do) perform better than governmental agencies, such as *verification* of *arms control* treaties, technical analysis and other expert study, and *environmental* and *human rights* monitoring. Moreover, by 2001 the majority of all nonmilitary foreign *aid* was delivered in the field by NGOs.

That was not entirely unproblematic. The sheer number of NGOs involved in aid delivery suggested a degree of breakdown of final donor accountability for what was done in the field. From the recipient point of view, NGOs were also seen as potentially far more interventionist, bypassing even local government oversight and policy to promote social and development programs that might be more reflective of the Western values, whether secular or religious, of the NGO's employees than of the recipient society, or at least of its *elite*. Some NGO activities were even said by critics to complicate and prolong violent conflicts, such as involvement in *refugee* relief into whose waiting camps armies might drive unwanted ethnic or religious minorities, or the anti-*slavery* campaign of some NGOs in Sudan that involved buying freedom for some, thereby worsening the overall problem by creating a ready market for slaves. Finally, like any other *bureaucracy*, NGOs have a propensity to *mission creep*, to expand into new areas of concern beyond their original brief and to become self-perpetuating, perhaps beyond the point where their aid and existence are no longer required. *See also* INGO; *nonstate actor*.

noninterference. (1) Respect for the *sovereign* rights of another *state*, in deed and word, as when a *Great Power* so respects the cultural, economic, legal, political, and *territorial* rights of a smaller power. (2) Often used as a euphemism for refusing to become involved in a foreign *dispute*, such as over respect for *human rights*, a *civil war*, or an interstate war that remains localized. *See also Brezhnev Doctrine; Congress system; Good Neighbor policy; Kuranari Doctrine; Monroe Doctrine; nonintervention; Organization of African Unity.*

nonintervention. The legal obligation to abjure involvement in the domestic *jurisdiction* of other *states*. It was significantly advanced as an international norm in the *Peace of Westphalia*, where it served to preserve religious independence from either meddling neighbors or the universal claims of popes and Holy Roman emperors. The *French Revolution* set up a new challenge by endorsing competing views of political *legitimacy* (*republicanism* versus *monarchism* and *absolutism*) that contended in the nineteenth century. Until after the mid-nineteenth century it was restricted in application to "Christian states" or "*civilized states*": the European states intervened at will in coastal Africa and throughout the Americas in the sixteenth through the eighteenth centuries; the Great Powers intervened in *Ottoman* affairs in Greece in 1827, in Lebanon in 1860, and repeatedly after that; they intervened in China and in Japan throughout the second half of the nineteenth century; and they penetrated into the interiors of India and Africa, overrunning dozens of indigenous states, from the eighteenth century onward.

In the twentieth century, just as the principle was expanded to include all states it was also eroded by the rise of *democracies* and *Communist* states to global prominence, as each proclaimed a right to *intervention* based on new and more exclusive interpretations of political *legitimacy*. Concerning *human rights*, claims that particular practices were protected by virtue of being *internal affairs* were routinely rejected by the end of the twentieth century, at least regarding such *basic rights* as freedom from *torture*. However, nonintervention was still respected on most issues that arguably remained a matter of culture or faith. *See also abatement; Brezhnev Doctrine; Comintern; Good Neighbor policy; Holy Alliance; intervention; armed humanitarian intervention; Monroe Doctrine; noninterference; Reagan Doctrine; spheres of influence; Woodrow Wilson.*
Suggested Reading: R. J. Vincent, *Nonintervention and International Order* (1974).

nonjusticiable dispute. An interstate dispute not amenable to settlement by reference to *international law*; a synonym for *political dispute*. *See also justiciable dispute.*

non liquet. A circumstance when the absence of clear *rules* makes it impossible to reach judgment based on the law.

non-offensive defense (NOD). *Jargon* only a military bureaucrat (or perhaps a political scientist) could love or decipher. Essentially, it proposes a *deterrence* policy based on deployment of weapons systems that are incapable of offensive action and are therefore psychologically nonthreatening to others. *See also defensive weapons; dual use; Maginot Line; offensive weapons.*

"non-person." A state of political and social limbo in the post-*Stalinist* Soviet Union, in which purged party members were not killed but disappeared from mention in the Soviet media; sometimes their images were even erased from photographs. Among others, this happened to *Khrushchev* and *Malenkov*. Even *Stalin* disappeared from official view for two decades, but only posthumously, which was not the same thing.

nonproliferation. Curbs on the spread of advanced weapons systems. *See also arms control; ballistic missile defense (BMD); IAEA; Nuclear Non-Proliferation Treaty; Nuclear Suppliers Group; prohibited weapons; proliferation.*
Suggested Reading: Henry Sokolski, *Best of Intentions* (2001).

nonrecognition. *See recognition.*

nonresident ambassador. A peripatetic *diplomat* accredited to more than one foreign capital. Because a person can reside in only one location, such a diplomat therefore travels back and forth to the other capitals. *States* have increasingly turned to this mechanism as a cost-cutting measure in regions where their interests or resources are not deemed sufficient to warrant individual representatives in each country. Some states also have begun to trade information and expertise. For example, Australia and Canada have agreements to exchange nonsecurity information on Asia and Europe, respectively, where each regards the other to be better informed and to have more dedicated resources.

nonstate actor. Any player in international politics that is neither a government nor an organization created by and serving governments, including *nongovernmental organizations* and *multinational corporations*.

nontariff barriers (NTBs). Any mechanism used to protect domestic markets and producers by limiting imports through means other than *excise*. They include *licensing; quotas; voluntary restraint agreements*; procurement policies that favor domestic suppliers; and purposeful obscurity in customs, regulations (especially on health and sanitation), or environmental standards. *See also GATT; Kennedy Round; World Health Organization.*

non-zero-sum game. *See game theory.*

Nordic Council. An association formed in 1952, aiming at a *free trade area* in *Scandinavia*. With the creation of the *European Free Trade Association* and application by Denmark and Norway to join the *European Community*, it evolved into a mainly cultural association. Its members are the *Nordic states*.

Nordic Passport Union. A *passport*-free zone permitting free travel among all five *Nordic states*. In 1995 it negotiated an associated status with the members of the *Schengen* zone.

Nordic states. Denmark, Finland, Iceland, Norway, and Sweden. *See also Scandinavia.*

norm. (1) In moral discourse, a principle or statement of general value. (2) In interstate relations, an accepted *rule* of state conduct that underwrites the workings of a given international *regime*. (3) In *international law*, the complex concept of *jus cogens*. *See also classical school; cosmopolitan values; ethics; justice; human rights.*

normalize relations. To restore formal, if not amicable, *diplomatic relations* after a period of elevated *tensions* over a *dispute* or a *crisis* or after a *war*.

Normal Trade Relations (NTR). A term substituted in 1998 in U.S. trade legislation for the vintage *most-favored-nation* (MFN), which was used for more than 200 years but which after the 1974 *Jackson-Vanik Amendment* was widely misunderstood and even abused, in particular by advocates of *protectionism* or of the imposition of *sanctions* on foreign violators of *human rights*. The status of NTR is, as the name implies, granted to virtually all trading partners; it confirms that most trade will take place on the same terms as are granted to other trading partners. Sometimes called Permanent Normal Trade Relations (PNTR).

Normandy invasion and campaign (June–July 1944). On "D-Day," June 6, 1944, in the greatest amphibious invasion to that point in history (*Okinawa* would later surpass Normandy), the Western *Allies* launched Operation Overlord, secured a beachhead in Normandy, and began to move inland to commence the *liberation* of Western Europe from *Nazi* tyranny and military *occupation*. D-Day began the climactic campaign that ended with defeat of *Nazi Germany* 11 months later and a historic linkup with the *Red Army* in the center of Germany and Europe. The landings were preceded by a series of brilliant ruses by British intelligence that partially deluded *Hitler* about where the troops would hit the beaches. *Montgomery* was put in command of the land forces, with *Eisenhower* as supreme allied commander. The Allies first heavily bombarded the Normandy coast from the sea and air, bombed the French rail and road network the Germans would use to *counterattack*, and put three divisions of *airborne troops* inland to capture strategic junctions and slow the inevitable German counterattack. Then they hit five distinct beaches along 60 miles of coastline. Utah beach fell relatively easily to the Americans, but the G.I.s were mauled on Omaha (most of the nearly 5,000 American casualties on D-Day were taken on Omaha, with just 197 suffered on Utah). British and Canadian troops pressed inland quickly from Sword and Juno beaches, respectively, but the British suffered heavier losses on Gold.

The Allies utilized some 12,000 combat aircraft (including 5,000 fighters) against fewer than 200 planes put up by the once mighty *Luftwaffe*. They also employed 6,500 transport ships (including 4,000 landing craft), and put ashore five full divisions in the first assault waves. By the end of the first day, 23,000 American troops had been landed on Utah alone. Facing the allies was a German beach defense force of just three divisions, supported by a paltry 169 aircraft. However, there were a total of 50 German divisions nearby, and resistance quickly stiffened. As German reinforcements arrived over the next days and weeks, Allied units began to take much heavier casualties. Still, the beachhead was secured and troops and war matériel poured ashore. Within 20 days a full 26 Allied divisions were in Normandy, with another 15 in

England waiting for transport. Fighting then centered on Caen, where the British faced the great bulk of the German armored divisions. *Patton* broke out with the Third Army into Brittany, then headed north, chasing the Germans who were running ahead of his lead units. The British and Canadians then turned south, hoping to trap the Germans at Falaise. Although 60,000 were captured, the gap was closed too late to trap all the German troops, though they left most of their equipment and heavy weapons behind. That caused bitter controversy over Montgomery's performance. A second landing in the south of France completed this prelude to the larger battle to *liberate* France, which preceded a full-scale invasion of Germany itself.

Normans. "Northmen." The Normans were descendants of pagan Scandinavian invaders (*Vikings*) who conquered, settled among, and were later Christianized by and assimilated into the pre-existing Gothic and Frankish peoples of Normandy. In 1066, under William I (1027–1087, "the Conqueror"), they began a lightning conquest of England and Wales, which soon became their new base of power; their descendants still form the core of the hereditary aristocracy of the British Isles. The Normans were empire builders, and for 200 years they were the dominant warrior people of Western Europe. In addition to the conquest of Normandy and of Britain and Ireland, they also pushed the Muslims from Sicily and from Malta, raided the Adriatic coast of the *Byzantine Empire*, and ripped southern Italy from Byzantine control. In the eleventh century, it was mainly Norman knights who led and manned the First *Crusade*. In time, this and other misadventures overstretched their *feudal* military system. They adapted by bringing new social classes to the battlefield to supplement the heavy, armored *cavalry* of the Norman nobility, and armed them with new weapons—notably the famous English longbow. However, even these expansive armies and technological innovations found limits in Scotland (where Edward I encountered *William Wallace* and where his son and grandson were beaten by Robert Bruce) and especially in France in the final years of the *Hundred Years' War* (where Norman armies were beaten back by "The Maid" and the armies of the *Capetian* kings), and Norman power was confined to Britain. *See also Albania; Holy Roman Empire; Kingdom of the Two Sicilies.*

Suggested Readings: Marjorie Chibnall, *The Normans* (2001); David C. Douglas, *The Norman Achievement, 1050–1100* (1969); Jack Lindsay, *The Normans and Their World* (1974).

normative approaches/theory. Those relating to, or derivative from, moral standards, rights and duties; the ethical content of foreign policy and world affairs. *See also classical school; ethics; justice; international society.*

North. (1) The *OECD* nations. (2) The *West* plus Japan. (3) The *Union* during the *American Civil War*. *See also First World.*

North Africa. The northern tier of African *states* comprising the *Arab* and *Berber* peoples of Algeria, Egypt (west of the *Suez Canal*), Libya, Morocco, Tunisia, and Western Sahara.

North America. *Central America*, Canada, Mexico, the United States, and various island attachments.

North American Aerospace Defense Command (NAADC). Founded in 1957 to oversee the *DEW Line*, it is headquartered in the United States but includes integrated Canadian Armed Forces personnel in its command structure. In 1981 the name was changed to NAADC from the original North American Air Defense Command (NORAD). *See also North Warning System.*

North American Air Defense Command (NORAD). *See North American Aerospace Defense Command (NAADC).*

North American Free Trade Agreement (NAFTA). A comprehensive agreement setting up a *free trade area* among Canada, Mexico, and the United States, distinct from the already existing Canada–United States *Free Trade Agreement*. NAFTA aimed at 99 percent *tariff* reduction to be phased in over 15 years, beginning January 1, 1994. It was signed in 1992, but it faced *protectionist* opposition in Canada and the United States (Mexico embraced it) before final acceptance in 1993. It created a free trade area second in combined *GDP* and population only to the *EEA*. Among its key provisions were elimination of all tariffs on automobiles and parts (10 years); phase-out of 100 percent of tariffs on *agricultural* products after 15 years, 94 percent after 10 years, and 57 percent immediately; removal of tariffs on *textiles* within 10 years; and opening up of *foreign direct investment* rules in Mexico, including banking, securities, and insurance. Side agreements set up two commissions with formal powers to impose fines and if necessary curtail trade privileges in cases of violation of environmental, worker health and safety, child labor, or minimum wage laws. In 1993 the *Rio Group* endorsed NAFTA as a step toward a hemisphere-wide trade agreement. In 2001 this initiative led to promises to develop a *Free Trade Area of the Americas (FTAA)*.

North Atlantic Cooperation Council (NACC). It was founded by *NATO* on March 10, 1992, to promote *Confidence and Security Building Measures (CSBMs)*, contacts on civil-military relations, air-traffic coordination, defense conversion, and *peacekeeping*. It involves all NATO and former *Warsaw Pact* states.

North Atlantic Council. Founded in 1949 along with *NATO*, it sits in permanent session, meeting weekly to discuss alliance business. Unlike the *De-*

fense Planning Committee, in which France did not participate between 1966 and 1993, it has always included all NATO members.

North Atlantic Treaty Organization (NATO). One cliché wrapped around a small grain of truth is that NATO was formed to "keep the Soviets out, the Germans down, and the Americans in [Europe]." In 1948 five West European signatories of the *Treaty of Brussels* (Britain, France, and the *BENELUX*) asked for U.S. security assistance and for an *alliance* in which some European members were then concerned as much with *double containment* of Germany as with military insurance for economic and political *containment* of the Soviet Union. The Brussels states joined Canada, Denmark, Iceland, Italy, Norway, Portugal, and, most critically, the United States in signing the North Atlantic Treaty in Washington, D.C., in 1949. Greece and Turkey joined in 1952. West Germany was admitted in 1955, prompting the Soviets to form the *Warsaw Treaty Organization* (WTO). NATO was a major departure by the United States from its historic abstention from *entangling alliances* in peacetime, although it insisted on at least *dual key* control of all strategic weapons and had sole control in most cases. During the *Eisenhower* years, and given the Soviet Union's enormous *conventional weapons* and troop advantages, the emphasis of NATO's *deterrence* policy was on *massive retaliation* with *nuclear weapons*. There was a shift toward *flexible response* under *Kennedy* and to *arms control* and *détente* under *Johnson* and *Nixon*.

France withdrew from the unified command structure in 1966 but remained in the political alliance, tacitly coordinating military policy as well. That crisis prompted the *Harmel Report*. Disputes in the Aegean and between Greece and Turkey over Cyprus forced Greece outside the unified command, 1974–1980. Spain joined in 1982. The end of the *Cold War* brought dramatic changes, starting in 1990 when NATO foreign ministers arranged for the inclusion of a reunited Germany. Moscow approved the plan, but only after the United States made a "gentlemen's agreement" with *Gorbachev* and *Shevardnadze* that NATO would not expand farther east (this was "violated" in 1999 with the admission of three former WTO states). It was then announced by NATO that the Soviet Union was no longer considered a hostile state. In the entire Cold War NATO never fired a shot in anger; however, through its deterrent posture it helped the West win a sustained geopolitical engagement lasting some 40 years. Also in 1990, NATO approved the *London Declaration*. With victory in the Cold War and the subsequent dissolution of the Warsaw Pact, NATO began to redefine its role. At a summit in Rome (November 1991), it elevated liaison with former members of the Warsaw Pact, agreed to develop a "European pillar" to handle regional problems and provide more equitable "burden sharing" with the United States, and endorsed establishment of a *rapid reaction force*. France resumed attendance at meetings of the military committee when *peacekeeping* was the topic, and NATO set up joint task forces with, and placed some of its assets at the disposal of, the *WEU*.

The *Clinton* administration cut U.S. forces in Europe significantly by 1995, to about one-third of 1989 levels, just before NATO undertook its first-ever combat mission: enforcing UN *no-fly zones* in Bosnia. It initially ruled out admitting East European countries to the distant future, instead offering them (and Russia) *partnerships for peace*. In March 1999 NATO admitted as members Poland, the Czech Republic, and Hungary, upsetting many in Russia who believed that an implicit promise not to expand toward the Russian border had been broken. Poland's inclusion, especially, was seen by the United States partly as counterbalancing the tendency of a French-led bloc within NATO to seek security autonomy for Europe outside the alliance. In 1998 NATO approved its first extensive "out-of-area" use of force when it intervened with massive *air power* in *Kosovo*. In response to the *September 11, 2001, terrorist attack* on the United States, for the first time in history NATO invoked Article 5 of its charter, thereby formally asserting that the attack on the United States constituted an attack on all members of the alliance. Thus, quite unexpectedly, did Europe come to the aid and defense of the United States through an alliance structure originally crafted to ensure that American aid would be sent to defend Western Europe. *See also EUROCORPS; first use; neutron bomb; SACEUR.*

Suggested Readings: Michael Brenner, ed., *NATO and Collective Security* (1998); S. Victor Papacosma et al., eds., *NATO After Fifty Years* (2001).

Northeast Asia. China, Japan, the Korean peninsula, Mongolia, Eastern Siberia, Taiwan, and various islands (Sakhalin, the *Ryukyus*, and several small groups). Along with *Southeast Asia*, it forms *East Asia*.

Northeast Boundary Dispute. *See Aroostook War; Webster-Ashburton Treaty (1842).*

Northern Expedition (1926–1928). With Russian arms and advisors, *Chiang Kai-shek* sent several combined armies of *Guomindang* and *Communist* troops from Guangzhou (Canton) against some 34 *warlord* strongholds in north and central China. This cooperation ended with the April 1927 *Shanghai massacres* of Communists in the cities by Chiang, which marked the start of the *Chinese Civil War*. The campaign did not go all Chiang's way: he suffered a serious defeat in July 1927 at Xuzhou. He then reformulated an alliance with warlords sympathetic to a unified republic and moved north again. He clashed directly with Japanese troops in *Shandong* in May 1928, losing badly at Jinan, but by 1928 his forces had captured territory as far north as Shenyang (Mukden). Such overall military success made national unification possible, with the new republican capital relocated to Nanjing. It also removed the common enemy that encouraged the original alliance between the nationalists and Communists and thus intensified the civil war. *See also Lin Biao; Mao Zedong; Zhu Dei.*

Northern Ireland. *See Ulster.*

Northern Marianas Islands. *See Marianas Islands.*

Northern Song dynasty/Liao Empire. *See Song dynasty.*

Northern War, First (1654–1660). *See Treaty of Andrussovo (1667).*

Northern War, Second (1700–1721). *See Great Northern War (1700–1721).*

North, Frederick (1732–1779). Lord North. British prime minister. *See also American Revolution.*

North German Confederation. It was assembled by *Bismarck* after the defeat of Austria in the *Seven Weeks' War.* The old *German Confederation* was broken apart and Frankfurt, *Hanover*, Hess-Cassel, Hesse-Nassau and *Schleswig-Holstein* were *annexed* to Prussia, although they retained limited and formal *autonomy.* The south German states of Baden, Bavaria, and Württemburg were connected by secret treaty, deliberately undercutting creation of a South German Confederation. In 1871 this assemblage was converted into the *Second Reich*, also incorporating the south German states.

North Korea. *See Korea, Democratic People's Republic of.*

North Sea. The waters lying between Britain and Europe, once called the German Ocean. It has been of great strategic importance to Great Britain for centuries, often as a locale of *blockade* of continental enemies. In *World War I* and *World War II* it saw desperate naval warfare. Large deposits of *oil* were discovered on its *continental shelf* in the 1960s. Norway and Britain got the lion's share; Denmark and the Netherlands also gained. An *ICJ* ruling (1969) expanded West Germany's zone. The North Sea has also been the locale of fierce *fishing* disputes.

North-South Disunion (220–589 C.E.). A revolt in North China in 220 C.E. overthrew the *Han Empire* and ushered in the era of the Three Kingdoms. In 220 there were three states in China: Shu Han in the southwest, Wu in the south, and Wei in the north. In 263 Wei absorbed Shu Han and subsequently conquered Wu. China was thus briefly reunified, 280–304, under the Western Jin dynasty. Then it split again on north-south lines until 589, this time into the Six Dynasties centered on Jiankang (Nanjing) in southern China, and the Sixteen Kingdoms of northern China. Into the midst of this political chaos rode barbarian invaders, as much of north and west China was overrun and occupied by older Turkic (Di, Qiang) and new *Mongol* and other hordes (Toba, Xianbei)) from *Inner Asia.* These invaders established their own kingdoms on the Chinese northern plains. Of these, the most important was the *Buddhist* Northern Wei dynasty (386–535), centered on Luoyang. Over time, they became Sinified by the superior civilization of the people they governed. However, the whole Chinese empire was not reunified until the *Sui dynasty* was imposed in 589 following a civil war won by a Xianbei aristocrat from north China, Yan Jian (Wendi).

North-South issues. Economic, cultural, political and, to some extent, security issues salient in relations between the *OECD* nations and the *Third World*. *See also aid; apartheid; debt crisis; decolonization; distributive justice; ECOSOC; G-77; GATT; International Bank for Reconstruction and Development (IBRD); International Monetary Fund (IMF); intervention; Lomé Conventions; NIEO; nonproliferation; stabilization program; UNCTAD; UNDP; UNGA.*

North Vietnam. *See Vietnam.*

North Warning System. An early-warning radar system, mostly automated, stretching from *Alaska* to *Newfoundland*. It is jointly operated by the United States and Canada. It was phased in between 1988 and 1993 and replaced the old *DEW Line*.

Northwest Frontier. The Pacific territories of North America were under constant dispute among Britain, Russia, and the United States during the first three-quarters of the nineteenth century. American and Russian claims to *California* were settled in a 1825 *convention*, and the United States purchased *Alaska* from Russia in 1867. The Northwest Frontier question exacerbated relations with Britain until the *Oregon Territory* settlement. It was finally put to rest with the *Treaty of Washington* (1870).

Northwest Passage. The frigid, dangerous passage from the Pacific to the Atlantic that runs through the Arctic Ocean above Canada. Before construction of the *Panama Canal* it was sought out by several mapping expeditions—not all of whose members survived—including several sent out by the *Hudson's Bay Company*. Its extremely harsh conditions and massive pack ice problem make it only marginally useful for commercial carriage. During the *Cold War* the U.S. insisted it was an *international waterway* and on occasion sent surface ships through it to maintain the claim. Canada counterclaimed the area as *internal waters*. American (and Soviet) *submarines* simply ignored the whole dispute by remaining submerged beneath the pack ice.

Norway. This Scandinavian nation was a *Viking* domain from the ninth century, interacting violently with other Viking states and exploring and settling or conquering (or both) Iceland, the Shetland Islands, the Orkneys, Scotland, northern England, northern France (where they and other Norsemen founded a great *Norman* state), and much of the Baltic region. Most Norwegians converted to *Christianity* as a result of contact with the already Christianized peoples they encountered in Western Europe, including English and Irish *missionaries*. Norway, Denmark, and England became embroiled in a recurring struggle in the eleventh century, culminating in the Norman invasion and conquest of Saxon England in 1066. The twelfth century witnessed Norway's progressive incorporation into the mainstream of life in the *res publica Christiana*, and the thirteenth century ushered in a Norwegian renaissance and expansion to Iceland and Greenland. In 1319 Norway and Sweden joined in a *union of crowns* under Magnus VII and, after a bitterly disputed succession, also with Denmark under Margaret I in a great northern compact known as the *Union of Kalmar*. Norway was for the next 400 years essentially a province of Denmark.

The *Protestant Reformation* arrived in the sixteenth century, otherwise Norway developed as part of the Danish kingdom until the upheaval all through Scandinavia of the *Great Northern War* (1700–1721). Norway was severed from Denmark during the *Napoleonic Wars*, gaining *autonomy* in 1807. With the defeat of Denmark (*Napoleon's* ally), it was attached to Sweden in 1814 by the *Great Powers* at the *Congress of Vienna*. During the nineteenth century it remained linked to Sweden via a personal *union* but enjoyed considerable *autonomy*. In 1905 it split peacefully from Sweden, and a Danish prince became its king (Haakon VII). It was neutral during *World War I*, although *Fridtjof Nansen* played a prominent international role during and especially after the war. In *World War II*, it was attacked by Germany in April 1940, in a complete surprise aided by Norwegian *Nazis* who served as *fifth columnists*. A British force that landed at Narvik was badly beaten by the Germans and pulled out when *Hitler* invaded France later that summer. Norwegian *partisans* kept up resistance to the Germans and the puppet regime of the traitor *Vidkun Quisling*.

The monarchy returned on *liberation* in 1945. In 1947 Norway joined in the *European Recovery Program*. It was a charter member of NATO in 1949. It joined the European Free Trade Association (EFTA) in 1960. It was admitted to the *European Community* in 1972 but declined membership after a *referendum*. During the 1980s it engaged in disputes with Britain and the Soviet Union over marine pollution and fishing. *Gro Harlem Bruntland* was prime minister for much of the 1980s and 1990s. In 1993 Norway received widespread criticism for a decision to resume *whaling*, but it also received praise for its use of *good offices* in brokering a peace agreement between Israel and the *PLO*. In 1994 Norwegians again voted against European Union membership.

Suggested Readings: Gwyn Jones, *A History of the Vikings* (1968, 2001); Ivar Libék and Øivind Stenersen, *A History of Norway from the Ice Age to the Age of Petroleum*, 3rd rev. ed. (1999).

note. *See diplomatic note; ultimatum.*

notification. When one state informs another state of some legally relevant fact, such as its intent not to renew a *treaty*, or an alteration in its interpretation of an extant agreement. *See also nullification.*

notoriety. A mostly archaic but once widespread international legal concept that pointed to publicity attendant on *occupation* of a *territory* preparatory to acquisition of title.

Novotný, Anton (1904–1975). President of Czechoslovakia, 1957–1968. He was a hard-line *Communist* whose repression and ineptitude in running (ruining actually) the economy did much to generate the opposition, which flowered into the *Prague Spring.* He directly provoked that crisis by calling in the army to repress peaceful demonstrations in February 1968. When it refused his orders, he resigned.

n-person game. *See game theory.*

NPT. *See Nuclear Non-Proliferation Treaty.*

NSC. *See National Security Council.*

NSC-68. *See National Security Council Directive #68.*

Nubia. The large *sudanic* region of the upper Nile Valley. It was politically and economically connected to *Egypt* for two millennia before the *Muslim* conquest of Egypt, sometimes as a province but sometimes (as the Kingdom of Kush), itself overrunning Egypt in the first two millennia B.C.E. Under the Pharaohs, Nubia was colonized to above the second cataract of the Nile, c. 2000–1780 B.C.E. In the eleventh century B.C.E. Egypt was disturbed by civil wars and dynastic succession disputes, and Nubia became independent as the Kingdom of Kush (the exact origins and makeup of the dynasty are unknown). In the eighth century B.C.E. Kush conquered Egypt and governed it, 770–666 B.C.E., until Egypt was conquered by the Assyrians. Kush then retreated southward along the Nile to a new capital at Meroe. This Egyptianized but also distinctly African kingdom was one of the first sizable states of Africa. Nubia left a legacy of kingship and state-building that permeated Nilotic civilization immediately south of Egypt for many centuries. Some scholars believe that it may have been a significant conduit for *diffusion* of *technology* and ideas about divine monarchy from the Mediterranean world into more distant parts of Africa beyond Kush and Nubia, though others argue that it remains possible that divine kingships systems developed on parallel lines farther south, as they did in many other human societies.

Much of the trade between Nubia and Egypt was in human cargoes, especially after Nubia was invaded by Arabs flush with the first generation of zealotry for *Islam*, 641–642 C.E. It was not conquered, but it henceforth faced constant border warfare and slave-raiding into its territories. A Christian kingdom in northern Nubia, with its capital at Dongola, made a treaty with Egypt in the seventh century to pay an annual *tribute* of slaves, for which it received corn and horses from Egypt. In short, as was the case in many ancient tributary systems, tribute concealed what was really an active trade. In addition, the Fatamid *caliphs* of Cairo regularly raided into Nubia and took from it more black slaves. In 1340 Dongola collapsed, and Arab slavers poured into Nubia. The medieval *Christian* kingdom of *Alwa* was located in southern Nubia. In the tenth century it was still able to keep Arab slavers from its borders, but it was pushed farther south by a Mamluk army in 1316. Afterward a new pressure existed throughout Nubia, as over time it became a primary source of the Arab *slave trade* to the Middle East and India, while still exporting slaves to *Mamluk* Egypt. From the thirteenth century Nubia as a whole was increasingly attached to Egypt as alternately a weak province or *frontier* area, although petty states existed there. Northern Nubia was known to the *Ottomans* as Berberistan. *See also Sudan.*

Suggested Reading: Adams, W. Y., *Nubia: Corridor to Africa* (1977).

nuclear deterrence. Preventing a nuclear attack by an adversary who also possesses *nuclear weapons* by threatening *retaliation* in kind, which will produce levels of unprecedented and unacceptable destruction on the territory of the attacking power. An emerging problem in the theoretical literature and in policy is that most thinking about nuclear deterrence done during the *Cold War* assumed an effectively *bipolar* nuclear world. Adjustments must now be made to the reality of multiple nuclear powers and the additional fact that in some areas (such as South Asia), the opposing sides may have assembled enough weapons to do vast damage to each other but too few to utterly destroy the other side, and thus perhaps not enough to deter through a *balance of terror*. *See also Assured Destruction; ABM Treaty; ballistic missile defense; credibility; deterrence; first strike; humane deterrence; opportunism;* qui desiderat pacem, praeparet bellum; *retaliation; second strike; submarines. war-avoidance strategy.*

Nuclear Non-Proliferation Treaty (NPT). Signed on July 1, 1968; in force from March 1970. It aimed at limiting *nuclear weapons* to a finite number of states, specifically the five long-standing *nuclear weapons states* that at the time the treaty was drafted had publicly acknowledged having such weapons: the United States, the Soviet Union, Britain, France, and China. The latter two at first refused to sign, but the others undertook not to help additional states acquire such weapons. The nonnuclear states signing and ratifying the NPT agreed, in turn, not to openly or secretly seek to acquire nuclear weapons or weapons-related materials and technology and to permit *IAEA* inspections of their civilian nuclear facilities. South Africa secretly built six weapons in the 1980s but then destroyed them, signed the NPT, and joined the IAEA in 1991. China and France joined the system in 1992. Ukraine, Belarus, and Kazakhstan, which became nuclear weapons states in fact with the dissolution of the Soviet Union, also agreed to be bound by the rules of the nonproliferation *regime*. Ukraine did so even though, for a time, it indicated an interest in retaining some of its weapons.

Iraq was found in violation of the treaty in 1991, following IAEA weapons inspections after the *Gulf War*. North Korea shocked the system by threatening to withdraw, giving the required six-months notice on March 12, 1993, just before an IAEA inspection deadline. It recanted "provisionally," then again refused cooperation. In January 1994, it agreed to the principle of *continuity of safeguards*, then refused inspections. Until Iraq showed that the old inspection regime was inadequate, the IAEA could visit only declared sites. In 1991 it was given new powers and thereafter could—in theory, at least—make special inspections of NPT states, including of research and production sites that were undeclared. However, attempting to use those powers was precisely what provoked North Korea's animosity toward the NPT. The greatest threat to the NPT arose in South Asia. From the outset, India criticized the perpetual nuclear monopoly the NPT sought to freeze in place and was the first nation to openly defy the regime. It exploded what its official press release called a "peaceful nuclear device" in 1974. In the land of *Mohandas Gandhi*, at first one did not say one had built an *atomic bomb*, even when one had. India never accepted the NPT system, although for another 24 years it maintained the fiction that it was not a nuclear weapons state. In 1998 India openly broke with the NPT when it test-detonated five nuclear weapons. That provoked its vigorous subcontinental rival, Pakistan, to do likewise. Nevertheless, the official nuclear weapons states refused to grant either South Asian nation formal status under the treaty, without them also accepting its full *verification* regime, which they were not prepared to do.

nuclear parity. *See essential equivalence; strategic nuclear parity.*

nuclear proliferation. *See proliferation.*

nuclear reactor (Osiraq, Iraq), attack by Israel (June 7, 1981). Israel fighter-bombers destroyed the Iraqi Tammuz 1 (Osiraq) nuclear reactor near Baghdad, the first—and only, to date—such direct attack on a state's nuclear facilities. None of the 16 Israeli aircraft involved in the attack were lost. The intention was to delay or forestall *Saddam Hussein's* acquisition of *nuclear weapons*. Israel regarded the Iraqi reactor and the nuclear weapons program it supported as a direct threat to its *national security* and justified the attack as permissible under *Article 51* of the *United Nations Charter*. The *Security*

Council condemned the attack. Even the United States was (publicly) equivocal, given that it was then supporting Iraq in the *Iran-Iraq War*. Iraq subsequently used *highly enriched uranium* to make weapons-grade material and dispersed and concealed its nuclear weapons program, as post–*Gulf War* weapons inspections revealed. Note: The *IAEA* inspected the Iraqi reactor in January 1981, without discovering Hussein's weapons program. Later realization at just how easily the IAEA's *verification* regime had been circumvented led to reform of inspection protocols. However, confidence remains low in the IAEA's ability to ferret out a nuclear weapons program that a given state or regime is determined to keep secret.

nuclear reprocessing. The process of separating nuclear spent fuel from fissile material. *See also plutonium.*

Nuclear Suppliers Group (NSG). Established in 1993, this informal association of most (excluding China) major suppliers of nuclear industry materials and equipment voluntarily banned all trade in such supplies with nonnuclear states that did not respect international ("full-scope") safeguards against *proliferation*. This went beyond the extant *NPT* ban on aiding in research or construction of *nuclear weapons*, to include potential *dual use technology* and even civilian reactor fuel, although in 1995 the NPT members also agreed to this ban. *Verification* of compliance is difficult, however, and perhaps impossible.

nuclear test ban. *See Partial Test Ban Treaty.*

nuclear umbrella. *See extended deterrence.*

nuclear war. A war fought with *nuclear weapons*, either besides or in lieu of *conventional weapons*. *World War II* was principally a conventional conflict but it ended as the first nuclear war, with atomic attacks on *Hiroshima* and *Nagasaki*. There have been many crises where the use of such weapons was a real possibility. Several occurred between the United States and the Soviet Union; others took place between the United States and China, and two serious, near-nuclear crises took place between the Soviet Union and China. India and Pakistan also may have come close to a nuclear exchange over *Kashmir* at various times. Nuclear confrontation also occurs on the Korean peninsula and in the Middle East, where some pairings of states (not necessarily host countries) possess nuclear weapons.

nuclear weapons. These come in many forms: bombs, *land mines*, *depth charges*, *missile* or *artillery* shell *warheads*, and nonexplosive *radiological weapons*. *Atomic* and *hydrogen bombs* are first- and second-generation nuclear weapons. They range from tactical battlefield devices with lower *yields* to massive hydrogen bombs many times more destructive than the weapon dropped on *Hiroshima*. Third-generation weapons include *neutron bombs*, which have been designed, built, and stockpiled, but not deployed, by the United States, and by 2001 were also under construction or secretly deployed by China. Fourth-generation weapons likely will include *charged particle beams* that channel for destruction the elemental products of nuclear explosions. The mere existence, let alone potential use, of such weapons dominated the mass psychology of the *Cold War* and greatly influenced the calculations of policymakers. Yet, in and of themselves such weapons may have had little to do with its outcome, other than to allow it to be determined by other means: the Cold War was decided largely by the economic and technological success of the West and corresponding stagnation of the *Soviet bloc* and by the triumph of free market and liberal-democratic ideas over a desiccated *Marxist* ideology and the fatal flaws of a *command economy*. As *Winston Churchill* said of the surfeit of nuclear weapons, "all they are going to do is make the rubble bounce."

A longer view is also illustrative: In the 1950s states newly acquiring nuclear weapons (Britain, France) did so primarily to balance power, support their claims to international *prestige,* and maintain the international status quo through *deterrence*, as conventional offense and defense alike became less viable and acceptable options. Moreover, nuclear weapons were a stabilizing force in world affairs at a time when Great Power hostilities (United States–Soviet Union, Soviet Union–China) were at such extreme levels that, under nonnuclear conditions, they likely would have led to war. By c. 1980 many states seeking to newly acquire nuclear weapons wanted them to upset rather than sustain some regional status quo, and perhaps also one day to use them against hated religious, ethnic, or regional enemies. Nuclear weapons thus appeared to become a source of grave regional, and more general international, insecurity and instability. On the other hand, and contrary to analytical fears and much popular perception alike, the evidence after a half century of living with the atomic bomb was that the introduction of such weapons to regional conflicts tended to sober national leaders and lead over time to progressive abatement of regional warfare. This was true in South Asia, where India and Pakistan began to experiment with agreement-to-disagree peaceably over Kashmir in the late 1990s, and in the Middle East, where suspicion of Israel's possession of hundreds of nuclear weapons ended public calls for its utter destruction by all but the most radical and marginal Arab leaders. *See also Assured Destruction; ballistic missile defense (BMD); IAEA; ICBM; limited nuclear war; Manhattan Project; Minatom; near-nuclear states; Nuclear Non-Proliferation Treaty; nuclear deterrence; nuclear states; Nuclear Weapons Free Zone; Peenemünde; plutonium; SALT; SDI; START.*

Suggested Readings: George F. Kennan, *Nuclear Delusion* (1982); Michael Mandelbaum, *The Nuclear Revolution* (1981); Richard Rhodes, *Dark Sun: The Making of the Hydrogen Bomb* (1995).

nuclear weapons–free zones (NWFZs). Regions where *nuclear weapons* are banned by international agreement and that ostensibly are "nuclear free": Antarctica, the South Pacific, Latin America, Southeast Asia, the ocean floor, and space. Of course, not all states respect or even acknowledge the legality of such bans. Also, some agreements ban transit by nuclear weapons transports, but others do not. Some municipal governments, including in *NATO* countries, declared themselves local "nuclear-free zones," often in defiance of national policy. Unlike state-to-state agreements, such local posturing has no standing whatever in *international law* or *diplomacy* and almost certainly no real meaning beyond emotional gratification. *See also* the *Antarctic, Outer Space, Seabed, Rarotonga,* and *Tlatelolco* treaties; *ZOPFAN.*

nuclear weapons states. States admitting to building and/or stockpiling or possessing *nuclear weapons*: United States (1945); the Soviet Union (1949), briefly succeeded by Belarus, Kazakhstan, and Ukraine (1991–1996); and by Russia (1991–); Britain (1952); France (1960); China (1964); India (1974), which tested one bomb, but claimed for the next 24 years not to have any more in stock; South Africa (1979) admitted that it had built six bombs starting in 1979 but had dismantled these before signing the *Nuclear Non-Proliferation Treaty* in 1991. By 1996 the post–Soviet Union nuclear arsenals inherited by Belarus, Kazakhstan, and Ukraine were all dismantled or physically surrendered to Russian control and U.S. inspection. In May 1998, India and Pakistan demonstrated their de facto status as nuclear weapons states by each detonating five nuclear weapons, though they were denied legal recognition as nuclear weapons states under the NPT, a status that remained reserved to the original five nuclear powers. Israel has been a de facto, though officially secret, nuclear power since c. 1967. The number of nuclear weapons controlled by various states has varied greatly. In 1947 the U.S. nuclear monopoly probably amounted to possession of no more than seven bombs. By 1948 the United States had perhaps 25 *atomic bombs,* and maybe 50 by 1949, the year the Soviet Union first acquired nuclear weapons. At the height of the Cold War the United States and Soviet Union each had arsenals of about 30,000 nuclear weapons of all types. *See also near-nuclear states.*

"nuclear winter." The thesis proposed by some scientists, and given wide publicity during the 1980s, that an all-out nuclear exchange between the *superpowers* would raise such an amount of dust and debris into the upper atmosphere that enough sunlight would be blocked to cause rapid global cooling, with a consequent dearth of plant life and breaking of the food chain, an effect roughly comparable to that theorized for a large asteroid impact. Other scientists countered that the result would more closely approximate a "nuclear autumn," such as is occasionally produced by large volcanic eruptions, which may equal several hundred atomic explosions and expel vast amounts of ash and dust into the upper atmosphere, bringing about a brief cooling of the planet but not inducing long-term climate change. In either case, much public opinion in the West in the 1980s embraced the notion as an inducement to nuclear *disarmament*. Governments were more skeptical.

nulla poena sine lege. "No punishment without a prior law." *See also* nullum crimen sine lege; *Nuremberg war crimes trials.*

null hypothesis. A proposition in which no relation among *variables* is specified, in contrast with one's working *hypothesis*, in which such a relation has been specified. *See also falsification.*

nullification. (1) In *international law*: cancellation of a *treaty*, or of a less formal interstate understanding; this is different than *notification*. (2) In U.S. history: an extreme *states' rights* doctrine holding that the individual states of the American *union* had the power to declare "null and void" any federal law based on powers not expressly listed in the U.S. Constitution as adhering to the federal government, which the states therefore might reasonably deem unconstitutional. This "compact theory" of the nature of the union of 1789 was a major issue at stake in the *American Civil War*, alongside *slavery*. The Civil War decided the matter, by force of arms rather than by reasoned judgment, in favor of the "implied powers" doctrine that subsequently dominated U.S. legal theory and political history. *See also Andrew Jackson.*

nullity of judgment. Some circumstances render void a *judgment* by an international court, such as *error* or *excess of authority*.

nullum crimen sine lege. "Where there is no law, there is no crime." A legal maxim held by some to have been violated by the procedures and charges brought at the *Nuremberg* and *Tokyo war crimes trials*. *See also* nulla poena sine lege.

nullum crimen sine poena. "No crime without punishment." A controversial, even mischievous, maxim promoted by the *Soviet bloc*. It was not widely accepted by states, and even less so among legal thinkers.

nuncio. "Apostolic Pro Nuncio." An *ambassador* (permanent representative) of the pope. This is the title peculiar to use by papal—after the *Lateran Treaty* of 1929, *Vatican*—ambassadors since at least the Italian *Renaissance*. The original nuncios were messengers without *diplomatic powers* to negotiate, and the term was widely used by secular powers in the Italian *city-state* system of the fifteenth century, as well as by the popes. If the papal ambassador is a cardinal rather than an archbishop, the title is simply "nuncio."

Nuremberg (*Nürnberg*) Laws. A series of decrees against the Jews announced at the 1935 *Nuremberg Rally*. They were later enacted by unanimous vote of the rubber-stamp, Nazi-controlled *Reichstag*. They stripped German Jews of all civil rights; forbade Jews from entering or practicing the professions (a decree welcomed by more jealous doctors, judges, lawyers, and academics eager for promotion than those professions yet feel comfortable admitting); and declared illegal all sexual intercourse or marriage between Jews and "*Aryans.*" This enforcement of a two-class citizenship system in Germany was just the beginning of the process of dehumanization that ultimately led to the *death camps* of the *Holocaust*. The 1935 laws were followed by hundreds of *anti-Semitic* decrees up to 1943, when the mere presence of a Jew in Germany was decreed a crime instantly punishable by death. *See also Roma.*

Nuremberg (*Nürnberg*) Rallies. Mass propaganda festivals held by the *Nazis* in and around the football stadium in Nuremberg, 1933–1938. They were famous for their torchlight parades, trumpet fanfares, and pagan extravagance; and for careful concentration on bending the young to the Nazi message. Many Germans later remembered them as thrilling events that evoked a sense of oneness with the *nation*. They culminated weeks of cultural and sports activities, including Wagnerian music festivals, athletic competitions, air shows, hiking, and other seemingly innocuous—but always Nazi-inspired and controlled—events. They gave full reign to the frustrated artistic longings of *Adolf Hitler* and revealed that he did indeed have a certain genius for political design and stagecraft. *See also Nuremberg war crimes trials.*

Nuremberg (*Nürnberg*) war crimes trials (1945–1947). The *United Nations alliance* set up a War Crimes Commission in 1943 in London and warned in the Moscow Declaration (October 30, 1943) of postwar retribution to come for the atrocities being committed by the *Nazis* inside occupied Europe. After the war, the *Allies* chose Nuremberg for the trials specifically because it had been the scene of the *Nuremberg Rallies* and the planned future capital of the Nazi state. American, British, French, and Soviet judges (that is, the main victors in Europe in *World War II*) sat in judgment of Austrians and Germans accused of *crimes against humanity*, *crimes against peace*, and *war crimes*. Of 177 tried, 142 were convicted and 35 acquitted. Of the convicted, 97 received varied sentences, 20 were given life sentences, and 25 "major criminals" were condemned to death. Two, including *Göring*, would cheat the hangman by committing suicide. Martin Borman was tried *in absentia*; in fact, he was already dead, but this was not known at the time. In addition, six "corporate accused" were cited as criminal organizations. The German *General Staff* and the *Sturmabteilung* were tried but were found not to be criminal organizations. The leadership corps of the *Nazi Party*, the *Schutzstaffel (SS)*, the *Sicherheitsdienst (SD)*, and the *Gestapo* were all convicted, and those organizations were deemed to be criminal enterprises, permitting the arrest of any member, on that basis alone, as a participant in a criminal organization guilty of crimes against humanity. The trials and executions were criticized in some legal circles as an example of *victor's justice* and as not being supported by the *international (public) law* of the time. Others counter, and most plainfolk appear to believe, that even if that is true, it was justice. *See also denazification; Karl Dönitz; Hans Frank; Rudolf Hess; Alfred Jodl; Krupp family*; nulla poena sine lege; nullum crimen sine lege; Joachim von *Ribbentrop*; *Albert Speer*; *superior orders; Tokyo war crimes trials.*

Suggested Readings: Airey Neave, *Nuremberg* (1978); Telford Taylor, *Anatomy of the Nuremberg Trials* (1992).

Nurgaci (1559–1626). A dynamic tribal leader who united the Jürchen clans of *Manchuria* into a martial culture and state. He instituted major military reforms (the *banner system*), including mass *conscription* which greatly enhanced Manchu military power, and incorporation of *artillery* in an effective system of *combined arms*. Once a *Ming* vassal, in 1610 he shook off this designation and in 1616 he proclaimed himself "khan" and his expanding domain an empire (Later Jin), modeled on the Manchu Jin (Golden) Empire, which had ruled northern China, 1122–1234. He then launched a prolonged war against the Ming, absorbing into his forces many Ming soldiers who surrendered and who were made to shave their foreheads and adopt the characteristic Manchu "queue" as an act of submission. In 1625 Nurgaci set his capital at Shenyang (Mukden). He was defeated the next year by a Ming counterattack while trying to invade China across the *Great Wall*. However, his eighth son (Hong Taiji) and later heirs conquered Inner Mongolia (1632), made Korea a *tributary* state (1638), and succeeded in establishing Manchu (*Qing*) rule over all China (1644 and after).

Nyasaland. Former name of the British Central African Protectorate, later *Malawi. See also Federation of Rhodesia and Nyasaland.*

Nyerere, Julius (1922–1999). Tanzanian statesman. He was active in the independence movement in *Tanganyika*, becoming prime minister in 1961. In 1964 he oversaw Tanganyika's *union* with *Zanzibar* and became president of the new nation of *Tanzania*. He championed *pan-Africanism* as well as a relatively humane nationalism. He developed a variant of *social democracy* called "*African socialism*" based on historic communal property patterns, which he laid out in the *Arusha Declaration* of 1967. He had many admirers in the West, including among aid agencies, who pointed to his emphasis on *self-reliance* and grass-roots rural development. He became an articulate international spokesman for a *basic needs* approach to Africa's development problems. He also had critics, however, who pointed to his less-than-stellar *human rights* record, and then during the 1970s to the worsening performance of the Tanzanian economy, even on a relative basis. On the other hand, surrounded by regional conflicts, he kept Tanzania relatively peaceful. He thus became a leader of the *frontline* states in their opposition to *apartheid* and to the *Unilateral Declaration of Independence (UDI)* in Rhodesia. He was a harsh critic, within the *Commonwealth*, of Britain's refusal to impose comprehensive *sanctions* on South Africa. Yet he was forced by geographical and economic reality to deal with the apartheid regime. He was one of a handful of African leaders to grant *recognition* to *Biafra*. He authorized a shift from *hot pursuit* of Ugandan troops who crossed Tanzania's border into an outright invasion that overthrew *Idi Amin*; for that he was heavily criticized within the *OAU* but much praised in the *West*. However, he followed up by reinstalling Milton Obote in power, which proved a disaster for Uganda and led to a prolonged civil war and much bloodshed and suffering. On his retirement in 1985 many of his domestic programs were overturned as Tanzania moved toward a *market economy*. Nyerere had the rare decency and grace to concede that he had been wrong on most economic matters. In 1993 the old man was called back to mediate a serious constitutional dispute between *Tanganyika* and *Zanzibar*.

Nystad, Treaty of (1721). This settlement ended the Russian-Swedish portion of the *Great Northern War* (1700–1721). Sweden ceded and confirmed *Peter I's* (Russia's) possession of Ingermanland, Livonia, Estonia, part of Karelia (Viborg), and certain islands. Sweden retained the province of Finland, from which Russia was required to evacuate its army of *occupation*. Other clauses in the treaty concerned *free trade*, freedom of religion, extradition of criminals, *diplomatic relations*, and other more minor matters.

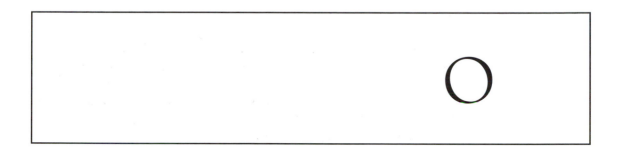

OAS. *See* Organization de l'armée secrèt; *Organization of American States.*

OAU. *See Organization of African Unity.*

obiter dictum. A judicial opinion not essential to a decision. *See also* stare decisis.

object (in international law). Any person or thing, such as a ship, plane, or firm, that is not a *state* or otherwise does not enjoy the status of an *international personality*, yet is regulated under *international law. See also flag of convenience; subject.*

objectivity. In the social sciences and in *history*, objectivity springs from conscious emotional, intellectual, and personal detachment from the facts in order to permit them to "speak for themselves." Of course, that is precisely what facts never do. Historical, political, and economic statements and assumptions are laden with the values of observers and analysts, even those who honestly strive for detachment rather than merely make a humbug bow in its general direction. This problem is a by-product of the inherent uncertainty of knowledge in these fields. "If you would know history, know the historian" is also sound advice concerning *economics* and *political science*. In the final analysis, the best guard against subjective distortion masquerading as objective truth is a critical intelligence and skeptical, but not cynical, attitude toward intellectual authority (including any pale authority imputed to entries in this work). In sum, one must strive to remain aware of the issues and prejudices of one's own moment and to uncover those of the times in which a given historian—or economist, or political scientist—lived and wrote, since these greatly influence interpretation. That does not mean that objective truth is impossible. It does mean that it is hard to attain, however, and that it must never be assumed. *See also critical theory; paradigm; positivism; postmodernism; relativism.*

obscurantism. Deliberate obscurity in speech or writing. This pernicious disease breeds in academe. It is often carried by professors and has been known to be communicable to bureaucrats, journalists, politicians, and students. It is advisable to keep exposure to a bare minimum. Note: Infection may be warded off through exercise—of a sense of humor. *See also critical theory; jargon; postmodernism; rational choice theory; theory.*

obscuritas pacti nocet ei qui apertius loqui potuit. "When there is ambiguity in a *treaty*, it works against the party that could have been more clear."

observation. An older term for *reconnaissance*, as in "observation balloon" or "observer corps."

observer mission. An international team with reporting powers alone, sent in to observe compliance with a given agreement such as a *cease-fire*. First instituted by the *League of Nations*, they have become a fairly common feature of *multilateral diplomacy*. *See also good offices; human rights; mediation; peacekeeping.*

observer status. A level of formal participation in meetings of *international organizations* below that of full dues-paying member, without voting rights. This status is sometimes accorded to accommodate *nonstate actors* in which the members have an interest, as when the *Palestine Liberation Organization* and *Amnesty International* were granted participatory rights by the United Nations. It is also a means to allow states to consider easing into full membership over time, as in the case of Papua New Guinea and Vietnam within *ASEAN*. It is sometimes used to permit important nonregional states to participate in regional organizations, such as allowing the United States to attend the *Berlin Conference* or Japan to attend meetings of the *OSCE*. It has also been extended to some international organizations by others. Thus, the *Commonwealth* was granted observer status by the *United Nations General Assembly* in 1976. *See also associated states.*

Occam's razor. Named for the English scholastic William of Occam (d. 1349?), this tight principle of argument suggests that the assumptions underlying an explanation ought not be multiplied beyond necessity. *See also parsimonious theory.*

occupation. (1) Physical control of part, or the whole, of an enemy's *territory* by military means. (2) Acquisition of legal title to a territory, by virtue of effective and sustained possession. *See also resistance; Spratly Islands; war crimes; war treason.*

occupation zone. An area of one state controlled by the military forces of another. This is a temporary situation occurring after *defeat* in a war (e.g., the Four Power divisions of Germany and Austria and U.S. occupation of Japan after *World War II*) or pending a *peace treaty* and restoration of an acceptable, to the occupier, local authority.

occupied territories. (1) In *international law: Territories* of one *state* controlled by a foreign military, but not *annexed.* (2) In the *Middle East:* The Arab lands captured by Israel but not annexed: the *Sinai* (since returned to Egypt), *Gaza,* and the *West Bank.* The *Golan Heights* were annexed by Israel, but in April 1993 Tel Aviv suggested it might return this area to Syria in exchange for a secure peace. *See also self-governing territories.*

occupying power. Any state whose army takes physical possession of a *defeated* or otherwise invaded state, but that does not (at least overtly) intend *annexation* or otherwise to extinguish the occupied state, such as the *Allies* in Austria, Italy, Germany, and Japan after *World War II. See also laws of war.*

Oceania. An alternate term for the South Pacific, used mainly in France, Japan, and by certain *multilateral* agencies. It refers to the south and central Pacific, including *Australasia, Melanesia, Micronesia,* and *Polynesia.*

O'Connell, Daniel (1775–1847). "The Liberator." Irish nationalist. He opposed the *Act of Union* joining Ireland to the *United Kingdom.* His great cause, and lasting impact, was to link Irish *nationalism* with *Catholicism,* under the rubric of *Catholic emancipation.* His election to Parliament in 1828, which left him unable to take his seat owing to the requirement of the "Test Act," requiring an oath of loyalty that violated his religious convictions, moved *Wellington* to repeal the Test Act and led to Catholic emancipation. His effective union of Catholicism and Irish nationalism isolated *Protestants* in Ireland, most of whom remained *Unionists.* O'Connell went on to found a broad, parliamentary movement for Irish *Home Rule.* Although his approach to the *Irish Question* was rudely pushed aside during the *Revolutions of 1848* and the Great Hunger in Ireland, by harder men such as the *Fenians,* his reformist politics greatly influenced *Parnell.* Thus, his Parliamentary impact was felt long after his death, indeed dominating British politics throughout the *Gladstone* era, though it failed to impress the more militant. *See also Irish Question.*

October Crisis (1962). *See Cuban Missile Crisis.*

October Crisis (1970). *See* Front de liberation du Québec; *Pierre Trudeau.*

October Days (1789). *See French Revolution.*

October Revolution (1917). *See Russian Revolution, November (October) 1917.*

October surprise (1980). *See hostage crisis.*

October War (1973). *See Fourth Arab-Israeli War.*

Octobrists. (1) Members of the constitutional movement in Russia, who split from the Kadets in 1905. (2) A huge Soviet youth organization, with compulsory membership, which emphasized athleticism that incorporated martial training.

Oder-Neisse Line. The border between Germany and Poland, as agreed at *Yalta* and confirmed at *Potsdam*. It followed the Oder and Neisse rivers, which had some historical basis as the old, medieval *frontier*. After *liberation* by the *Red Army* in 1945, some five million Germans were *ethnically cleansed* from what had been *East Prussia* (which was given to Poland) and parts of *Silesia*, while much the same happened to Poles in the eastern part of Poland (annexed by the *Soviet Union*). The *de facto* border gained some legal *recognition* from *West Germany* in 1970 as part of its *Ostpolitik* opening (*East Germany* had always accepted it). It was confirmed in 1990 in a formal agreement between Poland and Germany, made to ease early nervous tensions among Poles about possible German *revanchism*, resulting from the fact of German reunification in 1990.

OECD. *See Organization for Economic Cooperation and Development.*

offensive. A planned, coordinated series of advances or attacks aimed at bringing destructive capabilities to bear upon the enemy's armed forces, and/or capture of *territory*. *See also advance;* élan; *retreat.*

offensive weapons. Weapons whose primary use furthers aggressive or preemptive military action. For many weapons, until they are actually employed in warfare, any distinction from *defensive weapons* may be virtually meaningless. In short, "offensive" or "defensive" purpose most often lies in the eye of the beholder and whether that eye is looking down or into the barrel of a gun. *See also deterrence; first-strike capability; first use; nonoffensive defense (NOD); preemptive strike.*

Office of Strategic Services (OSS). The wartime, civilian *intelligence service* of the United States, set up in June 1942. It supported Yugoslav and Italian *partisans* as well as lesser partisan groups in Bulgaria, Hungary, and Rumania. Its more important activities lay in code breaking, although here U.S. Army and Naval *intelligence* was vastly more effective. The OSS made at best a marginal contribution to the war effort. It was disbanded in October 1945. The *CIA* succeeded it as the main U.S. civilian agency in 1947. *See also Việt Minh.*

officer. Any person holding a commission in a regularly constituted military force or a commander in a *guerrilla* army acknowledged by the troops as a legitimate *combat* or *logistics* authority with the right to issue orders. The term derives from the great military reform in France of 1444, wherein formerly *mercenary* leaders were replaced by men appointed at the pleasure of the king and who thus became office-holders, or officers, in the royal service. The idea that officers should also be nationals of the state that employed them arose much later, not until the *French Revolution*, and even then was not universal practice for several decades after that. *See also commissioned officer; flag officer; noncommissioned officer; military ranks; petty officer.*

officer corps. The whole body (corpus) of *officers* in a regularly constituted military force.

Official Development Assistance (ODA). Financial or technical assistance provided by a developed state, or an *OPEC* member, to a *developing nation* (or *LDC*), usually on a gratis or concessionary basis. It may be in the form of credits, grants, loans, material assistance, or expert personnel. Note: The *OECD* defines it narrowly as concessional grants or loans where interest is set below prevailing market rates. *See also aid.*

official financing. Financial transactions by a government, usually through its *central bank* but possibly including *International Monetary Fund* facilities, aiming at prevention of gross fluctuations in the value of the national *currency* occasioned by surpluses or deficits in the *balance of payments.* If deficits persist, *foreign exchange reserves* may become exhausted and/or *debt* increase.

Ogaden. A long-disputed region between Ethiopia and whatever power controlled it: Oman or independent sheikdoms, Italy, or Somalia. In 1954 Britain handed it to Ethiopia, despite claims to it by the Somalis. *See also Second Abyssinian War; Ethiopia-Somalia War.*

OGPU (*Obyedinyonnoy Gosudarstvennoe Politicheskoe Upravlenie*). "United State Political Administration." The *CHEKA*, or Soviet *secret police*, 1923–1934. It was later renamed *NKVD* and, later still, the *KGB*.

oil. Petroleum from ground or sea wells is a product of relatively recent importance. During much of the eighteenth and nineteenth centuries, lubricants, lighting, heating oil, and other oil products (tallow) came mainly from animal fats, including those harvested from *whaling*. The rising importance of petroleum was directly related to *industrialization* and an attendant rise in appetite for fossil fuels, the internal combustion engine, and the consequent invention of modern mechanized warfare. Oil became the most *strategic* commodity in the world from c. 1850, as it lubricated the global economy and sustained the ability of industrial states to wage war on a vast scale. The first American well was drilled in 1859 in Pennsylvania. American production dominated world oil supply until about 1950 and, although its consumption then surpassed domestic production, the United States remained a major producer into the twenty-first century. So too did Russia. The first well in the Middle East was drilled in 1908 in Persia, greatly elevating the strategic importance of that region. Oil was first struck in Iraq in 1927, in Saudi Arabia in 1935, and in Kuwait in 1938, elevating in turn each country's (or colony's) geopolitical importance. Similarly, oil fields that became available for exploitation in the Caspian basin after the *Cold War* made that a region of rising interest and important to outside powers. In 1992 China became a net importer of oil, greatly adding to upward pressure on world prices. The desire or need to control oil supplies has sparked intervention and *coups* (e.g., Iran 1953), *cartel* formation, and the *debt crisis* brought on by the *oil shocks* of the 1970s, and it has hugely affected major wars. In *World War II* Germany's eastern strategy required securing the only European oil fields within reach, at Ploesti in Rumania, and Japan decided to attack the United States at *Pearl Harbor* once *Roosevelt* added oil to the list of embargoed commodities. The *Gulf War* was more about keeping control of world oil prices out of *Saddam Hussein's* hands than it was about restoring *sovereignty* to Kuwait, though it was also about that principled position. *See also gold rush; natural resources; oil spills; OPEC; Seven Sisters; water.*

Oil Rivers Protectorate. A nineteenth-century British *protectorate* at the mouth of the Niger River, named for its production of palm oil, a major export crop. It was later incorporated into the *colony* of Nigeria.

oil shocks. Dramatic increases in the world price of *oil*, and related massive transfers of *capital* from *OECD* countries to *OPEC* members, starting during the *Fourth Arab-Israeli War* of 1973, and again in 1979–1981 with the *Iranian Revolution*. They initiated an enormous flow of wealth into the oil-producing states, high *inflation* in the industrialized world, and the rise of huge *debt* burdens in many *Third World* economies. Efforts to curtail consumption and develop alternative energy sources mostly failed, and oil prices continued to spike during times of crisis—such as the *Gulf War* in 1990.

oil spills. Efforts to regulate oil spills and assign liability include a 1954 convention, amended in 1962. *UNCLOS III* listed 42 articles concerned with marine controls, monitoring, pollution, and enforcement. These powers were assigned to a Seabed Authority, which was not generally accepted by the major maritime nations. Therefore, the proposals had little effect beyond suggesting international norms. *Bilateral* agreements on coastal spills and pollution later were agreed as stopgap measures.

Ojukwu, Chukwuemeka (b. 1933). "Ikemba Nnewi." President of the *secessionist* nation of Biafra, May 1967 to January 1970. He became military governor of the Eastern Region of Nigeria after the "Ibo coup" of 1966. After tens of thousands of other *Ibos* were massacred in the north he led his region into secession as Biafra and commanded it throughout the *Nigerian Civil War*. A greatly charismatic figure, he helped sustain Biafran morale long after any hope of *victory* had disappeared. As the ragtag Biafran Army finally succumbed, he fled to the Côte d'Ivoire, where he was granted *asylum*. Pardoned in 1982, he returned to Nigeria where he became a spokesman for Ibo grievances, especially over the poor development of the former eastern region and extraction of its oil resources for federal development purposes. In the 1990s he objected to introduction by northern Muslims of the *sharia* code and called for a renegotiation of the Nigerian union.

Okhrana. The tsarist *secret police*, founded in 1881. The Okhrana pioneered many techniques of *counterespionage* in its effort to monitor and repress the Russian democratic, as well as *anarchist* and *socialist*, opposition. It also developed a number of modern foreign *intelligence* methods, including early *sigint* in the form of *cabinets noirs*. The *Bolsheviks* inherited both traditions—repression and *espionage*—and carried them further in the *CHEKA*, *NKVD*, and *KGB*.

Okinawa. *See Ryukyu Islands.*

Okinawa, Battle of (April 1–June 21, 1945). This Japanese island, the largest of the *Ryukyus*, was invaded and captured by American (and some British and other Allied) forces after heavy fighting and much loss of life, including that of many civilians who committed suicide or were caught in the crossfire. The invasion of Okinawa was larger even than the *D-Day* assault that began the *Normandy campaign* on June 6, 1944: Operation Iceberg landed some 184,000 troops on the first day, of a total force of 545,000. Waves of nearly 2,000 *kamikaze* met the invasion fleet. They sank 38 United States warships and damaged nearly 200 in all. A suicide flotilla of 10 Japanese warships was also sent in, but was mostly sunk. Over the course of the battle the Japanese lost an astonishing 7,800 planes and a lesser number of pilots. The United States took 49,000 casualties, the highest rate in its military history. Japan lost 107,000 dead and 11,000 prisoners. About a quarter of all civilians on the island also died, many either encouraged or forced by Japanese officers to seal themselves in caves or hurl themselves and their children off cliffs into the sea.

Old Believers (*Raskolniki*). Russian *Orthodox* who refused to accept the reforms or rulings of the Council convened by Patriarch Nikon (1605–1681), symbolized by a change in the number of fingers used to make the sign of the cross, and clinging instead to the old rituals. Some estimates suggest they constituted as much as 20 percent of the Russian population at the end of the seventeenth century. They were severely persecuted in tsarist Russia, especially once *Peter I* simultaneously introduced centralizing and secularizing reforms. In turn, they found Peter a repulsive figure in his frequently vulgarian personal behavior and in his western attitudes and dress, which flouted much Orthodox tradition, and his decree of 1705 enforcing shaving of the beards "God had given men." Also giving offense were his semiprivate drunken mock Synods, Saturnalia that belittled the Church and all religious belief, old, new, Orthodox, and *Catholic*. The Old Believers objected as well to Peter's changing of the calendar to the Julian (though not the Gregorian) form and the day beginning the New Year from September to January 1st. In 1700 one of their leaders denounced Peter as the anti-Christ. From 1707 to 1709 Old Belief resistance to Peter helped feed a *Cossack* rebellion in Russia under ataman Kondratay Bulavin (c. 1660–1708), which also swept into arms perhaps 100,000 peasants. The cult-like character of the insurrection was revealed by several mass-suicides. The rebellion was crushed by Peter's better trained and more disciplined soldiers and ruthless generals. In 1716 Peter introduced double taxation of all Old Believers ("the beard tax") and required them to wear distinctive markings to subject them to public ridicule. Those were more effective methods over time than burning at the stake, or the knout, perhaps, but still proved insufficient to eradicate sincere if ignorant devotion. Many left to live in Siberia to escape the reach of the impious tsar; in 1724 Peter forbade that, too. See *fundamentalism*; *Pugachev Rebellion*; *Stenka Razin*; strel'sty.

Old Bolsheviks. The original *Bolshevik* leaders and party members. Most were *liquidated* by *Stalin* in the *Yezhovshchina* of the 1930s. *See also Vladimir Lenin*; *Leon Trotsky*.

Old Catholics. Catholics in *schism* from Rome over certain decisions taken at the first *Vatican Council*, 1869–1870, notably its proclamation of papal infallibility. They were especially prominent in Austria and Germany.

Old World. The Middle East, Europe, and North Africa (that is, the known world of the Mediterranean, Baltic, and Atlantic seaboards that constituted the limits of European geographical knowledge before the charting of the coasts of Africa, Asia, and the *Americas* in the *Age of Exploration*). At a popular level, and in politics, the term traditionally connoted to most Americans images of *Machiavellian* intrigue, lack of principle, conflict, and war in Europe. To many Europeans, who often incorrectly regard it as applying only to themselves, it often suggests cultural conservatism and traditional social values.

oligopoly. When several firms together control the production and pricing of a *commodity*. *See also monopoly.*

Olympic Games. A modern revival (13 countries competed in 1896) of ancient Greek, ritual athletic competitions. They have since expanded beyond recognition by the athletes of Athens and other Greek *city-states* (e.g., an inherent absurdity, "solo synchronized swimming," was an official event in 1992). The games were held every four years thereafter, except during *World War I* and *World War II*. They were intended to promote peaceful competition among *nations*, but in many years the games were highly politicized, as states came to see sports as a continuation of politics by other means. The most infamous example was the 1936 Berlin Olympics, where the *Nazis* attempted to illustrate their racial theories and bolster domestic opinion by achieving international prominence in sport. However, the triumph of the would-be *Herrenvolk* had to be postponed as a result of one of the greatest Olympic track performances of all time. Jesse Owens (1913–1980), a self-effacing black American, the grandson of a Georgia slave, won four gold medals—including by besting a great German competitor in the long jump; afterward, they became lifelong friends. That accomplishment caused *Hitler* to stomp out of the stadium in an *Aryan* huff. Still, he had his propaganda triumph: Nazi Germany won more medals than any other country in 1936, and the closing ceremonies took on the sinister aura and odor of the *Nuremberg Rallies*.

Less dramatic but just as political, the 1964 Tokyo Olympics were used by Japan as something of a national coming-out celebration, for its full reacceptance after World War II into the *community of nations*. The 1972 Munich Olympics were the most tragically marred, as Palestinian *terrorists* took *hostage* and then murdered Israeli athletes. *Mossad* took the next 21 years to hunt down and kill all of those involved. The 1976 Montreal Olympics were boycotted by African states protesting sport contacts with South Africa (itself excluded, 1960–1994) and by rejection of Taiwan in favor of the People's Republic of China (mainland China). The 1980 Moscow Olympics were boycotted by many Western and Islamic countries, protesting the Soviet invasion of Afghanistan; the next games, in Los Angeles, were boycotted by the *Soviet bloc* in retaliation. South Korea used the 1988 games to marginally improve relations with North Korea, enhance its global profile, and gain *prestige* as a rising economic powerhouse. China made an intense bid to host the 2000 Olympics in Beijing. It lost to Sydney, partly owing to a poor *human rights* record and the then recent memory of the massacre at *Tiananmen Square*. In 2001, however, it was awarded the Summer Games for 2008.

Individual protests also occurred at the Games: in 1896 Irish athletes on the British team held up their aspired-to national flag, rather than Great Britain's; in 1968 three African-American athletes gave a "black power" salute from the medal podium. During the *Cold War*, Americans and Soviets competed fiercely (1952–1988), while certain small countries sought to make up in sports achievement what they lacked in political *legitimacy* or national confidence. Of these, the most spectacularly successful was *East Germany*. Cuba, Rumania, and other Soviet bloc nations also placed a premium on the political prestige that came with Olympic success. The Winter Olympics, which began in 1924, have never been as popular or well-attended as the Summer Games: the Jamaican bobsled team notwithstanding, it is understandably hard to get the world's many warm weather populations to compete in (or watch) events such as luge and speed skating. Nor have the Winter Games been as political as the Summer Games. The notable exception was ice hockey, where politics came to the fore between the Soviets and Czechoslovakia at Grenoble in 1968 (after Moscow's crushing of the *Prague Spring*), and between Soviets and Americans at the Lake Placid Olympics in 1980.

Oman. Formerly Muscat and Oman. In 1650 the Omani threw the Portuguese out of Muscat. An Omani fleet captured the island of Zanzibar in 1652. Omani sultans then laid siege to Mombasa (Fort Jesus) in 1695, finally taking it in 1698. Portugal recaptured it briefly, 1728–1730, before it reverted to Arab control. Seyyid Said (r. 1806–1856) won an intense struggle for power with supporters of the *Wahhabi* movement. He subsequently introduced clove cultivation to Zanzibar and greatly diversified that island's economy. In 1840 he transferred his capital there from Muscat, mainly to escape from violent Arabian peninsular politics still reverberating from the Wahhabi revolt. Thus, from the end of the seventeenth century into the mid-nineteenth century an Arab-dominated trading system was restored in the western Indian Ocean that dealt mainly in *slaves* and *gold*. Oman became the most powerful state in *Arabia*, too, after it emerged as an independent *sultanate* in the mid-eighteenth century. It dominated the nearby seas with its extensive navy and ruled far off Zanzibar as a slave-gathering *colony*. Upon Said's death, in 1856 Oman and Zanzibar were split among his heirs. In 1861 the Omani sultan of Zanzibar lost control to the British, who ended its long *slave trade*. Tensions between interior *tribes* of Arab nomads and the mixed Arab and Indian population of the capital Muscat led to violence in the mid-1950s. This was repressed with British assistance. *Oil* was also discovered, changing the basis of the Omani economy and reinforcing the dominance of Muscat. In 1970 the old sultan was deposed by his son, who engaged in a more explicitly pro-Western policy. During the *Iran-Iraq War* Oman did as most *Gulf States* and supported Iraq. In the *Gulf War* it permitted the use of its airfields to the *Gulf coalition*, and thereafter moved closer in security affairs to the West and to Saudi Arabia. *See also Gulf Cooperation Council.*

Omdurman, Battle of (September 1–2, 1898). After the humiliation of the defeat by the *Mahdi* and the death of *Gordon* and his garrison at Khartoum (1885), the British trod lightly in Sudan for over a decade. The victory of Ethiopia under Menelik II (c. 1834–1913) in the *First Abyssinian War* and the humiliation of Italy at *Adowa* (January 1896) had changed the regional *balance of power.* To this concern was added fear of a French advance to the Nile. Thus, *Kitchener* was ordered into the country to secure British control of the Nile, and thereby of Egypt and the *Suez Canal.* In June 1896, he crossed the border into Sudan, but he then took his time about its conquest—over a two-year period he slowly advanced up the Nile, laying a railway to supply his forces as he went. In April 1898, a Mahdist force offered battle at Atbara and was defeated. Kitchener waited several months for reinforcements from Britain and then resumed the final advance on Khartoum, accompanied by the 23-year-old *Winston Churchill* and many other reporters. Most in Britain keenly followed his progress, as recounted in *jingoistic* stories in the daily newspapers. At Omdurman, the Mahdist capital built across the river from the Egyptian slave-city of Khartoum, Kitchener's 25,000 British, Egyptian, and Sudanese troops met the main Mahdist army, perhaps 50,000 strong. On the first day Kitchener shelled the city. On September 2nd, the Mahdist force attacked. Against the poorly coordinated Mahdist assault, Kitchener deployed vastly superior firepower, including steam gunboats on the Nile. The better-equipped, -disciplined, and -led British forces slaughtered the oncoming Mahdists, who attacked in a dense mass of infantry right into the teeth of long-range British rifles and *machine guns.* When it was over, 28 British were dead, but some 10,000 Sudanese corpses carpeted the desert, and many thousands more wounded crawled off to live or die later. Kitchener entered Omdurman and desecrated the Mahdi's tomb, casting his bones into the Nile. A handful of Mahdist survivors kept up a desultory *guerrilla* campaign in the western desert for another year and then dissipated. The victory was so complete it led to establishment of an Anglo-Egyptian *condominium* over Sudan. *See also Fashoda.*

omission. When a state fails to meet its *treaty* or other legal obligations through lack of positive action.

one-party state. Any state, regardless of ideological orientation, where only one political party is permitted by law or in fact. The one-party states of the *Soviet bloc* collapsed, 1989–1991. Subsequently, some *Third World* one-party regimes experimented (sincerely or not) with *democracy*, as *OECD* states made this a partial condition of *aid*.

Onin War (1467–1477). *See Japan.*

OPEC. *See Organization of Petroleum Exporting Countries.*

open city. (1) A city that is of little or no military importance and therefore not attacked or bombed. (2) A city abandoned by retreating military forces and declared "open" in the hope that an invading enemy will spare it destruction that is no longer necessary to its capture. Neither the Germans nor the *Allies* bombed Paris during *World War II* after open city declarations. However, the Japanese heavily bombed Manila, even though it was declared open to their advancing troops.

"open covenants of peace, openly arrived at." This slogan, coined by *Woodrow Wilson* in his *Fourteen Points* address, grew out of the *liberal peace program* before and during *World War I*. It was an idea championed in a qualified sense by Wilson at the *Paris Peace Conference*. The demand arose out of fear that secret *alliances* might lead to another world war (it was widely believed they led to the First). Also contributing was shock and disgust at publication by the *Bolsheviks* of secret *treaties* and cynical *territorial* swaps made by Britain and France with Italy, to get it into the war, and with Russia, to keep it in the war. The core idea of open diplomacy is that *public opinion* is inherently *pacifist* and thus can provide a powerful check on the putatively amoral and illiberal intrigues of *diplomats*. That conceit contributed to a new emphasis on *conference* over *quiet diplomacy*, including the permanent conferencing of the *League of Nations* and *United Nations General Assembly*. *See also Constantinople Agreement (1915); registration; Treaty of London (1915).*

open diplomacy. *See open covenants.*

Open Door. A principle of *free trade* championed by the United States toward China, c. 1850–1949, which called for treating all foreign nationals and firms on a *most-favored-nation* basis, or one of equality rather than special rights. It was made explicit in the *Open Door notes*. After Japan's *Twenty-one Demands* on China, Secretary of State *William Jennings Bryan* announced that the United States would not accept any alteration in Asia that adversely affected American rights, impinged upon the *territorial integrity* of China, or sought to close the "open door" of competitive trade. The Open Door was of cardinal concern in the *Lansing-Ishii Agreement*. The principle was internationalized in the *Nine Power Treaty* in 1922 and, in a distant sense, much later in *GATT*. Some scholars, those of the *Wisconsin school*, view the Open Door as mere cover for economic *imperialism* in Asia. Others, notably *realists*, view it as an example of naïveté in U.S. diplomacy in the face of actual European and Japanese territorial and commercial imperialism toward China. Liberal-nationalist historians tend to view it as an example of self-fulfilling moral exceptionalism in American politics and civilization or as an example of enlightened self-interest at the core of American foreign policy. *See also capitulations; free trade; unequal treaties.*

Open Door notes. These *diplomatic notes* were sent by Secretary of State John Hay (1838–1905) to the European powers and Japan in September and November 1899. They called on all powers with *spheres of influence* in China to respect the principle of the *Open Door*, not to stand in the way of China's collection of *customs* duties, and to cooperate with the United States in ensuring all other powers adhered to the Open Door. Only Italy, which had no sphere in China, embraced the notes. Most other powers were polite but noncommittal. Nonetheless, Hay declared that he had secured international respect for the *territorial integrity* of China. In fact, the hard realities remained that spheres of influence would be defended by force, as the *Russo-Japanese War* would demonstrate, and that *free trade* in Asia was not widely accepted. The 1899 notes revealed that American interests had already expanded greatly in Asia, even if U.S. policy in the region was as yet little more than a missal of ineffectual pieties. In 1900 Hay issued more notes, unilaterally declaring for the Open Door and China's territorial integrity. The other *Great Powers* were again more polite than they needed to be: the United States had in the past itself impinged on Chinese *sovereignty* and was at that moment closing the Open Door in the Philippines. The notes are perhaps most important for signaling a new engagement by the United States in world affairs. Unexpected by most, this had come about not through entanglement with the Great Powers of Europe, but via commercial interests in Asia. The notes also gave sign that, despite its new-found power and importance, the United States still intended to uphold the notion of its moral exceptionalism in dealings with the wider world. The national style of American diplomacy was thus to the fore: *national interests* were overdressed in a cloak of principle and escorted about in a hansom cab of abstractions. *See also* Idealpolitik.

Open Skies. A proposal for a *verification regime* to reduce tension over a possible *first strike* by either side, made by *Eisenhower* to *Khrushchev* at their 1955 *summit* in Geneva. It was elegantly simple: each side would allow surveillance overflights by the other. The Soviets rejected the proposal, fearing the United States would discover just how far behind their missile program really was and because of historic paranoia about foreign observance of Russian internal conditions. In a sense, the idea—which anticipated satellite technology—was implemented unilaterally by the United States in the form of *U-2* overflights. The rapid development of satellites by both sides in the 1960s rendered most aerial reconnaissance less important. In the altered climate of the late 1980s the United States revived the open skies proposal and, under *George H. Bush*, finally secured Soviet agreement. American and Soviet (later, Russian) overflights thereafter became almost routine. Russian observers were sometimes flown over American bases and missile silos in American planes, as their own equipment proved below standard or had ceased to function.

operational code. *Jargon* for the world view of a foreign policy *decision maker* or *elite*.

operationalize. *Jargon. See also variable.*

Operation Condor. A secret military plan initiated by Chile in 1975 to seek out and eliminate left-wing *guerrillas* on a regional basis, but also ordinary leftist political *dissenters*. This multistate effort was supported by use of American communications facilities to share intelligence among the *juntas*. Six Latin American military dictatorships were part of the program during the 1970s, arranging kidnappings and assassinations of one another's political opponents, regardless of where they were found, and cooperating in sending out *death squads* to kill critics throughout Latin America and beyond. The democratic governments that succeeded to power in the 1980s and 1990s launched an investigation into the Operation. Some U.S. intelligence and military agencies may have been involved. *See also Pinochet.*

Operation Desert Shield/Desert Storm. *See Gulf War (1990–1991).*

opino juris et necessitatis. The evolution of *international customary law* through frequency and habitual action by states, accompanied by declarations of acceptance of legal obligation, not mere ceremonial or courteous behavior, such that a given custom becomes generally binding.

opium trade. Opium became a major international commodity in the eighteenth and nineteenth centuries, as the *East India Company* imported to China large quantities of opium it cultivated in India to barter for Chinese porcelains and other goods it then sold in Europe in a highly lucrative *triangle trade*. "John Company" had turned to opium so that it would no longer have to pay for Chinese exports with silver, whose net loss was affecting the *balance of payments* in Britain and had become worrying to the British government. In China, mass opium addiction caused the usual social and economic problems that attend use of a popular narcotic. Hence, in 1800 its importation was banned by the *Qing*, and in 1813 even smoking opium was made a crime, punishable by public flogging and other humiliations designed to induce shame in addicts and persuade them to quit their habit. As with any *drug trade*, once opium was made illegal the profit margins to its importers—mostly

British—soared. (For perspective's sake, it should be recalled that opium was also imported to Britain, where use was legal and fairly common among the chattering classes.) By 1825 the specie pattern reversed: Chinese silver was flowing out to pay for British opium, causing a rise in domestic *inflation* that began to have disruptive economic and social effects, felt in forms as varied as a squeeze on state revenues to mass peasant rebellion. The main impact of this early international drug trade was felt in the First and Second *Opium Wars*. An international opium trade abolitionist conference was attended by 12 states at the Hague in 1912, but came to naught. *Yuan Shikai* continued late Qing anti-smuggling efforts, but millions of Chinese remained addicted as the dealers simply moved into the foreign *concessions*. After the *Communist Revolution* (1949), *Mao* and the *Communist Party*—both of whom frequently exhibited a puritanical streak—launched campaigns against opium addiction. An opiate derivative, heroin, remained a major international commodity into the twenty-first century, disrupting and distorting the development of several Latin American, Caribbean, and South Asian countries. *See also Qing dynasty.*

Opium War, First (1839–1842). As lopsided trade with China developed, with the *Ming* and *Qing* importing few goods but exporting large amounts of silk, tea, and porcelains, the Western powers developed a major *balance of payments* problem. To correct this, the *East India Company* began importing *opium* to China from its Indian plantations. It operated a *triangular trade* of opium from India; porcelains, tea, and silk from China; manufactured goods from England. Over time, to pay for the huge demand for opium, China exported so much silver it experienced a severe monetary crisis. In 1834 Britain's new commercial agent in *Canton* demanded to deal with the Imperial court on the basis of sovereign *equality*. That concession would have undermined China's *tribute system* and risked alienating the increasingly antiforeign Chinese gentry. For years, Chinese leaders had debated how to limit the number of addicts ("opium eaters") and stop further penetration by foreign traders and ideas. War finally broke out when a Qing minister (Lin Zexu) decreed the death sentence for opium trafficking, confiscated a shipment of opium that John Company merchants intended to market, and blockaded opium warehouses. Britain asserted the *extraterritoriality* of its laws, denied *jurisdiction* to China, and, with *Palmerston's* backing, demanded return of its seized opium and arrested merchants, and dispatched a war fleet to China.

Hostilities began with skirmishing between Chinese junks and British gunboats already on the scene, with the main British fleet arriving off China in June 1840. Several ships were left to institute a *blockade*, while the rest moved to the Dagu (Taku) forts, near Tientsin, where negotiations began. In August, fighting resumed around Guangzhou (Canton) between British marines and Chinese *militia*. The British fleet—of some 16 warships, including four steam-powered gunboats, which represented a *revolution in military affairs* in Asian waters—retaliated by shelling Guangzhou and seized an area of coast around the village of *Hong Kong* to settle merchants expelled both from Guangzhou and *Macao*. The next summer, the British fleet moved at will, unopposed by any Chinese navy along the coast; a more modern Chinese fleet—modeled on the British—was under feverish construction, but was not completed before the war ended. The British thus took Xiamen (Amoy) and Ningbo. Meanwhile, in 1842 land reinforcements from the *Indian Army* were put to work seizing control of key access points on China's *Grand Canal*. After heavy fighting, Indo-British forces captured several provincial cities, occupying Shanghai (June) and Zhenjiang (July 1842). In August, a British army moved inland to lay siege to Nanjing, and the Qing capitulated. The war ended in a diplomatic and geostrategic revolution in Asia, as China was compelled to accept hard terms in the *Treaty of Nanjing* (1842). It was further humiliated by having to pay *compensation* to British merchants for the opium destroyed. The opium trade thus continued, and even expanded, under the license offered to the British (and soon, also other foreign merchants) under the new *capitulations*.

Suggested Reading: Peter Fay, *The Opium War, 1840–42* (1975).

Opium War, Second (1856–1860). This conflict is sometimes called the Arrow War, after the British *casus belli*: China's boarding and seizure of the opium merchant ship Arrow in a Chinese port and arresting of its crew. Interpretations of the conflict from the British side differ. Some see the war as one in which peripheral interests determined policy; others, that London clearly set policy and defined British interests; and still others, that "gentlemen imperialists" brought about war for selfish reasons. On the Chinese side, it sprang from the same basic cause as the first: a clash over economic benefits related to the *opium trade*—exacerbated by a diplomatic crisis when the British tried to force China under the established system of *international law* and to revise the *Treaty of Nanjing* to add additional *capitulations* and clauses on *extraterritoriality*. Britain, joined by France, launched two punitive expeditions. The first came after an initial attack was repulsed and the British were held back by the military demands of suppressing the *Indian Mutiny*. It involved again sailing to and taking the Dagu (Taku) forts, near Tientsin. The second expedition came after China reneged on the onerous terms of the *Treaty of Tientsin* (1858), which had followed the first Anglo-French raid into the interior. Beijing was occupied in 1860, forcing the Imperial Court to stop resistance. Under terms of the Peking (Beijing) Convention, China ceded the Kowloon peninsula to the British in *Hong Kong*. The opium trade continued uninterrupted. Some experts estimate that by 1900 there were 40 million users in China, about 15 million of them addicted. *See also Gordon.*

Suggested Reading: J. Y. Wong, *Deadly Dreams* (1998).

Oppenheimer, J. Robert (1904–1967). Nuclear physicist. In 1942 he joined the *Manhattan Project* and the next year he headed its *Los Alamos* base, driving its scientists to completion of the world's first *atomic bomb* while playing liaison with the military. When the first bomb was tested, his internal reaction as he gazed on the fireball was to quote from the Bhagavad-Gita (*Hindu* scripture): "Now I am become death, the destroyer of worlds." He came to deeply regret the bombings of *Hiroshima* and *Nagasaki* and called for joint control of nuclear technology with the Soviet Union. Under a cloud of *McCarthyite* accusations, but also because of prudent suspicion of his past associations with known American Communists and approaches made to him by Soviet agents, and his lack of proper candor about those associations and contacts, he was suspended from all atomic research (1954). He was a man of exceptional intellect and considerable conscience, who died emotionally broken. Later revelations from *KGB* archives strongly suggest that he was a secret member of the American Communist Party, but while they show clear KGB interest in recruiting him they also contain no evidence that he was ever a spy or otherwise betrayed his country. *See also Edward Teller.*

Suggested Reading: Alan Weinstein and Alexander Vassiliev, *The Haunted Wood* (1999).

opportunism (in foreign policy). When a state with a generally *expansionist* thrust to its diplomacy bides time, advancing militarily only when meeting weak or no resistance, as opposed to embarking on frank and outright *aggression*. If it is concluded that this is an opponent's intentions and modus operandi, the logical counterpolicy is firm support for *deterrence* and *containment*. Many *intelligence* and policy analysts in the West during the *Cold War* saw this as the prime characteristic of Soviet policy. They rejected cruder, even hysterical, views that portrayed the Soviets as relentlessly aggressive and ever-ready to use force, as *Nazi Germany* had been. They also dismissed as naïve, or worse, portrayals that ignored or denied the expansionist motif in Soviet policy. *See also George Kennan; Peter I.*

opposable. In *international law*, a statement or act that one *state* may not regard as the exclusive concern of others.

optimize. *See game theory.*

Optional Clause (of the Statute of the International Court of Justice). Article 36. It stipulates that states may agree in advance to submit to *compulsory jurisdiction*. Those accepting do so on the basis of *reciprocity*. The United States made a *reservation* (the Connally Amendment, 1946), asserting a right to exclude disputes regarded as under *domestic jurisdiction*. This has been much criticized in legal circles by those who believe compulsory jurisdiction is highly desirable. Yet the Connally Amendment is in line with similar reservations taken by 90 percent of states accepting the clause so far. A further, more contentious modification was made by the *Reagan* administration in 1984, to deny the court *jurisdiction* in a case charging *indirect aggression*, brought by Nicaragua against the United States.

optional protocol. A substantive addendum to a *treaty* that signatories are not bound to accept, but may if they wish. *Adherence* to any such protocol is a separate act from *ratification* of the covenant to which it is attached.

optional rules. *See consent.*

oral history. (1) Historical lore passed from generation to generation by the spoken word. (2) Interviews, tape recorded or videotaped by historians, of persons thought to have led significant lives or who have been witnesses to important events.

Orange Free State. An independent *Boer* republic, 1854–1900, established during the *Great Trek*. It was renamed the Orange River Colony by the British in 1900. In 1910 it was incorporated into the Union (later Republic) of South Africa.

Orangemen. So-called after Prince *William III*, of Orange. (1) Members of a secret society organized in *Ulster* in 1795 to promote and defend political union of Ireland with Britain, promote *Protestantism* in Ireland, and exercise power over native, Catholic Irish. (2) Loosely, Ulster Protestants in general. (3) More precisely, a rough synonym for *Unionists*.

orderly market arrangements (OMAs). Alternative *jargon* for *voluntary export restrictions (VERs)*.

ordnance. Bombs, bullets, explosives, grenades, projectiles, shells, torpedoes, or any other lethal device dropped on or fired at the enemy in *warfare*.

Oregon Question (1843–1846). "Where to draw the western border between Canada and the United States?" The absence of settlers in the Oregon Territory meant its ownership and boundaries were left unresolved until the 1840s. Pressures then built in Britain to claim the whole Columbia River basin, and for some in the United States to assert extreme territorial claims, captured in the slogan "54–40 or fight!" in reference to the preferred latitude of settlement. The border dispute with Canada was aggravated by tensions over American expansionist pressure on Mexico, then a British *client state*. In 1846 agreement was reached by which the United States gained what later became Idaho, Oregon, and Washington, and Britain (Canada) received British Columbia and Vancouver Island. That left only the Alaskan panhandle as an outstanding border issue. It was settled in favor of the United States after a bit of *saber rattling* by *Theodore Roosevelt* in 1902. *See also Aroostook War; Hudson's Bay Company; Oregon Question; Rush-Bagot Agreement (1818); Webster-Ashburton Treaty (1842).*

organizational process model. Institutional routines and *standard operating procedures* of bureaucracies said by social scientists to skewer foreign policy decisions during the implementation phase in ways that may surprise and frustrate the *decision maker* or be misinterpreted by foreign leaders. *See also bureaucratic politics model; rational decision-making.*

Organization de l'armée secrèt (OAS). An illegal military cabal formed by French colonial officers and supported by *colons* from Algeria (the "pied noir"). The OAS refused to accept *independence* and tried several times to assassinate *Charles de Gaulle.*

Organization for Economic Cooperation and Development (OECD). It succeeded the *OEEC* in 1961, to expand beyond European recovery into a harmonization of economic policy in industrialized countries. Its main purposes are: (1) to facilitate *sustainable growth*; (2) to assist economic *development*, even for nonmembers; and (3) to encourage expanded *trade* among the world's major trading nations. It also serves as an important clearing-house of statistical data and economic analysis and sometimes as a powerful *caucus group* in international economic negotiations. It self-describes as a "club of like-minded countries," most of which are wealthy: in 2001 OECD states produced two-thirds of the world's total output of goods and services. Membership is limited to those states committed to a *market economy* and a pluralistic *democracy*. It had 30 member states in 2001, up from 20 original members. Unless otherwise indicated, membership dated from 1961: Australia (1971), Austria, Belgium, Britain, Canada, Czech Republic (1995), Denmark, Finland (1969), France, Germany, Greece, Hungary (1996), Iceland, Ireland, Italy, Japan (1964), Luxembourg, Mexico (1994), Netherlands, New Zealand (1973), Norway, Poland (1996), Portugal, Slovak Republic (2000), South Korea (1996), Spain, Sweden, Switzerland, Turkey, and the United States.

Organization for European Economic Cooperation (OEEC). It was set up in 1947 to facilitate delivery and oversee administration of massive *Marshall Plan* aid flowing into Western Europe from the United States. The phase-out of Marshall aid and the division of Europe into *EC* and non-EC members later undermined its rationale. In 1961 it was superseded by the *OECD*.

Organization of African Unity (OAU). It was founded in 1963 by 32 charter member states. In 2001 it had more than 50 members. It aimed first and foremost at continental stability, but also at speeding the *decolonization* of the continent, discouraging *secession*, encouraging *pan-Africanism*, and enhancing Africa's voice in *multilateral* negotiations. It found unity around the issues of decolonization of what remained of European rule, especially that of Portugal and Spain, and in opposing *apartheid*. It adopted two core principles to ensure stability: *noninterference* in members' *internal affairs*, and the inviolability of inherited colonial borders (*uti possidetis*). However, it quickly divided into two *blocs*: (1) a smaller "Casablanca bloc," led by *Kwame Nkrumah*, promoted *pan-African* solutions and upheld a confrontational style in relations with the *West*; and (2) the majority-formed "Monrovia bloc," led jointly by *Haile Selassie* of Ethiopia and various leaders from Nigeria, who took a more conservative and nationalist line on most issues. The OAU later divided over such regional conflicts as the *Nigerian Civil War*, the *Chad-Libya War*, and the Tanzanian invasion of Uganda in 1979. In the 1980s it was severely split over Libya's *aggression* against its neighbors, Moroccan refusal to allow self-determination for *Western Sahara*, the *Ethiopia-Somalia War*, secession by Eritrea, and civil wars in Angola and Mozambique. In fact, so bitter was the feeling over the admission of *POLISARIO* in 1982 that annual summits were temporarily suspended. In 1992 the OAU proved unable to mediate an end to Somalia's civil war, agreeing to United Nations and U.S. *intervention* as an "interim measure." The original core principles of the OAU fell by the wayside after the mid-1990s, when regional interventions and major wars broke out in Congo, Sierra Leone, Liberia, and Sudan. *See also Rwanda.*

Organization of American States (OAS). The regional organization for the Western hemisphere, founded in 1948 by 21 charter members. By 2001 it enjoyed universal membership of sovereign states in the *Americas*. Its precursor was the *Pan-American Union*. It is headquartered in Washington, D.C., and has the full paraphernalia of a council of ministers and assembly. For its first two decades it was preoccupied with the perception of a *Communist* threat to the region and was not always adverse to U.S. *intervention*. The apex of OAS cooperation on security issues came during the *Cuban Missile Crisis*, when it voted unanimously to support the U.S. response. In 1965 an OAS military mission also went into the *Dominican Republic* after U.S. assertions of a Communist threat. However, during the 1970s and 1980s the OAS divided over U.S. intervention in Central America and unanimously opposed the *invasion of Grenada*, on which it was not consulted. It also opposed U.S. intervention in Panama. Canada finally joined in 1990, as its foreign policy took a turn toward the Americas under *NAFTA*. The OAS played a constructive role in winding down several civil wars in Central America in the early 1990s. *See also Alliance for Progress.*

Organization of Arab Oil Exporting Countries (OAPEC). It was founded in 1968 by Kuwait, Libya, and Saudi Arabia. Most of the *Gulf States* have since joined, as did Algeria and Iraq. As its name suggests, it is confined to Arab states that export oil, thus excluding Arab countries such as Jordan (no oil) or oil nations such as Nigeria (non-Arab). Most members also belong to *OPEC*, an organization OAPEC led in imposing the *embargo* that led to the *oil shock* of 1973–1974.

Organization of Central American States (ODECA). A subregional organization founded in 1951 by Costa Rica, El Salvador, Guatemala, Honduras, and Nicaragua. The ODECA states were far too divided by internal and cross-border conflicts in the 1980s to advance their declared goals of enhanced economic cooperation and coordinated diplomacy. *See also Central American Common Market.*

Organization of Eastern Caribbean States (OECS). Founded in 1981 by the Treaty of Brasseterre by Antigua and Barbuda, Dominica, Grenada, Montserrat, Saint Lucia, Saint Vincent, St. Kitts-Nevis, and the Grenadines. Anguilla and the British Virgin Islands are associate members. Its declared purposes are to promote cooperation among members and preserve their *sovereignty*, *territorial integrity*, and *independence*. It was essentially an institutional response to the collapse of the *West Indies Federation*. In 1983 it requested U.S. intervention in Grenada, on the ground that events had begun to threaten regional *security* and *stability*. Four OECS states joined Barbados, Jamaica, and the United States in the *invasion of Grenada*.

Organization of Petroleum Exporting Countries (OPEC). It was founded in 1960 by Iran, Iraq, Kuwait, Saudi Arabia, and Venezuela to present a common negotiating front in talks on oil prices with major oil companies. Later, members developed an ability to coordinate production and thereby to exert a major influence on world prices. Subsequently joining were: Qatar (1961); Libya (1962); Indonesia (1962); Abu Dhabi (1967); Algeria (1969); Nigeria (1971); Ecuador (1973); and Gabon (1975). OPEC had minimal influence until 1973, when its Arab members (who also belonged to *OAPEC*) convinced the group to impose an oil *embargo* against Western states that supported Israel during the *Fourth Arab-Israeli War*. As prices leaped upward, several Western states shifted their diplomatic positions, leading some analysts to proclaim the arrival of an era of paramount "resource power." In 1978–1979 OPEC cut exports again, leading to another price rise and *oil shock*. This time Western states were less affected, as the earlier experience had stimulated new exploration and production by non-OPEC members such as Britain, Mexico, and Norway, and some conservation. The real losers were Third World importers: OPEC-induced oil price rises were among the major factors behind the *debt crisis* of the 1980s and the failure of numerous national development plans. OPEC's ability to act jointly was severely damaged by the *Iran-Iraq War*, which divided its membership: the *Gulf States* supported Iraq and thereby earned the *enmity* of Iran. The *Gulf War* exacerbated divisions by alienating smaller Arab exporters from Iraq as well. World oil prices were flat during the 1990s, but spiked upward again in 2000. Such fluctuations aside, OPEC has often suffered the instability inherent in a *cartel*. Also, for most of OPEC's history, Saudi Arabia's huge production capacity and reserves made it the "swing producer," able nearly on its own to set prices and determine OPEC pricing policy. That meant the United States and other Western states, especially after the Gulf War, had a close ally within OPEC, which tended to moderate prices. *See also Seven Sisters.*

Organization of Security and Cooperation in Europe (OSCE). From 1973 to 1975 all European states (except Albania) plus the United States and Canada met in Helsinki to discuss regional security. The Soviets wanted recognition of their postwar gains; the West Europeans wanted to expand *détente*, as did most *neutrals.* The United States was at first not that interested as *Nixon* and *Kissinger* preferred bilateral talks with the Soviets, but under *Ford, Carter,* and *Reagan* the United States grew into a leadership role. All participants agreed on the *Helsinki Accords,* explicitly linking the military, economic, and human dimensions of security in an ongoing Conference on Security and Cooperation in Europe (CSCE) process. Follow-up conferences were held on implementation of the Accords (13 between 1975 and 1989), but with little to no progress made on economic or *human rights* issues. After the Stockholm conference (1985), however, great progress was made on *arms control* and on introduction of *CSBMs.* After 1990 much changed, reflecting the end of the *Cold War* and collapse of the *Soviet bloc.* The *Charter of Paris* was adopted and a Conflict Prevention Center set up in Vienna. The CSCE thereafter implemented broad CSBMs, expanded activity in the "human dimension," and coordinated some *peacekeeping* and many election *observer missions.* Helsinki II (1992) set up new structures: a *Secretariat* and Permanent Committee in Vienna and an Office for Democratic Institutions and Human Rights (ODIHR) in Warsaw; the name was changed from "Conference" to "Organization" to reflect the establishment of its permanent structures. The OSCE accepted the *successor states* of the Soviet Union and Yugoslavia, rising to 53 members. It then *suspended* Serbia. Japan (and, for a time, also Macedonia, whose entry was initially vetoed by Greece under the *unanimity rule*) has observer status—it attends but does not speak or vote. The *European Union* often acts as a bloc, or *caucus group,* and thus also as a drag. The OSCE is a highly cost-effective international organization: before 1992 it operated on just $20 million per annum. That budget expanded with the creation of a permanent structure and with a proliferation of OSCE observer, mediation, and monitoring missions throughout its region of responsibility.

Orient. The eastern hemisphere. *See also Asia; East.*

Oriental exclusion laws. Racially discriminatory legislation introduced in the United States from 1880 to 1947, and in Canada from c. 1900 to the mid-1950s. Their purpose was to limit Japanese and Chinese settlement on the west coast of North America. In 1905, in the post–*Boxer Rebellion* mood of assertive *nationalism* in China, an *embargo* on all U.S. goods was declared in response. In 1924 the *immigration* code in the United States was changed to totally exclude Asians, by votes of 308 to 62 (House) and 68 to 9 (Senate). This deeply embittered relations with all Asian nations, especially Japan. Canada still legally discriminated against Asians, including native-born Asians, into the 1950s. *See also overseas Chinese; passport.*

Orientalism. An academic theory, originally and mainly associated with Edward Said, which holds that Western scholarship about the Middle East suffers from deep, often unconscious, bias that invents an Orient full of debauchery and fanaticism that does not in fact exist, in order to satisfy the psychological and political needs of *imperialism*. This overeasy charge is quite often leveled with gross inaccuracy and personal unfairness in order to exclude as unconsciously "orientalist," and thereby to deny as "illegitimate," research and commentary by scholars who are not personally of Middle Eastern ancestry or do not adhere to the preferred and "politically correct" interpretation.

Suggested Readings: A. L. Macfie, ed., *Orientalism: A Reader* (2000); Edward Said, *Orientalism* (1978).

orientation. *Jargon* for the broad thrust of a state's foreign policy. *See also alliance; isolationism; nonalignment; paradigm.*

Orlando, Vittorio (1860–1952). Italian statesman. Prime minister, 1917–1919. He led the Italian delegation to the *Paris Peace Conference*, led it out in protest when *Woodrow Wilson* refused Italy's exaggerated territorial claims, which went beyond even the secret *Treaty of London* in 1915, which was later published by the *Bolsheviks*, and then led it back in just before the closing of the conference. *See also Big Four.*

Ortega, Daniel (b. 1945). Nicaraguan *guerrilla* commander; president, 1985–1990. He fought in the long guerrilla war that finally toppled *Anastasio Somoza Debayle* in 1979. He then headed the *Sandinista* government in its 11-year confrontation with the United States and its *civil war* with the *Contras*. Seen as a charismatic reformer by some, he was in fact a rigid and doctrinaire *Marxist* ideologue. He reoriented the country toward the *Soviet bloc* primarily out of political conviction, though secondarily from economic necessity after a U.S. *embargo* was imposed. Defeated at the polls in 1990, and then more decisively in 1996, he remained a figure of considerable political influence within Nicaragua throughout the 1990s. In 1998 his stepdaughter, age 30 and also a member of the Sandinista Front, accused him of sexually abusing her from age 11.

Orthodox Church. The several national churches of Eastern Europe, including Russia, that follow the *Byzantine* rite and Nicene creed, a statement of fundamental principles set at the Nicene *Ecumenical Council* in 325 C.E., and whose members numbered approximately 250 million worldwide at the end of the twentieth century. The final *schism* with the Latin (Roman) Church had roots in the eighth century and hardened doctrinally during the eleventh century (1054). It was confirmed politically by the sack of *Constantinople*, the great capital and center of primacy of the Orthodox faith, by *Crusaders* in 1204. Kiev is another notable holy site, as it was the site of Prince Vladimir's conversion in 988 and is thus seen as the cradle of Russian Orthodoxy. The Russian branch grew progressively independent of Constantinople after that city was overrun by the *Ottomans* in 1453, and this pattern was followed in other jurisdictions (Bulgaria, Cyprus, Georgia, Greece, Rumania, Serbia). The Greek Church was not restored until the *Greek War of Independence* and by then was too small to reestablish dominance over other national churches. In most cases, national Orthodox churches have been subservient to the states that hosted them.

Even the powerful Russian church was subservient to the Russian state for most of its history. It was made markedly so even as it was elevated to an independent (but state-dominated) patriarchate by *Boris Godunov* in 1589 and made completely so under *Peter I*, who left the patriarchate vacant after the death of Adrian in 1700 and abolished it in 1721 in favor of a church synod directly controlled by the tsar. The Moscow patriarchate was not restored until the end of tsarism in 1917. The Russian Orthodox Church thus remained a creature of the state and a servant of tsarist *autocracy*, supporting among the peasantry and other believers the tsarist regime's claim to legitimacy and even to holiness—in a land of mass illiteracy, the priest as propagandist was a powerful force. This habit of subservience contributed to schisms within Russian Orthodoxy once the state began to secularize or, perhaps more accurately, ascribe to itself a sacral nature. This led to repeated rebellions by, and attendant savage persecutions of, *Old Believers* in Russia who refused to accept the changes either within the Church or in their relation to the state. As with *Confucianism* in China, Orthodoxy—unchallenged by *Reformation* thinking and long a coerced servant to tyrants—helped prepare the way in several countries for later justifying political doctrines of absolute authority residing in the state and thus was a pillar of the *ancien régime*. In Peter's time, fully one-fifth of Russia's peasants were owned by the Church. As such, the Russian Church was persecuted viciously by the *Bolsheviks*. However, during *World War II* it was found politic by *Stalin* to reopen the churches (and synagogues) as a spur to Russian nationalism and an inspiration to resistance against the age-old *Teutonic* invader.

After the collapse of the Soviet Union, the Orthodox Church in Russia experienced a revival of attendance, with *Boris Yeltsin* and other politicians also paying clumsy, ill-practiced homage to its renewed and lasting influence over the Russian people; *Shevardnadze* actually converted to Orthodoxy, sincerely or not. However, more schisms split the Ukrainian Church, with some even rejoining the Catholic world while maintaining distinct eastern rites (see *Uniate Church*). The largest branch of the modern Ukrainian Church accepts the jurisdiction of the Patriarch of Moscow, but maintains its own "Metropolitan" in Kiev. It views as schismatic a more nationalist but less numerous Ukrainian Orthodox Church, ruled by a Metropolitan known to his faithful, but not recognized as such by the Russian Church, as "Patriarch of Kiev." In 2001 the Catholic pontiff, *John Paul II*, formally apologized to the Orthodox world for past wrongs, especially the sack of Constantinople, in a historic effort at reconciliation. However, his visits to largely Orthodox countries, most notably Ukraine, were studiously ill-received by Orthodox clergy. Patriarch Aleksei II, head of the Russian Orthodox Church in Moscow, refused to meet the Catholic pontiff and warned him not to visit Moscow. In addition to the major national churches, minor branches of Orthodoxy exist in many countries, including Finland, Poland, the United States, Canada, and several countries in Latin America. *See also Third Rome*.

Suggested Readings: J. M. Hussey, *The Orthodox Church in the Byzantine Empire* (1986); J. Paraskevas and F. Reinstein, *The Eastern Orthodox Church* (1969).

Osnabrück, Treaty of (October 24, 1648). The second part of the *Peace of Westphalia* that, along with the *Treaty of Münster*, brought about a general peace settlement in Europe at the end of the *Eighty Years' War* (1566–1648) and the *Thirty Years' War* (1618–1648). Osnabrück was a heavily detailed agreement that resolved long-standing religious and territorial questions in Germany; for example, it clarified the legal status of the *Protestant* branch— Johanniter Orden—of the Knights of St. John as separate from the Order of Malta, clarified the titles and claims of various German princes and bishops, ended certain election provisions of the *Holy Roman Empire*, and confirmed as *sovereign* some 300 political entities in Germany.

Ossetia. A small region in the *Caucasus* bordering Georgia to the south and *Dagestan* and *Chechnya* to the east and north. It was divided upon the breakup of the *Soviet Union,* in which it was submerged for 70 years, into North Ossetia and South Ossetia (located in post-soviet Russia and Georgia, respectively). The northern half forms one of the "constituent republics" of the Russian Federation. In 1992 a movement for *secession* from Georgia began in South Ossetia, almost certainly with local if not official Russian connivance. As fighting increased, some Russian Army units directly supported the Ossetians. The *rebellion* abated in late 1993.

Ostpolitik. "Eastern policy." The opening to *East Germany* and to Moscow initiated by *Willy Brandt*; it led to *peace treaties* with Poland and the *Soviet Union,* acceptance of the *Oder-Neisse line* as the German border, and admission to the United Nations of the two Germanies in 1972. It was further developed within the *CSCE*. It went beyond *regulated coexistence* and completely overturned the *Hallstein Doctrine*.

Ottawa Agreements. *See imperial tariff.*

Ottoman Empire. The first Turkish empire (sixth through seventh centuries) was based in Turkestan and Mongolia. Turkic nomads subsequently dominated *Inner Asia* for centuries, mounting raids into China and north India and eventually overrunning Central Asia and most of the Middle East. The Seljuk Turks, ancestors of the Ottomans, defeated an army of the *Byzantine Empire* in 1071, at Manzikert, starting that great and rival Empire on its final decline. The Ottoman Empire arose from, and was centered on, Turkish power. One of the great *gunpowder empires*, it lasted from 1300 to 1919. It was ruled by the Ottoman (Osmanli) dynasty and named for its founder Osman (or Othman, 1259–1356). The Ottomans expanded out of their base in Anatolia nearly continuously from the thirteenth through sixteenth centuries, acquiring their first territory in Europe at Gallipoli in 1354. In the fourteenth century they conquered Asia Minor and portions of the Balkans, most of the *Islamic world* west of the Safavid Empire in Persia, and extensive Arab lands. In the fifteenth century the Ottomans again surged out of *Anatolia*. Under *Muhammad II* they battered down the walls of *Constantinople* with *artillery* in 1453, extinguishing Byzantium, and moved their capital there.

After 1492 the long contest between Imperial Spain and the Ottoman Empire in the Mediterranean ultimately left the *Barbary States* of North Africa—*Algiers, Tunis,* and *Tripoli*—only nominally under Ottoman control. In 1514 Sultan Selim I conducted a mass slaughter of dissident Muslims before launching a campaign against ancient Persian rivals, the *Safavid dynasty*. In 1516 the Ottomans took Damascus and in 1517 the new professional corps of firearm-bearing troops, the *Janissaries*, defeated the *Mamluks* of Egypt. The cultural peak of Ottoman civilization came under *Suleiman the Magnificent* (sultan, 1520–1566). He ruled a population nearly three times that of Spain, then the greatest power in Europe and soon to be the dominant power of the Age. He was succeeded by no less than thirteen weak and ineffectual sultans, under whom the Empire fell irretrievably behind the West in industrial and military technology, cultural and scientific innovation, social organization and cohesion, and economic productivity. This long-term trend was disguised by apparently continuing military strength, even after the great naval disaster at *Lepanto*. The Ottoman high tide came in 1683, when in a final surge Ottoman troops washed up against the walls of Vienna, only to begin a centuries-long recession from offensive power and an end to expansion into Europe.

In general, Ottoman decline was rooted in a failure to *modernize*, not just in terms of *technology*, but more importantly in terms of the organization, administration (bureaucracy), and political structures of the Empire. For example, the Ottoman military continued to be slave-based for many decades after the European *Great Powers* had already moved to *standing armies* of the modern, professional sort, which meant that even later military reforms failed to stay even with, let alone catch up to, Europe. In the seventeenth and eighteenth centuries the Ottomans fought mostly defensive campaigns, though not always losing ones, against Austria, Hungary, Poland, Venice, and Russia. The trend was clear, however: the Treaty of Carlowitz (1699) detached Hungary to Austria; Kuchuk Kainarji (1774) sent the Crimea to Russia; 1775 saw *Bukovina* lost to Austria; and in 1812 *Bessarabia* was ceded to Russia. More *Russo-Turkish Wars* followed. This led Sultan Selim III (r. 1789–1809) to undertake major military reforms, creating a new army on an essentially modern basis.

During the first quarter of the nineteenth century the Ottoman Empire's other major problems—its multinational character, lack of centralized political controls, and deep religious differences—continued to feed a deep internal decay. Social and military disintegration—first in Serbia, then in Egypt, and next in Greece—encouraged *secessionist* movements by provincial governors, invited foreign *aggression*, and led to further annexations of outlying provinces. *Mahmud II* (r. 1808–1839) also tried to reform the core structures of the Empire. Instead, he lost Greece in the *Greek War of Independence* (1821–1829), his navy at *Navarino*, and control of Palestine and Syria to *Mehemet Ali* of Egypt. In 1838 he was forced to accept *capitulations* under the Anglo-Ottoman trade convention, which pulled the Empire into the world market. Britain and France propped the Ottomans up as a bulwark against Austria and Russia during the prolonged disputes over the *Eastern Question* and the related *Straits Question*. That helped bring about the *Crimean War*, rebellion, yet another Russo-Turkish War, and major losses of territory under the *Treaty of San Stefano* (1878).

In the late nineteenth century, under *Abdul Hamid II*, Ottoman frustration was felt in atrocities against the Bulgarians and other Christian subjects, such that *Gladstone* and other Western liberals sought to intervene. These were also the years of the first *Armenian genocide* and a final effort, by the *Young Turks*, to remake and modernize an old Empire. Dismayed, humiliated, and damaged by the outcome of the *Balkan Wars*, and the discrete *Italo-Turkish War*, the Young Turks joined the Ottoman Empire to the *Central Powers*, attacking Russia on October 31, 1914. They were certain that Western "guarantees" of their neutrality and *territorial integrity* were not to be trusted, and instead bet all on a last, but in the end terribly losing, gamble to stop the fatal erosion of their Empire by striking at their mortal enemy, Russia. Turkey's entrance into *World War I* was not just a defensive maneuver however: Minister for War *Enver Pasha* indulged deeply *revanchist* grievances and motivations, as did most of the Young Turks and many ordinary citizens, and thought the war would further an imperialist vision of an expanded empire of unified Turkic peoples. Within a week the Turks found themselves also at war with Russia's allies, France and Britain. That cost them Egypt, Kuwait, and the Gulf emirates immediately. The British later helped spark and arm the *Arab Revolt* against Ottoman rule in Syria and Palestine. During the war, Imperial Germany dominated the Ottomans economically, diplomatically, and militarily, while the Western Allies plotted their permanent demise in the *Sykes-Picot agreement*.

As the war ended, the Ottoman Empire was stripped of all its non-Turkish territories and the Allies encouraged revolts and invasions by the Greeks, Kurds, and other peoples. The *Treaty of Sèvres*, dictated to Turkey at the *Paris Peace Conference*, was signed but never *ratified*. It would have created independent states in Armenia, Mesopotamia, and Syria and called for cession of swaths of ethnically and historically Turkish land to Greece, including *Smyrna*. It also would have created an independent Kurdish homeland (*Kurdistan*). It was rejected by the Turks, who were able to outwait Allied unity and outfight the Greeks, to gain the more favorable terms of the *Treaty of Lausanne* in 1923. It was *Atatürk*, above all others, who fended off Greek attacks, overthrew the sultanate, moved the capital to Ankara, and established the modern Republic of Turkey. *See also Crimea; Dodecanese; Gallipoli; Knights Hospitallers; pan-Islamicism; Sublime Porte;* and various lands and countries once part of the Empire, including *Albania; Algeria; Arabia; Armenia; Azerbaijan; Bessarabia; Bosnia; Bulgaria; Cyprus; Egypt; Georgia; Greece; Hejaz; Hungary; Iraq; Kuwait; Libya; Macedonia; Nagorno-Karabakh; Palestine; Roma; Rumania; Serbia; Syria; Transylvania,* and *Tunisia.*

Suggested Readings: Roderic H. Davidson, *Turkey: A Short History*, 3rd ed. (1998); Roderic H. Davidson, *Reform in the Ottoman Empire, 1856–1876* (1973); David Fromkin, *A Peace to End All Peace* (1989); Jason Goodwin, *Lords of the Horizons: A History of the Ottoman Empire* (1999); Marshall Hodgson, *The Gunpowder Empires and Modern Times* (1974); H. Inalcik, *The Ottoman Empire* (1978); C. M. Kortepeter, *Ottoman Imperialism During the Reformation* (1992); Stanford Shaw and E. K. Shaw, *History of the Ottoman Empire and Modern Turkey*, 2 vols. (1977); Andrew Wheatcroft, *The Ottomans* (1993).

Outer Mongolia. *See Mongolia.*

Outer Space Treaty (1967). Treaty on Principles Governing the Activities of States in the Exploration and Use of Outer Space. In 1961 the *United Nations General Assembly (UNGA)* declared in a nonbinding resolution that the principles of the *United Nations Charter* extended to space. Another, nonbinding *declaration* followed in 1963. Primarily reflecting an interest in snuffing out any extension of the *arms race* to space, this 1967 *treaty* stipulated: (1) prohibition of space-based *nuclear weapons*; (2) a ban on military uses of the moon or planets; (3) exploration of space to take place in accordance with the *common heritage principle*; (4) a ban on *territorial* or other *sovereign* claims; (5) cooperation on peaceful *exploitation* of space; (6) liability for harm caused by objects launched into space; (7) people in space, of whatever nation, are to be considered representatives of all humanity, and, as such, all states are bound to aid them in situations of duress; and (8) launching states retain ownership and *jurisdiction* over spacecraft, no matter where a vehicle rests after reentry. Adopted unanimously by the UNGA in 1966, it entered into force in 1967. However, it contains no *verification* or *adjudication* provisions. Related agreements exist on Rescue of Astronauts (1968); Liability for Space Objects (1972); and Peaceful Uses of Outer Space (1976). *See also ballistic missile defense (BMD); Moon Treaty; satellites.*

outflank. To maneuver around the *flank* of an enemy's position, thereby threatening lines of retreat and supply and a multi-sided assault.

outlaw state. (1) In international law: The remote possibility that a *state* might forfeit its status as an *international personality* if it persists in disrespect for the rule of law. (2) In foreign policy rhetoric: States that act outside accepted *norms*, for instance, by sponsoring *terrorism* or flouting *Security Council* resolutions. *See also pariah state; rogue state.*

outliers. Single observations that are anomalous compared to the other data used in a *regression* analysis. They are often extremely interesting cases in and of themselves, with much to teach about the nature of international relations. However, this point is often missed entirely by the *quantitative* minded, who insist that individual cases do not matter and that as researchers they are interested in *theory* rather than content.

out-of-area. Military *theaters* where a security organization has no legal *jurisdiction* or *geostrategic* interest in operations. For example, before 1993 *NATO* never operated outside its Atlantic-member countries zone. Since then it has agreed to a United Nations request to enforce a *no-fly zone* over Bosnia.

output. (1) In *economics*: Any *service* or *commodity* produced and put on the market for sale. (2) In *political science*: *Jargon* for the policy decisions that are yielded from a mix of considerations (*inputs*) fed into the *decision-making* process.

overkill capability. The ability, especially of a nuclear arsenal, to totally destroy an enemy force not once but several times.

overpopulation. When the number of persons in a given territory or state is too great for that area to support at subsistence levels. Beyond subsistence, this becomes a relative concept: how many people is too many depends on one's subjective sense of what level of *exploitation* of *natural resources* is possible and/or necessary and what is a desirable *standard of living*. *See also famine; Thomas Robert Malthus; migration; population.*

overproduction. Producing *goods* or *services* in excess of demand. *See also deflation.*

overseas Chinese. The Chinese *diaspora.* Not all Chinese migrants, pushed by a swelling population and huge internal disorders in the eighteenth and nineteenth centuries in particular, chose to move overseas. Most migrated overland—to Burma, Tibet, northern Vietnam, to the vast desert regions of Xinjiang, or north into Manchuria and Mongolia. Others settled on Taiwan. Overseas Chinese established communities along the main oceanic *trade routes*, mainly in Southeast Asia, Malaya, and what is today Indonesia. This was disdained and discouraged by most emperors, however, and so these communities existed both outside imperial control and imperial protection. They expanded after the lifting of the *Ming* ban on maritime commerce in 1567. However, leaving China was still regarded as an act of disloyalty: Chinese coastal populations were sometimes treated with great harshness for engaging in external trade, and official China maintained little contact with these communities or interest in their affairs, despite in theory claiming them as continuing subjects. Many thousands were massacred in the Philippines in the early seventeenth century by the Spanish. The *Qing* state showed no real concern for Chinese outside its borders (and arguably, in the late Qing, not that much for those inside China either) until 1873, when it established a consulate in Singapore as part of its overall effort to develop a modern diplomatic service. Chinese immigrant laborers were important in developing the west coast of North America in the nineteenth century, starting the *gold rush* in *California* in the 1840s, and then continuing through building of the transcontinental *railways* in both Canada and the United States. Then, starting in 1880, they were subjected to *Oriental exclusion laws* by the U.S. Congress, acting for California, and later also by Canada in behalf of its agitated white population in British Columbia. They also worked and settled in South America in the nineteenth century. In 1957 China finally *ratified* its first *dual nationality* treaty concerning overseas Chinese, with Indonesia. By the late twentieth century ethnic Chinese formed distinct and influential, but also very often persecuted, minorities in many countries. Many of the *boat people* who fled Vietnam after 1975 were persecuted ethnic Chinese. In 1999 murderous anti-Chinese riots convulsed Indonesia.

Suggested Readings: Wang Gungwu, *China and the Overseas Chinese* (1991); Lyn Pan, *Sons of the Yellow Emperor* (1990).

overseas departments (of France). Off-shore administrative units for lands incorporated under the French constitution that participate directly in French government through elected representatives. *See also French Guiana; Guadeloupe; Martinique; Mayotte; overseas territories; Reúnion; St. Pierre et Miquelon.*

overseas territories. (1) Colonial possessions not contiguous with a *metropolitan power.* (2) A type of direct *dependency*, in which certain islands are constitutionally part of the home country. *See also French Polynesia; French*

Southern and Antarctic Lands; Netherlands Antilles; New Caledonia (Kanaky); overseas departments; Wallis and Fortuna Islands.

overt-covert operations. A clumsy phrase to describe *covert* operations that are openly admitted because they are successful or publicly approved and therefore good for the *intelligence agency's* image, for example, CIA aid to Afghan *guerrillas* or *mujahadeen*, 1979–1989.

Oyo Empire. *See Nigeria; Yoruba.*

ozone depletion. The thinning of the protective ozone layer in the upper strata of the atmosphere, especially the opening of ozone holes over the poles as a result of natural release of volcanic gases, but also CFCs and other artificial chemical pollutants. In 1984–1987, the Vienna and Montreal Conventions on ozone depletion were negotiated and signed. A convention on climate change was also signed at the *Earth Summit.*

P

P-5. *See Permanent Members of the Security Council.*

pacification. (1) In general: A euphemism deployed by governments to conceal violent repression of armed resistance, usually in rural areas. (2) In military usage: A tactic used against *guerrillas* whereby one first secures urban areas, then fans out to control the countryside "like an oil slick" ("tache d'huile"), so that the local population seek security within the "pacified zone." The French used this technique to effect in Morocco and Algeria in the nineteenth century, but it failed them badly in the *French-Indochina War*. (3) In the *Vietnam War*: A U.S. policy of "nation-building" and winning back the countryside from the *Viêt Cong*, or National Liberation Front (NLF), by providing village-level security by physical elimination of the NLF through conventional military means and via a selective *assassination* program run by the CIA (code-named "Phoenix," which killed at least 26,000); directly protecting friendly infrastructure and newly pacified villages; and organizing intelligence networks, *propaganda*, and support for civic participation. This effort increased after the *Tet Offensive* and was intimately connected to *Vietnamization*.

pacific blockade. *See blockade; quarantine.*

Pacific Islands Forum (PIC). Originally, the South Pacific Forum (the name was changed in 2000). It was formed at the urging of Fiji to address political issues explicitly excluded from the *South Pacific Commission*. Its founding meeting was in New Zealand in 1971. Other island nations and self-governing *territories* were invited to join, but *Melanesian* members resisted the inclusion of non–self-governing territories (mainly French and American). In 1985 the Forum agreed to designate the South Pacific a *nuclear weapons–free zone*. That helped precipitate a crisis within *ANZUS*. In 1989 Britain, Canada, China, France, Japan, and the United States were invited (as "friendly states") to attend postforum regional discussions on an annual basis. The PIC has no charter, proceeding only by consensus. Consensus positions were reached condemning nuclear tests in the region and on the *law of the sea* (with a special regional interest in *Exclusive Economic Zones*), *decolonization* issues, the environment, and various *fishery* questions. Several regional, *functional agencies* dealing with aviation, fisheries, shipping, and pollution have been established under PIC auspices. Issues of concern are: (1) *deforestation* of atolls by Southeast Asian and other lumber operations; (2) exploitation of the area's rich fish stocks by "distant water fishing nations" (notably, Japan, South Korea, Taiwan, and the United States), which paid minimal compensation to sparsely populated island nations. The PIC is an official observer at *APEC* meetings. *See also Exclusive Economic Zone.*

Pacific Ocean. The world's largest ocean (70 million square miles), bounded by the west coast of the *Americas* and the east coasts of the *Asian* and *Australian* continents. It is divided by the equator into the North Pacific and South Pacific. *See also Pacific Rim.*

Pacific Rim. Geographically, all territories with a *Pacific Ocean* coastline. However, the term is used politically to depict the Pacific as a transportation freeway connecting states in *interdependent* relations, instead of holding them at vast distances as it once did. It is sometimes used to imply a regional community, parallel to the *Atlantic Community*, whether that exists in fact or not. Some prefer the term "Asia-Pacific" as a way to both focus on *Asia* and exclude *South America*. In Canada and Japan, but less so elsewhere, "North Pacific" is used to focus even more tightly on the seven northern hemisphere states of Canada, China, the two Koreas, Japan, Russia, and the United States.

pacific settlement of disputes. *See peaceful settlement of disputes.*

Pacific War (1941–1945). The preferred Japanese term for the naval and marine garrison combat in the Pacific, mainly against British and American forces, which Japanese historians tend to see as more apart from the larger story of *World War II* than do their Western counterparts. *See also China War.*
  Suggested Reading: Sabur Ienaga, *The Pacific War* (1978).

pacifism. (1) Simple nonresistance to *aggression*. (2) The principled position that all *war*, and involvement in war, must be resisted as a moral evil. Sentimental pacifism is common in peacetime, but usually dissolves rapidly as the ethnic, national, or religious passions of those holding such views are engaged and inflamed by war. Philosophical pacifism is more serious, and therefore more rare. Many individuals of refined conscience, including *Mohandas Gandhi* and *Albert Einstein*, have been pacifists; others have not. In terms of groups, pacifism is promoted most consistently by certain religious communities, usually offshoots of mainstream *Buddhism*, *Christianity*, or *Hinduism*, but rarely more militant faiths such as *Sikhism* or *Islam*. As among the earliest Christians, this is often the product of alienation from all earthly politics rather than a strictly principled abhorrence of violence. Quakers are prominent among modern pacifists and were among the first to respond with pacifist peace programs to periods of international violence and upheaval such as the *Napoleonic Wars* and *World War I*. Following the Great War of 1914 to 1918, in face of the awful carnage and political and military futility of that war, pacifism exercised great appeal to many, especially in Europe where the suffering had been greatest. This mood did not survive *World War II*, however, with its revelations of the *Holocaust* in Europe and everyday Japanese brutalities in China and throughout Asia. In light of such events, of the unmitigated evil of *Nazism* in particular, even many former pacifists concluded that some causes were worth fighting against, even though none might be worth fighting for.

Thus, in the postwar period the *just war tradition*, arguably the most sophisticated moral examination of the problem of war, enjoyed a historic revival. That tradition rejects absolute pacifism for failing to make key moral distinctions about just cause and right intention. It argues that there are crucial differences between *aggressor* and victim which may at times oblige direct action by the victim alone or even by third parties. Yet, pacifism appears nearly always to counsel passivity. Absolute pacifists reply that any notion of just war is an oxymoron, as all war is inherently unjust and morally unacceptable because it requires means too evil to contemplate or capable of advancing good ends. They therefore tend to support calls for general *disarmament* and *arms control*, to oppose military preparedness, and to propose such nonviolent means of conflict resolution as *arbitration* and *mediation*. During the *Cold War* a pacifism of fear was encouraged by concern over *nuclear weapons*. Such "nuclear pacifism" argued against any research, construction, or deployment of such weapons even for purposes of *deterrence*. However, with the end of the Cold War fear subsided among most populations and this form of pacifism lost its mass appeal. It appears, therefore, that rather than pacifists helping to raise awareness of the futility of war among modern *Great Powers*, it is the futility of modern, *industrialized*, and possibly also nuclear, wars which raises a consciousness of pacifism. *See also conscientious objection.*

pact. An alternate term for *treaty*. It is usually reserved for military agreements, *alliances* aimed at specific adversaries, or *multilateral* arrangements.

pacta sunt servanda. "Treaties are binding." Legal maxim affirming that *treaties* create firm legal obligations and rights and require contracting parties to observe all *terms* on which *reservations* have not been accepted. Furthermore, treaties bind *states*, not mere and transitory governments. This means that a successor government, even a revolutionary one, may not (legally) renounce binding international agreements except in accordance with the terms previously agreed which permit legal *termination* of the binding obligation incurred. Treaties also bind *successor states*, though with modifications according to the nature and degree of succession. Thus, the former Soviet republics each accepted shares of the rights and obligations of the *extinct* Soviet Union, but Russia assumed the main burden of obligation and the main advantages, such as the *veto* in the *Security Council*. For limitations, *see also validity*.

pacta tertiis nec nocere nec podesse possunt. "Treaties impose no burden and confer no benefits beyond contracting parties." A statement of the rule that *treaties* create rights and binding duties only for *states* which are party to them. *See also consent.*

Pact of Steel (May 22, 1939). A ten-year *nonaggression pact* signed by Germany and Italy in the run-up to *World War II*. It formalized the Rome-Berlin Axis. *See also Tripartite Pact.*

pactum de contrahendo. An advance agreement which announces the intention of states to draft a *treaty*.

Pahlavi, Muhammad Reza Shah (1919–1980). "Shah-in-Shah" of Iran, 1941–1979. He succeeded his father, who was deposed by the *Allies* during *World War II*. He allowed the Allies to tranship *Lend-Lease* from Iran. In 1946 he asked for, and received, Western help to resist Soviet *encroachment*. He nearly lost power in 1953 in a crisis over *nationalization* of Iran's oil facilities by *Mossadegh*. He hung on with the help of American and British *intelligence*. In 1955 he took Iran into the *Baghdad Pact* and built it into a major regional power. He continued *modernizing* and *secularizing* reforms of his father, but as domestic opposition grew, he turned increasingly to his *secret police* (SAVAK) to repress dissent. Sick with cancer, on January 16, 1979, he fled into *exile*, first to New York, then Mexico, next to Panama, and finally to *Anwar Sadat*'s Egypt, where he was given *asylum* and died. *See also Iranian Revolution.*

Pahlavi, Reza Shah (1878–1944). A Persian army officer who launched a successful *coup* against the Qajar dynasty in 1925 and, with the support of Great Britain, was crowned Shah of Persia. He began major *secularizing* and *modernizing* reforms ("White Revolution"), modeled on the reforms of *Atatürk*. He ruled Iran—the name was changed in 1935—until 1941, when his pro-

Axis sympathies led to joint British-Soviet military intervention which forced abdication in favor of his son, *Muhammad Reza Pahlavi*. He died in *exile* from Iran.

Pakistan. Pakistan was founded as a *Muslim* state (the name means "Land of the Pure") at the insistence of the *Muslim League* and *Muhammad Ali Jinnah*. In fact, its creation was more the result of long-standing subnationalisms in *Bengal* and *Punjab*, papered over with an Islamist ideology. Still, the result was *partition* of India in 1947 into three main parts, with *East Pakistan* (Bengal) and *West Pakistan* (Punjab and other attached territories) divided by 1,000 miles of Indian territory. That odd beginning was ostensibly designed to separate the *subcontinent's* Muslim from Hindu areas, but left more Muslims in India than the total population of Pakistan. The first *Indo-Pakistani War* immediately broke out over *Kashmir* (1947–1949), followed by the *Second* (1965) and *Third* (1971), which was by far the most damaging to Pakistan. Domestically, Pakistan stumbled from one assassination, coup, and state of emergency to the next. Throughout its history, Pakistan's Army enjoyed a privileged social and political position as a result of ongoing conflict with India. Pakistan became a republic in 1956 (it had been a *Dominion*). *Ayub Khan* introduced *martial law* and an aggressive swagger to foreign policy in 1958. Pakistan joined *SEATO* and *CENTO*, largely to gain access to American military aid.

Civilian rule returned in the wake of the loss of East Pakistan (*Bangladesh*) in 1971, when *Zulfikar Ali Bhutto* became president. Bhutto was overthrown in 1977 and subsequently executed by *Muhammad Zia ul-Haq*, who reintroduced martial law, 1981–1986. The Soviet invasion of Afghanistan and India's *tilt* toward the *Soviet Union* made Pakistan more important in the eyes of American strategists. Aid flowed in by the billions in exchange for facilitating arms supplies to the Afghan *mujahadeen*, whom Pakistan supported anyway out of fear of the Soviet thrust into Central Asia. Zia was assassinated in 1988, to be succeeded in time by the daughter of the man he had killed: *Benazir Bhutto*. She was sacked in 1990 on what may have been trumped-up charges and an unconstitutional process, but in 1993 she returned to power. Pakistan withdrew from the Commonwealth in 1972 after that organization admitted Bangladesh; and it continues to harbor ambitions of obtaining more or even all of Kashmir. In 1990 the United States suspended aid both because the Soviets had pulled out of Afghanistan and because Washington suspected Karachi of having constructed *nuclear weapons*. In 1998 this suspicion was publicly confirmed when India test-detonated five nuclear weapons and Pakistan responded in kind. In 1999 Pakistan sponsored a cross-border attack by militants in Kashmir which led to serious fighting and Indian retaliation. Also that year, General Pervez Musharraf took power in a coup, displacing Nawaz Sharif. Pakistan began a basic reorientation of its foreign policy after the *September 11, 2001, terrorist attack on the United States,* by which it played a key role in supporting the U.S. assault on the *Taliban* regime and *al Qaeda* bases in Afghanistan. Before that shift, Pakistan had sought to make up for a lack of political legitimacy and the minimal loyalty of the population in its western provinces by catering to *Islamists* in the Taliban and among its own Pashtun minority. Tensions with India rose sharply again at the end of 2001 after a *terrorist* assault on India's parliament by a Pakistan-based group, even while the campaign against al Qaeda in Afghanistan was still underway.

Suggested Reading: A. S. Ahmed, *Jinnah, Pakistan, and Islamic Identity* (1997).

palace coup. A seizure of power by one faction of a royal court (or *dynasty* or, most loosely, any dictatorial government) from another, with or without direct military assistance. *See also Catherine the Great;* coup d'etat; *Dowager Empress.*

Palau. After *World War II* this South Pacific island was made part of the *Trust Territory of the Pacific Islands,* administered by the United States. In 1978 it rejected *commonwealth status.* In a 1979 *referendum* it approved by 92 percent a non-nuclear constitution. The United States removed the anti-nuclear clauses and resubmitted, but this time only 30 percent approved. With anti-nuclear clauses restored, it passed by 78 percent in 1980. Palau then asked for self-government in *free association* with the United States, which insisted on a naval base agreement. Palau also agreed not to undertake *defense* arrangements incompatible with U.S. interests. In a 1983 referendum a majority approved the compact, which included a nuclear ship visitation clause, but the vote fell short of the 75 percent required by the Palau constitution. Although the *Federated States of Micronesia* and the *Marshall Islands* achieved free associated status by Senate consent in 1986, Palau did not. It had *autonomy*, but remained suspended in a legal limbo between the status of *trust territory* and independent *microstate*. In November 1993, it voted in another referendum (this one requiring only a simple majority and supervised by the United Nations) to accept free association with the United States. This arrangement entered into force in 1994.

Pale of Settlement. The area in Russia and Russian Poland where Jews were permitted to settle, and were confined, after their expulsions from Spain and Portugal.

Palestine. An ancient Asian country known in biblical times as Canaan. This territory, which included what was later divided among Israel, Jordan, and the *occupied territories*, became an *Ottoman* province in 1517. It remained under Turkish rule until 1918, when it was overrun by the *Arab Revolt* and the British advance on Damascus. *Zionists* began to migrate there in small numbers at the turn of the twentieth century. In 1917 its future was dramatically altered by the *Balfour Declaration*, promising a Jewish homeland in Palestine. It was made a British *mandate territory* in 1920, but the Balfour

Declaration and rising Jewish immigration henceforth dominated its increasingly sectarian internal politics. Arabs and Jews alike sparked and participated in sectarian riots in the 1920s and 1930s. More intense violence erupted, 1937–1939, and was repressed by British forces taking resort to draconian measures—which provoked retaliation by Jewish guerrillas such as the *Haganah*, *Irgun*, and *Stern Gang*. Independence was delayed by *World War II*, but in 1947 the United Nations voted to *partition* Palestine into Jewish and Arab states, with *Jerusalem* to become an *international city*. Britain walked away from the mandate on May 15, 1948, leading to three-way partition (Israel, the *West Bank* to *Transjordan*, and *Gaza* to Egypt) and to the *First Arab-Israeli War* and the exodus of hundreds of thousands of Palestinian Arabs to *refugee camps* in other Arab countries.

In 1967 the West Bank and Gaza, along with Sinai, were occupied by Israel following the *Third Arab-Israeli War*. The future of Palestine became a central issue in the *Camp David Accords*, and the focus of Egyptian-Israeli tensions following the peace treaty and return of the Sinai to Egypt. From 1988 Palestine experienced the rising violence of the *Intifada* and the counterviolence employed by Israeli forces and *Mossad*. Modern conceptions of Palestine range from the extreme Israeli view that Jordan is already a Palestinian state to the extreme Palestinian view that a new Palestinian state must be erected on the whole territory of the old mandate, requiring the utter elimination of Israel. More moderate voices at last prevailed in September 1993, with an agreement between Israel and the *Palestine Liberation Organization* for a trial period of *autonomy* in Gaza and Jericho, under the *Palestinian Authority*, with security guarantees to and from Israel. However, the peace process broke down completely in 2000, when *Yassir Arafat* rejected a generous *land for peace* offer from the Barak government. A second Intifada followed, along with a hardening of attitudes on all sides. *See also Arab League; Crusades; Hamas; Hezbollah; Jewish Agency; Jordan; Lebanese Civil War; Mamluks; Mehemet Ali; Ottoman Empire.*

Suggested Readings: Yoav Gelber, *Palestine: 1948* (2001); Ibrahim Abu-Lughod, ed., *The Transformation of Palestine* (1971, 1987); Wm. Roger Louis and Robert W. Stookey, eds., *The End of the Palestine Mandate* (1986); John Quigley, *Palestine and Israel* (1990); Abdul L. Tibawi, *British Interests in Palestine, 1800–1901* (1961).

Palestine Liberation Organization (PLO). Founded in 1964 and governed by the Palestine National Council, a quasi-parliament. Led by *Yassir Arafat*, the radical group *Fatah* formed the core of the PLO and took majority control after 1968. It led other *guerrilla/terrorist* groups in forming the PLO's armed wing, which conducted raids into Israel or against Israeli targets in third countries. It was expelled from Jordan after a bloody confrontation with King Hussein in 1970, settling in Lebanon, where it was effectively a state within a state and soon became heavily embroiled in the *Lebanese Civil War*. In 1974 the Arab states collectively announced that they regarded the PLO as the official body responsible for all Palestinian issues, after which most other states recognized it as the sole representative of the Palestinian people. In 1982 it was attacked in Lebanon by Israel and driven from Beirut and its outlying camps. The PLO was compelled to evacuate to Tunisia, where it moved its headquarters and where Israel bombed it again, in 1985. It was caught mostly unawares by the *Intifada* and, while trying to catch up to and then lead the accelerating *uprising*, found itself challenged within the *occupied territories* by *Hamas*.

The PLO lost key support within the Arab world by backing Iraq in the *Gulf War*, but never lost its status for most Arabs as the sole recognized voice of Palestine. Israel consistently refused to negotiate with the PLO, however, stating it would talk only to Palestinians who resided in the occupied lands. Israel was able to convince the United States to adopt the same policy for many years, which enormously complicated the peace process. However, behind the scenes of *multilateral* talks which got underway at the end of the Gulf War, the PLO in fact was formulating the Palestinian position, as both Israel and the United States knew. In September 1993, after months of *back-channel negotiations* in Norway, it agreed to an accord with Israel, which had begun to see the PLO as moderate, at least compared to the utter irreconcilables in Hamas. The PLO renounced its prior calls for the destruction of Israel and officially accepted a two-state solution to the problem of *sovereign* ownership of Palestine. It then became the dominant force within the *Palestinian Authority*. In 2001 Arafat declined a *land for peace* deal with Israel, which led to a second Intifada and rehardened Israeli attitudes toward the PLO as a partner in the peace process.

Suggested Readings: Diana Reische, *Arafat and the Palestine Liberation Organization* (1991); Barry Rubin, *The Transformation of Palestinian Politics* (1999).

Palestinian Authority. A governing body with *autonomous* powers, established for all major towns and cities of the *occupied territories*, but excluding Jewish settler communities and *Jerusalem*, under a peace agreement negotiated between Israel and the *Palestine Liberation Organization* in 1993, amended in 1995. It was initially headed by *Yasser Arafat*, who several times threatened to make a unilateral declaration of independence for Palestine, but in 2000 balked at a *land for peace* deal which would, in fact, have made Palestinian statehood a real possibility. At the end of 2001 its relations with both Israel and *Hamas* were badly damaged by a spate of suicide bombings and attendant reprisals.

Palestinians. (1) Pre-1948: All inhabitants of pre-partition *Palestine*, whether Jew or Arab. (2) Post-1948: The Arab population of pre-partition Palestine, now scattered in a *diaspora* of their own. There are approximately 5 million Palestinians, of whom some 2.3 million live in Israel or the *occupied territories*, many in *refugee camps*. Another 1.3 million live in Jordan, a number swollen by those expelled from Kuwait in 1991 for welcoming Iraqi invaders in 1990.

Palme, Olaf (1927–1986). Swedish statesman. Prime minister, 1969–1976, 1982–1986. A major figure in international *social democracy*, he was an active advocate of opposition to *apartheid* and of *arms control*, despite Sweden's record as a quiet but major *arms exporting nation*. He was critical of the United States during the *Vietnam War*. He headed the Palme Commission in 1980 on global *disarmament*. He also served on the *Brandt Commission* and on a United Nations *fact-finding* and *mediation* mission which sought an end to the *Iran-Iraq War*. He was shot on the way home from an outing with his wife. A deranged man was convicted of the killing in 1989 (later overturned). It is not thought to have been a political assassination.

Palmerston, Henry John (1784–1865). British statesman. First lord of the admiralty, 1807–1809; secretary for war, 1809–1828; foreign secretary, 1830–1834, 1835–1841, 1846–1851; prime minister, 1855–1858, 1859–1865. He made the transition from *Tory* to *Whig* in 1830. In his cabinet days, he served with *Liverpool, Canning,* and *Wellington*. He was out of office over the issue of *free trade* in corn, vital to the relief of the *famine* in Ireland, but back in during the *Revolutions of 1848*. In his several terms as prime minister, on occasion he promoted *liberal* causes, distancing Britain from the *reactionary,* continental powers by supporting Greek independence in the 1820s, securing Belgian independence in 1831 (also done to prevent Belgium becoming a French satellite), distantly supporting the *Risorgimento,* and then *recognizing* Italian unification in 1861. More often he acted out of a strict sense of British *national interest*. While joining the *Quadruple Alliance,* he supported the Ottomans against both *Mehemet Ali* of Egypt (in 1839) and, later, *Nicholas I* of Russia in the *Crimean War,* which his policy helped to extend even after it had clearly stalemated through his insistence on vigorous military action. He also oversaw the disaster of the *Anglo-Afghan War*. With more immediate success, he fought the *Opium Wars* against China and suppressed the *Indian Mutiny,* winning an election in 1858, which had been called over the former. His actions and rhetoric could be reckless, as when he approached war with the United States during the *Trent Affair*. Still, he kept Britain—and thereby, also France—out of the *American Civil War*. He moved to institute *direct rule* in India upon the Indian Mutiny. Through sheer longevity, and by bluster and repeated interventions and a sense that he was the nation's minister and not just his party's, he left a more lasting mark than anyone else on the diplomacy of the greatest *world power* of the nineteenth century.

Pamyat. A Russian, *fascist* political movement founded as the *Soviet Union* was collapsing and dedicated to *Slavophile* values and hostile to democracy. It even called for new *pogroms* against Russia's Jews.

Pan-African Congress (PAC). A radical splinter group which broke with *Mandela* and the *African National Congress* in 1959. There was a brief reconciliation in 1990. In 1993 the ANC and PAC again divided over the pace of change toward a multiracial society and the degree of acceptable *power sharing* with whites: PAC wanted no delay of either goal.

pan-Africanism. A social, cultural, and political movement which sought to span the political divisions of the African continent, sometimes applied exclusively below the Sahara, through appeal to a continental supernationalism. American black intellectuals, especially Marcus Garvey and W. E. B. Du Bois, were highly influential in stimulating the movement. Several pan-Africanist congresses were held from 1900 sponsored by Du Bois, but to little direct political effect. *World War II* changed that, creating the preconditions for African *decolonization* by draining Europe's resources and fatally weakening its empires. The pan-African conference held in London in 1945 made the movement influential in several *independence* drives. It received rhetorical support within the *OAU* in the 1960s, leading to formation of a minority bloc within that regional organization. Once real power was won by African elites on a national basis, the pan-African movement ceased to have political meaning and subsided into a cultural ideal. *See also* négritude; *Nkrumah*.
Suggested Readings: Immanuel Geiss, *Panafricanism* (1974); Ronald W. Walters, *Pan-Africanism in the African Diaspora* (1993).

Panama. In 1513 Vasco Núñez de Balboa stood on a Panamanian peak and looked west, the first European to see the Pacific coast. He thus confirmed that *Columbus* had discovered not Asia, but a *New World*. An *audiencia* was established in Panama in 1538; it was broken up in 1543 and then reestablished in 1564. After 1584 the small city of Portobello held an annual fair which was the chief method of entry for Old World commerce heading into South America. Although later surpassed by new cities and ports, it retained importance until 1740, when the last fleet sailed. In 1826 *Bolívar* invited leading South American nationalists to a congress in Panama to discuss his grand vision for a continental confederacy in alliance with Britain. The Panamanian Isthmus remained attached to Colombia throughout the nineteenth century, after the break with Spain. Accepting U.S. encouragement and naval support, it became independent in 1903 in the *War of the Thousand Days*, after which it agreed to allow the United States to build the *Panama Canal* and to control the *Canal Zone*. Until the advent of the *Good Neighbor policy*, U.S. marines routinely *intervened* in Panama's volatile domestic politics. During *World War I* the United States had a heavy military presence in Panama, protecting the vitally important canal. Relations with the United States were broken, 1963–1964, over Panama's demand for return of the Canal Zone (and its revenues). An agreement was reached with *Jimmy Carter*, 1977–1979, though not without a great deal of opposition to returning the canal from the *Republican* right ("It's ours. We built it!" said *Ronald Reagan* during the debate).

During the 1980s the Panamanian military, under Manuel Noriega, ran guns to the *Contras* in Nicaragua and drugs to the addicts of Miami, Orlando, and points north. In 1988 Noriega launched a *coup* and assumed the presidency after the properly elected president tried to fire him. The United States imposed *sanctions*, and Noriega was indicted by a Miami court on drug charges. Elections were set for May 7, 1989. When Noriega announced he had won, international observers cried fraud. It did not help matters that the real winner (Guillermo Endara) was beaten bloody by Noriega's thugs before a worldwide TV audience. An attempted coup on October 3rd failed, and there was considerable criticism of *George H. Bush* for failing to lend at least *logistical* support to the coup planners. In November and December, a U.S. marine from the Canal Zone was killed and others harassed by Panamanian soldiers. The war of words and mutual *saber rattling* intensified, with Noriega at one point ramming a resolution through his Assembly which seemed to *declare war* on the United States. On December 20th the United States obliged, with an airborne *invasion* of some 25,000 troops which included the first-ever combat use of *stealth technology* aircraft. Noriega sought *asylum* with the papal *nuncio*, but after 10 days he surrendered (January 3, 1990) and was taken to Miami to stand trial. Endara was installed as president, and American aid and advisers arrived to help with *reconstruction*. The Canal Zone was returned to Panamanian control as midnight passed on December 31, 1999.

Panama Canal. The first effort to build a canal across the Panamanian isthmus was made from 1881 to 1889 by the French builder of the *Suez Canal*, Ferdinand de Lesseps. Malarial fever and bankruptcy defeated that effort. The 40-mile-long passage was built from 1903 to 1914 by U.S. Army engineers, in response to strategic interests first made clear during the two-ocean *Spanish-American War*. A Panamanian revolt and *secession* from Colombia in the *War of the Thousand Days* was endorsed by *Theodore Roosevelt*. The United States quickly obtained rights to garrison the *Canal Zone*, but also accepted a *servitude* to keep the canal open to all ships in peacetime. It proved of great *strategic* importance, permitting the U.S. Navy to easily reinforce its Pacific from its Atlantic fleet and vice versa. The greater size and draft of *post–World War II* warships, tankers, and merchant ships reduced its significance. The original (1904) agreement was revised in two *treaties* in 1979. One promised to abolish the Canal Zone and remove U.S. troops by midnight of December 31, 1999. It gave Panama *jurisdiction* over most of the Canal Zone, including the ports at either end, but it also reserved the right of defense of the canal to the United States. The second treaty came into effect on January 1, 2000. It declared the canal *neutral* and assigned a right of defense to both Panama and the United States, to be exercised jointly or severally.

Panama, Congress of (1826). *See Simón Bolívar.*

Panama, Declaration of (1939). An effort by the American republics, led by the United States, to keep *World War II* in Europe, distant from the shores of the Americas. It declared a *neutral zone* 300 nautical miles around the Americas, excepting Canada, which was already a *belligerent*. This *declaration* was rejected by all the major naval powers in the Atlantic region (Britain, France, Italy, and Germany), which simply ignored it in their combat operations. *See also Battle of the Atlantic.*

pan-Americanism. Social, cultural, or political movements which seek to span the political divisions of the Americas. Historically, the term sometimes excluded Canada, the United States, and the non-Latin Caribbean. *See also Organization of American States.*

Pan-American Union. Founded in 1890 to promote cultural, technical, and other exchanges among the states of the *Americas*, from 1948 it was incorporated into the larger structure of the *Organization of American States*.

pan-Arabism. Social, cultural, or political movements which seek to span the actual division of Arab *peoples* into diverse *states*, sometimes with the object of creating a single Arab political community ("the Arab nation"). Where *fundamentalists* include an emphasis on the majority population's common *Islamic* religious and political traditions, *Copts* from Egypt, *Maronite Christians* from Lebanon, and other non-Muslim Arabs are by definition excluded. *See also Arab nationalism.*

Panipat, Battles of. Three major battles in modern Indian history were fought at this strategic site north of *Delhi*. (1) 1526: *Mughal* (Timurid) rule was established in *Delhi* by King Babur (1483–1530) of Kabul, a direct descendant of two earlier scourges of settled civilizations, *Tamerlane* and *Ghengis Khan*, following his victory over the *Delhi Sultanate* (1200–1526) at Panipat. (2) 1556: Troops loyal to *Akbar* defeated an Afghan army at Panipat, preserving Mughal rule in India. (3) The *Marathas* were decisively defeated by an Afghan (*Pathan*) army at Panipat, fatally weakening the Maratha state and opening the door to its conquest by troops of the *East India Company*, in a series of sharp wars and rebellions ending in 1818.

pan-Islamism. Within *Islam* in the nineteenth century, given the weakness of the *Ottoman Empire* and the growing *Eastern Question*, and during the *scramble for Africa* of the European *Great Powers*, a revivalist religious and political movement arose in opposition to the increasing encroachment by Christian powers on historically Muslim lands. It began in Turkey in the 1870s, where the recent unifications of Italy and Germany made a sharp impression. It gained adherents in Egypt after the British takeover in 1882; from there it spread through the Middle East and North Africa, to reach sub-Saharan Africa early in the twentieth century. The core idea that all Muslims belong to a single civilization, with common interests and enemies, did not survive—other than in more *radical* circles—the breakup of the Ottoman Empire (and, later, parts of several European empires) into discrete Muslim states. However, culturally it remains a powerful undercurrent in Muslim societies, capable of taking amorphous political shape whenever mass sentiment in the *Islamic world* is aroused by a symbolic issue or dispute.

pan-Slavism. (1) Social, cultural, or political movements which seek to span the political divisions of the *Slavs*. (2) A *tsarist* leaning—but not official foreign policy—in favor of support for Slav independence (always excepting Poland) in lands occupied by the *Ottomans* or *Austria*. Its purpose was to inspire *secession* by the Slav areas, and thereby weaken regional enemies and perhaps prepare territory for *annexation*. Its implicit appeal to *nationalism* undercut its utility to Russia, itself a multinational empire. *See also Slavophile.*
Suggested Reading: Barbara Jelavich, *Russia's Balkan Entanglements, 1806–1914* (1991).

Panzer. German *armor* divisions in *World War II* made up primarily of tanks, but also including mechanized support troops. They were capable of powerful assault and rapid advance in the early *Blitzkrieg* campaigns, 1939–1942. Their tactics and formations ultimately were imitated by the other major powers, however, and then turned against Germany. Also, they grew progressively weaker as the war went on: in 1939 a full-strength Panzer division boasted some 328 tanks; by mid-1943 they were down, on average, below 75 tanks apiece; and by 1945 a tank division had just 50 tanks. This came about through battlefield *attrition*, the failure of German industry to increase production, and a tendency for German designers—spurred also directly by *Hitler*—to gigantism, which led to production of fewer tanks but of multiple design, with some attaining enormous mass, in 1944 and 1945. *See also Battle of France; Charles André de Gaulle; Heinz Guderian; Battle of Kursk; Erwin Rommel; Waffen SS.*

papal nuncio. *See nuncio.*

Papal States (755–1870). Territories in central Italy under the temporal authority of the popes, granted by a succession of Carolingian kings of the Franks in the eighth century, but also based on a papal forgery, the infamous "Donation of *Constantine*," purporting to document an imperial—*Roman Empire*—fourth-century grant of vast central and south Italian lands to the popes. The degree of papal temporal power waxed and waned with the fortunes of the popes in their great struggle with the emperors of the *Holy Roman Empire*, in the tenth through thirteenth centuries, reaching a nadir with the

"Avignon Captivity," when several popes were prisoners of the French court, and then the *Great Schism*, in which three popes competed for Peter's crown and control of the See of Rome. During the Italian *Renaissance* the Papal States were led by warrior popes, who made frequent war and intrigued to expand, as did the princes of other *city-states*. They *declared war* on France in 1793, in opposition to the *French Revolution*'s radical *secularism* and confiscation of church property. *Napoleon I* occupied the Papal States (twice). They were restored, as was so much in Europe, by the *Congress of Vienna*. There were several rebellions against papal control in the nineteenth century, leading to a 20-year French *protectorate* in all but name. As late as mid-century the Papal States spanned 16,000 square miles and contained over three million souls (as the popes would say). Their takeover by the Italian state in 1870 caused a 60-year rift between Italy and the papacy, a new form of the old *Roman Question*. This was settled in the *Lateran Agreements* in 1929. Today, only the vestigial hectares of *Vatican City* remain under the temporal control of the popes. *See also Austria; Catholic Church; Charlemagne; Giuseppe Garibaldi; Holy See; Giuseppe Mazzini; Pius IX; Risorgimento.*

Papandreou, Andreas (1919–1996). Prime minister of Greece, 1981–1989; 1993–1996; son of *Georges Papandreou*. He was an economist by training, a socialist by conviction, and an erstwhile *naturalized* American (he renounced his U.S. citizenship). He was imprisoned in 1967 during the "colonels' coup," which overthrew his father. In exile, he became the focus of Greek opposition to the *junta*. He returned to Greece when the colonels' regime collapsed. His premiership was marked by rhetorical confrontation with, and radical chic posing toward, traditional Western *allies*. He practiced socialist economics at home and faced formal charges that he was redistributing rather a lot of the government's wealth to his own bank accounts and those of political cronies. He was also criticized internationally for a slack policy toward *terrorism*; for a time, some airlines avoided Athens airport. His government fell in a swirl of personal financial and sex scandals. Without demur, Greeks reelected him to a majority in 1993, and more of the same followed until his death.

Papandreou, Georges (1888–1968). Greek prime minister, 1944, 1963–1965. He was active in the anti-Nazi *resistance* during *World War II*. He was a popular politician, but one dogged by the problem of *Cyprus* and consistently opposed by the army. The latter launched the "colonel's coup" in 1967 to prevent his return to office.

Papua New Guinea. The Dutch claimed the western half of the island of New Guinea in the nineteenth century. The eastern half was divided by the British and Germans in 1884. The British transferred the southeast portion (Papua) to Australia in 1905, and Canberra seized the rest of eastern New Guinea from Germany in 1914. It was made a Class C *mandate* under Australian administration from 1920. In 1942–1944 it was *occupied* by the Japanese. Australia returned as the *trustee power*, 1946–1975, when Papua New Guinea achieved independence. It maintains close relations with the wider Commonwealth, but its diplomacy is largely local, focusing on relations with Australia, Indonesia, and Micronesia. Papua New Guinea keeps up a joint defense arrangement with Australia. In 1979 it signed a border agreement with Indonesia. In 1984 some 11,000 *West Irian* rebels fled into its *territory*. At the invitation of Indonesia, it became an observer at *ASEAN*. In 1988 relations soured when Indonesia made *incursions* into Papua New Guinea territory in *hot pursuit* of rebels from West Irian. By 1991 relations with Indonesia had warmed again, but the possibility of a flare-up of border conflict remained. Despite its poverty, Papua New Guinea has played a role in regional security affairs. In 1980 it sent 400 troops to *Vanuatu* to help suppress a *secessionist* movement in that neighboring state. It further took the diplomatic lead in *Melanesia* when it helped launch the *Spearhead Group* in 1986. And it fought its own long campaign against secessionists in the *Bougainville insurgency*, a problem which drew offers of aid and *good offices* from New Zealand and the Solomon Islands. In 1997 the government hired white South African mercenaries to put down a revolt. This backfired when elements of the Papuan military *mutinied*, causing the deal to be cancelled. In 1998 it was hit by a tsunami, which killed 3,000. Papua New Guinea remains desperately poor overall, underdeveloped, and premodern in some of its interior areas. It is a large country, however, rich in *natural resources* and with potential to emerge in time as one of the natural leaders in the South Pacific.

Paracel Islands (a.k.a. Xisha or Hoang Sa). These small islands and reefs lie in the South China Sea. They were formerly part of *French Indochina*, but were *occupied* by Japan during *World War II*. That confused past led Vietnam and China to fight a sharp battle over the Paracels (and their separate dispute over the *Spratlys*) in 1974. China pushed Vietnam out of the latter in another clash in 1982 and subsequently garrisoned some of the islands, but ownership remains hotly disputed. They have no indigenous population. *See also Exclusive Economic Zone.*

paradigm. An underlying, *grand theory* which guides research and the accumulation of scientific knowledge. The idea was developed in the 1960s by historian of science Thomas Kuhn to explain scientific revolutions such as the Copernican. He argued that scientific knowledge does not develop in a linear fashion. Instead, it builds up contradictions of an existing grand theory and then suddenly overturns it by serving as a better predictor of experimental outcomes and accounting for more known phenomena with greater elegance and simplicity. Both the orthodox view being challenged and the discomfiting theories threatening it, he called paradigms: ultimately incommensurate views of the same reality, which highlight different features of a subject of inquiry, point to dissimilar problems as the key ones, and potentially distort perception of puzzles and disconfirming evidence, even so far as to blind researchers to alternative explanations. The idea thus suggests that the sociological, non-objective component of even "hard science" knowledge is far more important than most researchers dedicated to the scientific method would like to admit. How much more true was all this of the social sciences! Yet, undeterred by this context, many social scientists declared that their subjects and efforts were "pre-paradigmatic" scientific inquiries, implying that full status as predictive sciences (and of course, full stature as scientists) awaited only further accumulation of a "critical mass of data," after which a true grand theory (full paradigm) would be sure to emerge. Kuhn never meant the term for the social sciences or *history*, because they represent a different form of knowledge and follow a different epistemology, or should. He regarded this usage as corrupted, inappropriate, and misleading, and said so. Nonetheless, a debate raged within the social sciences for nearly 10 years. It has since cooled, its origins largely forgotten. Today "paradigm" has deteriorated into little more than *jargon* for an academic's general theoretical perspective (*critical theory*, *behavioralism*, *neorealism*, *Marxism*, *postmodernism*, etc.), which may be used to select interesting (or not) problems for research.

Suggested Reading: Thomas Kuhn, *Structure of Scientific Revolutions* (1970).

Paraguay. The *indigenous* Indian population of Paraguay (then a territory four times its present expanse) was subjected to an overlay of Spanish settlement after 1535 and toiled under the *encomienda system* for most of the colonial period. In the 1630s the *Jesuits* succeeded in concentrating more than 100,000 Indians in Paraguay to keep them from the encomienda draft labor system. These Jesuit colonies were raided by slavers, but in 1641 the Indians were armed by the Jesuits and beat back the slave raiders, simultaneously blocking Portuguese expansion into Paraguay. The few Spanish who migrated to Paraguay took Indian wives or mistresses, quickly producing a *mestizo* population. Paraguay effectively broke from Spain in 1811, as part of the great upheaval, 1810–1825, which led to the independence of all other Latin American republics on the continental mainland. It was badly defeated in the *War of the Triple Alliance* (1864–1870), also known as the Paraguayan War, in which it lost so much territory and population it never recovered its previous position and was left economically destitute and politically unstable for decades. From 1811 to 1864 Paraguay had followed a more *dirigiste* and *isolationist* economic model, under a severe dictatorship, than had the rest of Latin America. That ended with the war. During the 1920s there was a series of border conflicts and crises with Bolivia which erupted into the bloody *Chaco War* in 1932, from which Paraguay gained some territory back but deepened its domestic problems. In 1954 General *Alfredo Stroessner* seized power. His stern rule was wielded through the compliant and long-standing Colorado Party, but relied ultimately on the military and support from major landowners in Paraguay's near-feudal rural areas. His style of state bribery, tactical reform, and widespread repression became known as "Stronismo." He was not deposed until 1989, by a *coup* led by General Andés Rodriguez, subsequently elected president. Multiparty elections were held in 1993, but with population and unemployment both rising, democracy's grip on Paraguay was a weak one into the twenty-first century.

Paraguayan War (1864–1870). *See War of the Triple Alliance.*

paramilitary. Any private (nonstate) armed force that is organized along military lines. *See also brownshirts; blackshirts; Freikorps; militia; Irish Republican Army.*

paratroops. *See airborne infantry.*

parent country. One where an MNC originated and is headquartered. *See also Calvo Clause; Drago Doctrine; host nation.*

pariah state. A *state* which steps outside accepted *international law,* for instance, by supporting *terrorism* or by flaunting established legal and diplomatic *norms, regimes,* or conventions. *See also international society; outlaw state.*

par in parem non habet imperium. "Equals hold no *jurisdiction* over one another." *See also equality; sovereignty.*

Paris, Charter of (1990). A *declaration* by all members of the CSCE which formally ended the *Cold War* between the *NATO* and *Warsaw Pact* alliances on terms wholly favorable to the Western alliance. It declared that future security relations within Eurasia would be based on liberal-democratic principles as enshrined in the *Helsinki Accords,* that is, upon the promotion of *market economies* and free flow and interchange of ideas, respect for *human rights,* and on the assumption of peaceful relations among law-abiding, free peoples. *See also convergence; cosmopolitan values; Immanuel Kant; two-plus-four talks.*

Paris Club. A "club" of lending states which hold outstanding capital loans to *debtor states.* Its purpose is to coordinate interstate lender rates and policies when negotiating with borrowers which are having difficulty making *debt service* payments. *See also London Club.*

Paris Commune (1871). Defeat in the *Franco-Prussian War* and the capture of *Napoleon III* at *Sedan* stimulated a radical rising in Paris in March 1871, which lasted until the last week of May. It was crushed by Marshal *MacMahon* after much bitter street fighting which left 20,000 Parisians dead, much of the heart of Paris burned and gutted, and France with a powerful legacy of mutual class mistrust and hatred. It also fed a legend of *proletarian* fervor important to revolutionary *socialists* throughout Europe, including *Karl Marx*. *See also Pierre Joseph Proudhon.*

Paris, Congress of (1856). *See Paris, Declaration of (1856); Paris, Treaty of (1856).*

Paris, Declaration of (1856). This was the first major effort by the *Great Powers* to set out the *rules* of naval warfare. It proclaimed four basic principles: (1) *privateering* was made illegal; (2) *neutral* flags protected enemy *goods*, except for *contraband*; (3) neutral goods other than contraband were exempt from *capture*; and (4) *blockades* had to be effective or they were not binding. Naval warfare was briefly addressed by the *Geneva Convention* (1864) and more fully by the *Hague Conference* (1907). A major conference was held at London (1908–1909). It laid out elaborate rules, but did not touch upon *submarines* and went unsigned by the major *sea power* of the day, Britain. *See also cruiser warfare; free ships.*

Paris, Pact of (1928). *See Kellogg-Briand Pact.*

Paris Peace Conference (January 18, 1919–January 20, 1920). As the victorious *Allied and Associated Powers* of *World War I* met in Paris to redraw the maps of the world, restore peace to its troubled regions, arrange the *postwar* settlement, and decide terms for the defeated *Central Powers*, much of Europe lay in ruins and faced social upheaval and chaos. The prospect of *famine* was widespread. There was general agreement that, unless people could be fed and order quickly restored, the new threat of *Bolshevism* in Russia might spread to Germany and beyond. The European powers were all gravely weakened by war and heavily indebted to the United States. By that same token, prosperity and security in America was now dependent on economic restoration and stabilization of Europe, including Germany. Recovery and the *reparations* question should have occupied center stage at the conference, and did for most of the European powers, along with questions of territorial swaps and colonial adjustments and *compensations*. On the other hand, the American president whose presence towered over the conference, *Woodrow Wilson*, focused most of his attention and hopes for a *liberal* new world order on two non-economic questions, the establishment of a *League of Nations* and *self-determination* of nations. He also allowed components of his peace program—in particular, his famous "peace without indemnities" pledge—to be decided in ways detrimental to Germany and the apparent liberal promise of the *Fourteen Points*.

The conference ultimately drafted the terms of five treaties, which brought a formal end to World War I for the *Central Powers* and most other participants: *Neuilly* (Bulgaria), *St. Germain* (Austria), *Trianon* (Hungary), *Sèvres* (Turkey), and *Versailles* (Germany). Though it began with great expectations of a *Wilsonian* peace, it ended in acrimony among the erstwhile Allied and Associated Powers. Why? An overwhelming parliamentary vote of confidence in French Premier *Georges Clemenceau* in France, *Lloyd George's* tough public line in Great Britain, and a midterm election in the United States showed that the populations of the Allied and Associated nations wanted a far harsher peace than Wilson was prepared to oversee. Furthermore, *Orlando* of Italy stormed out of the conference hall after failing to get his territorial demand for *Fiume*, even though Italy received everything else promised in the secret *Treaty of London* (1915) by Britain and France. Clemenceau and Lloyd George felt duty-bound to give Orlando everything promised in the Treaty of London, but joined Wilson in denying him Fiume. Italy rejoined the conference just before signature of the treaties. In its absence, the other major powers had already distributed the *mandates* (former German and *Ottoman* colonies) among themselves. Many Italians thereafter made *fascistic* or wounded *nationalistic* mutterings about their *mutilated victory*. Japan had been miffed over the defeat of its aggressive ambitions toward China, unmistakably framed in the *Twenty-one Demands* it had made in 1915. At Paris, it pushed for possession of the German islands in the North Pacific and the German economic concessions in *Shandong* and got them all. The failure to return Shandong to China sparked nationalist riots in that country and led to formation of the *May 4th movement*. Japan was needlessly humiliated by failure to obtain acceptance of the principle of the equality of races alongside that of nations, a point Wilson himself—who was not a liberal on the race question—blocked.

Also troubling the conference, *Weimar Germany* agreed to terms only under duress and over rising internal opposition from the *Freikorps* and other hard-right and veterans groups. The conference struggled with the issue of self-determination, granting *recognition* to (not creating, as is sometimes falsely charged) the weak *successor states* of the *Austro-Hungarian Empire*, several of which already showed signs of making renewed war to determine their desired borders. Lastly, Russia was in the throes of the *Russian Civil War* and thus sent no representative to Paris, at least none acceptable to the Allied and Associated Powers. Despite two efforts by Wilson to bring the warring Russian factions together, and to deflect or fend off efforts at French, British, and especially Japanese intervention in the civil war, Russia was never a party to the postwar settlement. When Russia finally emerged intact in 1921, its Bolshevik masters were rigidly opposed to the settlement framed at Paris and determined on a policy of *subversion* of it and its sponsoring powers. And of course, and most damaging of all, having played the most important part in determining the shape of the peace, the United States failed to *ratify* the treaties and thus never joined the planned instrument of their enforcement, the League of Nations, since the *Covenant of the League of Nations* had been foolhardily incorporated into the text of the Treaty of Versailles, at Wilson's insistence. The United States later, under *Warren Harding*, signed a separate peace with those states with which it had been at war.

Why did Wilson play the role he did? Partly, he was required to compromise by a weakened domestic position resulting from election losses in Congress. Even more importantly, the great gamble of *Ludendorff* and *Hindenburg* in launching *unrestricted submarine warfare* had forced Wilson away from *neutrality* and into the war, and then their failed spring offensive in 1918 led to the total collapse of German military power. That meant that the "peace among equals" he had proposed to broker while still neutral was no longer possible, since the two sides were no longer equal in fact (Germany had been beaten). Wilson therefore was more open to harsh council on questions of reparations and the *Rhineland* and the *Saar*, when faced with determined Allies who had closer and harder interests in those matters and who had in any case accepted his Fourteen Points with reservations recorded by the French and British on reparations and *freedom of the seas*, respectively, as the basis for negotiations. In spite of protestations of republican virtue coming from the new leadership in Berlin, Wilson thus agreed to a number of measures which, to liberal opinion in Germany and abroad, appeared to violate the spirit of his own Fourteen Points.

Yet, each time he compromised he in fact succeeded in moderating the harshest demands of the Allies. Among the most controversial of such decisions, he accepted permanent *demilitarization* of the Rhineland and a fifteen-year French occupation of that region. That arrangement was in fact designed to forestall outright annexation by France or the creation of a separate Rhenish state. He then agreed to heavier reparations than he thought wise, but which he thought had to be accepted or risk failure of the whole conference. He also agreed to delay Weimar Germany's entry into the League, but did so anticipating that it would become a fully integrated member in due course. On the other hand, he stood firmly against territorial adjustments in Germany which did not fit with the Fourteen Points or his pragmatic interest in seeing Germany survive as a counterweight to the worst ambitions of the Allies and to Bolshevik Russia. He was so committed to the defense of Germany's *territorial integrity* that he once threatened to leave the conference should Clemenceau persist in plans to annex the Saar. And he accomplished all that in spite of active opposition, even outright disloyalty, from within the ranks of his own administration and delegation. Wilson felt able to accept such compromises because he was supremely confident of the role the United States and the League would play in moderating their implementation and that *world public opinion* was on his side and would accept nothing less than his full peace plan. As importantly, he took a long-term view of the role to be played by Germany in the *balance of power*, of its eventual rehabilitation, and the desirability of its incorporation into a community of liberal, trading nations.

Ever the optimist, Wilson placed his hopes on the prospect that the assigned reparations were not beyond Germany's ability to pay and that the *occupation* of German territory in the west was for a specified time period only; territorial adjustments in the east he oddly regarded as in keeping with the Fourteen Points. When he achieved Allied acceptance that Weimar Germany in time would join the League, it was not in fact unreasonable to hope that *prudence* might reassert itself over vengeance in the councils and actions of the Allies, even if the immediate price was bitterness and a sense of national humiliation and rejection in Germany. Above all, Wilson had an unshakeable belief in the positive impact of the League of Nations because he fully expected the United States to be the linchpin of that organization and the new world order it would represent and guard. Where the French strove at Paris to tie America to a League of victorious powers whose principal aim would be to repress German attempts to revise the Versailles settlement, Wilson aimed at a universal League in which a democratized Germany one day would cooperate in sustaining a liberal concert of power. Therefore, he reasoned, it was not so very much to ask that Germany assuage real and deep French and Allied fears in a probationary period before membership. Besides, he thought many of the rough edges to the Treaty of Versailles could be worn down later through American influence under the auspices of the League once public anger dissipated. To conclude, as embittered liberals and others did then and after, that Wilson betrayed his own principles at Versailles is to seriously misread the man and his ideas. He was certainly blameworthy for the ultimate failure of the conference, through his tactical error of insisting that the Covenant of the League of Nations be inserted in the text of the treaties, to which he later failed to obtain Senate consent. That is a different matter and responsibility, however, than failing to defend or to act on principle.

In the end, Germany probably received the best it realistically could have expected from Wilson, who consistently moved to moderate harsher demands made by the Allies, while remaining willing to use force to impose the terms of the draft Treaty on a still resisting and embittered Weimar leadership. Germany's governors had asked for much more from Wilson and the conference than was in any sense possible, in effect insisting that the final peace reflect the power realities and opportunities of 1917 rather than 1919. They do not seem at all to have understood or appreciated to what extent Wilson did moderate terms harmful to Germany, in an effort to preserve enough of German power that it could serve as a counterbalance to French ambitions and the Bolshevik threat alike. Germany's new and democratic rulers were also firm nationalists. What they perceived as unreasonably harsh terms and a betrayal of the promise of the Fourteen Points Wilson saw as simply short-term tactical concessions in the context of a successful, larger liberal peace which left Germany substantially intact, territorially and economically.

When Weimar's leaders balked at the terms of the draft treaty, Wilson naturally responded with resentment at their accusations of his putative betrayal of principle, and anger at their resistance to what he saw as a Treaty reflecting the historic triumph of his policy on the League and on national self-determination. Hence, by the end of the conference the fragile young democracy in Weimar and the confident democratic colossus of the United States were already moving apart, alienated from and disappointed in one another. In Germany, the most pro-American and clearly liberal republican of the early Weimar parties, the Democratic Party, suffered a significant electoral setback; and all the liberal and social democratic parties and forces associated with the Armistice or with Versailles were marked with a heavy burden of defeat and national shame which helped destabilize the Republic with false accusations of a "*stab-in-the-back*." Meanwhile, back home Wilson came under pressure from the Republican right to cut back American commitments in Europe and return to the prewar status quo. He threw himself into the bitter Treaty fight with the Senate in an effort to save the League and his vision of America's key role in twentieth-century world affairs. He eventually lost that battle, with tragic consequences for the United States and for Europe which continue to reverberate down through time.

Consider that, for a moment in 1919, something of the promise of Wilson's vision of the critical importance of the end of American *isolationism* about world affairs was already evident in Europe. U.S. troops were still there, forming part of a buffer force between France, Germany, and the Low Countries along the Rhine; and Americans were active participants in the important (and later acrimonious) deliberations of the Reparations Commission and the Supreme Council. The United States also held much of the world financially dependent in 1919, and Wilson stood poised to use that power to insist upon a world economic system which genuinely kept open the door of *free trade*. The potential stabilizing power of U.S. economic bounty was everywhere in evidence, most obviously in the massive famine and medical aid effort of the *American Relief Administration* (ARA), which kept alive millions of Europeans. And consider as well that the ARA would, from 1921 to 1923, provide aid to some 30 million starving Soviets, in a profound gesture of sincere humanitarianism and potential reconciliation among great nations.

With the first vote against the Treaty of Versailles in the Senate in November 1919, and its second and final defeat in March 1920, however, all that promise faded away. Americans had signaled that they wanted no part of the international responsibility required of them under a Wilsonian peace. A withdrawal from remaining military, economic, and diplomatic commitments ensued, with deleterious consequences for U.S. interests and for the interest of peace and stability in Germany and Europe. American troops were pulled out of the Rhineland in 1923, after the French occupied the *Ruhr*, and the U.S. representative was withdrawn from the Rhineland Commission. That left France feeling exposed to possible German *revanchism*, but also free to harden the terms of the settlement through direct occupation of territory.

During the 1920s the United States had no official presence on the Reparations Commission and had almost no leverage on the question, despite its critical linkage to the problem of Allied *war debt* repayments, which American presidents all later vehemently, and quite incorrectly, denied existed. As a result, failure to deal with the interrelated problems of reparations, war debts, and reconstruction loans would contribute to friction among Western democracies up to the outbreak of the *Great Depression*. And without their traditional Russian and new American allies, the European democracies would prove incapable of restraining Germany when its national ambition rose again in the 1930s. Yet, in 1919 Europe was still too proud to admit that it had lessons to learn from America about how enemies might be tamed, and the balance of power reinforced, by consciously developing a community of nations with shared political values and linked economic interests.

What example did the United States really offer Europe, however, after its failure to ratify the Treaty and to join the League? Wilson was soon gone from the world scene, and his country seemed as tragically immobilized as its gravely ill, former president. The United States abandoned Wilson's early effort to secure and sustain in Germany a stable and prosperous democracy as a keystone of a wider liberal international order. Instead, it turned inward, grasping at spurious explanations of its entry into World War I which served as convenient rationalization for a wider withdrawal from responsibility as the *preponderant power* in world affairs. Indeed, so sharp was the falloff in concern for foreign affairs that a separate *peace treaty* with Germany was not signed until 1921, more as a passive formality than an activist bridge to improved relations with a young and struggling democracy, but also so that American firms could trade with Germany under legally regularized conditions. Americans thus revealed that they too were unprepared for, and unwilling to accept, the leadership role the facts of WWI and the inspiration of Woodrow Wilson had thrust upon them. In a recoil from that bloody encounter with Europe, they sought only to return to the comfortable past of hemispheric political and military, though not economic, isolation. America thus would remain falsely secure for two decades more and then pay a high price indeed for its failure to live up to demands the times themselves made of its citizens.

Wilson and internationalist liberals had pegged hope on the influence of "world opinion," a nebulous concept at best, to bring about a "people's peace," whatever that meant. On that notion at least, the last word went to Clemenceau, Wilson's perpetual sparring partner at Versailles: "God gave us the Ten Commandments, and we broke them," he said, "Wilson gave us the Fourteen Points. We shall see." The war had been just too long and too bloody, and its ending too unclear, for a sustainable peace to be reached. Moreover, the several leading peoples of Europe turned out to be more vindictive than Wilson and *liberal-internationalists* had anticipated, and those of America less generous than hoped. The world would have to go through another, even greater war—*World War II* would cost nearly 60 million lives—

before it again turned to the transformative proposals about sustainable peace first vetted at Paris in 1919. *See also John Maynard Keynes; Spartacists.*

Suggested Readings: Michael Dockrill and J. Good, *Peace Without Promise* (1981); Erik Goldstein, *Winning the Peace: British Diplomatic Strategy, Peace Planning, and the Paris Peace Conference, 1916–1920* (1991); William R. Keylor, *The Legacy of the Great War: Peacemaking, 1919* (1998); Margaret MacMillan, *Peacemakers* (2001); Arno Mayer, *Politics and Diplomacy of Peacemaking* (1967); Harold Nicolson, *Peacemaking, 1919* (1933); Klaus Schwabe, *Woodrow Wilson, Revolutionary Germany, and Peacemaking, 1919–20* (1985); Alan Sharp, *The Versailles Settlement* (1991); Arthur Walworth, *Wilson and His Peacemakers* (1986).

Paris Peace Talks/Accords (1973). A set of complex negotiations, 1968–1973, ended in agreements completing the American phase of the *Vietnam War.* A cease-fire and U.S. withdrawal agreement, negotiated by *Henry Kissinger* and *Lê Ðuc Tho,* was signed on January 23, 1973, by the United States, the Republic of Vietnam (RVN, or South Vietnam), the Democratic Republic of Vietnam (DRV, or North Vietnam) and the Provisional Revolutionary Government (PRG, formerly the National Liberation Front, or *Viêt Cong*). The accords came on the heels of the Christmas bombing of the DRV ordered by *Richard Nixon,* who claimed that action forced the DRV back to the table. In fact, the deal reached was only marginally different from one offered by the DRV in October 1972. It permitted 300,000 People's Army of Vietnam (PAVN, or North Vietnamese) troops to remain inside the RVN, reasserted the unity and territorial integrity of Vietnam as recognized in the *Geneva Accords* (and all along the DRV position), and called for the return of all *prisoners of war* and MIAs and the withdrawal of all foreign troops from Laos and Cambodia. The pact was torn up within two years, as the DRV completed its unification of the country by a final, full-scale invasion of the RVN, the *Pathet Lao* took power in Laos, and the *Khmers Rouges* overran Cambodia.

Paris, Treaties of (1947). After six months of negotiations, *terms* were agreed in February 1947 for the five minor *allies* of *Nazi Germany* in *World War II:* (1) Bulgaria was returned to its frontiers of January 1941, before its participation in the *invasion* of *Yugoslavia.* (2) Finland ceded part of *Karelia* to the Soviet Union, but otherwise returned to the frontiers of 1940 set upon its defeat in the *Finnish-Soviet War.* (3) Hungary was limited to the frontiers set in the *Treaty of Trianon,* except for some territory surrendered to Czechoslovakia. (4) Italy ceded some Adriatic islands and small peninsular territories to Yugoslavia, transferred a border area to France, and relinquished the *Dodecanese* to Greece; *Trieste* was declared a *free city.* (5) Rumania had the cession of *Bessarabia* and *Bukovina* to the Soviet Union confirmed; otherwise, Rumania returned to its boundaries of the interwar years. The *Japanese Peace Treaty* was negotiated separately in 1951. No *peace treaty* was signed with Germany: with its *de facto* division by the *Cold War* there was no single German government capable of signing, nor the possibility of Allied agreement on terms. An interim settlement was achieved much later in the *Helsinki Accords*.

Paris, Treaty of (1763). Britain, France, and Spain made a peace to end the *Seven Years' War* in which France regained the Caribbean sugar islands it lost in earlier fighting but Britain acquired title to *Québec* and Nova Scotia, along with Dominica, Grenada, St. Vincent, Tobago, and Senegal, all from France. In addition, Spain was pushed out of south Florida, which also went to Britain, while *Louisiana* went to Spain in *compensation*. French power was thus expelled from North America after nearly a century of Anglo-French warfare. That opened the way to a rising dispute—in the absence of a common enemy—between Britain and its American colonies, but turned French attention back to the European continent. England also pared France's possessions in *French India* to a tiny, *demilitarized* presence, permitting the British to dominate the subcontinent for the next two centuries. Five days after the Treaty of Paris was signed (February 15, 1763), Austria and Prussia signed the Treaty of Hubertusburg, ending their part in the great war.

Paris, Treaty of (1783). This treaty ended the *American War of Independence*. Britain accepted the *sovereignty* of the United States, agreed to frontier borders at north Florida, the Mississippi River, and the Great Lakes, and granted the United States fishing rights off *Newfoundland*. It also made minor concessions to its European enemies in Minorca and Tobago, but these in no way reversed the enormous geopolitical gains England had made in the *Treaty of Paris* (1763). The creation of the United States had two major consequences for world history: (1) Britain (and eventually, also Russia) was henceforth flanked geopolitically by the existence of an independent and increasingly powerful nation in North America, whose latent potential was increasingly included in the calculations of the *Great Powers*; and (2) over the next two hundred years the United States developed as an alternate to Europe as a source of economic strength, trade, and industrialization, and eventually military power as well, fundamentally changing the world *balance of power* and shifting the center of the *international system* away from Europe.

Paris, Treaty of (1856). This agreement ended the *Crimean War* on terms of the territorial *status quo ante bellum*, except for the loss of south *Bessarabia* and control of the mouth of the Danube by Russia. It dissolved the Russian *protectorate* over, but confirmed the *autonomy* (including from Austria) of the *Danubian principalities*; and it *neutralized* the *Black Sea*, with neither the Russians nor the *Ottoman Empire* permitted to maintain forts or navies there. It also declared the Black Sea part of the *high seas*, except for its coastal, *territorial waters*. Russia broke the *demilitarization* clause of the treaty when it pressed ahead with naval construction on the Black Sea after 1870, while Europe was being alternately appalled and dazzled by *Bismarck's* remarkable victory in the

Franco-Prussian War. The treaty also abolished the right of *reprisal* by individuals, reserving it to the *states* alone, and thereby ended hundreds of years of quasi-legal, private warfare at sea. Also, it set out the law of *blockade* in modern terms and abolished *privateering* in the *Declaration of Paris*. Finally, it began legal expansion of the *community of nations* (that circle of *civilized states* bound by *international law*) beyond Europe by admitting the Ottoman Empire as a full member. *See also Straits Question.*

Suggested Reading: Winfried Baumgart, *The Peace of Paris, 1856* (1981).

parity. (1) The established *exchange rate* for converting a given currency to *gold* or to a dominant currency (sterling, the U.S. dollar). (2) Rough equivalence or correspondence in military force levels, equipment, and weapons. *See also essential equivalence; strategic nuclear parity.*

Park Chung Hee (1917–1979). South Korean general. He took power in a *coup* in 1961 and was president until 1979. He ruled harshly, with diminished respect for *human rights*, but oversaw a dramatic expansion of the economy and the country's emergence as an *Asian Tiger*. In 1979 he was assassinated by the head of his own *KCIA*. *See also Augusto Pinochet.*

parley. Talks with an enemy during a *truce*, to arrange exchanges of the wounded and/or *prisoners of war* or perhaps to discuss *terms* of *surrender*.

Parnell, Charles Stuart (1846–1891). Irish nationalist. A *Protestant*, he was nonetheless deeply influenced by the Irish *Catholic* reformer and parliamentarian, *Daniel O'Connell*. In the Irish Land War, 1879–1882, Parnell pioneered the tactic of *boycott* and thereby won significant concessions from *Gladstone*. He stood against the radical *Fenians* in favor of parliamentary reform of Ireland's grievances. His campaign for *Home Rule* through parliamentary politics was building steam when it was ruined by personal scandal. In a predominantly Catholic country, he could not survive politically once it was made known he was having an affair with (and had fathered children by) a married woman, Kitty O'Shea, who was the wife of a friend. Parnell's failure was a tragedy for Ireland.

parole. When a *prisoner of war* was allowed to go free, upon giving his or her word not to resume the armed struggle. In an age when chivalry and personal honor were still thought to matter in times of war, particularly in the eighteenth century (which fell between the hard *Wars of Religion* of the sixteenth and seventeenth centuries and the fierce wars of *ideology* and *nationalism* which commenced with the *French Revolution*), this method was used to dispose of enemy prisoners one could not carry along with the baggage, but preferred not to kill. For example, as a young officer, *George Washington* was paroled by the French after his capture at Fort Duquesne (Pittsburgh) in 1754. In the

American Civil War the *Union* and *Confederacy* paroled troops, at first. When this was stopped, as part of the North's campaign of attrition against the South, and prisoner of war camps were instead established, appalling conditions—which arose mostly from neglect, rather than malice—needlessly took many lives.

parsimonious theory. One which explains much with little, like this.

parsimony (law of). *See Occam's razor.*

Parsis. Followers of the Zoroastrian faith of ancient Persia. After the conquest of Persia by militant *Islam* in the seventh century C.E., most fled to India. There many belonged to an elite merchant community centered at Bombay.

Partai Kommunis Indonesia (PKI). It was founded in 1920 as a *Communist*, but also *nationalist*, movement to agitate for *decolonization* from the Dutch. During *World War II* it joined other Indonesians in *guerrilla* resistance to the Japanese. In 1948 fighting broke out between the PKI and Indonesian nationalists (republicans). The PKI enjoyed solid electoral success after independence, but could not form a majority. Even while engaging in electoral politics the PKI never renounced its doctrinaire *Marxist* call for violent *revolution*. It attempted an armed uprising in 1965 ("the year of living dangerously"), but this was put down with ruthless brutality: hundreds of thousands were rounded up and slaughtered by the Indonesian Army—including many innocents. That destroyed the PKI, which until then was the third largest *Communist Party* in the world.

Partial Test Ban Treaty (1963). Signed by Britain, the United States, and the Soviet Union in the *thaw* which followed the *Cuban Missile Crisis*, it limited signatories to underground tests of nuclear weapons, banning tests in the atmosphere, the oceans, and space. France unilaterally ceased atmospheric tests in 1974; China continued them until 1980. After that, no nation tested above ground. Negotiations on a comprehensive test ban treaty (to include cavern tests) were stymied by the felt need of most nuclear powers to maintain a margin of *deterrence* credibility, and weapons safety, by occasional testing. Sophisticated computer modeling mitigated this need by the mid-1990s, leaving mainly political obstacles to a general test ban. A two-year, unofficial *moratorium* on all testing was broken in 1993 when China detonated a device. In 1999, India and Pakistan each tested five weapons (all underground), more to increase their *prestige* by displaying their status as nuclear powers than to refine their nuclear technology.

Parti Québecois (PQ). A *secessionist* party in *Québec* founded in 1968 by journalist René Lévesque (1922–1987) and others. It formed a government in the province in 1976. It held a *referendum* in 1980 on what it called "sovereignty-association" with Canada, a form of halfway *independence* which would retain such links as a common *currency, passport,* and army. Despite this proposal to have one's gateau and eat it too, the referendum was defeated 40 percent Oui to 60 percent Non. After that rebuff, the PQ split into a minority of irreconcilable nationalists and a majority reconstituted into a moderate *social democratic* party. That looked to be the future of the party. However, with the failure of constitutional reform in Canada in a national referendum in 1992, the PQ enjoyed a revival. It gained an ally in the form of a large bloc of *separatist* members of parliament in the federal parliament from 1993. In 1994 it again formed a government in Québec. A second referendum was defeated in 1995. A third referendum in 1999 (an eventual "Oui" vote will mean independence, but each "Non" appears to mean only "let's try that again") came within a half percentage point of passing. *See also Front de Libération du Québec (FLQ).*

partisan (partizan). *Guerrillas* fighting behind the enemy's *frontline.* The term originated with the Parteigänger, or Partisanen, of the *Austrian Empire.* These were mostly Croat, Serb, Greek, or other *irregulars* used against the Turks in the sixteenth and seventeenth centuries, on a frontier where cross-border raids and warfare became endemic, even a way of life. *Habsburg* Partisanen fought with effect against *Frederick the Great* during the *War of the Austrian Succession.* Colonial *militia* performed a similar function during the *American Revolution.* The term became attached to Russian units which harried *Napoleon's* formations and *supply lines* during the *retreat from Moscow,* and thereafter it acquired a general meaning. During *World War II* partisan units sprang up from remnants of broken Soviet divisions which took refuge in the vast, impenetrable *Pripet Marshes* behind German lines. These erstwhile regulars were joined by volunteers from White Russia and Ukraine, for a total of perhaps 2.6 million fighters. Both partisans and resident civilians paid a terrible price for guerrilla attacks, while inflicting relatively minor damage on *Wehrmacht* and SS formations. They were dealt with especially harshly by the Germans, who killed and burned out civilians indiscriminately, and often with savage pleasure, in partisan areas.
Suggested Reading: J. A. Armstrong, *Soviet Partisans in World War II* (1964).

partition. Dividing *sovereign* control of a given *territory.* Most partitions historically were by agreement of *Great Powers* over the heads of the population of the territory concerned. Others were carried out by unilateral *force.* In the twentieth century, however, a new method was introduced: partition to meet the principle of *self-determination,* usually following a *plebiscite,* as in *Cameroon* or *Schleswig-Holstein.* This democratic innovation should not be overestimated: where a plebiscite is impossible or not desired by one or more sides, the old, forceful ways still are favored as a means of firmly settling territorial disputes. The most horrific case of partition was division of Pakistan from

India in 1947. In the *Punjab* and *Bengal,* a forcibly rushed division of people and assets followed a best guess at sectarian divisions on the ground by a boundary commission appointed by *Mountbatten.* India was to receive 82.5 percent of assets and Pakistan was to receive 17.5 percent; this included the entire civil service, the armed forces, rolling stock and vehicles, and so on. Probably 10 million Muslims, Hindus, and Sikhs fled or were driven across the new borders, with at least one million *refugees* dying by sectarian murder, with millions more injured and raped, and with their possessions looted, in one of the larger human calamities of the twentieth century. *See also Abkhazia; Bosnia; Eritrea; Eastern Question; ethnic cleansing; Kashmir; Nagorno-Karabakh; Nazi-Soviet Pact; Ossetia; partitions of Poland; Québec; secession; Third Balkan War; Ulster.*

partition of Africa. *See scramble for Africa.*

partitions of Poland. By the 1770s Russia saw Poland as a *satellite state* and undermined any effort to reform or strengthen it. Although it wanted to dominate Poland, it was forced to accept partition by two neighboring powers. Prussia also coveted Polish territory, which lay between its central and eastern provinces. Austria insisted on territorial *compensation* to preserve its relative position in eastern Europe. Thus, the three partitions of Poland: (1) 1772: Portions of Poland were *annexed* by Austria, Prussia, and Russia, with Poland losing one-quarter of its territory and five million subjects. (2) 1793: Austria was excluded from a round of annexation by Prussia and Russia, with the latter acquiring the lion's share of *territory.* (3) 1795: the rump of Poland was extinguished, again divided among the three eastern powers. This *extinction* of one of Europe's largest states smashed the eighteenth-century belief that the *balance of power* system was a natural and benevolent mechanism working to preserve the *independence* of *sovereign* states. Instead, it was revealed to be, at best, a device for preserving *equilibrium* among the *Great Powers* and, at worst, an excuse for their common aggrandizement. They also reconfigured the map of Europe more than at any other time between the *Ottoman* invasions of the fourteenth century and the rise of *Napoleon.* There were more partitions to come. (4) 1815: From 1807 to 1814 a French vassal state, the Duchy of Poland, made a brief appearance, but it was promptly eliminated at the *Congress of Vienna.* In 1815 Prussia and Russia rearranged their Polish holdings, with most territory going to Russia. (5) 1939: Germany and Russia again divided Poland (which had reemerged in 1918, in the wake of the *Russian Civil War*) in the *Nazi-Soviet pact.* A few weeks later, *Stalin* ceded eastern Poland to *Hitler* in return for Lithuania. (6) 1944–1945: Poland was moved 200 miles west and north, at the behest of Stalin. It was compensated for its eastern losses with western provinces taken from Germany. The respective German and Polish populations were expelled, or *ethnically cleansed.* Poland's present borders were accepted by Germany in 1990 and are additionally protected from violent revision (an unlikely event in any case) under rules of the *OSCE*. *See also East Prussia.*

partnerships for peace. *Bilateral* agreements offered as of 1993 by *NATO* to the former members of the *Warsaw Pact*, and as well to some *successor states* to *Yugoslavia* and the *Soviet Union*. They permit participation in some NATO functions, such as *war games* and conferences, but do not offer a firm security commitment by the alliance. They appeared to offer an entry vehicle into the alliance, but were really designed to slow down the clamor for, and the initial rush toward, NATO enlargement during the 1990s. This backfired, as the partnerships encouraged early and formal applications for full membership. After initial objections, in 1994 Russia signed a partnership agreement, thereby tacitly foregoing its claim to exercise a *veto* over NATO membership for former *Soviet bloc* allies. *See also WEU.*

party line. Cleaving to the doctrine of a party or leader on a given issue of the day, and shifting positions in tandem with that leader or party, no matter in how tortuous a position one ends. It was also used about the rigid loyalty (from about 1920 to 1970) of many foreign *Communist parties* to doctrines laid down by Moscow. *See also Eurocommunism; Hundred Flowers campaign (1956–1957); Nazi-Soviet Pact; socialist realism.*
   Suggested Reading: George Orwell, *Nineteen Eighty-Four* (1947).

Pašić, Nikola (1845–1926). Serb statesman. Ambassador to Russia, 1883–1889, 1893–1894; Serb prime minister, 1891–1892, 1904–1908, 1910–1918; chief minister of Yugoslavia, 1921–1926. He led Serbia during the *Balkan Wars*, the confrontation with Austria in 1914, from exile during much of *World War I*, in negotiating the *Corfu Pact*, and at the *Paris Peace Conference*. His policy after 1921 always favored the Serbs, striving for *Greater Serbia* at the expense of other Balkan and Yugoslav peoples.

Passchendaele, Battle of (1917). *See Third Ypres.*

passive defense. Any measure taken to protect military or other *strategic* targets by dispersal, *hardening*, or *camouflage*.

passport. The modern passport is a document issued to private citizens, but which remains the property of the issuing government and *state*, authenticating a person's identity, affording limited *diplomatic protection*, and requesting other states to extend to bearers and their legitimate property "due courtesy" and respect before the law. That was not always the case. The initial purpose of passports was to identify to which *jurisdiction* an individual belonged; that is, to which state a subject owed political and legal loyalty—and taxes, and perhaps also military service. Passports developed as part of an effort by states to control, or even to stop, *migration*. Among European nations this pattern has been traced to the *French Revolution* and *Napoleonic Wars*, both of which scattered *refugees* (and spies and "subversives") across the Continent. This was a time when private travel was still rare, even among the greatly privileged, and during which near-constant war made travel seem an almost criminal activity. With expanding commerce and then *free trade*, private travel was decriminalized by mid-century in most of Europe and expanded rapidly thereafter in Europe and also globally, especially with innovations in steam locomotion such as *railways* and steamships. This new mass mobility led in places to new passport restrictions, however, such as in the late nineteenth century in the United States, where stiff passport laws that aimed at limiting Chinese and Japanese immigration portended later *Oriental exclusion laws*. In Russia, in 1722 *Peter I* introduced required internal passports for use by peasants while traveling inside the borders of the empire. This use of passports to severely restrict peasant mobility and monitor other social classes was also the practice in Japan under the *Tokugawa*. The move by most other states to a modern passport system came with *World War I*, when tens of thousands of *aliens* were caught by the start of the war on what overnight became enemy territory. This posed a special problem for the United States, thousands of whose *dual citizens* were visiting their native lands in the summer of 1914. Many were dragooned into military service. Virtually all states reintroduced temporary passport laws which, after the war, remained in place and became universal. During the mid-twentieth century, in *totalitarian* states internal passports again were made mandatory. In Nazi Germany they were additionally used to cull from the population all those slated for *genocide*. An internal passbook system was also employed to restrict movement and residence for all nonwhites in South Africa under *apartheid*. By the end of the twentieth century, encouraged by the efficacies of *free trade* and the success of *democracy* in many lands, a number of countries moved to eliminate the need for passports for citizens of specified second countries: the five Nordic states maintained a Nordic Passport Union; Canada and the United States abolished bilateral passport controls; citizens of the *European Union* moved freely among 15 countries; and in 1995 the *Schengen Agreement* enlarged the zone of passport-free travel in Europe to include specified non–*European Union* states. *See also Nansen passport; visa.*

Suggested Reading: John Torpey, *The Invention of Passports* (2000).

Pathans. A Muslim people straddling the mountainous borderlands of Afghanistan and Pakistan. Pathan raiders frequently savaged northwest Indian states such as *Punjab* during the decline of *Mughal* power, tying the fortunes of Afghanistan to that of north India for several centuries. There has, from time to time, been agitation for a separate Pathan state.

Pathet Lao. A Laotian *Communist-nationalist* movement which sponsored *guerrilla* resistance to a post–*World War II* return of French rule in Laos and later launched attacks against the government set up in Vientiane by the *Geneva Accords*. During the *Vietnam War* the Pathet Lao allied with the *Việt Cong* and the Democratic Republic of Vietnam (DRV, or North Vietnam) and helped maintain and operate the *Hô Chí Minh Trail*. In 1975 it seized power in Laos in the wake of the collapse of the Republic of Vietnam (RVN, or South Vietnam) and American military and political withdrawal from southeast Asia.

patient capital. Long-term *capital* invested abroad in the expectation that *profit* taking will not occur for some years. *See also foreign direct investment.*

patriotism. Devotion to the values, symbols, and cause of one's own country. This may, or may not, be an attitude which is uncritical and unthinking. *See also chauvinism; jingoism; nationalism.*

Patton, George (1885–1945). "Old Blood and Guts." American general. Patton represented the United States at the 1912 *Olympics* in Stockholm. He studied at the French *cavalry* school at Saumur and at the U.S. cavalry school in Kansas. In 1916 he was part of General *Pershing's* futile chase of *Pancho Villa* in Mexico. During *World War I* Patton undertook training on the new armored cavalry weapon: the tank. He became an enthusiast of *armored* warfare and commanded a U.S. tank school, hurriedly established in France. He led a massed tank assault at St. Mihel, September 12–17, 1918, an engagement during which he was slightly wounded. Patton stayed with tanks after the war. He served on the *general staff*, 1923–1927, and as chief of cavalry, 1928–1931, and returned to the general staff in 1935. He helped plan the Operation Torch landings in North Africa in 1942, where he landed his armored corps in November. Patton took over command of U.S. forces in North Africa briefly in March 1943, but quarreled with his British allies and was relieved. He already showed signs of becoming one of the best field commanders in the U.S. Army, and on the entire *Allied* side, in *World War II*. He has been roundly criticized for disregarding casualties in the interest of spectacular maneuvers, but he delivered results: in North Africa, Sicily, and then in southern France and Germany and into Czechoslovakia, forces under his command smashed German defenses, took territory, and killed or captured more than a million enemy troops.

Patton has been criticized for a lack of concern for Allied units on his *flanks*. His retort was that he took "calculated risks." That is quite different from being rash." He believed in his own destiny and in his repeated reincarnation. He was frequently in trouble with superiors for off-the-cuff remarks and off-the-field behavior. In Sicily, he slapped a soldier in a field hospital who was suffering from *battle fatigue*, thinking the man a coward. He was relieved by *Eisenhower*, reprimanded, ordered to apologize to the soldier and his troops, and then packed off to England in disgrace. Patton thus was not part of the initial *Normandy invasion*. Instead, a phantom army was built around his presence in southern England, to decoy the Germans into thinking the invasion would come at the Pas de Calais. The ruse worked: *Hitler* held back his armor until it was too late to throw the allies off their beachhead in Normandy. Patton was then given command of the U.S. Third Army, arriving in France one month after *D-Day*. He led the all-important breakout by the Third Army from the Normandy pocket and raced across France cutting off German armies. He performed an extraordinary feat of battlefield maneuver during the *Ardennes Offensive* in December 1944, relieving the besieged American garrison at Bastogne the day after Christmas. Patton and the Third Army crossed into Germany on March 22, 1945, and advanced rapidly into Bavaria and Czechoslovakia. Upon Germany's surrender (May 8, 1945), he was not sent to fight the Japanese as he hoped, but remained in-country as military governor of Bavaria. He was relieved of that command in October 1945, after making impolitic remarks about the Soviet Union and for not proceeding with *denazification* with due speed. He died in Germany, two weeks after breaking his neck in a car accident.

Pax Americana. "The American Peace." The international security guaranteed to parts of Europe and Asia by the military and economic power of the United States during the *Cold War* and reasserted post–Cold War in *Bosnia* and *Kosovo*. *See also hegemony; long peace; preponderant power.*

Pax Britannica. "The British Peace." The relative lack of *Great Power* conflict, c. 1815–1853. If this is solely attributed to British *preponderance*, then it is credited falsely because general peace among the Great Powers was underwritten by the *Concert of Europe* as a whole and aided as well by a diversion of expansionist and other European tensions into extracontinental expansion. As for the rest of the century, a nation cannot fairly be described as "peaceful" which fought the *Crimean War*, the *Afghan Wars*, the *Zulu Wars*, the *Indian Mutiny*, two *Boer Wars*, the *Mahdi* in Sudan, and numerous small colonial conflicts. *See also British Empire; hegemony; imperialism; preponderant power; Royal Navy; Zulu Wars.*
  Suggested Reading: Muriel E. Chamberlain, *Pax Britannica? British Foreign Policy, 1789–1914* (1988).

Pax Hispanica. "The Spanish Peace." (1) The condition of *demilitarization* and relative absence of warfare in Italy after 1560 which resulted from the policies of *Philip II* and his successors. (2) The period of retrenchment of Spanish power, 1598–1621, as a result of *peace treaties* or *truces* signed with England, France, and the Netherlands by Philip III. (3) The absence of violent interstate conflict in *New Spain* and *Peru* under Spanish colonial rule and, indeed, throughout much of Latin America. It was punctuated by Indian rebellions, but there was no interstate wars such as were then common in European affairs and would occur in the nineteenth century after Latin American independence. *See also Black Legend; Roman Empire.*

Pax Romana. "The Roman Peace." *See also Roman Empire.*

Pax Sovietica. "The Soviet Peace." The relative order and peace imposed by Soviet military power on the lands conquered by Russia and on some bordering regions, in particular the *Caucasus* and parts of *Central Asia* and *Eastern Europe*, varying region-by-region between 1922 and 1988. It ended with the *Armenia-Azerbaijan War* and a blaze of brush wars within Russia (*Chechnya, Dagestan*) and in the so-called *near abroad. See also Sonnenfeldt Doctrine.*

payload. Any kind or amount of *ordnance* carried by an aircraft or *missile.*

peace. (1) *De facto:* A prolonged lull separating armed conflicts, though without benefit of a formal *armistice, cease-fire,* or *peace treaty.* The satirical essayist Ambrose Bierce caustically defined this form of peace as "a period of cheating between two periods of fighting." (2) *De jure:* The condition of normal legal relations re-established among erstwhile *belligerents* upon *signature* and *ratification* of a *peace treaty.* (3) Colloquial sense: The end, and absence, of armed *hostilities,* whether this comes about by consent or *conquest.* (4) Comprehensive: The absence of *war* and the expectation of war, corresponding to general acceptance by the *Great Powers* that the status quo is not to be changed by force, so that *diplomacy* and *international law* displace war as the prime mechanisms of resolution of interstate *disputes.* (5) Ideal and perpetual: A sustained period of general security and order, where international law and *human rights* are broadly respected and disputes are settled by *adjudication, arbitration, conciliation,* diplomacy, and *negotiation* and the only force used or legally permitted in relations among nations concerns cases of limited *reprisal* or law enforcement.

Peace Corps. Established by *John F. Kennedy* in 1960, this program sent young Americans to developing, and later to former *Communist*, countries to teach or assist in social or economic *development* projects. Other nations developed similar programs (CUSO in Canada, the VSO in Britain, among others).

peace dividend. Fiscal and productive resources freed for civilian investment, production, and consumption by the end of a war or by the close of a prolonged *arms race* such as that accompanying the *Cold War.*

peace enforcement. (1) Historically: For most of recorded history *peace* was enforced by *force majeure,* and thus often with great brutality, by clear *victory* in war, or through *conquest.* In the extreme, it was maintained by means of *hostage-taking* and enslavement of conquered peoples and even by *ethnic cleansing*, *genocide*, and other such draconian methods associated with many a *Carthaginian peace*. This was still true in much of the world well after *World War II*. With the *Peace of Westphalia*, however, *international law* and the *balance of power* began to joust for influence as two key ideas debated by those devoted to peace. The nineteenth century relied on them both, plus sophisticated *diplomacy* and the principle of *compensation* among the *Great Powers* during the *Concert of Europe*. Efforts were also made at *demilitarization* of border posts and whole *frontiers*, as in France in 1815. The twentieth century brought a sustained, grand experiment with various forms of *collective security* and new thinking about *deterrence* and *international security*. Many less destructive measures than the classical means were tried over the course of the twentieth century, including *disarmament* but not dismemberment of defeated enemy states. Sometimes this enjoyed real success (Germany and Japan after 1945), but not always (Germany after 1919). Other ideas largely failed as principal means of keeping the peace, although they enjoyed some successes at reducing tensions at a lower level of conflict: *arbitration*, *mediation*, and *arms control* rank high on that list. By the start of the twenty-first century a new international consensus was developing around an old *Kantian* and *Wilsonian* idea, whether right or wrong, that encouraging and even exporting *democracy* and respect for basic *human rights* is the ultimate means of peace enforcement.

(2) Post–*Cold War*: The notion that the Great Powers, and other states of the *community of nations* which already enjoy peace, should act through the United Nations to end civil wars and other conflicts even if not requested to do so by the contending factions. This notion asserts that the UN should not simply seek to keep warring parties apart (*peacekeeping*) or prevent them from expanding through the use of UN forces as police and relief workers and offers of *good offices* (*peacemaking*), but should actively seek to suffocate civil or smaller interstate conflicts by military *intervention* and imposition of a political solution. In Bosnia, 1992–1995, and after, the UN used force to this end on the largest-scale since it intervened and was bloodied in the *Congo crisis*, and not merely as *interposition forces* but to provide real humanitarian relief and a modicum of civil order. In Somalia, 1992–1993, forces under the UN flag were involved in heavy fighting as they sought to disarm warring Somali factions (clans) and provide *famine* relief. UN diplomats simultaneously conducted mostly unsuccessful talks on rebuilding Bosnian and Somali civil society. In 1993 *Boutros-Ghali* called for the creation of Peace Enforcement Units (national forces on standby for UN duty), but the idea was received with little enthusiasm by member states. The UN again intervened with significant force, in Sierra Leone, in 2000.

Suggested Readings: Jane Boulden, *Peace Enforcement: The United Nations Experience in Congo, Somalia, and Bosnia* (2001); David Carment and Frank Harvey, *Using Force to Prevent Ethnic Violence* (2001).

peaceful coexistence. A security doctrine openly enunciated by *Khrushchev* in 1956, but part of Soviet practice before that date. It adjusted the orthodox *Marxist* prediction of ineluctable conflict between *capitalism* and *socialism* to the reality of the Soviet Union's nuclear confrontation with the West. It gave birth to a policy of support for *wars of national liberation*, by which the capitalist world could be prodded at its (putative) weakest point, colonial *dependencies*, while the socialist motherland and the *dialectic* of history were alike spared from ending in a puffery of mushroom clouds. *See also regulated coexistence; Sino-Soviet split.*

peaceful settlement of disputes. A United Nations term for all techniques of nonviolent conflict resolution. *See also adjudication; arbitration;* compromis; *compulsory jurisdiction; conciliation; diplomacy; good offices; fact-finding mission; justiciable dispute; legal dispute; mediation; negotiation; nonjusticiable dispute; observer mission; political dispute; treaty.*

peacekeeping. The use of *interposition forces* by United Nations member states, inserted by mutual consent as a buffer between contending parties. During the *Cold War* it was standard to exclude troops from the *superpowers*, and to "balance the ticket" by troops from *NATO*, the *Warsaw Pact*, and the *Nonaligned Movement*. UN peacekeeping forces were used under restrictive *rules of engagement* and could be withdrawn upon the request of one of the warring parties, as in *Suez* in 1967. They were used mainly in conflicts, such as *Cyprus*, not central to the Cold War. UN peacekeepers were awarded the *Nobel Prize* for Peace in 1988. After 1988 requests for peacekeepers (and the peacekeeping budget) increased exponentially, and strictures on using American or Russian units were discarded. Also discarded were narrow rules of engagement, the light equipment and small size of previous forces, and the idea that prior consent of contending factions was required to legitimate *intervention* by a UN force. Even as peacekeeping began to shade into *peacemaking*, some countries (notably the United States) warned against the UN assuming too many burdens, at too bloody and dear a cost. In 1993 Russia first joined UN peacekeeping operations, in Bosnia, and the United States sent "blue helmets" to Macedonia and Somalia. China, too, tentatively became involved with a small contingent of *PLA* engineers sent to Cambodia. From 1992 to 1994 Germany and Japan eased into peacekeeping duties. In 1994 post-*apartheid* South Africa participated, in a small way, in UN efforts in Rwanda. Peacekeeping is not confined to the UN. Regional bodies also undertake missions. They may use variations of UN methods and rules or not. Also, on occasion *Great Powers* act unilaterally (sincerely or not) in the name of *abatement* or peacekeeping, as in multiple French interventions in Africa, and Russia within the *CIS* region. *See also ECOMOG; failed states; Dag Hammarskjöld; mission creep; Lester Pearson.*

Suggested Readings: John Hillen, *The Blue Helmets* (2000); United Nations Department of Public Information, *The Blue Helmets* (1985, 1990, 1996).

peacemaking. This concept remains ill-defined, but seeks to go beyond merely keeping opposing sides in a conflict apart with *peacekeeping* forces. Instead, it searches for a United Nations–brokered, political solution to the underlying conflict. This means abandoning the tradition (some would say fiction) of outside *nonintervention* in favor of *conciliation, mediation,* and *good offices* by the *Secretary-General* and various UN agencies. It may also mean a significant military deployment to establish law and order in an anarchical situation, provide assurances of security to all sides, insist on a cessation of fighting even when the *United Nations presence* is not welcomed on the ground, and see to the material and medical needs of the *civilian* population. *See also peace enforcement.*

Suggested Reading: I. William Zartman et al., eds., *Peacemaking in International Conflict* (1997).

peace process. Any continuing negotiations aiming at settlement of a long-standing dispute. *See also peace talks.*

peace research. Activist-driven studies which seek to establish empirical bases, scholarly credibility, and policy relevance for preexisting normative prescriptions thought to be desirable and usually already fervently believed in by the activists doing the research. Most social science peace research explores either the structures of the *international system* thought to conduce to conflict resolution or the psychological realm, which it presumes harbors obstacles to the only conceivable (to peace researchers) rational condition in human public affairs and relations among nations: *peace. See also war.*

peace support measures. United Nations *jargon* for such efforts as *armed humanitarian intervention, collective security, crisis management, peacekeeping, peacemaking,* and *preventive diplomacy.*

peace talks. *Negotiations* ostensibly or actually aimed at ending *armed hostilities;* they may result in an *armistice, cease-fire, truce,* or even a *peace treaty. See also war termination.*

peace treaty. The only mechanism, other than *subjugation* or a formal and joint *declaration* preparatory to a peace treaty, by which a *war* or a *state of war* may be legally terminated. It re-establishes *diplomatic relations* on a full peacetime basis in terms of legal rights and obligations between or among formerly hostile *states.* Unless the *terms* of a peace treaty state otherwise, all prior agreements (usually suspended during hostilities) resume their full legal status and effects. A peace treaty thus goes well beyond any provisions contained in an *armistice, cease-fire, truce*, or declaration which may have preceded it. And it has the additional character of the full, binding force accruing to any *treaty*. Many wars, such as the *Korean Conflict, World War II* concerning Germany and Japan, and the various *Arab-Israeli Wars*, ended without peace treaties, leaving the *combatants* in a legal state of war for decades. This anomaly was corrected for Japan and most other belligerents in the *Japanese Peace Treaty* (1951). Concerning Germany, the legal state of war was terminated only during 1990 and 1991, with negotiation, signature, and ratification of the Treaty on the Final Settlement with Respect to Germany, which included a unified Germany's formal renunciation of war as an instrument of national policy and recognition of the extant 1945 border with Poland. This agreement also ended the *occupation* rights of the *Allied* powers, who subsequently withdrew from *Berlin. See also Kellogg-Briand Pact; POWs; war termination.*

Peacock Throne. The extraordinary throne of India's *Mughal* emperors, specifically Shah Jahan (1592–1666), builder of the Taj Mahal. It was made of solid gold and encrusted with sapphires, emeralds, rubies, diamonds, and pearls. In 1739 a Persian army sacked Delhi, butchering 20,000 of its inhabitants, and took the *Peacock Throne* back to Persia. There, it upheld the posteriors of Qajari emperors, 1794–1925. In the twentieth century it was mounted by the *Pahlavis.*

peak tariffs. Extremely high *protective tariffs*, by convention those pegged at 15 percent or higher. They were a special target of the *GATT* process.

Pearl Harbor (December 7, 1941). The U.S. Pacific fleet was moved to this shallow harbor in *Hawaii* from its normal fleet base at San Diego as a *deterrent* to a Japanese assault on *Southeast Asia*. Instead, the U.S. fleet was caught unawares by a naval air attack on a sleepy Sunday morning. The Japanese fleet had sortied from the *Kurils* on November 26th, flying the famous Z flag, which fluttered above naval victories over Russia in 1904 and 1905. As early as July 2nd, an Imperial Conference in Tokyo had decided on a drive into Southeast Asia. On November 1st, Admiral *Isoroku Yamamoto*, who opposed the war, ordered the attack on Pearl Harbor. He was fatalistic about Japan's eventual defeat, but he intended to immobilize the Americans during a period of consolidation of the gains to come in Indochina, Indonesia, the Philippines, and so forth. Even so, he warned, he could only promise victories for six months to one year. Washington had broken the Japanese diplomatic (but not military) code and sent warnings to Pearl Harbor and Manila of an anticipated assault; but the attack was expected by all to fall on the Philippines, with no one considering that the Japanese might be so daring as to hit Pearl Harbor. Attacking without a *declaration of war*, which was delayed by lengthy transcription and decoding by the Japanese Embassy in Washington, the Japanese Navy struck. They launched several waves of attack aircraft just minutes after 7:00 A.M. on Sunday morning, December 7th, 1941.

Surprise was total. Within hours of the first explosions, nineteen U.S. *warships* were afire, sunk, or badly damaged, more than 120 aircraft had been destroyed, and some 2,400 Americans were dead. Among the major capital ships, the battleship Arizona was destroyed, the Oklahoma was overturned, and the California, Nevada, and West Virginia were sunk. The Japanese lost a mere 29 planes. The American *aircraft carriers*, the primary targets sought by Yamamoto, were fortuitously at sea and thus were spared. In asking Congress the next day for a declaration of war against Japan, *Franklin Roosevelt* said of December 7, 1941, this day "will live in infamy." Four days later, for largely quixotic reasons, Germany and Italy declared war on the United States, even though Japan remained out of the war with the Soviet Union until attacked by Russia on August 8th, 1945, three months to the day after Germany had surrendered. The attack on Pearl Harbor was accompanied by Japanese attacks on European colonial outposts all across Southeast Asia, and it was indeed followed by a half-year of uninterrupted Japanese victories in the Pacific as Japan enjoyed brief freedom of naval maneuver. However, within just six months, after the evasive American carriers and fleet won decisively at the *Battle of Midway*, Japan found new victories elusive.

In the United States, immediate recriminations followed the attack. There were even suggestions that Roosevelt had connived to allow the attack as a means of bringing the United States into *World War II* via the Asian backdoor. In fact, he was deeply worried that the Japanese attack might deflect public attention away from the real threat, which was clearly from Germany, toward the secondary threat from Japan in the Pacific. Moreover, there is simply no solid evidence to substantiate the charge, and much which refutes it. As with most complex conspiracy theories, it turns out that confusion and chaos are better explanations. Note: Pearl Harbor was not, in fact, the opening shot in the Pacific War. Japan attacked in other locales in Southeast Asia an hour earlier, but because of the International Date Line those attacks are recorded as occurring on December 8th, 1941.

Suggested Readings: James William Morley, *The China Quagmire: Japan's Expansion on the Asian Continent, 1933–1941* (1983); James William Morley, *Fateful Choice: Japan's Advance Into Southeast Asia, 1939–41* (1980); James William Morley, *Final Confrontation: Japan's Negotiations With the United States, 1941* (1994); Roberta Wohlstetter, *Pearl Harbor* (1962); Gordon Prange, *At Dawn We Slept* (1981).

Pearson, Lester B. (1897–1972). Canadian statesman. Ambassador to Washington, 1945; minister for external affairs, 1948–1957; prime minister, 1963–1968. He was always a strong proponent of *multilateral diplomacy*, and especially of the *United Nations*. He was critical of the U.S. decision to push north during the *Korean Conflict*. He won the *Nobel Prize* for Peace for his *peacekeeping* initiative, taken along with *Dag Hammarskjöld*, during the *Suez*

Crisis. In the 1963 elections he ran on a pro–*nuclear weapons* platform, but later declined to so arm Canadian *missiles*. He broke sharply with the *Johnson* administration in 1965, when he delivered a speech at Temple University critical of U.S. policy in *Vietnam*. It has been reported that the next day, on a balcony outside the Oval Office, Johnson repeatedly shouted and cursed at Pearson, once lifting him off his feet (Pearson was much the smaller of the two men) to do so.

Peenemünde. Baltic site of German development and testing of the *V-1 and V-2 rockets* during *World War II*; work was also done on the world's first jet fighters and on an *atomic bomb* for *Hitler*. *Slave labor* was used extensively there. Some heroic Jews and other prisoners were able to *sabotage* rockets and other equipment, slowing weapons production; the *Allies* also heavily bombed Peenemünde. Most of the German scientists were captured either by the Americans or Russians after the war and were instrumental in the American and Soviet space and *ICBM* programs. *See also Los Alamos; Manhattan Project; Minatom.*

pegging. (1) Attaching a weak *currency* to changes in the *exchange rate* of a stronger one rather than letting it *float* independently, for example, the Irish pound's sometime pegging to sterling or African *CFAs* being pegged to the French franc. (2) When a government artificially fixes the price of bonds and other securities, say, during a *war*, to guarantee itself a steady and abundant supply of cheap money.

Peking (Beijing), Treaty of (1905). It confirmed Chinese acceptance of the gains Japan had made in *Manchuria* and North China as a consequence of the *Russo-Japanese War*.

Peloponnesian War (431–404 B.C.E.). It was fought mainly between Athens and Sparta and resulted in Sparta's triumph and the overthrow of the Athenian empire. The great history of this conflict was written by Thucydides (c. 460–400 B.C.E.), whose version is widely read. Students of international relations are usually exposed only to the short "Melian Dialogue," wherein representatives of the city of Melos appeal unsuccessfully to the better nature of the Athenians. Their city is sacked anyway after futile resistance. This morality tale is held up by *realists* as an example of the persistent amorality of politics, in which "the strong do what they will and the weak suffer what they must." Other readers note that the Melian prediction came true: the other *city-states* of the peninsula grew to fear and distrust Athens for what it did to Melos, so that the imperial democracy of the classical age was thereby left to face Sparta alone and was itself conquered and enslaved. Usually, international relations theorists assert that Thucydides is the progenitor of modern realism and therefore that its conclusions and "laws" are timeless.

That is a bald caricature of Thucydides, who was far more concerned with the role of *ethics* and with notions of community and reciprocal obligation in international relations than are most contemporary realists.

Suggested Reading: Lowell Gustafson, ed., *Thucydides' Theory of International Relations* (2000).

penal colonies/settlements. *Colonies* initially peopled by convicts and/or political *dissidents* sent into *exile*. These were usually founded by naval empires. Large land powers such as Russia or China tended to settle convicts internally, in distant unpleasant corners of the empire. *São Tomé and Principe* were settled by Portuguese convicts in the 1490s, and Cape Verde also received criminal deportees from Portugal. The French maintained an infamous penal colony on Devil's Island in French Guiana, to which they sent *Dreyfus*, among others. In the seventeenth century the British shipped criminals to Virginia, including Irish and Scots rebels. Some were sold as indentured laborers. In the eighteenth and nineteenth centuries, with the American colonies lost to the *British Empire*, the British set up two main penal colonies in the South Pacific: Botany Bay in Australia (1786–1840) and Hobart in *Van Diemen's land* (1812–1853). They sent to them ordinary criminals, as well as prisoners from the rebellion of the *United Irishmen*, *Fenians* arrested in 1867, and sundry other rebellious Irish. *See also Gulag Archipelago.*

Penal Laws. *See Catholic Emancipation.*

penetration agent. A *spy*, *terrorist*, or other agent of a foreign power or movement sent or recruited abroad but left inactive for many years. Also known as "sleepers," if spies, these agents seek by careful career choice and promotions to one day be insinuated into a position of trust, influence, or power or to gain access to *classified information*. If terrorists, they may await a prearranged signal or contact from their controllers before taking any action or they might be instructed to act with full independence should a defined sequence of events occur.

penetration aids. Any device, such as chaff, dummy warheads, or *stealth technology*, which helps an aircraft or missile penetrate enemy defenses.

Peninsular War (1807–1813). In Spanish history, it is known as the War of Independence. The broader name refers to the wider contest and bloody *campaign* fought by Spanish and Portuguese irregulars (the term *guerrilla war* originates with this conflict), with support from the British under *Wellington* (then still Arthur Wellesley), against French invasion and *occupation* forces sent into Iberia by *Napoleon I* to mount his family members on the Iberian thrones. It was sparked by Portugal's refusal (it was an old, British ally) to implement his *Continental System* against England, which provoked Napoleon to invade Portugal with a Franco-Spanish force in 1807 and that country's monarch, John VI, to flee on a British warship to Rio de Janeiro. He returned in 1808 as British forces landed that August to help the Portuguese hold the highlands. The war spread to Spain when Napoleon cavalierly forced his brother Joseph onto the Spanish throne as King José I, deposing Ferdinand VII, who was taken as a prisoner to France, where he remained until 1814. That humiliation sparked an extraordinary *nationalist* and *liberal* revolt. A national *junta* was formed in September 1808, which declared itself the real government of Spain and its world empire. In 1810 the junta yielded some power to a new Cortes (parliament), which met in Cadiz, a city Spanish forces still held, while the French held court in Madrid. The Cortes of Cadiz had representatives not just from Spain but also its overseas colonies, and in 1812 it produced Spain's first written, and also liberal-democratic, constitution.

At first, Wellington kept his small force in the highlands and let the French hurl themselves uselessly and bloodily against well-prepared fortifications. He then moved onto the plains, where he joined with Spanish officers and men and won battle after battle, liberating territory as everywhere the Spanish rallied to the cause of their own liberation. For the first time, one of Napoleon's opponents was fighting a war of careful and superior position, and of bloody-minded *attrition*, rather than the rapid movement at which the French emperor and his marshals excelled. The contest drained French finances and *reserves*: by 1811 France had 350,000 troops in Spain, most of whom were tied down fighting Spanish rather than English troops. This acute problem was further aggravated when Napoleon unwisely overstretched his army and alliances by invading Russia in 1812. That allowed Wellington to take the offensive. He won a major victory at Salamanca (July 1812), clearing Spain of French armies. Napoleon was informed of this defeat while in Russia, and the news prodded him to make the fateful decision to *retreat from Moscow*. In early 1813, Wellington invaded southern France. British historians generally regard the Peninsular War as a major cause of the final defeat of Napoleon; continental historians are not as impressed. Napoleon himself later said: "It was the Spanish ulcer which ruined me." In addition, this war opened Brazil to *free trade* and, by gravely weakening Portugal and Spain and opening for debate the fundamental issues of *sovereignty* and *legitimacy*, it stimulated the revolutionary upheavals and wars of independence waged in Latin America, 1810–1825.

Suggested Readings: D. Gates, *Spanish Ulcer* (1986); M. Glover, *The Peninsular War* (1974).

Pentagon. The building housing the *Department of Defense*. The term is often used as a synonym for the U.S. military *high command* and its policies.

Pentagon Papers. A *classified* study of U.S. involvement in the *Vietnam War* leaked to the "New York Times" by Daniel Ellsberg, a Pentagon employee who asserted a crisis of conscience as his motivation. The office of Ellsberg's psychiatrist was later burgled by the White House "plumbers" of *Watergate* fame, trying to find information with which to smear him. Publication revealed a pattern of government deceit about the costs of the war and private doubts among high officials about the possibility of *victory*. In turn, that raised public doubts about the wisdom of U.S. involvement and stimulated even stronger opposition to continued American involvement in Indochina.

peonage. *See slave labor.*

people(s). The entire body of persons who form, or feel they belong to, a given ethnic community, such as a *nation* or *tribe*, whether living in the same political community or *territory* or as part of a larger *diaspora*.

People's Bureaus. Under *Muammar Quadaffi*, this was the quixotic term used by Libya for its foreign *embassies*.

People's Liberation Army (PLA). The *communist* army led by *Zhu De, Zhou Enlai,* and *Mao Zedong*. It was called the Red Army when first founded in the 1920s. Its major wing was renamed the Eighth Route Army during the *Second Sino-Japanese War* (1937–1945), when for a time it was nominally under the united command of the *Guomindang;* later in the war it also formed a New Fourth Army. It was reorganized and renamed People's Liberation Army immediately after *World War II*, as fighting with the Guomindang resumed in the culminating phase of the *Chinese Civil War*. The PLA became the armed forces of the People's Republic of China (PRC) with the *Communist Revolution* of 1949. It included all the armed forces of China, not just the army. It was the mainstay of the communist ascent to power and a pillar of the regime afterward. Mao called in the PLA to suppress the *Red Guards* during the *Great Proletarian Cultural Revolution*. In 1988 local PLA divisions balked at crushing pro-democracy demonstrators in *Tiananmen Square*, but more distant units were brought in to do the bloody work. Subsequently, divisions of the People's Armed Police were stationed near Beijing and other major cities, as the first line of defense of the people's government against the people. At more than four million strong in the mid-1990s, the PLA was the largest armed force in the world. However, its equipment and doctrine were outdated, a fact made clear by the utter destruction of a similarly armed and commanded force during the *Gulf War*. For that reason, and as a reward for loyalty at Tiananmen in 1988, it was rearmed in the early 1990s under the *four modernizations*. The PLA thus became a major player in China's economy, running a vast number of industries, firms, and farms. It also controlled medium-range *missiles* and *nuclear weapons*.

people's war. In *Maoism*, the doctrine that a *communist* movement did not have to wait for social conditions to produce an industrial *proletariat*, but could instead ride to power on the back of an aroused peasantry educated in revolutionary tactics and mobilized ideologically for war by party *cadres*. Once the *Communist Party* took power, the doctrine was adapted to make a military virtue out of China's huge population: its lack of technical expertise and advanced weaponry was downplayed by the typically Maoist romantic claim that *people*, not armies, are decisive in warfare. Some apply the term to any leftist *guerrilla warfare* or spontaneous leftist uprising such as the *Paris Commune*. The political angle is important: few who favor the term would admit that a population employing violence toward right-wing rather than left-wing goals could truly represent the people. Others might argue that point. *See also Algerian War of Independence*; *Boer War*; *Chinese Civil War*; *Enver Hoxha*; *Irish War of Independence*; levée en masse; *nationalism*; *national liberation, wars of*; *Spanish Civil War*; *Russian Civil War*; *Vietnam War*.

peremptory norms. *See* jus cogens.

Peres, Shimon (b. 1923). Israeli statesman. He emigrated to Israel in 1934 at age 11. A few years later he joined *Haganah*. He held a series of ministerial posts after 1948, including foreign affairs and finance. He was deputy minister of defense, 1959–1965; minister of defense, 1974–1977; and prime minister, 1984–1986. He was more moderate than *Menachem Begin* or *Ariel Sharon* and kept close ties to France and the United States. He was a strong advocate of Israeli military superiority in the region and of its secret *nuclear weapons* program. By 1992 he was ready to trade *land for peace*, joining in the U.S.-sponsored, *multilateral* peace talks which followed the *Gulf War*. He also oversaw an improvement of relations with Russia. In July 1993, he authorized shelling of southern Lebanon in response to *Hezbollah* rocket attacks, creating many thousands more Arab refugees. The next month he met secretly with *PLO* officials to arrange a historic breakthrough on Palestinian *autonomy*, for which he was jointly awarded the 1994 *Nobel Prize* for Peace with *Yasser Arafat* and *Yitzhak Rabin*. In 2000 he lost his bid to cap his career by becoming Israel's president.

perestroika. "Restructuring." A term used by *Mikhail Gorbachev* to describe his (rather vague) plans to reform, modernize, and partly decentralize the Soviet economy. Although he introduced more *glasnost*, or intellectual openness, there was little to no fundamental restructuring of the economy before the collapse of the *Soviet Union*. *See also* tanzimet.

Pérez de Cuéllar, Javier (b. 1920). Peruvian and world statesman. *Secretary-General* of the United Nations, 1982–1992. He made little headway with an offer of *good offices* to resolve the Argentine-British dispute which led to the

Falklands War. He was much more successful brokering an end to the *Iran-Iraq War*, the phased Soviet withdrawal from Afghanistan, resolution of Namibian independence, and *mediation* of the civil war in El Salvador. Overall, his efforts brought new prestige to the office he occupied and made diplomatic activism by the secretary-general not merely an accepted but an expected innovation.

perfidy. Deceptions and tricks in war which are considered illegitimate, and possibly *war crimes*, such as concealing oneself in a hospital for purposes of advantage in combat, or feigning *surrender. See also espionage; treaty; violation.*

peripatetic courts. Prior to 1500 most European courts (unlike those of China, the *Inca,* or *Aztecs,* but similar to many in Africa) were impermanent. There were few national capitals—London and Paris were notable exceptions. Instead, the court and capital moved to wherever the *sovereign* was physically located. Sovereigns needed to move about their domains in order to display their authority, to act as a roving court of justice, or to impose their rule by force. As central authority became more firm, and roads and communications improved during the sixteenth through seventeenth centuries, permanent courts were established.

periphery. In *dependency theory,* the outlying areas of the *world capitalist system* comprising the poor countries of Africa, Asia, and Latin America. It is depicted as controlled, and its resources and labor as cruelly exploited, by the *elites* which control the *core. See also comprador class.*

Permanent Court of Arbitration. This arbitral body was set up by the first *Hague Conference* in 1899. Its creation led to a spate of bilateral *arbitration treaties* before *World War I.* Although that great cataclysm dampened more naïve enthusiasm for such agreements as a realistic means of avoiding *war,* the court survived because of its utility in resolving *disputes* which did not touch upon *vital interests. See also Root Arbitration Treaties.*

Permanent Court of International Justice. Also known as the World Court. The world's first standing international court. It operated under the auspices of the *League of Nations,* 1922–1946. Up to 1940 it delivered decisions in 29 cases and gave 27 *advisory opinions* to the League. It was replaced by the *International Court of Justice.*

Permanent Members of the Security Council (P-5). There are five permanent seats on the *Security Council,* but in a sense there have been seven occupants: Britain; the *Republic of China* (Taiwan) before October 25, 1971, the People's Republic of China (mainland) after that; France; the Soviet Union to the end of 1991, and Russia since then; and the United States.

These states are the only ones with the ability to exercise a *veto* through casting a "no" vote on issues of substance (not procedure). Essentially, they were the five major powers on the victorious side (*United Nations alliance*) in *World War II*, when the United Nations was founded at the *San Francisco conference*.

Permanent Normal Trade Relations (PNTR). *See most-favored nation; Normal Trade Relations.*

permanent revolution. The policy backed by *Trotsky* and the Left Position in the *Bolshevik* Party during the great power struggle which followed *Lenin's* death. It argued for permanence in two senses: first, the *revolution* should proceed directly from its democratic (*bourgeois*) phase to its socialist (*proletarian*) phase; and second, it posited that *socialism* in Russia would fail without a transition from a national to an international stage if it did not lead to socialist revolutions in other countries. The implication was that Soviet foreign policy should aggressively export revolution, almost as a means of *self-defense*. Trotsky lost the debate (and later his life) to *Stalin* and the doctrine of *socialism in one country*. In China, *Mao* essentially adopted Trotsky's policy, but under the modified slogan "continuing revolution."

Perón, Juan (1895–1974). President of Argentina, 1946–1955, 1973–1974. In 1943 he was part of the *junta* which seized power in Argentina and established a semi-*fascist* regime. Perón was an admirer of *Mussolini*, and to an extent of *Franco* and *Hitler*. Perón was elected president in 1946. With his famous wife Eva ("Evita," 1919–1952) he ran a populist regime which employed left and right policies in an eclectic mix whose catalytic ingredients were personal power and opportunism. He made no real effort to challenge the dominance of the latifundio cattle-breeders. His foreign policy was mainly rhetorical, emphasizing opposition to the involvement of Britain (with which Argentina disputed the *Malvinas*) and the United States in Latin American affairs. Deposed in 1955, he spent two decades in Spanish exile before returning to a hero's welcome in 1973. His third wife, Isabel, briefly succeeded him as president after his death. She too was ousted by a coup (March 1976). *See also Juan Manuel de Rosas.*

Perry, Matthew C. (1794–1858). American naval officer. He served on the Great Lakes during the *War of 1812*, where his then more famous brother, Oliver Hazard Perry (1785–1819) made his reputation. Matthew then served off Africa in the 1840s, helping to suppress the *slave trade*. He played a key role in shifting the navy to steam from sail and in establishing the Naval Academy at Annapolis in 1845. He fought in the *Mexican-American War*, twice leading riverine *search and destroy* expeditions into the Mexican interior. From 1848 to 1852 he organized mail steamer service on the nation's major waterways. He is best remembered for his actions in Asia. American interest in succor for shipwrecked sailors and in coaling stations for the new steamships led to a visit by two U.S. ships to Edo in 1846, but their initiative was spurned. On July 2, 1853, Perry's four-ship squadron of "black ships" (with 61 guns and nearly 1,000 men) steamed into Edo (Tokyo) Bay, where Perry—acting under official instructions—refused to sail to *Nagasaki* and instead demanded trade and visitation concessions from Japan and that his letter from the president be delivered to the emperor in Kyoto. A military confrontation was a real possibility. Perry left to resupply in China while the Japanese considered his demands. He returned in March 1854, prepared to carry out his violent threats against the city, and Japan therefore accepted the *Treaty of Kangawa*. This forced opening hastened the demise of the *Tokugawa shogunate*, starting a chain reaction of events which led to the *Meiji Restoration* and then to Japan's *modernization*. Perry remained an avid overseas expansionist, later lobbying (unsuccessfully) for the United States to acquire the *Bonins*, *Ryukyus*, and *Taiwan*.

Suggested Readings: Peter Booth, *Yankees in the Land of the Gods* (1990); Tyler Dennett, *Americans in Eastern Asia* (1922).

Pershing, John J. (1860–1948). "Black Jack Pershing." Commandant of the American Expeditionary Force in France during *World War I*. He first saw action in the Great Plains *Indian Wars* in the 1880s and was present in the aftermath of the massacre at Wounded Knee (December 28, 1890). During the mid-1890s he commanded a regiment of "buffalo soldiers" (black cavalry, so-called by American Indians in apparent reference to their tight, curly black hair). That posting earned Pershing the nickname "Black Jack." He fought in Cuba during the *Spanish-American War*. In 1899 he was posted to the Philippines, where he fought the Moro rebellion for the next four years. He served as a military attaché in Tokyo during the *Russo-Japanese War*. That brought him to the attention of *Theodore Roosevelt*, who promoted him multiple ranks to Brigadier General. Pershing served again in the Philippines for eight years after 1906. On August 26, 1915, his wife and three of his four children died in a fire, a spiritual and emotional blow from which he never recovered. In March 1916, *Woodrow Wilson* ordered Pershing into Mexico in pursuit of *Pancho Villa*. Ten months later, he returned to the United States, and on May 12, 1917, he was named to command U.S. forces in Europe. He oversaw the U.S. troop buildup from a scrub force into an army of two million men. He commanded this army in defense during the great German spring offensive of 1918 and in offense during the great Western counteroffensive that summer and fall. He and his fresh and even eager army were instrumental in winning the war for the *Allied and Associated Powers*. However, Pershing was dissatisfied: he had wanted to press on for *unconditional surrender*, but was overruled. Unlike prior and later commanders of great American armies, Pershing's stern personality left him unable to convert his military success into a ticket to the White House. *See also George C. Marshall; George Patton.*

Suggested Reading: Gene Smith, *Until the Last Trumpet Sounds* (1998).

Persian Empire. *See Iran.*

Persian Gulf. An arm of the Arabian Sea, some 600 miles in length, lying between Iran and Arabia. It is highly *strategic*, as it is the passage for much of the world's supply of *oil*. *See Gulf War; Iran-Iraq War.*

Persian Gulf War. *See Gulf War* (1990).

persona grata. A *diplomat* acceptable to one state as a representative of another, or any other person who may enter freely.

persona non grata. A *foreigner* deemed unacceptable by a state, for criminal or political reasons. The term is also used as a euphemism for *diplomats* apprehended as *spies* and signals that they have been, or are about to be, expelled. *See also legal agents.*

persuasive precedent. In *international law*, when in support of a decision a judgment relies on the internal logic and force of argument—not the formal existence—of a previous judgment. *See also* stare decisis.

Peru. In pre-Columbian times Peru was the seat of *Inca* power (at Cuzco), presiding over a vast South American *empire*. Starting in 1532 with the arrival of *Francisco Pizarro*, Spanish *conquistadores* began costly raids into Peru in search of gold and precious stones. That exacerbated an ongoing Inca *civil war*, then toppled the empire, and led to outright conquest when Pizarro captured and then killed the Sapa Inca, Atahualpa. The leaders of the various conquering bands soon quarreled over the spoils, however, and most conquistadores suffered violent deaths. In 1542 new colonial laws were passed forbidding enslavement of Indians. This provoked a rebellion in 1544 by slave-owning settlers led by Pizarro's half-brother, Gonzalo (1506–1548). He won a quick victory over the newly instituted Spanish viceroy, whom he beheaded, and some rebels urged him to proclaim a Peruvian kingdom. A replacement viceroy suspended the *New Laws* and offered pardons to most rebels; this led to collapse of the rebellion and the execution of its leaders in 1548. In the interim, an *audiencia* had been established in Lima in 1543. From 1569 to 1581 Don Francisco de Toledo was *viceroy* in Lima. He expanded the *encomienda system* ("mita") and worked the great Potosí mine to feed silver into the European wars of *Philip II*. In 1581 an old conquistador, Lope de Aguirre ("the Wanderer"), led a mutinous expedition into the Amazon in search of *El Dorado* and made wild plans to seize Peru back from the viceroys. The mission failed, and he died at the hands of his own men. During the colonial period Lima was one of the two great urban centers of *New Spain* (the other was Mexico City). *Creoles* overtime evolved as the ruling class, but not one always in agreement with Spain. From 1780 to 1781 Peru was rocked by the largest Indian rebellion within *Spanish America* in the eighteenth century, a bloody *jacquerie* in the high Andes led by *Túpac Amaru II*. Meanwhile, in northern Bolivia a simultaneous Indian rising, by the Aymará, raged from 1780 to 1782. In 1821 *San Martín* proclaimed Peru an independent *republic* and proclaimed liberal reform of its Indian tribute system (in the form of a head tax) and an end to *slavery*. This was not entirely welcomed by the notables in Lima, which had long seen themselves as the ruling class not just of Peru but much of *Spanish America*. After all, Lima had been the seat of the only Viceroyalty south of Mexico City into the eighteenth century, when some of its administrative authority was transferred to new Viceroyalties in *New Granada* (1739) and *Río de la Plata* (1776). Northern Peru was not fully secured by *Bolívar* until victory over the last Spanish army in Peru at the Battle of Ayacucho (December 1824). During the overall Latin American independence struggle, 1810–1825, Peru played a conservative, indeed a resistant, role. In the end, it did not so much rebel as it was forced to depart the Spanish Empire by outsiders—or at least, its coastal, Creole population was; as Túpac Amaru had shown, its highland Indian peoples were more than ready to rebel against Spanish labor laws and Indian *tribute*. This tension between highland areas and the coast, both political and racial, remains a deep legacy of Peru's colonial history.

Peru was in turmoil for much of the 1830s, with region pitted against region such that there was no well-organized central opposition, though there was much negative sentiment, to the Bolivian proposal to federate with Peru made in 1836 by Andrés de Santa Cruz (1792–1865). The new state appeared so threatening to the *balance of power* in South America, however, that Chile and Argentina both declared war on the Confederation and broke it apart, with Chile the prime mover of events. Peru was internally reassembled during two moderate conservative presidencies by Ramón Castilla (1797–1867). He was a *mestizo* with a lengthy military background (in short, a *caudillo*) who served as finance minister in the early 1840s. He was keen to *modernize* Peru economically and understood that required social change as well, and securing some political stability. He was president from 1845 to 1851 and again from 1855 to 1862. He promoted economic diversification and partial industrialization, financed by guano exports. This permitted him to also promote improvements in transportation via commissioning a steamship line and embarking on major *railway* construction. His second presidency followed a short but sharp civil war in 1854, during which he finally accomplished what San Martín had tried but failed to do: end Indian tribute (government head tax revenues could be made up by new taxes on expanding commerce and on guano exports) and Indian slavery. The economy went into steep decline after its loss of territory to Chile in the *War of the Pacific* (1879–1884), but recovered as Peru—along with most Latin American countries—enjoyed a prolonged export-fed boom which lasted until the start of the *Great Depression* collapsed commodity prices and compressed export markets starting in 1929. Peru kept up a long and sometimes violent boundary dispute with Ecuador, fighting localized wars over part of the Cordillera del Condor region, known as Tiwintza, in 1941, 1981, and 1995. In 1998 an accord was agreed ending this dispute.

Peru was ruled conservatively for most of the twentieth century, until a left-wing *coup* in 1968 placed in power a *junta* which tried to *nationalize* foreign industries and assets. Civilian rule did not return until 1979, just as Peru experienced a severe *debt crisis* born of excessive spending by the outgoing government, further aggravated by the *oil shocks* of 1973 and 1979. The 1980s were marked by a consolidation of democracy and swings between the austerity of adjusting to a *stabilization program* and radical initiatives such as bank *nationalizations*. There was also the persistent violence of the quirky, *Maoist* movement *Sendero Luminoso*. President Albert Fujimori, an elected *autocrat*, reintroduced *International Monetary Fund*–inspired austerity and stabilization programs in 1990, including a *debt rescheduling* agreement. Investor confidence was further increased with the 1992 capture of Sendero Luminoso's founder, Abimael Guzmán. That curtailed killings by the radical left for awhile, but it did not end *human rights* abuses by the state, which grew worse as Fujimori was revealed to be no lover of civil liberties. A constitutional crisis and a massive corruption scandal brought Fujimori down in 2000. He fled into exile in Japan, which declined to *extradite* him.

Suggested Readings: Victor Alba, *Peru* (1977); Peter Bradley, *The Lure of Peru* (1989); Richard Keating, ed., *Peruvian Prehistory* (1988); Scarlett O'Phelen Godoy, *Rebellions and Revolts in 18th Century Peru and Upper Peru* (1985); David Scott Palmer, *Peru: The Authoritarian Tradition* (1980); Frederick Pike, *The Modern History of Peru* (1967).

Peru, Viceroyalty of (1544). The Spanish administrative area, until 1739, which encompassed all Spanish possessions in South America, including Brazil, 1580–1640, when Portugal and its empire were annexed to Spain, and what is today Panama but was then part of Colombia. The other Viceroyalty was *New Spain*. *See also* audiencia; *Black Legend*; *Christopher Columbus*; conquistadores; *Council of the Indies*; encomienda; *Inca Empire*; real patronato; requerimiento; *Túpac Amaru*.

Pescadores. An island chain off the southeast Chinese coast, ceded to Japan after the *First Sino-Japanese War*. They were returned to China after the *defeat* of Japan in 1945.

Pétain, Henri Philippe (1856–1951). Marshal of France; president of *Vichy*, 1940–1944. Unlike most French officers, he did not believe in offensive operations at the outset of *World War I*. Yet, he seemed indifferent to casualties and thus performed well during the hard retreat of the *First Battle of the Marne* in August 1914 and again at Arras (May 9–16, 1915). He made his reputation at *Verdun*, France's enormously costly defensive victory, even though his disregard for casualties caused *Joffre* to assume real command there. His defiance at Verdun was remembered in the ringing phrase: "Ils ne passeront pas!" ("They shall not pass!"). Pétain emerged as the hero of that battle and, later, as the admired successor to *Foch* and to General Robert Nivelle. He was given overall command of French forces in April 1917. He had to deal with the *French Army mutinies* almost immediately. By the end of the war, *propaganda* had made him the embodiment of France's determination to resist German aggression. In private, he succumbed to *defeatism* as early as 1918.

Promoted to marshal, he headed the French Supreme War Council in the 1920s and put down the *Rif Rebellion* (1921–1926) in Morocco. He was briefly in government in the early 1930s, but grew contemptuous of the Third Republic and civilians in general. He was recalled from Spain, where he was ambassador from 1939, to head a desperate defense and new government in the wake of the German triumph over the French Army in the *Battle of France* (May–June 1940). His pessimism had grown with his years, however, and led him to accept quick *surrender* and later outright *collaboration* with the *Nazis*. He headed the Vichy regime until 1944. Even as France was being overrun (that is, *liberated*) by the Western Allies during the *Normandy campaign*, Pétain continued to collaborate. He was compelled to retreat to Germany as the Allies and *Free French* advanced; he next fled to Switzerland, but returned to Paris after the war. He was sentenced to death for *treason* in 1945, but his age and past services to the nation led to commutation of the sentence to life imprisonment. *See also Léon Blum; Charles de Gaulle; Pierre Laval; Maginot Line.*

Peter I, of Russia (1672–1725). "The Great." Peter was made co-tsar with his elder half-brother Ivan (d. 1696) at age ten (June 25, 1682), under the regency of his sister, Sophia (r. 1682–1689). The *strel'sty* (the traditional guard of the tsar) revolted, killing dozens right inside the *Kremlin*, including one of Peter's uncles. This event preyed on his thinking about dynastic and personal security for the rest of his life in the way a comparable revolt—the Frondes—and flight affected *Louis XIV* of France. Peter was forced to flee Moscow (August 6–7, 1689), but took sole power the following month, at age seventeen, after deposing his sister from her regency with the help of foreigners in the Russian service: Sophia was confined to a convent, where she died in 1704. Russia was essentially a slave state, with a small service nobility and a huge population divided among *serfs* and "state peasants," and deep traditions of theocratic *absolutism*.

As co-tsar, at first Peter traveled widely, leaving most administration to his officials and all heavy rituals required by the *Orthodox Church* to the devout, half-wit Ivan. He made a sort of play war on Turkey in 1695, failing miserably in a first try to take Azov; and then he grew more serious and seized Azov the next year, later confirming his victory in treaties of alliance with *Venice* and the *Austrian Empire*. He then traveled abroad on his Grand Embassy, 1697–1698, sometimes pseudo-incognito, to Latvia, Brandenburg, Hanover, and the Netherlands where he worked for a time as a shipwright in Amsterdam. He spent four months in England, visiting factories and the *Royal Navy* yards at Plymouth. During all this he repeatedly sought Western allies for an intended war against the Turks, but found no takers. These voyages confirmed his extant sympathies as a *Westernizer*. Beyond fondness of the West, it must be noted that from a young age Peter exhibited an active contempt for many things Russian, as in his infamous "All-Drunken, All-Jesting Assembly," which indulged ostentatiously pagan mockeries of himself but also of the deepest religious values of "Old Russia." He forced many to participate in these affairs, including Tsar Ivan in his full Orthodox regalia. Nor was this just some adolescent pranksterism—Peter kept it up all his adult life, oddly instituting mock offices, including a mock tsar whom he paraded around his court and to whom he bent and paid homage. Peter tamed the real Orthodox Church too. He left the patriarchate vacant after the death of Adrian in 1700 and abolished it entirely in 1721 in favor of a church synod directly controlled by the tsar. Similarly, the official imagery of the regime changed from the tsar as Orthodox saint to tsar as new Roman emperor, on coins and in court portraits. A man of his times, Peter did not like Jews. A man of his country, he also distrusted *Catholics* and despised *Jesuits*.

Ill-made and full of restless tics, Peter's private habits had both feet planted firmly in the bizarre. Beyond bowing to a mock tsar and hosting eccentric, often cruel bacchanalia, he kept a menagerie of unfortunate physical "freaks," had a morbid fascination with stillbirths and the details of executions, was intrigued by odd genetic mutations, sometimes delayed funerals to better observe human decomposition, and enjoyed pulling bad teeth from, or operating on the wounds of, living people. Peter failed badly in one area where most later Russian leaders excelled: he did not set up a *police state*. His *autocracy* was profoundly personal, rather than institutional. Indeed, much of Russia remained lawless under Peter, governed by the knout and whip of some landlord's overseer who was restrained only by temperament and personal conscience (if possessed). What few roads existed were not safe for unarmed travel. Provincial towns, commerce, and civilized life all suffered impoverishment accordingly. If anything, Peter's Russia might have benefited from a few more police.

After his initial failure at Azov, Peter grew serious about reform, devoting himself to *modernization* of all aspects of Russian national life, though concentrating foremost on the army and navy, building the latter essentially from scratch to a force which at his death boasted 36 *ships-of-the-line*, 86 additional major significant warships (*frigates* and *galleys*), and 280 supporting vessels. So dedicated was he to the navy he made chopping down an oak tree a capital offense. He imported hundreds of foreign artisans, engineers, and *mercenaries* and sent Russian nobles abroad to study. He began several great factory, construction, and educational projects; founded several key schools, universities, and medical institutes; and in general began the long-term modernization of Russia. He crushed the *boyar* gentry and strel'sty, who had revolted again while he was abroad in 1698, returning to slaughter many and symbolically shave the beards of the rest—to show them there was no going back to their old, *Slavophile* ways—and ordered them to wear western dress.

Through all this upheaval Peter did not neglect foreign affairs. Indeed, expanding the empire and propelling Russia into the front rank of the *Great Powers* was his ultimate ambition as tsar, drove all his diplomatic and domestic reforms, and was his single greatest and most subsequently influential accomplishment. He was no visionary, however, and had no *grand strategy* of empire. Peter was more of a seat-of-the-pants *opportunist*. His hopes for a long-term alliance with Austria against Turkey were dashed by Austria's "betrayal of Russia" at Carlowitz in 1698, when Vienna made a *separate peace* with the *Ottoman Empire* in order to prepare for war with France. Instead of a southern war, in 1700 Peter now signed a 30-year truce with the Ottomans. Secure to the south, he attacked Sweden, starting the *Great Northern War* (1700–1721), which forever altered the balance of power in north Europe. That year, he was also first denounced as the anti-Christ by *Old Believers*. He sought to gain Livonia, but was badly defeated at the Battle of *Narva* (November 30, 1700) by a much smaller force under *Charles XII*. In the wake of that defeat, and given some relief by the outbreak of the *War of the Spanish Succession* (1701–1713), Peter reorganized and modernized the army, including importing military technology from the West. In 1702 he won several small battles against Swedish and Polish forces in the Baltic.

To secure these victories, in 1703 Peter began to build his great new capital, *St. Petersburg*, while Charles was busy in Poland. The city cost many thousands of lives, but served Peter's desire to have a "window on the West," as well as to remove himself from the claustrophobic political memories of Moscow. Once again he emulated Louis XIV, who had escaped Paris by building *Versailles*. In 1704 Peter finally captured Narva. The Swedes, having done with Poland, now counterattacked. Peter lost skirmish after skirmish and once was nearly captured, as he made the deliberate decision to avoid a *battle of encounter* and instead practiced *guerrilla warfare* and *scorched earth*. His army was pushed all the way to the Ukraine by the invading Swedes. Peter then won all in a dramatic victory over the vastly overextended Swedish army in the great and decisive battle at *Poltava* (July 8, 1709). He finished the job in 1714, capturing from Sweden the Baltic territories of *Livonia*, *Estonia*, and *Karelia*. That victory was so complete it expelled Sweden from the ranks of the Great Powers and established Russia as its replacement, in the Baltic and in Europe as a whole, a shift confirmed in the *Treaty of Nystad* (1721). Peter also turned on the Ottomans, but he was less successful in the south than he had been in the north: he lost Azov to the Turks in 1711.

Domestically, he ruled with a mailed fist while maintaining a veneer of enlightenment and admixture of policies which *Rousseau* might have said "forced Russians to be free": in 1705 Peter forbade the wearing of beards; in 1714 he made education for nobles compulsory and ordered 1,000 to move to St. Petersburg; in 1718 he ordered double taxation of Old Believers; and in 1721 he banned the sale of individual serfs (an edict without real effect beyond the two capitals), but the next year he introduced a *passport* system required for any peasant travel. And he taxed almost anything imaginable. He had his own son, Alexis, who conspired against him, tried for *treason* and probably also had him murdered in his cell (1718). In 1721 the reversal of relative power vis-à-vis Sweden was confirmed by formal cession of the *Baltic States* and the Karelian isthmus of Finland. In 1722 he declared war on Persia, seeking again to expand to the south; the next year, he captured Baku and made peace. Peter spent his final years in more enlightened pursuits, but that was largely due to the greater security enjoyed by Russia owing to his ruthless destruction of its (and his) enemies, rather than to his native temperament. Still, after Peter came decades of chaos, which always causes tyrants to be recalled more fondly.

Historians continue to quarrel over Peter's legacy to Russia. Some view him as the progenitor of *Stalinism*, of a system of centralized command administration which cast a mold for all subsequent tyrants, including the *Bolsheviks*. Others see him as a heroic figure and principal shaper of modern Russian nationalism. He was, of course, both and neither: he left a large footprint on Russian history, in particular on its role as a Great Power for the first time fully engaged with the wider world (he opened relations with every country in Europe and some in Asia), and respected by it; but those who came later made decisions all their own. It is therefore best to judge Peter in light of the limits and possibilities of his own times, and his successors by the light of theirs. *See also Alexander I; Alexander II; Catherine II; cultural revolution; Ivan IV; Gorbachev; Mahmud II; Nicholas I; Nicholas II; revolution from above; Josef Stalin.*

Suggested Readings: James Cracraft, ed., *Peter the Great Transforms Russia* (1991); Lindsey Hughes, *Russia in the Age of Peter the Great* (1998); Robert Massie, *Peter the Great* (1980); B. Sumner, *Peter the Great and the Emergence of Russia* (1940).

Petersburg missions. *See Western European Union (WEU).*

les petites riches. "The little, rich ones." Cultivated 1980s slang for the small and wealthy countries of the *EFTA* who were not, but were welcome to become, members of the *European Union:* Austria, Finland, Iceland, Norway, Sweden, and Switzerland. *See also deepening versus widening.*

petition. A formal request from an individual, group, or state for a hearing of a grievance by an international *human rights* body. Few international *covenants* permit petition from groups other than states, and those which do often require adherence to an *Optional Protocol*. Thus, few states afford this legal option to their citizens. Yet, several countries enacted legislation in response to international criticism of a specific practice after the issue arose in an individual petition, among them Canada, Finland, and Sweden.

petitum. The *object* of an international legal claim.

petrodollars. U.S. *currency* held by *oil*-producing states, but redeposited in Western banks and financial institutions. The term was widely used in the 1970s and 1980s, when *OPEC* price increases led to a massive transfer of *hard currency* to OPEC states from the *OECD* countries and oil-poor *Third World* states. *See also oil shocks.*

Petrograd Soviet. *See Soviet (Petrograd).*

petty officer. The naval equivalent of a *noncommissioned officer* in the army.

Peul. *See Fulbe.*

Phalange. A right-wing Lebanese *militia* founded in the 1930s to defend against Syrian *annexation*. In 1975 it fought the *PLO* in Lebanon. In 1982 it allied with Israel in the *Lebanese Civil War*. It was the main loser in that war, forced in the end to accept a lesser share of power and a Syrian presence.

Philip II, of Spain (1527–1598). Son of *Charles V*; king of England, 1554–1558; king of Naples and of Spain, 1556–1598; king of Portugal (as Philip I), 1580–1598. Philip first exercised power as regent in Spain at age sixteen. As his father declined, despaired, and was defeated in Germany, Philip was made king of Naples in 1554 and the next year king of the Netherlands. In 1556 he succeeded Charles as absolute ruler of Spain and therefore also of much of South and Central America. His conquest of the Philippines in 1565 made him ruler of the first true, world empire in history, albeit one only superficially united and which severely lacked geographical cohesion. At the height of his powers, in 1580 he invaded and annexed the neighboring kingdom of Portugal, where the throne had fallen vacant and was in dispute, adding its overseas empire—coastal Brazil and several key African and Indian territories—to his own.

The Spanish Empire was now a vast undertaking, and its finances became Philip's main concern. Somehow, he had to find the money to maintain a hugely expensive *standing army* of some 90,000 in Flanders during the *Eighty Years' War* (1556–1648) against the Dutch, reinforced via the *Spanish Road*, with another 70,000 troops holding garrisons throughout the overseas empire. And he needed to build and support an immense navy required to hold together an empire which at his death girdled the globe, and he was usually at war on several oceans and continents at once. That meant not merely building ships, but also harbors, warehouses, overseas bases, and all the paraphernalia of world naval power. The best recent scholarship argues that Philip indeed pursued a grand strategy of empire and that he well might have succeeded but for the independent and often chance course of events, and the restraints of his personality, which allowed lesser powers—in particular, Holland and England—to frustrate his grand design and defeat his plans. Among those personal traits was an inability to let go the minutest detail of administration: Philip spent the greatest part of every day of his adult life diligently reading and signing in person literally hundreds of petitions and itemized bureaucratic orders; in the end, this tendency to micromanagement overwhelmed him and slowed Imperial Spain's responses to mounting crises on several fronts.

Like most monarchs of his day, Philip failed to understand state finance. As a result, and despite the flow of treasure ships carrying *New World* gold and silver to his coffers, he faced constant money worries and repeated bankruptcies which undermined his strategic plans and led to mutinies in the military. Most famously, the Army of Flanders mutinied and sacked Antwerp in 1576, in an act of wanton murder and mayhem remembered still in the Low Countries as the "Spanish fury." That same army mutinied 46 times between 1572 and 1607, mainly over the inability of Philip (and then his son) to pay promised wages. At times, such concerns so overwhelmed Philip that he took recourse in feigned illness and prolonged bed rest: on one occasion, consumed with war and fiscal worries and the details of plans for dispatching an armada to invade England, he stayed in bed from February to July 1587.

A devout *Catholic*, with all that meant on the part of a sixteenth-century monarch, Philip believed that he and Spain had a divinely appointed imperial *mission* to crush *Protestantism* in Europe. This faith extended to reliance on hoped-for miracles where planning or resources were clearly insufficient and to baffled interpretation of defeats as a form of divine judgment on his statecraft. He once chided an official whose zealotry was lapsing: "You are engaged in God's service and in mine—which is the same thing." To this end, he supported the work of the *Jesuits* in their many missions throughout his overseas empire, and the *Inquisition* in Flanders, along with its special and largely *anti-Semitic* form, the Spanish Inquisition, at home in Spain. He ordered the Inquisition to his *New World* empire in 1565, and it was in place there by 1570 in Lima and Mexico City. This did not mean that Philip always got on well with the popes. Far from it: in 1557 Pope Paul IV actually excommunicated Philip and declared war on Spain. That particular pope was forced to terms within a few months, when Philip's armies starved Rome of grain from

Sicily. Thenceforth, Philip was deeply involved in church politics and the *Papal States* to prevent election of unfavorable popes.

Philip's grand design was encouraged by a paralysis of French diplomacy resulting from 30 years of confessional civil war between *Huguenots* and Catholics in France known as the *Wars of Religion*. That left Philip free to intervene in France when he chose, rather than face France as the foe of Habsburg designs it long had been, and free to prosecute his long war against the Dutch rebels in Flanders. Even as that war expanded, in *Granada* a major rebellion by the Moriscos (Muslims compelled to convert to *Christianity* after the defeat of Granada in 1492) broke out, and in 1570 the *Ottoman Empire* resumed a naval offensive in the eastern Mediterranean, attacking Cyprus. Even so, Philip failed to take advantage of the Wars of Religion to hamstring France more permanently. He was instead repeatedly drawn into futile conflict with the Ottoman Empire, as his father had been, and with the *Barbary States*. At the *Battle of Lepanto* (October 7, 1571) Philip's modern fleet destroyed the Ottoman slave-galleys in the Gulf of Corinth, achieving the great victory in the eastern Mediterranean which had for decades eluded his father. However, again Philip did not follow-up. Instead, his attention was drawn to wars in other parts of his empire. The Ottomans remade their losses remarkably quickly and forced a truce on Philip by 1578. The triumph of Spanish naval arms thus proved ephemeral. Philip had appeared a new colossus, but rapid rebuilding of the Ottoman Navy and the subsequent loss of his own Armada off the English coast in 1588 eliminated any advantage gained at Lepanto, as did his repeated bankruptcy and the continued success on land and at sea of the Dutch "beggars" in the chronic Eighty Years' War.

In 1554 Charles had made for Philip a *dynastic marriage* of policy with Mary Tudor ("Bloody Mary," 1516–1558), Catholic Queen of England, which thereby encircled *Bourbon* France with Habsburg power. Philip spent 14 months in England, king of yet another new realm, but failed to woo his Protestant subjects. For centuries England had allied with Castile against France and Scotland, an alliance structure whose last gasp was the short-lived marriage of Philip to Mary. With Mary's death (1558), the outwardly Catholic but in fact Protestant *Elizabeth I* ascended the English throne. She demurred on Philip's tepid offer of marriage, as she did also and later with many other royal suitors over her long and successful reign. At first Philip supported the young English queen. However, as her Protestantism emerged and she *established* the Church of England, Elizabeth's ascension and reign led to a diplomatic revolution which aligned Protestants in Scotland and England with Dutch rebels against Philip. As a *cold war* between England and Spain deepened, Philip began to indulge a mounting messianism that it was God's plan that he annex England and to plot against Elizabeth's life and throne, including with Mary Stuart, Queen of Scots (1542–1587), whom Elizabeth had under close arrest. These plots were discovered and, as one eminent historian has put it: "turned England from a neutral observer into a covert enemy."

Several times Philip considered invading England, but pulled back. Then in 1587 he made the decision and the next year dispatched the "Invincible Armada" to carry out what in weak private code he called the "Enterprise of England." This *Spanish Armada* was met and scattered by English fire ships and cannon and by the North Sea winds. Much of it was lost on the return trip. The next year, an Anglo-Dutch fleet put ashore landing parties in Spain to damage war stores and terrify the population. Philip rebuilt the fleet, at great cost, to try again. Meanwhile, he was drawn into the climactic battles of the Wars of Religion in France.

God too now failed Philip. This was a crushing blow, for Philip genuinely believed in direct divine intervention in the affairs of nations (he had no dealings with *Machiavellian* notions of "fortuna"), and indeed often had relied on this, hoping that God would "find a way" when material resources were lacking and men proved wayward. Yet, battles had been lost and fleets sunk as storms blew unpredictably on the high seas. By 1596 Philip's treasury was empty, and the next year his armies in France and the Netherlands mutinied yet again, as did his navy, and soon both refused to fight. To employ the famous imagery of one of Philip's own soldiers, Miguel de Cervantes (1547–1616), Philip's lifetime of tilting at Protestant windmills had not just proved futile, it had ruined Spain. And it was not over. Philip had set Imperial Spain on a course that led to 80 years of hugely expensive and losing war in Flanders, and another 20 with England, even as Spanish armies and navies were sent out on major expeditions against the still-powerful Ottoman Empire and the peskier but unbowed Barbary States in the Mediterranean, and to consolidate older conquests in the Americas and Asia. These wars proved too many, and so costly in expenditures of blood, treasure, and not least also of good will and international trust, that Spain never recovered. Its mid-seventeenth century fall from *preponderant power* to second-rate kingdom, and then in the eighteenth century its humiliation as a mere vassal of Bourbon France, resulted in the main from Philip's failures. To be sure, these were repeated and compounded by his son and other successors, who might have chosen differently. Yet, throughout the great caldron of confessional and Great Power warfare that was the seventeenth century in Europe, Spanish kings cast policy from moldings Philip had earlier set. *See also Henri IV; Hongwu emperor; Louis XIV;* Pax Hispanica; *Peace of Augsburg; Peter I;* real patronato.

Suggested Readings: Henry Kamen, *Philip of Spain* (1997); Geoffrey Parker, *The Grand Strategy of Philip II* (1998).

Philippines. The *indigenous people* of the Philippines migrated there from several locales over many thousands of years, including from Borneo, Sumatra, and Malaya, as well as various parts of Polynesia and from China. *Islam* arrived with the trade winds from India and perhaps also the Arabian Gulf. It made inroads in the southern part of the archipelago from the fourteenth century. Possession of the Philippines was disputed by Portugal and Spain during negotiations on the Pacific extension of the *line of demarcation*. They went to Madrid (on paper), despite lying inside Lisbon's sphere, since they were discovered in 1521 by Ferdinand Magellan (1480–1521) while in service to *Charles V*. They became a Spanish colony in fact upon conquest and acquisition by *Philip II* in 1565. An *audiencia* was established at Manila in 1583. The settlement was fortified by the Spanish in 1585 and became their central legal, administrative, and military base. Large numbers of *overseas Chinese* began to settle in the late sixteenth century. They played a key role in the Asian trade, but were also severely maltreated by the Spanish. The Philippines remained a Spanish colony until their capture by the United States in 1898 in the *Spanish-American War*. Filipinos had been conducting a *guerrilla war* against the Spanish, and not all regarded the arrival of U.S. ships and marines in Manila Bay as an unmitigated blessing.

Emilio Aguinaldo (1870–1964), leader of one of the many factions opposed to Spain, rather than the national resistance leader he is usually portrayed, at first welcomed assistance but soon rejected the Americans as simply a change of colonial masters. The guerrilla campaign switched to American targets. Fighting lasted until 1902 and saw the United States adopt some tactics (*concentration camps*) which had been its *casus belli* against Spain in Cuba. Could the United States simply have granted the Philippines *independence* in 1898? Not in the world as it then was: a weak and internally divided Filipino state—and there was no other possibility at that time—it would have simply attracted the vultures of imperialism then circling over all Asia, and would almost certainly have faced interference and even annexation by some other empire. In the light of those considerations, even the most liberal members of the *McKinley* and *Roosevelt* administrations thought the wisest course of action was for the U.S. Navy and an American political presence to remain in the archipelago. The foresight of this decision was shown after 1914: with Europe distracted by *World War I*, had the United States been fully withdrawn from Asia an independent Philippines would likely have become an early victim of Japanese expansionism, added to the trophy case beside Korea and northern Manchuria, and the grants Tokyo sought in 1915 from China in the *Twenty-one Demands*.

Nevertheless, the United States began moving toward a grant of *autonomy* almost immediately, and an anti-imperial reaction among the American public led to early acceptance of the idea of independence for the Philippines (Jones Act, 1916; Tydings-McDuffe Act, 1934). *World War II* interrupted the process. The Philippines were attacked nearly simultaneously with *Pearl Harbor* and brutally occupied by Japan until 1945. Guerrilla resistance to the Japanese continued throughout the occupation, unlike elsewhere in the Pacific theater, and Japanese rule and reprisals were correspondingly brutal. In 1943 the United States formally committed to full independence upon *liberation* of the Philippines, which came with Allied landings and a bloody campaign from June 1944 to July 1945. The United States fulfilled its promise on July 4, 1946. Emilio Aguinaldo became the first president of the Philippine Republic. Until 1950 the Philippines faced the *Huk Rebellion*, but Filipino conservatives—a landed plutocracy—retained control of most of the country. In 1965 *Ferdinand Marcos* was elected and thereafter became an entrenched dictator. He ruled under *martial law*, 1972–1981. In the 1970s a left-wing *insurgency* resumed in the form of the *New People's Army* (NPA). In 1986 Marcos was overthrown by a peaceful, grassroots rebellion ("people's power") led by *Corazon Aquino*. With the end of the *Cold War*, and minor land reform, the NPA insurgency faded. However, that left another Muslim insurgency smoldering on the southern island of Mindanao. A pact was signed with the Muslims in 1993, but intermittent fighting continued throughout the 1990s. Filipino *nationalism* also grew more assertive vis-à-vis the United States. In 1992, with much controversy and despite the loss of foreign *currency* earnings, the leases on the U.S. bases at Clark Air Field (which was then destroyed by a volcano anyway) and Subic Bay were left unrenewed. In 2001 another constitutional crisis erupted when the military intervened in a popular, bloodless coup to topple Joseph Estrada from the presidency. The Philippines retained a claim to part of the *Spratlys*. *See also Bataan death march; Douglas MacArthur; open city.*

Suggested Readings: Brian M. Linn, *The Philippine War, 1899–1902* (2000); Ivan Musicant, *Empire by Default* (1998); Samuel Tan, *A History of the Philippines* (1987).

Phoenicia. The Greek name for the coastal region of what is now Syria and Lebanon.

Phoenix Program. *See CIA; pacification.*

Phony War (September 3, 1939–May 10, 1940). The period of inactivity along the *western front* after the expiration of British and French *ultimata* to Germany over its *invasion* of Poland. The British at least began the fight at sea and assembled a force to help Norway. The bulk of the French Army sat or drilled in the deep bunkers and fortifications of the *Maginot Line*, a picture of magnificent ineffectiveness in their sky-blue tunics. This futile activity frittered away morale, cost the French Army its fighting edge, and infected the British Expeditionary Force keeping it company on the Belgian *flank*. The Germans were content, as their main force was in Poland and then in winter quarters, resting for the spring campaign to come against France. It ended with the Nazi *Blitzkrieg* in May and June 1940, which captured Paris and knocked France out of the war, and Britain off the continent. *See also Sitzkrieg.*

Physiocrats (*les économistes*). An eighteenth-century French economic school which rejected "colbertisme," or the *mercantilism* pursued by *Jean-Baptiste Colbert*. They argued that *land* was the basis of productive wealth, and against Colbertist doctrines which stressed the role of international trade and captive overseas markets in national economic policy. Their ultimate vision was of a single world market in which trade occurred peaceably among nations and firms, and to the mutual benefit of all. They also averred a *laissez-faire* attitude toward internal *tariffs* and the merits of economic liberty which greatly influenced *Adam Smith* and other *classical liberal* writers toward the development of a rational discipline of political economy.

Piedmont-Sardinia, Kingdom of. These Italian territories were united in 1748. They formed an independent Italian kingdom, 1720–1860, which included Genoa (after 1815), *Sardinia*, and *Savoy*. They were conquered by *Napoleon I* in 1796, but restored to independence in 1814 by the *Congress of Vienna*. After 1850 Piedmont was active in the drive for Italian unification (*Risorgimento*), under the foreign policy guidance of *Cavour*, though most often in a hurried effort to preempt *Garibaldi* and *Mazzini* rather than from a central conviction or *nationalism*. With the help of a French alliance in a war with Austria in 1859, unification was largely achieved by 1861. It was completed with the incorporation of Rome into the new Kingdom of Italy in 1870. *See also Crimean War; Roman Question.*

Pierce, Franklin (1804–1869). U.S. president, 1853–1857. As a congressional leader he supported admission of *Texas* to the Union as a *slave state*. As president he upheld *slavery* and the controversial fugitive slave law by which slaves on free soil could be forcibly returned, as the property of their owners. He encouraged repeal of the Missouri Compromise and pushed instead for the Kansas/Nebraska Act which helped precipitate the *American Civil War* a few years later. In foreign affairs, he opened new commercial relations with Britain and sent Commodore *Perry* to force open the door to trade with Japan. He also oversaw the actions of *filibusters* in Central America and Cuba.

pike. A long-shafted infantry spear, used by pikemen formed into squares to defend against charging *cavalry*. Swiss pikemen upset the military balance in Europe when they formed in squares to first block and then defeat the heavy cavalry of Charles the Bold at Morat and Nancy (1476). Pike squares also became the main offensive infantry formation in fifteenth- through seventeenth century warfare in Europe, pushing aside whatever resistance they met from archers or *artillery* while axmen followed to hack to death overrun and broken enemy formations. During the *Renaissance* pikemen were used to protect early gunmen, whose rate of fire was poor. The pike was merged with the musket when the socket *bayonet* was invented by *Vauban* in 1687. Thereafter, pikemen were displaced by musketeers who could also stab from, or bristle in defense of, their own position.

pillage. To rob with violence; to *plunder*. Pillaging has been carried out by countless armies over the centuries. Indeed, it was often used as the prime reward for soldiers. It was forbidden in law by the *Hague Conventions*, a theoretical prohibition impossible of enforcement that was nonetheless repeated in a 1977 Additional Protocol (II) to the 1949 *Geneva Conventions*. *See also requisition; sack.*

Pilsudski, Josef (1867–1935). Polish statesman. From 1887 to 1892 he was exiled to *Siberia*. He asked Japan to support a Polish rebellion, 1904–1905, during the *Russo-Japanese War*, but the effort fizzled. During *World War I* he led a Polish unit in the Austrian Army against Russia. When Germany showed before and at *Brest-Litovsk* that it was more interested in its own eastward expansion than Polish emancipation he protested, was arrested, and briefly imprisoned. He was elected president of Poland after Germany's defeat in 1918 and confirmation of Polish independence at the *Paris Peace Conference*. He commanded Polish forces in the *Polish-Soviet War* (1919–1920). In 1926 he returned to power via a *coup d'etat*. After 1926 he was increasingly dictatorial, and his voice alone spoke for Poland in foreign affairs. It was raised early and often about the danger which *Hitler* posed, but his repeated warnings fell on deaf ears in the West.

pincer movement. A military maneuver which seeks to encircle an enemy force by flanking it on both sides at once, often with cavalry or armor, ultimately joining one's advance forces to close the circle behind the trapped enemy units. *See also Blitzkrieg; encirclement; infiltration tactics.*

ping-pong diplomacy. (1) The preliminary softening-up of American, and to a lesser extent (because it made little to no difference to government policy) also Chinese, *public opinion* preparatory to the Sino-American *rapprochement* of 1971, by a series of ping-pong matches held in 1971. China handily won almost every game. The invitation was approved by *Mao*, who was growing evermore worried over the *Sino-Soviet split*. This was the first direct exchange between the United States and China since the cease-fire negotiations of the *Korean Conflict* and the talks which led to the *Geneva Accords*. (2) Derived from the above: Use of interstate sports contacts to break down hostile *images* of opponents and soften public opinion before some diplomatic *démarche* or *coup de théâtre* which might shock "plain folks" were they not so prepared.

Pinochet, Augusto (b. 1915). Chilean dictator, 1973–1989. He led the *coup* which overthrew *Salvador Allende* in 1973. He set up a cruel dictatorship which arrested more than 100,000 persons, tortured many, and killed thousands of *desaparacidos*. However, his *monetarist* economic policies made Chile's economy one of South America's fastest growing and developed. In a *plebiscite* in 1988 Chile rejected his bid to be installed as president-for-life.

Despite the economic progress of his tenure, he was a widely despised and feared man. To obtain his agreement to free and fair elections it was necessary to pardon the military criminals, if not the crimes, of his officers and regime and to retain Pinochet as head of the army (to 1998), and later as a senator with lifetime immunity. In 1989 elections he was defeated by Patricio Aylwin. In 1999 a Spanish judge indicted him for crimes committed in Chile, sparking an international incident over *jurisdiction*. British courts ruled in favor of his *extradition to* Spain, but also that he was too ill. He was allowed to return to Chile, which then stripped him of immunity and brought charges, but it was again determined that he was too ill to stand trial.

piracy. In *economics*, "piracy" is the practice—but just as often, merely a rhetorical charge—of illegal or "unfair" trade practices, such as *dumping*, which aim at securing a *monopoly* over a given market. Under *international law* there are two main forms of piracy. The first is setting up illegal (private and unlicensed) commercial *radio* or TV stations off a nation's *territorial waters* in order to broadcast to that country free of taxation or regulation. A number of states took forceful action against pirate radio stations—which were popular with listeners—in the 1970s and 1980s. Nature itself acted against others by sinking ships or overturning oil rigs from which the stations operated. The second sense of "piracy" under international law is the use of private force to kidnap persons or detain a vessel on the *high seas*, in the air, or anywhere else outside the *territorial jurisdiction* of states, where the intention is to *plunder*. In 1841 Britain, France, Russia, Austria, and Prussia signed a treaty extending this legal logic to make the *slave trade* an act of piracy. This interpretation later was universally adopted. In modern international law there are two subtypes: {i} statutory piracy: defined variously in discrete, national legal codes; and {ii} piracy *jure gentium* ("under the law of peoples"): defined in a 1934 decision as "any armed violence at sea which is not a lawful act of war," and amended under *UNCLOS III* (1982) to mean any such acts committed "for private ends."

Piracy in practice is as old as shipping. Wherever on the seas moved goods that might be stolen or people who might be held for ransom, pirates appeared to prey upon them. The only security against pirates in history has been armed force wielded by states to root them out of their home ports or burn their ships from under them and enforce the rule of law. When such states have not existed, pirates have flourished. One of the greatest accomplishments of the *Roman Empire* was to end the scourge of piracy in the Mediterranean, thereby permitting commerce to expand and securing for Rome peaceable, wealthy provinces and *tributaries*. When Rome fell, piracy returned to the Mediterranean. Indeed, it obtained support by some coastal states, notably the Muslim emirates of North Africa known widely as the *Barbary States*. The Mediterranean continued to be a bastion of pirate navies, mostly *galleys* rowed by Christian *slaves*, into the early nineteenth century. *Thomas Jefferson* lost the *Tripolitan War* to the Barbary pirates, and they remained an international problem until a multinational effort to clean them out was made following the *Napoleonic Wars*, in 1815. In 1842 the British and Americans agreed to maintain two naval squadrons specifically to suppress pirates.

The *Vikings* started out as not much more than pirates, though later they became a much more deadly threat: invaders and conquerors. However, piracy was curbed in most of the Baltic from the twelfth century by the success of the *Hansa*. Piracy, or private warfare, was endemic elsewhere in the sixteenth and seventeenth centuries. In the Caribbean, pirates were mostly French, Dutch, and English, preying on the richer Spanish colonies and the *flota*. In Jamaica, Henry Morgan (c. 1635–1688) was so successful as a pirate he was knighted and made governor. The Mosquito Coast of Central America was infested with English *pirates* from the 1630s to the 1780s, when they were driven out by the Spanish. Groups of English pirates, also known as *filibusters*, crossed the Central American isthmus to steal ships from Spanish ports and use them to harry other Spanish shipping from 1680 to 1681, and again from 1685 to 1689. More than 50 Spanish ships were lost to these English buccaneers, who were not turned away until the local population raised funds to buy two *frigates*. In times of war among Spain, England, and the Netherlands, a state of affairs that dominated much of the last half of the sixteenth century and first half of the seventeenth century, many English and Dutch pirates became *privateers* and enjoyed official support from London and Amsterdam. The Caribbean was awash in French and English pirates who were broadly tolerated by the loose colonial governments of the islands (and who sometimes were the "government"). This changed as the island populations expanded and the local economy became more stable and reliant on trade rather than on a share of sea-borne plunder brought back to port to be eaten, drunk, and whored away. Thus, in the second half of the century Spain, France, England, and the Netherlands signed a series of treaties formally recognizing each other's island possessions. Further crippling piracy in European-controlled areas was a concentration of naval force in the hands of the states—in short, the rise of modern *navies*.

In East Asia, Japanese *wakō* terrorized Korea and China for many decades, sometimes mounting large-scale inland invasions. The arrival of advanced European navies in these waters helped suppress piracy, but it did not end it. Indeed, high seas piracy continued to be a significant problem, especially for weak archipelagic states or those with tangled coastlines as in West Africa, into the twenty-first century. Thousands of Vietnamese *boat people* were killed or abducted into *slavery* by pirates in the 1980s and 1990s, decades when pirates also operated with newly swift craft (motorized gunboats) but ancient casual brutality off the coasts of West Africa, Thailand, Indonesia, and the Philippines, as well as off Vietnam and southern China. Hundreds of attacks were reported to the *International Maritime Organization* in 2000, with Indonesian waters far and away the most dangerous. *See also buccaneer; corsair; fisheries; hijacking; international criminal law; Japan; Maroons; Trucial Oman.*

Suggested Readings: James G. Lydon, *Pirates, Privateers, and Profits* (1970); C. R. Pennell, *Bandits at Sea: A Pirates Reader* (2001); Neville Williams, *The Sea Dogs: Privateers, Plunder and Piracy in the Elizabethan Age* (1975).

Pitcairn Island. The last British *dependency* in the *South Pacific.* In 2001 this tiny, isolated island had a population of fewer than 100, most of them descendants of the survivors of the HMS Bounty who settled there after the *mutiny.*

Pitt, William (1708–1778). "Pitt the Elder." First Earl of Chatham. British *Whig* statesman. He was driven by a vision of English national greatness, but also an awareness of England's weakness and vulnerability, which necessarily clashed with the interests of the *Bourbons.* From 1756, during the *Seven Years' War* (and *French and Indian War* in North America), Pitt pursued a traditional English "maritime strategy" of seeking to sustain the *balance of power* in Europe while employing Britain's great advantage in *sea power* to expand overseas. He resigned briefly in 1757 over the king's uncertainty about a strong war policy, due to the Hanoverian connection, but was quickly reappointed and prosecuted a vigorous war. Whether or not Pitt had a grand strategic vision or merely reacted to events, he shrewdly supported this effort by raising the militia, building new fleets, and making large *subsidies* to *Frederick the Great* of Prussia. He also maintained a *mercenary* army in Hanover. In North America, he ceased to treat the colonists as mere subordinates and accorded them instead the status of near-allies and made an alliance with the *Iroquois Confederacy.* The result was decisive defeat for France on several continents and oceans. He resigned in 1761 over the issue of war with Spain. In 1766 he was again prime minister. He sincerely wanted to compromise with American dissenters, but when the issue came to war he voted in favor of using force. He dragged himself from a sickbed to make that speech and vote (April 2, 1778), collapsed in the House of Lords—he had been appointed Earl of Chatham—while rising to take a question, and died five weeks later (May 11, 1778).

Suggested Reading: Marie Peters, *The Elder Pitt* (1998).

Pitt, William (1759–1806). "Pitt the Younger." British statesman. Son of *William Pitt* (1708–1778). Prime minister, 1784–1801, 1804–1806. Pitt was chancellor of the Exchequer at 23 and the youngest ever prime minister, at 24. He began as a reformer of public offices and the *East India Company,* though most of his early measures (at the Exchequer) were blocked. Overcoming fierce Parliamentary opposition, Pitt quickly proved an extraordinary debater, coalition-builder, and favorite of the king. He immediately passed major Parliamentary reforms, elevating the role of the Commons and repressing "rotten boroughs." He also revised and reformed trade and taxation policy. Pitt was a firm supporter of the new doctrine of *laissez-faire*, at home and abroad, concluding a trade agreement with France; he failed, however, to gain *free trade* with Ireland and was additionally unsuccessful in reforming the Irish Parliament or ending anti-*Catholic* abuses. Pitt supported the anti–*slave trade* campaign, telling the gentlemen of the House of Commons in 1792: "No nation in Europe . . . has plunged so deeply into this guilt as Great Britain." He passed the *India Act* (1784) and reforms in Canada (1791).

Pitt is best remembered for taking a superb *Royal Navy* and financially sound government and using both to lead Great Britain brilliantly in the difficult and dangerous years of its great contest with France after the *French Revolution* and in the early *Napoleonic Wars*. At first *neutral*, his anti-*Jacobinism* grew apace with the radicalization and export of the revolution. This led him to restrain reform and then turn to active repression at home, lest economic unrest and social change encourage a similar rebellion. Pitt put down the revolt by the *United Irish Society* (1798). He then pushed through the *Act of Union* with Ireland in 1800 and tried for *Catholic Emancipation*. However, he failed to resolve the *Irish Question* owing to profound royal opposition in the person of *George III* and deep division within the country over what to do about and with Catholic Ireland. Like his father, in the French wars at first Pitt used British *sea power* to fight France anywhere save on the continent. The Royal Navy captured *Cape Colony* and *Ceylon* for the *British Empire*, as well as territories in the Caribbean, and as prime minister Pitt saw the great naval victories at *Abukir Bay*, *Trafalgar*, and *Copenhagen*. He then died of broken health, at just 47 years. *See also Peace of Amiens.*

Suggested Readings: Jennifer Mori, *William Pitt and the French Revolution, 1785–1795* (1997); Paul W. Schroeder, *The Transformation of European Politics, 1763–1848* (1994).

Pius IX, né Giovanni Ferretti (1792–1878). Pope, 1846–1878. He was in constant struggle with the Italian state over control of the *Papal States* and, after 1870, over the temporal status of the *Vatican*. He was forced to flee Rome during the *Revolutions of 1848*, but returned with French military backing. *Napoleon III* supported him, 1850–1870, until Rome was joined to Italy in the wake of France's defeat by Prussia in the *Franco-Prussian War*. Pius called the *First Vatican Council*, which declared him (and his successors) "infallible" on matters of faith and doctrine. That and the "Syllabus of Errors" he promulgated caused severe political problems in Austria and Germany. In general, Pius was something of a throwback to the days of the "church militant" and much at odds with the new *nationalism* in Italy. "It is an error," he once declared, "to believe that the Roman Pontiff can and ought to reconcile himself to, and agree with, progress, liberalism, and modern civilization." Later pontiffs did not, on the whole, emulate his irascible style, even while supporting his doctrinal claims. *See also Kulturkampf; Old Catholics.*

Pius XI, né Achille Ratti (1857–1939). Papal *nuncio* to Poland, archbishop of Lepanto, cardinal of Milan; pope, 1922–1939; *sovereign* of the *Vatican State*, 1929–1939. A fierce anti-*Communist*, he roused worldwide *Catholic* opposition to the *Soviet Union*. He signed the *Lateran Treaties* with *Mussolini* (1929) and a *concordat* with *Hitler* (1933). In 1937 he protested against Nazi violations of the concordat. He prepared a major encyclical condemning *anti-Semitism* in Nazi Germany but died before he could publish it. It was suppressed by his successor, *Pius XII*.

Pius XII, né Eugenio Pacelli (1876–1958). Pope, 1939–1958. Pacelli was a career *Vatican* diplomat, rising to cardinal and serving as secretary of state to the *Holy See*. He lived for many years in Germany, where he negotiated the *concordat* signed by the Vatican with *Hitler*. His failure to speak publicly against the *Holocaust* has been greatly criticized by those of acute moral sensibility, whether *Jews*, *Protestants*, *Catholics*, or church historians. Although Pius was informed about the Nazi *genocide* underway against Jews, *Roma*, and others, he never spoke publicly against *Nazism*. Nor did he try to marshal Catholic opinion against the mass murder of those peoples then underway across Europe. He did not even publish the major condemnation of *anti-Semitism* prepared by his predecessor, *Pius XI*. More pointedly, while tolerating the hiding of Jews and others in Catholic monasteries and convents, he never commanded Catholic clergy to speak out against *fascism* generally, despite its clear anti-religious and even pagan predilections. Nor did he command the faithful to oppose to the best of their moral abilities and the limits of personal courage, as he might have done, the murderous policy of the Nazi regime, not even when SS death brigades came into Rome itself in 1943 to cart off Italian Jews to the *death camps*.

Pius' reticence was motivated by a complex of factors. First, he was concerned with political calculations relating to the vulnerable position of the *Catholic Church* in Nazi-occupied Europe. Second, he and the Curia were powerfully influenced by a deep detestation of *communism* and of the *Soviet Union*, probably more so than by any personal antipathy for Jews, though that possibility may not be discounted entirely. Finally, Pius feared the destruction of his life's work, which had been to consolidate papal power over national Catholic churches in Italy and Germany and worldwide. Even if all that is true, his silence still deafens. And there lingers the possibility that his passivity had darker, more sinful motivations of anti-Semitism.

On the other side of the moral ledger, the Vatican intervened to help Allied *prisoners of war* and aid civilian victims of *World War II*. When it was all over, in September 1945, Pius XII asked *Dwight Eisenhower* to permit creation of a Catholic nation in southern Europe comprised of Austria, Bavaria, Saxony, and the other Catholic parts of southern Germany, to be headed by Archduke Otto, heir to the *Habsburg* throne. The Catholic parts of Czechoslovakia, Poland, and Hungary attracted him, but were excluded as they lay within the Soviet *occupation zone*. The plan was never effected. During the early *Cold War* Pius enjoyed a renewed international acceptance as he led a vehement crusade to persuade lay Catholic opinion that opposition to communism amounted to an almost absolute religious duty. Would that he had done likewise with regard to Nazism, that other *totalitarian* scourge of the twentieth century.

Suggested Reading: John Cornell, *Hitler's Pope* (1999).

pivotal states. States deemed to occupy pivotal points of strategic importance upon whose turning, by way of the *balance of power* or *alliance* or *ideology* or *conquest*, much depends. Examples include Cambodia between Thailand (Siam) and Vietnam; Belgium between France and Germany; Poland between Germany and Russia; and Turkey between Christian Europe and the Muslim and Arab Middle East.

pivot of history. *See geographic pivot of history; Halford Mackinder.*

Pizarro, Francisco (c. 1478–1541). He was part of expeditions to coastal Colombia in 1509 and to Panama in 1519. He first encountered *Inca* outposts in northern Peru in 1528. He returned to Spain to gain permission, and a royal contract, for a conquest. In early 1531 he led an expedition of conquest to Peru, departing from Panama with just 183 men, including several brothers, 37 horses, and some small cannon. He moved with caution, not advancing down the Andes until September 1532. Unbeknown to him, but of fundamental importance in explaining his subsequent success, the Inca were in the midst of a major civil war and succession struggle. On November 16th Pizarro surprised and seized the Sapa Inca, Atahualpa, who had invited him to a parlay. The Spanish slaughtered some 2,000 Inca guards with their artillery and firearms, swords and pikes. Pizarro extorted a massive ransom for Atahualpa's release (a large room literally filled with gold) and then murdered him anyway in July 1533. Pizarro next marched on the capital at Cuzco. Subsequently reinforced, his *conquistadores* fanned out from Cuzco to conquer the rest of Peru and most of southern Chile, while Pizarro founded Lima.

One brother, Juan, was killed in an Inca insurrection in 1537. Another conquistador, Diego de Almagro, who had led the expedition into Bolivia and Chile, lifted the Inca siege of the small Spanish garrison in Cuzco and occupied the city. Pizarro sent his brothers to defeat this rival, who was then garroted and beheaded (1538). Pizarro was then killed in his home in Lima in 1541 by rebellious conquistadores allied to Almagro and enraged at his murder. A climactic battle between the factions took place at Ayacucho (Huramanga) on September 18, 1542, with more beheadings of the losers. Next, surviving conquistadores refused to submit to the authority of the royal viceroy, who was trying to limit the excesses of the *encomienda system* under the *New Laws*. Pizarro's half-brother Gonzalo led an attack on Lima in 1546 and won a victory over the Spanish viceroy, whom he beheaded. Some rebels urged Gonzalo to proclaim a Peruvian kingdom, with himself as king. However, a replacement viceroy suspended the New Laws and offered pardons to most of the rebels. This caused the rebellion to collapse and led to the beheading of its leaders, including Gonzalo, in April 1548. Another Pizarro brother, Hernando—who had earlier killed Almagro—was imprisoned upon his return to Spain, until 1560.

Plains of Abraham, Battle of (1759). This elevated field lies outside the fortress walls of Québec City, abutted by a steep cliff. An English army scaled the heights to achieve *victory* over French forces and decide the fate of *New France*. Both commanding generals, James Wolfe (an arrogant, pompous martinet) for the British and Louis Montcalm for the French, were mortally wounded. Their imagined death scenes were memorialized in several romantically heroic paintings. The battle opened the way to Montréal and secured *Lower Canada* (*Québec*) for England, a transfer confirmed in the *Peace of Paris* (1763). The defeat for France reverberated throughout North America, determining that Canada would evolve as a British colony and removing the common enemy which bound the otherwise distinct interests of the American colonists and the *British Empire*. The acquisition of Canada was also Britain's first large-scale addition to the empire by direct conquest. *See also American Revolution.*

planned economy. Where major decisions as to *capital* and *labor* supply are not left to the market, but are set and controlled according to certain social objectives or with bureaucratic interests foremost in mind. Typical examples were the *Soviet bloc* economies to 1989 and China before c. 1978. *See also command economy; five-year plans; market economy; mixed economy; rationing.*

Plassey, Battle of (June 23, 1757). *See Clive.*

Platt Amendment (1901). This act was written by *Elihu Root* but shepherded through Congress by Senator Orville Platt. It granted the United States a right of *intervention*, thus making Cuba an effective *protectorate*. It also limited Cuba's treaty-making powers and gave the United States rights over *Guantánamo*. *See also Good Neighbor Policy; Monroe Doctrine.*

Plaza Agreement (September 1985). A key meeting was held in the Plaza Hotel in New York, attended by American, British, French, German, and Japanese *central bank* officials. They agreed to cooperate on management of international *monetary policy*. This was highly significant because: (1) it ended a post–*Bretton Woods* era of U.S. neglect of global economic management; and (2) it represented the definitive entry of Japan as a full partner in international economic management. *See also G-5.*

plebiscite. A synonym for *referendum*. The use of plebiscites (usually rigged) as a means of providing a constitutional veneer to effective personal dictatorship was pioneered by *Napoleon I*. The method was later used by various *fascist* and *Communist* states, as well as individual dictators. Uses vary from ratifying domestic constitutional changes to certifying and providing false legitimacy to external conquests. *See also democracy; popular sovereignty.*

plenipotentiary. A diplomatic representative of *ambassadorial* or *cabinet* rank, with full powers to negotiate substantive agreements on behalf of the state he or she represents. The term was commonly used by the seventeenth century, when it replaced the older "procurator," which predated the *Renaissance*.

PLO. *See Palestine Liberation Organization.*

plunder. When an army steals massively from the people of an area it passes through or *occupies*, either to provision itself or just for profit. It does not carry the connotations of murder, rape, and other violence which *pillaging* or *sacking* does. *See also requisition.*

pluralism. (1) A view of foreign policy *decision-making* in democratic states which argues against the control of policy by *elites*, in favor of the competition of *public opinion* and *interest groups* in developing a grand compromise which informs policy. (2) A view of the *international system* as populated by many more *actors* than just the *states* and which does not necessarily see *security* as the main issue in *world politics*. *See also elitism; MNCs; nongovernmental organizations (NGOs); transnational actors; turbulence.*

plural nationality. *See dual nationality.*

plutocracy. Rule by a wealthy *elite*. *See also kleptocracy.*

plutonium. Named for the Greek god of the underworld, plutonium has a fissionable isotope of prime importance in the *nuclear age*: PU^{239}, the deadliest, most poisonous substance known. Plutonium is similar to uranium in its atomic chemistry and is formed by bombarding the element neptunium with deuteron. This creates an artificial, radioactive element (within pitchblende, slow decay of neptunium produces U^{235}, a natural element, which is also fissionable), which can sustain a chain reaction leading to a *fission* explosion. Uranium has two main isotopes: U^{235} and U^{238}. The first is bomb-grade material. For the second to be used in weapons it must first be enriched with U^{235}, producing highly enriched uranium (HEU). Like HEU, plutonium can be used for power generation or to make *nuclear weapons*. Plutonium may also be refined: so-called ivory plutonium is almost pure PU^{239}. It is found mainly in Russia, which during the *Cold War* built new nuclear *warheads* with fresh stocks of fuel while storing old bombs, plutonium, and all. Both types of fission devices may also serve to trigger the *fusion* process within *hydrogen bombs*. It takes about 35 kg (77 lbs.) of civilian-grade plutonium to make a *Hiroshima*-sized bomb, but only about 5 kg (11 lbs.) of military grade metal. In the mid-1990s there was about 1,000 metric tons (2,200,000 lbs.) of plutonium and 2,000 metric tons (4,400,000 lbs.) of HEU in the world. Some 95 percent of all HEU was held by the American and Russian militaries combined. Thus, only 1 percent fell under *IAEA* inspections and safeguards.

Similarly, the majority of plutonium was in civilian hands, with only about 30 percent coming under IAEA or other safeguards. Since it would take only 220 kg of HEU (and less than 45 kg of plutonium), or 0.01 percent of the total stock to make a new *nuclear state*, fears about *proliferation* were widespread. Military plutonium production began to abate with the end of the *Cold War*: the United States and Russia agreed to cease making any new plutonium by 2000. In 1994 the United States agreed to buy 500 tons of surplus Russian HEU for civilian use over a 20-year period. Civilian production, however, continued to expand as "fast" or "breeder" reactors were used to enrich plutonium and HEU for use in power generation. Coincidentally, this process also made new supplies of weapons-grade metal. Some analysts proposed developing mixed-oxide fuel (MOX), in which plutonium would be blended with HEU for civilian reactors. All this spoke to the paradox of post–Cold War nuclear *arms control*: some 700–800 metric tons of HEU formerly in *warheads* was released through dismantling of old missile systems under *START*. There was no safe place to put it either in terms of the environment or security from theft; without MOX, there would be no commercial use for it either. From the 1940s to 1970s, most plutonium waste was dumped or buried without separating the plutonium or taking due precautions. This problem was acute in the Soviet Union but also occurred in the United States. After 1987, the United States began to retrieve this plutonium preparatory to permanent burial in a repository 2,150 feet deep in Carlsbad, New Mexico. *See also radiation effects; radiological weapons.*

pocket battleship. A *battleship* in all respects except tonnage. They were developed to meet limitations on battleship displacement (ship size) in several arms control treaties after *World War I*. *See also battle cruiser.*

pogrom. "Devastation." This Yiddish term entered most Western languages after physical attacks on Jews and their property in *tsarist Russia* in 1881–1882, when Jews were blamed for the assassination of *Alexander II* (a false charge). The carnage engaged European and American attention as a result of a massive outflow of destitute *refugees*: from 1881 to 1920 more than two million Jews fled to the United States. The pogroms increased in ferocity after the *Russian Revolution* (1905), under the *Black Hundreds*. Pogroms also took place in Poland, Rumania, Hungary, and the Soviet Union in the 1920s and

1930s. Some were spontaneous, springing from peasant bigotry and superstition, but many were government inspired. During 1990 there were rumblings from *Pamyat* about a new pogrom, but none materialized. The term is also used retroactively, to refer to attacks on Jews such as those throughout Spain in 1391 and after the expulsion order of 1492. *See also anti-Semitism; Kristallnacht.*

Suggested Reading: J. Klier and S. Lamboza, eds., *Pogroms* (1991).

Poincaré, Raymond (1860–1934). French statesman. Prime minister, 1912, 1922–1924, 1926–1929; president, 1913–1920; foreign minister, 1922–1924. He improved France's alliance with Russia and its *entente* with Britain before *World War I.* As president, he stood above the turmoil of wartime policy by organizing a *national front.* Although he had opposed the harsher terms of the *Treaty of Versailles,* he approved *occupation* of the *Ruhr* in 1923 to compel Germany to pay *reparations.* With neither U.S. nor British approval he could not buttress that position and resigned. *See also Georges Clemenceau.*

poison. Poison has long been considered a *prohibited weapon* of war, both in practice and within the *just war tradition*: records show that as early as 1100 B.C.E. in India there existed prohibitions against poisoned weapons in war. The ancient Greeks also prohibited the use of poisons. The *Romans*, on the other hand, frequently used it as an adjunct to *siege warfare.* Under terms of the *Hague Conventions*, poison (for instance, for use against a city's water supply system) was formally made illegal. This sense later attached to *poison gas*, which came to be viewed as heinous. Yet, the limited utility of poisons, rather than their "illegality," is probably the main cause of their restricted use in warfare. *See also chemical weapons; nerve weapons; radiological weapons.*

poison gas. *See gas weapons.*

Poitiers, Battle of (1356). *See Hundred Years' War.*

Poland. Most of the population in Poland, primarily of *Slavic* origin, was converted to *Catholicism* in the ninth century, and Poland formed a widely recognized kingdom from the eleventh century. Poland numbered among the *Great Powers* of the European Middle Ages, expanding across the great plain between the then concentrated power of the *Holy Roman Empire* to its west and the fractured chaos of Appanage Russia in the east. Poland reached new heights under Casimir III, the Great (1310–1370, r. 1333–1370), who made peace with Bohemia and the *Teutonic Knights*, consolidated the monarchy, codified Polish laws, and improved the lot of Jews and peasants in a just and benign reign, by the standards of the Age. Poland added Royal Prussia to its holdings after that area revolted against the Teutonic Knights in 1454. Poland came under pressure from the expanding *Ottoman Empire* and other Muslim forces, and though scoring defensive victories, suffered a long, tortuous decline. In an effort to arrest this decline it formed a Commonwealth with Lithuania in the Union of Lublin in 1569. There were moments of renewed expansion and hope, too, such as when the Poles occupied Moscow, 1608–1613. Overall, however, internal stagnation and political and military decline resumed, so that Poland found itself in the seventeenth and eighteenth centuries as the barley caught between the great millstones of the rising power of *Prussia* and *Russia*.

Poland's chronic weakness was confirmed in the *Great Northern War* (1700–1721), where *Peter I's* decisive victory at *Poltava* (July 8, 1709) pulled Russia deep into Polish affairs, and again in the *War of the Polish Succession* (1733). In 1772 Poland was still the third largest state in terms of territory in all Europe, but that fact belied its fatal internal weaknesses, greatly contributed to by the *liberum veto*. It disappeared from the map with the three *partitions of Poland,* 1772–1795. It was redivided and occupied by France and Russia at *Tilsit,* but went largely to Russia after 1815 with decisions taken at the *Congress of Vienna.* Two great rebellions in the nineteenth century, in 1831 and 1863, were crushed by Russia.

An independent Poland did not reappear until 1918. It was enriched with a strip of territory taken from Germany at the *Paris Peace Conference* to create the *Polish Corridor.* It then made its presence felt in the east with a successful expansionist war, the *Polish-Soviet War.* It joined the *Little Entente* and allied with France during the interwar years. Until 1934 General *Pilsudski* dominated Polish politics and foreign policy. In all discussions of collective defense in the 1930s, Poland refused to consider transit for the *Red Army* heading for the Czech-German frontier to repel a German *invasion.* That was one reason no eastern defense pact was agreed. Instead, Poland became the main target of the *Nazi-Soviet Pact,* which cleared the way for Germany to attack on September 1, 1939. Two weeks later Russian troops crossed the border not as defenders, but as collaborators in conquest with the Germans. The *NKVD* followed, and following them, the awful massacre of the Polish officer corps at *Katyn.* The Nazi occupation was horrific: millions of Polish *citizens,* including most Polish Jews, were murdered. Not all Poles mourned the loss of the Jews, and some even *collaborated* in their extermination: Poland's history was stained with *pogroms* and other manifestations of a deep *anti-Semitism* on the part of many. During the war, Poland maintained, in exile where it was equipped by the Allies, one of the largest armies fighting the Axis.

The Red Army returned to Poland in 1944, this time as liberator and occupier rolled into one. It was cynically paused by *Stalin* to permit the Germans to crush the *Warsaw Rising* and then used to install a *communist* government at Lublin, which would displace the *government-in-exile* in London after the war. Poland was a major issue of contention at *Teheran, Yalta,* and *Potsdam.* In 1945 it was reconstituted on the *Oder-Neisse Line* in the west and the *Curzon Line* in the east. Millions of Poles moved westward, expelling the Germans of *East Prussia* and *Silesia,* the innocent along with the guilty, in punishment for what their Nazi masters had done to 10,000 Polish towns and villages and six million or more compatriots (three million of whom were Jews). By the end of 1946 Poland was firmly within the *Soviet bloc,* with successive governments toeing the *party line* as set in Moscow.

Poland joined the *Warsaw Pact* in 1955 and participated in the invasion of Czechoslovakia in 1968. Serious rioting occurred across Poland in 1956, and again in 1970, both times leading to merely cosmetic political changes. A tidal shift came after 1976, when a Polish cardinal, Karol Wojtyla, was elected to be Pope *John Paul II.* A surge of *nationalism* combined with pent-up economic frustration to give birth to the extraordinary national reform movement *Solidarity,* led by *Lech Walesa.* In 1980 more strikes and violence erupted, culminating in fear of Soviet invasion and displacement of the *Communist Party* by the Polish military under General *Jaruzelski,* declaration of *martial law,* and U.S. trade *sanctions.* The Communist façade had cracked, revealing a crumbling foundation as well.

In 1989 Solidarity was legalized, multiparty elections held, and effective Polish independence re-established. In 1990 Walesa was elected president. After three years of economic *shock treatment* on the way to a *market economy,* by 1993 *inflation* began to recede and Polish GNP and industrial output began to grow again. Solidarity moved back into opposition as it and Polish national unity shattered into the inescapable quarreling and factions of "normal politics." That was made clear in 1993 when a coalition government was formed of two parties with roots in the old Communist system, in a clear reaction against the harsh—though probably unavoidable—deprivations of the transition period. In March 1999 Poland was admitted to *NATO.*

Suggested Readings: M. B. Biskupski, *The History of Poland* (2000); R. F. Leslie, *The History of Poland Since 1863* (1980).

polar regions. *See Antarctic; Arctic.*

police action. A euphemism for the use of force to bring about compliance with *Security Council* resolutions. Most famously, the *war* in Korea was called a "police action," thereby avoiding the need to *declare war,* which would involve time-consuming debate, and the even more difficult diplomatic task of identifying, formally and legally, the *aggressor.* The term also implies for some suggestions, welcome or not, of the United Nations as "globocop."

police activities (on the high seas). *See hot pursuit; piracy; slave trade; visit and search.*

police state. One in which *secret police* or the military enforce draconian restrictions on civil, political, and personal liberties. *See also Gestapo; KGB.*

POLISARIO. The *independence* and *guerrilla* movement formed in 1973 in *Western Sahara*, which forced Mauritania to abandon its claim, 1976–1979, and fought a protracted war with Morocco after that. Its prime backer was Algeria. In 1974 it was *recognized* by many *OAU* and *United Nations* members as the legitimate *government-in-exile* of Western Sahara, which it called the "Sahrawi Arab Democratic Republic."

Polish Corridor. A narrow strip of *territory* cutting through *East Prussia* near the Vistula, given to Poland at the *Paris Peace Conference*. It permitted Polish goods access to the seaport of *Danzig*. It was a serious irritant in German-Polish relations during the *interwar years*. *Nazi* demands for *liberation* served as the excuse for the German attack of September 1, 1939, which was the proximate cause of *World War II*.

Polish-Soviet War (1920). With Russia in the throes of the *Russian Civil War*, the Poles struck east in a bid for more territory for their revived state, which had reappeared for the first time since the *partitions of Poland*. Led by *Pilsudski* and in *alliance* with Ukrainian *Whites*, Polish units overran much of Ukraine, briefly capturing Kiev in May 1920. They were repulsed and driven deep into Poland by the *Red Army*, fresh from its victories over Crimean *Cossacks* and Ukrainian Whites and under orders from *Lenin* to foment a Polish *revolution*. A second Polish offensive, in August, pushed the Russians back and retook much eastern territory lost in the spring. In the Treaty of Riga (March 18, 1921) Poland received portions of western Byelorussia, Lithuania, and Ukraine. These areas were not recovered by the *Soviet Union* until it attacked Poland in September 1939, were lost again in 1942, but recovered to Russia—along with much more territory—in 1945. *See also Curzon Line; Nazi-Soviet Pact.*

Politburo (*Politichekoye*). "Political Bureau." (1) The compact, governing council (inner circle) of the Soviet *Communist Party* and other soviet-style Communist parties. It was master of the Soviet governmental system. In 1952, just before *Stalin's* death, it merged into the Presidium. That represented a cosmetic change only, as the inner circle continued to meet and set policy separately from the larger body. With *Khrushchev's* demise, it was changed back. In the Chinese Communist Party, the inner sanctum of the Politburo, the absolute center of power, is its Standing Committee. *See also Central Committee; Zhou Enlai.*

political asylum. *See asylum.*

political capital. A metaphor wherein political influence is likened to *capital* reserves, in that its present sum and future purchasing power decline with expenditure (use or application). However, it should be noted that political capital is rather more like money kept in a mattress than a portfolio: if not invested or spent, it will only depreciate and very rapidly, as *George H. Bush* learned, 1991–1992.

political dispute. One which by its contentious nature is considered inappropriate for legal settlement. A synonym is *nonjusticiable dispute*. *See also legal dispute*.

political economy. (1) In the era of *mercantilism*: A body of thought about how best to manage national society to maintain wealth, relative to other states. (2) In the nineteenth century: A social science which evolved into the modern discipline of *economics*. (3) In modern usage: {a} Study of the interrelatedness of *politics* and *economics*, whether at the domestic or international levels; {b} the use of economic models of rational choice to explain political decisions and actions; and {c} the actual structures of interrelated, global (or regional or national) political and economic activity and phenomena, including but not limited to world markets, production and consumption patterns, global financial and trade institutions, *multinational corporations*, and the *states*, their governments, and myriad economic regulations. *See also Bretton Woods institutions; classical school; Jean-Baptiste Colbert; dependency theory; General Agreement on Tariffs and Trade; globalization; gold standard; hegemonic stability theory;* laissez-faire; *Marxism; mercantilism; most-favored nation; NIEO; Physiocrats; Adam Smith; World Trade Organization.*

political offenses. Offenses by individuals against the laws of some (usually, but not always, highly repressive) state for which other states will not *extradite* a fugitive. Political offenses are usually identifiable as threats to the *national security* of the targeted state and are committed mainly by members of identifiable groups, or in behalf of group claims, rather than merely as acts of individual protest. They may be acts normally considered criminal (robbery, destruction of property, even killing) if committed by individuals, but given circumstances of group conflict in the country in which they were in fact committed, reasonably may be seen as having a political motivation and effect. A "purely political offense" is one in which there is no underlying criminal activity of any kind under the laws of the state being asked to extradite. For example, the United States would not consider or conduct extradition of a person accused of "slander against the state" or some similarly *Stalinist* or *Maoist* notion of a political crime. *See also asylum; dissident; espionage; hijacking; political prisoner; prisoner of conscience; sedition; terrorism; treason; war crimes.*

political prisoner. A person incarcerated for political beliefs or acts, not for any criminal behavior. Legality is broadly unimportant in this concept, as repressive societies often ban in law actions which in a free society are taken as normal or at least as protected, exercise of civil rights (printing and circulating pamphlets, organizing political rallies, or joining a strike). A political prisoner may or may not, therefore, have advocated the use of violence against a repressive system. This term is not generally used in reference to democratic states, where mechanisms of free speech, assembly, and political representation exist and offer reasonable hope of effecting political and social change, and where violent actions taken in opposition to an existing state of political affairs is therefore widely (and correctly) viewed as criminal and illegitimate. This judgment might have to be qualified, however, wherever such civil freedoms were merely formal, or suspended, or not applied evenly across religious or ethnic groups with real grievances. *See also Amnesty International; GULAG archipelago; Nelson Mandela; prisoner of conscience.*

political science. A social science concerned with the systematic study of public affairs. Its methodology is necessarily eclectic, drawing on such fields as economics, geography, history, law, philosophy, psychology, sociology, and statistics. It is conventionally subdivided into comparative politics, international relations, political economy, political philosophy, and constitutional theory. At its best, it draws questions from the conversation across time of the great political thinkers as well as from current policy debates and examines these through a rich, humanistic discourse which is both historically and philosophically aware. At its modern (and also postmodern) worst, however, it is too often prone to methodological throat-clearings which substitute for real political analysis and spends a great deal of time and effort striking elaborate *scientistic* poses about arcane topics of interest only to its "professional"—that is, its academic—practitioners. All of this is most often rendered in impenetrable prose which has the effect—and in many cases also deliberately seeks—mainly to obscure from those outside the discipline its lack of real political content, practical utility, or intellectual originality.

This is a great pity, as in its classical concerns with matters of governance, *power, ethics,* and *diplomacy,* the study of politics is a hugely rich and important scholarly endeavor—far too important, in fact, to be left to political science (to paraphrase *Georges Clemenceau*). Fortunately, a minority of political scientists understand all that and continue to produce works of genuine quality and value. For example, S. E. Finer's "History of Government From the Earliest Times," 3 vols. (1997) is a genuine masterpiece of humanistic and historically informed political analysis. In international relations, the works of Martin Wight, Hedley Bull, Hans Morgenthau, Stanley Hoffmann, and Robert H. Jackson, among others, are also likely to stand the tests of time and scholarly scrutiny. *See also anarchical society; anarchy; behavioralism; bureaucratic politics; case study; cognitive dissonance; critical theory; cybernetic theory; decision-making theory; dependency theory; deterrence; economics; end of history; events data; falsification; game theory; geopolitics; grand theory; George Friedrich Hegel; hegemony; hegemonic stability theory; history; Thomas Hobbes; idealism;*

input; instrumental rationality; international organization; international system; jargon; Immanuel Kant; levels of analysis; liberal-internationalism; long-cycle theory; Niccolò di Bernardo Machiavelli; Karl Marx; Marxism; Marxism-Leninism; misperception; mirror image; neorealism; objectivity; obscurantism; organizational process model; paradigm; pluralism; postbehavioralism; postmodernism; power; qualitative analysis; quantitative analysis; rational decision-making; realism; realist; regime; regression analysis; Jean-Jacques Rousseau; standard operating procedure; structuralism; systems theory; taxonomy; theory; traditionalism; turbulence; units; variables.

politics. The art and science of governance, *power*, *ethics*, and *diplomacy*, as conducted through consent, force, intrigue, manipulation, and stratagem, and embracing the whole complex of public affairs within and among societies. Alternate definitions include: (1) "Who gets what, when, how" (Harold Lasswell); (2) "The authoritative allocation of values" (David Easton); and best of all, (3) "That realm where conscience and power meet, where the ethical and coercive factors of human life interpenetrate and work out tentative and uneasy compromises" (Reinhold Niebuhr).

polity. (1) A synonym for both state and a given regime. (2) Any organized political community.

Polk, James Knox (1795–1849). U.S. president, 1845–1849. He was elected as an *expansionist* who promised to facilitate admission of *Texas* to the Union as a *slave state*. Despite an atmosphere redolent with sentiments of America's *manifest destiny*, Polk settled the *Oregon Question* peacefully with Britain. Polk is most remembered for deliberately provoking the *Mexican-American War* by advancing troops to the border, among other incitements. He played upon submerged, romantic and expansionist sentiments (which later surfaced as the idea of *manifest destiny*) among the public. His private objectives were more prosaic: he wanted to obtain the deep water harbors of *California* (San Diego and San Francisco) for the United States, to use as stepping stones to its ultimate destiny as a great commercial nation plying the Pacific trade, as it already was in the Atlantic. He succeeded, through a shatteringly one-sided war which permanently scarred U.S.-Mexican relations but brought vast new territories under American sovereign control, including most of the southwest and California. However, that was a mixed blessing which soon led to a national crisis over *slavery* by raising the question of how to admit new states carved from the Mexican lands, as *slave state* or *free soil*. See also *Winfield Scott; Zachary Taylor.*

pollution. *See acid rain; Bhopal; Chernobyl; deforestation; desertification; dumping; environmental issues; global warming; greenhouse effect; nontariff barriers; ozone depletion; plutonium; oil spills.*

Pol Pot, né Saloth Sar (1926–1998). Cambodian *Communist* and *genocidal* maniac. He was a commander in the *Khmers Rouges* campaign against the *Lon Nol* regime in Cambodia through the 1960s into the 1970s. On April 17, 1975, capitalizing on the collapse of American-supported regimes in Cambodia and in neighboring South Vietnam and Laos at the end of the *Vietnam War*, his *guerrilla* troops entered the capital of Phnom Penh. Vicious murderers and savage ideologues, recruited young and trained in his image, under his orders immediately set about deurbanization and deindustrialization of the entire country and commenced the mass slaughter of the "killing fields" of the *Cambodian genocide* that ultimately killed at least half the population. This he proclaimed as the start of "Year Zero" of the new era of the Democratic Republic of Kampuchea, of which he was premier until driven from power in 1979 by the *Cambodia-Vietnam War* (1977–1991). He took refuge in Thailand, along the border, from where he continued to direct Khmers Rouges attacks and atrocities. In 1997 he gave his only interview to a Western reporter, in which he affirmed that "even now . . . am I a savage person? My conscience is clear." He was subsequently seen in a Khmers Rouges video being denounced by hundreds of erstwhile followers in a jungle *show trial*. He may have simply died (he was terminally ill), but rumors persist that he was killed by rivals in a final power struggle over the remnants of the Khmers Rouges.

Suggested Reading: Ben Kiernan, *The Pol Pot Regime* (1996).

Poltava, Battle of (July 8, 1709). June 27, 1709, in the old calendar. A Russian army led by *Peter I* deliberately avoided battle for nearly two years, instead practicing *scorched earth* all the way from the Baltic to Ukraine, pursued by an invading Swedish army under *Charles XII*. The Swedes became badly overextended while, living off the land, they were drawn toward the fatter pastures of the Ukraine. There, expected *Cossack* allies were destroyed in a great massacre of some 6,000 Cossacks and their families at Baturin in October 1708, when the Russian commander learned that hetman "treachery" was afoot. This destroyed a vast depot of supplies and reduced the Cossack force which ultimately joined Charles to some 3,000–4,000. The next summer Peter finally turned to face the Swedes near the Ukrainian city of Poltava. He brought 40,000 *regulars*, now much better trained and equipped than the troops he had led to defeat at *Narva* in 1700, along with 5,000 *irregulars* and modern *artillery*. The Swedish Army had been reduced by winter storms and summer heat, and by forced marches, disease, and *partisans*, to about 28,000 men. Charles left nearly 7,000 dead or wounded on the field, and another 2,000 *prisoners of war*. The Russians lost just under 1,400 killed and 3,300 wounded. Three weeks later the rump of the Swedish Army surrendered at Perevolochna. The loss knocked Sweden from the ranks of the *Great Powers* and confirmed Russia as its replacement. It also sent Charles and a few hundred of his royal guards scurrying by horse to seek the protection of the

Ottoman sultan in *Constantinople*. Poltava thus effectively decided the *Great Northern War* (1700–1721), even though that contest dragged on with additional battles for another dozen years. Finally, the battle permanently ended the Swedish threat to Peter's new capital at *St. Petersburg* and to Russia's northern frontier. It is notable that neither the Baltic territories which it secured, nor the bloody field itself, remained attached to Russia after 1991.

polyarchy. Useless social science *jargon* for *democracy*.

polycentrism. (1) Archaic: Allowing for national differences in the implementation of *communist* theory. (2) As *jargon:* A synonym for *multipolarity,* though not quite as excessive a bit of *obscurantism* as *bipolycentrism*. *See also Eurocommunism*.

Polynesia. The sea and islands east of *Melanesia* and *Micronesia,* extending north-south from Hawaii to Australasia. Its *indigenous peoples* are ethnically distinct.

Pompidou, Georges (1911–1974). French statesman. Prime minister, 1962–1968; president, 1969–1974. A loyal follower of *de Gaulle* (he served on his staff with the *Free French*), he negotiated an Algerian *cease-fire* in 1961. He was elevated to premier by de Gaulle in 1962 and served for several years as de Gaulle's faithful and compliant prime minister. As president and successor to the great man, however, he took the important step of reversing the old general's earlier *veto* of Great Britain's entry into the *European Community*.

pontoon bridge. A floating, makeshift military bridge, where track is laid over boats or other floats. It permits rapid crossing of riverine obstacles by an advancing force.

pooled sovereignty. The partial surrender of decision making over traditionally domestic matters to consensus procedures with other states. *See also European Union*.

Popular Front. Coalition governments of *liberals, socialists,* and *Communists* formed in France, Spain, and other West European countries in the 1930s in response to the *Great Depression* and the advent of right-wing coalitions which attended the rise of *fascism*. *See also Léon Blum; National Front; social fascism*.

popular sovereignty. (1) An *Enlightenment* political doctrine derived from *natural law* and launched into the political world with the *American Revolution* and, more importantly, the *French Revolution*. It holds that a *sovereign's* right to rule derives solely from the people and rejects the older, absolutist notion of a *divine right of kings*. It revolutionized international relations by challenging the *ancien régime* with ideas of democracy and *self-determination*. (2) In the pre–*Civil War* United States this term was used by *states' rights* advocates to deny federal jurisdiction over *slavery* issues in states applying for admission to the Union, by upholding the doctrine that the status of slavery in the territories could only be decided by settlers in those territories. It proved, at best, a temporary compromise on a fundamentally irreconcilable difference. *See also authoritarianism; autocracy; enlightened despotism; mandate of heaven; totalitarianism; Emerich de Vattel.*

population. By convention, the number of people residing in a given territory is widely considered one of the tangible components of national *power*, with the operating equation assumed to be the simple proposition that a larger population equals increased power. That notion is historically based, but not always historically accurate. It recalls the intense military competition within Europe in the nineteenth century, and particularly the experience of France, which fell behind Germany in its rate of natural increase and fretted openly as its relative military power declined as a result of fewer potential *conscripts* in each intake year. However, the impact of population on national power cannot be evaluated discretely from the ability of the country to sustain it. That is one reason, among many, why China and India introduced draconian population control programs in the latter half of the twentieth century. India soon abandoned its in favor of voluntary controls and incentives, but China's one-child policy was rigidly enforced with more than 20 million forced sterilizations from 1981 to 1982 alone. Ways could be found around such measures, of course, if one came from a privileged *cadre* or could afford the requisite fine or bribe. Nor may the impact of population be divorced from crucial intangibles such as *national morale*, the quality of one's *diplomacy*, access to *natural resources, standards of living, productivity* of the economy, and so forth.

More generally, understanding population growth and decline is one key to understanding the largest cycles (*logistic*) of war and peace and of economic prosperity or decline. The *Roman Empire* at the height of its power and vibrancy had reached from 80 million to 100 million persons, with Rome itself reaching one million (citizens and slaves). At that time, China's population was still less than 50 million. Centuries of war, pestilence, and economic decline followed in the wake of Rome's collapse, however, so that Western Europe—including Scandinavia but excluding *Byzantium*—about 1000 C.E. had barely 20 million people. Then a great surge in population occurred, so that by 1300 Western Europe had nearly 70 million people. This was mainly due, it is thought by demographers, to improvements in nourishment, an expansion of trade, and a decline in warfare as 600 years of barbarian invasions finally drew to a close. Meanwhile, by 1300, Chinese emperors ruled more than 100 million subjects. That may be instructively compared to Japan, where 300 years later only about 12 million people lived. Cities everywhere but China remained small until very recently, in historical terms. Paris and Milan were the largest in Europe, at about 200,000 by the end of the fourteenth century; but London at that time still had only 40,000 residents, and most other urban areas were little more than large towns.

The rapid growth in Christendom's population had an enormous impact on its economy and surely also contributed to the *Crusades*, which were first launched in 1095 C.E. and lasted for some 200 years in the Middle East, and even longer in eastern Europe and Iberia. In addition to the Crusades to the *Holy Land*, during the first West European "logistic" crusader expansion also took place into eastern Germany, Lithuania, and Poland, and wars of expansion and conquest were fought with the Moors of Spain and Muslim states in Sicily, North Africa, and the Balkans. During the peak of this time of renewed European confidence and military aggression, the *Black Death* arrived in Western Europe via the *Silk Road* and by ship, and the *Hundred Years' War* and other conflicts stunted population growth and sapped Europe's expansionist energies. Europe's population declined dramatically as a result during the thirteenth and fourteenth centuries. In the mid-fifteenth century, however, the larger wars ended and resistance to the plague had developed so that the population began to grow again, as did the economy in attendance. This period also witnessed the consolidation of several national states under strong kings, starting in France and England, partly because the old feudal order had collapsed with the huge loss of population to the Black Death, to be replaced by rising wages for laborers who were fewer in number and thus more greatly in demand. In the sixteenth and seventeenth centuries Europeans killed each other in large numbers over such issues as the nature of transubstantiation, the selling of indulgences, and whether priests were a necessity for the salvation of the souls of the faithful. From the eighteenth through the twentieth centuries Europe's population again grew at an explosive pace, feeding a new and larger migration—internally to the cities and overseas to the Americas, South Africa, and even to Asia. This phenomenon paralleled European *imperialism*, as the export of surplus population in part relieved economic and social pressures in metropolitan countries.

The rest of the world did not begin to achieve Europe's level of population growth until the mid-nineteenth century, just as European growth began to taper off. This overall effect resulted from declining birth rates and rising life expectancy. In 1800 world population was about 900 million; in 1900 it was 1.6 billion; in 2000, it was six billion. Everywhere, population growth led to greater urbanization and upset traditional societies, classes, and social and political orders. In the Americas, the indigenous population had been tragically suppressed—by 90 percent or more in many areas—by epidemic diseases brought by the *conquistadores* and later settlers. The *Aztec Empire*, for example, was severely undermined, and its military collapse furthered, by smallpox and measles epidemics which preceded the final Spanish (and allied Indian) assault. Subsequently, epidemics led to a complete demographic collapse of the

Indian population throughout the Americas, as nonresistant natives first encountered measles, mumps, smallpox, typhus, and the plague, among other new diseases to which they had no natural resistance at all. However, as Latin American economies began to enjoy an export boom which lasted from c. 1850 to 1929, and the start of the *world depression*, the total population of Latin America grew by 250 percent in just over 60 years (1850–1912), from c. 30 million to c. 78 million. In the twentieth century the Latin American population exploded: by 2000 it was more than 460 million.

In Africa, population was additionally depressed by many centuries of supplying the *slave trade* across the Atlantic, into Arab-Indian Ocean markets, and across the *Sahara Desert*, and by all the wars and death in Africa attendant on that trade. Then came the *Mfecane*, which depopulated much of the south, and the continent was constantly churned by internal wars which both flowed from and aggravated *famines* and other disruptions. This produced an internal labor shortage which contributed to Africa's underdevelopment well into the twentieth century. Then its population exploded: between 1970 and 1990 Africa's population rose from 275 million to more than 450 million, straining resources and infrastructure of newly independent countries, absorbing otherwise impressive economic advances, and causing a whole new set of development problems. At the close of the twentieth century, however, *AIDS* began to ravage and depress African populations. *See also food; industrialization; infant mortality rate; Thomas Robert Malthus; Malthusian; ZPG.*

Suggested Readings: Carlo Cipolla, *Economic History of World Population*, 7th ed. (1978); Sherburne Cook and Woodrow Borah, *Essays in Population History*, 3 vols. (1971–1979).

population explosion. A crude metaphor holding that uncontrolled population growth will lead to calamitous economic, social, and political effects. *See also Thomas Robert Malthus; Malthusian; population.*

Port Arthur (a.k.a. Darien, a.k.a. Ryojun). A major *warm water port* on the *Liaodong peninsula* in northern China. Russia based its far eastern fleet there after 1897; that was where the Japanese found and sank most of it in a surprise attack in 1904. Japan took possession under the *Treaty of Portsmouth* and forced China to issue a 99-year lease. The Soviets retook the port in 1945. It was returned to China in 1955.

portfolio investment. When foreign investors buy shares in national firms, or government bonds and loans, but do not take control or provide *infrastructure*. *See also foreign direct investment.*

Portsmouth, Treaty of (1905). The *peace treaty* which concluded the *Russo-Japanese War*. Russia was racked by *revolution* in 1905 and ready to make peace. Tokyo had humiliated and defeated the Imperial Navy twice, at *Port Arthur* and *Tsushima Straits*, and made some headway on land, but it was nearly bankrupted by its war effort. The Japanese therefore asked *Theodore Roosevelt* to mediate an end to the conflict. The parties gathered at Portsmouth, New Hampshire, to negotiate terms. *Manchuria* was returned to nominal Chinese control; that is, neither side won its major aim, which was to secure Manchuria. Russia agreed to acknowledge a Japanese *sphere of influence* in Korea, transfer *Port Arthur* and the *Liaodong peninsula* to Japan, as well as southern *Sakhalin Island*. No *indemnity* was paid, as Japan had demanded and its people expected, based upon the example of the *First Sino-Japanese War*. That led to anti-American "Hibiya" riots throughout Japan, which took more than 1,000 lives, because Tokyo had exaggerated the scope of its victory and concealed the extent of its financial problems. A concerted *propaganda* effort successfully transferred the blame, and with it public anger, to Roosevelt and America. This contributed to a long, and ultimately deadly, deterioration in Japanese-American relations.

Suggested Reading: Eugene Trani, *The Treaty of Portsmouth* (1969).

Portugal. Portugal has been independent since the twelfth century, though with occasional interludes of Spanish and French occupation. In the early thirteenth century it completed conquest of the Algarve. From 1383 to 1411 it fought off neighboring *Castile*. By 1400 it was united under the Avid dynasty (John I, 1385–1433). In the fifteenth and sixteenth centuries it was the leader among all maritime powers, capitalizing on its location (close to Africa and the as yet undiscovered South America) and the initiative of Prince Henry "*the Navigator*" (1394–1460). He captured *Ceuta* in 1415 and founded a school of navigation from which later explorers graduated to map the coasts of Africa, India, and South America, all in search of *gold*, *spices*, and *slaves*. These expeditions of exploration were followed by traders, missionaries, soldiers, and then settlers, as the barely one million people of Portugal—which had been ravaged by the *Black Death*—built an overseas empire on the coasts of three continents. Madeira was colonized in 1419; the Azores, from 1439. It again fought Castile, 1474–1479, with the war ending in agreement to leave the Azores and Madeira with Portugal and give the Canaries to Castile.

Portugal's king might have formed a *union of the crowns* with *Castile*, had not *Ferdinand* of Aragon won Isabella in *dynastic marriage* instead, catapulting "Spain" to world prominence after its completion of the *Reconquista* and the fall of *Granada* in 1492. The Portuguese controlled the early Atlantic *slave trade* and initially also much of the maritime *spice trade* running from Cape Verde to Mozambique, India, China, and Japan. In 1493 the pope granted Portugal a monopoly on trade in the eastern half of the globe marked by the *line of demarcation*. Hampered by a small population, Portugal did not generally penetrate or settle the interior of Africa or Asia before the late nineteenth century. Instead, it was content to control the sea lanes and ocean-borne trade and to raid for slaves or trade into continental interiors from fortified coastal settlements. In southern Africa, the Portuguese destroyed virtually every local state into which they came in contact, including *Kongo*. The Portuguese only slowly penetrated and settled Brazil, but otherwise did not sustain their full territorial claim in the *New World*. Portugal was not a major power within Europe either. It was annexed to Spain by *Philip II* in 1580. Caught up in the *Eighty Years' War*, from 1631 to 1641 Portugal lost Pernambuco, Elmina (Ghana), Luanda (Mozambique), Ceylon, and Malacca to the Dutch. Portugal rebelled in 1640, as Spain was facing defeat in the final years of the Dutch war, the *Thirty Years' War*, and its even longer war with France.

Constantly threatened by continental powers, and having lost its monopoly over the eastern trade, Portugal developed a lasting alliance with Great Britain (after 1600, itself an important maritime power). As an English ally it was invaded by the Spanish *Bourbons* in 1762, in aid of France. Lisbon was decimated by an earthquake in 1755, which led to the assumption of extraordinary powers by the city's rebuilder, the Marquis of Pombal, who governed while Joseph I (r. 1750–1777) reigned. Portugal was invaded and occupied by *Napoleon's* troops in 1807, forcing King Dom Joao VI (John VI) and his court to move to Rio de Janeiro via British warship, arriving on January 22, 1808. British troops came to Portugal's aid during the protracted *Peninsular War*, and the court was able to return to Portugal along with a British landing party under *Wellington*. The monarch, however, remained in Brazil (until 1821): an appetite for monarchy was thus established in Brazil, and a parallel taste for Brazil whetted in the monarchy. The French were finally fully driven out in 1811 and Portugal resumed both its independence and its historic alliance with Britain, yet still its king would not return. In 1815 he elevated Brazil to equal status with Portugal, as a kingdom. In 1819 a *mutiny* in the army overthrew the king's regents in Lisbon. Portugal's Cortes (parliament) in 1821 ordered the king to return. He did (March 7, 1821), but with great reluctance. The Cortes next revoked Brazil's trade privileges (attempted to reimpose a *mercantilist* regime) and otherwise treated Brazil as a colony, not an equal. When it tried to force the prince regent, Dom Pedro, to return (September 7, 1822), he replied "fico" ("I remain") and was crowned as the first emperor of Brazil the next month.

Portugal had lost Brazil in 1822, but managed to cling to its other colonial possessions in Africa and India into the late twentieth century. Domestically, its own economy remained backward and unproductive. The monarchy was overthrown by a republican revolution in 1910. Portuguese colonial forces fought in *German East Africa* during *World War I*, and Portugal joined the Allies in March 1916. In 1926 Portugal's nascent democracy was overthrown by the military. In 1932 it fell under the quasi-*fascist* dictatorship of *Salazar*. It was neutral in *World War II*. It finally gave up neutrality during the *Cold War* to become a charter member of *NATO*. In 1961 it lost *Portuguese India* to an Indian takeover. From 1964 to 1974 it faced protracted *guerrilla wars* in all its African colonies (Angola, Guinea-Bissau, and Mozambique). It allied itself with white, minority, and racist regimes in Rhodesia and South Africa, becoming a pariah among *Third World* countries and to a degree also in the West. Portugal underwent great domestic turmoil and a democratic revolution, 1974–1976, from which it finally emerged as a stable democracy and during which it shed its African colonies and *East Timor*. It retained only *Macao*, until 1999. It enjoyed increased prosperity after 1975 and joined the *European Community* in 1986. In 1999 it helped oversee an independence *referendum* in its former colony of East Timor.

Suggested Readings: C.R. Boxer, *The Portuguese Seaborne Empire* (1969); Carlo Cipolla, *Guns and Sails* (1965); Gervase Clarence-Smith, *The Third Portuguese Empire, 1825–1975* (1985); Richard Hammond, *Portugal and Africa, 1815–1910* (1966); Malyn Newitt, *Portugal in Africa: The Last Hundred Years* (1981).

Portuguese East Africa. A *colony* of Portugal, later independent as *Mozambique*.

Portuguese Guinea. A *colony* of Portugal, later independent as *Guinea-Bissau*.

Portuguese India. A composite *colony* consisting of the tiny *enclaves* of Daman, Diu, and Goa. The first foothold came at Diu, where the Portuguese bested an Arab navy in 1509. In 1510 Goa was seized by the architect of Portugal's Indian empire, the religious fanatic Viceroy Dom Affonso d'Albuquerque (1453–1515). In 1542 the *Jesuits* arrived in Goa, where they introduced the *Inquisition* in 1560. *Philip II* of Spain took control of all overseas Portuguese possessions in 1580. Portugal recovered these bases after 1650. All three territories were retaken for India by *Nehru* in 1961.

Portuguese West Africa. A *colony* of Portugal, later independent as *Angola*.

positive action links (PALs). *See positive controls.*

positive controls. Military *jargon* for *fail-safe* systems, or those which require a clear and definite "go" command which must be authenticated as coming from appropriate civilian authorities before *nuclear weapons*, or other *weapons of mass destruction,* may be launched.

positive law. Law which is written down, or otherwise clearly established or recognized by governments, usually in *treaty* form. *See also customary law; natural law.*

positive sum game. *See game theory.*

positivism. In *international law*, positivism is an approach to determining the validity of laws which insists that legal *rules* exist and are binding only if states have given their explicit *consent* to them and that new rules cannot be made by reasoning alone or be said to lodge in the supposed eternal verities of *natural law*. In *history*, positivism was a nineteenth century empirical theory holding that history was a true science in which there should exist a complete separation of subject and object and that the job of historians was to ascertain and assemble all relevant facts before drawing any conclusions from them. Most modern historians reject this view as vulgarly empiricist, as neglecting the inescapable role of historians in selecting which facts are historically relevant facts, and as falsely denying the reality that interpretation therefore enters into every so-called fact of history.

In philosophy, positivism is a general theory about knowledge which rejects all intuition as mere metaphysics and is unconcerned with, or at least distrustful of, eschatology (final ends), the origins of things, and (whether Platonic or Hegelian) philosophical speculation about ideal forms. It holds instead that the only reliable, or even possible, knowledge is based on *empirical* study of phenomena which exist positively ("objectively"); that is, which have a reality distinct from the prejudice, influence, or preference of any particular scholarly observer. A more recent and widely influential variant draws heavily on the work of Auguste Comte (1798–1857), who argued that all human understanding historically progressed by three distinct stages: theological, typified by mysticism and irrationality; metaphysical, marked by reasoning but not empirical testing; and "positivist," in which all knowledge worthy of the term had to be scientific, or knowledge that was empirically testable and verifiable. Comte added that entire societies might be characterized by these labels, corresponding to modes of historical development they had or had not achieved.

In Latin American development positivism was a nineteenth-century theory of social development, with one toe in the racist waters of *social Darwinism*, which held that, since European countries were then much more advanced than any others, importing European people would necessarily promote Latin social and economic progress, as well as relieve a growing shortage of skilled laborers and unskilled urban workers. It also promoted what later came to be called "social engineering," or large-scale efforts by government to provide incentives (and disincentives) in law and tax policies to steer people's behavior in what the government deemed to be desirable directions. In contemporary social sciences, positivism is a rapid descent from positivist philosophical epistemology, and always welcome calls for greater *objectivity*, into a crude empiricism that is mostly ignorant of, and indifferent to, the insights of history, humanism, and the grand traditions of political thought. It stresses *quantification* and promises predictability and "policy relevance." It too often delivers arid and often irrelevant treatises on the obvious, the banal, and the trivial, as in *rational choice theory*. *See also behavioralism; classical school; Thomas Hobbes; Hugo Grotius; Immanuel Kant; Jean-Jacques Rousseau.*

postbehavioralism. (1) A general trend in the social sciences away from strict *behavioralism* as an approach to the study of world affairs, toward a mix of methodologies and theoretical *paradigms*. Postbehavioralism has shifted contemporary research from an often fruitless and contentious debate over methodology back to a concern with substantive matters. In the process, it has carried along a number of *quantitative* techniques and uses these alongside more traditional, or *qualitative*, approaches, though this eclecticism should not be mistaken for synthesis. (2) An effort within the academy to hive off *international relations* as a distinct field of study, drawing upon *economics*, *history*, *political science*, and other disciplines, but separate from them in its central questions and interests. (3) A rather pretentious term for otherwise welcome calls for philosophical, historical, and policy relevance and the use of less arcane methods and language in political science and other academic research about world affairs.

post-boost vehicle (PBV). *See bus.*

post-dependency theory. *See dependency theory; postimperialism.*

post hoc ergo propter hoc. "After this, therefore because of it." A famous logical fallacy in which the mere fact that one event precedes another leads to the assumption that the first caused the second. For example, it is true enough that arms manufacturers tend to profit from an *arms race* preceding, and increased *military spending* during, a war. Yet, it does not necessarily follow that the *"merchants of death"* had a hand in bringing about the arms race or war. Similarly, because a nation acquires *territory* as part of the settlement of a war it has just won, it does not necessarily follow, though it may and certainly often in fact does, that acquisition of the territory was the main reason for going to war in the first place. In short, it may or may not be true that prior event A caused subsequent event B; but it is always wrong to assume it is true.

postimperialism. An academic theory developed after c. 1975 in response to: (1) major changes in the world economy attendant on the OPEC *oil shocks* and the rise of the *NICs*; (2) the growing unattractiveness of *dependency theory* for *Third World* elites (and for different reasons, not a few academic *radicals*); and (3) the abject failure of dependency prescriptions (such as *autarky* from world markets) in practice. Its basic premise is that *imperialism* was a historic phase which is now effectively finished. Hence, it suggests, theories which depict the Third World as locked into perpetually exploitative relations by *neocolonial* structures generated by modern *capitalism* are at odds with reality. The continuing expansion of capitalism is not to be seen as necessarily imperialistic. Instead, MNCs, *foreign direct investment*, and other features of

North-South economic relations are viewed in a much more positive light than that cast by dependency theorists. Capitalism is portrayed as potentially unifying Third World national economies and reorganizing them to participate in the world economy according to the mutually beneficial dictates of *comparative advantage*. It is also already acting as the main source of *technology transfer* and *capital*, and the capitalist nations are the main markets for Southern exports. Many *developing countries*, especially the NICs, are described as run by elites which appreciate the mutuality and positive *interdependence* of North-South connections. This stands in stark contrast to the dependency-Marxist view of such elites as *comprador classes*. Note: Some "postimperialist" writers represent the above, fairly traditional and *liberal* view of capitalism as relatively benign. Others remain quite radical, employing this thesis not to point out that dependency theory has overplayed its negative portrayal of the effects of capitalism so much as to note development of a global capitalist class, which they view as ultimately harmful to human welfare and against which they direct political and analytical fire.

postlaunch survivability. The ability of an aircraft or *missile* to survive enemy defenses and complete its mission of attack. *See also prelaunch survivability.*

post liminium. Returning an *occupied territory* to its previous legal status.

postmodernism. Originally, a late-1960s French philosophical school, of which the most widely quoted (though largely indecipherable) authors were Michel Foucault and Jacques Derrida. It later became a broad cultural and artistic—especially architectural—movement. The ideas of these latter-day, or rather would-be, philosophes became intellectually fashionable (chic) in the Anglo-American academy during the 1980s—not entirely coincidentally with the decline of leftist political fortunes in Britain and the United States in that decade and a concomitant felt need to turn against what was seen as a declining *liberalism*. Essentially (is essence possible or desirable? who constructed it? does it exist), postmodernists reject the assumption that material progress through *modernization* is a positive good. Like *critical theorists*, with whom they share an incestuous sociological and academic ancestry, they also reject the formal rationalism of the *Enlightenment* and the scholarly ideal of explaining objective reality, in favor of *relativism*. However, their pretense of normative neutrality in fact masks a remarkable dogmatism most akin to the spirit of the *Marxist* and other radical ideals many once cleaved to, but which they later abandoned and denounced as misguided because they are also rooted in Western rationalism and the false idea that progress was possible. Postmodernists thus seek to "deconstruct" the "metanarratives" (*grand theories*) of international relations to remove the "bias" ("class, gender, race" are the usual suspects) of the theorists who "constructed" it in the first place, especially bias in favor of the state in the case of *realism* and of *neorealism*.

Insofar as postmodernists seek to puncture balloons of arrogant proclamation and *scientistic* pretension floated by other "international relations theorists," or expose spurious claims to universality—as opposed to real *cosmopolitan* values—which serve as cover for parochial or other material or sectoral interests, they might conduct a welcome and potentially useful exercise. Sadly, that is not the case. The central premise of postmodernism is ineluctably self-contradictory: it cannot produce a better or more accurate approach to the field of international relations, or any other field of scholarly inquiry, since if its claim is true that *all* knowledge is fatally tainted by considerations of power then *no* "truth" about international relations (or anything else) is truly knowable, not even to postmodernists. As a result, what is substituted for the putative bias of more traditional researchers, who are at least striving for *objectivity*, is the unexamined bias of the postmodernist poseur and casual (and casuistic) deconstructionist who denies objectivity is even possible and therefore feels free to substitute for it whatever peculiar preference they may have—usually, a sneeringly elitist disposition against market democracies and "bourgeois values." That may play well at Princeton, but not in Peoria. And in the case of postmodernism, Peoria is surely more right.

In practice, many purported deconstruction exercises become merely nihilistic, even fetishistic, and the vaunted moral purpose proclaimed ad nauseam by adherents is lost—insofar as it ever really existed—in the cacophony and babel produced. With some, however, there is more than a whiff of *fascism* detectible in the dehumanizing contempt with which any and all opposition is received, the sheer violence of the language of denunciation employed, and the cultlike behavior exhibited by devotees at symposia, which usually reduce to soliloquies on solipsism. Postmodernism's tyrannical impulse would be more dangerous for its utter inability to recognize itself as such, except that it is fortunately confined to the trivial stakes of academic politics. It thus remains dangerous solely to junior colleagues and better graduate students who do not share its spoiled temperament and cultivated cynicism—or its faux sophistication and concern with clever conversations about nothing—and who thus live uncertain because untenured lives in constant threat of being *purged*. In sum, by the early twenty-first century postmodernism had been exposed as just one more self-indulgent, jargon-laden academic fad and sterile moral pose, with little to nothing of value to say about the real world of issues of power, justice, and politics among peoples and nations. It was *Stalinist* in temperament, relativist by conviction, and nihilist in its outcome.

Suggested Reading: Marshall Berman, *All That Is Solid Melts Into Air: The Experience of Modernity* (1988).

post-traumatic stress disorder. A psychoneurosis, or other severe psychological reaction, sometimes mistaken for moral or personal cowardice but in fact resulting from prolonged exposure to combat, including a natural fear of death and the horrors of violent dismemberment of one's friends, comrades, or other fellow human beings. Formerly called *shell shock* or *battle fatigue*, it is now recognized that virtually anyone, if exposed to fire and danger long enough, may crack psychologically. In response, modern armies routinely rotate soldiers out of combat zones and now also provide counseling and treatment.

postwar. (1) A cultural marker for an extended period following a great or *world war*, where politics and/or social life are broadly and notably changed from the antebellum period. (2) The period immediately following any war, usually characterized by political uncertainty, even instability, in at least the losing country and often on both sides. This is caused by a lack of clarity about what the outcome of the war actually is. As far more wars end in relative shifts in the *balance of power* than in total *victory* for one side (e.g., *World War I*), it takes time to figure out just what the degree of shift is. And those few wars which do end in absolute victory (e.g., *World War II*) also cause uncertainty, by rendering unclear the relative gains and losses of each member of the winning coalition and their new relationship toward one another. Furthermore, for some years there may be no one in the losing state(s) sufficiently acceptable to the winners with whom to make the inevitable and necessary *rapprochement*. *See also* diktat.

Potemkin, Grigori Alexandrovich (1739–1791). Russian field marshal and statesman. Potemkin came to the notice of *Catherine II* (1729–1796; r. 1762–1796), as a handsome, young (he was ten years younger than she), one-eyed officer in the Horse Guards. He played a role in the *palace coup* which involved the murder of her husband, Tsar Peter III, and consolidated her hold on the throne. He performed well in the *First Russo-Turkish War* (1768–1774) with the *Ottoman Empire*, and he probably first found his way into Catherine's bed in 1774. He continued in sexual service to Catherine and public service to the state for twenty years and, as a result of both endeavors, was promoted commander of the army and governor of Ukraine, among many other titles. As Catherine's trusted adviser, he exerted influence over most Russian affairs and was in effect tsar in all but name. His special charge was the southern lands which he and Catherine had taken from the Turks. He reformed the armed forces and personally participated in several more southern wars. He was in nominal command over *Suvorov*. For Russia and for himself, he conquered the *Crimea* and much of the Black Sea region, founded the great port city of *Sebastopol*, and began the building of the *Black Sea Fleet*, 1784–1787. From 1788 to 1790 he led a Russian army against the Turks in *Moldavia*. Potemkin was vain and endlessly ambitious. His relationship of "amitie amoureuse" with Catherine gave full rein to both vices, and to others (with her doting permission, he also bedded five of his own nieces). The famous story of his erecting false towns ("Potemkin villages") to deceive Catherine, Emperor Joseph II of Austria, and King Poniatowski of Poland, who together toured the south lands in early 1787, as to the condition of the peasants is partly apocryphal. However, it also usefully illustrates both Catherine's distance from the Russian people and Potemkin's political sagacity and talent for self-promotion. Potemkin and Catherine also conspired together on the "*Greek Project*," a fanciful foreign policy ambition to conquer the Ottoman Empire and re-establish a great Christian empire with its capital at *Constantinople*. It came to naught with Potemkin's death, despite Catherine's grooming of her grandson to sit on the "Greek throne."

Suggested Reading: Simon Sebag Montifiore, *Prince of Princes* (2000).

Potsdam, Conference of (July 17–August 2, 1945). The final wartime conference of the *Big Three* in *World War II*, held just outside the ruins of Berlin. While *Josef Stalin* was an old hand at wartime *diplomacy*, it was *Harry Truman*'s first conference. Upon losing a general election, *Winston Churchill* found himself replaced halfway through by *Clement Atlee*. One day before the meetings began the first *atomic bomb* was detonated in the New Mexico desert. When Truman informed Stalin of this (on July 25th) he was perplexed that the great dictator was not surprised—it was learned later that Stalin knew of the secret *Manhattan Project*, if not of the actual test, through Soviet *agents* who had penetrated it. Truman and Churchill agreed that the news about the bomb meant the vast reserves of Russian troops would no longer be needed to defeat Japan; but Russia would enter the eastern war anyway, an agreement confirmed at *Yalta*. It was decided to *disarm* and *demilitarize* Germany, as well as *purge* it of Nazis and set up *war crimes* tribunals, but to treat it as a single economic and political unit. There was a deep and continuing quarrel over the degree of *reparations* to be exacted from Germany and related arguments over final interpretation and the carrying out of the Yalta agreements on Eastern Europe. A particular problem was the *Oder-Neisse Line*, which the Western allies refused to recognize as other than temporary.

The discussion of all these issues assumed that a set of *peace treaties* would follow in due course; they did for the smaller *Axis* powers, but never for Germany and separately for Japan. Also rejected by the Western powers were Stalin's demands for control of the *Dardanelles* and of the Italian *colony* of *Tripoli* (Libya). In Asia, the United States was to receive the Japanese *surrender* in Korea south of the 38th parallel, in the Pacific Islands, the Philippines, and Japan itself. The Soviets were to take control of the *Kurils* and *Sakhalin*, Korea north of the 38th parallel, and *Manchuria*. The Chinese were to accept surrender of all Japanese forces in China, and in Indochina to the 16th parallel. The British were to receive all surrenders in Southeast Asia. Finally, it was agreed to issue the *Potsdam Declaration* on the war against Japan. Potsdam was conducted in an air of deepening acrimony and revealed many of the *Cold War* divisions to come. *See also Klaus Fuchs; Japanese Peace Treaty; Paris Treaties (1947); Ethel and Julius Rosenberg.*

Suggested Readings: Herbert Feis, *Between War and Peace* (1960); James Gormley, *From Potsdam to the Cold War* (1990); Martin Sherwin, *A World Destroyed* (1987).

Potsdam Declaration (July 26, 1945). *Stalin* did not join in this declaration (the *Soviet Union* was not yet at *war* with Japan) issued at the *Potsdam Conference*, but it was endorsed by *Harry Truman*, *Clement Atlee*, and *Chiang Kaishek*. It promised that the *Allies* would occupy and disarm Japan, called for *occupation* policies to purge it of *militarism*, and proposed to limit its defense forces to the *home islands*. The declaration's central demand was for Japan's *unconditional surrender*, barring which it could expect "prompt and utter destruction." The threat was, of course, to use the *atomic bomb*, successfully tested just 10 days prior. However, the Japanese could not, and did not, know that.

poverty. In crude economic terms, poverty is a condition in which personal or national income falls below the level needed to provide food and shelter. In historical and political reality, the perception of poverty beyond mere subsistence is a much more subjective and relative concept varying within each society and by place and era. Why? Because it also reflects wants and desires compared with the relatively privileged status of others in that society, and not just one's physical needs. Thus to be poor in Germany or Japan is quite a different matter from being poor in Bangladesh or Mali. Most poor living in twenty-first-century developed nations thus enjoy significant welfare benefits and access to health care, food, and other material goods, and even comforts, which few other than the wealthiest enjoyed in earlier centuries. *See also capitalism; development; famine; industrialization; population.*

power. A relationship of economic, military, ideological, technological, or other superiority (inequality), which gives one state (or other political actor) an ability to sway the policy or de facto behavior of other states and thereby to produce the range of foreign policy outcomes it desires. Relationships of interstate inequality are usually based upon possession by one state of greater *capabilities* relative to other states. These vary greatly in utility, however, from issue to issue. An alternative definition, from the great twentieth-century political scientist Hans J. Morgenthau: "Whatever creates, and helps one maintain, control over the minds and actions of men and women." In Morgenthau's schema, the sources of national power were split into "tangible" and "intangible" components, thus: {A} Tangible sources of national power: *food supply*; economic strength (*competitiveness, productivity*, wealth, *industrialization*); geography (*size, location, climate, topography*); military capability; *natural resources; population;* and *technology;* {B} Intangible sources of national power: generalship; *ideology; national morale; prestige;* and the quality of one's *diplomacy.*

To simply divide power into ostensible components, as if the sum of power equaled the whole of its measurable parts, overestimates its material basis and misses the point that sheer material power does not determine the course of diplomacy or success in war. As Morgenthau pointed out, skill, vision, ignorance, cunning and duplicity, arrogance and vanity, and other human qualities, as well as dumb luck, play as large (or an even larger) role—this is what he meant by maintaining that the quality of diplomacy is the decisive factor in the conduct of international politics. Moreover, there is no single recipe for power; its ingredients will mix in ways both unforeseen and unforeseeable by statesmen, intelligence officers, or academics. Why? Because any component of power, or any given admixture of its components, must result in different outcomes under varying circumstance of time and place.

Power is thus best understood as a relationship, as mostly indirect and limited influence over people, decisions, and events, and as arising from a complex host of sources. It is always relative to the power of others and always contextual (historical), dependent on specific time and place. And it is forever transitory: power cannot be hoarded. If unused, it dissipates; if overused, it dilutes. Finally, it must be recalled that all *politics* involves relations of power and competing values because all political actors, even the weakest, have at least some degree of power (influence) in relation to others—once again, varying greatly with time and circumstance—and seek to use this to implement whatever values they hold. Hence, all politics concerns both power relations and ethical considerations, and that means all international politics involves diplomacy (negotiation) at its core, at all times. *See also Lord Acton; coercion; influence; leverage; propaganda; soft power.*
Suggested Reading: Hans J. Morgenthau, *Politics Among Nations*, 5th ed. (1978).

power politics. The approach to international relations analysis or to *statecraft* which sees *states* as ends in themselves, grades them according to their *capabilities*, and stresses the use of whatever means are necessary and at hand to the dedicated pursuit of the *national interest*. It is especially identified with the threat or use of force. *See also* Idealpolitik; *Niccolò di Bernardo Machiavelli;* Machtpolitik; raison d'etat; *realism;* Realpolitik.
Suggested Reading: Martin Wight, *Power Politics* (1979).

power sharing. A constitutional division of powers which modifies strict democratic representation with a preserved bloc of seats for a given group. During *decolonization* it was tried in *Rhodesia and Nyasaland* to ease white acceptance of *majority rule.* It was proposed by some for South Africa, but not adopted until the end of *apartheid.*

power transition theory. In international relations *theory,* the idea that wars are more likely as one state passes another in relative *power.* The trigger is casually assumed to be this or that crisis, treated by the theorist as unimportant in itself, but the fundamental *cause* is assumed to be refusal of the "declining" state to accept a loss of power and *prestige* to the "rising" state and its fear that passivity while still in a superior position may cause it to be overcome by the rising rival at a later date. *See also anarchy; hegemonic stability theory.*

Praetorian Guard. (1) An elite military corps with distinct interests of its own, which were almost never coequal with the interests of ancient Rome. Tiberius Claudius Germanicus (10–54, r. 41–54 C.E.), who reigned as Claudius I, was located by the Praetorian Guard hiding behind a curtain during the assassination of Caligula (12–41, r. 37–41 C.E.), cowering in fear of also being put to the sword as a descendant of Augustus. Instead, Claudius was proclaimed emperor by the army. The Praetorian Guard was not elevated to principal power for another hundred years, during the reign of Lucius Aurelius Commodus (161–192, r. 180–192 C.E.). This is generally identified as the point at which the Western *Roman Empire* entered its prolonged and final decline into military despotism, civil war, and failure to resist barbarian invasion. (2) The term subsequently was used to identify any similarly elite military force which protected a despot or wielded despotic power of its own, up to and including deposition of one tyrant in favor of another. *See also Janissaries; KGB; Republican Guard; SS.*

Pragmatic Sanction (1717). *See Maria Theresa; War of the Austrian Succession; War of the Polish Succession.*

Prague Spring (1968). An unofficial term for the 1968 liberalization movement in Czechoslovakia under *Alexander Dubček*. It was crushed by an *invasion* by the *Warsaw Pact*. The reforms presaged the cultural, press, and individual liberties which *Gorbachev* would introduce in the Soviet Union itself 20 years later—when they proved precisely as mortally threatening to the *communist* system as *Brezhnev* feared in 1968.
  Suggested Reading: H. Gordon Skilling, *Czechoslovakia's Interrupted Revolution* (1976).

Pravda. "Truth." This infamous newspaper was the mouthpiece of the *Communist Party* of the Soviet Union for seven decades, without ever living up to the claim of its masthead. *Boris Yeltsin* banned it in October 1993, after a failed, hardline *communist* uprising led to street fighting in Moscow. *See also* Izvestia.

preamble. The prologue to a *treaty* or *final act*, usually dwelling on matters of general principle.

precedent, in international law. *See persuasive precedent; self-defense;* stare decisis.

preemptive strike. A surprise attack on the enemy, provoked by the belief that one is about to be attacked or to remove a basic threat, as in Israel's attack on Arab airfields at the beginning of the *Third Arab-Israeli War* (1967) or its attack on the Iraqi "Tammuz 1" (Osiraq) *nuclear reactor* near Baghdad on June 7, 1981. It may also be aggressive, designed to achieve *strategic* superiority with a single blow, as in the Japanese attack on *Pearl Harbor*. *See also first-strike; preventive war.*

preferential tariff (preferential trade). Granting special *terms of trade* to certain trading partners by means of lower *tariffs* on their *imports* than apply to others. *See also customs union; free trade area; GATT; GSP; imperial tariff; Lomé Conventions; most-favored nation; PTA; reciprocity; STABEX.*

Preferential Trade Area for East and Southern African States (PTA). It was established in 1981, partly in response to the *independence* of Zimbabwe, by the *frontline states* and other regional countries. It sought lower *tariffs* within the region, with a long-term view to cooperative regional *development.*

prelaunch survivability. The ability of a weapon to survive a direct attack and still launch. *See also postlaunch survivability.*

preliminary objection. The first notice by a *state* of objection to a legal proceeding, on grounds (procedure or *jurisdiction*) unrelated to the merits of the case.

preponderant power. A *state* which is markedly superior in economic or military power and hence dominates all such arrangements in its region as a result of its sheer presence and expansive interests. It may also do this deliberately, in which case *imperialism* flows from its preponderance. Note that preponderance, even dominance, and imperialism may not be the same thing: the former may be unintentional or unavoidable; the latter is neither. Examples of preponderance, imperial or not: Japan in East Asia, 1895–1945; Germany in Central Europe, 1870–1943, 1989– ; India in Southwest Asia, 1965– ; Russia in the Caucasus since c. 1780; the United States in the Western hemisphere since c. 1885, and globally since c. 1917. *See also primacy; primus inter pares.*

prescription. Uninterrupted *occupation* of a *territory* which formerly belonged to another *state*, leading to a *recognized* legal claim after the passage of time. It assumes the previous state is *extinct* or acquiesces in the occupation. The necessary period for prescription to take hold remains highly moot.

Presidium. *See Politburo.*

press-gang. *See impressment.*

Prester John, legend of. *See Crusades; Age of Exploration.*

prestige. Where a nation ranks in the pecking order among states. Seeking acknowledgment and/or enhancement of one's prestige is common to most diplomatic endeavors, even if seldom the prime goal of any given initiative. Yet, prestige is nonetheless best understood as an aspect, rather than a mere representation of *power*. It may be sought for domestic purposes—to provide an inflated sense of national importance among the general public which is *fungible* into support for certain foreign policies or for a given regime, dynasty, dictator, or political party. The concern of Chinese emperors, and later communist dictators, to preserve the *mandate of heaven* was an example of this latter function, in support of primary domestic interests. Or foreign acknowledgment of a state's power ranking may be sought because it is convertible into acceptance of one's own foreign policy preferences or to reinforce *deterrence*. Prestige thus both reflects and influences the power evaluations made about one state by all other states, and this has a real impact on foreign policy behavior. States are therefore about as jealous of their prestige (and as sensitive to slights against it) as, for instance, street gang leaders, junior cabinet ministers, or many recently tenured associate professors. *See also Ethiopian-Eritrean War; face;* force de frappe; *imperialism;* kowtow; *May Day; middle power; Olympic Games; Partial Test Ban Treaty; power transition theory; preponderance; primacy;* primus inter pares; *protocol; scramble for Africa; soft power; space race;* SPUTNIK; Weltpolitik.

Pretorius, Andries (1799–1853). *See Great Trek; Natal; South Africa.*

preventive diplomacy. Closely associated with *Dag Hammarskjöld*, it was originally the idea of *diplomatic intervention* in conflicts concerning areas not of direct concern to the major protagonists in the *Cold War*. It was designed to try to exclude the *superpowers* from carrying their competition into new areas and regions. Since the end of the Cold War, it has shaded somewhat into the idea of *peacemaking*. It still means a primary emphasis on *advisory services, mediation, good offices,* and so forth, rather than *multilateral* military action. *See also OSCE peacekeeping; United Nations.*

preventive war. A near synonym for a *preemptive strike*, but implying a much more extensive use of *force*, for example, Israel's destruction of Arab air forces and subsequent land attacks during the *Third Arab-Israeli War*, in contrast, with its sharp but more limited attacks on *PLO* or *Hezbollah* bases in Lebanon. *See also first strike.*

price controls. Regulatory *intervention* in the marketplace to freeze prices, usually at artificially low levels. They are often used concerning *food* staples, especially bread, as a means of dampening political unrest by maintaining a minimum "social bargain" with the poorest members of society. *See also black market; free market; stabilization program.*

price elasticity. The rate at which, and the range within which, demand for *goods* or *services* changes in response to price. *See also elasticity of demand.*

price revolution (of the seventeenth century). A spectacular and prolonged inflation which beset all economies in Europe after the discovery of the *New World* and all through the great *Wars of Religion* from c. 1500–1660. Its causes and effects remain subject to intense academic debate. Certainly two causes are uncontroversial: the influx of *gold* and silver from the Spanish colonies of the *New World* vastly increased Europe's supply of monetary metals, while decades of war and deficit financing encouraged debasement of currencies. In general, the seventeenth century witnessed a steady rise in commodity prices, a situation aggravated by a rising population *logistic* and a decrease in real wages. The price revolution helped undermine the political and social position of landed aristocracies and further impoverished peasants, whose lot was declining with rising population and agricultural changes anyway. It benefited rising merchant classes and centralizing monarchs. It destabilized industries and entire economies; aggravated social, religious, and international conflicts; turned the expanding city populations into deep pools of immiseration and thus potential revolution; and in significant measure underlay the larger political, social, and religious crisis of the seventeenth century that wracked European civilization.

price supports. When a government *intervenes* in the marketplace to inflate the price of a *commodity* as an aid to domestic producers.

primacy. The condition of being first in *power* and *prestige*. Sometimes inaccurately used to mean *hegemony*. *See also preponderant power;* primus inter pares.

primary producer. (1) A state whose economy is heavily dependent on the *export* of *primary products* rather than manufactured *goods*. Such states must often reimport at much higher prices manufactured or processed goods made from their own lower-priced primary exports. This exploitative relationship was a mainstay of colonial economics. For instance, *Gandhi* opened many eyes about the underlying economic nature of the *Rāj* with a *boycott* of British cloth made from Indian cotton, then re-exported to India. This is not always the case, however. Canada is a leading example of a primary producer nation which enormously benefits from its place in the world economy. (2) In *dependency theory*, primary producer nations invariably are portrayed as exploited by the structure of the *world capitalist system*, whether they are or not, and as incapable of benefiting from reform of that system, which several *NICs* have done in fact.

primary products. Unprocessed or minimally processed *goods* drawn directly from nature; for example, *oil* which is sold or exported unrefined; or selling or exporting logs, rather than paper; or selling or exporting raw fruit, rather than tinned fruit.

primary sector. A conventional category of description of economic activity, referring to all *production* which draws products directly from natural sources, including *agriculture, fishing,* forestry, and mining. For most of human existence, the vast majority of people labored in the primary sector. This remains true in *underdeveloped* economies, but is no longer the case in more advanced economies. *See also primary producer; primary products; secondary sector; structure; tertiary sector.*

Primo de Rivera, Miguel (1870–1930). Spanish general; dictator, 1923–1930. His command in the Philippines was defeated by U.S. forces during the *Spanish-American War.* He was brought to power by the humiliating defeat of Spanish arms at Anual during the *Rif Rebellion* (1921–1926) and the constitutional crisis which followed. He took power in a *coup* in 1923, after which he tried to establish a *fascist* regime on the Italian model. His efforts inspired formation of the *Falange,* founded by his son, José. He suppressed the Rif in 1926, with aid from France.

primus inter pares. "First among equals." (1) The greatest among the *Great Powers*; the one enjoying the most *power* and status, such as the United States in power since 1917, and power and *prestige* since 1945; or Britain, France, and Spain in earlier eras; or China in a different region and era. (2) The leading state in a region or on an issue, in any identifiable group of states. *See also preponderant power.*

Princely States. Some 700 traditional statelets of greatly varying size scattered over the subcontinent. They were targets of *Mogul* and then British expansionist ambitions. After their individual conquest or intimidation, they were controlled by the *East India Company,* and later the British *Rāj,* by treaties securing limited *autonomy.* After the *Indian Mutiny* they came to be seen as conservative bulwarks against more radical forces for change in India's relations with Britain. British negotiators also used them to cynically deflect claims that the *Congress Party* represented a single Indian nation. They were divided among, and dissolved into, India and Pakistan in 1947; most joined India, as few were located inside Pakistan. A small state with a Hindu majority population and a Muslim *nawab,* Junagadh, acceded to Pakistan but was isolated and subverted by India. Two much larger princely states caused special problems: *Hyderabad* and *Kashmir*. *See also James Dalhousie; Punjab.*

Prince Rupert's Land. *See Hudson's Bay Company.*

principality. A state governed by a prince, duke, or some lesser nobility, but not a king; for example, *Monaco.*

Principal Organs (of the United Nations). There are six: (1) the *Security Council*; (2) the *General Assembly*; (3) ECOSOC; (4) the *Trusteeship Council*; (5) the *Secretariat*; and (6) the *International Court of Justice.*

principal power. (1) A synonym for *Great Power.* (2) In some academic—and even then, highly idiosyncratic—usage, states said to be "principal" in importance to some other country(ies), without themselves being Great Powers, as in the relationship of Australia and New Zealand to some of the South Pacific *microstates.*

principal state. One which accepts to exercise delegated authority over foreign policy and security, granted by an *associated state,* such as the United States in its capacity toward the *Marshall Islands* or New Zealand vis-à-vis the *Cook Islands.*

Pripet Marshes. A vast area of natural wetland southwest of Moscow, and sometimes within Poland's frontiers, forming the only natural barrier between Germany and Russia. Their location determined that historically there were three distinct invasion routes into Russia: along the Baltic coast to *St. Petersburg*; north of the Pripet Marshes to Moscow; and south of the Marshes into Ukraine and the Crimea. *Napoleon I* took the Moscow route in 1812, in both directions. The *Brusilov Offensive* of the Tsarist Army broke down at Pripet in 1916. *Hitler* sent troops along all three routes during *Barbarossa* in 1941. During *World War II* scattered remnants of broken *Red Army* divisions fled into the Pripet Marshes and set up *partisan* units there. The Germans sent in sweep operations to kill everything alive, military or civilian. The *resistance* in the Pripet Marshes was a main theme of Soviet wartime propaganda, but was militarily far less significant than usually reported.

prisoner of conscience. An *Amnesty International* (AI) designation for political *dissidents*; it carries the proviso that they must not have advocated or used violence to advance their cause. This definition troubles those who might view this or that *war* for *self-determination,* or an *uprising* against an unjust government, as quite moral and its practitioners as deserving of defense from persecution (or even prosecution). However, the restrictive definition has the merit of allowing AI to avoid having to make such difficult, and inherently political, judgments about the causes dissidents espouse. It is widely believed that AI's resulting reputation for objectivity increases its persuasiveness, at least with some governments. *See also political prisoner.*

prisoner of war (POW). Historically, in most premodern societies captives in war were held for ransom or enslaved, a fact of warfare which continued in parts of Africa into the late nineteenth century. Elsewhere, prisoners who were not massacred but could not be cared for might be *paroled*—allowed to go free upon giving their word not to resume armed struggle. This was the case for much of the *American Civil War*, for example. After the *Crimean War*, European states began to codify the rights of prisoners of war. This led to a new legal status in which military personnel captured by the enemy have specific rights and duties under the *Geneva Conventions*, distinct from the rights and duties of *civilians*. These rights are conditional upon *belligerents* being party to the conventions, and even then are frequently ignored in the cruelty of combat and captivity. During *World War II* the Japanese severely mistreated nearly all POWs in their custody. The Germans generally respected the Geneva Conventions with regard to Western prisoners, but refused to apply it to Russian POWs. Instead, millions of Russians were worked, many to death, as *slave laborers*. In turn, the Soviet Union mistreated and retained hundreds of thousands of German POWs (and even some *Allied* prisoners liberated from the Germans) after the war. As a form of unilateral *reparations*, they were put to forced labor on *reconstruction* work. Many died; most were not allowed to return to their homes for more than 10 years, until *Stalin* died. Others married local women and settled in the Soviet Union. The issue of postwar exchanges of POWs frequently complicates *peace* negotiations, delaying resumption of *normalized relations*. Thus, disputes and recriminations over forcible return of POWs drew out the *Korean Conflict* negotiations for many months. India and Pakistan argued over POWs after each of their wars; and some Arab countries refused to return and instead executed Israeli prisoners. United States–Vietnam relations remained strained for 20 years by unresolved cases of *MIAs* and reports (mostly unsubstantiated) of sightings of American POWs. *See also biological warfare; Cossacks; EPW; mercenaries; Vietnam War.*

Suggested Readings: Geoffrey Best, *Humanity in Warfare*, 2nd ed. (1983); Geoffrey Best, *War and Law Since 1945* (1994).

prisoner's dilemma. *See game theory.*

privateer. (1) A merchant ship, armed and converted to wartime use. (2) A privately owned *warship*, hired by a state to harass, *capture*, or destroy the enemy's shipping under *letters of marque*. During *Elizabeth I's* war with *Philip II*, more than 100 English privateers preyed on Spanish shipping. Dutch and English privateers also raided Chinese junks in the seventeenth century, from the Philippines to Southeast Asia. Hundreds of privateers raided French shipping during the *War of the League of Augsburg*, and France returned the favor by supporting dozens of privateers against its enemies' ships during the *War of the Spanish Succession*. The French (and Spanish) *Bourbons* also paid back the favor during the wars of the eighteenth century by commissioning *buccaneers* to raid English seaborne commerce in the Caribbean. Privateers remained important as supplemental *commerce raiders* into the period of *Napoleonic Wars*. They were made obsolete by changes in international law which reflected the trend toward a state monopoly over war at sea and the banning of private navies and fewer safe harbors in which to hide from the *Royal Navy*, but also the sheer size and expense of nineteenth-century warships: *ironclads*, in particular. Privateering was declared illegal in the *Declaration of Paris* (1856).

Suggested Readings: James G. Lydon, *Pirates, Privateers, and Profits* (1970); Neville Williams, *The Sea Dogs: Privateers, Plunder and Piracy in the Elizabethan Age* (1975).

private international law. *See international law (private).*

private sector. All economic activity other than government purchases and expenditures.

privatization. Returning to private control the economic activities or facilities previously run by the state. During the 1980s *Margaret Thatcher* undertook extensive privatization in Britain, reversing an economic trend within the *OECD* which dated back several decades. By the 1990s privatization and other *neoliberal* policies were in vogue from Africa to China and India, in the former *Soviet bloc*, and throughout the OECD. The main arguments made in its favor were to increase overall economic *efficiency* and to reduce the destabilizing role of governments in what were seen as naturally self-regulating private markets. *See also command economy*; laissez-faire; *monetarism*; *nationalization*; *shock treatment*.

prize. Enemy *goods* or vessels seized or *captured* at sea in wartime. *See also booty*.

prize court. An ad hoc, international court established to decide conflicting claims over what is, or is not, *contraband*. Prize courts were originally established to assess the competing claims of *privateers* and merchants and to give the state a stake in any goods seized during naval warfare.

Procrustean bed. From Procrustes, a mythical Greek robber who cut off the limbs of victims to make them fit his bed; said of *theories* which try to do the same to the facts: produce conformity by arbitrary means.

product cycle theory. The idea that the motive force behind firms expanding into *multinational* activity is a threat to their existing *export* markets; they supposedly respond by building *subsidiaries* near these markets to lower prices and raise their access. *See also internalization theory.*

production. The process wherein the various *factors of production* are brought together to create *goods and services.* Production is most often measured in terms of raw output of finished units of any given product or in terms of the monetary value of those units. *See also GDP; GNP; productivity; mode of production.*

productivity. The amount of product created over a given period as related to a single component of production such as *capital* or *labor* (labor productivity). It measures economic *efficiency* and depends on the underlying quality of the *factors of production* which are brought to bear. Relative national productivity is an important measure of economic *competitiveness.* In addition to its obvious importance for peacetime economics, productivity plays a key role in waging war. For example, during *World War II* the Japanese and German economies were not just much smaller than the American economy, they were much less efficient: respectively, one-fifth and one-half the productivity per worker-hour. In some respects, they were even less efficient than the Soviet economy. This was a burden neither the Japanese nor the German military overcame. *See also human capital; law of diminishing returns.*

profit. A net positive return on an *investment* as a result of an excess of return over expenditure. This is the form compensation takes for entrepreneurs (and investors), as distinct from wages earned by workers or income from rent earned by landowners. Moral acceptance and legal protection of the idea of profit was a key change underlying the shift from a *feudal* to modern *capitalist* economies. Medieval thinkers in Europe had eschewed profit in their theories of prices, since they believed money was merely a medium of exchange of no value in itself and that prices should reflect only the cost of production of goods, including a fair wage to laborers. Profit became morally acceptable as credit systems developed to support expanding investment and commerce resulting from the discovery of the Americas and from European population growth, which provided some of the preconditions for capitalist development of Europe. Once an early banking system was in place, other economic diversification—including the shift to capitalism—proceeded over time. *See also Adam Smith.*

pro forma. "As a matter of form (alone)." When a thing is done, such as a *diplomatic protest*, without serious intent to *influence* the other party, but merely to satisfy legal ritual or mislead *public opinion.*

prohibited weapons. The effort to prohibit certain weapons from use in warfare is ancient. *Poison* (as added to a besieged city's water supply or applied to arrow tips) was banned by the ancient Greeks, but the Romans, Byzantines, and Ottomans all used it at different times. During the *Crusades*, European Christians first encountered the Muslim crossbow and recoiled from the devastation it wrought among the knights. The *Catholic Church* tried to ban the crossbow in war among Christians (while permitting its use against Muslims), but it was too effective a weapon to suppress and soon was in wide use. Similarly, when the English longbow appeared in the thirteenth century, it was banned at first; but it was far too efficient a killing system to suppress for long: it too was soon widely deployed and nearly proved decisive during the early part of the *Hundred Years' War*. After the middle of the nineteenth century there were near-constant attempts to prohibit the use of weapons which developed out of the chemical and textile (dyes) industries of the *industrial revolution*. An effort was made in the St. Petersburg Declaration (1868) to place limits on the destructiveness of weapons, but this failed to include, or prevent development of, either automatic weapons or high-explosive projectiles. Similarly, aerial bombardment (from balloons) was banned at the first *Hague Conference* in 1899, but this was soon rendered ineffective by the subsequent invention of heavier-than-air craft. After *World War I* several weapons—especially gas—first encountered on the battlefields of 1914 to 1918 were restricted, and a few were banned outright.

Such prohibition efforts met with mixed results, with the general rule applying that if a weapon had proved mostly useless (e.g., poison gas) it was banned and not used, but if it was thought useful or suspected that some other state was stockpiling it, then it was stockpiled and deployed on all sides, including by otherwise peaceful states. The logic is simple: it is just not prudent for a state to forgo possession even of a legally prohibited weapon unless there is fair (verifiable) assurance that no other state will continue to possess it. In 1981 a UN Protocol banned certain uses of *land mines*, updated by a separate *Land Mine Treaty* in 1997, and booby traps. One class of weapons for which there is not even a minimalist normative convention in *international law* limiting use, and no general convention outlawing production or stockpiling, remains *nuclear weapons*. That is true despite efforts to contain *proliferation* through the *IAEA* and the *Nuclear Non-Proliferation Treaty*. For the nature and legal state of other weapons types, *see also biological weapons; Biological Warfare Treaty; chemical and biological warfare; chemical weapons; Chemical Weapons Convention; gas weapons; Geneva Protocol; incendiary; just war tradition; mustard gas; nerve weapons.*

Suggested Reading: Jozef Goldblat, *Arms Control: A Guide to Negotiations and Agreements* (1994).

proletarian revolution. In *Marxism*, a *revolution* to overthrow the *mode of production* of *capitalism* and replace it with a *socialist* mode, by the ultimate winner of history, the *proletariat* or working class.

proletariat. (1) Members of the industrial working class, or persons who labor in exchange for wages. (2) In *Marxism*, the class of wage laborers produced and exploited by *capitalism*, which is destined by the "iron laws of history" to be expanded by capitalism's repression of all other classes until just two remain: the workers and their exploiters. At this point, classical Marxists expected a spontaneous revolution in which the proletariat arose to violently overthrow the capitalist *mode of production* (carry out a *revolution*), institute a socialist mode, and thereby transform society into the *communist* nirvana. *See also vanguard.*

proliferation. The spread of military technology concerning advanced weapons systems, particularly *weapons of mass destruction*, to additional countries. (1) Horizontal: Acquisition of weapons systems by additional *states* or *terrorists*. (2) Vertical: Quantitative increases in available weapons by extant military powers. *See also arms control; BMD; diffusion; IAEA; MIRV; near-nuclear states; nonproliferation; Nuclear Non-Proliferation Treaty; revolution in military affairs.*

propaganda. The deliberate spread of ideas, images, and information which may (but need not) be untrue, to advance one's cause and undermine the interests of opponents. The term derives from the sixteenth-century Catholic committee "Congregatio de Propaganda Fidei" (Congregation for the Propagation of the Faith). It was established by Pope Gregory XV (1554–1623) to supervise foreign missions and proselytize among native populations. Propaganda is an ever-present element of international relations. All *states* (and not a few *international organizations*, MNCs and even NGOs) engage in propaganda to some degree. Governments will always put the best possible light on their own actions and policies and frequently will also use heavy-handed, even coarse, distortion of the views and actions of enemies to advance their own interests. Propaganda is a potentially highly effective means of *influence*, given the right message and audience, and that can mean virtually anything and anyone. It is thus generally viewed by states as an integral component of *power*, though they almost always call such public persuasion campaigns something else. *See also atrocity; biological warfare; disinformation; doublethink; Josef Goebbels; Greenpeace; national morale; NWICO; Pravda; psychological warfare; public opinion; Radio Free Europe; soft power; UNESCO.*

propinquity. Geographical proximity, or nearness. Some *states* have used this as justification for claiming special rights in a neighboring *territory*: Japan regarding China in the *Lansing-Ishii Agreement*; the United States in the *Monroe Doctrine*; post-Soviet Russia in its stance toward the *near abroad*. Declared or not, it is an underlying assumption behind almost all claims to a *sphere of influence. See also regionalism.*

proportionality. In *international law* and in the *just war tradition*, a *rule* by which a *state's* right to use *force* in *self-defense* or *retaliation* is limited by a requirement that the compulsion used correspond to the danger still posed or the harm already done. Under the *jus in bello* this controls the type of weapon permitted, while under the *jus ad bellum* it is the total good and evil expected to flow from a contemplated action. *See also carpet bombing; Charles Maurice de Talleyrand.*

protecting power. In *international law*, a *neutral* acting to protect the nationals or property of a *belligerent*; or like Switzerland, protecting *prisoners of war* on all sides though itself remaining neutral.

protection. A cover term widely used by the *Red Cross* and other NGOs, and by governments, for the legal rights and obligations incurred under the *Geneva Conventions.* *See also hospital ships; prisoners of war; war crimes.*

protectionism. Any effort to hinder the free flow of *trade*, especially by use of *protective tariffs, nontariff barriers,* and *subsidies* which aim to defend domestic producers from more efficient foreign producers. From 1846 to 1870 trade liberalization, led by the United Kingdom, broke down protectionist systems. After 1878 protectionism resumed, until it peaked during the *Great Depression,* which it hugely aggravated. After *World War II,* led by the United States within *GATT,* protectionism was progressively broken down among OECD nations. With the collapse of the *Soviet bloc* and global embrace of *free trade,* by 2000 all major economies were (officially) opposed to protectionism. *See also free trade; mercantilism; neomercantilism; new protectionism; secular trend; Smoot-Hawley Tariff; World Trade Organization.*

protective tariffs. Taxes on *imports* which aim to shelter favored domestic producers by excluding more efficient foreign competition from the home market. These are different from normal *tariffs,* which aim at extracting revenue for the government from foreign producers in exchange for the privilege of trade. An important historical example is the Corn Laws in Britain in the early- to mid-nineteenth century. These aimed at excluding imports of bread grains in order to protect domestic farmers, but they did so at the great expense of urban consumers. In 1841 the *Whig* government fell over its attempt to reduce the tariff. When *famine* struck in Ireland—then part of the United Kingdom—beginning in 1845, the crisis became acute and the damage to the public interest obvious. The Corn Laws were repealed in 1846. *See also peak tariffs.*

protectorate. A territory declared, or agreed by treaty to be, dependent on and defended by a more powerful state. The proclamation of protectorates was one way imperial powers limited the chance of coming to blows over competing claims, through knowledge that certain areas of uncertain jurisdiction would be defended by force although not formally annexed or colonized. They also may be legitimately thought of as a kind of pre-*colony*, since larger or more valuable protectorates were often converted to formal colony status after long possession led to acceptance of claimed authority by other colonial powers. A new form of protectorate is the *associated state*. In the 1990s, the United Nations and NATO established de facto protectorates in Bosnia and Kosovo, but did not use this term. *See also First Abyssinian War; Anglo-Russian Entente (1907–1917); Annam; Ashanti; Berlin Conference; Botswana; British East Africa; Brunei; Bukhara; Burma; Cambodia; Cameroon; Comoros; Cook Islands; Côte d'Ivoire; Cyprus; Dahomey; Danubian Principalities; dependency; East Aden; East India Company; French Indochina; French Polynesia; Ionian Islands; Kamerun; Khiva; Kiribati; Kokand; Korea; Kuwait; Laos; Lebanon; Lesotho; Madagascar; Malawi; Malaya; Maldives; Marshall Islands; Mauritania; Monaco; Napoleon; Nigeria; Niue; Oil Rivers; scramble for Africa; Qatar; Samori Touré; Sarawak; Sierra Leone; Sikkim; Slovakia; Solomon Islands; Somalia; Sudan; Swaziland; Tanganyika; Tibet; Tientsin; Togoland; Tonga; Tonkin Wars; Trinidad and Tobago; Trucial Oman; Tunisia; Tuvalu; Twenty-one Demands; Uganda; Vietnam; Wallis and Fortuna Islands; Yemen; Zambia; Zanzibar.*

protest. *See diplomatic note; diplomatic protest;* pro forma.

Protestantism, and international relations. *See Calvinism; Catholic Church; Counter Reformation; Eighty Years' War; Jesuits; manifest destiny; missionaries; Protestant Reformation; Thirty Years' War; Westphalia; Wars of Religion.*

Protestant Reformation. A great sixteenth-century shattering of the unity of Latin *Christian* civilization—the Christian world had already split into *Catholic* (Latin) and *Orthodox* branches centuries earlier. It was both an extension of the *Renaissance* and a reaction against it. The Reformation took different national form in several core countries, from which it later spread (unevenly) across the Christian commonwealth. It took deep root in Germany, but had independent origins in Holland, Switzerland, and, though more out of the dynastic and personal financial interests of Henry VIII (1491–1547), in England as well. It was occasioned by new economic, social, and political developments which created the opportunity to present an alternative to the political and intellectual dominance of the *Catholic Church*. Many challenges to Catholic orthodoxy were made between c. 1340 and 1648. The most intense phase of religious ferment and demand for reform, leading to a permanent division in the Church, began in 1517 when *Martin Luther* (1483–1546) nailed 95 theses protesting the sale of "indulgences" (promissory notes on reduced punishment in the afterlife) to a church door in Wittenberg. By 1521 parts of the German church were in de facto *schism* from Rome; they broke openly with the promulgation of the Augsburg Confession of basic principles in 1530.

Given the translation of the Bible into vernacular languages (the German translation was made by Luther) and its mass production on the new Gutenberg printing press invented c. 1450, Protestantism spread rapidly. It drank deeply from disgust at Church corruption, but also fed on economic and national grievances, as well as on ancient apocalyptic traditions which painted the Catholic Church—with its attachments to secular power—as the "whore of Babylon" and any reigning pope as the anti-Christ. Protestant soon also fought Protestant, as militant *Calvinism* rejected *Lutheranism* and Catholicism in near-equal measure. Protestantism quickly became a many-colored cloak, adding new patches with the repeated rise of some locally charismatic preacher who fixed on this doctrinal point or that and worried it into an absolute moral claim around which formed a faction of followers. Still, its main tenet remained that individual souls needed no intermediary between themselves and God—no established and corruptible priesthood with a monopoly on interpreting scripture, no hierarchy of doctrinal or administrative authority, and most certainly no pope. Not all Protestants were that radical in the changes they sought or the new doctrines they preached. That was the general form Protestantism took as decades of bloody struggle burned all bridges to Rome and fanatics condemned each other as heretics on all sides of every fiercely debated angelic, apostolic, catechistic, or doctrinal question.

For 150 years confessional conflict led to war between and among Catholic and Protestant princes, states, and peoples. Of these, the *Eighty Years' War* (1566–1648) and the *Thirty Years' War* (1618–1648) were the greatest and longest. From the point of view of secular international history, the Reformation was vitally important because church quarrels and priestly revolt quickly turned into overt political rebellion and then into far-reaching *revolution* and civil and interstate war. For instance, it overturned the existing diplomatic system in northwestern Europe. For centuries England had allied with Castile against France and Scotland, an alliance structure whose last gasp was the short-lived *dynastic marriage* of *Philip II* of Spain to Mary Tudor (1516–1558) in 1554. The ascent of the Protestant *Elizabeth I* to the English throne in 1558 constituted a diplomatic revolution of the first order: it ultimately aligned Protestants in Scotland and England with Dutch rebels against Philip. The Reformation had similar effects in Germany. In consequence, European civilization was shaken to its core and violently tossed and torn for more than a century. This bloody series of contests damaged Europe inwardly and hardened its states and its politics.

The Protestant Reformation also drove energies outward, ultimately to engage much of the wider world as well in a search for profit and martial advantage of use in mortal combats at home. The Americas became open battlegrounds among Iberian Catholics and English and Dutch Protestants and their navies. The coasts of Africa and India were penetrated by rival traders, but also by rival *missionaries*. Even faraway China was buffeted by Reformation winds as European *privateers* attacked ocean-going and coastal junks, and each other, seizing cargos and seeking to monopolize China's ocean-borne trade. The *Jesuits* and like orders in the frontline of the Catholic *Counter Reformation* fanned out over Asia in a fierce competition for converts, bringing the *Inquisition* with them to places such as the Philippines. Protestant and Catholic traders, diplomats, and missionaries also vied to curry favor with the profoundly suspicious *Tokugawa shoguns* of Japan. Moreover, Europe eventually emerged from the Reformation flush with political energy released by a new emphasis on *individualism*, already with mastery established over far-flung lands and divers peoples, an appetite for still more profit and land that grew with the eating, and armed with navigational, technological, and commercial innovations born of decades of cutthroat warfare and ferocious economic competition.

Such great change reinforced a new intellectual openness born of the earlier Renaissance, which was itself partly stimulated by contacts with the heritage of the classical world via Arab translations, and with China. This helped Europe become the first civilization to embrace a scientific (empirical) world view and then to adopt *secularism* as a core principle of its political and interstate affairs. Together, these vast changes greatly empowered the rising states of Europe, enabling them to conquer most of the rest of the world and to impose upon it the state system itself—along with all the anti-ideological presumptions and international rules established at *Westphalia*, originally intended to keep religious peace inside Europe. That great settlement finally brought confessional peace to Europe, but only by elevating the state to a near absolutist position in relation both to claims of superior religious authority and over subject populations. Through this radical innovation, and with the blood and conquest of the coming imperial age, for good and for ill the entire world ultimately would be politically united. In sum, the Protestant Reformation so changed Europe it greatly enabled Europeans to set the pace of global change for the next 500 years. Properly understood, it was a key act in the great play of world history, not merely a cultural upheaval native to the European region. *See also Charles V; Confucianism; Elizabeth I; Habsburgs; Holy Roman Empire; Orthodox Church; Philip II; res publica Christiana; Max Weber.*

Suggested Readings: Owen Chadwick, *The Reformation* (1972); G. Elton, *Reformation Europe* (1963); Richard Marius, *Martin Luther* (1999); Steven Ozment, *The Age of Reform, 1250–1550* (1981).

protocol. (1) An international agreement supplementary to an existing *treaty*. (2) Ritual, ceremony and formal courtesies used to signal the state of relations among nations and assist in the clear conduct of *diplomacy*. Elaborate measures are engaged not person-to-person, though that is how it may appear, but nation-to-nation. Giving deliberate offense to an *ambassador*, for instance, by missing appointments or speaking brusquely, is therefore intended (and received) as a snub to the nation he or she represents. Conversely, flowery accolades have the opposite effect. Ritual and minute agreement is the essence of diplomatic negotiation. It is usually condemned by outside observers as effete or immoral, as when arguing over the shape of a negotiating table while a war rages. Such discussions may well be essential to deciding how the war is framed (interstate war? insurrection? civil war?) and thus which parties are to be allowed a say in its formal ending. Progress or failure at that stage often indicates whether the moment for peace has in fact arrived or not. Symbols and ritual behavior are thus essential to diplomatic (as to most human) communication, and detailed debate over their deployment and significance advances broader understanding of an opponent's position. On occasion, diplomatic courtesy may be extended to nondiplomatic persons as an indication of a desire to elevate relations or to signal a desire for a change in the political map of another country. For example, the West continued to receive ambassadors from the *Baltic States* during the *Cold War*, though those countries had been annexed by the Soviet Union; and France starting in the late 1960s extended full diplomatic courtesy to the premiers of *Québec*, to signal support for independence without provoking an open confrontation with Canada. More subtle variations in the proper use of protocol may signal disapproval of another government's policy or an impending shift in one's own. *See also prestige; provocation.*

"Protocols of the Elders of Zion." An infamous forgery by the tsarist *secret police* (the *Okhrana*), purporting to document a Jewish conspiracy to set up a world dictatorship, used as *disinformation* to stir up *anti-Semitism* and justify *pogroms*. It was later seized upon by the *Nazis* for use in their hate campaigns against the Jews, and later still, it was employed by Arab governments and groups to the same purpose. Despite thorough and complete exposure as a forgery, including by a Swiss court in 1935, the Protocols continue to be cited by *neo-Nazis* and other latter-day anti-Semites as putative evidence that their fear and loathing of Jews is in fact well-grounded. *See also "final solution to the Jewish problem"; Holocaust.*

protracted war. A *Maoist* concept of war-making in which a *guerilla* force stretches out a military conflict with opposing *conventional* forces until the enemy's political will cracks. *See also people's war.*

protraction. *See people's war; protracted war.*

Proudhon, Pierre Joseph (1809–1865). French *anarchist.* He participated in the *revolution of 1848* in Paris and was elected to the Assembly. He was imprisoned for his *radical* views by *Louis Napoleon* and took refuge in Belgium, 1858–1862. There he further developed his view of anarchism as liberation, famously saying that "property is theft." He was active again during the *Paris Commune*. He split with *Karl Marx* during the *First International*. His writings remained influential in many countries into the middle of the twentieth century.

Providence, belief in. *See Alexander I; caliph; Calvinism; Catholic Church; Charles V; Christianity;* conquistadores; *Hernando Cortés; Oliver Cromwell; Crusades; Ferdinand and Isabella; fundamentalism; Adolf Hitler;* imam; *Ismaili;* jihad; *Knights Templar; Louis XIV;* mahdi; *mandate of heaven; manifest destiny; missionaries; mission, sense of; Old Believers; Philip II; Protestant Reformation;* requerimiento; res publica Christiana; shi'ite; *Taiping Rebellion; Third Rome; Thirty Years' War; Teutonic Knights;* Wahhabi; *Wars of Religion; Westphalia, Peace of; White Lotus Rebellion; Woodrow Wilson.*

provisional government. (1) One set up in the wake of *liberation, defeat,* or *revolution,* pending establishment of a new constitutional order. (2) The revolutionary, democratic government in Russia from March 12 to November 6, 1917. It was nearly overthrown by a right-wing *coup,* launched a disastrous summer offensive while delaying domestic reforms, and in November was overthrown by the *Petrograd Soviet,* by then fully controlled by the *Bolsheviks. See also Alexander Kerensky.*

provocation. A public act or official gesture, such as a breach of *protocol,* which violates the *comity of nations.* If severe (for example, a pattern of military *incursions*), it may be responded to with force. In almost all cases, a provocation will call forth a *diplomatic protest.* In some, it may be sufficiently severe to trigger war. Provocations sometimes have been exaggerated, or even staged, in order to justify military action or *aggression. See also Ems Telegram; Gulf of Tonkin Resolution; Mukden incident.*

proxy wars. Wars in which *Great Powers* or *regional powers* fight indirectly through sponsorship of smaller powers or local insurgents. During the *Cold War* it was widely believed that in an age of *nuclear deterrence*—where direct use of force against one another was denied to the Great Powers—many small wars could be explained as proxies for larger *superpower* conflicts. Although this reasoning was applied far too frequently to conflicts which often had deep local causes, there is some evidence that this was indeed the case in special situations. Soviet support for North Korea and the Democratic Republic of Vietnam (DRV, or North Vietnam) certainly was, in part, a form of proxy conflict. As new archival information revealed in the late 1990s shows, it also arose from real ideological affinity for the cause of international socialism. On the other side, various sponsored interventions in Third World conflicts—the *Reagan Doctrine* and logistical support for the Afghan *mujahadeen*—were examples of the United States using proxies as an extension of the policy of *containment*. In earlier centuries, other Great Powers used other proxies, often in variations of containment policy of some great enemy state or to advance imperial interests of their own. However, it is not just the Great Powers which use proxy fighters. Inter alia, Israel helped maintain proxy militias in southern Lebanon for many years, as did Iran and Syria; South Africa supported proxy rebellions in neighboring African states during the era of *apartheid*; and numerous African states backed proxy rebels in Congo during the bloody regional conflict which broke out in Central Africa in 1997. *See also Cambodia-Vietnam War; Eastern Question; Ethiopia-Somalia War; "merchants of death."*

prudence. (1) In *realism*: The cardinal political virtue, requiring restraint, taking only those limited actions necessary to pursuit of the *national interest*, and implying respect for the national interests of other *recognized* political communities. (2) In the *just war tradition*: The moral requirement that before resort is had to *force* to correct some evil a calculation must be made as to whether *intervention* will likely cause an even greater evil, such as: "Will massive military intervention to stop *ethnic cleansing* (in some given state) save lives or lead to a widened conflict and greater destruction?"

Prussia. This north German state (called "Brandenburg-Prussia" upon the acquisition of Brandenburg and *East Prussia* by Albert of *Hohenzollern* in 1618) was a rising but still fairly minor Baltic power before the eighteenth century. As late as 1750 Prussia was only about the size of Connecticut, with a small and impoverished population of just 2.5 million. Its ascent to the ranks of the *Great Powers* coincided with a series of interrelated events: the *Protestant Reformation*; the *Thirty Years' War* (1618–1648) and the *Peace of Westphalia* (1648); expulsion of the *Huguenots* from France (1685); the decline, eventual *extinction*, and *partitions of Poland* (in which Royal, or Polish, Prussia was annexed to Prussia and renamed West Prussia); and the geopolitical eclipse of its Baltic rival Sweden by more distant Russia under *Peter the Great*. During this extended period, *Frederick-William of Brandenburg* and his immediate successors managed to raise the resource-poor, northern state of Prussia slowly from obscurity, based largely on its highly professional *standing army*. This crucial fact was wretchedly captured by a disgruntled Prussian liberal, Freiherr von Schrotter, in c. 1800: "Prussia," he lamented, "was not a country with an army, but an army with a country which served as headquarters and food magazine."

Prussia's rise also resulted from the most spectacularly successful policy of economic centralization in history. Its leaders concentrated on developing a professionalized administration (bureaucracy), strictly collected taxes, were fiscally prudent, and were devoted to cultivation of the army while seldom committing it to battle. In the mid-eighteenth century Prussia finally struck: under *Frederick II* ("the Great") it contested by force of arms with Austria for control of *Silesia* in the *War of the Austrian Succession* and the *Seven Year's War*. Having annexed and held Silesia, and then participating in the *partitions of Poland*, Prussia was accepted as a *Great Power* by the time of the *French Revolution*. After suffering initial defeat at the hands of French Revolutionary armies, Prussia abandoned its allies (Austria, Britain, and minor Italian and German states) and retreated into neutrality while France, and *Napoleon*, destroyed these once-and-future allies (except for Britain) one-by-one. Then, picking the worst possible moment, following Napoleon's utter humiliation of both Austria and Russia, Prussia *declared war* on France in 1806. Within a month it was nearly extinguished by Napoleon, at *Jena*. A new Prussia emerged only slowly and only after experiencing French military occupation and the burning of *Berlin*. Those humiliations moved *Frederick-William III* to adopt wholesale economic, social, and military reforms which enabled Prussia to strike back hard, 1813–1815. More territorial gains at the *Congress of Vienna*, and the continuing weakness of the *Austrian Empire*, helped propel Prussia to predominance within Germany by the mid-nineteenth century.

From 1815 to 1866 Austria and Prussia competed for influence over the central and southern states of the *German Confederation*. Then *Bismarck* settled the issue of who would rule Germany once and for all, though in the process raising a new question about Prussia's place in Europe. He did so through three sharp Prussian victories: (1) over Denmark in 1864; (2) over Austria in the *Seven Weeks' War* (1866), which dismantled the old German Confederation and temporarily set up the *North German Confederation*; and (3) by crushing France in the *Franco-Prussian War* (1870–1871), and thereafter annexing most of north, central, and southern Germany to create the German Empire under the Hohenzollern Prussian king, who henceforth was also *kaiser* of the *Second Reich*. In the 1860s and 1870s Prussia extended its control over the *North German Confederation* and under *Bismarck* rapidly defeated Denmark, Austria, and France to become the foundation state of Imperial Germany. Most of what had been eastern Prussia was divided among Lithuania, Poland, and the Soviet Union after *World War II*. *See also Baltic States; Karl Maria von Clausewitz; diplomatic revolution; Franco-Prussian War; Frederick I; Frederick III; General Staff; Germany; August Wilhelm von Gneisenau; Junkers; partitions of Poland;* Realpolitik; *Gerhard Johann von Scharnhorst; Schleswig-Holstein; Seven Weeks' War; Sonderweg; Tilsit; Voltaire; Wilhelm II.*

Suggested Readings: F. Carsten, *The Origins of Prussia* (1954); Michael Howard, *The Franco-Prussian War* (1981); H. Rosenberg, *Bureaucracy, Aristocracy, and Autocracy* (1958); Geoffrey Wawro, *The Austro-Prussian War* (1996).

psychohistory. The attempt to apply psychological methods and theories to the interpretation of historical events and/or to the analysis of historical persons.

psychological warfare. Techniques of *disinformation, propaganda,* publicity, threats, and other measures designed to influence or intimidate a foreign population, and by that undermine an enemy's *national morale*. It may be *covert* or *overt*.

public contracts. Contracts for goods or services made between states and private firms or individuals.

public debt. The total of government debt from all levels, federal, state, and local. *See also national debt.*

public goods. (1) In economics: Facilities such as communications, transportation, electricity, and other publicly funded and regulated services necessary to conduct economic activity. A near-synonym is *infrastructure*. (2) In international relations theory: The idea that a *hegemon* provides services of common utility to a regional or global *international system* which it dominates. For instance, Great Britain is often said by international relations theorists to have provided the nineteenth-century world with global political stability, an open international economy, and secure *global commons* and public goods such as *free trade* and open international *trade routes*. Few, if any, international historians would agree with that bald assessment of British benevolence.

public international law. *See also international law; private international law.*

public international unions. These were the first major *functional* organizations to develop. They did so in response to the extraordinary outburst of commercial and other *transnational* activity in the latter half of the nineteenth century. They were in no way the product of visionaries. Instead, they were the invention of bureaucrats reacting to pragmatic administrative needs by setting up contacts with their counterparts in other *states*, even those their political masters might not favor. The public international unions fed directly into the functional stream of modern international organization. *See also International Telegraph Union; Universal Postal Union.*

public opinion. The collective opinion of a national community, or, more properly, of the "attentive public" (those who pay attention to issues of politics and foreign policy). Traditionally, *diplomacy* took place without regard for public opinion, which before the advent of mass literacy—around the middle of the nineteenth century—was virtually nonexistent concerning *foreign affairs*. With increasingly literacy, travel, and the rise of several *democracies* to *Great Power* status, public opinion began to play a more important role in international relations. Contrary to original *liberal* assumptions, quite often the function of public opinion is negative and warlike rather than peaceful and progressive. Public opinion is most often aroused to block initiatives or change, rather than to bring change about, as it is easier to get large masses of people to dislike a policy than it is to persuade them to support one. Public opinion will thus more likely stir in order to oppose some proposed policy, such as initiating *diplomatic relations* with a new but unsavory regime, engaging in a far-off war, or dispatching *peacekeeping* troops to a long-troubled region, or accepting *free trade* and regional *integration*.

On occasion, public opinion may spur a government to do something positive it otherwise is reluctant to undertake, such as intercede in behalf of *human rights* or in relief of *famine* or some other humanitarian disaster. Sometimes, though the evidence is mixed, it may pressure a government into ending a war. This was at least partly true of the *Vietnam War* and the *Afghan-Soviet War*. Aroused opinion has also on occasion propelled reluctant governments into starting a war, as was partly the case in the *Crimean War* and the *Spanish-American War*, and almost wholly the case with *Gladstone* during the *Zulu War*. Atavistic *nationalisms* with broad public support lurk behind numerous conflicts, including the decade-long fighting in the 1990s of the *Third Balkan War*.

Most often, however, public opinion simply follows the lead a government or elements of the national elite provide, which usually means that all armies in most wars are initially cheered off to battle by their respective publics. In day-to-day foreign policy decision-making, public opinion is not supposed to trump *raison d'etat*, but many a democratic leader is in fact more attuned to the public mood than to any longer-term vision of what is good for the country. They will as a result go through all sorts of political, moral, and analytical contortions to arrive at a policy which speaks to the fickle public mind while remaining at least arguably an approximation of the *national interest*. *See also CNN; donor fatigue; mood theory; national morale; propaganda; world public opinion.*

public sector. The total governmental portion of a national economy, federal, state, and local, excluding all private expenditure and transactions.

Pueblo Affair. On January 23, 1968, the USS Pueblo (a spy ship) was seized by North Korea. The United States insisted the ship had been on the *high seas* and protested vehemently, with *public opinion* demanding forceful action by the *Johnson* administration. After 11 months of bitter negotiations, the United States signed an apology and the crew (but not the ship) was released. The apology was vitiated by an advance declaration that it had been coerced and was immediately renounced by Washington upon release of the crew.

Puerto Rico. This Caribbean island was inhabited by Arawak Indians when Columbus landed there in 1493. It was claimed for Spain in 1509 by Juan Ponce de León (1460–1521), who also brutally suppressed an Arawak rebellion. Within a few years most of the Arawak population succumbed to disease and oppression. The Spanish then imported African slaves to work the sugar fields (*slavery* was not abolished until 1873), over time giving the island its distinctive, mixed-race population. The Dutch and British both tried to seize Puerto Rico in the late sixteenth century, but Spain defended it until it fell to the United States in 1898 after the *Spanish-American War*. In 1916 its inhabitants were granted U.S. *citizenship* (Jones Act). In 1952 Puerto Rico was granted status as a self-governing commonwealth attached to the United States. Puerto Ricans remain divided over whether they should seek U.S. statehood: they have no representation in Congress, and no electoral votes for president. Extreme advocates of independence sometimes conducted bombings and assassinations on the U.S. mainland to advance their cause, notably in New York in the 1970s. In November 1993, in a *referendum*, they decided 50 percent in favor of the status quo as a commonwealth, in which they pay no individual federal income tax, and headquartered corporations also receive tax breaks which make the island attractive for direct investment, to 46 percent for statehood. A mere 4 percent voted for *independence*.

Pugachev rebellion (1774–1775). A major peasant uprising led by the *Cossacks*, under the peasant Emelian Pugachev (c. 1744–1775), a veteran of the *Seven Years' War* (1756–1763) and of the *Russo-Turkish Wars*. Pugachev claimed to be a reincarnation of the assassinated Tsar Peter III, whom many believed had been murdered by *Catherine the Great*. Many nobles were slaughtered by peasant mobs. The uprising was put down with the usual extreme ruthlessness of the tsars. Pugachev was taken in an iron cage to Moscow, where he suffered public torture and execution. *See also Great Fear*; jacquerie; *Nian Rebellion*; *Stenka Razin*; *Túpac Amaru*.

pump priming. When a government stimulates an economy by spending borrowed money. *See also Keynesian economics*.

Punic Wars. A protracted conflict for control of the Western Mediterranean, Iberia, and North Africa, between the *Roman Empire* and the Carthaginian Empire.

(1) First Punic War (264–241 B.C.E.): It arose from the struggle between the North African empire of Carthage, which controlled most of the trade in, and otherwise dominated, the western Mediterranean in the third century B.C.E., and the Roman Republic. Its proximate cause was internal strife among two *city-states* of Sicily—Messina and Syracuse. This quarrel among minor regional powers drew in the Punic Army from Carthage and then the Legions and Navy of Rome. The Romans scored a naval victory at Mylae (260) and progressively occupied Sicily. Their attempt to invade North Africa (256) failed, however. Another naval triumph, at the Aegadian Isles (241), blocked Punic reinforcements from Sicily and gave the victory to Rome.

(2) Second Punic War (218–202 B.C.E.): The great Carthaginian general, Hannibal (c. 247–182 B.C.E.), who had been raised to hate Rome by his general father (who made him swear implacable hostility to Rome at age nine)

now took the war into Spain, where Roman and Punic armies sometimes skirmished. He attacked and overran Rome's allies in Iberia, 221–218 B.C.E. Then he brought the fight to Italy, crossing the Pyrenees to defeat the Gauls and then crossing the Alps in just 15 days with an African army that included war elephants and heavy *cavalry*. He left many thousands of men and beasts dead in the high passes, but as he marched he gathered new allies and conscripted new levies from among the tribes and cities Rome had earlier subjugated. On the Plain of Trebia, he scattered a Roman army, then wintered along the Po. When spring came, in 217 B.C.E., he crossed the Apennines, burned out most of Etruria, and marched on Rome itself. He defeated another Roman army at Lake Trasimeme. He paused, living off the fat of Roman lands and wintering at Gerunium. In the spring of 216 he destroyed a third Roman army, at Cannae.

Hannibal was far from home, however. His *supply lines* were greatly overextended and easily interrupted, by land or sea, and in any case the politicians of Carthage did little to support their great general, possibly from fear that his victory over Rome would later give him one at home, over them. For years Hannibal's army lived off the land and campaigned in Italy, wearing down over time while Rome raised new armies to send against him. In 207 his brother sought to bring him a relief force of fresh Punic troops via Spain, but he was intercepted and killed, forcing Hannibal to withdraw to the high ground of Italy and onto the defensive. In 203 Hannibal was recalled to Carthage, which by now itself faced invasion by a Roman army. In 202 he was decisively defeated by the Roman general Scipio Africanus (236–183 B.C.E.) at Zama. Mighty Carthage was stripped of its navy and Spanish provinces and became a mere *tributary* of Rome. Hannibal was briefly in power, but with Carthage uncaring of his efforts at reform he went into exile (195). As Rome continued to expand he found fewer places to hide. The end came with Rome out for his blood and a price on his head: he committed suicide by poison.

(3) Third Punic War (149–146 B.C.E.): Some in Rome wished to reduce Carthage utterly, and in 149 B.C.E. they located an excuse to do so in a diplomatic incident between Carthage and a minor Roman ally. War was declared and Carthage blockaded by sea, then invaded by land. The city and its hinterland was methodically razed and much of its population enslaved. It later revived as a commercial center within the *Roman Empire*, but was never again a threat to Roman power. *See also Carthaginian peace.*

Suggested Readings: Brian Caven, *The Punic Wars* (1980); Adrian Goldsworthy, *The Punic Wars* (2001).

punitive damages. *Damages* exceeding the harm actually done, exacted as punishment by one state for another's illegal behavior. *See also indemnity; reparations.*

Punitive War (1979). The preferred term in China for the *Sino-Vietnamese War* (1979).

Punjab. A region of the *subcontinent* of India seared by violent division in 1947 between India and *West Pakistan*, with most *Muslims* going to Pakistan. The Punjabis of Pakistan have dominated that country's national politics and life more often than not. Those of India were subdivided in 1966 into *Hindu* and *Sikh* administrative areas. Among the Sikhs there has been considerable agitation for *secession* to form "Kalistan." That led to mass violence in 1984 and smaller outbreaks thereafter.

puppet regime (puppet state). Often pejorative as well as descriptive, this term refers to a *state* which is not free of the direction of a more powerful state in its foreign policy, despite maintaining the fiction of *independence*. Positions it adopts, *wars* it fights, and so on are decided in a foreign capital. *See also Manchukuo.*

purchasing power. A method of comparing national income (or production) which seeks to go beyond simply translating per capita *GNP* figures into a standard *hard currency* and then measuring the differences. Instead, it assesses purchases which might be made before comparing the relative buying power of each currency. Often, the results indicate a greater purchasing power in poorer countries than per capita income figures suggest.

purge. Mass elimination of political opponents from within the government, or one's own party, power base, or political movement. *See also cultural revolution; Gang of Four; Great Proletarian Cultural Revolution; Hongwu emperor; Khmers Rouges; Mao Zedong; Night of the Long Knives; purge trials; Red Guards; reeducation; rehabilitation; Maximilien de Robespierre; Josef Stalin; Terror; Yezhovshchina.*

purge trials. Criminal-political proceedings, especially if rigged, used to remove, imprison, or kill opponents of a given *regime*, whether the opposition was real or imaginary. Their most important function was to provide *propaganda* makers in *totalitarian* states with a set of scapegoats upon whom all failings of the promised *revolution* could be fastened, and through which the new *party line* was communicated by excoriation and example, even to a far-flung and illiterate peasant audience. They were, when all was said and done, a form of political theater in which anticipation was built by baiting the defendant (victim), and the climax came with a confessional breakdown, arranged in advance by threats or *torture*. The denouement of sentencing hardly mattered—although death sentences were usually carried out, in some cases *reeducation* and *rehabilitation* was permitted to reinforce lessons of the purge-morality play. The most spectacular took place in the Soviet Union in the 1920s and 1930s, when star chambers condemned the usual suspects, on testimony from the usual witnesses, who were then callously purged in their turn. In this way, the anger and frustration of urban workers—who were being squeezed by *Stalin's* exaggerated *five-year plans* on the one hand, and whose *standard of living* was plummeting as a result of *collectivization* on the other— was focused on "wreckers," "saboteurs," and other supposed *counterrevolutionary* villains. *See also Lavrenti Pavlovich Beria; cultural revolution; Felix Dzerzhinsky; Gang of Four; GULAG; KGB; Mao Zedong; NKVD; OGPU; Pol Pot; strel'sty; Andrei Vyshinsky; Yezhovshchina.*

Putin, Vladimir Vladimirovich (b. 1952). President of Russia, 2000– . He was trained to the doctoral level as an economist, though at a time when Soviet orthodoxy dominated Russia's educational system. He served as a *KGB* officer from 1975 to 1990. With the *extinction* of the Soviet Union, about which Putin subsequently expressed considerable regret, he became active in politics in *St. Petersburg*. He moved into national politics in 1996, working under *Yeltsin*. In 1998 he was appointed to head the *Federal Security Service* (FSB), successor to the KGB. In 1999 Yeltsin appointed Putin prime minister of Russia, at age 47. Putin immediately launched an all-out war effort in *Chechnya*, which while greatly costly in lives and treasure was also wildly popular in Russia, at first. He then turned on Yeltsin, who had become utterly decadent, inept, and corrupt, sharply criticizing him for Russia's continuing economic decline and for mishandling the Chechen war. Putin promised that he would deliver a quick, and if need be also ruthless, victory. The public was enthusiastic, as *terrorist* bombs had just been detonated in Moscow, taking many civilian lives. This cowardly act was officially blamed on Chechens, who were then rounded up and deported from the cities. Whether Chechen rebels had in fact planted the bombs or they were the work of some *agent provocateur* remained unclear and unproven. Nonetheless, Putin rode a rising tide of anti-Chechen and anti-Yeltsin anger into the presidency in elections held in March 2000. As president, he moved quickly to recentralize Russia's chaotic bureaucracy and tax system and pushed through some additional liberalizing economic reforms. And he kept his promise on Chechnya, delivering a savage series of punishment blows to the Chechens, if not quite outright military victory to Russia. Putin's foreign policy rhetoric at times was deeply *nationalistic* and confrontational with the West, somewhat in the *Slavophile* tradition on matters of culture and *prestige*. On the other hand, he also proved capable of singular pragmatism in working with Western leaders, especially *George W. Bush*, on issues they supported but he opposed, such as *ballistic missile defense* and *abrogation* of the ABM Treaty. This new pragmatism in Russian-U.S. relations bore fruit for both sides after the *September 11, 2001, terrorist attack on the United States*, as Putin forged a series of cooperative agreements with Bush on trade, security, and technology cooperation. He also appeared to have a firmer grasp of modern economic realities than any Russian leader since before the *Russian Revolution of 1917*. Whether or not that would be enough to permit him to reform and heal a deeply corrupt and fractured nation remained to be seen, at the end of 2001.

Suggested Reading: V. Putin, *First Person* (2000).

Putsch. A near synonym for a *coup*, but referring also to a sudden revolt or uprising. It is used especially about the several extreme right-wing attempts to take power in the *interwar* period in Germany. *See also Beer Hall Putsch; Kapp Putsch.*

Pu Yi (1906–1967). "The Last Emperor." Known as "Henry Pu Yi" in the West, to Chinese he was Hsuan T'ung. He later was crowned—but was widely unrecognized—as K'ang Te (Kangde) emperor, a nominal head of Japanese-run *Manchukuo*. Proclaimed the tenth (and last) *Qing* emperor of China at age two, in 1908, he reigned without ruling until the *Chinese Revolution* (1911) forced his abdication on February 12, 1912, at age six. In 1917 a former Qing general briefly took Beijing and declared the eleven-year-old Pu Yi reinstated. The restoration was suppressed, and the Republic ordered that Pu Yi be educated in Western ways. In the abdication agreement the remnant of the Qing court had been assigned the *Forbidden City* for life. Pu Yi was now essentially confined there until 1924, when he was evicted by yet another *warlord* and moved to the Japanese *concession* at Tientsin in 1925. After the *Mukden incident* in 1931, at age 25, he made the fateful decision that made him a traitor in the eyes of most Chinese: he bowed to his *Manchu* and regal origins and agreed to be smuggled from Tientsin to *Manchuria*. There, he became the figurehead ruler of the Japanese *puppet state* of Manchukuo; he was proclaimed K'ang Te emperor in 1934. Again, he reigned without ruling. With Japan's defeat in 1945 he abdicated his second imperial throne. He tried to flee to Japan but was captured by invading Soviet troops and interned in the Soviet Union until 1950. He was handed over to the Chinese *Communists* after the *Chinese Civil War*. Proclaimed a *war criminal*, he underwent political *reeducation* and nine years of hard imprisonment in forced labor camps. After his "conversion" (sincere or not is unclear) to *Maoist* communism, in 1959 he was allowed to settle into quiet, closely guarded retirement in a botanical commune.

Pyrenees, Treaty of (1660). This was the decisive settlement which essentially mapped out the modern border between France and Spain. It signified Spain's defeat after 160 years of warfare in an effort to establish *hegemony*, and *Habsburg* acceptance of the primacy of France within the European state system. *See also* Île des Faisans.

pyrrhic victory. One obtained—whether in politics or in war—at a cost in assets, lives and treasure so great that *victory* may not be distinguishable from *defeat. See also Iran-Iraq War; Verdun; World War I.*

Q

Qaddafi, Muammar. *See Quadaffi, Muamar.*

al Qaeda. "The Base." In Peshawar, Pakistan, the Makhtab al Khadimat was formed in 1984 by *Usama bin Laden* to recruit Arabs and other non-Afghan Muslims to fight alongside the Afghan *mujahadeen* waging *holy war* against the *Red Army* and other *communist* forces in Afghanistan. In 1986 this organization merged with *Egyptian Islamic Jihad* to form al Qaeda, an umbrella outfit some compare to a *terrorist* holding company. It was dedicated to fomenting *Islamist* revolution in all Muslim countries—although its leadership principally aimed at fomenting radical change in Egypt, Pakistan, and Saudi Arabia. The explicit anti-Americanism of al Qaeda derived from two key sources: (1) mujahadeen victory over the Soviet Union in 1979 gave rise to a false sense of confidence and assumption of divine assistance to the cause; and (2) U.S. troop deployments into Saudi Arabia during and after the *Gulf War* came to be seen as an effort by another Western *superpower* to establish *hegemony* over the core Muslim lands. U.S. support for Israel was a lesser, though reinforcing and aggravating, grievance. In 1996 al Qaeda formed a symbiotic alliance with the *Taliban* in Afghanistan, to which land it again imported tens of thousands of *Afghan Arabs* for training as Islamist fighters and terrorists.

Al Qaeda proved early on that it was prepared to use any and all terrorist tactics to bring about U.S. withdrawal from Arabia as the initial step in its planned *fundamentalist* reformation of the Islamic world. In 1992 it lent support to clansmen in Somalia who attacked and killed U.S. Rangers supporting the UN humanitarian relief mission there, which was successfully feeding millions of starving Muslims and attempting to assist in *nation-building* efforts. Al Qaeda was involved in planning the car bomb attack on the World Trade Center in New York (February 26, 1993), which killed six Americans and injured thousands. It may have been involved in an attack on U.S. military advisors to the Saudi National Guard that killed five Americans in Riyadh on November 13, 1995. Al Qaeda was behind another attack in Saudi Arabia, on the Khobar Towers barracks on the King Adbul Aziz Air Base, which killed 19 Americans on June 25, 1996, once again without provoking a serious or effective response from the *Clinton* administration.

Next came two massive truck bombs aimed at the U.S. embassies in Nairobi, Kenya, and Dar Es Salaam, Tanzania, on August 7, 1998. These coordinated attacks killed 12 Americans and 232 African employees or civilian bystanders and injured several thousand more. Clinton responded with cruise missiles fired into Sudan and Afghanistan. This had no effect on al Qaeda while reinforcing the image of the United States as both feckless and reckless in its use of punitive force. Over the next year, the *State Department* ordered "duck-and-cover" practice drills to be carried out at U.S. embassies and consulates and reinforced embassy security. The Justice Department indicted bin Laden along with 22 other terrorists for the African attacks; some of the lesser players were extradited and tried in New York, but not the al Qaeda leadership. On October 12, 2000, an al Qaeda suicide team carried out an attack against the *destroyer* U.S.S. Cole, which was making a port-of-call in Yemen. Seventeen U.S. sailors died, and several hundred million dollars in damage was done to the warship. Clinton again made threatening public statements but took no forceful action, as al Qaeda continued to be treated as a criminal, rather than a military problem. In private, Clinton signed *findings* authorizing lethal force against al Qaeda's leaders, but repeatedly demurred about actually using the larger-scale force the U.S. military told him would be necessary to ferret bin Laden and al Qaeda out of their Afghan caves. With this refusal to put "boots on the ground," no further or effective action was taken during the remainder of his administration.

Al Qaeda rose to world historical significance with a single act: the *September 11, 2001, terrorist attack* on the United States, which killed more than 3,000 (mostly Americans, but including 80 different nationalities) and wounded several thousand more. The attack inflicted $100 billion in direct physical damage, savaged the world's stock markets, and plunged the global economy deeper into an already well-advanced recession. The U.S. response was a powerful and sustained military, financial, *intelligence*, and diplomatic campaign that aimed at nothing less than ruthless, permanent destruction of al Qaeda. By the end of 2001, al Qaeda had already lost several thousand of its fighters to U.S. and allied bombing and strafing, and its leaders had been driven from their caves and from power in Afghanistan. *See also George W. Bush; Tony Blair; Shanghai Cooperation Organization; Uighurs.*

Qajar dynasty (1794–1925). *See Iran.*

Qatar. Located in the *Arabian peninsula*, the modern state is coterminous with a small peninsula, jutting eastward from Arabia proper, known by the same name. It is a member of the *Arab League, OAPEC, OPEC,* and the *United Nations.* It shares most of its history with that of the larger peninsula. Its population converted to *Islam* along with the rest of Arabia in the seventh century. It shared the history of much of Arabia in subsequent centuries, including being for several hundred years a minor province of the *Ottoman Empire.* It was also wracked by the revolt of the *Wahhabi* and by anti-Wahhabi intervention by the son of *Mehemet Ali.* It confronted Britain, 1882–1883, and again in 1887, without Ottoman support, as that empire's decline accelerated. In 1893 a rebellion broke out as a result of *Bedouin* raids from neighboring sheikdoms, which fatally damaged Ottoman rule. In 1916, during *World War I,* it became a British *protectorate.* London thereafter decided its foreign policy. As Britain prepared to withdraw from its *Persian Gulf* commitments in the late 1960s, Qatar sought *federation* with other former British protectorates. When this fell through, it declared itself an independent *sheikdom* in 1971. During the *Gulf War* it opened its territory to *Gulf coalition* forces. Subsequently, it realigned more closely with the United States and settled a minor border dispute with Saudi Arabia, its larger and dominant neighbor. By 1997 exploration made it clear that Qatar's natural gas reserves were so huge that only those of Russia and Saudi Arabia were larger.

Qianlong (Ch'ien-lung) emperor (1711–1799). The reign name of Hongli (r. 1736–1795), the longest-reigning emperor in Chinese history, and grandson of the similarly long-reigning *Kangxi.* He made Tibet a *protectorate* and briefly advanced *Qing* control as far west as Turkestan (Xianjang, or the "New Territories") in the 1750s. That put an end to 150 years of *frontier* warfare with the Zunghar, whose last forces were systematically slaughtered, and led to additional agreements with Russia on where to situate the common border. Then he settled *banner troops* along the frontier, with their families, as military colonies. He initiated the compilation of one of the greatest works of Chinese classical culture, the massive "Four Treasuries," yet this also led to significant distortion of the history of the *Manchus,* as Hongli commanded a revisionist dynastic history and destroyed copies of any work deemed slighting or unfavorable (at least 2,000 such works have never been recovered). Faced with a series of late-reign crises, Qianlong lost effective control to a powerful but utterly corrupt minister, Heshen (1750–1799), who rose from the ranks of the Plain Blue Banner regiment to win the emperor's lifelong, but ill-chosen, confidence.

In 1788 Qianlong was drawn into a succession dispute and major civil war in Vietnam, sending an army to invade the north (*Tonkin*) to restore the familiar Viêt dynasty, which had long paid China *tribute.* This army took

Hanoi, but then one of the Tây Són brothers, Nguyên Huê (or Quang Trung, d. 1792) defeated the Chinese in a series of historic battles remembered in Vietnam as the Ngoc Hôi-Dông-Da (1789). Qianlong recognized Huê as king of *Annam*, ending China's many centuries of intervention in Vietnamese *internal affairs*. He had more luck in Tibet and Nepal, where his troops defeated the *Gurkhas* in 1792 and forced them, too, to pay tribute. Within China, his final decades in power were wracked by spontaneous peasant uprisings, including by "White Lotus" *Buddhists* near Beijing in the 1770s, Muslims in the west in the 1780s, and on Taiwan in 1788. Qianlong famously dismissed the *East India Company's* effort to widen trade relations during the *Macartney mission* to China in 1793, preferring to keep the strictly limited and state-controlled *Cohong* system in place. Following his resignation (1795) and continuing after his death (1799), China was convulsed by the *White Lotus rebellion*, 1796–1804, a much larger and more dangerous affair than the Buddhist uprising of the 1770s. Heshen did not long survive him: he was compelled to kill himself by Qianlong's son and successor, Jiaqing (1799–1820).

Suggested Readings: Pamela K. Crossley, *A Translucent Mirror* (1999); R. Guy, *The Emperor's Four Treasuries* (1987); Harold Kahn, *Monarchy in the Emperor's Eyes* (1971).

Qing (Ch'ing, or Manchu) dynasty (1644–1912). The Manchus were an *Inner Asian* border people (Jürchen), numbering fewer than two million in the mid-seventeenth century but possessing advanced bureaucratic skills learned from the Chinese. Together with their superior military system, this greatly enabled their takeover of *Ming* China. *Nurgaci* organized the tribes in the first quarter of the seventeenth century into a mass army (the *banner system*) and led them out of *Manchuria* to attack China. In 1644 his son and successor breached the *Great Wall* when a protracted civil war and *warlordism* in China led a Ming "traitor," General Wu Sangui, to ask the Manchu for military aid in suppressing a massive rebellion by the warlord Li Zicheng, who had already taken Beijing, causing the last Ming emperor to hang himself. Once through the wall, Manchu regiments defeated or bribed many into submission. Millions more were drawn to Manchu service. Even so, all resistance was not overcome for fully 17 years: banner campaigns against the Ming princes lasted from 1644 to 1661. The last Ming prince sought refuge in Burma, where his retainers were slaughtered and he and his family were kept prisoner by the king. They were handed over to Wu Sangui, who invaded Burma in 1661, and strangled to death.

The new dynasty that slowly secured its grip on China was alien, a Jürchen (renamed Manchu) dynasty that called itself Qing (Pure or Clear). It would last to 1912. After 1644 Manchu emperors governed from Beijing. While preserving their "racial" separation from the *Han*, immediately in 1644 the Qing ordered all Chinese males (only Muslims were exempt) to shave their foreheads and grow the distinctive Manchu battle queue, upon pain of execution; this decree was withdrawn for civilians but was kept for Chinese troops serving under Qing banners. Then in 1645, the decree was reinstated for all Chinese males. Over succeeding centuries, cutting the Manchu queue, the central symbol of alien rule, was often the first act of open rebellion by Han Chinese. In 1673 the Three Feudatories of south China (provinces governed by Chinese collaborators, including the now double-traitor, Wu Sangui) rebelled. Despite his tender years, the *Kangxi* (K'ang-hsi) emperor (1661–1722) sent his generals to brutally subjugate the southern rebellion (War of the Three Feudatories, 1673–1681). At the same time he himself struck north to complete more Manchu conquests, in which he overran Mongolia and secured China's frontier with Russia in the *Treaty of Nerchinsk*. He also added Taiwan to China's holdings (1683) and intervened militarily in Tibet (1720). To hold such a vast empire, the minority Qing inducted large numbers of Chinese (and others) into new regiments in the banner system. Kangxi named no heir, leading to the troubled reign of Yongzheng (r. 1723–1735), considered by many at the time to be a usurper. From 1726 to 1735, Yongzheng prosecuted a major campaign against the Zunghars of western China. Even while issuing edicts to legally free oppressed occupations and minority ethnic groups, he engaged in severe religious persecution and executed *opium* dealers. Kangxi's grandson, the *Qianlong* (Ch'ien-lung) emperor (1736–1796), made Tibet a *protectorate* and pushed into Turkestan. At the same time, Qianlong rebuffed the *Macartney mission* from Britain. His diplomatic rebuff to the British was not immediately consequential, however, because the *Napoleonic Wars* distracted all European nations from Asian affairs until after 1815.

Qing China suffered from continuing growth in population (to about 300 million by the 1790s) without a corresponding increase in agricultural or industrial productivity. This contributed to immiseration of the peasantry, repeated famine and attendant religious millenarianism, and mass rebellion, beginning in the 1780s and continuing through much of the nineteenth century. The Qing repressed the major *White Lotus Rebellion* (1796–1804) but faced more uprisings among western Muslims (1821–1835) and indigenous Miao tribesmen. Nor were Qing emperors able to fend off foreign influence. They rejected two early *East India Company* diplomatic and trade missions (1793 and 1816) but were forced open to the outer world after humiliation in the *Opium Wars* (1839–1842 and 1856–1860), which led to acceptance of the *unequal treaties*. For a quarter century after 1850 the Qing lost effective control of large parts of China to four separate rebellions. The largest and most destructive of these was the *Taiping Rebellion* (1850–1864), which was put down only by surrendering central power to regional gentry and local militia. Muslims also rebelled in several areas in the west and south (1855–1873), and the *Nian Rebellion* (1851–1868) directly threatened the dynasty. In the 1860s the Qing (Tongzhi) Restoration was approved by *Dowager Empress Cixi*. It sought to resist the *treaty system* and reform the dynasty through partial Sinification and "self-strengthening." By 1873 the countryside was at last pacified, though at a price of the loss of some 60 million people in under

25 years, and China appeared to be modernizing, if only slowly. Any progress was interrupted, however, by the disaster of the *Sino-Japanese War* (1894–1895). The Dowager Empress made a final attempt to expel the hated foreigners in the *Boxer Rebellion*, but when that too failed it became clear not only that fundamental reform was inescapable, but also that the Qing were largely incapable of it.

In any case, the Qing would not be permitted by Chinese nationalists—who increasingly saw them as a foreign, "Manchu" dynasty—to carry out reforms that would keep them in power. Although the Qing in fact sought to modernize the army and build a national *railway* system, they were increasingly seen by nationalists to be merely seeking to hold on to power and to be willing to appease foreigners to do so. The Chinese as a whole were now prepared to fight for their national independence. After a few years of failed and frustrated reform, the Qing dynasty—in the person of the last Qing emperor, the child *Pu Yi*—was cast aside as archaic and irrelevant by the *Young Turks* of the nationalist movement. When the military mutinied in 1911, the regency abdicated. That signaled the start of the *Chinese Revolution* of 1911. Next came military dictatorship, warlordism, a bitter and protracted civil war, foreign invasion, and the extraordinary disasters that flowed from the *Chinese Revolution* of 1949. That amounted to three-quarters of a century of human catastrophe and suffering on a scale so vast it remains essentially ineffable.

Suggested Readings: Jacques Gernet, *China and the Christian Impact* (1985); Immanuel Hsu, *Rise of Modern China*, 4th ed. (1990); Evelyn Rawski, *The Last Emperors* (1999); Jonathan Spence, *The Search for Modern China* (1990); Jonathan Spence, *Treason by the Book* (2001).

Qin state (221–206 B.C.E.). Qin emerged from the *Warring States* period as the sole surviving state, and as the unifier of China. It was strategically located on the western frontier and benefited greatly from its reformed bureaucracy. It made effective use of *cavalry*, adapted from the nomad tribes of *Inner Asia*, and of massed *infantry* rather than traditional Chinese chariots to push back the Rong and Di in the north and west and to climb the greasy pole of regional dominance during the Warring States. The last Qin king, Yin Zheng (259–210 B.C.E.), became China's First Emperor, Qin Shi Huang, in 221 B.C.E. He built roads, canals, and other public works; reformed the bureaucracy and the military; imposed central rule on China by bashing down the fortified defenses of rival potentates among the aristocracy; and in general ruled ruthlessly and cruelly. He is reputed to have murdered hundreds of *Confucian* scholars and burned libraries of books recording history unfavorable to the Qin state, and he is known to have slaughtered tens of thousands who opposed him. He also spent much energy and resources searching for an elixir to give himself eternal life. He constructed walled fortifications on China's northern frontier (which were added to by later dynasties), but contrary to popular belief he did not construct the *Great Wall*, most of which is *Ming* construction. His tomb at Xi'an was unearthed in 1974, astonishing the world with its sculpted army of nearly 10,000 life-size terra cotta soldiers, but also revealing the bones of the workers who were slaughtered upon its completion in order to keep its secret. Qin was succeeded four years after his death by the first *Han* ruler. It was highly illustrative of the character of *Mao Zedong* and many in the Chinese *Communist Party* (CCP) during the *Great Proletarian Cultural Revolution* that, during the mass campaign against Confucianism, propagandists for the CCP wrote tomes arguing that Qin had no choice but to burn the Confucian books, and even the scholars, as this was essential to his political goals.

Quadaffi, Muammar (b. 1942). Libyan dictator. An admirer of *Nasser*, Quadaffi led the 1969 coup that overthrew the Libyan monarchy. Some analysts questioned his mental stability, but he was astute enough to cling to power most of his adult life. Domestically, he tried to develop and implement an administrative system of leftist, politicized *Islam* based on a personal epiphany about how to blend Islam with *popular sovereignty, capitalism,* and *socialism,* which he laid out in a "Green Book." He used Libya's *oil* wealth to elevate his own international profile far beyond Libya's (or his) real geopolitical importance, not least by supporting *terrorism* against several countries, including Britain and the United States. In the 1970s he was behind several assassination attempts against other Arab leaders, including *Anwar Sadat* of Egypt and King Hassan of Morocco. Quadaffi's persistent attempt to reassert ancient *Tripolitan* claims to dominance in the *sudanic* region of the lower Sahara led to clashes with most of Libya's neighbors, including Chad, Egypt, Morocco, Sudan, and Tunisia. He aided the coup plotters who ousted Nimieri in Sudan in 1975, but most of his other stratagems came to naught.

Among Quadaffi's major setbacks were sending troops to aid *Idi Amin* against Tanzania in 1979; losing the *Chad-Libya War;* losing the *Auzou strip,* first militarily then under ruling of the *International Court of Justice;* and repeated failure to construct a *pan-Arab* federation in North Africa. He perennially sought to acquire *chemical, nuclear,* and other *weapons of mass destruction.* Quadaffi was accused by the *Reagan* administration of sponsoring terrorist attacks. On April 15, 1986, the United States bombed Libyan military installations and Quadaffi's personal living quarters in *retaliation,* during which his young adopted daughter was killed in error. After the raid, he was far less active abroad. During the *Gulf War,* for instance, Quadaffi gave merely rhetorical support to Iraq. In 1999 he at last agreed to permit two intelligence officers accused of the Lockerbie (Pan Am) airliner bombing to stand trial at The Hague. He also pledged not to sponsor terrorists and in general sought rapprochement with Western states. During the 1990s Quadaffi authorized $25 billion to build 2,000 miles of interconnecting tunnels. He claimed these were for irrigation, but given their size and direction—four meters diameter and reaching almost to Sudan and Chad in the south and to Tunisia and

Egypt in the west and east, with underground storage and warehouses at various points—they appeared designed to conceal and carry military vehicles, on the model of North Korea's military tunnels under its border with South Korea. See also *line of death; Gulf of Sidra.*

Quadrilateral. A system of Austrian fortifications in north Italy based on the towns of Legnano, Mantua, Peschiera, and Verona. It was designed to hold French power back from the peninsula. It figured prominently in the *Napoleonic Wars*, in the *revolutions of 1848*, and the French war in 1859. It became strategically irrelevant with the unification of Italy in 1861.

Quadruple Alliance. Also called the Grand Alliance. (1) The powers which defeated France, 1813–1815, namely, Austria, Britain, Prussia, and Russia (along with minor German, Italian, Iberian, and Nordic allies). (2) The alliance of the four main victors of the *Napoleonic Wars* (Austria, Britain, Prussia, and Russia), dating from November 20, 1815 (Second Treaty of Paris), a revised compact made in the wake of the *Hundred Days*. Its purpose was to maintain the terms of the settlement imposed on France. It survived for some 20 years. Note: This alliance should not be confused with the *Holy Alliance*. *See also Congress System; Quintuple Alliance.*

quagmire. A metaphor dating to U.S. engagement in the *Vietnam War*, 1964–1973, used as shorthand for unanticipated entanglement in a prolonged military conflict which distracts from the nation's larger foreign policy purposes, drains financial and military resources, and badly divides domestic *public opinion.* As such, it is probably the single most overused and abused cliché in contemporary journalism and instant academic punditry, where it is almost always accompanied by a baritone warning against being drawn into "another Vietnam." It was so applied, with some merit, to the similar Soviet experience in the *Afghan-Soviet War*, but ever after it has been trotted out by Cassandras—in government as well as without—to warn against taking action in virtually any circumstance where the use of force was being contemplated by the United States. Yet as early as the start of the 1980s it was already a hoary chestnut that ignored the special circumstances of Vietnam, where the enemy was bordered and massively supplied by two major powers (China and the Soviet Union) and the United States never invaded its home territory. In fact, in virtually every significant military conflict engaged in by the United States since the Vietnam War the use of force was precise, limited, of short duration, and highly effective. *See also Afghanistan; Granada; Gulf War; Kosovo; Panama; September 11, 2001, terrorist attack on the United States.*

Quai d'Orsay. A common reference to the French foreign ministry, from its site on the south bank of the Seine. *See also Foggy Bottom; Forbidden City; Kremlin; Sublime Porte; Whitehall; White House.*

Quaker gun. A sham gun so emplaced as to fool the enemy into thinking the defensive strength of a *fortification* or ship is greater than it is in fact; coined in open mockery of the renowned *pacifism* of Quakers.

qualified majority voting. In the *European Community* the *unanimity rule* applied until this form of *weighted voting* was introduced by the *Single European Act*. Under the qualified majority system, it took two large countries and one small one to block new single-market laws. In the *European Union* most votes thus were weighted so that on internal functions of the common market the four large states could not block propositions or rule changes by themselves; they needed three small states to join them to sustain an effective *veto* of 23 votes.

qualitative analysis. In *political science,* analysis that seeks to penetrate to the core nature or essence of events or phenomena, or their constituent parts, using eclectic methodologies and expressing conclusions as general principles or judgments. For example, "Based on a close reading of archival material, interviews, and public documents, it can be said that the main motives of the key participants in the crisis were. . . ." Such analyses are often accused of delivering up subjective judgments about what should be objective phenomena. However, their great strength is to incorporate the real role of accident, *volition,* and the subtext of human motivation and psychology into explanations of *economics, history,* or *politics.* Some qualitative analyses also happily use *quantitative* techniques, but usually only when it is clearly useful and appropriate, not out of a predilection to *scientism. See also behavioralism; post-behavioralism; rational choice theory; traditionalism.*

quantitative analysis. In political *science* approaches to international relations, analysis that seeks to assess the proportional weight of different causes of events or phenomena (*variables*), or their constituent parts, using statistical and other numerical devices and expressing conclusions in formulae and measurements. For instance, "$X(t)$ expenditures by nation X for conventional weapons in year t. $S_x(t)$ stock of conventional weapons at time t. This can be reduced to: $S_x(t) \ X(t) + S_x(t-1)$." [That is an actual quotation.] For some, this approach promises "scientific" (verifiable) conclusions and a predictive *model* of economic or political life that will allow social engineering on a grand scale. At its best, quantitative analysis may on occasion deliver precise conclusions. However, most often it does so about strictly limited and even trivial (but quantifiable) issues, which are far less important than the humanistic elements in international relations that are the primary cause (determinant, or variable) in the course and shape of most public events. The concept is also subject to gross misapplication to real-world events, in which it utterly misconceives a given subject matter in a strained search for a *rational choice* model of human behavior. As if convoluted causality and ahistorical argument was not awful enough, the inherent obscurity of much quantitative analysis and language renders it of little or no use to real-world policymakers and makes it impenetrable by most students and fellow researchers. Lastly, claims to a rapier-like methodology are frequently blunted in the application, leading to spurious or specious conclusions delivered in language so *obscurantist* as to remove the offending analysis, and researcher, beyond normal political discourse (or criticism, which may be the whole point in terms of academic careerism). At its worst, quantitative analysis tends to reduce the richness of political behavior and issues of complex *causation* to reductio ad absurdum formulae. *See also behavioralism; classical school; events data analysis; jargon; Robert S. McNamara; outliers; post-behavioralism; qualitative analysis; traditionalism.*

quarantine. (1) Confinement of persons, animals, or plants infected with communicable diseases in order to contain any spread of infection and prevent consequent harm to persons, livestock, or crops. This prudential practice was traditionally governed under *international customary law*, which suggested detaining diseased ships at anchor and distant from all other ships for 40 days. A 1959 convention updated the practice to account for civilian air travel. (2) A merely rhetorical policy of *Franklin Roosevelt*, announced in 1937, in which he proposed to "quarantine" arms sales to the *fascist* states. (3) A variant of *blockade*, invented by the United States during the *Cuban Missile Crisis* to permit interception of Soviet ships bearing missiles to Cuba. It fell somewhere between a pacific blockade and a hostile, or belligerent blockade. That is, it did not reflect a direct intention to perform *acts of war*, but neither did it exempt third-party ships from *visit and search*. *See also* cordon sanitaire; war contagion.

quarantine flag. A yellow flag flown to signal that a ship is under medical quarantine because it is carrying diseases communicable to humans, or that the ship has insects or plant diseases on board that might infect a port country's agricultural production or forestry.

quarter. Mercy, in the form of a refusal to fire on or kill a defeated enemy who is attempting to *surrender* or has already done so. This is a basic expectation of the *just war tradition* and the *laws of war*. However, there are permitted exceptions in both theory and law: (1) when no quarter is offered by an enemy, none need be given either; (2) one is not required to give quarter twice. Thus, if a foe fakes *surrender*, fire may be resumed and continued until the enemy position is utterly repressed (all defenders killed or *hors de combat*). *See also* guerre mortelle.

quasi delicts. International legal breaches that do not amount to *torts* but are analogous to such acts. *See also delict.*

quasi–international law. Legal relations in which an *object of international law* is treated on a factual footing with a *subject*, but where the ultimate *jurisdiction* is *municipal law*, as in private bank loans to a foreign government.

quasi states. The idea that weak states, particularly in Africa, are at times sustained not by the old structures of "positive sovereignty," as generally applied in the *Westphalian* system, but by *international law* and *international morality*. Although such states lack some or all of the empirical (*de facto*) aspects of *sovereignty*, they are buttressed by "negative sovereignty" (invented to accommodate rapid decolonization), which derives from, and is mainly sustained by, juridicial (*de jure*) and moral acceptance of their continued legal existence. *See also failed state.*

    Suggested Reading: Robert H. Jackson, *Quasi States* (1990).

Quasi War (1797–1800). In 1795, and then again from 1797 to 1800, France seized hundreds of U.S. vessels trading in the West Indies, a policy related mainly to France's ongoing conflict with England in the *Napoleonic Wars*. The United States retaliated in kind, although its naval resources were meager. Neither side *declared war*, though more radical *Federalists* wanted to do so. The *Directory* in France responded to the election of *John Adams* by raising the stakes close to war. The crisis worsened with the *XYZ Affair. Talleyrand*, who saw no advantage to France in a wider war with distant America, finally facilitated settlement.

Québec. For its pre-1960s history see *Canada; Lower Canada; New France.* Québec is the second largest (after Ontario) and the second most populous province of Canada. In the 1960s agitation among its predominantly *Francophone* population began, seeking broad government promotion of the French language. As the movement spread beyond artistic and intellectual communities it developed a broad nationalist attraction. Reforms were legislated in what became known as the Quiet Revolution. Things turned briefly violent by 1970, with *terrorist* bombings and political kidnappings (and one murder) by the extremist *Front de Liberation du Québec* (FLQ). Prime Minister *Trudeau* responded with *martial law* (the War Measures Act), shocking most Canadian and international opinion. The mainstream of the nationalist movement rejected violence, turning instead to the *Parti Québecois* (PQ). It won a majority in 1976 but lost a *referendum* on *secession* (or *separatism*) in 1980. From 1980 to 1992 efforts focused on entrenching legal changes that gave preference to the French language even in some private affairs of non–French speakers and set up a linguistic monopoly in all public affairs. Federally, efforts were made to revise the constitution to make it acceptable to Québec without alienating other provinces, mainly by devolving powers to all of them. In 1992 these efforts came to naught: in a national *referendum* a majority of all citizens in a majority of the provinces, including Québec, rejected the compromise constitution devised by the politicians. A referendum on sovereignty in Québec alone in 1999 fell just shy of majority approval.

Queen Anne's War (1702–1713). The North American extension of the much larger and more important conflict in Europe, the *War of the Spanish Succession*. That wider war between England and France, then under *Louis XIV*, was joined by American colonists and English *regulars*, who fought French regulars, *Québec* colonists, and France's Spanish and Indian allies. The French invaded New England, an action notable mainly for a massacre of the citizens of Deerfield, Massachusetts (1704). As in *King William's War*, American colonists from the northern colonies responded with angry demands to invade Québec, while southerners wanted to attack south and west into French holdings in the Floridas and across the Mississippi. An invasion of Québec failed, but *Acadia* was taken. In the *Treaty of Utrecht* (1713) the British gained permanent control of Acadia and the *Hudson's Bay* territory, as well as French recognition of British control of *Newfoundland*. That loss of strategic territory so emasculated *New France* geostrategically that it appeared to be only a matter of time until French power in North America was extinguished by Britain. Other wars followed, notably *King George's War* and the *French and Indian War*, which saw the final acts in a century-long drama for control of *New France*.

Quemoy and Matsu crises (1953–1954, 1958). "Crises of the Taiwan (Formosa) Strait." Quemoy (Jinmen) and Matsu are the main islands of an offshore group retained by the *Nationalists* after their evacuation to Taiwan. The People's Republic of China (PRC) was repulsed in its effort to take Quemoy in October 1949. In 1953–1954 the PRC heavily shelled the islands, from which Nationalists had launched several *commando* and air raids against China's coastal installations. That led to a U.S.-Taiwan defense pact in December 1954. Undeterred, China retook some minor islands in the group in January 1955 but stopped short of attacking Quemoy or Matsu. A second crisis over possession erupted when China began shelling again on August 23, 1958. It was resolved when *Eisenhower* threw a naval screen around the islands and made clear that the Republic of China (ROC, Taiwan) had full U.S. backing. *Mao* probably never intended an invasion. More likely, he saw these island outposts as a locale where he could apply pressure on Taiwan and the United States at will, rather as *Khrushchev* was then doing in *Berlin*. The Soviet failure to support China to the hilt during the crisis further disillusioned Mao about Moscow's leadership role in the *Communist* world, whereas to the Soviets Mao was seen as dangerously reckless. This contributed to the *Sino-Soviet split*. Note: in 2001 the ROC and PRC agreed to permit limited direct travel and trade between the PRC and Quemoy and Matsu.

qui desiderat pacem, praeparet bellum. "Whosoever wants *peace* should prepare for *war*." Flavius Vegetius Renatus, c. 375 C.E. This is the main principle underlying all *deterrence*. Compare Aristotle, "We make war that we may live in peace." "Nicomachean Ethics," Book I, Ch. 7. *See also disarmament.*

quieta non movere. "Do not disturb settled affairs." A legal maxim suggesting that one should let lie sleeping international *disputes*.

quiet diplomacy. Using direct, government-to-government channels of communication when making an appeal or *diplomatic protest* or when pressing for better *human rights* treatment of another nation's citizens, rather than using open or public channels. This approach assumes that recalcitrant governments will respond better to criticism if they may do so behind the scenes, so that in public they save *face*; and it argues that interstate *negotiation* is most effective when not conducted in the glare of media attention and subjected to the pressures of aroused *public opinion*. It may therefore involve secret recourse to *mediation*, *good offices*, or the like. It is the preferred path of most governments when dealing with highly contentious and emotional issues. *See also open covenants.*

Quintuple Alliance. The *Quadruple Alliance* plus France, after its readmission to the *Great Power* club at *Aix-la-Chapelle*.

Quisling, Vidkun (1887–1945). Norwegian traitor. *Military attaché* in Russia, 1918–1919, and Finland, 1919–1921; minister of war, 1931–1933. Quisling worked under *Nansen* in Russia, 1922–1926. He conspired with *Hitler's* plans to invade Norway and subsequently headed a Nazi *puppet regime*, 1942–1945. Immediately after the war he was tried for *treason* and shot (October 1945). His name thereafter entered many languages as a synonym for treachery and betrayal. In English it rivals that of *Benedict Arnold. See also Pierre Laval;* Uštaše; *Vichy; Wang Jingwei.*

Quito. The colonial-era name of Ecuador.

quota. A type of *nontariff barrier*. There are two main types: (1) *Import quota*, a blanket limit to the total amount of an import permitted in a specified period. (2) *Tariff* quota, a specified amount of imports are permitted in at one price, and subsequent volumes are subjected to higher tariff rates. *See also Cod Wars; GATT; voluntary export agreements (VERs).*

R

Rabin, Yitzhak (1922–1995). Israeli statesman. Chief of staff, 1964–1968; ambassador to Washington, 1968–1973; prime minister, 1974–1977, 1992–1995. Rabin joined the *Haganah* and fought in the *First Arab-Israeli War* as commander of an elite strike force near *Jerusalem*, where he was born. He remained in the military but did not see action during the *Second Arab-Israeli War* (1956). He served as chief of staff, 1964–1968, including during the *Third Arab-Israeli War* (1967). In 1984 he oversaw Israel's partial withdrawal from its politically disastrous intervention in Lebanon and definition of a unilateral "security zone" in south Lebanon manned by local Christian militia allied with Israel. Rabin long opposed efforts to trade part of the *West Bank* for a peace settlement with Palestinians. Yet in September 1993, he agreed to do just that after secret *back-channel* talks in Norway with the *PLO*. He was awarded the 1994 *Nobel Prize* for Peace jointly with *Yasser Arafat* and *Shimon Peres*. On November 4th, 1995, he was assassinated by a *radical* Jewish nationalist, an act of native-born *terrorism* which stunned Israel.

"race to the sea" (August–September 1914). After the *Battle of the Frontiers* the *British Expeditionary Force (BEF)* and the French Army began a fighting retreat against advancing Germans. However, after an Allied counterattack (*First Battle of the Marne*) the German Army broke off its effort to carry out the *Schlieffen Plan* and instead dug in and began to fortify along the line of the Marne and Aisne. There were as yet no troops between the Aisne and the sea, except a Belgian redoubt at Antwerp. The "race for the coast" which followed was actually a succession of efforts by each side to flank the other. This serpentine maneuvering ended when the Germans took Antwerp, and its Belgian garrison retreated to positions along the Allied line. Full-blown *trench warfare* then commenced, as all armies dug in for what became a brutal war of *attrition*.

rachat. The purchase of domestic *slaves* for use in military formations. It was an ancient practice among slave empires such as the *Mamluks* in Egypt. The French used this system to swell the ranks of the *Tirailleurs Sénégalais*. The British also used it in their West African recruitment.

racism (in international relations). "Race" is a highly contentious, dubious, essentially unscientific categorization of groups of people based on observable differences in superficial facial or other surface features, such as pigmentation levels, which evolved over prehistoric millennia as minor adaptive responses to local environmental conditions by isolated populations. Nonetheless, economic, political, or social discrimination against individuals or groups based on their race—or, more broadly, their ethnicity or *tribe*—has been a frequent, woeful, and baleful occurrence in human history. Discrimination based on race has also frequently correlated with class discrimination: as manual labor came to be seen as degrading by ruling *elites* in different societies at various times, it often took on class and racial overtones. This was especially marked where conquering peoples depended on the slave, indentured, or otherwise exploited labor of the conquered—which was virtually everywhere before the eighteenth century. Thus, racially based social and economic differentiation occurred in south India and precolonial Africa centuries, indeed millennia, before the arrival of Arab or European conquerors, undergirding and partly shaping the *caste system* in the former and sustaining vast, slave-based empires (such as *Mali, Songhay, Sudan,* or that of the *Tuareg* of the deep desert) in the latter. Race-based *slavery* developed a new coloration for *New World* Indians after 1500 under the Spanish and Portuguese, but it had existed on a tribal basis for centuries before that, with cannibalism and human sacrifice (as in the *Aztec Empire*) sometimes as further horrors added to the lives of defeated peoples. Race slavery subsequently spread everywhere in the Americas where the *encomienda system* was applied, or later, where black slaves were put to work as chattel labor. On a lesser scale, racism coupled with inequitable labor conditions and pay characterized life for Chinese "coolie" laborers in the United States and Canada, and the deeply abused *Roma* in Rumania (where it was combined with slavery) and elsewhere in eastern Europe in lands that broke free of the *Ottoman Empire* in the nineteenth century. And it was standard fare for ethnic or linguistic minorities in many countries in the twentieth century in lands too numerous to list.

Often lurking just beneath the surface of interstate relations, racial tension only recently intruded into diplomatic relations in legal if not historical terms. Until the nineteenth century, naked exploitation and mistreatment of distinctive populations was ubiquitous, and so on both pragmatic and *Westpha-*

lian legal grounds it was considered by most states to be a matter of *internal affairs* on which they would neither comment nor act. A new view—which in extremis argued for and permitted *sanctions* aimed at coercing changes in internal state behavior, or even *armed humanitarian intervention*—took shape starting with the nineteenth-century campaign to end the *slave trade* and then to abolish slavery as an institution. Concern for race in international relations often commingled with *religion* in the latter nineteenth century, as a real rather than theorized *clash of civilizations* brought to the forefront issues such as mistreatment of *Christians* and foreign *missionaries* in Japan and China, persecution of distinct nationalities and religious minorities within the decaying Ottoman Empire, and *pogroms* and other mistreatment of *Jews* within Tsarist Russia. *The Indian Mutiny* marked a decisive turning point in the history of the *British Empire*, and *colonialism* in general, by greatly raising not only cultural and racial tensions but also awareness on the subcontinent. Spurious notions of *social Darwinism* now mingled with self-deluding myths of "*manifest destiny*," or the "*white man's burden*," or "*la mission civilisatrice*," or some other sense of putative *mission*, to racialize thinking about geopolitics and empire. At the same time, largely ignored by the European powers were numerous and often severe abuses against native populations within their various empires, while American protests about mistreatment of Jews in Russia or Christians in Japan were met with derisive notation of the annual number of lynchings of blacks in southern states. An important exception to this neglect of European transgressions was King Leopold II's appalling record in the *Congo*, which reached *genocidal* proportions in its effects and culminated in an unusual (and in many quarters, notably German, also humbug) international outcry and campaign against his continued personal rule there. The Belgian government interceded in 1908, ending the worst atrocities of the *concessionaire companies* but far from ending all abuses derived from a system of raw racial hierarchy and exploitation. Meanwhile, in *German Southwest Africa* the *Herero-Nama War* (1904–1907) had been prosecuted to a genocidal conclusion.

Japan's surprising defeat of Russia in the *Russo-Japanese War* (1904–1905) shattered myths of white racial superiority, stunning Europe and many of its nonwhite possessions into thinking hitherto forbidden thoughts about the possible end of imperial-colonial relations. American (and Canadian) *Oriental exclusion laws* in the first half of the twentieth century were a significant irritant in relations with Japan before *World War I* and again during the interwar years. Meanwhile, Japan's own severe exploitation of Koreans after 1910 damaged its reputation, as did its massacre of thousands of Koreans in 1919. That alerted the Chinese and other Asian peoples to Tokyo's intended threat to their national development. It also left a lasting and bitter residue in Japan's relations with Korea, which was only exacerbated by several more decades of gross exploitation and then post-1945 discrimination against ethnic Koreans born and living in Japan, where their forebears had been brought as sex slaves or forced laborers. Hypocrisy is an equal-opportunity vice, however, and so it was Japan which formally raised the issue of racial equality at the international plane as a diplomatic issue at the *Paris Peace Conference* (1919–1920). Japan failed to gather interest or support beyond the handful of non-European delegations that were present, and the initiative was actively opposed by *Woodrow Wilson* and several of the *White Dominions* of the British Empire.

The interwar years witnessed some effort to organize for a more positive agenda on a "racial basis," as in the competing ideas of *pan-Africanism* and *négritude*, which convulsed elite opinion among (and led to a half-century of international conferencing by) predominantly black leaders, many of whom later led their colonies to nationhood. Then the world experienced its darkest hours of racist barbarism during *World War II*. That conflict cannot be properly understood if it is forgotten that, as well as being a mortal combat among the *Great Powers* fought with the full capabilities of modern industrialized nations, it also took on the character of a genocidal race war in Eastern Europe after 1941, where Germany attempted the industrialized slaughter of unarmed peoples. Racial animosity also infused fighting in China and the Pacific theater, in particular concerning mistreatment of *prisoners of war*, brutal *reprisals* taken against populations of occupied nations, and *biological warfare* by Japan which included lethal targeting of children with infected candies. Meanwhile, inside the Soviet Union *Stalin* internally deported entire populations—Tartars, "Volga Germans," Koreans from Sakhalin Island, and others—to Siberian or Central Asian exile or destruction solely based on "suspect" ethnicity. Far less brutally, but racially motivated and damaging nonetheless, Americans and Canadians *interned* their ethnically Japanese citizens for most of the war.

After World War II, *decolonization* of Asia and Africa took on immediate and deep overtones of racial tension and frenetic violence, as in the vicious Dutch war in Indonesia, France's return to *French Indochina*, and the British response to the *Mau Mau* rising in Kenya. Nor were Great Powers immune from such tensions: Chinese-Soviet relations leading to the *Sino-Soviet split* were marked by racial grievances and animosities, as well as by ideological disagreement. Overall, however, international concern to end racial violence and discrimination, and identification of racism as a *human rights* issue of legitimate and permanent interstate concern, accelerated after 1945. This legal and normative development was spurred by revelations of the full horrors of the *Holocaust* and of Japanese atrocities in the Pacific theater, and burgeoning issues of rapid decolonization and national *self-determination*. Racism became of increasing international diplomatic and rhetorical concern in interstate relations once a non-Western majority dominated membership of the *United Nations General Assembly*, c. 1965. This group demanded that regular attention be paid to the racial aspects of decolonization struggles, notably in *Rhodesia, South Africa*, and several territories of the Portuguese Empire, where *guerrilla* campaigns were underway. Shamefully, it also forced through a contentious resolution identifying *Zionism* as a form of racism. After sharp Western objection and bitter and angry debate, this was retracted some years later.

In other areas, too, once again hypocrisy competed with genuine concern among states on the issue of racism, as the same automatic majority which condemned *apartheid* or the *Unilateral Declaration of Independence (UDI)* remained silent on discrimination by one of their own, such as Malaysian and Vietnamese persecution of discrete communities of *overseas Chinese*, or *Idi Amin*'s rough expulsion of Uganda's Asians. Nevertheless, the sense of absolute *sovereignty* on matters of race began to break down as concern for, and a growing consensus about, basic human rights as a legitimate area of foreign policy interest slowly developed among the democratic nations. Liberal states, supported by the Third World majority in the General Assembly, elevated this concern to the level of a governing international *norm* in the second half of the twentieth century, starting with inclusion of respect for human rights in the *United Nations Charter* as a basic obligation of UN membership. This new norm held that fundamental human rights, ultimately including a right to be free from racial discrimination, were in fact *cosmopolitan* principles that underpin *international security* relations in the longer term. In 2001 this rhetorical consensus was affirmed at the World Conference Against Racism, held in Durban, South Africa, but then the usual political poison was added by singling out Israel alone among nations for direct condemnation, along with an effort to revive miscategorization of Zionism as a form of racism.

In sum, by the start of the twenty-first century racism was identified in international law and interstate relations as an unforgivable sin, and one that might call forth concerted multilateral action to bring about its end, even if from time to time the issue was invoked more as a propaganda club than with sincere intent. On the other hand, whatever the legal and rhetorical promises, racism had not been eradicated in fact from the corrupt hearts of men and women, of all races, the world over. *See also Aborigines; Ainu; anti-Semitism; assimilation; Armenian genocide; black legend; boat people; Bosnia; Boxer Rebellion; Burundi; California; Cambodia-Vietnam War; colons; Houston Chamberlain; Creoles; cultural imperialism; Cyprus; Dumbarton Oaks; East Timor; Ethiopian-Eritrean War; ethnic cleansing; fascism; Fiji; Franz Fanon; Geopolitik; Guyana; Adolf Hitler; imperialism; Indian Wars; Kosovo; Lebensraum; Minorities Treaties; Benito Mussolini; Nanjing, rape of; National Socialism; New Left; New Order; Friedrich Nietzsche; Nigerian Civil War; Paris Peace Conference; positivism; power-sharing; Cecil Rhodes; Russification; Rwanda; tribalism; "untouchability"; white slavery; "yellow peril"; Zimbabwe.*

Suggested Reading: Paul G. Lauren, *Power and Prejudice* (1988, 1996).

radiation effects. The immediate, as well as lingering, lethality and physical harm caused by the flash (blindness) and a range of other radiation released in a nuclear explosion. Radiation sickness is typified by extreme nausea, vomiting, cramps, bloody diarrhea, and so forth. Later, genetic mutations and cancers are also common. *See also blast effects; fallout; neutron bomb; radiological weapons.*

radical. Concerned with fundamental, even revolutionary change, which goes to the "root" of public affairs. Note: Although this may occur at either end of the political spectrum, in *Cold War* discourse "radical" was reserved to the far left. In the People's Republic of China (PRC) "radical line" was the term used by the *Gang of Four* to indicate a policy of cleaving to the peasant communes established for the peasantry during the *Great Leap Forward*, and expanded to the factories and even the bureaucracy during the *Great Proletarian Cultural Revolution*. *See also reaction.*

radio. The invention of radio revolutionized naval command at sea, from about 20 miles maximum using *flag* signals to several thousand miles by *World War II*, to globally today. This helped make modern navies a highly flexible instrument of national policy. A similar improvement in communications on land came much later. In land warfare radio was first extensively and effectively used by the *Wehrmacht*, which tied its *armor* and air cover together by radio as an integral aspect of the tactic of *combined arms* and *Blitzkrieg*. The British did this first, at *Cambrai* in 1917, but having won the Great War had less incentive than did the losing Germans to develop the technique further. Radio similarly made it possible for aircraft to fight as larger units, under a single command, rather than individually. The first international effort to regulate radio came in 1906, with founding of the International Radiotelegraph Union. A conference in 1927 set the rules whereby civilian radio broadcasters ever after were required to obtain licenses from national authorities, regulations were set on the use of commercial and ham frequencies, and certain frequencies were reserved for emergency and navigational communications. In 1932 radio and other telecommunications were brought under the regulatory authority of the *International Telecommunications Union (ITU)*. The ITU made rules against jamming legal broadcasts, *piracy*, and related matters. A major supplementary convention on telecommunications came into effect in 1982.

Radio Free Europe. A CIA-funded, though technically private, broadcast service set up during the *Cold War* to send news and other programming into the censored countries of the *Soviet bloc* in various languages. Accused by Moscow of carrying merely Western *propaganda*, but listened to by many millions anyway, its signal was jammed until the presidency of *Mikhail Gorbachev*. A parallel service was Radio Liberty. And for Cuban listeners, the United States maintained Radio Marti into the twenty-first century.

radiological weapons. Nonexplosive *nuclear weapons* which emit high levels of harmful radiation to *poison* people, and/or render useless other targets by making them radioactive. Armor-piercing shells tipped with depleted *uranium* are not radiological weapons. In their case, minor levels of radiation attending the spent shell and pieces of its exploded target is a side-effect of its penetrating power (uranium is a denser metal than steel, which is why it is used to penetrate heavy *armor*) not its main, intended effect. *See also dirty bombs; radiation effects.*

Rafsanjani, Ali Akbar Hashemi (b. 1934). Iranian statesman; deputy speaker of the *Majlis*, 1980–1989; head of the armed forces, 1988–1989; president, 1989–1997. He was the moderate leader the *Reagan* administration thought it could deal with in *Iran-Contra*. Although he manifested more pragmatism than his predecessors, either from conviction or necessity he also bent to pressures from *fundamentalists* and *xenophobic* nationalists. He publicly condemned the introduction of Western troops into the region during the *Gulf War*, but he privately welcomed the destruction of Iraqi military capability. While seeking domestic liberalization in several areas, he toed a harder line on symbolic policies, including refusing to lift the *Ayatollah Khomeini's* infamous fatwa (edict) calling for the faithful to murder *Salman Rushdie*.

Rahman, Sheikh Mujibur (1920–1975). Prime minister of Bangladesh, 1972–1975; president, 1975. He led the Awami League's bid for independence for *East Pakistan*. After winning an overwhelming victory in the 1970 election he called for independence for *Bangladesh* but was soon arrested. That occasioned riots and West Pakistani military *intervention*, which sparked the *Third Indo-Pakistani War*. Rahman then set an unfortunate precedent for the country's future by governing as a dictator. He was assassinated in 1975 by elements of the army.

railways. The "Age of Railways" as the literal locomotive of *industrialization* began in Great Britain in 1825. By 1830 the first commercial line was open, and by the middle of the nineteenth century Britain was crisscrossed by rails. Belgium followed suit, then France, Switzerland, the Netherlands, and Germany. *Bismarck* and the German high command poured funds into railways and drew up *mobilization* plans to make full use of them. They speeded troop deployments; erased the ancient problem of wartime *logistics*, which had reached spectacular levels in the *retreat from Moscow*; kept reinforcements fresh; and permitted harnessing of the whole national economy to the war effort.

Railways first demonstrated this *revolution in military affairs* during France's 1859 war with Austria in Italy, then again in the *American Civil War*, the *Seven Weeks' War*, and the *Franco-Prussian War*. Latin Americans and Turks also began serious building in the second half of the nineteenth century. The

British ruled India and South Africa, and much else besides, from the network of railways they built after midcentury to connect colonial garrisons, and along which they conducted and guarded imperial trade. In the last quarter of the century the *scramble for Africa* was facilitated by railways which bypassed the absence of navigable rivers and opened the interior to commercial exploitation. Concern that Germany might build a line to Baghdad importantly influenced British policy in the Middle East before 1914.

The United States outstripped all other powers in railway construction in the later nineteenth century, spanning the continent several times by the 1890s and tying its vast *hinterland* to a commercial and territorial empire which fully exploited the benefits of industrialization and the *agricultural revolution*. Canada was assembled as a new nation in 1867 on a commitment to build a transcontinental railway to cement and complete the promise of its national union; the Canadian Pacific Railway was completed in 1885. The tsars built railways deep into Siberia and Central Asia in a race against American, European, and later also Japanese builders eager to link China's cities and penetrate its interior. The Chinese at first viewed railways with *Confucian* disdain as disruptive of the natural harmonious order and traditional occupations, such as barge haulers on the *Grand Canal*. However, in the last days of the *Qing dynasty* China embarked on a railway-building campaign that was largely financed with foreign capital.

Europe's railways became a key feature of the *war plans* of all the major powers before *World War I*, and rail timetables importantly affected the *mobilization crisis* of July 1914. Conversely, Russia deliberately did not build railways in western Poland, which it expected to lose early in any war with Germany and Austria. In the event, all over Europe the same railways that had enabled nineteenth-century European civilization to make extraordinary advances carried millions of young men—and the *ancien régime* itself—to destruction. Railways were key to *Bolshevik* victory in the *Russian Civil War*. The Japanese assault on China during the *Second Sino-Japanese War* was launched along the inland railways. After 1945, Chinese *Communists* used the same tactic—fanning out from rail routes—to defeat the Nationalists. By the twenty-first century railways were less strategically important, but they remained major contributors to lower prices and economic development the world over. *See also Berlin–Baghdad railway; passport; Tukolor Empire.*

Suggested Readings: Denis Bishop and Keith Davis, *Railways and War*, 2 vols. (1972); Michal Freeman, *Railways and the Victorian Imagination* (1999); George Rogers, *The Transportation Revolution, 1815–1860* (1951); Dennis Showalter, *Railroads and Rifles* (1975).

Rainbow Warrior incident (1982). A *Greenpeace* vessel (the *Rainbow Warrior*) was sunk by French *intelligence* agents in Auckland Harbour in July 1982, killing one crew member. France hoped to prevent Greenpeace from protesting against *nuclear weapons* testing in the South Pacific. Arrest of the French agents led to a diplomatic quarrel with New Zealand, which convicted the agents but then agreed to allow them to serve sentences in French custody. After a token incarceration in France they were released, decorated, and resumed their careers. The incident heightened awareness of Greenpeace and provided it a martyr and focused critical attention on French atmospheric testing.

raison d'état. "For reason of state." A classical justification (*Romans* called it "public safety") for policies that must (or merely do) depart from accepted norms of moral conduct or look past mere *dynastic* or class interest, actually or ostensibly to promote the "public good" or *national interest*. The idea asserts that conventional moral categories should not apply to, and private interests—including those of the *sovereign*—should not be served by, the state. Three central claims form the core of the doctrine: (1) that statecraft is an autonomous realm in which distinct rules of moral judgment apply; (2) that the *vital interests* of the state, and their protection through the instrument of foreign policy, is supreme over the interests of civil society; and (3) that, as with the restraints of morality, the restrictions of legality must give way in times of need to the dictates of necessity. In sum, the idea of "reason of state" upholds a dual ethical standard which is more forgiving of the actions of states and of statesmen than of moral choices made by ordinary citizens, which thereby serves to justify forceful action against perceived foreign and domestic enemies of the state. It also advances a claim to autonomy by the state and weds this to the notion of the supremacy of the state's *vital interests* (security, independence, survival) over such values of domestic society as liberty or constitutionalism, and over weak international norms such as certain laws or prior treaties or agreements. Republicans have tended to see the doctrine as being closely associated with *despotism* and the more deleterious features of *power politics*, and with concentration of domestic power within centralized national institutions. Some proclaim that republics are a morally superior form of government because they supposedly do not permit a distinction between private and public virtue. *See also Machiavelli; realism; Armand Jean Richelieu.*

Rāj. "Royal Rule." (1) An ancient Indian kingship tradition. (2) The *British Empire* in India, some three-quarters under *direct rule* with another 700 *Princely States* paying obeisance to the *East India Company* and later, the British Crown. *See also India.*

Rajputs. From "rajaputra," or "son of a chief." A martial caste of *Hindu* warriors. They established themselves under local potentates in various locales, mainly in western India. Their precise origin is disputed. Some assert they arose from original clan/communal formations (traditionally, there were 36 Rajput clans) which climbed to local prominence through warfare and offering protection to the peasantry, to then found discrete states and kingdoms.

These histories ascribe to the Rajputs what they claimed for themselves: a vedic pedigree as the "first kshatiyas" in the *caste system*. Others argue they most probably descended from early Central Asian invaders of India (Hunas). If so, these early Central Asian peoples, and the small states they founded in western India, were subsequently Indianized and Hinduized and transmuted into Rajputs who laid claim to the vedic tradition, possibly with the aid of hired Brahman scribes. Certainly *untouchables* were drawn to the Rajputs, as military service was one method to rise within the caste system. Whether home-grown or imported, their states and chiefs strenuously resisted later Central Asian invasions of India by Turkic and *Muslim* peoples from the eighth to the thirteenth century. During those centuries the Rajputs successively, but ultimately unsuccessfully, fought invasions of north India, which they held into the tenth century, by the Ghaznavids, the Ghurids, the *Mamluks*, and the Khaljis, who took control of Delhi in 1290. Sultan Ala-ud-din (r. 1296–1316) for a time overran the Rajputs and thus was able to invade the even more ancient Tamil states to their south. Conflict with Muslim India continued for centuries. Sometimes it was horrific. In 1568, for example, when *Akbar* threatened to conquer their states, some Rajput warriors massacred their women rather than allow them to fall into Muslim hands. Meanwhile, some Rajputs allied with Akbar, who then practiced a policy of broad religious toleration. Any who still resisted were exterminated. Thus, Akbar reduced the Rajput city of Chitor and ordered the slaughter of 30,000 of its inhabitants. With the Muslim fanatic *Aurangzeb*, however, it was another matter. His restoration of the *jizya* and interference with *autonomous* Rajput territories proved intolerable. While he was tied down by war in Afghanistan, the Rajputs rose against his rule. In the early eighteenth century Rajput fortunes revived in proportion as *Mughal* fortunes declined, but only in time for all India to then succumb to the invading British.

rake. Firing along the length of a *flanked* position of enemy troops or line of ships. This avoided exposing oneself to a volley or *broadside*, while bringing maximum fire to bear on the enemy. This was standard naval tactics of the *line ahead*, until the *American Revolution* revealed the utility of new tactics and *Nelson* used daring and rapid-firing gunnery to break the French line at *Trafalgar*. *See also ironclad; turret.*

Ramadan. *See Islam.*

ramification. In *functionalism*, the idea that after states cooperate in technical areas, such cooperation may *spill over* into security issues.

rampart. A raised earthen or stone structure which shields defenders from enemy fire.

Rand. "Witwatersrand." The *gold*-producing region of South Africa. By far the world's largest known deposit of gold ore was discovered there in 1886, when the area was still part of the small *Boer* republic of *Transvaal*.

Rapallo, Treaties of. (1) 1920: Italy and Yugoslavia (United Kingdom) agreed to set aside their *disputes* over control of certain islands in the Adriatic and pledged to oppose any effort to restore the *Habsburgs* in Austria or Hungary. (2) 1922: This is the more important treaty, between *Weimar Germany* and the *Soviet Union*. It re-established *diplomatic relations*, breaking the isolation of each nation; it mutually renounced all financial claims, which spoke to German resentment over *reparations* and Soviet refusal to pay Russia's *war debts* or *compensation* for *nationalized* property of foreigners; and it opened trade relations, vitally important to both. It also contributed to the development of secret military cooperation, which enabled Germany to get past the *disarmament* provisions of the *Treaty of Versailles*.

rape. *See Battle of Berlin;* "*comfort women*"; *crimes against humanity; torture; war crimes;* "*white slavery.*"

Rapid Deployment Force (RDF). A highly mobile force poised to deploy in the *Persian Gulf*, set up by the United States after the *Iranian Revolution* and the start of the *Afghan-Soviet War*. It included prepared bases and equipment stockpiles in the region, to permit quick air transport of troops. It was used to great effect in Operation Desert Shield preceding the *Gulf War. See also Gulf Cooperation Council.*

Rapid Reaction Force (RRF). After the end of the *Cold War*, this was part of a "new strategic concept" within *NATO*, replacing *forward defense*. It called for a smaller, high-technology and mobile force to be ready for *intervention* in trouble spots, rather than to meet an enemy along a broad and prepared front.

rapprochement. Instituting improved, even cordial, relations after a period of *conflict* or *war. See also détente.*

Rarotonga, Treaty of (1987). South Pacific Nuclear Free Zone Treaty. An agreement making the *South Pacific* a *nuclear weapons free zone*, drafted by members of the *South Pacific Forum*. Most states in the region signed it, excepting Tonga. It arose in response to nuclear testing in the South Pacific by France. It thus banned nuclear tests, along with ocean dumping of nuclear waste. None of its signatories was in a position to enforce its terms, however, so its effects remained mostly symbolic. Nor did the treaty ban port calls by, for example, French or American nuclear *warships. See also ANZUS;* "*Kiwi disease.*"

Rasputin, Gregori Yefimovich, né Novykh (1871–1916). Priest and mystic. Tsarina Alexandra's belief in his ability to control the hemophiliac condition of her son, Tsarevich Alexi, gave Rasputin nearly controlling influence over her, and through her over *Nicholas II*, and thereby also over Russia's foreign and domestic policies—especially via corrupt government and civil service appointments. It is even thought that he may have interfered with some military decisions during *World War I*. Infamous for drunkenness and debauches, he was murdered by aristocrats who wanted to end his hold over the tsar. He took awhile to die: he was poisoned, stabbed, shot, and finally thrown into the Neva River to drown.
Suggested Reading: Edvard Radzinsky, *The Rasputin File* (2000).

Rassemblement Démocratique Africain. A collaborative movement of French African political parties whose representatives worked together in the French National Assembly prior to, and on behalf of, independence for their colonies in the aftermath of *World War II*. Suppressed at first for its parliamentary association with the French *Communist Party*, it was led in a new direction by *Félix Houphouët–Boigny* (1905–1990), later president of Côte d'Ivoire, 1960–1990, who broke with the Communists and instead offered to support any French party that would advance the agenda of *decolonization*. In one French colony it was never very strong: Senegal, where *Léopold Senghor* and the competing doctrine of *négritude* held sway.

Rathenau, Walther (1867–1922). German statesman. He directed the German economy during *World War I* and *Weimar*'s reconstruction from 1921. As minister of foreign affairs, in 1922 he arranged reduced *reparations* and negotiated *Rapallo* with Russia. A Jew, he was assassinated by a fanatic *anti-Semite*.

ratification. (1) International: When the *executive* authority of a state formally confirms that it accepts a *treaty* by delivering *instruments of ratification* to the other signatory, if the agreement is *bilateral*, or to an appropriate body such as the United Nations if the treaty is *multilateral*. (2) Domestic: Legal acceptance by the requisite constitutional authority of a state's *adherence* to a treaty. This usually requires legislative approval and executive signature, with the process varying according to specific constitutional provision. The U.S. process is among the most complex and can be highly troublesome (because it is uncertain) for other states. It is also frequently misstated, as in "the Senate ratified the treaty." Actually, the Senate gives "advice and consent" regarding treaties, but the president (chief of the executive branch) negotiates, signs, and ratifies them. Yet a president may ratify a treaty only if it is left unamended by the Senate. The Senate may attach amendments (*reservations*), which will in turn affect the decision of the president to ratify. If the treaty is amended, he must renegotiate it to obtain *consent* to the Senate's revisions from all other signatories. If he does not accept the revisions, or is unable to obtain consent of the other parties, he may refuse to ratify it. In the event the Senate withholds consent (rejects a treaty), the matter of ratification never arises.

ratio decidendi. "Reason for the decision." The legal principle on which a court rests its *judgment*.

ratio legis. "Reason for the law." The reasoning which led to the *rule* used to decide a case.

rational actor. *See rational choice theory.*

rational choice theory. A social science approach to international relations which assumes all individuals are "rational actors" who purposively seek in their political decisions and actions to maximize specific interests. This approach seeks a universally applicable, deductive theory of politics modeled on modern academic approaches to economics, where similarly mindless mathematization has had little explanatory success. It thus eschews detailed historical or philosophically informed case study in favor of reduction of politics to formal models and mathematical generalizations. These most often engage extreme simplifications about *causation* and are additionally couched in a nearly impenetrable, *obscurantist* and *scientistic* terminology of testable *hypotheses* and *variables*. The worst feature of this common academic approach is that the resulting models almost always "explain" what was already known, or is obvious, or else are so vaguely defined that they explain nothing at all. Over that thin substance is then spread a thick veneer of superficial and, too often, false rigor, all packaged in a formal mathematical language which is sometimes found humorous by serious statisticians but is—and is intended to be—quite intimidating to the uninitiated. Left out of all this is the reality that much of importance in human and political affairs may only be explained not by "rational choices" made to maximize hard individual interests but by *ideology* and ignorance, blundering and stupidity, courage and self-sacrifice, or blind luck. Finally, often adding injury to passing intellectual insult, rational choice theorists (and other formal modelers) tend, as a group, to profound intolerance of other, especially *classical* and humanistic, approaches to the study of international relations, to the point that rational choice may be fairly accused of seeking scholarly *hegemony*—to use a favored term. See especially *decision theory; game theory; jargon. See also bureaucratic politics; cognitive dissonance; decision-making theory; group think; image; misperception; security dilemma; standard operating procedure (SOP); organizational process model.*
  Suggested Reading: Michael Brown et al., eds., *Rational Choice and Security Studies* (2000).

rational decision-making. The assumption, basic to most analyses of foreign policy, that *decision makers* are for the most part agreeable to reason; that is, that they assess, rank, and then choose on a logical basis from a range of policy options those which are the most satisfactory (or the least unsatisfactory) and likely to advance their hard interests. This assumption has been challenged by evidence that other factors come between leaders and a purely rational choice, yet it remains an essential starting point in most efforts to explain complex human motivation and public affairs. *See also misperception.*

rational player. *See game theory.*

rationing. Strict apportionment of food, fuel, and other necessities of life among a population, whether civilian or military. This is a common practice during *war*, when great call is made on the nation's resources to sustain a military endeavor at the *front line*, or because of a *siege*. It may also occur during peacetime as a result of *depression* in *market economies*, or crop failure or natural disaster in poorer countries. It was endemic in all countries with a *planned economy*, amounting to a basic feature of such inefficient systems.

raw intelligence. *Intelligence* information which remains to be analyzed for significance and accuracy and vetted for *disinformation*. Because it may be unreliable, it is not normally shown to top *decision makers*.

raw materials. Any material in its natural or preprocessed state: iron ore, not iron; wheat, not flour; wool, not yarn; and so forth. An abundance of raw materials, or at least viable access to such materials, is widely considered a prerequisite of great national *power*. The drive to acquire raw materials was a major component of *wars* and of *empire* building over the centuries.

raze. To burn or otherwise destroy a conquered fortress, village, town, or city. *See also Carthaginian peace; Napoleon; Sherman; Tamerlane.*

Razin, Stenka (c. 1630–1671). He led a Don *Cossack* revolt, 1670–1671, which also swept along numerous *serfs* and other peasants with grievances against the *boyars* and other landowners. Razin assembled an army—or perhaps more accurately, an ill-trained rabble with diverse grievances and limited military ability—of some 200,000. This huge rural mob exploded into a campaign of landlord-killing, terror, and destruction from the lower Volga to the Caspian Sea. Although the rebels were joined by some runaway Russian troops and even a few disgruntled nobles, the rebellion soon ran its course. It was finally crushed, with all due brutality, by troops loyal to the tsar. Razin was publicly tortured to death in Moscow. As in the later *Pugachev rebellion*, Cossack and peasant grievance was not so much anti-tsarist as organized around the assertion that the reigning tsar (or tsarina, in the case of *Catherine*

II) was a "false tsar" against whom the Cossacks and *Old Believers* proposed an alternate or a pretender, or that "German influence" had diverted the true tsar from the True Faith, and he might be persuaded back by an appeal to restore the Old Belief. Many Cossacks and serfs thus died under Russian sabres or on the execution block with surprise and prayer on their lips.

razzia. "Raid." A traditional style of Arab warfare in which small units—usually of light *cavalry*—would sweep into a town or other built-up area in search of *plunder* or as a form of ritualized warfare intended to humiliate and demonstrate the weakness of the enemy. The French adapted this practice in Algeria and elsewhere from the 1840s, using *flying columns* to fall upon Algerian villages to burn them out and terrorize the inhabitants.

reaction (reactionary). Pejorative terms suggesting favoritism for the far (but not revolutionary, or *fascist*) *right wing* of the political spectrum, or those whose prime political motive is a negative reaction to some great change which has taken place. It originally referred to those who responded with hostility to the *liberal* ideals of the *French Revolution*. Of course, what "far right" (or left) really means is dependent on time, context, and speaker. *See also conservative; radical.*

Reagan Doctrine. A promise made by *Ronald Reagan* in his 1985 State of the Union address to aid all anti-Communist *insurgents*, whom he referred to as "freedom fighters" and compared to the *minutemen* of the *American Revolution*. It served to justify martial and other assistance already underway to *guerrillas* in Afghanistan, Angola, and Nicaragua. *See also authoritarianism; totalitarianism.*

Reagan, Ronald (b. 1911). *Republican* president of the United States, 1981–1989. A member of the *Democratic Party* until 1952, after a long career in film he was twice elected Republican governor of California and served from 1967 to 1974. He won a landslide victory over *Jimmy Carter* in the 1980 presidential election. He followed *monetarism* in his economic policy, whereas blanket anti-*communism* formed the core of his approach to security policy. He was not loathe to use limited unilateral force to advance foreign policy goals, in Grenada (1983), Lebanon (1983–1984), and Libya (1986); or indirect force through aid to governments (El Salvador, Guatemala, Honduras); or *covert* aid to *insurgents* (the *Contras* in Nicaragua, the *mujahadeen* in Afghanistan, and *guerrillas* in Angola and Mozambique). He relaxed Carter-era *human rights* strictures on aid to *Third World* allies while increasing them toward the *Soviet bloc*. His main concern was always the Soviet Union. During his first administration he continued the *arms buildup* begun in 1978 by Congress and carried over in the final Carter budget, until by 1985 both the U.S. armory and the federal *deficit* were bulging. From 1981 to 1985 there was extreme, though mainly rhetorical, confrontation with Moscow over Afghanistan, Central America, and Poland. Also, a major leadership crisis within *NATO* occurred in the early 1980s over Pershing and *cruise missile* deployments Reagan wanted to counter a prior Soviet deployment of SS-20s. At the time, Reagan was widely criticized for avoiding *summits*. He did so because of the rapidity with which Soviet leaders were dying and being replaced (*Brezhnev, Andropov,* and *Chernenko* all died between 1982 and 1985), but also because it was his preferred tactic to complete the arms buildup before negotiating from strength with Moscow.

When *Mikhail Gorbachev* assumed power in the Soviet Union, he and Reagan struck a new chord in American-Soviet relations. Reagan's second term saw a winding down of the confrontation over Afghanistan and major breakthroughs in *arms control* and resolution of regional disputes. They achieved an *Intermediate-Range Nuclear Forces (INF) Treaty* (December 8, 1987), which eliminated all U.S. and Soviet *intermediate ballistic* and cruise missiles in Europe. Along with the missiles, nearly 500 U.S. and 1,600 Soviet nuclear warheads were dismantled in the first agreement to eliminate an entire class of nuclear weapons. Reagan's second term was badly marred, however, by the *Iran-Contra* scandal and by federal budget deficits, which continued to rise, seemingly out of control. His more uncritical admirers assert that he "won the *Cold War*," implying that he did so nearly single-handedly. It is true that the collapse of the Soviet empire, and Union, began on his watch and was surely hastened by several of his policies, but such an exclusive claim ignores decades of sustained *containment* by eight presidents, Congress, and numerous foreign allies, all of which combined to hem in the Soviet Union until its internal economic and political contradictions led to fissures in its legitimacy, which then widened to canyons of social discontent. After his presidency Reagan retired into complete privacy, as he suffered the progressive debilitation of Alzheimer's disease. *See also authoritarianism; Reagan Doctrine; SALT I and II; Strategic Defense Initiative; START I and II.*

Suggested Readings: Coral Bell, *The Reagan Paradox* (1990); Lou Cannon, *Role of a Lifetime* (1991); Don Oberdorfer, *From the Cold War to a New Era* (1998). For those who enjoy fiction, there is also the "memoir" by Edmund Morris, *Dutch* (1999).

realism, classical school. A broad approach to international politics and history which focuses on the role of *power* and the *national interest*, with special concern for *national security*, admiration for the *balance of power*, and hardheaded respect for the utility of both *force* and *diplomacy*. In consequence, it is less concerned with issues of *low politics* or *distributive justice*, at times to the point of apparent indifference. Classical realism stems from a pessimistic assumption about the flawed nature of humanity (its penchant for evil) and the consequent absence of reliable trust or any *harmony of interests* among human societies. It consequently assumes and observes that all politics is—whatever the surface appearance—at root a *struggle for power* under conditions of threat and fear, wherein power is the coinage of measurement and defense of the national interest. Less well understood or appreciated is the argument made by classical realism that the balance of power ultimately rests on shared social and moral bases and practices among national communities, in what amounts at the least to an *anarchical society*. The constant search for equilibrium within this structure requires of wise leaders cultivation of the virtues of *prudence* and self-restraint. It is merely a caricature (sometimes purveyed by cruder, self-proclaimed, and proudly amoral realists themselves) which portrays political realism as necessarily advocating *Machiavellian* ethics. Nor is realism unconcerned with *international law* or *international organization* or inarticulate about *human rights* and national, political, or civic community—as its coarser adherents and critics too often make out. At its best, realism supports law and organization as central mechanisms of diplomacy, as ends desirable in themselves, and as means advancing world order and civilization. In sum, in realism as in any other serious approach to politics, there exists a perpetual tension between analytical and historical description and normative prescription. *See also democracy; end of history; idealism;* Idealpolitik; *international society;* Leviathan; *liberal-internationalism;* Machtpolitik; *neo-realism; Peloponnesian War*; raison d'etat; *realist;* Realpolitik.

Suggested Readings: Hedley Bull, *Anarchical Society* (1977); Hans Morgenthau, *Politics Among Nations* (1948, 1978); Hans Morgenthau, *Scientific Man vs. Power Politics* (1946); Joel Rosenthal, *Righteous Realists* (1991); Robert Tucker, *The Inequality of Nations* (1977); Martin Wight, *Power Politics* (1978).

realist. (1) A person who analyzes and views the world the way it truly is, not giving in to sentimentalism or wishful thinking about how they might like it to be. (2) A person who thinks that they analyze and view the world the way it truly is, because they lack the imagination to conceive that it might be different, already or in the future, from how they perceive it to be. (3) A person who approaches the analysis of *international relations* or the conduct of *statecraft* and *diplomacy* according to the principles and predilections of *realism*.

real patronato. "Royal patronage." This was a grant of extraordinary governing powers by the *Spanish Monarchy* to the *Catholic Church* in Latin America, but nowhere else in the Spanish Empire. This mechanism intertwined the politics of various Catholic orders—notably Augustinians, Dominicans, Franciscans, and *Jesuits*—with the interests of the crown, but also with the politics of settlement, Indian *missionary* conversion and physical welfare, and all other thorny issues raised by the *encomienda system*. The Church's "Christianizing mission" among the Indians was deepened, broadened, and subjected to more clear hierarchical authority under instructions issued by *Philip II* in 1574. In return, the state claimed the right to name bishops and archbishops, and thereby control the social, class, racial, and indirectly also the doctrinal makeup of the Church hierarchy.

Realpolitik. The practice of *diplomacy* based on an assessment of *power*, material, and prudential matters, without undue concern for theoretical considerations or restraint by ethical worries. The term was first used by the liberal journalist and historian August Ludwig von Rochau. It later came to best characterize the foreign policy of *Otto von Bismarck*, whom Rochau and others saw as abjuring the pursuit of abstract principles (*Idealpolitik*) to be guided instead by "the reality of the natural law of power." Rochau said Bismarck's pursuit of *Prussia's* interests was conditioned as much by limitations as by *capabilities* and saw him as being free from either soft sympathies or hard antipathies for other states. Whether regarding Bismarck or others, avoidance of sentimentality about relations among nations should not be mistaken for amorality, although it often is. As a result, the term acquired a pejorative implication of core *Machiavellianism* about both means and goals. That is a subtle shift in emphasis perhaps reflecting more than anything a distaste felt by *liberal* observers for the necessities, and not just the excesses, of traditional diplomacy. Still, clear-headed detachment is a key component of any policy that aspires to Realpolitik. *See also Winston S. Churchill; Grotian; international society; Immanuel Kant; liberal-internationalism; Niccolò Machiavelli;* Machtpolitik; *power politics; prudence;* raison d'etat; *realism; realist.*

rear echelon. Transport troops and other support personnel, such as cooks or hospital staff, not in the *front line.*

rear guard. Part of a larger military force detached from and charged with defense of the rear of a moving army, especially if the army is in retreat. Its role is to buy time for the main body of the army to escape destruction or to re-form, if retreating. If advancing, its job is to detect and prevent enemy encirclement.

rearmament. (1) Building up the armed forces after a period of *demobilization* or *arms control*, either in preparation for *war* or to reinforce *deterrence*. (2) Upgrading the quality of a nation's armed forces, particularly their weaponry and equipment. Some examples: The interwar period, 1919–1939, was deeply concerned with the issue of German rearmament, which was forbidden under terms of the *Treaty of Versailles*; after *World War II*, the issue of German rearmament played a key role in early debates over the formation of *NATO*; in the 1990s the United Nations was concerned with preventing Iraqi rearmament in the wake of the *Gulf War. See also arms control; disarmament.*

rebellion. Armed *insurrection* in resistance to an established government. The term is usually employed when the violence is on a greater scale than a simple *mutiny* but has not reached the point of *civil war* or *revolution*; or when the governing side wishes to delegitimize the rebels and underplay the threat they pose. *See also Boxer Rebellion; guerrilla war; Nian Rebellion; prisoner of war; Taiping Rebellion; White Lotus Rebellion.*

rebus sic stantibus. *See* clausula rebus sic stantibus.

recall the ambassador. (1) For consultations: A tactic used to show displeasure with another government's policies or actions. It falls short of breaking *diplomatic relations* and is more easily reversed. (2) Permanently: This occurs when fully severing diplomatic relations or on a formal *declaration of war*. *See also recognition;* relations officieuses.

recession. A short-term decline of economic activity, notably falling industrial *production*, declining *investment* and *growth*, falling capacity utilization, and a corresponding rise in unemployment. By convention, a recession is an economic downturn lasting a minimum of three consecutive fiscal quarters. *See also business cycle; depression; recovery.*

reciprocity. (1) In *international law*: A basic principle that allows *reprisal* and bases procedures on a notion of equal rights and duties among *states*. (2) In *extradition*: Advance agreement to surrender one's own citizens for trial in other countries in exchange for the right to try citizens of those countries for offenses committed within one's own *jurisdiction*. (3) In *foreign policy*: Treating the actions of other states in a tit-for-tat manner, be this positive or negative. (4) In *trade*: Mutual lowering or raising of *tariff* and other *trade barriers. See also GATT; most-favored-nation (MFN); normal trade relations (NTR).*

recognition. A fundamental principle of *international law* involving legal acceptance of the *international personality* of foreign political communities, and thereby of their requisite rights and duties under the law. Recognition may be express or implied; it is sometimes only *de facto*, but usually it is also *de jure*. The sine qua non of recognition is "effective rule" of a given territory (although there are exceptions even here, such as the *Baltic States*, 1940–1991), a fact which stems from the core understanding of the purpose of government on the part of the states: maintenance of internal order and a real ability to carry out international relations and keep international commitments. Its abiding characteristic is pragmatism.

Despite its legal significance, recognition remains essentially a political act with legal consequences: states are not obligated to extend recognition to an entity simply because it attains all the de facto or even de jure attributes of statehood; they retain discretion. Similarly, recognition is not constitutive of statehood (an older idea); instead it acknowledges (declares) de jure status and opens up legal relations with a de facto state. In the twentieth century efforts were made to establish new principles in addition to effective control, including popular support, democratic *legitimacy*, and *good faith* treaty keeping. None of these took hold, and pragmatic realism remained the common standard.

Recognition may be extended implicitly by signing a *treaty*, or in an announcement followed by formal ceremonies where *diplomatic credentials* are exchanged. A special form of recognition is sometimes extended to successful *insurgencies*, elevating them to a status of *belligerent* ("belligerent community"). This may occur—again, the decision is political rather than legal—when the rebels demonstrate clear control and substitute government functions in a portion of the territory of the affected state. Recognition in this form does not confer the status of international personality on the rebels, nor does it proffer to them other rights or incur obligations under peacetime international law. It does afford them legal protections (and incur obligations) under the *laws of war*. Britain extended this type of recognition to the *Confederacy* during the *American Civil War*, and some states recognized the belligerent status of antigovernment rebels in the El Salvador civil war of the 1980s. "Nonrecognition" is usually a feeble, symbolic policy sometimes adopted to express displeasure with or disapproval of a changed political situation in another territory (e.g., most states refused to recognize *Manchukuo*).

It is noteworthy that nonrecognition of a government is distinct from withholding recognition from a *state*: Western refusal to recognize the *Bolshevik* regime in Russia in the 1920s, or China after 1949, did not imply a lack of legal acceptance that states called Russia and China existed. Similarly, general international withholding of recognition from the Vietnamese-supported regime in Cambodia, 1979–1992, did not mean that recognition of the state of Cambodia was at an end by the *international community*. On the other hand, refusing recognition to *Kurds* in their long aspiration for *Kurdistan* denies them legal status, international protections, and the other rights they would obtain were they in possession of a sovereign state. Similarly, *Biafra* never obtained sufficiently widespread recognition to permit Biafrans to also obtain adequate matériel or moral or legal help to sustain their political claims to independence from Nigeria during the *Nigerian Civil War*. This was also true for numerous other secessionist provinces and movements.

"Derecognition" of states is possible but rarely occurs. The best-known and most important case was the derecognition by the majority of members of the *community of nations*, from 1972 and later, of the Republic of China (ROC), or Taiwan, in favor of the People's Republic of China (PRC). When ROC delegations appeared before the credentials committee of the United Nations, its *credentials* were rejected and it could not be seated in the *United Nations General Assembly (UNGA)* or the *Security Council*. In both cases, there were multiple abstentions on the issue of accepting Taiwan's credentials. The same procedure was followed at the *International Monetary Fund*, the *International Bank for Reconstruction and Development*, and other international organizations. In contrast, not even South Africa during its *apartheid* years was derecognized, though some African states called for this, just as most Arab states called for derecognition of Israel. Instead, the *letter of credence* presented to the credentials committee of the UNGA by South Africa was refused, and it was not allowed to take its seat until apartheid was completely dismantled in the early 1990s; but it was not even *expelled* from membership, let alone derecognized. *See also legitimate government; recall the ambassador;* relations officieuses; *sovereignty; two-Chinas policy.*

Suggested Reading: M. Peterson, *Recognition of Governments* (1997).

recommendation. A nonbinding *resolution* passed by the *United Nations General Assembly* or some other *IGO*.

reconnaissance. The active search, at the *tactical* level on the field of battle, for useful military information. Historically, this was carried out by advance parties of scouts, light *cavalry*, or more recently, light armored cars or small aircraft.

reconnoiter. To spy out an enemy's battle strength or position, or one's own possible line of movement.

Reconquista. In 711 C.E. Muslim Moors from North Africa advanced into and conquered *Iberia*. Their migration threatened southern France as well, until they were defeated and forced south of the Pyrenees by the Franks, 732–737, under Charles Martel ("The Hammer," c. 688–741). For the next 800 years Christians and Muslims waged war for control of Iberia. For centuries Muslim states dominated southern Iberia, creating a magnificent and prosperous urban civilization (notably in Cordova and *Granada*) which advanced learning and served as a conduit of classical knowledge to the West. In the tenth century, northern Christians accelerated the "reconquest" of Iberia, just as *Norman* raiders took back Sicily from the Muslims and the *Crusades* to the Holy Land got underway. A turning point came in 1092 when "El Cid" (Ruy Díaz de Vivar) captured Valencia for *Castile*. Another major Christian victory came at Las Navas de Tolosa (1212). Fifty years later, Muslim Spain was largely confined to Granada. Despite the warfare, the Reconquista also saw long periods of mutual toleration and social, intellectual, and economic interaction. Intense religious hostility increased as the final conquest approached, led by the warrior caste of Castile. It all ended with the negotiated surrender of Granada, after a 10-year siege, and the procession of *Ferdinand and Isabella* into that city on January 2, 1492. This event was read as a divine blessing, which the *Catholic* ideologue Isabella celebrated by expelling the Jews from Spain and financing the first voyage of *Christopher Columbus. See also* conquistadores.

Suggested Reading: Hugh Kennedy, *Muslim Spain and Portugal* (1996).

reconstruction. (1) The period immediately following any destructive war, in which economic, political, and social order is rebuilt or made over. (2) In American history, the period from c. 1865 to 1877, when recovery from the *American Civil War* and partial adjustment to the end of *slavery* took place, under conditions of such corruption and retribution that permanent bitterness marked the South for several generations. Southern whites who supported Reconstruction were known by their opponents as "scalawags," whereas northerners who moved south to profit from public office were widely known as "carpetbaggers," from their cheap luggage. Confederate veterans added terror and murder to the mix as "night riders" and Klansmen.

recovery. A return to pre-*recession* levels of economic activity, production, investment, and *growth* and a corresponding rise in employment. By convention, a recovery is underway when an economic upturn lasts three consecutive fiscal quarters.

recruit. A newly enlisted soldier, whether a *conscript* or a volunteer.

Red Army. The army organized by *Leon Trotsky* to defend the *Bolsheviks* during the *Russian Civil War*. The Red Army put down the *Kronstadt mutiny* in 1921 and assisted in expropriations from and forced *collectivization* of the Soviet peasantry. Its officer corps became a primary target of *Stalin*'s paranoia and vengeance at the height of the *Yezhovshchina* before *World War II*. The Red Army was thus commanded at the senior and middle levels by numerous incompetents who demonstrated their lack of management and combat skills in the opening months of the *Finnish-Soviet War*. It next suffered astonishing losses as it fell back under *Hitler*'s massive attack in 1941, code-named *Barbarossa*. This compelled a return to merit as a means of selecting officers, giving more room to brilliant commanders such as *Zhukov* and *Rokossovsky* to oversee the Red Army's recovery and re-formation. Under Stalin's overall (and sometimes, direct and interfering) command, the Red Army counterattacked the *Wehrmacht* in the hugest battles of World War II, the most important of which were *Stalingrad*, *Kursk*, and *Berlin*. On the *eastern front*, the Red Army took staggering losses but ultimately prevailed. By the end of the war, it was the largest and one of the best-equipped armed forces in the world.

During the *Cold War* the Red Army continued as one of history's most formidable militaries, adding *nuclear weapons* to its arsenal from 1949. It remained a pillar of the *communist* order in the Soviet Union and enforcer of the cohesion of the *Soviet bloc*. The Red Army enforced the allegiance of *Warsaw Pact* countries to the *Soviet bloc* in Hungary in 1956, Czechoslovakia in 1968, and elsewhere by the implicit threat of those examples. It was badly divided over the *Afghan-Soviet War*, losing some internal cohesion and much of its popular reputation. Some units supported the 1991 *coup* attempt against further decentralization of the Soviet federation, but others supported *Yeltsin*, thus dooming the coup. The Red Army was then ordered back from its forward posts in the *Baltic States* and former Warsaw Pact countries, though some troops failed to return due to a lack of housing to receive them, and perhaps also lingering imperial interests in certain quarters of the old *nomenklatura*. The Red Army, too, split apart with the breakup of the Soviet Union, with units joining the national armies of the post-Soviet republics. Some units, renegade or not, joined in fighting to support ethnic Russians in *Moldova*, and to support secessionists in *Abkhazia*. Others gave support to rebels in *Ossetia*. The long-term attitude toward reform of the renamed Russian Army remained a matter of conjecture. In 1993 *Duma* elections the Russian Army vote went heavily to the neo-*fascist* party of *Zhirinovsky*, but it was less cohesive in subsequent elections.

Note: The army of the Chinese *Communist Party* (CCP) was also called the Red Army until the name of its main formation was changed to Eighth Route Army during the *Second Sino-Japanese War*. Before the *Chinese Revolution* (1949) it was renamed the *People's Liberation Army* (PLA).

Suggested Readings: David M. Glantz, *Stumbling Colossus* (1998); John M. Macintosh, *Juggernaut* (1967).

Red Brigades. An *anarchist* and *terrorist* group active in Italy in the 1970s and 1980s. It was responsible for multiple bomb attacks and political murders, including that of Prime Minister Aldo Moro (1916–1978).

Red China. A colloquial term for the *People's Republic of China*. It fell into disuse in most circles after c. 1972.

Red Crescent. National organizations which derive their inspiration from, and work closely with, the *International Committee of the Red Cross*, but which operate mainly in *Islamic* countries.

Red Cross. See *International Committee of the Red Cross*.

Red Guards. Fanatical, mostly teenage, youths stirred up and unleashed by *Mao Zedong* to *purge* the Chinese *Communist Party* (CCP) during the *Great Proletarian Cultural Revolution*, but including spontaneous associations of workers as well, who organized to voice long-standing grievances over pay or work conditions. Many of the student Red Guards began as childish idealists. They were taught to be ideologically driven, *fundamentalist* bullies and even killers. Given social license, others just discovered within themselves a predilection and talent for vicious thuggery. Together, they publicly humiliated, harried, beat, and on occasion also murdered those whom they accused of *counterrevolution*, *revisionism*, "capitalist-roadism" and other ideological crimes. Ultimately numbering nearly 20 million, and organized into military-style units, they persecuted tens of millions, caused untold cultural and economic destruction—a favored pastime and instruction was desolation of China's classical buildings and heritage—and not a few deaths. Red Guards rejected all tradition and authority, whether real or symbolic, including that of all teachers, intellectuals, and even high CCP officials. Their targets were the "Four Olds" (old ideas, culture, customs and habits, and thinking). They recognized only the personal authority of Mao and drowned themselves in his *cult of personality*. There were scenes of hundreds of thousands of teenage Red Guards in Tiananmen Square frenetically chanting praise and loyalty to Mao—who stood looking down on them with a false fatherly approval—while waving in unison the "little red book" of his political sayings compiled by *Lin Biao*. Six such orchestrated demonstrations were staged, each sending chills through Chinese society, the CCP, and indeed the world.

In 1966 all schools and universities in China were closed and many faculty members were purged and publicly humiliated, so that even more millions could join the Red Guards and commit mayhem. This was social recklessness on a colossal scale. In January 1967 the Red Guards seized control of the cities, ousting CCP officials and taking over the administration; the bureaucrats were then sent to the country for *reeducation*. Most of the Red Guards were ignorant children, full of inchoate rage. They thus menaced China with *anarchy* and even *civil war*. Reacting against the *terror* and mass-conformist and orthodox state which Mao had constructed, with its permission and utilizing its tools and slogans, their rage was a measure of the distance between *communist* rhetoric and communist reality in China. It could not last: as class and other divisions among the Red Guards emerged they turned their feral impulses against each other. Rival formations of Red Guards formed, partly reflecting China's two-tiered educational system, which disadvantaged any identified as having a suspect family, class, or former *Guomindang* background. Then began the battles in the streets. Mao also heedlessly urged the Red Guards to purge the *People's Liberation Army* (PLA). Toward the end of 1967 Mao recognized that he had lost control of the Red Guards and might lose control of the PLA next (units of Guards had already fought large-scale battles with the PLA and with each other). Before that happened, he ordered the PLA to cooperate with workers' organizations to repress the Red Guards. Many hundreds of thousands of young people who should all along have been in schools or universities thus became members of China's "lost generation," who never returned to complete their interrupted studies and were instead betrayed to rural exile and political banishment by the "Great Helmsman" himself. These hapless children were shipped off to rural labor camps and collective farms to taste for themselves the bitter flavors of the political "reeducation" they had forced on so many others, as innocent as they or more so. Meanwhile, the father of all the chaos, bloodshed, and senseless destruction the Red Guards had wrought in the cities reclined into a renewed personal mastery in Beijing and began to consider what to do about the PLA next.

Suggested Reading: Anita Chan, *Children of Mao* (1985).

Red Orchestra. "Rote Kapelle." One of several *communist* spy rings operating in Western Europe before and during *World War II*. It was so named by *Admiral Canaris*, head of the German *Abwehr*. It was active in feeding information concerning German and Italian military *capabilities* to Moscow during the *Spanish Civil War*. Most of its operatives in Germany were caught by 1942 and were tortured to death; female members were guillotined. Their information was accurate enough, but although it had been obtained at the cost of their lives, *Stalin* did not always believe it.

redoubt. An isolated fortification defending an important position; or a small and self-contained fortification built within a larger structure as part of its layers of defense.

Red Scare (1919). In the wake of the *Bolshevik Revolution* in Russia a hysteria about possible *communist* plots and agitation swept the popular press and imagination in America. Some employers and government officials actually believed it; others used it as a pretext to smash unwanted unions, deport undesirable *aliens* or, in the South, target blacks who might organize others politically. A similar phenomenon occurred in Canada, where a *general strike* in the western city of Winnipeg led to bloodshed and death.

Red Sea. An extension of the Indian Ocean between Arabia and Africa, connecting to the Mediterranean via the *Suez Canal*.

Red Terror. (1) Indiscriminate *summary executions* carried out by the *CHEKA* in the wake of an *assassination* attempt against *Lenin* which left him badly wounded. Inside two months, 15,000 were murdered, mainly in the cities, in the first mass example of *secret police* ruthlessness and reliance on *terror* which would characterize the Soviet Union's politics for decades. (2) A savage campaign of repression (*counterrevolution*) in *Ethiopia* in the 1970s and 1980s, under the orders of Mengistu Haile Mariam (b. 1941). As in Russia, assassination of government officials was used as a pretext for *state terrorism*, and *torture* was ubiquitous. As many as 100,000 were summarily executed or hunted down by *death squads*. *Famine* was also used against *guerrillas* and other dissidents, killing several million more. With the usual callous brutality of a typical twentieth-century revolutionary regime, families in mourning were made to pay for the bullets used to murder their loved ones. *See also collectivization; Felix Dzerzhinsky; KGB; NKVD; OGPU; war communism; war crimes trials.*

reduce. To break down the defensive walls of a fortified position. *See also fortification; trench warfare; Sébastien Vauban.*

reductio ad absurdum. "Reduction to the absurd." Taking an analogy or argument to the absurd extreme, simply by extension of its own logic. This is a frequent feature of social science *theories* of international relations. *See also critical theory; game theory; postmodernism; rational choice theory.*

reductionism (reductionist). Reducing an explanation, for example of foreign policy, to a single factor through gross *abstraction* or oversimplification. In international relations theory, the charge of reductionism was famously made by Kenneth Waltz against virtually all who came before him. Yet his own theory of international relations (1979) was crudely, indeed spectacularly, reductionist: it attributed all *causation* to the "structure" of the international system and denied any role to individual decision making or social, political, ideological, military, or economic forces at the state ("unit") level. *See also mode of production; neorealism; systems theory.*

reeducation. (1) A euphemism for indoctrination, and even brainwashing, used by *communist* states about their treatment of political and social *dissidents*. The assumption is that deviation from the *party line* is caused by ignorance or "false consciousness," not rational or defensible disagreement. This was considered a merciful assessment, compared with the punishments meted out for willful *revisionism* or, worst of all, *counterrevolution*. (2) Public education campaigns undertaken by the *occupying powers* in Austria, Italy, Germany, and Japan after *World War II*, whose aim was to eradicate *fascism, Nazism,* and *militarism* and substitute attachment to Western democratic values and ideals. *See also Cultural Revolution; denazification; GULAG; Laos; rehabilitation; Vietnam.*

referendum. When a population is asked to answer a specific question, for example on *secession* or *union*. In the twentieth century referenda grew in use, until virtually no question about *self-determination* was considered fully legitimate without popular ratification by *plebiscite. See also Cameroon; Denmark; Palau; Saar; Schleswig-Holstein; Switzerland; totalitarianism; Québec.*

reflation. Deliberate *inflation* caused by government spending which aims to stimulate economic *growth.*

reflexive development. When the process of *modernization* responds, like a reflex, to external conditions; that is, when an economy has high *vulnerability* to external economic factors which can alter its development despite local decisions.

Reformation. *See Protestant Reformation.*

reformism. An approach to *North-South issues* which argues the violent overthrow of the *world capitalist system* is not required, because it can be reformed. *See also dependency theory; postimperialism.*

reform liberalism. A revision of *classical liberalism* which became dominant in the twentieth century. It accepted the premise that the most *efficient* and desirable economic system is a *free market.* Yet it argued that a completely free market does not lead to inevitable harmonious results as classical liberal theory supposed, but to maldistribution of wealth and resources. Adherents thus accepted government *intervention* in the economy as fitting and necessary to more fairly distribute wealth, but rejected *central planning* as suffocating the sources of wealth creation. *See also capitalism; command economy; individualism; Keynesian economics; market economy; planned economy.*

refugee camp. Makeshift living quarters for *refugees* who await relocation to a country of final settlement, or merely wait to return home once a natural disaster or *war* subsides, or until a political solution is found to some *human rights* problem or civil disorder which restores them to their homeland and proper national status.

refugees. Persons who flee a situation of economic distress, persecution, or war to seek refuge in another part of their own country (internal refugees) or in a foreign country (external refugees). By convention, refugees are additionally classified as (1) economic refugees: not officially counted, to whom little *aid* is offered, and who are subject to *deportation*; (2) political refugees: for whom a welcome of varying warmth or coolness awaits in different host countries, but who are looked on with relative favor; and (3) wartime refugees: who may receive international assistance but are seldom offered relocation, as they are expected to resettle in their home countries once the fighting dies down. Internal refugees also are not officially counted and do not come under international mandates except when faced with *famine* or *genocide.* In 2001 the *United Nations High Commissioner for Refugees* identified 15 million refugees worldwide, up from 8 million in 1980 and just 2.5 million in 1970. Not included in that figure were another 25 million internal refugees (not legally refugees under *international law*) and an untold number of economic migrants. *See also asylum; boat people; Economic and Social Council (ECOSOC); internally displaced person (IDP); Kurds; migration; Nansen; Palestinians; partition; refugee camp; statelessness.*

regency. Government by an appointed regent, or council of regents, in the event of a minority succession by a monarch, or when an adult monarch is disabled, as in Great Britain, 1811–1820, when *George III* suffered his final madness.

regime. (1) Domestic: A synonym for government; often pejorative, it implies lack of respect for democratic rights, as in the usage "*Nazi* regime." (2) International: An umbrella term for any set of *rules*, *norms*, and procedures which focus common concerns and are used to manage an issue (or "*issue area*") of common interest, as in "*nonproliferation* regime," or "*free trade* regime." It may incorporate *treaty* rules but implies as well both a broader and more informal set of understandings than the precise index of *terms* in a treaty. *See also interdependence.*

   Suggested Reading: Stephen Krasner, *International Regimes* (1983).

regional banks. *See African Development Bank; Asian Development Bank; Inter-American Development Bank.*

regionalism. (1) A policy favoring regional over universal associations as the optimum path to *international organization*. Some analysts view regional *integration* as merely an interim step to construction of global organizations; others see it as a possible serious obstacle to *universalism* should regional trade and/or political blocs develop. (2) A claim to exclusive *jurisdiction* over an issue or conflict, based on *propinquity*. Thus, African states might call for an "*OAU* solution" to a *civil war*; Arab states might prefer an *Arab League* solution to a regional crisis; the *Organization of Security and Cooperation in Europe (OSCE)* and *NATO* assert primary responsibility for *peace* and *security* in Europe; the *OAS* claims special rights in the Americas; and *ASEAN* and *Asia Pacific Economic Co-operation (APEC)* do the same in Asia.

regional power. A state which can effectively project influence within a given region, but not globally: Nigeria in West Africa, Vietnam in *Southeast Asia*, Egypt or Israel in the *Middle East*.

regional war. One which expands beyond just two *states* to include some or all neighboring states but which does not draw the *Great Powers* directly into the fighting. *See also Arab-Israeli Wars; Balkan Wars; Indo-Pakistani Wars.*

registration. Depositing a copy of a signed and ratified *treaty* with a public registrar, such as the United Nations, for purposes of publication and open dissemination. The idea was spurred by the *liberal peace program*, which insisted that there should be *open covenants, openly arrived at* as a means of avoiding a repeat of the calamity of *World War I*, thought by many, correctly or not, to have been caused by secret prewar *alliances*.

regression. A statistical technique for identifying a functional relationship between two or among several *variables*, drawn from *empirical* examination of a set of data where the relationship is expressed in the natural units of the variables. It is used by *quantitative* analysts to predict values for "dependent variables" based on known values of "independent variables."

regular army. The permanent, professional force that forms the core of a *standing army*. It can be rapidly expanded should *reserves* be called up or *conscription* introduced.

regulated coexistence (*geregeltes Nebeneinander*). A West German adjustment to the physical and political reality of *East Germany*, enunciated in 1967 and thereafter moving the country on a pragmatic basis roughly halfway from the rejectionist *Hallstein Doctrine* toward the later accommodation of *Ostpolitik*. *See also peaceful coexistence.*

rehabilitation. When, in a *communist* political system, a former official or leader who had been *purged* was brought back into public life, after a (almost always coerced, by *torture*) confession of wrongdoing, or the proclamation of a new *party line* which the official was now prepared to sing in tune. *See also reeducation.*

Reich. An *empire* of Germanic peoples. The "First Reich" was a retroactive name given by German nationalists to the *Holy Roman Empire*. The Second Reich was Bismarck's creation: Imperial Germany, from the proclamation of a new German Empire in the Hall of Mirrors at Versailles following Prussia's defeat of France in January 1871, to the abdication of Kaiser *Wilhelm II* in November 1918. "Third Reich" was the propaganda name *Hitler* gave to Nazi Germany, to identify the Nazis as the linear inheritors of Germany's imperial tradition and their empire as its completion. It was used about his ascent to power in January 1933, until *unconditional surrender* and *occupation* in May 1945. Hitler boasted that his Reich—like the first German Empire—would last 1,000 years, but it was overthrown in just twelve. *See also Austria; Germany.*

Reichstag. (1) The electoral college of the *Holy Roman Empire*, which met at Ratisbon from 1356 to 1806. (2) The parliament of the *North German Confederation*, 1867–1871. (3) The lower house of the German legislature, which met in Berlin, 1871–1945. On February 27, 1933, the Reichstag was set afire, probably by the deranged Dutch *Communist* who was actually blamed by the *Nazis* (and later beheaded by the *Gestapo*), although some still suspect the Nazis started the fire. The "Reichstag fire" proved a milestone on the path to *totalitarian* dictatorship. *Hitler* used it as an excuse to ban the German *Communist Party*, suspend all political rights, and justify the Enabling Act, which allowed him to bypass all democratic institutions, including the legislature. Within months the Nazis banned all political parties but their own and proclaimed the *Führerprinzip*.

Reichswehr. "State defense." The German military, 1871–1933. The "Black Reichswehr" was an illegal force, organized in secret, to supplement the 100,000-man armed forces permitted Germany under the terms of the *Treaty of Versailles*. Units of this force rebelled in 1923, and it was disbanded. The Reichswehr was renamed the *Wehrmacht* in 1933. *See also Bundeswehr.*

reify. To regard an abstract notion as if it were something material or concrete.

Reinsurance Treaty (June 18, 1887). A secret German-Russian agreement which gave Russia freedom of maneuver toward Bulgaria, in return for guaranteeing German *neutrality* in all events save a Russian war with Austria or a German war with France. It was a hasty arrangement by *Bismarck* to pacify Russia after Austria's refusal to extend the *Dreikaiserbund*; Bismarck simultaneously blocked its effects by secretly encouraging the *Mediterranean Agreement*. It was repudiated by a foolhardy *Wilhelm II* in 1890.

***relations officieuses*.** "Official relations," even in the absence of *recognition*. This condition arises when there is no *de jure* recognition and political obstacles arise to extending it, but a pressing, practical need yet exists to resolve common problems or *disputes*. For example, despite not recognizing its *communist* regime, the United States participated with China in negotiating the *Geneva Accords*. Similarly, before its recognition of the Soviet Union (1934) the United States dealt with an unaccredited Soviet trade representative, including using him to pass noncommercial *diplomatic notes* back to Moscow. Even further back, during the *American Civil War* Great Britain maintained "relations officieuses" with the *Confederacy*. Also see *special interest section*.

relativism. The philosophical position that ethical and social truths depend on the individual (moral relativism) or group (cultural relativism) upholding them. Some argue that any search for universal standards of *international law* or morality, such as concern for *human rights* or *distributive justice*, is inherently misplaced and even "imperialistic." *See also critical theory; universalism.*

religion, in international affairs. The progressive and formal *secularization* of international relations since the *Peace of Westphalia* (1648) notwithstanding, religion has had, and continues to have, an enormous influence on the affairs of nations and states: in most societies it helped shape the collective imagination which constitutes much of what it means to be a nation; it sacralizes certain claims to political *legitimacy* over others; it configures alliances as well as disfigures enmities among states and between nationalisms; it can determine international *boundaries*; it permeates the world view of most national leaders, at least in a deeper cultural sense; and over the centuries it has sometimes promoted peaceful relations but far more often has encouraged and legitimized "*holy war.*" The role of religion in modern world affairs—in the affairs of secular states—is most often wholly overlooked by "theorists" of international relations, who are used to thinking in terms of alike *units*; but then in fact, so is almost everything else truly interesting about how and why states behave the way they do. It can be underestimated and misunderstood by real-world leaders as well. During a visit to Moscow before *World War II*, to try to arrange a new Franco-Russian front against Germany, *Pierre Laval* (who would later betray his country to the *Nazis*) asked the *communist* dictator *Josef Stalin* if he could ease up a bit on doctrinaire religious persecutions, as this would assist with *Catholic* opinion in France and with the Pope. Stalin famously replied, "The Pope! How many divisions has he got?" In the short term, of course, Stalin was right: in any *Realpolitik* analysis of the *correlation of forces* in the mid-1930s the Pope was not a player on the military stage, which everyone suspected was soon to become the only one that mattered. In the longer run, however, as Stalin's successors found out in the 1980s, another answer was "as many as may be filled by all the Poles in *Solidarity.*" *See also Lord Acton*; *Akbar*; *anti-Semitism*; apartheid; *Arab-Israeli Wars*; *Aurangzeb*; *assassin*; *Augsburg, Peace of*; *ayatollah*; *Aztec Empire*; *Balkans*; *Bolshevism*; *Boxer Rebellion*; *Buddhism*; *Byzantine Empire*; *caliph*; *Calvinism*; *caste system*; *Catherine II*; *Catholic Church*; *Charles V*; *Christianity*; *clash of civilizations*; *concordat*; *Confucianism*; *conservatism*; *convergence*; conquistadores; *Coptic Church*; *Hernando Cortés*; *Counter Reformation*; *Crimean War*; *Oliver Cromwell*; *Crusades*; *Daoism*; *devil theories of war*; *diplomacy*; *Druse*; encomienda; *Edict of Nantes*; *Eighty Years' War*; *Elizabeth I*; *Enlightenment*; *fanaticism*; *Ferdinand and Isabella*; *Ferdinand II*; *Four Freedoms*; *Frederick the Great*; *French Revolution*; *fundamentalism*; *Mohandas Gandhi*; *Great Schism*; *Guelphs and Ghibellines*; *haj*; *harijans*; Hejaz; *Henri IV*; *Hinduism*; *Hirohito*; *Holocaust*; *Holy Land*; *Holy Places*; *Holy Roman Empire*; *Huguenots*; *human rights*; *Toyotomi Hideyoshi*; *imam*; *Inca Empire*; *Indian Mutiny*; *Indo-Pakistani Wars*; *Inquisition*; *Iranian Revolution*; *Islam*; *Ismaili*; *Jacobites*; *Jerusalem*; *Jesuits*; jihad; *Ali Jinnah*; *jizya*; *John Paul II*; *John XXIII*; *Judaism*; *just war tradition*; *Knights Templar*; *Kulturkampf*; *Lateran Treaties*; *liberation theology*; *mahdi*; *mandate of heaven*; *manifest destiny*; *Marxism*; *Mecca*; *Mehemet Ali*; *militarism*; *missionaries*; *mission, sense of*; *mullah*; *Münster, Treaty of*; *natural law*; *New Laws*; *Nigerian Civil War*; *nongovernmental organizations (NGOs)*; *Nystad, Treaty of (1721)*; *Old Believers*; *Old Catholics*; *Orthodox Church*; *Ottoman Empire*; *pacifism*; *Papal States*; *Peter the Great*; *Philip II*; *Pius IX*; *Pius XI*; *Pius XII*; *Protestant Reformation*; *al Qaeda*; *racism*; *Rajputs*; *Renaissance*; requerimiento; res publica Christiana; *rites controversy*; *Roman Empire*; *Roman Question*; *Russification*; *Russo-Turkish Wars*; *Salāh-ed-Dīn*; *sati (suttee)*; *Scotland*; *sharia*; *shi'ite*; *Shinto*; *Sikhism*; *Sinification*; *slavery*; *slave trade*; *Solidarity*; *Sovereign Military Order of Malta*; *sunni Islam*; *Taiping Rebellion*; *Taliban*; *terrorism*; *Third Rome*; *Thirty Years' War*; *thugi (thuggee)*; *Tokugawa shogunate*; *Teutonic Knights*; *Uniate Church*; *Vatican*; *Ven-*

dée rebellion; Wahhabi; Wars of Religion; White Lotus Rebellion; William Wilberforce; Zionism.

remedy. When a state agrees to make legal redress for some action it has taken which has been deemed unfair or illegal and has caused harm to an *alien.* Under *international customary law,* an individual seeking *damages* against a foreign *state* must first seek redress by all available local means ("exhaustion of local remedies") before his or her government is entitled to appeal under rules of *diplomatic protection.* There has been a recent modification in multiple cases, by the practice of lump-sum or general settlements between governments. *See also imputability; responsibility.*

remilitarization of the Rhineland. *See Rhineland.*

remittances. *Profits* from foreign *subsidiaries* of *multinational corporations* (MNCs), or wages from migrant workers to their families and accounts in their home country, *repatriated* from wherever they are earned abroad.

remonstrance. A synonym for *diplomatic protest. See also diplomatic note;* pro forma.

Renaissance (Italian). A profound intellectual and cultural efflorescence, as well as a political and diplomatic revolution away from the *res publica Christiana* toward the modern, secular *state,* which began in Italy but influenced all Europe and then all the world. It can be traced as far back as the life work of Francesco Petrarch (1304–1374), among others in the high Middle Ages, but it reached its vital and brilliant peak in the late fifteenth century. Some consider it to have spread beyond Italy, lasting through the life of René Descartes (1596–1650). The Renaissance is closely identified with events in *Venice* and Florence and other northern Italian polities, but in fact it affected most of the peninsula before spreading over the Alps to influence all of Europe and to shape the character of the modern age. Culturally, it was distinguished by a revival of classical learning—in particular in the natural sciences, but also in theological criticism and moral philosophy—inspired in part by lost or newly translated texts acquired through Muslim middlemen in great centers of Islamic scholarship such as Sicily, *Granada,* and Seville. Its profound impact on cultural life arose from a new, secularist celebration of humanism, empiricism, and rationalism, which would find full flower in the *Enlightenment.* It is justly famous, although historically less important, for its extraordinary advances in the fine arts and literature. Commercially, it marked a dramatic expansion of commerce by credit, in which the Medici political and banking family of Florence played a central role as the single most important financial institution in Europe from its founding in 1397 to its end in 1494, the year after the French invasion of Italy.

The most direct and world-changing influences of the Renaissance concerned *diplomacy, international law*, and *war*: Italian thinkers changed political perceptions forever, while Italian diplomats and soldiers fanned out into Europe, especially after the French invasion of 1493, selling new services such as resident diplomacy and refined espionage to powerful foreign monarchs. And Europeans flocked to Italy to study in the new "Italian school" of war and diplomacy, as well as the new Italian style in painting, poetry, and sculpture. The Renaissance witnessed the "golden age" of the Italian peninsular system of independent *city-states*, whose unique political patterns were later copied and helped supplant more general *feudal* relations in Western Europe. And it helped overturn the old sense of universal community in Christendom in favor of more narrow definitions of political loyalty to individual secular states, and to the lusty exercise of power by the new "princes" who governed their exciting, and often also illicit, relations. It was these city states which first explicitly formulated the idea of the *balance of power*, around the middle of the fifteenth century, as a description and then as a theoretical justification for the equilibrium which developed in fact among the five larger Italian powers (Venice, Florence, Milan, Naples, and the *Papal States*). The machinations and wolf-like relations of this insulated subsystem, isolated by Alpine borders and the distant preoccupations of the *Great Powers* during most of the fifteenth century, gave rise to the central ideas of *Machiavellian* ethical and political theory, including a revival of interest in constitutional *republics*.

The new, permanent diplomacy of the Italian Renaissance took clear form roughly between 1420 and 1493. It would become the model for all subsequent diplomacy, first in Europe and then globally. When the movement passed north of the Alps it reinforced a shift in power already underway from the Mediterranean to the Atlantic states: from *Byzantium* and the *Holy Roman Empire* to England, France, the Netherlands, Portugal, and Spain. In sum, the Renaissance marked the transition from the ancient and feudal eras to modern times, not just for Europe but through the subsequent expansion and global dominance of Europe in the age of *imperialism*, for the entire world. In addition, its rational curiosity and impulse toward change in *economics, politics, religion*, and *technology* echo familiarly to modern hearing down to the present day. *See also Muhammad II; spice trade.*

Suggested Readings: Jacob Burkhardt, *Civilization of the Renaissance In Italy* (1995); G. Gash, *Renaissance Armies* (1975); John R. Hale, *War and Society in Renaissance Europe* (1985); John R. Hale, *Machiavelli and Renaissance Italy* (1960); Niccolò Machiavelli, *The Prince* (1532); Garrett Mattingly, *Renaissance Diplomacy* (1955).

rendition. Surrender of an individual between *states* which have an *inter se* relationship. *See also extradition.*

reneversement des alliances. "Reversal of alliances." For examples, whole or partial, *see Aztecs; Brest-Litovsk; diplomatic revolution; Frederick the Great;*

Prince Metternich; Napoleonic Wars; Nazi-Soviet Pact; Seven Years' War; Tilsit; Triple Alliance.

reparations. (1) During peacetime: Money or goods delivered abroad to make redress for a prior *illegal act*. In this form, reparations are usually minor sums paid to foreign interests in compensation for *damage* to private or governmental property, or for harm done to another state's citizens, or for transgressions against that state's legal rights. For instance, in 2001 the United States paid for unintentional damage and deaths it inflicted on the Chinese embassy in Serbia during the *NATO* bombing campaign over *Kosovo*, while China paid to repair retaliatory damage to the U.S. embassy in Beijing caused by riotous Chinese. (2) As a result of war: Money or goods extracted from a defeated power to defray the cost of repairing war damage done to the victor, often but not always based on the claim that the losing side provoked the war. Inter alia, Great Britain compelled *Qing* China to pay reparations after the *Opium Wars*, and multiple powers demanded reparations from China for damages done during the *Boxer Uprising*; Japan insisted on reparations from China after the *First Sino-Japanese War* (1894–1895); Germany extracted reparations from Russia at *Brest-Litovsk*; at the *Paris Peace Conference* following *World War I*, the *Allies* demanded reparations from the *Central Powers*; the Soviet Union and France took heavy reparations, in cash and in kind, from Germany after *World War II* (the Soviets also unilaterally took reparations from Manchuria); and the *United Nations* forced Iraq to pay reparations immediately after the *Gulf War* (1990–1991) to Kuwait and other Gulf War victims. In 1999 a UN commission ordered that Iraq also pay compensation to Israel for damage done by unprovoked Scud missile attacks.

The most famous case of reparations was for damages authorized in the so-called *war guilt clause* of the Treaty of Versailles with Germany and in related treaties with other defeated Central Powers. In a complex interplay of inter-Allied *war debts* and reparations, payment issues dominated international relations in the 1920s and, when compounded by the effects of the *Smoot-Hawley Tariff*, helped unravel and depress the world economy in the 1930s. German reparations were divided into categories: cash payments; payments in kind (principally coal, timber, chemicals, and pharmaceuticals); and credits for occupied or lost territories. The issue was complicated by *Lloyd George*, who intruded the issue of British widow and veteran pensions into Allied demands, since Britain had little to no actual war damage to claim, unlike France; this increased the British share of the total, but contrary to the calculations of *John Maynard Keynes*, it did not increase the overall burden. Later research demonstrated that *Clemenceau* put forward quite moderate demands and that France in the 1920s was open to economic cooperation with Germany in ways which presaged the post–*World War II* formation of the *European Community*. The United States did not seek or accept any reparations at Paris. In the end, Germany was assigned a level of payments it could well have made, because assessments were based not on Allied claims but on calculation of the German ability to pay.

As a nation, however, Germany later chose not to pay in full, and the *Weimar* government may well have deliberately caused a *hyperinflation* in order to pay its reparations bills in reduced-value Reichsmarks. That demoralized the middle classes, radicalized the working classes, severely undermined any chance for democracy to take root in Germany, and thereby ultimately destroyed the Weimar Republic itself. Since German reparations payments were used by Britain and France principally to pay war debts still owed to the United States, and since *Coolidge* and other American presidents refused to waive those debts, the German reparations crisis affected the entire international economic system, which ultimately collapsed in the *Great Depression*. The Lausanne Conference (1932) recognized this hard reality and brought reparations to an effective end, presaging the collapse of the entire Versailles system. Austria, Hungary, and the other *successor states* of the *Austro-Hungarian Empire* were treated like Germany with regard to reparations. Bulgaria was assigned a fixed sum, later reduced. Turkey received the lightest reparations burden of any defeated power, mainly because it lost so much territory in the *Treaty of Sèvres*. In the renegotiated *Treaty of Lausanne*, Turkey's reparations bill was erased as part of a more generous peace. Note: Reparations should not be confused with either *indemnity* or *restitution*. *See also Aix-la-Chapelle; apology; Caroline Affair; Dawes Plan; liberal peace program; Lusitania Notes; prisoner of war; treaties of Rapallo; remedy; Antonio López de Santa Anna; underdevelopment; war termination; Young Plan.*

Suggested Readings: Bruce Kent, *The Spoils of War* (1989); William R. Keylor, ed., *Legacy of the Great War: Peacemaking, 1919* (1998); Anthony Lentin, *Lloyd George, Woodrow Wilson, and the Guilt of Germany* (1984); Marc Trachtenberg, *Reparation in World Politics: France and European Economic Diplomacy, 1916–23* (1980); Stephen Schuker, *American "Reparations" to Germany, 1919–1933* (1988).

repartimiento. *See encomienda system.*

repatriate. To return someone (e.g., *persona non grata* or *refugees*) or something (e.g., *profits* or *remittances*) to his, her, or its state of *citizenship* or origin. *See also boat people; Cossacks; deportation; extradition; prisoner of war.*

representation. The right of *international personalities* (and very rarely, other entities) to send and receive agents abroad to represent their positions and interests as a member of the *community of nations*. The most recent *codification* of these rights came in 1961, with the *Vienna Conventions*. The main functions of such representatives, or *diplomats*, are information gathering (but not *espionage*) about the affairs of state, commerce, science, the military, and so on in the host country, and communication of accurate reports to his or her *foreign ministry*; *negotiation*; *protocol*; seeing to due process and fair play for nationals in legal or other trouble with the host country; and representation of the *sovereign* power and the policies of his or her government to the host government, and at times also to the host population. In return for *diplomatic immunity* a diplomat must refrain from *subversion*, espionage (many engage in this nonetheless), smuggling, counterfeiting, and other merely criminal acts. A second category of representation involves *consuls*. These are commercial representatives. Historically, in the late Middle Ages in Europe and early in the *Renaissance*, they were chosen by and from the corps of foreign merchants in a given city. Consuls are official representatives of governments, but they do not normally enjoy diplomatic immunity. Their main functions are facilitating commercial and other transactions; administering travel documents, *passports*, and *visas*; aiding fellow nationals in difficulties and before local courts, if necessary; and reporting on economic and other activity in the host country. *See also ambassador*; attaché; chargé; *envoy*; *envoy extraordinary*; *minister plenipotentiary*; *nonresident ambassador*; persona grata; persona non grata; *plenipotentiary*; *special interest section*.

reprisal. (1) In *international law*, an act normally illegal, but permitted if taken to punish the prior *illegal act* of another *state*; e.g., applying discriminatory *tariffs*, deportation of *diplomats* for cause as *persona non grata*, and so forth. (2) In *war*, reciprocal punishment; e.g., Israel's bombing southern Lebanon in reprisal for *guerrilla* or rocket attacks launched from there. *See also letters of marque*; *Treaty of Paris (1856)*.

republic. (1) In classical usage, a constitutional *state* where the citizenry is said to be bound in a single community by a *social contract*, is regularly consulted on matters of governance, and exercises power (or thinks it does) through chosen or appointed representatives. (2) In modern usage, any state headed by a president, elected or not, rather than a hereditary *monarch*; not necessarily a constitutional *democracy*.

Republican-Democratic Party. The original name of the *Democratic Party*. It was founded by *Thomas Jefferson* and *James Madison* in 1792 and retained the name until 1830, when under *Andrew Jackson* it was known simply as the Democratic Party. Four Republican-Democratic presidents were elected in succession: Jefferson, Madison, *James Monroe*, and *John Quincy Adams*.

Republican Guard. The *elite* corps of armored and other units within the Iraqi Army which backed the *Ba'ath* coup in 1968; supported *Saddam Hussein* in power and in his internal repressions; was bloodied but escaped destruction in the *Gulf War*; repressed the *Kurds* and southern *shi'ites* after the war; and continued to sustain Saddam in power into the twenty-first century.

republicanism. Clear preference for constitutional government and an elected president and/or supreme legislature, rather than a personal *sovereign*. *See also absolutism; American Revolution; democracy; divine right of kings; Enlightenment; French Revolution; Immanuel Kant; Niccolò Machiavelli; monarchism; nonintervention; popular sovereignty; Jean-Jacques Rousseau; social contract.*

Republican Party (United States). The second of the modern American political parties, it was founded as successor to the *Whigs* in 1854 in order to oppose the extension of *slavery* to the new western states of Kansas and Nebraska. Originally based in the west and still strongest there, it supported *free soil* farmers and rapid western settlement. Its opposition to any extension of slavery (an institution inimical to free farming in the west) appealed to eastern abolitionists even as the issue tore apart the rival *Democratic Party* on north-south lines. The first Republican president was *Abraham Lincoln*. During *Reconstruction* and under *Grant*, the party adjusted so that its base included general business and industrial, as well as western and agrarian interests. It continued to dominate national politics for over three decades, losing the presidency only rarely before 1912. *William McKinley* took the United States into the *Spanish-American War*, and under *Theodore Roosevelt* the Republican Party made the United States into a Pacific power and led it through a dalliance with overseas *imperialism*. The party split badly over *Taft's* reelection bid but remained powerful in Congress, where select Republicans helped block the *Treaty of Versailles*. After *World War I* its nativist and *isolationist* wing commanded, and it became home to most *conservatives* outside the "solid South," where the Democrats held sway. In the *White House* again, 1920–1932, under *Harding, Coolidge*, and *Hoover*, it governed passively. In opposition, 1933–1953, and with many grassroots Republicans still convinced that social, in addition to economic, *laissez-faire* was next to godliness, it opposed the *New Deal* reforms of *Franklin Roosevelt*.

However, during *World War II* most Republicans—along with most Americans—abandoned isolationism to embrace the United Nations and a more active American global role, especially toward China, although many remained uncomfortable with postwar *Keynesian* initiatives such as those taken at *Bretton Woods*. Also, an isolationist and "strict constructionist" minority hovered on the *right wing* of the party and in Congress, impeding *Eisenhower's* activist foreign policy by seeking a constitutional amendment (the Bricker Amendment) to hamstring the president's ability to employ *executive agreements*. During the *Cold War* most Republicans were fiercely anti-Soviet. Unlike the Democrats, most of whom were also anti-Soviet but who as a party had a pronounced inclination toward *Atlanticism*, the Republican Party was drawn by its historical western roots into an emphasis on waging the Cold War in Asia. That led to a grand compromise in which blanket anti-communism in the Party platform concealed regional tensions. After 1968 the Republicans again dominated presidential elections. The Party endured the fiasco of *Watergate*, during which its leaders did the right thing and told *Nixon* directly he must resign, and then *Ford's* perceived ineptitude. The conservative wing of the party was ascendant in the 1980s under *Ronald Reagan*, emphasizing *monetarism* and *supply-side* policies in the country's foreign economic policy, although this was less the case under the moderate-centrist *George H. Bush*. With the end of the Cold War, the Republican foreign policy consensus was broken, and old divisions reappeared between a nativist and isolationist minority and the conservative-internationalist majority. The party was also damaged by two third-party efforts in the 1990s which split its base and helped elect *Bill Clinton*. Following the *Gulf War*, moderates and conservative-internationalists in the party again clashed with the neo-isolationists and social conservative wing. After eight years of Clinton, however, they reunited to elect *George W. Bush* to the White House in 2000.

Republic of China (ROC) on Taiwan. *See Taiwan.*

reputation. *See apology; face; prestige; protocol; restitution.*

requerimiento. *Ferdinand* of Aragon summoned a panel of leading theologians to advise on the status of natives in the *New World*. They drew up the "requerimiento," which was supposed to be read aloud by all *conquistadores* prior to making war on the Indians of the Americas. It demanded that natives accept the authority of the *Catholic Church* and the United Crowns of Spain, and that they permit *missionaries* to move and preach freely in their lands. If these demands were refused or ignored, the conquistadores might lawfully—and with full religious sanction—commence slaughter and conquest with a clear and a good conscience. It was first read out, to baffled native Americans who could not understand its language, in 1514. *See also encomienda system; just war.*

requisition. When an invading or other foreign army demands *billets*, foodstuffs, and other matériel necessities from the civilian population, with or without full payment.

res communis. "Common things." Those things held to lie outside any *sovereign* authority, such as the air as opposed to *airspace*, the *seabed*, the *Moon and planets*, *satellite* parking orbits, and *radio* band broadcast frequencies. This notion lies at the core of the *common heritage principle*.

reservation. A statement reserving *sovereign* rights by withholding *consent* from specific provisions of a *treaty*. It operates only if other parties to the treaty agree. If they do not, the reserving state must accept the whole treaty without reservation, or decline the treaty. *See also derogation; ratification; understanding.*

reserve currency. Holdings of *hard currency* used to finance trade arrangements and pay the *national debt*. *See also foreign exchange reserve.*

reserves. (1) In *war*: That portion of an armed force held back from combat for emergency defense or *counterattack*; or in a prolonged conflict and wider sense, potential *conscripts* or *war matériel* available to replace battlefield losses. (2) In *peace*: that portion of the military enrolled but not on active duty, and maintaining respectable levels of training and preparedness. (3) In finances: A state's financial holdings, including *gold, reserve currency, International Monetary Fund* credit, and *Special Drawing Rights.*

res extra commercium. In *international law*, a thing excluded from the sphere of private transaction.

res inter alios acta. In *international law*, a thing which is the exclusive concern of others. *See also noninterference.*

resistance. (1) A generic term for *partisans* actively opposed to foreign occupation by force of arms. *Winston Churchill* placed great hopes in local resistance to *Nazi* occupation, but these rarely materialized. For France and several other European countries, "the Resistance" during *World War II* later assumed near-mythical proportions, sometimes obscuring the competing reality of extensive *collaboration.* In fact, during the first half of 1942 fewer than 150 German soldiers and officials were assassinated in France. When France was liberated in July and August 1944, in the whole country there were only 120,000 Resistance fighters. Such small numbers exacted a minimal strategic cost on the *Wehrmacht,* which by 1944 had fully 60 divisions in France to face the landings in Normandy. Only in the German rear on the *eastern front,* in Yugoslavia, Norway, and Italy, was resistance more than an irritant to the Wehrmacht or local *fascists,* and even then the damage done was strategically minor and paled compared with the price the Nazis exacted in savage and indiscriminate reprisal. In several Asian states, with the defeat and departure of the Japanese, national resistance shifted against a reimposition of European colonial rule. Note: French Resistance fighters on Corsica and in the south were called "Maquis." (2) More recently, and especially in studies of African history, "resistance" has been inflated to refer to any and all opposition to *colonialism,* including psychological and cultural, drawing on *Franz Fanon,* not just armed opposition to the imposition of foreign rule. *See also Chetniks; Free French; guerrilla warfare; Katyn massacre; national liberation, wars of; Pripet Marshes; Tito; Viêt Cong; Warsaw Rising.*

res judicata. In *international law*, a thing which is decided.

res nullius. In *international law*, a thing without ownership.

resolution. A consensus statement by a *multilateral* body, whether the *United Nations General Assembly* or a regional or *treaty* organization. Within the United Nations, General Assembly resolutions are nonbinding but remain only *recommendations*. They have at most quasi-legislative authority under *international law* and their intentions require formal *consent* in a follow-up *convention* to have any binding force. Only the *Security Council* can make "binding resolutions," and not all of its resolutions fall into that category. Other *international organizations* have different *rules* concerning how their members are bound by resolutions and recommendations. *See also declaration; qualified majority voting; weighted voting.*

Resolution 242, Security Council (November 22, 1967). It called for a "just and lasting peace" in the Middle East, based on "secure and recognized boundaries," with Israeli withdrawal from *occupied territories* in exchange for *recognition*. *See also land for peace.*

Resolution 338, Security Council (October 22, 1973). Often cited in tandem with *Resolution 242*, it called for an immediate *cease–fire* in the *Fourth Arab-Israeli War*, to be followed by implementation of Resolution 242 and *negotiations* leading to a final settlement.

Resolution 660, Security Council (August 2, 1990). It found Iraq's *invasion* of Kuwait a breach of the law and of *peace*, condemned it, and demanded immediate and unconditional withdrawal. The resolution also called for follow-up *negotiations* with Kuwait over outstanding Iraqi grievances.

Resolution 678, Security Council (November 29, 1990). This resolution authorized members to use "all necessary means" to implement *Resolution 660* should Iraq fail to withdraw from Kuwait by January 15, 1991. It did, and so they did. *See also Gulf War.*

resolutive condition. In *international law*, a future event which, if it occurs, will have the effect of abrogating an existing right.

resources. In economics, the "land" (territory) available for *exploitation*, as well as the quality of that land in terms of agricultural usability, *natural resources*, and sometimes topography and climate. *See also power.*

resource wars. Wars waged, ostensibly or in fact, primarily to resolve disputes over control of scarce and valuable *natural resources*, such as the *War of the Pacific*. *See also oil; war; water.*

res petita. The object of an international legal claim.

responsibility. A central principle of *international law* by which *states* must make *compensation* for any *illegal act* they make. This does not extend to harmful acts against *aliens* made by private firms or citizens, unless the state in question fails to provide access to local remedies ("denial of justice") to the injured alien through which that party may seek redress of their grievance. *See also apology; imputability; remedy; reparations; restitution.*

res publica Christiana. "Christian Commonwealth." This West European, medieval concept expressed an admixture of pride in the *Roman* heritage of Latin law and civilization, and genuine faith in the unity and existence of a godly community of all Latin Christians which overarched *feudal*, political, and *dynastic* ties. It withstood the *schism* with the *Byzantine Church*, but began to break down with the "Avignon Captivity" of the Roman pontiffs. It provided deep cultural resistance to the idea and emergence of the modern, secular *nation-state*. It did not survive, other than as a romantic memory and papal pipe-dream, the Italian *Renaissance*, the sixteenth century breakup of Latin Christianity during the *Reformation*, and the attendant rise of self-seeking states and powerful centralized monarchies. Yet, the modern idea of the *European Union* that all Europeans belong to a single cultural community, and should also belong to a single political community, may be traced to historical memory of the Christian commonwealth which once actually existed. Politically, the res publica Christiania also contributed to development of a common body of law, much of which was incorporated by *Grotius* and others into modern *international law*. *See also clash of civilizations; Islamic world; Niccolò Machiavelli.*
   Suggested Reading: Garrett Mattingly, *Renaissance Diplomacy* (1955).

restitutio in integrum. *See restitution.*

restitution. (1) In *international law*: Returning some *object* of the law to the condition it enjoyed before a state committed an *illegal act* which harmed it. (2) Concerning *human rights* abuses: Formal state *apology* and financial "restitution" made for violations of human rights by prior governments. Restitution agreements aim to remove from the international (or domestic) agenda a long-standing and contentious issue which harms a state's reputation, by providing formal acknowledgment of the truth of the violations and symbolic compensation. This practice gained salience in international relations after *World War II*, and again during and after the 1990s. A precedent for restitution was set when *Konrad Adenauer* agreed to West German payments to Israel for acts committed against European Jews during the *Holocaust*, ultimately amounting to $50 billion paid to Israel and its citizens. In 2000 a multi-billion-dollar settlement was made by Swiss banks concerning deposits made by Holocaust victims they had hidden ("lost") for half a century. Other former *Axis* states also made payments, though less generously. Into the twenty-first century unresolved claims stood against Japan for severe personal harm done to so-called *comfort women* during World War II. Similarly, some 50,000 Chinese made claims against their use as *slave laborers* in Japan, 1937–1945. Australia, Canada, and New Zealand all settled *aboriginal* land claims in the 1990s based on earlier *treaties*, including restitution payments to native groups. Claims for restitution to blacks and to African nations for the manifold adverse effects of *slavery* in the Americas were also made, but they failed to gain political traction. *See also remedy; Truth Commission.*

Restoration. (1) The return to France of the *Bourbons*, in the (enlarged) form of *Louis XVIII*, with the aid of foreign armies in 1814, and so again after *Waterloo*. (2) The governmental system in Spain from 1875 to the *coup* of *Primo de Rivera* in 1923. (3) Any return to power of the old order and regime following a revolutionary interregnum. *See also Meiji.*

restrictive interpretation. Narrow, literal interpretation of the text of a *treaty*.

retaliation. (1) In *international law*: When one *state* suspends compliance with a *treaty* on the ground that another contracting party is not living up to its *terms*. (2) In *nuclear deterrence* theory: The threat of massive counter-destruction with *second strike* forces should an adversary contemplate or launch a *first strike*. *See also massive retaliation; retorsion.*

retorsion. Acts taken by states in *retaliation*, which in themselves are quite legal but might be considered unfriendly, such as closing access to markets, withdrawing *aid*, expelling *persona non grata*, and the like.

retreat. The withdrawal of a military force as a result of enemy action. A "forced retreat" is a withdrawal compelled directly by an attacking enemy force. A "strategic retreat" might be made in order to rest, repair, and preserve forces to fight another day, or to gain a subsequent positional or other advantage. A "rout" is a pell-mell retreat in which all military discipline and order collapse and units and individuals look to their own safety first and foremost. *See also advance.*

retreat from Moscow (1812). The Grand Armée of *Napoleon I* captured Moscow in September 1812, after the bloody battle of *Borodino*. They found the city empty, abandoned by its inhabitants. Within a day, fires broke out which swept through Moscow's tens of thousands of wooden buildings. The conflagration was most likely deliberately set by Russian *partisans* in an ultimate act of the *scorched earth* policy Russia had followed all summer and fall. The fire left the French with few billets and less sustenance. To escape the smoke and heat, Napoleon fled the Kremlin to shelter outside the city. He grew worried as news arrived of a failed coup attempt against him in Paris and of defeat of his army in Spain by *Wellington*. With *Alexander I* refusing to meet or talk, Napoleon ordered a general retreat on October 18th. His Grand Armée, weighed down now with cartloads of booty and having lost all sense of regular discipline, was denied the southern route by an approaching Russian army of reinforcement. Napoleon thus left by the same northern route by which he had invaded Russia, retracing lands already scorched by Russian partisans and scoured by his own foragers. As a result, his troops and horses alike were unable to live off the land. Winter weather, and *Cossack* raiders, took an immense toll on the shuffling, straggling, and ill-disciplined French. Napoleon was nearly captured as he fled ahead of the main body, racing for Paris before news of the catastrophe could be used to unseat him. Barely 1,000 French were still fit for fighting when the Grand Armée reached the border at the Beresina. Of more than 600,000 French and allied troops with which Napoleon entered Russia, fewer than 25,000 made it out: 300,000 were dead, 200,000 had been taken prisoner; the rest had deserted even before Napoleon reached Moscow. He also lost 80 percent of his *artillery* and, most damaging of all, 200,000 wholly irreplaceable, trained *cavalry* mounts. His comment on this ruinous defeat, which aroused a legion of enemies against him, was "from the sublime to the ridiculous is but a step." Smelling blood, the Great Powers of Europe gathered for a final campaign to be rid of him. They crushed his last army in the *Battle of Leipzig* (1813), where the lack of French cavalry hurt the French Army badly, and took Paris in early 1814. *See also Hundred Days.*

Suggested Readings: The pathos, and horror, of this great event is richly captured in Leo Tolstoy's classic novel *War and Peace*, and in A. Brett-James, *1812: Napoleon's Defeat in Russia* (1966).

retrenchment. An interior fortification within a larger fortress, to which a defending force can retreat if the outer walls are breached.

retrofit. Upgrading weapons systems by fitting them with advanced modifications. The main benefit is cheapness.

Réunion. This island located northwest of Madagascar became a French possession in 1665. Settlers imported *slaves* from Omani traders in *Zanzibar* and on Madagascar to serve its plantation economy. It is today an *overseas department* of France.

revaluation. Changing the official (as opposed to *black market*) rate of a *currency*, as measured against the *gold standard* or the value of *hard currencies*.

revanchism. From the French for "revenge," a policy of seeking to recover *territory* lost in an earlier *war*. *See also Alsace-Lorraine; irredentism.*

reverse course. Changes in U.S. *occupation* policy in Japan brought about by the exigencies of the *Cold War* in Asia. Essentially, the *Truman* administration determined in 1947 that it lacked the resources to simultaneously pursue *containment* of the Soviet Union and continue to suppress the defeated *Axis* powers, Germany and Japan. *George Kennan* was dispatched to convince *Douglas MacArthur* and *SCAP* of this and of the need to switch to a policy of rapid economic growth in the defeated Axis states. Leftist historians blame this decision for the "failure" of *denazification* in Germany and for the "failure" to develop a more liberal democracy in Japan and to complete the breakup of the *zaibatsu*. That charge must be balanced against the long-term emergence of stable, free societies in both countries.

revision. Reconsideration of a *judgment*, or the redrafting of a *treaty* to take account of changed circumstance.

revisionism. (1) Any foreign policy which seeks to amend a given regional or global status quo. (2) A generic term for histories which challenge established interpretations of events, from whatever point of view. (3) A term commonly used about the *Wisconsin school* of interpretation of U.S. foreign policy, and other histories which portray the United States as primarily responsible for the *Cold War*. (4) A pejorative term used by the orthodox about those who reassessed or revised the basic tenets of *Marxism*. It was a common charge in Russia during the *Yezhovshchina*, and again in China during the *Great Proletarian Cultural Revolution*. It was later used by China regarding the ossifying internal system of the Soviet Union and its foreign policy shift to *peaceful coexistence*. *See also aggression; imperialism; Sino-Soviet split.*

revisionist power. Any *state* which seeks to alter, especially by forceful means, the *territorial* or political status quo of a *peace* settlement or *balance of power*. The antonym is *status quo power*.

Revolt of the Netherlands. *See Eighty Years' War.*

revolution. The term descends from the great work by Nicolas Copernicus, "De Revolutionibus" (1543), which overturned the Aristotelian worldview of an earth-centered, static universe by establishing mathematical proofs for planetary revolutions around the sun. Political revolutions are the forcible overthrow not merely of a given government, but of an entire political and/or social system, usually by a significant portion of a population—though seldom a majority, and occasionally merely by a self-appointed *vanguard* or some revolutionary clique—and are usually accompanied by mass violence. They frequently result in *civil war*, and may also spark an international war or series of wars. Conversely, foreign wars—particularly when lost—may also lead to internal revolutions, as in Russia in 1905 and again in 1917. Internationally, revolutions greatly disrupt normal relations among states by bringing to power governments which do not necessarily accept the old diplomatic and legal rules which help sustain peaceable relations among nations. Once dedicated revolutionaries consolidate their power in a given country they typically, and zealously, seek to export their enthusiasm for change and their *radical* creed, which they often sincerely believe is the only conceivable one upon which *legitimacy* may henceforth rest, and which therefore justifies their effort to violently remake the world. In turn, this zealotry usually provokes formation of counterrevolutionary alliances composed of *status quo powers* and threatened social elites, or just discomfited neighboring states, which may well intervene if they believe they are seriously threatened by a spillover of radicalism or overt efforts to export revolution. More often, they will act in concert to *contain* the revolutionary state until its people "return to their senses" and their government returns to law-abiding membership in the *community of nations*. More positively, the example of revolution may stimulate reform in other countries which are compelled to at last recognize that they, too, have a festering social or political problem, but one by which reform efforts will permit them to avert comparable internal turmoil.

Most revolutions are of only local importance, displacing a given regime and perhaps, but far from always, increasing the quotient of social or political justice in a single society. Some have wider significance primarily because they occur within a sizeable *regional power* and therefore affect surrounding countries; for example, the several *Chinese Revolutions* of the twentieth century and the *Iranian Revolution*. A rare few have had world historical significance, for two reasons: (1) they propounded universal claims about their new conception of political legitimacy while simultaneously rejecting all legitimacy claimed by states of the extant *ancien régime*; and (2) they took place within a *Great Power*, which gave the ideologues in control a real capability to effect change or simply to cause trouble on a grand scale. The most powerful examples of such revolutions were the *French Revolution* (1789–1799) and the *Russian Revolution* (1917). These great upheavals affected the entire *international system*, upsetting and breaking apart existing alliances, altering the geopolitical importance and affecting the security of all nearby countries, leading to perceptions of conflict with other Great Powers on a global scale and over irreconcilable differences, raising overall levels of international tension, lending material and moral support to ideological admirers and *fellow-travelers* in other countries, provoking insecurity among foreign elites through *subversion*, and sometimes taking direct military action to advance their national cause under the guise of exporting revolutionary principles at point of bayonet. Proponents of such grand revolutions—of calculated and cataclysmic upheaval and destruction as a prerequisite and remedy for social, political, or economic injustice—almost always assert that they are really about the business of radical transformation not just of a given society, even if a Great Power, but of human nature itself.

Major revolutionary movements thus usually begin by proclaiming dedication to the highest plateau of human *liberation* yet sought or achieved in history, but then devolve into rank and harsh persecution of any who stand in the way of the purifying changes the revolution proposes. This phase is *The Terror*, as it was called in France in 1793 and has been known in every major revolution since then, in which the pure of heart and intention begin with the "necessary" eradication of "enemies of the people," but ultimately turn their puritanical fury against ordinary individuals who "willfully and perversely" display counterrevolutionary tendencies by clearly wishing to continue in the old habits of their daily lives. At this point, an organized reaction may occur led by the principal beneficiaries of the changes the revolution has made, but who fear its growing radicalism will cost them their lives or property. This *Thermidorian reaction* (again, the model is French) will seek to overthrow the radicals in order to lock in real gains. This awful, bloody pattern in France was repeated, with variations, during distinct phases of the later Russian, Chinese, and Iranian Revolutions, among others. *See also American Revolution; Catholic Counter Reformation; class struggle; collectivization; communism;* coup d'etat; *Oliver Cromwell; cultural revolution; Enlightenment; fascism; Industrial Revolution; insurrection; kulaks; Marxism-Leninism; Meiji Restoration; modernization; Naziism; paradigm; Protestant Reformation; rebellion; Renaissance; revolution from above; revolution in military affairs; revolution on horseback; rising expectations; totalitarianism; Emerich de Vattel.*

Suggested Readings: David Armstrong, *Revolution and World Order* (1993); Edmund Burke, *Reflections on the Revolution in France* (1790); Fred Halliday, *Revolution and World Politics* (1999); Mark Katz, ed., *Revolution* (2000).

Revolutionary Alliance. An anti-*Manchu* coalition arranged in 1905 between *Sun Yixian* and Chinese students studying in Japan. It was active in anti-*Qing* agitation, *subversion*, and *propaganda*, but also in military adventures in the lead up to the Wuhan revolt and *Chinese Revolution* (1911). *See also Wang Jingwei.*

Revolutionary Guards. *See hostage crisis; Iran; Iran-Iraq War.*

Revolutionary War. *See American Revolution.*

revolution from above. Any major social or economic upheaval or fundamental reform instituted by the reigning political authorities in a country, often against lower-level resistance. For example, *Peter I* and *Stalin* forced major changes on resistant social groups in Russia, Peter on the *boyars* and Stalin on all those he identified as "class enemies," but especially the *kulaks*. Such "revolutions" can be just as permanent and violent as mass phenomena that overturn existing power structures from below. In the twentieth century, "revolutions from above" have sometimes been imposed by foreign powers in *occupation* of a defeated opponent. The most spectacularly successful examples of this were the American and Allied occupations of Japan and Germany, respectively, after World War II. *See also* bakufu; *Bismarck; Lucius Clay; collectivization; communism; cultural revolution; Deng Xiaoping; dictatorship of the proletariat; Mikhail Gorbachev; Vladimir Ilyich Lenin; Mao Zedong; Douglas MacArthur; National Socialism; vanguard; war Communism.*

revolution in military affairs (RMA). The original theory of a "revolution in military affairs" (c. 1950) located it in early modern Europe, c. 1560–1650, and specifically in the Netherlands and Sweden. Subsequent studies stretched the term to cover the fifteenth through eighteenth centuries. It was especially identified with the expansive use of *infantry*, drill and professional discipline, the adoption of firearms and *artillery* arising from the *gunpowder revolution*, the corresponding adoption of heavy *fortifications*, and above all, the rise of professional *standing armies* and navies. The latter was key, because it required not merely tactical adjustments to new technologies employed on the battlefield, but a wholesale reorganization of early modern societies to develop the professional discipline and organization characteristic of modern warfare that so distinguished it from the *feudal* period in Europe and elsewhere. The exemplars of the change were the Netherlands, which saw great innovations by *Maurice of Nassau* in waging the *Eighty Years' War* (1566–1648); Sweden under *Gustavus Adolphus* and in the *Thirty Years' War* (1618–1648); and the New Model Army in England during its Civil Wars (1642–1646 and 1650–1651) under *Cromwell*. A second great revolution in military affairs arrived with the *French Revolution*, but one primarily political and organizational rather than technological in nature. The weapons of 1792–1815 were little changed from those of 1689–1713. It was changes in the makeup of society itself brought about by the French Revolution which wrought enormous changes on the battlefield, as carried forward by the *levée en masse* and by *Napoleon* and his imitators. These underlying social, political, and ideological changes ended Europe's era of *dynastic wars* and inaugurated a vastly more destructive era of national wars, prior to the impact of *industrialization* on warfare in the nineteenth and twentieth centuries. More generally, a revolution in military affairs may be characterized as a radical shift in the military balance of power which occurs when new technologies combine with changes in war-fighting doctrine to make obsolete an existing weapons system—or to create a wholly new weapons system—which is key to the military capability of one or more of the *Great Powers*. This also requires that militaries learn how to make use of the new technology and/or doctrines, a fact which usually results in a time lag between the invention of some technology and when its full impact is felt upon a real battlefield.

Classic examples include (1) the Muslim crossbow, which devastated *Crusader* armies and then revolutionized warfare in Europe, so much so that the

Catholic Church considered making it a *prohibited weapon*; (2) the impact of the English longbow during the *Hundred Years' War* (1337–1453); (3) the move toward national armies, heavy artillery, and mass building of expensive warships and professional navies which marked the era of *Phillip II* and *Elizabeth I*, during the Eighty Years' War and on into the Thirty Years' War, though it is noteworthy that Imperial China, which might easily have done the same, forwent naval artillery in favor of retention of the old methods of ramming enemy ships followed by grappling and boarding by marines; (4) the new doctrinal and practical emphasis in *Napoleonic warfare* on rapid movement, light artillery, and *cavalry*, and reorganization of armies into *divisions* and *corps*; (5) increased speed and easier logistics at sea and in land warfare made possible by steam engines in the mid-nineteenth century, which created such *dual use* technologies as steamships and *railways*; (6) advances toward instant, detailed communications and command and control technologies in the twentieth century. As *World War I* began in August 1914, the main forms of battlefield communication were still word-of-mouth couriers and *flags*, with only limited use of telephone or telegraph (which had been available for many years but had not been fully incorporated into the command structure of armies). Just 30 years later *radio* dominated the battlefield and warfare at sea. Radar and sonar also signaled the arrival of the electronic age in warfare. A generation after that *satellites* orbited above high-technology, electronically integrated battlefields. This was a common feature in the twentieth century RMA: increased exploitation of information technologies (C^3I), together with planning for near-continuous operations and threats to an entire *theater of war*, so that enemy forces are denied relief or sanctuary in what were once considered deep, *rear echelon* areas. RMAs often trigger major geopolitical upheavals, as when technology arrives via *diffusion* in new geographical areas. Thus, firearms introduced to Japan by European traders became the instrument of unification of that divided land in the sixteenth and seventeenth centuries. In Africa, firearms tipped the balance away from the armored cavalry of the Sahel peoples toward hitherto dominated coastal tribes, which were the first to acquire the new weapons. This did not happen in North or South America, however, where other factors (disease, relative population, and rapid external conquest of the major Indian states) dominated.

Great military powers continuously pursue "RMA technologies," both in a search for new military advantage and out of concern that any extant advantage they may possess could be undercut by someone else's technological breakthrough. This raises a basic problem with the concept: if in fact military research is an ongoing activity, and new technologies are incorporated as they arise, then the process is accretive rather than "revolutionary." Even so, in its strong suggestion of an essential difference between large-scale modern war and most previous warfare, and its urgent reminder of the vital links among technology, organization, and military and political culture, the concept remains highly instructive. *See also aircraft carrier; air power; armor; ballistic missile defense; biological warfare;* Blitzkrieg; *chemical weapons; cruise missile; Dreadnought; ICBM; infantry; ironclads; machine gun; mercantilism; neutron bomb; nuclear weapons; rifled-bore; smart weapons; smooth-bore; stealth technology; Strategic Defense Initiative; terrain contour matching; Sébastien de Vauban; weapons of mass destruction.*

Suggested Readings: Brian Downing, *The Military Revolution and Political Change* (1992); Ian Glete, *Navies and Nations: Warships, Navies, and State-Building in Europe and America, 1500–1860* (1993); MacGregor Knox, *The Dynamics of Military Revolution, 1300–2050* (2001); Geoffrey Parker, *The Military Revolution,* 2nd ed. (1996).

"revolution on horseback." The idea that social, economic, political, and even moral progress may be advanced and instituted by a military dictator with a progressive bent. An essential part of the myth of *Napoleon I* was the notion that, despite a clear and pronounced tendency to *despotism*, he represented powerful moral and ideological forces of reform and consolidation of the gains of the *French Revolution*, at least until his coronation as emperor in 1804. That clearly was not the case from the point of view of London, Vienna, Berlin, or Moscow, but there was some truth to it in the *Rhineland* and other parts of the German Confederation, and in northern Italy, where the arrival of Napoleon and his armies was greeted as liberation from stuffy *autocracies* or outdated constitutional orders. Later figures who brought about revolution at point of bayonet played on this theme, most notably *Simón Bolívar* and *Garibaldi.*

Revolutions of 1830. Several European countries, and several parts of Italy, experienced social and political unrest, but most incidents were minor—more liberal reform efforts than *revolutions.* The exceptions were in France, where the *Bourbons* were displaced by the *July Monarchy;* Belgium, which seceded from the Netherlands with the acquiescence of the *Great Powers;* and Poland, where a full-scale *insurrection* was bloodily put down by *tsarist* troops in 1831.

Revolutions of 1848. The clashes of this remarkable year arose from dislocation between the new *industrial* sectors of national economies and an exodus of peasants from the countryside in search of jobs and *goods* which did not yet exist in abundant *supply.* That set a match to the tinder of urban political dissent in Northern Europe and national discontent in Southern Europe. The situation was aggravated by the failure of Europe's potato crop. It was not just Ireland which experienced successive years of blight and food shortages in the "hungry '40s." Although Ireland suffered more than most, there were "potato riots" in several centers, including Berlin itself. An additional cause of the outbreak was the frustration of *liberals* with the stultifying effects of *Metternich's* system. Nearly every country in Europe experienced profound unrest, or outright *revolution,* with only the outbreaks in Hungary (where

Russian troops of the *Holy Alliance* briefly intervened) and northern Italy extending into 1849. The exceptions were (1) Belgium and Britain, where *industrialization* and (partial) representative government blunted the economic crisis and vented frustration into reform rather than revolutionary movements; and (2) Russia, which was so backward the dynamic of *rising expectations* did not occur. In short, the most liberal and the most repressive societies alone escaped the unrest. Elsewhere, the middle classes led the poor into the streets, then shuddered at what they had done and turned to the old, conservative order to save them from their folly and their less fortunate countrymen. All the uprisings failed, some after bloody clashes and repression (Berlin, Milan, Prague, Rome, and Venice) by sovereigns who regained their confidence as the rebellions sputtered out or shifted into *anarchy*. The one lasting success was in Paris, where the *Second Republic* was set up, if that benighted experiment may be rightly deemed a success. Flaubert said of the exuberance of 1848, "It was an outburst of fear. . . . Intelligent men were made idiotic by it for the rest of their lives." *See also Communist Manifesto; Lajos Kossuth; Karl Marx; Pierre Joseph Proudhon; serfdom.*

Suggested Reading: Robert Evans, *The Revolutions of 1848–49* (2000).

Revolutions of 1989. The *Soviet bloc* began to collapse as reformist governments took power in several East European countries, and greater freedom of movement and expression was allowed in response to *Gorbachev's* trumpeting of *glasnost* and *perestroika* in the Soviet Union. That undercut the *legitimacy* of the stagnant, repressive, gloomy *satellites* of the East, and released decades of pent-up animosity to their *Communist Parties* and *nomenklatura*. The essential event of this historic year came with *de facto*, and the next year also *de jure*, unification of Germany beginning on November 9th, 1989, when the *Berlin Wall* was first breached by thousands of German civilians. After that, the *communist* regimes of Eastern Europe crumpled with great speed and remarkably little violence. *See also Albania; Baltic States; Brezhnev Doctrine; Bulgaria; Nicolae Ceauşescu; clash of civilizations; Charter '77; Czechoslovakia; East Germany; end of history; Václav Havel; Helsinki Accords; Helsinki watch groups; Erich Honecker; Enver Hoxha; Hungary; Poland; Prague Spring; Rumania; samizdat; Solidarity; "Sinatra doctrine"; Tiananmen Square; Yugoslavia; Velvet Revolution; Lech Walesa; Warsaw Treaty Organization.*

Suggested Readings: George H. Bush and Brent Scowcroft, *A World Transformed* (1998); Timothy Garton Ash, *The Polish Revolution* (1983, 1991); Bernard Wheaton and Zdenek Kavan, *The Velvet Revolution* (1992).

Rhee, Syngman (1875–1965). Korean statesman. President of South Korea, 1948–1960. He was a longtime proponent of Korean *independence* from Japan, which imprisoned him, 1897–1904. He traveled to the United States, where he was influenced by *Woodrow Wilson*. He returned to Korea in 1910 but left again after a failed *insurrection* in 1919, heading a *government-in-exile*. He became the principal political figure in the U.S. *occupation zone* after 1945 and was elected president in 1948. He was dissatisfied with the levels of U.S. commitment to his government and was bitterly opposed to *partition* of the Korean peninsula. He led the South in the *Korean Conflict.* Following the near-total collapse of the South Korean Army and the flight of his government from Seoul, and following the United Nations landing at *Inchon,* he enthusiastically endorsed *Truman's* decision to cross the 38th parallel and unify the country by force. He proved a significant obstacle to *peace,* refusing for months to agree to forced *repatriation* of Northern *POWs.* He was ousted in 1960 after widespread rioting, and went into *exile* for the third and last time. He died in Hawaii.

Rhineland. The historic region of Germany bordering France and the *Low Countries,* lying along the course of the Rhine. Long sought after by *Louis XIV* and occupied by *Napoleon,* it was part of the territory ceded to *Prussia* by *Great Power* agreement in the great settlement of the *Napoleonic Wars* made at the *Congress of Vienna* (1814–1815). Over the course of the nineteenth century it became an area of paramount industrial importance. It served as a jump-off point for three German *invasions* of France: 1870, 1914 and 1940. At the *Paris Peace Conference* France sought to detach the Rhineland and create a separate Rhenish state, as a *buffer* between itself and Germany. That scheme was opposed by *Woodrow Wilson.* He proposed the compromise clause in the *Treaty of Versailles* permitting a 15-year French military *occupation* and permanent *demilitarization* of the right bank of the Rhine, along with a 30-mile-wide strip on the left bank. In 1923 a Rhenish *republic* was declared with French connivance, but it soon failed for lack of popular support. British troops withdrew in 1926. The French, who could not stand alone, pulled out in 1930. In March 1936, *Hitler* sent in just three battalions of troops to remilitarize the Rhineland. Although it was a daring violation of Versailles and *Locarno,* the troops had secret orders to pull out if opposed. When the Western powers did nothing, Hitler was emboldened to overturn other features of the Versailles settlement with even greater speed. After *World War II* France again sought to detach the Rhineland from Germany, and was again opposed mainly by the United States. The dispute appears to have been permanently resolved by *integration* of France and Germany, including the Rhineland, within the *ECSC* and the *European Union. See also Spanish Road.*

Suggested Readings: J. Emmerson, *Rhineland Crisis* (1977); Walter McDougal, *France's Rhineland Diplomacy* (1978).

Rhodes, Cecil (1853–1902). British imperialist. Sent to live in Africa at a tender age, Rhodes made his fortune in South African diamonds (De Beers Co.) and *gold* from the *Rand.* A heart attack at age 19 gave him an urgent drive that never abated. Deeply avaricious, he was premier of *Cape Colony,*

1890–1896, a position Rhodes used to advance his personal interests after he obtained a Royal Charter for the British South Africa Company (BSAC). He also worked to disenfranchise those few blacks who enjoyed the vote in Cape Colony, reducing them to the controlled labor force for his mines and other enterprises he regarded as their "rightful place" and as an economic necessity for the white colonists to prosper. In 1890 Rhodes's reputation was such that he met with Queen *Victoria* at Windsor. In fact, he had become almost a *sovereign* power unto himself, replete with a private police force and army. In 1891 the BSAC moved north of the Zambezi to what became Northern Rhodesia (Zambia), and comprised part of the composite colony of *Rhodesia* (later Zambia and Zimbabwe). Rhodes's vision was essentially racist: he was a *social Darwinist* who decided that the forward march of progress in Africa required a single political power from Cape Town to Cairo. He thought this was possible only under white mastery and with *railway* development, with Britons and Boers working together in southern Africa and expanding northward under the flags of the British South Africa Company and the *British Empire*.

Blocking that grand vision was *Transvaal*, which Rhodes needed to deal with first. At the end of 1895 he therefore dispatched a ragtag force of some 500 men on a misconceived adventure which aimed at the overthrow of the government of the Transvaal. This was seen internationally as naked *aggression*, and Rhodes was forced from office over his complicity in this "*Jamieson Raid*," which shattered his imperial policy and his reputation alike. Public opinion (and Victoria) remained anti-Boer, however, and an army of the British Empire would soon be dragged into a heavy military commitment by this action of a feckless *filibusterer*. Rhodes died at age 48. He left his fortune to the University of Oxford to fund the Rhodes Scholarship program. For many years, in the spirit of Rhodes's life and public philosophy, that program barred application by blacks and women. Rhodes was buried in a pretentiously African tomb in the Matopos Hills in what is now Zimbabwe, an area for centuries regarded as sacred ground by the local population. In 1970 black *guerrillas* tried to blast him out with dynamite, but failed. In 1998 a campaign was started by a student radical to have him removed, but the local people objected: Rhodes had become one of the country's main tourist attractions, and a brisk trade was being done in trinkets and keepsakes. He thus brought more real benefit to black Africans dead than he had ever contemplated doing in life. *See also Kruger Telegram; Malawi; scramble for Africa.*

Suggested Reading: John Flint, *Cecil Rhodes* (1976).

Rhodesia. *See Zimbabwe.*

Rhodesia and Nyasaland, Federation of (1953–1963). Also known as the Central African Federation. A composite British colony in East Africa. It was formed as a balance to the regional dominance of South Africa and was intended by the British to be a multiracial state. Settler political power blocked real *power sharing*, however, and the Federation broke into Malawi, Rhodesia (now Zimbabwe), and Zambia on January 1, 1964.

Ribbentrop, Joachim "von" (1893–1946). *Nazi* diplomat. Ambassador in London, 1936–1938; foreign minister, 1938–1945. He claimed an aristocratic background, but this was widely disputed. He helped negotiate *Hitler*'s ascent to power in 1933. He negotiated the *Anglo-German Naval Agreement* in 1935. He carried his sincere if perverse belief in Nazi *ideology* into German diplomacy in agreements such as the *Anti-Comintern Pact*, the *Axis* agreement, and the *Tripartite Pact*. With *Molotov*, Ribbentrop negotiated the *Nazi-Soviet Pact* of August 1939, which opened the floodgates to *World War II*. During the war his role in foreign policy was limited, although he took a direct and personal interest in advancing the *Holocaust*. He was convicted by the *Allies* as a major *war criminal* at the *Nuremberg trials* and was hanged.

Ricardo, David (1772–1823). *See comparative advantage.*

rice riots. *See Japan.*

Richelieu, Armand Jean (1585–1642). "Éminence Rouge." Cardinal of the church, statesman, and molder of the modern state and modern *diplomacy*. Richelieu trained for military service, but he became a cardinal to secure his family's hereditary claim to a French bishopric. He became a bishop in 1607 at age 22. In 1616 he was made secretary of state for foreign affairs. He was made cardinal in 1622 and became the king's first minister six years later. His life's work was to subordinate local and provincial government to, and centralize political authority under, the monarchy. Richelieu did this through a system of direct rule by officials (intendants) who reported directly to the crown. Provincial estates councils, and medieval towns previously governed by free charters, came under the authority of the intendants. He revoked the special political and military privileges enjoyed by French Protestants under the *Edict of Nantes*, issued by *Henri IV* in 1598. Defeated at La Rochelle, which Richelieu seized in violation of the terms of the Edict of Nantes, many *Huguenots* scattered to Holland, England, *New France*, and southern Africa.

When Richelieu was finished consolidating the home front, the absolute monarchy in France was nearly unchallenged and pursued a new concept in governance and statecraft: the justifying notion of *raison d'état*, or the *national interest*, was the new order of the day. France now had a national army and a powerful navy, and Richelieu used these means to break the *Habsburg* encirclement of France, destroy its foreign enemies, and make it preeminent in Europe. He did so without regard for the ideological content of the great war between *Catholics* and *Protestants* which marked his day. Richelieu was a "Father of the Church" but no Catholic ideologue: Paris, not Rome, hosted his true cathedral and commanded his deepest loyalty. He bested the Habsburgs at their own game of *dynastic marriage* and through rapier-like use of war-by-proxy as an adjunct and instrument of diplomacy. In 1630 Richelieu oversaw yet another French invasion of Italy, and conquered and annexed *Savoy*. He then courted the Swedish king, *Gustavus Adolphus*, his greatest anti-Habsburg proxy, and financed other leading Protestant allies before the "French phase" of the *Thirty Years' War* against Habsburg (and also Catholic) Austria and Spain. In 1635 Richelieu finally took France into the war, setting it on the path to a victory and *hegemony* which he did not himself live to see. Richelieu's legacy was complex, including a powerful and centralized crown and state. Alongside this absolutist state he also left a new codification of *international law* and reformed and advanced the forms and practices of modern diplomacy, and of *espionage*. *See also éminence grise.*

Suggested Reading: J. H. Elliot, *Richelieu and Olivares* (1984).

Riel (Red River) rebellion (1869–1870). *See Indian Wars (North America).*

rifled-bore. A gun or cannon with a grooved, spiral bore, which spins the projectile and gives greater accuracy and range (by a factor of five) to marksmen or gunners. For its revolutionary impact, *see gunpowder revolution* and *smooth-bore. See also case shot.*

Rif Rebellion and Republic (1921–1926). The Rifs were Moroccan tribesmen who rose against the Spanish in 1921, under Abd al-Qrim (1880–1963), greatly surprising that colonial power by killing 12,000 of its troops at Anual and setting up a republic. The defeat had major political repercussions in Spain. *Franco* commanded Spanish forces fighting the Rif, which provided him a power base from which he later would invade Spain and start the *Spanish Civil War.* The Rif Republic also implicitly threatened French control of Morocco, and on occasion sent raiding parties across the *frontier.* Hence, Paris and Madrid combined to overthrow it in 1926 with a joint force commanded by *Pétain* and *Primo de Rivera.* Abd al-Qrim was exiled to Réunion.

"right deviationists." A pejorative term used by *Stalin* against opponents of his *collectivization* scheme led by Bukharin, Rykov, and Tomsky. Real or imaginary, hundreds of thousands of accused "right-deviationists" were *liquidated* in the *Yezhovshchina* and other *purges. See also Old Bolsheviks; Leon Trotsky.*

"righteous Gentiles." Non-Jews who, during the *Holocaust*, risked their own lives to save Jews from *summary execution* or the *death camps.*

"right of initiative." An international right claimed by the *Red Cross* (for which this phrase is a term of art) and other "impartial humanitarian bodies" to offer its services in situations of humanitarian concern, wherever it deems these might be useful, including on issues states might otherwise regard as strictly their own *internal affairs*.

Rights of Man and Citizens, Declaration of. This influential statement of the original principles of the *French Revolution* was promulgated on July 27, 1789. Owing something to the American revolutionary example, but more to the French *Enlightenment*, it inspired generations of *liberal* thinkers and reformers. Besides proclaiming basic civil and individual rights, its most important assertion was the idea of *popular sovereignty*. In the twentieth century this declaration found resonance in the *Universal Declaration of Human Rights*.

right-wing. *See Convention.*

Rimland. From the *geopolitical* theory of Nicholas Spykman (1893–1943), developed as a modification of the idea of the *World Island* promoted by *Halford Mackinder*. Spykman saw not *Eurasia* but its outlying promontories (Africa, the Middle East, India, and Southeast Asia) as the key to world political dominance. He thus revised Mackinder's famous formulation about the influence of geography on history to read, "Who rules the Rimland rules Eurasia; who rules Eurasia controls the destinies of the world."

Rio de Oro. *See Spanish Sahara.*

Rio Group. A forum in which Latin American *heads of state* or *government* meet to discuss common problems and regional issues.

Rio Pact (September 2, 1947). Inter-American Treaty of Reciprocal Assistance. A regional defense *alliance* was set up at American behest. It includes all the major Latin American countries and is coordinated through the *OAS*. Cuba was barred from participation, also at American insistence, in 1962. Echoing the *Monroe Doctrine*, the Rio Pact called for mutual action not only against a direct extra-hemispheric attack but against "indirect threats" as well. It arose out of initial cooperation against German and Japanese naval forces in the Western Hemisphere *war zones* during *World War II* and was extended to speak to security concerns of the burgeoning *Cold War*. It was invoked after the *September 11, 2001, terrorist attack on the United States. See also isolationism.*

rising expectations, crisis of. This was (is) a phenomenon of the industrial age. During the first decades of *modernization* the vast mass of rural poor, displaced from the land or simply seeking fuller lives under bright city lights, found their expectations unfulfilled due to a shortage of jobs, housing, and so forth. The cause was a delay in the ability of the modernizing sectors of the economy to meet the new demands of a rising consumer society, and extant needs no longer being fully met by the collapsing traditional economy. This created a vast reserve of frustrated, needful people, and much potential for social violence, as *Karl Marx* noticed outside the windows of the Reading Room in the British Museum. On the other hand, the history of the nineteenth and twentieth centuries in Europe was to demonstrate that although short-term unrest increased with early *industrialization*, contrary to the predictions of orthodox *Marxists* social discontent actually decreased with full industrialization. That was because industrialization generally has been accompanied by social reform and welfare spending, supported by new wealth being created in the factories and through expanding trade. As that astute French observer, *Alexis de Tocqueville*, noted about the *ancien régime* in France, and the Soviets learned firsthand about their empire, 1985–1991, there is a parallel to this phenomenon in politics; to wit: a bad government is never in so much danger as from the moment it begins to reform itself. *See also fundamentalism*; *Industrial Revolution*.

Risorgimento. "Resurrection." A broad-based, nationalist movement working for unification of all the states of Italy into a single country. It achieved its goal in the second half of the nineteenth century. *See also Camillo di Cavour*; *Giuseppe Garibaldi*; *Giuseppe Mazzini*; *Piedmont-Sardinia*.

rites controversy. A major dispute between the *Catholic Church* and the *Qing* emperors over the ultimate allegiance owed by Chinese *Christians* to the Chinese state. The Qing court maintained that ancient *Confucian* rites of ancestor worship were civil, not religious, matters and hence outside the concern of foreign clerics. Therefore, Chinese Christians could be ordered to continue these practices, which were important to cultural and political unity of the empire. That position was supported by the *Jesuits* but was opposed by other Catholic orders. The controversy came to a head in 1705–1706 in the form of a clash between the *Kangxi* emperor and a legate representing Pope Clement XI. As a result, Christian preaching was severely limited and Catholic *missionaries* were expelled. Missions were later banned from China, 1724–1846. This prolonged China's relative technological and scientific backwardness by limiting access to Western science, philosophy, and technology that would have flowed into China via mission schools, albeit at the price of tolerating disruptive foreign religious doctrines. *See also Voltaire*.

Robespierre, Maximilien de (1758–1794). "The Incorruptible." French *Jacobin* (of Irish descent) and a dominant figure in the *French Revolution*. A lawyer by training and revolutionary leader and puritanical megalomaniac by temperament, he believed he personally embodied the "general will" of France. In 1791 he was appointed "public accuser." His ascent to absolute power came by way of the mob, which adored him. He opposed the *Girondins'* call for war early in 1792. He then resigned his post as public accuser to make more powerful and dangerous accusations within the Jacobin Club. In August

1792, he petitioned the Assembly to convene a new Revolutionary Tribunal and National Convention. The September Massacres (September 2–6, 1792) further radicalized the mob and engaged its blood lust, but it is not clear that Robespierre was directly responsible for inciting them. He was next elected to the Convention, where he formed a close alliance with *Danton*. Robespierre's preeminence in the Revolution came about concerning the question of what to do with the king, *Louis XVI*, once the monarchy had been abolished. Robespierre blocked the Girondins from putting the question to the country, and thereby saving the king's life. He instead pushed for, and voted for, Louis' execution (January 21, 1793). A deadly struggle for power between the Jacobins and the Girondins ensued.

The means to victory, Robespierre saw, was the Committee of Public Safety set up in April 1793. He took charge of the Committee, wielding its increasingly tyrannical powers until he achieved final victory by June, upon which the leading Girondins scattered to *exile* or were put under the blade. From that point, Robespierre was a key—although not yet completely dominant—figure in the collective leadership of France ("The Twelve"). Over the next year he sent legions of enemies, real and imagined, to the guillotine, as Jacobin power was consolidated and expressed by the terrible retribution of *The Terror* against all identified as "enemies of the people" or of the Revolution. For Robespierre, that came to include his erstwhile ally and fellow Jacobin, Danton, who lost his head on Robespierre's order in April 1794. For a few months after that, Robespierre was the absolute ruler of France at age 35. He and his fellow Jacobins rained down merciless judgments through decrees and the summary proceedings of Revolutionary Tribunals.

Robespierre's severely *radical* dictatorship now also became increasingly erratic. He altered the months of the year and the years of the Age, proclaiming the start of a whole new and revolutionary era. He then created new national holidays based on the altered calendar to celebrate a state religion made up from whole cloth, though couched in the rational deism of the *Enlightenment*. By decree, he insisted that this replace French holidays derived from tradition and the calendar of the *Catholic Church*, and that the Mass and other Catholic rites familiar to the French be supplanted by a cult of the Supreme Being. This outraged Catholics and contributed to a cleric-led peasant revolt in the *Vendée*, which Paris met with savage punishment and massacre. The far more dangerous—to Robespierre—reaction to this zealous *secularism*, however, was the gales of laughter with which it was received by most French. That response baffled the dour and humorless Robespierre, but it was a sure sign that his days as dictator were numbered. The denouement came when he tried to compel the Convention to suspend all rights of defense or appeal from decisions of the Revolutionary Tribunals, while Saint-Just and other toadies among ultra-Jacobins hollered to have him formally and lawfully elevated to dictator, the title taken by *Julius Caesar* after crossing the Rubicon and marching on Rome.

The threat of utterly arbitrary judgment at the whim of a pale, half-mad *fanatic* frightened nearly everyone, including those who had gained power, position, or wealth by Robespierre's earlier bloodletting. The move toward total dictatorship therefore instead provoked calls for his arrest within the Convention, and a conservative reaction within the country. His fall from power was dramatically swift. The National Guard moved to protect the Convention from the Jacobins. During the armed confrontation which ensued, Robespierre's jaw was shattered by a musket ball. The following day, July 28, 1794 (10 *Thermidor* on the Revolutionary calendar), he and 21 Jacobin allies were beheaded on the same guillotine to which so many citizens had been sent to die by their orders. Robespierre did not go well to meet his Supreme Being—he was a frail specimen and a physical coward; in his final minutes this was clear to all who watched. Robespierre was for many decades a hero of the radical and revolutionary *Left*, but he was and remains a repulsive figure to most moderates and all *conservatives*. *See also Vladimir Ilyich Lenin; Leon Trotsky*.

Suggested Readings: Colin Haydon and William Doyle, eds., *Robespierre* (1999); J. M. Thompson, *Robespierre and the French Revolution* (1973).

Rodney, George, Baron (1718–1792). British admiral. He first went to sea in a warship at age 14, took his first commission at 17, and captained a 60-gun ship at 24. He fought in the *War of the Austrian Succession* (1740–1748), the *Seven Years' War* (1756–1763), and the *American Revolution* (1775–1783). He was governor of *Newfoundland*, 1748–1752. In 1758, during the Seven Years' War, he led an expedition against the mighty French fortress of Louisbourg on Cape Breton Island, which effectively controlled the entrance to the St. Lawrence and hence the northern riverine route to the interior of North America. He also fought in Europe, off France. In 1761 he took command of British naval forces in the Caribbean. He successfully raided and captured a number of important islands in the French West Indies, as well as Cuba. From 1771 to 1774 he returned to the Caribbean, sailing out of Jamaica. He had squandered his vast wealth and had also spent much of his energy and that of the fleet in acts which amounted to *privateering*. After a brief exile in France he again took up a commission and returned to the Caribbean in 1779, relieving a siege of *Gibraltar* en route from England. During the American Revolution he variously supported the British Army in North America and continued his private fortune gathering in warmer seas to the south, raiding French and Spanish merchants. He was greatly distracted by law suits and *prize court* decisions related to his earlier semi-privateering activity. He returned after a leave of absence to defeat a French fleet off Martinique, on April 12, 1782, in the last sea engagement of the war of the American Revolution. His exploits and victories earned him a signal place in the pantheon of *Royal Navy* heroes.

"rogue states." A U.S. State Department term for states believed to act outside the boundaries of normal state behavior, such as by sponsoring *terrorism*. The United States identified these in the 1990s as Cuba, Iran, Iraq, Libya, North Korea, Sudan, and Syria. *See also ballistic missile defense (BMD); outlaw state; pariah state.*

Röhm, Ernst (1887–1934). *See Night of the Long Knives;* Sturmabteilung (SA).

Rokossovsky, Konstantin Konstantinovich (1896–1968). Polish-born "Marshal of the Soviet Union." He fought at *Stalingrad* and *Kursk*, although not in supreme command. It was his army which paused to watch the *Nazis* crush the *Warsaw Rising*. He led one prong of the final assault on Berlin. He was Poland's defense minister, 1945–1956, and used troops to crush worker uprisings in 1956. He returned to Moscow and served as deputy minister of defense before taking a final active command in *Transcaucasia*.

Roma. Predominantly Romani-speaking nomads, originally of mixed *Hindu* and Indian origin, who migrated to Europe as a warrior caste in service to the *Ottomans* (although, like the *Janissaries*, they remained non-*Muslim*). In 1054 they fought with the Ottomans against the *Byzantine Empire*. As one of Europe's last nomadic peoples, they suffered persecution and ill will for centuries. They were enslaved in Rumania until 1864. During *World War II* the Roma of Eastern Europe were rounded up and ghettoized, then murdered, by the *Nazis*. *Hitler* targeted them, along with Jews, in the *Nuremberg Laws*. Half a million Roma perished in the *death camps* of the *Holocaust*, known to the Roma as "Porramous," or "The Devouring." Collaborators in some Western European countries, notably Belgium and France, helped deport them. In contrast, many were hidden and survived in Denmark and Norway; others remained untouched in the British Isles. The Roma population of the *Baltic states* was virtually eliminated. In Croatia, a *fascist* regime acting independently completely wiped out the Roma. In Bulgaria they were better treated and sometimes protected. Their plight disappeared from international view for much of the *Cold War*. In 1994, however, anti-Roma sentiment resurfaced in official form in post-Soviet Eastern Europe, as they were openly persecuted by a crudely nationalist government in *Slovakia*. That led the *European Union* to propose formal, international legal protections. About six million survived in Europe at the end of the twentieth century, located mainly in the east but also in Spain and as far west as Ireland. Most lived unschooled and in deep poverty. "Gypsies" is widely used in place of Roma (although not all Gypsies are Roma); the term carries in most places a pejorative suggestion of thievery, superstition, and personal and sexual immorality, all of which typifies and feeds into anti-Roma prejudice.

Suggested Reading: Guenter Lewy, *The Nazi Persecution of the Gypsies* (2000).

Roman Empire. (1) The Republic: Romans credited the founding of their city, on the banks of the Tiber River, to Romulus c. 753 B.C.E. At first, Rome was one among several *city-states* on the Italian peninsula and was not a major power even in that region. Toward the end of the sixth century a republic was founded, governed by an *aristocracy* (patricians) but peopled mainly by a far larger class of ordinary citizens (plebeians), all served by a still larger côterie of *slaves*—at the height of the later Empire at least 40 percent of the population of Italy was enslaved. In theory, and often also in practice, power was shared by the Aristocratic party of the large estate-owning patricians, which controlled the Senate, and two consuls elected by the plebeians but often also drawn from the educated patrician class. However, the Roman Army was composed of citizens who elected their senior officers (tribunes), and there were additional civil offices to protect plebeian rights against abuse, as by unjust or corrupt magistrates. During the fourth and third centuries B.C.E., Rome expanded within Italy, progressively taking control of the surrounding peninsula with its legions while tentatively also sending triremes (slave-rowed *galleys*) along the coasts of the Adriatic and then into the Mediterranean on expansive missions of trade and sometimes of naval warfare.

Rome's intention to become a great Mediterranean power was signaled by the great struggle with its North African rival, Carthage. In three *Punic Wars* (264–241, 218–202, and 149–146 B.C.E.), Rome and Carthage struggled over control of Sicily, then of Spain and the whole western Mediterranean. Although the great Carthaginian general Hannibal (c. 247–182 B.C.E.) invaded and waged war in Italy for many years during the Second Punic War, from 217, Carthage was defeated and reduced to a *tributary* by 202. It was utterly destroyed by a vengeful Roman army in the wholly punitive Third Punic War, in 146 B.C.E. As a result of that total victory, by the middle of the second century B.C.E. the Roman Republic dominated the western Mediterranean along its European and African shores, and all the island territories it contained—including the large islands of Sicily and Sardinia and many smaller ones. Rome was now a self-confident, expansionist *sea power*. And with its strong and battle-hardened army, it was a rising *land power* as well. As such, even before it had finished with Carthage it turned to the eastern Mediterranean, its trireme navy ferrying amphibious expeditions to conquer coastal towns, with its army also marching overland to conquer most of Syria, too, by 190. Greece, Macedonia, and Egypt all were made tributaries of the Republic by 168. Rome also expanded into southern Gaul (France) and the lower Balkans. The Roman second century B.C.E. was filled with domestic strife, including several localized slave rebellions. Mainly, however, it was marked by the continuing political struggle between plebeian interests and representatives and the real (but not total) power wielded by leaders of the Aristocratic party in the Senate.

General Lucius Cornelius "Felix" Sulla (138–78 B.C.E.) became consul in 88 and pressed home a successful defense of Rome against a new threat from

Asia Minor, pushing back invading armies to the east. In 83 B.C.E. civil war broke out between Sulla's returning legions and rival generals (the "Marian faction") Marius and Cinna. The next year, upon his victory, Sulla was proclaimed dictator. Henceforth, the Republic would be repeatedly threatened by potential or real outbreaks of civil war, as this or that general returned from fresh foreign conquests and tried for supreme power in Rome itself, or it was feared that he might just because he could. Momentarily, plebeians and patricians were united by fear as from 73 to 70 B.C.E. a great slave and gladiator rebellion broke out. Led by a former robber and gladiator, but also natural military leader, Spartacus (d. 71 B.C.E.), it coursed up and down Italy and was only suppressed with a major military effort followed by massive brutality and executions. Next came Gnaeus Pompeius Magnus, or Pompey (106–48 B.C.E.), Sulla's greatly favored lieutenant and effective heir. Pompey completed the expurgation of the Marian faction from Italy and Spain and helped put down the Spartacist rebellion. Loved therefore by the mob, he was elected consul as reward (70). From 67 he campaigned at sea, truly making the Adriatic and Mediterranean *mare nostrum* by mercilessly chasing *pirates* from those waters. This aided the water-borne commerce that would sustain Rome for several centuries as one of the great empires and civilizations in world history, and united Mediterranean trade and bordering economies—stretching down the Nile and Euphrates and up the Danube and Rhine as well—in a way that has never since been seen. Pompey next conquered Armenia and Antioch, repressed the Jews, and entered *Jerusalem*. By 61 he enjoyed his third "Triumph" in Rome. The Aristocratic party in the Senate was impressed but ungrateful. Pompey made alliance with the younger *Gaius Julius Caesar* and with a powerful plutocrat, Crassus, to form the First Triumvirate in 60 B.C.E.

Caesar moved north for the next 9 years to complete the conquest of Gaul and attempt invasion of Britain, while Pompey remained in Rome and Crassus campaigned in Asia, where he died in 53 B.C.E. Over time, Pompey was slowly eaten by jealousy of the more popular Caesar—who, although a patrician, headed the Democratic party in Rome. In Caesar's prolonged absence Pompey was drawn into intrigues with the Aristocrats and finally was convinced by them to break the Triumvirate. He *decommissioned* Caesar and removed him from command in Gaul, whose conquest Caesar had completed, at last adding that vast land to the Republic. He then ordered Caesar's legions to be broken up and Caesar to return to Rome, where he surely would have been assassinated. Civil war thus broke out as Caesar crossed the Rubicon (49) with his legions intact and in tow. This changed Rome forever, propelling it more rapidly down a path it had been traveling for some time, toward personal dictatorship. Pompey's forces were scattered across the Republic's distant provinces and could not be assembled in time to block Caesar before Rome, from which Pompey fled. Caesar then cleared Spain of legions loyal to Pompey and the Senate, and cowed the latter into elevating him to dictator. He pursued Pompey to defeat him in Greece, Asia Minor, and Egypt. The decisive encounter came at Pharsalia (or Pharsalus, August 9, 48 B.C.E.), where Caesar crushed Pompey's (and the Senate's) army. By 46 Caesar had cleared Africa of the last senatorial generals and then put down a rebellion in Spain led by Pompey's sons.

Back in Rome, Caesar was made imperator and consul, was confirmed as dictator for life, and just for good measure was proclaimed a divine. He planned, commissioned, and began major public works and improvements to the city and Republic. His tenure was cut short, however, on March 15, 44 B.C.E. ("the Ides of March") by 60 "republican" (Aristocratic) assassins in the Senate who feared Caesar might found a hereditary monarchy and strip them of their traditional privileges and properties. After Caesar came the Second Triumvirate, formed by Gaius Octavianus (later, "Augustus," 63 B.C.E.–14 C.E.), Marcus Antonius (or "Mark Antony," c. 83–30 B.C.E.), and Marcus Aemilius Lepidus (b. ?, d. 13 B.C.E.). They divided Rome's dominions among themselves: Octavian retained Rome, Africa, Sardinia, and Sicily; Antony received Gaul; and Lepidus was given Spain to govern. Together, they then destroyed the last republican opposition, led by Brutus and Cassius, at Philippi (42 B.C.E.). Then Antony and Octavian, now related by marriage, re-divided the imperial holdings, with Antony taking the eastern half and Octavian the western half; Lepidus was consoled with Africa. With Antony consumed by infatuation with the Queen of Egypt, Cleopatra (69–30 B.C.E.), Octavian moved the last chess pieces on the board: he stirred up feeling among the Roman mob against the "presumption" and "plotting" of Cleopatra and declared war on Egypt—then still a tributary, independent kingdom, not a province of Rome. After a great naval victory by Octavian at Actium (31), Antony and Cleopatra committed suicide; Octavian put all of Antony's known children to death and emerged as sole and absolute master of the whole Mediterranean world. In 29 he returned to Rome, having spent 2 more years suppressing lingering dissent in Egypt and the eastern half of the Republic's extensive empire, and proclaimed peace across the Roman world.

(2) The Empire: Octavian now became "Augustus" ("Venerable"), a title that became a name which subsequently was regarded as senior even to "Caesar." Although he did not take the formal title of emperor, and Rome's republican titles were retained for show, he is properly regarded by history as the first emperor of Rome. He continued expansion of the Empire, sending armies to Asia Minor, Dalmatia, Gaul, and Germania, where a Roman army under Varius was destroyed in 9 C.E. Augustus was not just a warrior: he was a lawgiver and a builder, significantly improving public works in Rome and erecting new and Romanized cities throughout the now consolidated and unified Empire. A succession of lesser emperors followed the death of Augustus in 14 C.E. Worst of all was Gaius Caesar Germanicus, better known by his camp name of Caligula, or "Boots" (12–41, r. 37–41). Caligula was a pervert and a sadist, whose depravity only deepened with absolute power: he

had people tortured to death as he dined and opined publicly about slaughtering the whole population of Rome. He stole property and he murdered the same way he rutted, promiscuously. Contemptuous of all prior republican tradition, he elevated his horse to the Senate and proclaimed himself a god. He was, of course, fairly quickly assassinated.

The underestimated, ill-formed, and scholarly Emperor Claudius I (né Tiberius Claudius Drusus Nero Germanicus, 10–54, r. 41–54) was discovered by the Praetorian Guard hiding behind a curtain during the assassination of Caligula, cowering in fear of also being put to the sword as a descendant of Augustus. Instead, Claudius was proclaimed emperor by the army, which then upheld his claim. Claudius oversaw the conquest of much of Britain and its addition to the Empire, and the further consolidation and settlement of the eastern provinces. Through his lavish rewards to the soldiers who spared his life and elevated him to supreme power, however, Claudius cemented a direct relationship between the emperor and the army which over time converted Rome into a military despotism. On the other hand, he extended citizenship to those of merit throughout the Empire, stretching it toward universality. Claudius was poisoned by his wife, Agrippina, to bring her natural and his adopted son, Nero (37–68, r. 54–68), to the throne. The favor was not returned: Nero was an ingrate who subsequently had Agrippina murdered. A debaucher akin to Caligula, and nearly as cruel, Nero was the first of several emperors to fix upon adherents of the new eastern sect of *Christianity* as scapegoats for natural calamities or his own failings. Christian teachings had by then found their way—as did everything of note—to Rome, where Christianity was making converts among the slaves, and also among some citizens. Public torments and executions were carried out by Nero against Christians who would not renounce their faith, and persecution spread across the Empire. In Judea, the Jewish War broke out in 66, following an appalling massacre of Jews by Roman soldiers in Jerusalem. Also during Nero's reign, Rome itself burned in a great fire (64). With Nero's death by his own hand during a *mutiny* of the legions, the Augustan family line ended.

Under Titus Flavius Vespasian (9–79, r. 69–79) Rome's finances and moral probity alike were restored. Construction began on the Coliseum while Vespasian's son, Titus (39–81, r. 79–81), completed the Jewish War, a revolt which had broken out in Judea (Palestine). Titus drove the Jews from their historic homeland (70), thus beginning their prolonged and sorrowful *Diaspora*, whose consequences reverberated down through the next two millennia. Titus did not succeed his father for long, but in that time he completed the Coliseum, built great public bath houses in the center of Rome, and provided succor to victims of the great eruption of Vesuvius (79) and another great fire which scorched Rome for 3 full days. His brother, Titus Flavius Domitianus, or "Domitian" (r. 81–96), was on the throne while Rome's holdings in Britain were pushed further north, but he failed to conquer Dacia (Rumania) and took cruel revenge for that humiliation on innocents throughout the Empire. Such indiscriminate savagery led to his assassination. Marcus Ulpius Trajanus, or "Trajan" (53–117, r. 98–117), waged war widely in Germania, completed the conquest of Dacia (105), and partly resettled it with Roman colonists. In 113 he departed Italy to make war in the east, against the Parthians. He subdued Mesopotamia and Armenia but faced Jewish refugee revolts in Cyprus and Cyrene. In Trajan's absence, conspiracies bred in Rome, forcing his return. He did not make it, dying during the journey home.

Trajan's greatest accomplishments were not won on the field of battle but in improvements to governance of an Empire that now contained some 100 million subjects (twice as many people as lived in contemporary China) and was by far the largest and most advanced state and civilization of the Age. He regularized administration, punished corruption even at the highest levels of appointed office, permitted all Roman citizens to serve at the peak of the Empire regardless of ethnic or geographical origin, and built extensive new roads, along with many new aqueducts, bridges, canals, and towns. On the other hand, under Trajan official persecution of early Christian communities deepened. This was partly because Christians would not make sacrifice in Roman temples to propitiate pagan gods, a refusal seen as subversive by the majority of Romans, and one which also had a real economic impact in the marketplace and slaughterhouses of Roman cities and towns. With this important exception of persecution of Christians, which from Rome's point of view was fundamentally a political rather than a religious matter and motivation, Rome was broadly tolerant of religious differences and customs. It did not govern so as to maintain doctrinal uniformity—as several subsequent empires would do, at great cost to themselves and their subjects.

Publius Aelius Hadrianus, or "Hadrian" (76–138, r. 117–138), was proclaimed emperor by the army, to which he was well familiar as a capable commander in the east under Trajan. The army was now facing the first in what was to be a series of barbarian invasions out of Central Asia. Hadrian thoroughly reorganized the army for defense rather than further conquest, fended off some barbarian tribes and *appeased* others, then made peace with the Parthians, who had taken the chance of trouble on the border to revolt against Roman rule. He thus determined to set a firm limit to the eastern boundaries of the empire—a striking decision to avoid *imperial overreach* and retrench and consolidate those extant holdings most distant from the center of power in Rome, and thus hardest to govern and secure. He returned to Rome to firmly establish his authority, and narrowly survived a patrician-inspired assassination plot. Hadrian then set out to tour the western borderlands, visiting in turn Gaul, Germania, and Britain. In the west, too, Hadrian was determined not to be drawn into chronic and unwinnable warfare with border peoples over distant or scrubby lands not vital to the interests or the future of Imperial Rome. He therefore ordered construction of a line of defensive fortifications ("Hadrian's Wall") across northern Britain, from Solway to Tyne, to keep back the wilder Gaels. Proceeding south, Hadrian visited the provinces of Spain, Africa (Mauritania), Egypt, and Asia Minor, and thence traveled to Greece, before returning to Rome in 126. From 132 to 134 he crushed yet another revolt in Judea.

The next great emperor was the philosopher-king Marcus Aurelius Antoninus (né Marcus Annius Verus, 121–180, r. 161–180). A pacific and scholarly man by temperament, his reign nonetheless witnessed plagues, earthquakes, and other natural disasters, and endless wars in Asia Minor, Britain, but most especially along the Rhine *frontier* with still unconquered and fierce Germanic peoples. Major victories in Germania came in 168, 173, and 176, but never peace. Even so, other than the border wars and the occasional imperial despot, from Augustus to Marcus Aurelius was recorded the height of the "Pax Romana," or "the Roman Peace." The Pax Romana was a hard but a long-lasting peace, that was both imposed and conferred on the subject peoples of the Mediterranean world. It lasted until great waves of barbarian invaders poured over Rome's borders in later decades and centuries, and civil wars broke up the Empire from within. It was based on the unparalleled and unchallenged military power of Rome.

Yes, Rome ruled harshly at times, even ruthlessly and cruelly; but what ancient kingdom or empire did not? It was more important that under the protection of Roman arms and laws, traveling along Roman roads or back and forth across mare nostrum, "Our Sea," or among prosperous towns and entrepôt, there flourished one of history's most successful civilizations. The Empire's wealth and power—which was as much or more the product of peaceful farming and commerce than it was of imperial theft or exploitation of far-off colonies—made possible great feats of engineering and sustained a level of far-flung commerce which would not be matched in Europe for 1,000 years after its fall. The trade and influence of this great state stretched deep into Africa and along the *Silk Road* to India, with which there was an extensive trade, and even to far-off China. The Pax Romana ensured that the Mediterranean and its tributary regions in North Africa, Europe, and what was later called the Middle East enjoyed a prolonged era of expanding production, comparative peace, good government, and considerable prosperity. And yes, this also was an empire where many were enslaved, but again, of what ancient empire (or even modern empire, including several in the twentieth century) was that not true?

Rather than stop at ahistorical scorn, it is important to recall and appreciate as well the enormous political and cultural accomplishment that was the Roman Empire at its height, compared with both what had existed before and what was to come after. The Mediterranean world under Roman rule was not just free for the most part of internal or interstate war, it was just as importantly free of private warfare and had seen off (under Pompey) that ancient scourge of all seafaring civilizations, pirates. Rome thus governed the Mediterranean as though it truly were "mare nostrum," a demilitarized *Great Lakes* of the ancient world. And it built a remarkable road and aqueduct system to enable it to also rule and develop its ethnically and culturally varied contiguous provinces, whose many differences it tolerated even if it celebrated only Rome itself. Control of the sea provided the Empire with *interior lines* of communication and defense (it was possible to travel to Egypt from Rome by sea in a week) and allowed for a commerce which was more or less uniformly policed and taxed. Good roads meant ease of military reinforcement by reserve legions, but also safe conduct for merchants and a vital internal trade. This encouraged economic specialization and urbanization, and with that, also high civilization. And not least, Rome took the great ideas it found among the detritus of the classical civilization of the Greeks and progressively universalized them, notably during the first century C.E. It thereby planted seeds of ideas of citizenship, good government, and even liberty, which would sprout anew in its many successor societies, but especially in the Latin West during the *Renaissance* and after.

(3) The Fall of the Western Empire: The reign of the son of Marcus Aurelius, Lucius Aurelius Commodus (161–192, r. 180–192), is generally identified as the point at which the Empire entered its prolonged decline. Commodus was, in the words of one impassioned historian, "one of the most worthless and bloody wretches that ever disgraced a throne." He completed what Claudius began, giving reign to the army over the law and the Senate, especially the *Praetorian Guard*. Henceforth, like the *Janissaries* of the later *Ottoman Empire*, the political fortunes and even the lives of emperors were decided by an elite military corps with distinct interests of its own, which were almost never coequal with the interests of Rome. More than one emperor succumbed to an assassin's dagger or poison, as competing frontier armies put forward rival candidates to be emperor. This habit led to constant civil war among the legions in which some emperors fell in battle, but others took one of their own soldier's blades in the belly or back while serving in the field: Caius Messius Trajanus, or "Decius" (200–251), a savage persecutor of Christians, was killed fighting the Goths near Abricium; in 253 Trebonianus Gallus (r. 251–253) was butchered by his own troops; in 260 Emperor Publius Licinius Valerianus, or Valerian (c. 193–260, r. 253–260) was captured by the Persians and tortured to death; his son, Publius Licinius Gallienus (218–268), was murdered by some of his own officers. And so on, in what the great historian Edward Gibbon described as a procession from "the barracks, to the throne, to the grave."

The Empire effectively broke apart by the mid-260s, with the western provinces declaring their independence as "Imperium Galliarum" (the "Gallic State"), the eastern provinces under a Syrian potentate, and the Kingdom of Palmyra also independent of Rome. The Empire was—quite remarkably, in many respects—reassembled in the 270s by Lucius Domitius Aurelianus, or Aurelian (c. 212–275, r. 270–275), but only at the highest cost to its values and the quality of its civilization, for it became nothing less than an absolute military dictatorship presided over by emperors who asserted legitimacy based on *divine right*. A brief respite from this chaos came with Gaius Aurelius Diocletianus, or "Diocletian" (245–313, r. 284–313), a man who rose to the throne from humble origins: he too was chosen by the army. The Empire in Diocletian's time was being assailed on all fronts—by a revived Persia to the east, and all across the northern borderlands by aggressive and numerous German nations—and was suffering though a major crisis of *inflation*. His "solution" was to divide the Empire in two, that each half might better govern and defend itself, or so he thought. He retained the title "Augustus" and the eastern provinces, while raising a second "Augustus" to rule the west: Marcus Aurelius Valerius Maximianus, or "Maximian" (b. ?, d. 310). Maximian was a capable and experienced general, whom Diocletian made "Caesar" (a title roughly corresponding to "subordinate emperor") in 285 and then "Augustus" (full co-emperor) the next year. In 293 Diocletian raised up two new "Caesars": Constantius Chlorus, or "Constantius I" (c. 250–306, r. 305–306), and Caius Galerius Valerius, or "Galerius" (b. ?, d. 310, r. 305–310). Under this awkward quadripartite arrangement, the eastern lands of the Empire were split from Italy and Africa, which in turn were separated from Britain, Gaul, and Spain, while Illyricum and the lands of the great Danube valley were administered by a fourth potentate.

In 303 persecution of Christians sharpened in the lands under Diocletian and Galerius. Then he and Maximian abdicated in 305, in favor of the two Caesars, who became the new co-emperors. "Augustus" Constantius I took charge of the Western Empire and the campaign in Britain, where he died the next year, while "Augustus" Galerius ruled in the east. Flavius Valerius Aurelius Constantine (274–337 C.E.), who would ultimately rule the whole Empire as *Constantine I*, "The Great," was named successor by his father Constantius, whose death he attended at York. Galerius granted Constantine the lesser title "Caesar," but not the grander title "Augustus." Even that succession was contested once Galerius died in 310. At one point in this Diocletian-inspired chaos Rome had no fewer than six claimant emperors, including Maximian and his son, who alternately were allies and deadly rivals. All the claimants, Constantine among them, took up arms to secure the throne. During the multi-sided civil war which followed, Constantine converted to Christianity (312). The next year, he issued the Edict of Milan granting full civil and religious rights to Christians within the Empire. The persecution of Christians was over. In time, persecution of "heretics" and non-Christians would begin. In 314 Constantine overcame but spared the last claimant in the east, Licinius, and spent his next years reforming the law, reducing corruption, and campaigning along the German frontier.

In 323 civil war again broke out with Licinius. This time, Constantine put him to death and thereafter was the sole emperor of Rome. In 324 he declared Christianity the state religion of the Empire, although paganism and other faiths were still tolerated. The next year he called the Council of Nicaea, the first of the great *Ecumenical Councils*, to deal with the Arian "heresy": the union of faith and state was complete and set the pattern for centuries of religious conflict and persecution in both the western detritus of the Empire and its longer-surviving eastern half. In 330 Constantine moved his capital to the ancient Greek city of Byzantium and renamed it *Constantinople* ("City of Constantine"). Having united the Empire in blood, in an act of final foolhardiness he divided it again among his three surviving sons (he had earlier executed a fourth), who then fought a civil war over the succession, from 337. Upon the death of Theodosius I (346–395) the Roman Empire was permanently divided. Its western half succumbed to barbarian invaders over the course of the fifth century: Rome itself was sacked in 410 and again in 455. The last Roman Emperor in the west was deposed in 476 by the Goths.

The *Catholic Church* thereafter claimed the imperial-sacral heritage and authority of Rome. In 800, *Charlemagne* would be crowned Emperor by the popes, and later still the *Holy Roman Empire* in Germany would claim to be the true imperial successor. That was all chimera or propaganda. The popes had no legions; Charlemagne was a great king, but his empire was but a pale shadow of what Rome's had been, in terms of wealth, literacy and culture, or military power; and as *Voltaire* caustically said, the Holy Roman Empire was "neither holy, nor Roman, nor an empire." It did not boast the roads and prosperity of Rome, it could not match Rome's reach or culture, or repair crumbling aqueducts or even the rusting plumbing of the public baths Rome left behind.

At the Roman Empire's greatest extent, far to the north a frontier zone of forts and garrisons had stretched across Germania, northern Gaul, and Britain, with even more elaborate fortifications in the more populous east. This line, set by Hadrian, contained something of a "zone of peace" in the ancient world, called "The Empire." After the fall of the Western Empire such orderly conditions would not be enjoyed by European merchants for a thousand years, and have never since been realized in the Mediterranean basin. Instead, for the next 600 years Western Europe faced wave upon wave of invaders: Goths and Vandals, *Magyars* and Huns and many others from Central Asia, *Arabs* and allied Muslims from the south and east, and *Vikings* from the north. Its response everywhere was a hunkered *fortification* and *militarization* of society, including foreshortened commerce and de-urbanization as people fled en masse from the prime targets of besieging and marauding armies. That led to breakdown of the road system and a corresponding rise in brigandage and the cost and duration of travel, and decline into a near-subsistence agricultural life and militarized social and political system that was characterized by gross material poverty for the immiserated masses, overlordship by a class of mounted ignoramuses, and frequent *famine* and outbreaks of murderous religious hysteria. In short, Europe after Rome would turn in its desperate need for defense to the development of *feudalism*. Meanwhile, the African and Asian lands of the broken and abandoned Empire were scoured by repeated dynastic wars among the Muslim peoples who inherited those lands, from the seventh century onward. In the east, however, the Empire survived—and at times also prospered and revived—for another thousand years. With its great capital at Constantinople a Hellenized, eastern polity preserved much of the glory that had been Rome, under the name of the *Byzantine Empire*. *See also mission.*

Suggested Readings: John Boardman et al., eds., *Oxford History of the Roman World* (1991); John Boardman et al., eds. *Oxford History of the Classical World* (1988–); Edward Gibbon, *The Decline and Fall of the Roman Empire*, abridged to 2 vols. by D. M. Low (1960, 1985); Adrian Goldsworthy, *The Punic Wars* (2001); Michael Grant, *From Rome to Byzantium* (1998); Michael Grant, *History of Rome* (1978); Donald Kagan, *The End of the Roman Empire* (1992); Ramsay MacMullen, *Roman Government's Response to Crisis, 235–337 AD* (1974).

Romanov (a.k.a. Romanoff) dynasty. The ruling house of the Russian Empire for more than 300 years, 1613–1917, founded after the "Time of Troubles" by Michael I (1596–1645, r. 1613–1645). Romanov rulers alternated as *Westernizing* reformers and *Slavophile* isolationists. Several were bloody despots. *Peter I* was the greatest of the Westernizers, but he was followed by several weak tsars and tsarinas, until *Catherine II* took power after the murder of her husband. *Alexander I* also took power following a murder, of his father, Tsar Paul. His brother, *Nicholas I*, was a severe Slavophile. Some Romanovs—such as Peter and Catherine—claimed the title "The Great." Others were accorded it as the judgment of history, in particular *Alexander II* for his sustained effort to reform and modernize Russia politically and economically, and for his *emancipation* of the *serfs*. His successors failed to build on these crucial initiatives or to fend off powerful forces of rural and nationalist reaction against reform. The dynasty ended in ineptitude, defeat, shame, and savage and bloody tragedy. *Nicholas II* was a fatally weak tsar who failed to rise to the crisis of domestic reform or of *World War I*, and contributed directly to that awful national calamity. During the *Russian Revolution of March (February) 1917*, he was forced to abdicate. When the *Bolshevik Revolution* tipped the country into civil war from November (October) 1917, Nicholas was made a prisoner of the state. He was later murdered and buried in secret by the Bolsheviks, along with his wife, their five children (who were shot and then finished off by bayonet), several servants, and the family doctor. That the atrocity took place on *Lenin's* personal order was finally confirmed from Soviet archival sources in 1993. After the fall of the *Soviet Union*, the bodies of the royal family were exhumed and re-buried, in graves which became touchstones of controversy among *monarchists*, *republicans*, and aging *communists*. Some continue to believe that the tsar's eldest daughter, Anastasia, escaped the massacre, and there were many claimants to her name and fortune. The most famous, and possibly genuine, was Anna Anderson. Her claim was rejected by a German court in 1967 after several decades of litigation. She settled in Charlottesville, Virginia, and died in 1984. *See also Bourbons; Habsburg dynasty; Ivan III; Ivan IV; Josef Stalin.*

Roman Question. "What should be the relationship of the papacy to the Italian state?" For more than 14 centuries, with some breaks, Rome was under the temporal control of the popes, and beyond Rome, so were the *Papal States*. However, from 1850 to 1870 *Pius IX* was kept in Rome only by French troops. When these were pulled out for use in the *Franco-Prussian War*, Italian troops assaulted the city and incorporated it into Italy, making it the capital. The popes did not accept this until a compromise with *Mussolini* was agreed in the *Lateran Treaty* (1929), which established the *Vatican* as a *sovereign* entity.

Roman Republic. *See Roman Empire.*

Rome, Treaty of (1957). Six West European *nations* (Belgium, France, Italy, Luxembourg, the Netherlands and West Germany) met in Rome in 1957 to sign a *treaty* setting up *EURATOM* and the *EEC*, and intending to "establish the foundations of an ever closer union among the European peoples." It provided for creation of a *common market* within 15 years, while permitting smaller *customs unions* to operate as well, such as the *BENELUX*. It committed signatories to free movement of *capital* and *labor*, progressive elimination of *tariffs* and other *trade barriers*, and common *investment* and social welfare policies. *Agriculture* was exempt but was later brought under the *Common Agricultural Policy* (CAP). The treaty established four major organs: (1) the *European Commission*, a semi-executive; (2) the *Council of Ministers*, to coordinate national governments (connected to the Commission by a consultative committee); (3) the *European Parliament*; and (4) the *European Court of Justice*.

Rommel, Erwin (1881–1944). "The Desert Fox." A hard-charger who always chose attack over defense, thought by some to be a brilliant tactician. He was wounded twice during *World War I*, during which he saw action in the *infantry* on the *western* and *eastern fronts* and with mountain troops in Italy. He was first noticed by senior officers for his innovative tactics during the *Battle of Caporetto* (October–November 1917). After the war he stayed in the truncated *Wehrmacht* and wrote a widely read book on infantry tactics, published in 1937. He commanded *Hitler's* bodyguard during the march into the *Sudetenland* in 1938 and the Polish campaign of 1939. He served as a *Panzer* commander in the *Battle of France* (May–June 1940). He earned his reputation, his nom de guerre, and the grudging respect of his opponents while leading the Afrika Korps against the British in North Africa, 1941–1943. Although the military effect of his African campaign was minimal, he was made a great war hero by Nazi propagandists after he captured Tobruk in June 1942. His reputation survived in Germany even after the decisive defeat at *El Alamein* later that year. He next commanded in Italy, then took charge of Hitler's Atlantic defenses, greatly strengthening them for the invasion everyone knew was coming. After *D-Day*, convinced the war would be lost, he asked Hitler to sue for an *armistice*. This idea was dismissed out of hand. Rommel at last came to believe that if Hitler remained in power Germany would lose the war, and he finally talked to conspirators planning the *July Plot* to kill the German dictator. He hoped the coup to follow would lead to a separate peace in the West. It is uncertain if Rommel overtly supported the assassination plot; he may only have argued for Hitler's arrest and trial. Still, his name became attached to the coup attempt, extracted under torture of the other plotters, and Hitler ordered him killed. To preserve Rommel's reputation as a propaganda support for the war effort, rather than simply execute him Hitler threatened his family to convince the field marshal to commit suicide by poison. He did. It was later announced that Rommel had died of battle wounds, giving his all for Germany. He was then given a *state funeral*—a cynical curtain call for a corpse, even by Nazi standards.

Roosevelt, Franklin Delano (1882–1945). U.S. statesman. Assistant secretary of the navy, 1913–1920; *Democratic* president, 1933–1945. His first administration was preoccupied with the national calamity of the *Great Depression*, to which Roosevelt responded with the *hundred days* of "New Deal" legislation—public works spending and projects in agriculture and industry, social security and unemployment programs, and much else. This ameliorated some effects of the Depression, but overall his domestic efforts were undermined by a failure of his economic diplomacy, as during the *World Economic Conference* in 1933. Hard times and high unemployment continued until America went on a full *war economy* footing from 1939. In foreign affairs Roosevelt opened relations with the Soviet Union and affirmed the *Good Neighbor policy*. After 1936 he grew increasingly concerned with events in Europe and Asia, but he offered only such rhetorical support as his *quarantine* policy to proposals for *collective security* measures against Italy, Germany, or Japan. He funneled minor secret aid to the Republican side in the *Spanish Civil War*, which placed him in opposition to most American *Catholic* opinion (not for the last time), which was pro-*Franco*. Roosevelt sought to convince Britain and France to work with *Stalin* against *Hitler*, but to no avail, since he insisted at the same time that the United States would remain *neutral*. In 1940 and 1941, however, he jumped ahead of *isolationist* public opinion with the *destroyers-for-bases* deal, *Lend-Lease*, and the *Atlantic Charter*, which virtually declared defeat of the *Axis* as an American *war aim* although the United States was still a neutral power, and authorization of the top-secret *Manhattan Project*. In sum, Roosevelt embraced a policy up to 1941, as one historian has put it, of "all aid to Britain short of war." This also helped America achieve a full war economy even before its formal entry into *World War II*, which is what finally began to pull the country out of the Depression, rather than the New Deal as is often claimed.

Meanwhile, in the Far East Roosevelt increased pressure on Imperial Japan by applying additional sanctions after Tokyo joined the Axis alliance (1940).

Ultimately, *Pearl Harbor* brought the United States into the war. Despite public pressure to concentrate on the war against Japan, Roosevelt agreed with *Churchill* and Stalin to concentrate on defeating Germany first. That decision was not initially popular with the American public but was one of the most important and sound decisions Roosevelt ever made. He sided with Churchill against his own generals in the decision to land American forces in North Africa in 1942 to support the British campaign in Egypt and Tripoli, but he overruled his British ally in pressing for a landing in France at the first opportunity. He has been heavily criticized—fairly or not—for declaring the *unconditional surrender* policy at *Casablanca* that so affected the final months of World War II, although after the experience of 1918 and given the character of the Nazi regime it seems an entirely defensible position. Roosevelt is criticized by others for distrusting Britain almost as much, and perhaps more on certain issues, than he did Stalin and the Soviet Union. Also, he developed an intense and personal dislike of *Charles de Gaulle*, which had a lasting negative impact on Franco-American relations.

FDR negotiated personally at *Tehran* and *Yalta*, for which he has received much unfair criticism for a supposed "sell-out" of Eastern Europe to Stalin, when all he did was accept to live with the reality of a *de facto* Soviet *sphere of influence*, as any American president would have had to do. With more justice, he was criticized for overestimating the importance of *Chiang Kai-shek* to China's future and America's *national interest*, and in general for too often basing his foreign policy assessments mainly on personalities and faith in his own "Tammany Hall" arm-twisting skills and great personal charm. He pushed for creation of the *United Nations Organization*, 1944–1945, but he died while the *San Francisco Conference*—in which he stored great hope—was still underway. He remains an enigmatic figure. At his best, he was a pragmatic idealist of the first order. He was on occasion genuinely naïve, but he could also be tough with opponents to the point of cruelty and perhaps even cynicism. He reacted to events rather than seeking to shape them, but he shaped them anyway by virtue of the extraordinary power of the great nation he led. He hated poverty as he hated war, and in the end his historic greatness lay in coming to understand that it was crucial for America to lead an international effort to limit both. Bringing America permanently out of its historic isolationism to assume a positive world role was surely his greatest and most lasting achievement.

Suggested Readings: Robert Dallek, *Franklin D. Roosevelt and American Foreign Policy* (1979); Robert Divine, *The Reluctant Belligerent* (1965, 1979); Robert Divine, *Roosevelt And World War II* (1969); Warren Kimball, *The Juggler* (1991).

Roosevelt-Litvinov Agreements (1933). A set of paper understandings on consular arrangements, limited religious liberty, retrenchment of activities of the *Comintern*, trade, and *war debts*, all negotiated by *Franklin Roosevelt* and

Maxim Litvinov. They paved the way to U.S. *recognition* of the Soviet Union after 15 years of severed relations.

Roosevelt, Theodore (1858–1919). U.S. statesman. Assistant secretary of the navy, 1897–1898; vice president, 1901; *Republican* president, 1901–1909. At home he was an energetic "square deal" reformer. He established forest reserves and national parks, "busted" trusts (monopolies), and was generally sympathetic to the interests of labor—especially roundly exploited coal miners—although he was also capable of taking tough anti-union, or at least anti-strike, action if he deemed it in the higher *national interest*. It was Roosevelt who coined the phrase "the lunatic fringe in all reform movements." He was a determined opponent of concentrations of power in the hands of large corporations. In foreign policy he was an enthusiastic imperialist who led the country part way out of its historic *isolationism*. He saw American, and to a lesser extent also British, imperialism as essentially progressive, as leading primitive areas from backwardness into the enlightened and law-governed spaces occupied by the democratic *Great Powers* of the West. He was far less sanguine about German imperialism, either overseas or in the gathering threat to the *balance of power* in Europe which he saw taking shape from the erratic *Weltpolitik* of *Kaiser Wilhelm II*. And he viewed Japan with growing suspicion about its long-range ambitions in Asia and the Pacific. Given his sophisticated strategic perspective, Roosevelt actively pursued American *hegemony* in the Caribbean.

As assistant secretary of the navy, and in his presidential statecraft, Roosevelt was a persistent "big navy" advocate. He knew *Alfred T. Mahan*, but he appears to have come to his views on *sea power* independently. Roosevelt's emphasis was on finishing the *battleship* fleet begun by his predecessors, and on using it assertively—as they had not—to project power on a worldwide basis. Roosevelt got his main chance before the *Spanish-American War* (1898), when he sent the Pacific Fleet to patrol near the Philippines in anticipation of acquiring those islands should war break out as expected. When it did, *George Dewey* and the fleet proceeded to Manila, where they destroyed an entire Spanish battle fleet—which was badly obsolescent—and captured the city (May 1, 1898), without a single American fatality and fewer than 10 wounded. Dewey then imposed a *blockade* on the Philippines and enforced it—including against several German warships—while awaiting an invasion force from the United States. The naval victory at Manila and follow-up ground campaign made the United States a colonial and Pacific power, to the great surprise and subsequent considerable discomfort of most Americans, as it saddled them with an overseas empire most quickly discovered they did not really want. Back in Cuba, where rebellion against Spain was the original *casus belli* of the war, Roosevelt resigned from the navy to organize and lead to war a volunteer *cavalry* unit called the "Rough Riders." Most famously, the unit charged up Kettle Hill and San Juan Hill, taking them while suffering heavy casualties. That secured his national reputation and won him the New York governorship. His record in New York gained him a place on the Republican ticket alongside President *William McKinley*, and then election as vice president in 1900.

Roosevelt was sworn in as president a few months later, at age 42, when McKinley was assassinated by an anarchist (September 14, 1901). Roosevelt subsequently was elected on his own accord (1904). His most famous admonition was to "speak softly and carry a big stick," by which he meant that the United States should abstain from bellicose rhetoric, of which the kaiser and other bombasts were fond, while nonetheless maintaining a powerful navy to back up the claims of the *Monroe Doctrine*, see to its newfound imperial obligations, and—not least of all—gain the international *prestige* and influence which were America's due as a rising power. At the dawn of the age of the *Dreadnought*, both prestige and influence were widely thought to flow from possession of a first-class fleet of battleships. In the longer term, Roosevelt thought that the preponderant weight of combined American and British naval power was beneficent for *international security* and peace. The two "righteous nations" of Western civilization, he believed, had similar strategic interests, a common bond of democratic values and culture, and a shared moral obligation to secure a more just international order. Having thus secured the "big stick," Roosevelt consistently tried to follow his own advice about walking softly in foreign policy. Even when intriguing to create Panama during the *War of the Thousand Days* so that the United States could build a canal across it, although his exact role remains a matter of passionate controversy, he did not intervene with massive or blunt force. Indeed, he exhibited a deep reluctance to intervene militarily in Central America or the Caribbean, except when it was unavoidable to achieve *abatement* of some spillover conflict. (In contrast, *Woodrow Wilson* would intervene in the region far more frequently than the *realist* Roosevelt, in the name of *legitimacy* and *idealist* principle.)

In extra-hemispheric diplomacy, Roosevelt prudently concealed his antipathy to Germany and concerns about Japan, working diligently to preserve at least a surface harmony with both. In this he was largely successful, even as he helped to find a peaceful pro-French solution to the *First Moroccan Crisis* (1905–1906). He brought U.S. diplomacy into the "First Division" with a successful *mediation* of the *Russo-Japanese War* (1904–1905), helping to negotiate in detail the terms of the *Treaty of Portsmouth*, an achievement for which he won the 1906 *Nobel Prize* (for Peace). In 1912 he split the Republicans by running against *Taft* on the "Bull Moose" ticket ("I am strong as a bull moose, and you can use me to the limit"). Beginning in 1914 he argued for early entry into *World War I*, against what he saw as Wilson's excessive caution. He opposed the latter's call for a "peace without victors," arguing instead for a deliberate military *occupation* of Germany and the other *Central*

Powers, and an Anglo-American–led postwar order. His last words were "Put out the light." *See also Alaska; Great White Fleet.*

Suggested Readings: H. W. Brands, *TR: The Last Romantic* (1998); Richard H. Collins, *Theodore Roosevelt's Caribbean* (1990); John Milton Cooper, *The Warrior and the Priest* (1983); Louis L. Gould, *The Presidency of Theodore Roosevelt* (1991); Edmund Morris, *Theodore Rex* (2002); William N. Tilchin, *Theodore Roosevelt and the British Empire* (1997).

Root Arbitration Treaties. U.S. secretary of state *Elihu Root* believed that even weak *arbitration* agreements were better than none, and he negotiated 24 *bilateral* treaties (renewable at five-year intervals) with most leading states, except Germany. That added to the 10 which *John Hay*, his predecessor, had negotiated. *See also cooling-off treaties.*

Root, Elihu (1845–1937). U.S. statesman. Secretary of war, 1899–1904; secretary of state, 1905–1909. He served under *William McKinley* and *Theodore Roosevelt*. That meant he was closely—though never definitively—involved in such salient events as the *Spanish-American War* (1898) and the Filipino rebellion which followed. He wrote the *Platt Amendment* concerning *intervention* in Cuba and was engaged in securing *recognition* of Panamanian independence in 1903 as a result of the *War of the Thousand Days*, and permission to start construction of the *Panama Canal*. His main concentration as secretary of state, however, was on the legalistic and formalistic device of the *Root Arbitration Treaties*, for which he was awarded the 1912 *Nobel Prize* for Peace. He also negotiated the *Root-Takahira Agreement* with Japan confirming that empire's acquisition of Korea. He resisted, unsuccessfully, a precipitous decline in American-Russian relations that led a few years later (1912) to *abrogation* by Congress of a 72-year-old *commercial treaty* over the issue of Russian persecution of American Jews. He subsequently served in the Senate. In 1912 he broke with Roosevelt to support *Howard Taft* for president. He remained an internationalist all his life, supporting membership of the United States in the *League of Nations* and the *World Court*.

Root-Takahira Agreement (1908). U.S. Secretary of State *Elihu Root* and Japanese ambassador Baron Takahira agreed to confirm Japan's paramountcy in Korea in return for a Japanese affirmation that it had no designs on the Philippines. Two years later, having thus eased the way, Japan *annexed* Korea.

Rosas, Juan Manuel de (1793–1877). A *Creole* from a landed family of long lineage in Buenos Aires, he rose to power as a leader of the "gauchos" (Argentine herdsmen), whom he molded into a labor and *militia* force in the 1820s. He then made alliance with the cattle barons and major landowners ("estancieros") and forced his way into power as governor of Buenos Aires in 1829. He was governor twice: 1829–1832 and 1835–1852. Despite this lower-level official position, he was an effective ruler of Argentina. A sort of early

Perón, he was a populist who also wooed and attracted urban workers, but also governed them by force, including use of a secret society of thugs organized as *death squads* (which perhaps killed 2,000 persons) and dedicated to enforcing *terror* against the opposition. He was overthrown by a tripartite invasion of Argentina (whose borders remained ill-defined) by forces from Brazil, Uruguay, and Entre Ríos. He fled into exile and was taken on a British warship to Great Britain—where he spent the rest of his life.

Rosenbergs, Ethel (1916–1953) and Julius (1917–1953). American *Communists*, convicted in 1951 of being atomic spies for the *Soviet Union* at the Los Alamos research facility where crucial work was done on the *Manhattan Project* during *World War II*. Julius's espionage activities were discovered during the unraveling of a Soviet spy ring following the *Fuchs* trial in Britain. They were both executed (by electrocution) at Sing Sing prison. Their family understandably, and critics of their trial less so over time, vehemently rejected the verdict and/or the death sentence, charging that they were innocent victims of *McCarthyism*. Then the fall of the Soviet Union opened access to *KGB* archives, which, along with other intercepts, definitively proved Julius Rosenberg was engaged in atomic espionage. However, although Ethel Rosenberg probably knew what her husband was up to, it is not clear, but it is unlikely, that she was herself a spy. Her execution was therefore probably a miscarriage of justice. Deep division over the case existed between American *liberals* and *conservatives* for decades, when they should have been more united in waging the *Cold War* against the Soviet Union, which conducted real *purge trials* and *Yezhovshchina*.
   Suggested Reading: Alan Weinstein and Alexander Vassiliev, *The Haunted Wood* (1999).

Rote Kapelle. *See Red Orchestra.*

Rothschild, House of. A German-Jewish banking family. Its great fortune was made by Meyer Rothschild (1743–1812), who started as a money-lender and coin dealer in Frankfurt. Rothschild and his sons earned commissions and gained influence during the *Napoleonic Wars* by floating loans to several combatant powers, including Denmark, and arranging subsidies and government bond issues for England's continental princes and allies. They had close and cordial relations with the Bank of England. During the *Peninsular War* they channeled English money to *Wellington* in Spain. Having backed the right side against *Napoleon*, the five Rothschild sons were made barons in the *Austrian Empire* in 1822. They established branches of the bank in Frankfurt, London, Naples, Paris, and Vienna and were succeeded in turn by their sons. Much of the *industrialization* of the nineteenth century was financed by the House of Rothschild. Lionel Rothschild (1808–1879) took up the cause of Jewish emancipation in Britain, and the family was influential in aiding the early *Zionist* movement. The Rothschilds opposed aid to Tsarist Russia before and during *World War I*, owing to its deep *anti-Semitism*. They were a favored target of *Nazi* propaganda, which focused on their Jewishness and on the internationalism of their banking interests. *See also Balfour Declaration; House of Fugger.*

Suggested Reading: Niall Fergusson, *The House of Rothschild*, 2 vols. (1998–1999).

Round Table Conferences (1930–1932). A set of initially abortive talks between the British and various Indian leaders, including *Gandhi*, on self-government for India. (1) 1930: The First Round Table Conference took place after the *salt march* and was held over the objections of a minority of Conservatives led by *Winston Churchill*. It took place with no representatives from the *Congress Party* present—Gandhi and *Nehru*, among others, were in jail or boycotted the conference. It led nowhere. (2) 1932: Gandhi agreed to attend as the sole delegate from Congress, in return for ending the civil disobedience campaign which attended the salt march, to negotiate possible *dominion status* which would leave a united India within the British Commonwealth. Some in Congress, such as *Subhas Bose*, saw this as a betrayal. *Ali Jinnah* represented the *Muslim League*. Along with *Sikh*, "*Untouchable*," and other representatives, Jinnah demanded the separate communal and caste electorates which the British also favored. The conference ended in bitter disagreement. Shortly afterward, Gandhi was rearrested and Congress was banned. (3) 1932: Britain held a third conference in November, pressing ahead with effectively unilateral and nearly universally opposed "reforms" which culminated in the *India Act* of 1935.

Rousseau, Jean-Jacques (1712–1778). Swiss philosopher of the *Enlightenment*. He was abandoned by his reprobate father, and his mother died in childbirth. He became an autodidact while indentured to, and maltreated by, an engraver in Geneva. At age 16 he ran away. He was taken in, and thence to bed (he was a well-turned youth) by a wealthy shopkeeper's wife in Turin. This set a pattern for Rousseau, who moved from the bed of one wealthy patroness to another's. In 1741 he moved to Paris. Although he would famously write with passion and sensibility about childhood and education, he abandoned five of his own children to a foundlings' home. His influence spread widely, at first based on several popular operas he composed, later when many of his ideas were publicized by *Voltaire* and later still, when they were apparently embodied or tested by the *French Revolution*. He was one of several *social contract* theorists whose views later helped the doctrine of *popular sovereignty* surmount that of *absolutism*. Unlike *Hobbes*, however, Rousseau viewed *war* not as humanity's natural state in the *state of nature* but as an aspect of its international social condition, as the ineluctable result of the creation of a *states system* and thereby of social relations of conflict and cooperation among separate states. Rousseau wrote much and, like any prolific author, frequently appeared to contradict his earlier self. One may locate in his writings soaring and inspirational paeans to the "natural condition" of human freedom and the essential and reliable goodness of human nature ("Man is born free, yet everywhere we find him in chains"), as well as darker yearnings for political and social compulsion to perfection ("men must be forced to be free"), that great temptation to all radical idealists and wildly dangerous guide to social policy. Both were impulses which might be located in the formative puritanism and absolutism of his *Calvinist* youth in Geneva, to which he returned several times in later life, physically and spiritually.

Rousseau's key political concept was the idea of the *sovereign* or "general will"—roughly, the collective will and public good of a whole society—to which most individuals voluntarily surrender in order to construct social order, and which is therefore unconcerned with sectarian divisions or private interests or pursuits. It is when people willfully defy the "general will," which after all seeks their own best good and interests, that Rousseau argued they must "be forced to be free." Therein lay the seeds that others—though not Rousseau personally—such as *Robespierre* would cultivate into *The Terror* of the French Revolution. Later still, the *Bolshevik Revolution* would again try to "force men to be free"—of their normal individual wants, desires, and impulses arising from the vagaries of human nature, the fruits of personality, and the uniqueness of circumstance—in the name of a "general good" arbitrarily determined by self-righteous ideologues utterly persuaded of their own moral purity and clear grasp of absolute truths. His work also influenced *Kant* and *Hegel*, although in different directions—Kant toward moral Idealism, but Hegel toward Idealism as embodied in an *authoritarian*, if not *totalitarian*, state. Rousseau's views on "natural religion" were not well received by *Catholics* or *Protestants* in his day, and he was forced to seek protection from his fellow Swiss under the wing of the putative "*enlightened despot*" of Prussia, *Frederick the Great*. Rousseau went erratically but progressively insane in his final years. He was buried beside Voltaire in the Panthéon in Paris. *See also Hugo Grotius; Immanuel Kant; Leviathan; Niccolò Machiavelli; Thomas Robert Malthus; Peter I.*

Suggested Readings: Jean-Jacques Rousseau, On the Origin of Inequality (1754); Jean-Jacques Rousseau, The Social Contract (1762); Jean-Jacques Rousseau, Confessions (1781).

Royal Navy (RN). By consensus, the pedigree of the Royal Navy dates to the English navy assembled by *Elizabeth I*, which consisted of both royal (that is, commissioned) ships as well as *privateers* sailing under *letters of marque*. Both types of ship gathered and sailed together to meet and defeat the *Spanish Armada* in the *English Channel* in 1588. However, the Royal Navy as a permanent instrument of English (later, British) national power and policy is not generally regarded as having been established until c. 1649–1660. The RN demonstrated its value and its rising professionalism and martial superiority during the hard-fought *Anglo-Dutch Wars*. For the next 350 years the RN remained the principal expression of British military power and island security, and the key to its imperial reach and hugely successful overseas expansion. It fended off or deterred invasion attempts by *Louis XIV* in 1692 and 1708. It made possible decisive defeat of France in the Americas and in India during the eighteenth century, prevented another planned invasion of Great Britain, 1745–1746, and again in 1759 during the culmination of the struggle in the *Seven Years' War* (1756–1763). By 1757 it boasted 90 *ships-of-the-line* and 149 additional warships of all classes. By 1759 the RN had completed a careening facility in Halifax, Nova Scotia, where ships could be rolled so that barnacles might be scraped off, and thus improve battle speed. This enabled the RN to keep a full squadron in North America, as ships no longer needed to cross the Atlantic for regular scraping and refit at Portsmouth, the home port of the fleet. In the next century, copper-bottomed hulls were introduced and this procedure became redundant.

By 1770 the RN had 126 ships-of-the-line, but it still could be challenged by the combined fleets of its enemies, France and Spain, which together could put 121 ships-of-the-line to sea that year. This naval *arms race* continued past the end of the decade, creating a near-balance in numbers of top rates at sea. This told the tale during the *American Revolution*, in which the RN was badly overstretched by having to fight simultaneously in several oceans while also performing home defense and escort duties. Britain itself was at risk of invasion as a result. The RN had a great advantage, however, not in numbers but in organization and the skill and daring of individual captains. One such great captain, *George Rodney*, met and bested a French fleet in the West Indies and captured several of the sugar islands of the Caribbean. Nonetheless, that war was lost. The threat to Britain abated for a decade. Then came the *French Revolution* and the gravest danger to Britain since the Armada, but also the finest days of the Royal Navy. The RN's greatest victories were won during the *Napoleonic Wars* by *Horatio Nelson*, first at *Abukir Bay* (1798) and then at *Trafalgar* (1805). Nelson broke *Napoleon's* battle and invasion fleets and ended the threat of a French invasion of Britain. Subsequently, the RN *blockaded* French-occupied Europe, smuggled goods through the porous *Continental System*, raided French and Spanish commerce on all the world's oceans, and captured the overseas possessions of any declared enemy of Britain. It protected vital *convoys* from French raiders and privateers, and it ferried provisions to British armies in the Iberian Peninsula, and later in Flanders. In short, the RN made it possible for Great Britain to survive against France, until the Grand Alliance of 1813 was assembled to finish Napoleon.

In 1815 the Royal Navy had 214 ships-of-the-line and close to 800 smaller warships—an unprecedented accumulation of naval power. During the nineteenth century the successor ships of this formidable force excelled in policing the British ban on the *slave trade*, off both the east and west African coasts after 1833. In the second half of the nineteenth century it policed the oceans and guarded a globe-girdling empire and British commercial dominance. In the South Pacific islands the RN often acted as a protective buffer of indigenous populations from rapacious settlers, whom many of its officers saw as "white savages." This attitude of civilizing *mission* extended to its war against piracy as well. The British Empire was beginning to feel the strains of democratic pressures and the attendant rise of an imperial conscience. The Royal Navy, as both the hardest point and flag-bearer of the Empire, carried this moral burden to its highest and furthest limits.

Following the *Crimean War* and the advent of the *ironclad*, Britain was drawn into a half-century naval arms race with France and Russia, maintaining more or less its desired *two-power naval standard*. By the mid-1890s the RN had a new focus: the *Anglo-German naval arms race*. Along with the *Entente Cordiale*, the *Anglo-Japanese Treaty* of 1902 represented a new British strategy born of the expense of the naval race: a grand scheme to reduce what was increasingly seen in London as serious imperial overcommitment and to "recall the legions" of the Royal Navy from the Pacific to home waters. This was made necessary by the need to defend Britain itself against the threat arising from the Kriegsmarine. The naval legions were also recalled from the Caribbean after 200 years of deployment there. That was possible because of a deepening Anglo-American rapprochement, the good will toward the British Empire exuded by *Theodore Roosevelt*, and the concomitant advent in the Caribbean, as in the Pacific, of a powerful and friendly American Navy. The old policy of the two-power naval standard was abandoned in fact, though not officially or publicly, in 1912 in the face of growing German naval strength and the enormous expense of naval construction incurred by the *Dreadnought* revolution.

During *World War I*, at Coronel, off the coast of Chile on November 1, 1914, Britain suffered its first battle lost at sea in over 100 years. Revenge was taken shortly thereafter on some of the same German cruisers which fought at Coronel, in the Battle of the Falkland Islands. After that, the RN enforced an effective blockade of Germany during World War I, beating back the only full fleet challenge by the Kriegsmarine at *Jutland*, in 1916. Before the war the RN had cleaved to the idea of a single imperial navy, but as the *Dominions* began to develop their own navies during the war, clear value was recognized in departing from the old imperial scheme. In addition, the Royal Air Force (RAF) developed as an adjunct to the Royal Navy during the Great War. The RAF was then spun off from the RN in 1919.

The RN formally dropped the two-power standard when it accepted parity with the U.S. Navy at the *Washington Naval Conference* in 1922. Before *World War II* a serious misunderstanding of the relative importance of *aircraft carriers* and *submarines* was evident in RN planning, as was also the case with several other navies. During the interwar years the RN therefore continued to build and put to sea mainly *battleships*, *cruisers*, and *destroyers*. When war came, with significant assistance from the Royal Canadian Navy (RCN) and then the American Navy, the Royal Navy fought to a desperate victory over the *U-boats* of the Kriegsmarine in the *Battle of the Atlantic*. The RN lost two prized battleships early in the Pacific war to Japanese aerial attack, but for most of World War II it deferred to the United States in that theater of operations, instead concentrating its major effort in the North Atlantic, the North Sea, and the Mediterranean (where it engaged the French and Italian fleets, as well as the Kriegsmarine).

After World War II the Royal Navy shrank in tandem with Great Britain's reduced geopolitical role, but it remained a mainstay of *NATO*. It demonstrated its continuing high quality and professionalism during the *Falklands War* (1982), although that was also a contest which revealed serious and even fatal flaws in its ship design and materials. The Royal Navy subsequently took part in multiple actions in support of UN *sanctions* and NATO policy, including enforcement of various *embargoes*, blockades, or mine-clearing operations in the Mediterranean and the Persian Gulf. At the turn of the twenty-first century the Royal Navy was one of just a handful of *nuclear weapons*–capable navies. *See also Continental System; John Fisher; Gibraltar; impressment; mutiny; sea power; War of 1812.*

Suggested Readings: Paul Kennedy, *The Rise and Fall of British Naval Mastery* (1976); N. A. M. Roger, *Safeguard of the Sea*, Vol. I (1997).

Ruanda-Urundi. A *trust territory* in Central Africa under Belgian control, 1946–1962, when it was divided into the independent states of Rwanda and Burundi.

Ruhr. A major mining and industrial region of Germany, centered on the Ruhr Valley—the largest coal field and related industrial area in the world. It became important with German *industrialization* after 1850, surpassing *Silesia* and the *Saar*. By 1914 it was supplying fuel to a German steel industry which was twice as big as Britain's. It was occupied by French and Belgian troops, 1923–1925, in an effort to compel *reparations* payments. That contributed to the *hyperinflation* which bedeviled *Weimar* and set the stage for *Hitler* to attempt the *Beer Hall Putsch*, at the time considered a minor incident. The occupation gained little for France that was concrete, and lost it valuable diplomatic support from Britain and the United States.

rule. In *international law*, a binding general measure existing between or among *states*. The binding character of rules is derived mainly from *consent*, but also from the premise that there is broad agreement under *international customary law* as to the existence of commonly binding *norms* of state conduct. Certain rules have universal application (have been widely accepted by the states); others are specific to certain regions. *See also declaration;* jus cogens; *resolution; treaty.*

rule of 1756. Now archaic, this maritime *law of war* was promulgated by British *prize courts*. It said that trade between a *metropolitan power* and its *colonies* was designated "enemy trade" in wartime, even if it was carried by *neutral* shipping. *See also blockade; neutral rights; visit and search; War of 1812.*

rule of double criminality. Of recent vintage, this *rule* now written into many *treaties* on criminal *extradition* holds that extradition of a fugitive may occur and a trial proceed if the charges concern an act which is a crime in both countries concerned, even in the absence of its specific listing in any enumeration of extraditable offenses in the treaty.

rules of engagement. The operational orders under which a military unit is authorized to use *force* in a *war zone.* Rules of engagement may be liberal (at the extreme, akin to "shoot whatever moves"), or highly restrictive (at the extreme, "fire only if directly fired on and can identify the shooter and the gauge of weapon used, and then return fire only with the same gauge of weapon and using as many rounds as the perpetrator"). Worst of all from the defending soldier's point of view is when rules of multilateral engagement forbid return fire due to the political delicacy of a situation. To troops on the ground, that may amount to the order "duck." Highly restrictive rules were the usual ones for United Nations *peacekeeping* forces during the *Cold War,* but became much more liberal over the course of the 1990s with the UN's move into *peace enforcement* in places such as Somalia and Bosnia.

rules of the game. *Norms* of conduct tacitly agreed between or among *states* otherwise engaged in serious conflict, whose violation will gravely escalate the conflict. *Nonintervention* in each other's *spheres of influence* is a grand rule; not *assassinating* foreign *heads of state* or *heads of government*, or killing foreign *intelligence agents* is a lower-level example.

Rumania. Rumania was a province of the *Roman Empire* (Dacia) until the third century C.E. Like most other outlying provinces of Rome, over the next seven centuries it was subsequently, and alternately, overrun and settled by various barbarian peoples. In the thirteenth century the *Mongols* reached Rumania. Finally, the *Ottoman Empire* acquired the largely *Christianized* territories that make up the core of modern Rumania and governed them into the late nineteenth century, as the *Danubian Principalities* of Moldavia and Wallachia. During the seventeenth century they were briefly de facto independent of Ottoman rule after a sustained rebellion, but this did not last. Russia repeatedly intervened in the Danubian Principalities during the first half of the nineteenth century. It tried to make them into *protectorates* in 1856. Instead, they were given a joint guarantee of *autonomy* by the *Great Powers* in the *Treaty of Paris* (1856). In 1858 they formed "Rumania," though still within the Ottoman Empire. Rumania became fully *sovereign* in 1878 as a result of the *Russo-Turkish War* of 1877–1878, under terms of the *Treaty of San Stefano.* This was confirmed at the *Congress of Berlin.*

Rumania entered the *Second Balkan War* looking to add to its territory. Ionel Brătianu (1864–1927) was prime minister intermittently, 1909–1927, and at first tried to stay out of *World War I*. Rumania remained *neutral* in 1914, but it was bribed into the war on the side of the *Allies* on August 27, 1916, following the *Brusilov Offensive,* by promises (actually made in bad faith by France and Russia) it would receive *Bukovina,* part of Galicia, and *Transylvania* from Austria-Hungary. Instead, it was mostly overrun by Bulgarians, Austrians, Turks, and Germans and was forced to make a *separate peace* in March 1918. By re-declaring war in November, just days before the German *surrender,* it was able to sit as a "victor" at the *Paris Peace Conference.* Thereby, it gained huge new territories, including *Bessarabia* and Transylvania.

Rumania joined the *Little Entente* in the *interwar years,* but a large Rumanian *fascist* party (the *Iron Guard*) pulled it toward *Nazi Germany,* a process completed after the destruction of *Czechoslovakia.* King Carol II (1893–1953; r. 1930–1940) admired *Mussolini* and sought to appease *Hitler* with access to Rumanian *oil.* With Hitler occupied by his invasion of France, *Stalin* took Bukovina and Bessarabia from Rumania in 1940. Carol also lost territory to Hungary and Bulgaria and was forced to abdicate. Embittered, Rumania joined the *Tripartite Pact* in 1940 and joined the Nazi assault on Russia in 1941 in a bid to reclaim Bessarabia. Had it not joined the *Axis,* Rumania surely would have been invaded by Hitler: its oil, located in the Ploesti fields and the only major reserve in all Europe, was a critical strategic ambition of his all through *World War II.* As the *Red Army* crossed the Dniester from Ukraine in August 1944, King Michael dismissed Ion Antonescu (1882–1946), Rumania's fascist dictator (he was later shot, in 1946). Rumania *declared war* on Germany the next day, trapping nearly 200,000 German troops in the Carpathian Mountains. That provoked Hitler to bomb Bucharest but also permitted Rumania to escape full Soviet and other Allied vengeance. Still, the Red Army advanced into Rumania and by early 1945 a *Communist* regime was imposed, in violation of the *Yalta Accords.* Rumania remained within the Soviet orbit for the duration of the *Cold War.* Under the secure dictatorship of Gheorghe Gheorghiu-Dej (1901–1965), it negotiated the withdrawal of Soviet troops in 1958.

Nicolae Ceausescu succeeded as Communist dictator in 1967. He ran a ruthless regime at home which yet won favor in the West for its occasional, and wholly symbolic, foreign policy independence from Moscow. In the 1980s he intensified discrimination against ethnic Hungarians, forcing many to flee to Hungary and further embittering historically bad relations with that *Soviet bloc* neighbor. In 1989 his "Securitate," a particularly brutal group even by the usual standards of *secret police,* savagely repressed demonstrations in the provincial city of Timisoara. That set off a general uprising. Ceausescu's family dictatorship was overthrown in four days, and he and his wife, his lifelong partner in corruption and brutal repression, were shot. However, old Communists in democrats' clothing rallied to win the 1990 elections and retard movement toward genuine reform, which retarded Rumania's progress all through the 1990s. Rumanians were also distracted by fighting in Bessarabia, left by the post–Cold War borders as an ethnically Rumanian part of Moldova with a sizable Russian population as well, and where Russian "rogue units" supported ethnic Russian *secessionists* from *Trans-Dniestra* against the majority ethnic Rumanians.

Rumelia. A *Balkan* subdivision of the old *Ottoman Empire*, including Albania, Macedonia, and Thrace. Eastern Rumelia later became southern Bulgaria. Modern Turkey retains a small portion, abutting Istanbul (historic *Constantinople*).

ruse. A deliberately deceitful policy; a clever *stratagem* designed to delude in politics or diplomacy. As concerns military operations, "ruses de guerre" has a special and indeed a legal meaning. It is any deception or trick in the course of combat which is illegitimate, and possibly a *war crime*, by virtue of its abuse of the laws of war designed to protect *noncombatants*. Such ruses de guerre might include concealing oneself in a hospital for purposes of advantage in combat, or feigning *surrender* then firing on oncoming enemy troops, or flying the flag of a *neutral* state to lure ships into range, and so on. *See also grave breaches.*

"ruses de guerre." *See ruse.*

Rush-Bagot, Treaty of (1818). Acting U.S. secretary of state Richard Rush and British minister (ambassador) Charles Bagot negotiated this first-ever naval *disarmament* agreement. It limited both nations to light naval craft, sufficient only for police and *customs* duties, concerning the Great Lakes and Lake Champlain. During the *American Civil War* the United States considered giving the required six-months notice of renunciation. It was reacting to the use of Canadian soil as a base for *Confederate* raids into Vermont, New York, and other far northern states. The treaty passed from Britain to Canada and still remains in force. It underwrites part of the world's longest undefended frontier, some 3,800 miles of the Canada-U.S. border. *See also Aroostook War; Oregon Question; Webster-Ashburton Treaty (1842).*

Rushdie, Salman (b. 1947). British novelist. In February 1989, *Ayatollah Khomeini* condemned as blasphemous his allegory novel "The Satanic Verses," issued a fatwa (edict) calling for Muslims to strike him down, and offered a substantial gratuity for the act. Refusal by Iran to revoke this incitation to murder soured relations with Britain and the West, just as they had begun to improve. Rushdie spent many years in British protective concealment.

Rusk, Dean (b. 1909). U.S. secretary of state, 1961–1969. He had a long career in the *State Department*, at the United Nations, and as an adviser to presidents on Asian-Pacific affairs. A firm believer in the *domino theory* and in the *Munich analogy*, he was a strong supporter of using U.S. military power to block local Asian *Communist* movements in *Korea* and then in *Indochina*. He saw these as threads in a larger tapestry of *subversion* and *expansion* woven by Moscow. He was intimately connected with policy toward the *Korean Conflict* and the *Vietnam War*. He reputedly did not warm easily to opinions different from his own.

Suggested Reading: Dean Rusk, *As I Saw It* (1990).

Russia. This great and diverse nation has had an agonizingly complex history, one marked by repeated invasion as well as a sustained impulse toward aggressive *expansion*, sometimes defensive, but most often opportunistically aggressive. Russia has also vacillated between periods of intense internal reform and efforts at *modernization* and *Westernization* versus even longer periods of brutal domestic repression and *xenophobia*.

(1) From Kievan Rus to Muscovy: The first identifiably Russian state was Kievan Rus (c. 882–1240 C.E.), a loose *feudal* association of *Slavic* peasants organized as a state by Scandinavians, migrant *Vikings* who settled in Ukraine, possibly as hired defenders of the local population, who are known in Russian history as "Varangians." They are traditionally said to have been led by Rurik (b. ?, d. 879?) of Novgorod. The capital was subsequently moved to Kiev, from which the first "Russian" state derived its name. Kievan Rus then developed political and commercial ties (911) to the *Byzantine Empire*, even as it retained economic and cultural ties to Scandinavia. This initial contact was quickly followed by extensive cultural and religious connections from the late tenth century, when the Kievan Rus population was converted to the *Orthodox* faith under, and by, Grand Duke ("Saint") Vladimir (b. ?, d. 1015). Kievan Rus was severely weakened by repeated *civil wars* and by Cuman (a Central Asian Turkic people) raiding and border wars. It was overrun by *Mongol* invaders, 1237–1240. In 1242 Alexander Nevsky (1220–1263), Prince of Novgorod, defeated the *Livonian Order*, preventing their further penetration east at the expense of what was left of Kievan Rus, and firmly linking the development of those lands to the fate of Novgorod. The Mongols (*Tartars*) ruled what would become Russia for two centuries, establishing the Golden Horde and several khanates. They took everything, but gave almost nothing in return. This was the time of social chaos of "Appanage Russia," named for the splintered landholding (udel, or appanage) system which kept each local prince weak but independent of the others. A strong state (Muscovy) slowly emerged in the north around the city of Moscow. When Muscovy broke the "Mongol yoke" in 1480 it looked to Byzantium, not Mongolia, as its model and inheritance, except in one regard: Russia was to be a harsher state and society for its centuries of subjugation by those hard masters, the "Great Khans."

(2) Tsarist Russia (1480–1917): The empire established by Muscovy was

ruled by the *tsars*, who for 450 years went virtually unchallenged, from the renunciation of vassalage to the Mongols by *Ivan III* (the Great) in 1480, to the abdication of *Nicholas II* in 1917. Under Ivan III, his immediate successor Vasily III (1479–1533, r. 1505–1533), and *Ivan IV (the Terrible)* Russia expanded in all directions: south against the Tartars, where the khanates of Kazan (1552) and Astrakhan (1556) were overrun; west (less successfully) against Balts, Poles, and Lithuanians; and east into the vast expanses of *Siberia*. From 1604 to 1613 was the "Time of Troubles" ("Smutnoe Vremia"), defined by *dynastic* struggles with the "False Dmitri" during the reign of *Boris Godunov*, social unrest, *famine*, peasant *uprisings*, and harsh repression. It ended with the establishment of the *Romanov* dynasty under Michael I (1596–1645, r. 1613–1645). The mid-seventeenth century saw further westward expansion, at the expense of the Polish Empire in the First Northern War (1654–1660), which brought Kiev and its hinterland into the Russian Empire in the *Treaty of Andurussovo* (1667), a result ratified in 1686. The *Cossacks* of the Don and the "Little Russian Cossack Host" remained fickle: *Stenka Razin* led a Don Cossack revolt in 1670–1671; other Cossacks toyed with alliance with Sweden during its invasion of Russia, 1708–1709.

Russia was changed enormously by the reign and reforms of *Peter the Great*. Peter's wars ensured that it replaced Sweden among the *Great Powers*, and his reforms ensured that Russia at least began an effort at *modernization*. He also added new territories in the south, but more importantly *Karelia* to secure his new capital at *St. Petersburg*. And he added the rich *Baltic States*, which he incorporated in the empire on the basis of a special status, reflecting the fact that they were non-Russian and non-Orthodox provinces. Peter's reign was followed by another four decades of dynastic intrigue, but also continuing influence by *Westernizers* and Russia's further development as a Great Power and expanding empire, as its ancient competitors and bordering empires—Persia, Sweden, Poland, Turkey, and China—all faded as major powers. Its foreign policy was anchored by a 1726 treaty with Austria, which proved a foundation of the eighteenth-century diplomatic system in southern and eastern Europe. Next came *Catherine the Great* and more expansion, in the first of several *Russo-Turkish Wars* with the *Ottoman Empire* and through the *partitions of Poland*. Catherine's *Potemkin* enlightenment was further dimmed by the crushing of the *Pugachev Rebellion* (1774–1775). It was followed by the even briefer enlightenment period of *Alexander I*, before his great struggles with *Napoleon* and France during the *Napoleonic Wars*—and with his own internal demons—contributed to a return to deep *despotism*.

After the failure of the *Decembrist revolt* came the descent into full *reaction* under *Nicholas I*, a return to *isolationism*, *Slavophilism*, and *anti-Semitism*, but also continuing expansion through yet more Russo-Turkish wars. Defeat came in the greatest of these, the *Crimean War*, at the hands of Turkey's allies of the moment, Britain and France. That shook Russia from its long lethargy and led to the great reforms of *Alexander II*, notably his *emancipation* of the *serfs* (1861). Alexander's assassination in 1881 in turn propelled Russia part way back to reaction yet again and began several decades of the worst official indulgence of its deeply rooted anti-Semitism and tolerance of *pogroms*, which ultimately drove some two million persecuted and destitute Russian Jews abroad, mostly to the United States, leading to international opprobrium and a pronounced deterioration in relations with a country that had long been a "distant friend" of Russia. Dissent grew among the educated classes as well. Many intellectuals were so frustrated by the paternalism and repression of the Russian state they turned to radical political theories, including *anarchism* and *Marxism*. Others, such as the sadly naïve *narodniki*, looked inward in the Slavophile tradition. More importantly than the changing fashions of intellectual dissent, real class change and class conflict were on the rise due to the *industrialization* that now was coming to Russia, bringing with it growth of new social classes and a rapid expansion of its cities, and attendant and rising demands for urban and political reform.

With a new and powerful Germany under *Bismarck* at the center of Europe, Russia under Foreign Minister and Chancellor *Alexander Gorchakov* was at last freed from the constraints imposed by the *Treaty of Paris* (1856). It joined the *Dreikaiserbund* but also looked to the Far East—to *Manchuria* and Korea— for additional gains. Russia built *railways* through Siberia, pushed development into Kamchatka, and began to press into Manchuria. By 1900 Russia was the fifth largest industrial power in the world and threatened to surpass both Great Britain and Germany in time. In 1904–1905 Russia's long eastward expansion into Asia ran into Japan's aggressive young imperialism, then moving west. Russia was humiliated at sea, twice, during the *Russo-Japanese War*, losing entire fleets to the Japanese Navy. It fared better on land, but it still settled for a bitter peace at *Portsmouth*. Defeat propelled the empire into the *Russian Revolution of 1905*, the first of several great upheavals which were to shake tsarism until it finally collapsed in 1917. Yet the tsarist regime was only finally destroyed when things fell apart during *World War I*. Massive defeat followed upon massive defeat, bringing extraordinary casualties: at least two million dead and perhaps five million taken prisoner. Three years of terrible *attrition* broke the back of the army, the will of the nation, and the political and economic capabilities of the tsarist system. The regime collapsed into the *Russian Revolutions of 1917*. The center would not hold; years of savage civil strife, starvation, terror, and *anarchy* were loosed upon a vast empire.

(2) Soviet Russia (1918–1991): Despite defeat in World War I and in the *Polish-Soviet War* of 1920, Russia emerged from its revolutions still in command of the lion's share of its great empire. It would hold this vast area between the world wars. The *Bolsheviks* under *Lenin*, with *Trotsky* in command of the *Red Army*, won the *Russian Civil War* (1918–1921), despite much opposition, including foreign interventions in the far north (Murmansk) and Siberia. They had lost several of the tsars' provinces—the Baltic States, Fin-

land, and Poland—but retained tsarist gains to the empire in the Caucasus, Central Asia, Ukraine, and Siberia. Although the Bolsheviks never acknowledged the fact, the *Allied and Associated Powers* at Paris had also kept their western borders intact, returned to them the vast lands and populations they had signed away to Germany at *Brest-Litovsk*, and had even placed tsarist gold reserves in an escrow account. Nonetheless, the Russian Empire was now reconstituted as the Soviet Union (officially, the Union of Soviet Socialist Republics, or USSR) and was dedicated to *subversion* of, and permanent hostility toward, the West. In theory, this was a great, voluntary federation of 15 "independent" republics, plus other quasi–autonomous zones. In reality the USSR was a *unitary*, overcentralized, and highly repressive continuance of the Russian Empire. Russia was the largest of the constituent republics, itself containing 16 "autonomous republics" and still more "autonomous regions." For decades this composite state wore a cloak of *Marxist* internationalism. At one level this was an ideological fig leaf to cover the naked verity that the Soviet Union was fundamentally an imperial extension of the Russian nation. At another, the Marxist internationalism was sincere on the part of all members of the *Politburo* and many *apparatchiki*. Thus, the central question for contemporary observers then, and historians now: to what degree did Marxist internationalism merely cover over a more basic imperial drive in Russian history, and to what degree did it independently lead Moscow into seven decades of sustained hostility toward the West, and later also toward Japan, China, and all other immediate neighbors it did not directly control?

With the failure of orthodox Marxist predictions of revolutions to follow in the West, and internal defeat of Trotsky's notion of *permanent revolution*, the Soviet Union withdrew into a paranoid isolationism under *Stalin*. It pursued *socialism in one country* and successive *five-year plans*, and suffered the extraordinary torments of forced *collectivization*, artificial *famine*, the *Yezhovshchina* and the *GULAG*. Soviet Russia sensed the danger from Nazi Germany and Imperial Japan somewhat earlier than the West, but it was rebuffed in the mid-1930s in its efforts to form a collective front against *fascism*, partly because it refused to give up its own subversive efforts through the *Comintern*. Excluded from the *Munich Conference*, Stalin looked to a separate deal with *Hitler*, agreeing to the *Nazi-Soviet Pact* in August 1939. In October, after war had begun in the west and Stalin had a month earlier—in partnership with Hitler—conducted yet another violent partition of Poland, *Churchill* said, "I cannot predict to you the action of Russia. It is a riddle wrapped in a mystery inside an enigma." After dividing Poland with the other great tyrant of Europe, Stalin took advantage of German preoccupation with war in the west to launch the *Winter War* against Finland (1939–1940), annex the Baltic States (1940), and force *cession* of *Bessarabia* and *Bukovina* from Rumania. The Soviet Union lost all that territory, and one-third of European Russia, including Ukraine and the Crimea, when Hitler launched *Barbarossa* in June 1941. With *Lend-Lease* aid and with an extraordinary industrial and military effort of its own, by the end of *World War II* the Soviet Union retook all the territory lost between 1918 and 1920, all that lost between 1941 and 1942, all it had gained by the Nazi-Soviet Pact, plus a good deal more: it re-annexed the Baltic States and annexed parts of northern China, Czechoslovakia, eastern Germany, Finland, Hungary, Japan, Manchuria, Mongolia, Poland, and Rumania. By those actions it alienated all those nations to some degree.

This postwar behavior was not seen by the West as the realization of the agreements hammered out at *Tehran, Yalta,* and *Potsdam* to permit "*friendly states*" along the Soviet border, but as their disavowal. The *Cold War* therefore dominated the next, and last, four decades of Soviet history. It was highlighted, 1947–1968, by the *Berlin airlift* and *Berlin Wall* crises, the *Korean Conflict,* the *Hungarian Uprising,* the rank *adventurism* of *Khrushchev* before and during the *Cuban Missile Crisis,* indirect but prolonged confrontation with the United States through proxies in the *Vietnam War,* direct and increasingly dangerous confrontation with China in the *Sino-Soviet split,* and an invasion of Czechoslovakia to end the *Prague Spring.* In response to West Germany joining *NATO* in 1955, Moscow put together the *Warsaw Pact;* in response to the *Non-Aligned Movement* and U.S. *deterrence* policy, it promoted *wars of national liberation* and *peaceful coexistence,* respectively. The 1970s brought *détente* and the *SALT* treaties and setbacks in the Middle East, but also Soviet geopolitical thrusts into the Horn of Africa and the Arabian peninsula. The *Afghan-Soviet War* marked both a departure and the beginning of the final erosion of the communist system and Soviet power. For 40 years the Soviet Union had ignored the single greatest outcome of World War II, a worldwide trend toward *decolonization,* by pretending even to itself that it was not an empire. With the response of the Afghans to their "liberation" by Moscow, that myth was shattered. An intellectual "domino effect" began, as one by one the sacred myths of the Soviet system came under fundamental question, and the views of dissidents started to look not traitorous but truly patriotic. The subject peoples of the empire began to stir. Then, fatally for the Soviet idea, the Russian people remembered that they, too, were a nation and demanded back their old symbols, name, and institutions.

The early 1980s thus witnessed a core crisis of confidence in the Soviet mission, compounded by a protracted crisis of leadership as *Brezhnev, Andropov,* and *Chernenko* all were enfeebled and died within three years of each other. They were followed by *Gorbachev,* who stumbled from bold beginnings in 1985 to economic and political collapse, 1989–1991. A coup attempt by the old guard in the *Communist Party* and the Red Army failed in August 1991. The empire was collapsing from the weight of its loss in Afghanistan, its stagnating economy, and the weak and vacillating personality of Gorbachev, who was unable to decide which were the critical issues facing the Soviet Union or what to do about them. Mostly, however, it was collapsing because of the utopian nature of the regime, which could no longer convince its people or deny to itself that it was a failure on its own terms, and not just relative to several former allies and enemies who had surpassed it economically and technologically. There was nothing inevitable about this collapse: it shall remain an enormous mystery to future historians, who would do well to recall the astonishment of contemporaries who witnessed these events in a state of apprehended disbelief, why the Soviet Union ended when and how it did. It disintegrated at the peak of its power and world influence, with not a shot fired and most "expert observers" convinced to the very last moments that it was a stable regime. End it did, however: on December 25, 1991, the Soviet Union became *extinct* by nearly universal internal demand and international consent. Fifteen independent *successor states* formed from its breakup. Despite this huge loss of territory, the Russian state remained by far the largest in the world.

(3) Contemporary Russia (1991–): Even post-Soviet Russia sprawled over *Eurasia,* incorporating 21 "constituent republics" and spanning 11½ time zones. Under *Boris Yeltsin,* Russia confirmed a broad change in its foreign policy from confrontation and obstruction to more creative engagement and facilitation of international cooperation. It ceased to use its *veto* at the United Nations to block *collective security* or *peacekeeping* actions. Indeed, it supported UN use of force during the *Gulf War* and in *Somalia* and *Bosnia.* It began tentative cooperation with *NATO* and played a more positive role within the Organization of Security and Cooperation in Europe (OSCE). It applied to join the *International Monetary Fund* (IMF) and the *Group of Seven,* both for reasons of economic need and desire for *prestige* in a time of sinking *national morale.* It drew upon some Western aid but struggled into 1994 without completing the transition to a *market economy.* Russia also announced a liberal policy toward the 25 million Russians living in the *near abroad:* the best way to protect their rights, the Foreign Ministry said, would be to encourage local governments to respect *human rights* and democracy while securing both in Russia itself. It was an astonishing change, welcomed by the world in the early 1990s.

Old habits die hard: by 1993 Russia sent troops into Tajikistan to intervene in a civil war, and was accused by Georgia and Moldova of allowing Russian Army units to support *secession* movements. Its worst quarrel was with Ukraine, over the division of the *Black Sea Fleet* and the disposition of 1,800 *nuclear weapons* left in Kiev's hands with dissolution of the old union. An interim settlement, mostly on Russia's terms, was reached after Ukraine's economy collapsed to an even worse extent than Russia's. In October 1993, the last important vestiges of old-line communist power were crushed during a day of street fighting in Moscow. In subsequent years, however, large numbers of extreme right-wing delegates were returned to the *Duma,* including a fair number of unreconstructed communists. Also, Russia's central institutions and key political positions were taken over by members of the old *apparatchiki,* especially the former *KGB* (renamed the FSB), in corrupt cahoots with a criminal class which stifled entrepreneurial endeavor and strangled a hoped-for conversion to market democracy in its cradle, to instead erect a cynical *kleptocracy* just beneath the formal apparatus of a constitutional state. This process was aided by a new constitution introduced by Yeltsin which affirmed strong, centralized presidential power. That permitted abuse and corruption on a grand scale. Russia had not quite exhumed its tsarist tradition, but after seven decades of communist misrule it had returned to the path of pre-Soviet history and tradition: rule by central decree, nonconsultation of the populace except in pro forma elections and through a hamstrung Duma, and formal adoption of modern Westernized political forms without the West's corresponding civic and political values.

For the remainder of the 1990s the nation as a whole drifted in a chaotic and increasingly lawless condition. Internal conflict broke out in *Chechnya* and was met with a combination of ineptitude and savage repression. By the end of Yeltsin's presidency he was widely seen—at home and abroad—as unstable and ineffective. Russian relations with the West also deteriorated badly, over *NATO* expansion into former Warsaw Pact countries and direct intervention in *Kosovo*, and the brutality of Russian methods in the war in Chechnya. Yeltsin left much of Russia essentially unreformed, especially its chronic problem of agriculture. Its financial markets and economy were near outright bankruptcy and corrupted to the highest levels, including members of his own family. After this chronicle of wasted years, Russia turned for results to a harder man: *Vladimir Putin*, an ex-chief of the KGB, who promised to win the war in Chechnya and restore Russia's standing in the world. Both looked to be tall orders, at least in the shorter run. In January 2002, Russia ended some 40 years of military presence in Cuba when it withdrew the last of its forces from the island. *See also Mikhail Bakunin; Lavrenti Beria; Birobizhan; Black Hundreds; CHEKA; CIS; containment; Coordinating Committee on Multilateral Export Controls (COCOM); Felix Dzerzhinsky; Eastern Question; Sergey Kirov; Kurils; Minatom; Vyacheslav Molotov; NKVD; nomenklatura; OGPU; Old Believers; Pamyat; Port Arthur; purge trials; revolution from above; Russian America; Sakhalin Island; space race; SPUTNIK; START; Straits Question; Third Rome; Tilsit; Andrei Vyshinsky; X article; Vladimir Zhirinovsky; Giorgii Zhukov; Gregori Zinoviev.*

Suggested Readings: John Ledonne, *The Russian Empire and the World, 1700–1917* (1997); Dominic Lieven, *Empire: The Russian Empire and its Rivals* (2001); Martin Malia, *The Soviet Tragedy* (1994); Martha B. Olcott and Anders Aslund, *Russia After Communism* (1999); Richard Pipes, *Russia Under the Bolshevik Regime* (1993); Nicholas Riasanovsky, *A History of Russia* (1984); Robert Service, *Russia: A History* (1998); Hugh Seton-Watson, *The Russian Empire, 1801–1917* (1990); Adam Ulam, *Expansion and Coexistence: Soviet Foreign Policy, 1917–1973* (1974); Adam Ulam, *History of Soviet Russia* (1976); Warren B. Walsh, *Readings In Russian History*, 2 vols. (1963); J. N. Westwood, *Endurance and Endeavor: Russian History, 1812–1992* (1973, 1993).

Russian America. *See Alaska; California.*

Russian Civil War (1918–1921). Immediately upon the *Bolshevik* seizure of power in Russia, military opposition to their rule began. The first organized resistance came from *Cossack* units, traditional supporters of the *tsars*. Other *White* military units, often led by former tsarist *officers*, began to skirmish with the *Red Army* then being hastily assembled by *Trotsky*, which fanned out along the *railways* linking up the provincial *soviets*. Whereas the Reds fought under a unified and ruthless command, the Whites never formed a single force and repeatedly fell out with, and sometimes fought, one another. Balts and Finns (the latter under *Mannerheim*) from 1918 to 1920 succeeded in forcing the Bolsheviks to accept the loss of several tsarist provinces. In the Ukraine, Whites under Denekin, Reds, and Poles tangled in a bloody and confused mêlée. There and elsewhere, independent militia units of "Greens," some of them *anarchists*, joined the fray. In the *Crimea* armies of Cossacks seemed ready to fight everyone, with some units penetrating Ukraine proper before being defeated by the Reds. The special areas during the civil war were North Russia near Murmansk, the *Caucasus,* and *Siberia.* In North Russia Finns and Germans fought Russians, and the Western *Allied and Associated Powers* intervened, including a small U.S. backup force sent, with great reluctance, by *Woodrow Wilson.* The initial Allied plan was to prop up the *eastern front* and prevent the Germans from capturing large military stockpiles. With the *Treaty of Brest-Litovsk* that purpose evaporated and the Americans soon withdrew, forcing the Allies out too. In the Caucasus, French and British intervention helped prop up independent governments in Armenia and Azerbaijan, until the Reds moved in en masse, 1920–1921.

In Siberia, 1918–1922, motives for intervention were more varied: some in Britain (with *Winston Churchill* in the lead) and France wanted to intervene on a large enough scale to overthrow the Bolsheviks, and thereby exact vengeance for Brest-Litovsk. Japan, on the other hand, sought to detach part or all of Siberia from Russia, intending its own imperial penetration of that area and *Manchuria* during Russia's moment of weakness, and sent in by far the largest contingent of troops (more than 70,000). The United States again refused a forward role but went along with intervention in Siberia, providing a strategic rearguard mainly to keep an eye on the Japanese, whom it suspected of wanting to close the *Open Door* throughout the Far East. A secondary aim was to aid the *Czech Legion.* Intentions aside, the intervention drew the Allied and Associated Powers deeply into the war until Siberian Whites, under *Kolchak*, were finally defeated by the Red Army in 1920. Meanwhile, in the *Polish-Soviet War*, which was integrally related to the Russian Civil War, Polish units overran much of Ukraine, briefly capturing Kiev in May 1920. They were repulsed and driven deep into Poland by the Red Army, fresh from victory over the Cossacks and Ukrainian Whites and under orders from *Lenin* to foment a Polish *revolution* at bayonet point. However, a Polish counteroffensive in August pushed the Red Army back and retook most of the eastern territory the Poles had lost in May. In the Treaty of Riga (March

18, 1921) Poland received portions of western Byelorussia, Lithuania, and Ukraine from the Bolsheviks. The consensus estimate of the war dead is 7–10 million, or five times Russian casualties in *World War I*. In the *famine* which accompanied and followed the civil war another five million died.

Suggested Readings: Francesco Benvenuti, *The Bolsheviks and the Red Army, 1918–1922* (1988); John Bradley, *Allied Intervention In Russia* (1968); Vladimir N. Brovkin, ed., *The Bolsheviks in Russian Society: The Revolution and the Civil War* (1997); Michael Carley, *Revolution and Intervention* (1983); W. Bruce Lincoln, *Red Victory* (1989, 1999); Evan Mawdsley. *The Russian Civil War* (1987, 2000).

Russian Empire. *See Russia.*

Russian Revolution (1905). Discontent with the *reactionary* and incompetent rule of *Nicholas II* built for years, especially with rising rural taxes used to finance *industrialization* and with *Russification* in the outer provinces. Fuel was added by defeats in the *Russo-Japanese War* (1904–1905), but the tinder was lighted by a massacre of demonstrators on *Bloody Sunday* (January 9, 1905). Strikes, a naval *mutiny*, and creation of the *St. Petersburg soviet* under *Trotsky*, compelled the tsar to agree to set up the *Duma*. The right wing then turned on the Jews, and Russia was swept by a wave of *pogroms* more violent and vicious than any seen in 150 years. Russian *liberals* accepted reforms which seemed to promise a constitutional *monarchy*, but the soviet did not and was bloodily repressed, as were the peasants. When the crisis eased, the tsar returned to a more *autocratic* style. The Revolution had a real impact on China, too, where close analogies were drawn by *Marxists*—but even more so by *nationalists*—between the tsarist system and the *Qing dynasty*.

Suggested Readings: A. Ascher, *The Revolution of 1905* (1988); Solomon M. Schwarz, *The Russian Revolution of 1905* (1967).

Russian Revolution, March (February) 1917. Its immediate roots lay in the *rising expectations* brought about by the pace of *industrialization* Russia was experiencing at the turn of the twentieth century. Also important was the frustration among Russian *liberals* and reformers who saw the gains of the *Russian Revolution of 1905* eroded to nothing by a tsarist regime increasingly distant from the reality of the nation, and lost in a mystic miasma cast over the royal family by *Rasputin*. However, the *sine qua non* of the revolution of March 1917, was the fact that Russia was losing the war against Germany—taking insupportable casualties, as two million had been killed and millions more wounded or made *prisoners of war*—and was suffering runaway *inflation* and home-front deprivation. As workers were returned to the factories and mines to service the booming war economy, peasant troops forced to remain in the lines grew ever more bitter. They lost confidence in their officers and in the personal supreme command assumed by Tsar *Nicholas II* in 1916, and in 1917 they began to "*vote with their feet*" for peace and then for radical political change. All this was exacerbated by a severe food shortage in the cities. The professional revolutionaries, of which Russia had many, moved to seize the moment.

The majority were liberals or *democratic socialists* who sought varying degrees of constitutional and social reform and an expanded role for middle classes and for the *Duma*. Many also were nationalists who supported the war effort, though no longer the regime. More *radical* were the *Bolsheviks* and their allies of the moment, especially *Trotsky*, the Social Revolutionaries (SRs), and the many *soviets* which began to spring up in cities and towns. It was the liberals who made the March Revolution (February in the old Julian calendar). The affair was relatively bloodless: a *general strike* spread rapidly, troops sent to shoot down the strikers *mutinied* instead, then joined in defense of the public against the still-loyal *Cossacks* and tsarist *secret police*. Nicholas II was forced to abdicate, after failing to abolish a Duma which had finally stiffened its back after years of docility. Subsequently, the great political struggle was between the *Provisional Government* under *Kerensky* and the *Petrograd Soviet*, with the first deciding to continue the war and the latter obstructing policy in the hope of further radicalizing events. The *Bolsheviks* moved to take control of the once-spontaneous soviets, but when they contemplated a *coup* in July they were faced down, and *Lenin* fled to Finland. The decision to launch the so-called *Kerensky Offensive* in June proved disastrous. It broke the will of the army, split the Provisional Government, and opened the door to Lenin's return and a successful Bolshevik coup in November.

Suggested Readings: Sheila Fitzpatrick, *The Russian Revolution*, 2nd ed. (1994); T. Hasegawa, *The February Revolution* (1981); Richard Pipes, *A Concise History of the Russian Revolution* (1996).

Russian Revolution, November (October) 1917. *Lenin* and the *Bolsheviks* launched their long-planned *coup* on November 6, 1917. It succeeded where their July effort had failed, mainly due to the exhaustion of the Russian population caused by a pervasive sense that the *Provisional Government* would not quit the war, but instead wanted to continue a fight for which the nation no longer had the stomach. The Bolsheviks capitalized on this mood in brilliantly effective slogans, such as "All power to the *soviets!*" and most famously, "Peace, Land, and Bread!" By promising and then delivering peace, albeit the humiliating *diktat* of *Brest-Litovsk*, Lenin persuaded components of the conscript armed forces (excluding most officers) to support the Bolsheviks in their seizure of the major cities. Soldiers and workers came together in the All-Russian Congress of Soviets to sanction Bolshevik policy and vote support for the *Red Army* in the *Russian Civil War*, 1918–1921. Real power rapidly passed into the hands of Lenin and his closest associates, among them *Trotsky* and *Stalin*. By quickly enacting land reform the Bolsheviks gained a measure of peasant support despite their essentially urban agenda, and more importantly took the peasants out of the coming fight with the *ancien régime*.

That was crucial, as in 1918 the peasants rose—in some areas in the fashion of a *jacquerie*—seizing the great estates from nobles, who were killed or had already fled. The various subject, non-Russian nations also rose in discrete rebellions, along with Siberia, isolating the Bolsheviks in control of the heartland of central Russia. Peace waited until 1921, after the terrible ravages of the Civil War finally ended in the triumph of the Red Army. In the meantime, by promising to correct the food shortages in the cities the Bolsheviks gained support among industrial workers and their families. To accomplish this, they sent confiscation squads into the countryside to forcibly seize supplies of meat and grain; all available food was brutally confiscated from the peasants to feed the Bolsheviks' worker base in the cities, under the policy of *war Communism*. Anyone disaffected with these or other policies dictated by the Bolshevik "*vanguard*," and desperate or foolish enough to say so, was *summarily executed* during the *Red Terror* or sent to swell the *forced labor* system that was already developing into the *GULAG*. This contributed to a massive famine that continued after the Civil War, and was only relieved with a major charitable effort by the *American Relief Administration* under the guidance of *Herbert Hoover*.

The land, too, would be taken back from the peasants in the 1930s through forced *collectivization*. Nor did the workers fare much better: in their near-term future lay *terror* and *five-year plans*. A measure of how quickly disaffection set in came in the *Kronstadt mutinies*. Russian sailors at the Kronstadt naval base had helped spark the *Russian Revolution* in 1905, and had mutinied against the tsarist system again in 1917. During the Russian Civil War they had supported the *Bolsheviks*. Now, as they watched the democratic promises of 1917 corrupt into mass murder and summary injustice on a scale that made the tsar's offenses pale in comparison, they rose against Lenin's emergent tyranny. Their rebellion was bloodily suppressed by the Red Army and the *Cheka*, the new *secret police* force which carried out the meanest tasks ordered by the top Bolshevik leaders. The betrayal was complete.

Suggested Readings: Vladimir N. Brovkin, ed., *The Bolsheviks in Russian Society: The Revolution and the Civil War* (1997); John Daborn, *Russia: Revolution and Counter-Revolution, 1917–1924* (1991); I. Getzler, *Kronstadt, 1917–1921* (1983); Richard Pipes, *The Russian Revolution* (1990); Richard Pipes, *A Concise History of the Russian Revolution* (1996).

Russian Revolution (1989–1991). *See Gorbachev; Russia; Yeltsin.*

Russification. A policy practiced on and off by both tsarist and Soviet Russia, aiming at assimilation of ethnic and religious minorities by insisting on the use of the Russian language and the imposition of Russian over minority or local culture.

Russo-Japanese War (1904–1905). This conflict arose most directly from competing Russian and Japanese imperialist interest in penetrating and thereafter controlling and exploiting Manchuria, and to a lesser extent also

Korea. The Japanese Navy launched a surprise attack which destroyed the Russian fleet at anchor at *Port Arthur* on February 8, 1904. The Japanese Army then laid siege to Port Arthur, June 22, 1904–January 2, 1905. The Japanese lost 100,000 casualties (58,000 killed in action) before overcoming the Russian defenses, a casualty rate reflecting the fact that this was the first war where *machine guns* were heavily used by both sides. Russia responded by invading Manchuria and Korea. In late 1904 St. Petersburg dispatched the Baltic fleet on a seven-month journey to the Pacific, made necessary because it was refused passage through the *Suez Canal* by Japan's ally, Britain, following the *Dogger Bank incident*. When it arrived in the Far East it was quickly annihilated—with much loss of life—by the waiting Japanese, at the *Battle of Tsushima Straits*. Meanwhile, a stalemate had developed on land after the initial Japanese victories. Once the siege of Port Arthur succeeded, however, the Japanese beat the main Russian force at Mukden (85,000 Russian casualties, 70,000 Japanese), and forced its withdrawal during February and March 1905. These successive, humiliating defeats tipped Russia into the *Revolution of 1905*. Despite large American loans—many from Jews deeply opposed to Russia due to the *pogroms* underway there since 1882—Japan was nearly bankrupted by its war effort and anyway was unable to make further headway on land against the huge manpower reserves of the tsarist army. Tokyo therefore appealed to *Theodore Roosevelt* to mediate an end to the war. The parties met in New Hampshire, where they negotiated the *Treaty of Portsmouth*.

Suggested Readings: I. Nish, *Origins of the Russo-Japanese War* (1985); J. N. Westwood, *Russia Against Japan* (1986); J. White, *The Diplomacy of the Russo-Japanese War* (1964).

Russo-Polish War (1920). *See Polish-Soviet War.*

Russo-Turkish Wars. Russia and the *Ottoman Empire* fought repeatedly in the several centuries preceding the eighteenth, including under *Peter I*, but their great contest for control of Central Asia and the Balkans took on a new intensity after c. 1750.

(1) First (1768–1774): This started as another in a long line of Russian expansionist thrusts into lands long held by the Ottoman Turks, which partly responded to and in part underlay the deterioration of that great Muslim and Turkish empire and the attendant *Eastern Question*. By 1774 the armies of *Catherine the Great* had defeated the Turks but also were bogged down in the Balkans. Turkey was exhausted and ready to make peace, doing so in the Treaty of Kuchuk-Kainardji (1774). This treaty secured nominal independence for the *Crimea* and Russian claims to all territories east of that peninsula, including Azov, Kuban, and Terek. The Ottomans guaranteed *Orthodox* rights in *Constantinople*, where Russia was permitted to erect a church. Turkey regained Moldovia and Wallachia (the *Danubian Principalities*), but Russia retained a right of intervention in their affairs, effectively establishing a *protectorate* over their Christian populations. The Crimean *Tar-*

tars were proclaimed *autonomous*, while still acknowledging the *suzerainty* of the *caliph*. Russia also gained a right of commercial navigation of the *Straits*.

(2) Second (1787–1792): Russia penetrated deeper into the *Caucasus*, taking the key port of Odessa. Further penetration—the ultimate goal was Constantinople—was delayed by Russia's war with Revolutionary France, and then by the outbreak of the *Napoleonic Wars*. Russian gains were codified in the Treaty of Jassey (1792). Still, Russia's failure to conquer Turkey brought an end to one of Catherine's more far-fetched fantasies: the *"Greek Project."*

(3) Third (1806–1812): A halt in the war with France arranged at *Tilsit* permitted Russia to resume its offensive drive into the Turkish empire and its annexation of both eastern (1801) and western (1803–1810) *Georgia*. By the time *Napoleon* invaded Russia in 1812, most of Bessarabia had also fallen to Moscow, and the next year parts of Persia and other areas in the Caucasus were gained (Treaties of Bucharest, 1812, ending the Russo-Turkish War over Georgia, and Gulistan, 1813, which ended the Russo-Persian War, fought over the same cause).

(4) Fourth (1828–1829): Russia continued its southward pressure, achieving its objective of taking Adrianople. It also acquired the rest of Bessarabia and a slice of Armenia (Treaty of Adrianople, 1829), adding to its gains made just months earlier at Persia's expense (Treaty of Turkmanchai, 1828), in a brief war over the final disposition of Georgia.

(5) Crimean War (1853–1856): Russia's aggression against Turkey expanded into the *Crimean War* with France, Britain, and Piedmont, ending in massive casualties, a humiliating defeat for Russia, and hard terms imposed at the *Congress of Paris* (1856).

(6) War of 1877–1878: This conflict, which began as a revolt in Bosnia but quickly spread to other *Slavic* provinces under Ottoman control, was seized upon by Russia to resume its southward drive. It quickly demonstrated that Russia had recovered and improved its military capabilities following defeat in the Crimean War. It led directly to major territorial adjustments in the *Treaty of San Stefano* (1878) and at the *Congress of Berlin*.

(7) World War I (1914–1918): The culminating Russo-Turkish war took place inside *World War I*, a hurricane of a conflict which destroyed the Ottoman Empire and severely hobbled the Russian Empire, stripping away several outer provinces. It sprang from Turkish alliance with the *Central Powers* and began with a Turkish attack on Russia in the Crimea and the Caucasus, October 31, 1914. Thereafter, both empires were swept into a maelstrom of carnage and destruction. *See also Bessarabia; Balkan Wars; Bukovina; Disraeli; Greek War of Independence; Mikhail Kutuzov; Mahmud II; Mehemet Ali; Navarino, battle of; Grigori Potemkin; Alexander Suvorov.*

Ruthenia. An alternate name for Carpatho–Ukraine. It was given to *Czechoslovakia* in the *Treaty of Trianon* in 1920. Ceded to the Soviet Union in 1945, after 1991 it became a region of eastern Ukraine.

Rwanda. This small, densely populated territory was peopled by peasant-farmer Hutus (or Bahutu) before the sixteenth century. Pastoralist Tutsi (or Batutsi) then migrated to Rwanda, eventually establishing *tributary* chieftaincies which dominated the Hutu majority (90 percent of the population), from whom the Tutsi were visibly distinct, just as they did in *Burundi*. Early in the seventeenth century Rwanda came fully under Tutsi control. In the mid-nineteenth century well-armed *Nguni* refugees from the *mfecane* tried to enter Rwanda but were fought off. In 1890 Germany claimed the territory and incorporated it into German East Africa. In 1916 it was captured by Belgian forces, and after *World War I* it was made a *mandate territory* (as *Ruanda-Urundi*) under Belgian control. It was converted into a *trusteeship territory* after *World War II*. With independence looming, in 1959 a bloody, even genocidal, Hutu *revolution* overthrew the Tutsi monarchy in favor of a Hutu-dominated republic. In July 1962 it became an independent republic, separate from Burundi.

Ethnic conflict continued throughout the 1960s and 1970s, with the Hutu retaining the upper hand and practicing a politics of exclusion of the Tutsi minority as oppressive as the prior domination of Hutus by the Tutsi monarchy. In 1990 exiled Tutsis in the Rwandan Patriotic Front (RPF), led by direct descendants of the overthrown monarchy who had been based in Uganda since 1959, attempted an *invasion*. They were repelled, but only with direct Belgian and French assistance. In 1992 continued fighting created one million *refugees*, nearly one-seventh of the total population. In 1993 a *demobilization* agreement was signed under United Nations auspices, but ethnic relations remained taut. The situation was exacerbated by new massacres of Hutu in Burundi, where a major genocide of Hutu had taken place in 1972. With Burundi's Tutsi military abusing *hot pursuit* to drag Hutu back across the border to kill them, war threatened with Rwanda. In April 1994, the Rwandan and Burundian presidents (both Hutu) were killed when their aircraft was shot down. That sparked a *genocidal* frenzy of killing—but one which in fact had been methodically planned months in advance—of all Tutsi and also of moderate Hutus, by fanatical Hutu militia ("Interahamwe") and large segments of a stirred-up Hutu population, in an effort to arrive at a "*final solution*" to the Tutsi problem.

In response, the RPF advanced rapidly on Kigali. An airlift was mounted to get most foreigners out, while all around perhaps 800,000 Tutsi and moderate Hutu were butchered inside 100 days, and refugees from both tribes poured over Rwanda's borders. With the baleful experience of Somalia a recent memory, and "led" by the *Clinton administration* in the United States, the *Security Council* declined to intervene. Indeed, it pulled out UN *peacekeeping* forces already in the country under Canadian command, even as the massacres were accelerating in fury and scope. It later reinserted troops, once the main carnage ended and only after France had threatened a unilateral intervention. The RPF took control by midsummer, causing a million Hutu (many thousands of whom, known as "génocidaires," were guilty of the most horrific acts of murder of women, children, and infants, among other innocents) to flee. They settled in Uganda, Tanzania, Burundi, and Congo (Zaire), where starvation and cholera took their toll in hastily improvised *refugee camps*. International assistance to the camps was late in arriving, and the death rate rose further as defeated Hutu fanatics—who needed human bargaining chips—frightened many refugees into remaining in disease-infested camps instead of returning to Rwanda under UN protection. The RPF then pursued the génocidaires into the camps, indiscriminately killing tens of thousands of Hutus during their hunt for the guilty, and as revenge.

This conflict spilled over into Rwandan and multinational involvement in the civil war that overwhelmed Congo (Zaire) after 1997. In 1999 an OAU report caustically but not wholly inaccurately blamed the United States and the Security Council for their timidity toward what it called a "preventable genocide" in Rwanda.

Suggested Readings: David Brimingham and Phyllis M. Martin, *History of Central Africa* (1983); Wm. Roger Louis, *Ruanda-Urundi, 1881–1919* (1979); Christian Scherrerl, *Genocide and Crisis in Central Africa* (2001).

Ryswick, Treaty of (1697). The general settlement which ended the *War of the League of Augsburg* (and in North America, *King William's War*) and temporarily checked the ambitions of *Louis XIV*. It left large questions of territory and of the overall *balance of power* between England and France unresolved. Louis was forced to make temporary concessions since he had failed to prevail militarily, but his ambition remained unchecked. The peace made at Ryswick thus broke down four years later, with the start of the *War of the Spanish Succession*.

Ryukyus. This chain of 55 islands was long a possession of China. In 1609 the *daimyo* of Satsuma in southern Japan invaded the Ryukyus, and thereafter the joint fiction was maintained for some time that they still belonged to China, when in fact they were governed from Edo. In 1879 the indigenous monarchy on *Okinawa*, the largest island in the chain, was abolished and the whole Ryukyu chain was formally annexed to Japan. Tokyo retained only "residual *sovereignty*" over the Ryukyus after *World War II*, in the *Japanese Peace Treaty*. The United States occupied Okinawa until its return to Japan in 1972. The United States thereafter retained important military bases there. From the 1990s, opposition to these U.S. bases, in particular to their *extraterritorial* exception from local criminal laws, rose among the local population.